FREDERICK THE SECOND

FREDERICK THE SECOND
1194-1250

BY
ERNST KANTOROWICZ

Authorized English Version by
E. O. LORIMER

With Seven Maps

FREDERICK UNGAR PUBLISHING CO.
NEW YORK

Republished 1957
by arrangement with Constable and Co., Ltd., London

First published 1931

Printed in the United States of America

Library of Congress Catalog Card Number 57-9408

TO MY FRIEND

WOLDEMAR COUNT UXKULL-GYLLENBAND

IN GRATEFUL ACKNOWLEDGMENT

PREFATORY NOTE

WHEN the Kingdom of Italy, in May 1924, celebrated the seven-hundredth anniversary of the University of Naples, a foundation of the Hohenstaufen Frederick II, a wreath might have been seen on the Emperor's sarcophagus in the Cathedral of Palermo with this inscription :

SEINEN KAISERN UND HELDEN
DAS GEHEIME DEUTSCHLAND

This is not to imply that the present Life of Frederick II was begotten of that episode . . . but that wreath may fairly be taken as a symbol that—not alone in learned circles—enthusiasm is astir for the great German Rulers of the past : in a day when Kaisers are no more.

TRANSLATOR'S NOTE

THE English edition of Frederick II differs from the German in the following points : it has been provided with maps, with a table of contents, and with page headlines which are not in the original ; also with a few unobtrusive footnotes [signed *Tr.*].

A brief Summary of Sources has been appended, kindly supplied by the author himself.

Occasionally an allusive passage has been made clearer to an English reader by the insertion of an author's name or the quotation of an exact phrase. In a few passages a paragraph has been compressed or a recondite allusion omitted.

The translator is deeply indebted to F. J. E. Raby, who generously placed at the disposal of an amateur a scholar's expert knowledge of medieval literature and religion, and to D. L. R. Lorimer for a similar service in oriental lore ; to both for constructive criticism and suggestion. The translator's responsibility for any errors or mistranslations remains undivided.

E. O. L.

TABLE OF CONTENTS

TABLE OF CONTENTS

LIST OF MAPS

xix

CHRONOLOGICAL TABLE

1190. Death of Barbarossa
Emperor Henry VI

1194. December 26th.   Frederick II born in Jesi

1197. September 28th.   Death of Henry VI

1198. Innocent III becomes Pope
Welf-Hohenstaufen rivalries

1198. May.   Frederick II crowned in Palermo as King of
Sicily

1198. November 28th.   Death of the Empress Constance
Innocent III Regent of Sicily and Guardian of
Frederick II

1201. Markward of Anweiler ruling in Palermo

1204. Conquest of Constantinople by the Crusaders

1208. June 21st.   Murder of King Philip of Swabia
December 26th.   Frederick II comes of age

1209. Marriage with Constance of Aragon
Otto IV crowned Emperor in Rome

1210-11. Otto IV in the Kingdom of Sicily

1211. Frederick II elected German Emperor

1212. Arrival in Constance of the Puer Apuliae

1215. Coronation in Aix
Takes the Cross
Fourth Lateran Council

1216. July 16th.   Pope Innocent III dies at Perugia
Honorius III as Pope

1218. Death of Otto IV

1220. Diet at Frankfurt
Henry (VII) elected King of the Romans
Frederick crowned Emperor in Rome
Diet of Capua

1221-23. Subjugation of Sicily

1224. Foundation of the University of Naples

1225. Crusade Negotiations with the Curia
Treaty of San Germano
Marriage with Isabella of Jerusalem

1226. Diet of Cremona
Renewal of the League of Lombardy
Order of Teutonic Knights
Death of Francis of Assisi

1227. Death of Honorius
Pope Gregory IX
Preparations for Crusade
Plague in Brindisi
First Excommunication of Frederick II

1229. March. Coronation in Jerusalem
Return to Sicily
Rout of Papal Troops

1230. Peace with the Curia

1231. Constitutions of Melfi
Augustales
Development of the Sicilian Monarchy

1232. Visit to Venice
Diet of Friuli
King Henry VII

1233. Penance Movement in Italy

1235. King Henry's Rebellion
Frederick's March to Germany
Court of Justice at Worms
Marriage with Isabella of England
Diet of Mainz

1236. Obsequies of St. Elizabeth
First Lombard Campaign
Conquest of Vicenza
Campaign against Austria
Winter Camp at Vienna
Conrad IV elected King of the Romans

1237. Second Lombard Campaign
Cortenuova
Triumph in Cremona and Rome

1238. Third Lombard Campaign
Siege of Brescia
Marriage of Enzio

1239. Camp at Padua
Excommunication
Fourth Lombard Campaign
Reorganisation of Sicily
Foundation of the Italian State
Invasion of the Patrimonium

1240. March on Rome
Return to Sicily
Campaign in the Romagna
Capture of Ravenna
Siege of Faënza

1241. Capture of Faënza
Victory at Sea
Capture of the Prelates
Tartar Invasion of Silesia
New Campaign against Rome
Death of Gregory IX

1241-43. Papal Chair vacant

1243. Innocent IV as Pope
Negotiations for Peace
Defection of Viterbo

1244. Peace with the Curia
Flight of Pope to Lyons

1245. Council of Lyons
Deposition of Frederick II

1246. Camp at Grosseto
Conspiracy
Campaign in the Kingdom of Sicily
Henry Raspe Anti-King in Germany

1247. Re-organisation of Italian State
March on Lyons
Defection of Parma
Rise of Guelf Party in Italy
Parma besieged
Building of Victoria

1248. Defeat of Parma

1249. Arrest of Piero della Vigna
Doctor's attempt to poison Frederick
King Enzio taken Prisoner

1249-50. Crusade of Saint Louis

1250. December 13th. Death of Frederick II at Florentino

1265. May 8th. Birth of Dante

1266. King Manfred killed at Benevento

1268. Execution of Conradin

1272. Death of King Enzio

SUMMARY OF SOURCES

(The actual documents and references to the sources on which this book is based form a second volume of the German edition, which has just been published by Georg Bondi, Berlin. These *pièces justificatives* will no doubt be consulted in the original tongues by serious students of the subject. In the meantime Professor Kantorowicz has kindly written for the English edition the following note as a guide to the general reader.)

THE most important sources for the history of Frederick II are the *Regesta imperii*, vol. v: *Die Regesten des Kaiserreichs unter Philipp, Otto IV, Friedrich II, Heinrich (VII), Conrad IV, Heinrich Raspe, Wilhelm und Richard*, 1198-1272, edited by Boehmer, Ficker and Winkelmann (Innsbruck, 1881-1901). Letters and documents have been collected by Huillard-Bréholles in *Historia diplomatica Friderici secundi* (Paris, 1852-61). Constitutional documents, edicts, etc., relating to the Empire are to be found in the *Monumenta Germaniae Historica : Constitutiones et acta publica imperatorum et regum*, Tom. II (1198-1272), ed. L. Weiland (Hanover, 1896). The Letters of Petrus de Vinea were last edited by Iselin (Basle, 1740); there is no more modern edition. Further documents and letters will be found in J. F. Boehmer's *Acta imperii selecta* (Innsbruck, 1870); Julius Ficker's *Forschungen zur Reichs- und Rechtsgeschichte Italiens* (Innsbruck, 1874); E. Winkelmann's *Acta imperii inedita saeculi XIII* (Innsbruck, 1880-85); and also in Italian and German periodicals, especially in *Quellen und Forschungen aus italienischen Archiven und Bibliotheken*, published by the Preussische Historische Institut in Rome (Rome, 1898 ff.). Karl Hampe has printed a large number of important letters; the publications in which these have appeared are enumerated in *Quellen und Forschungen aus italienischen Archiven*, etc., vol. xx, p. 40.

The authoritative edition of the Emperor's Sicilian laws is that of C. Carcani : *Constitutiones regum regni utriusque Siciliae, mandante Friderico II imperatore* (Naples, 1786); the Greek translation and the fragment of the Register of 1239-40 will be found in the same place. The edition by Antonius Cervonius : *Constitutionum regni Siciliarum libri III* (Naples, 1773) is also useful on account of containing the Glosses. The Laws in chronological order will be found in Huillard-Bréholles, *op. cit.*, vol. iv, pp. 1 ff. The courtiers' letters are in an appendix to Huillard-Bréholles : *Vie et correspondance de Pierre de la Vigne*(Paris, 1865).

The number of chronicles and annals relating to the period of Frederick II is extraordinarily large ; an excellent summary of them will be found in the *Regesta imperii*, vol. v, 9, pp. lxxxvii ff. The important biography of Frederick II by Bishop Mainardinus of Imola has unfortunately perished ; it has been as far as possible reconstructed from surviving fragments by F. Gueterbock in *Neues Archiv*, vol. xxx (1905), pp. 35-83. The most outstanding Italian chroniclers are : Richard of San Germano, edited by A. Gaudenzi in *Monumenti storici, serie prima* : *Cronache* (Naples, 1888) ; the Guelf and Ghibelline *Annals of Piacenza* in the *Monum. Germ. Histor.* : *Scriptores*, vol. xviii, a volume which also contains the important *Annales Januenses* ; the Chronicle of Rolandin of Padua, *ibid.*, vol. xix, and the Chronicle of Fra Salimbene of Parma, *ibid.*, vol. xxxii. The most important German chroniclers are : *Burchardi Praepositi Urspergensis Chronicon*, ed. Holder Egger and B. v. Simson in *Scriptores rerum Germanicarum* (Hanover, 1916), and the *Chronica regia Coloniensis*, ed. G. Waitz, in *Scriptores rerum Germanicarum* (Hanover, 1880). A further main source is Roger of Wendover, *Flores historiarum*, ed. Coxe (London, 1841), and Matthew Paris, *Historia maior*, ed. Luard (London, 1872 ff.). Both of these are Englishmen. The Arabic sources have been edited and translated into Italian by Michele Amari, *Bibliotheca arabo-sicula* (Turin-Rome, 1880 ff.). The most important of the papal letters have been printed in *Monum. Germ. Histor.* : *Epistolae saeculi XIII e regestis pontificum Romanorum selectae*, ed. C. Rodenberg (Berlin, 1883 ff.).

Among secondary authorities Schirrmacher's *Kaiser Friedrich der Zweite* (Göttingen, 1859-65) is superseded by E. Winkelmann : *Jahrbücher der deutschen Geschichte, Philipp von Schwaben und Otto von Braunschweig*, 2 vols. (Leipzig, 1873-78), and *Kaiser Friedrich II*, 2 vols. (Leipzig, 1889-97), which, however, only extends to the year 1233. A concise and more recent account is given by Karl Hampe's *Deutsche Kaisergeschichte in der Zeit der Salier und Staufer*. Other attempts to give a complete portrait are : Wolfram von den Steinen's *Das Kaisertum Friedrichs II nach den Anschauungen seiner Staatsbriefe* (Berlin-Leipzig, 1922) ; Antonio de Stefano : *L'idea imperiale di Federico II* (Florence, 1927) ; further, Otto Vehse : *Die amtliche Propaganda in der Staatskunst Kaiser Friedrichs II* (Munich, 1929). A number of single questions relating to the history of the Emperor have been handled in smaller monographs in the *Heidelberger Abhandlungen zur mittleren und neueren Geschichte* (Heidelberg) for the medieval section of which Karl Hampe is the editor. The two following books are indispensable for a study of the culture and intellectual life at the court of Frederick II : Hans Niese's *Zur*

Geschichte des geistigen Lebens am Hofe Kaiser Friedrichs II, Historische Zeitschrift, vol. 108 (1912), pp. 437 ff., and the supremely excellent researches of Charles Homer Haskins, the bulk of which are collected in his *Studies in the History of Medieval Science* (Cambridge, Mass., U.S.A.), 1924.

E. K.

I. FREDERICK'S CHILDHOOD

Prophecies——Birth in Jesi, Dec. 26, 1194——Character of Henry VI——Hohenstaufen conception of Empire——Baptism——Death of Henry VI——Philip of Swabia ; Otto of Brunswick——Sicilian hatred of Germans——Papal policy towards Sicily——Constance's Concordat with Rome ; death, 1198——Innocent : Deliberatio super facto imperii——The Sicilian myth——Markward of Anweiler ; Walter of Palear ; Walter of Brienne——The Saracens of Sicily——Pisa and Genoa——San Germano ——Frederick of age, 1208——Episcopal elections——Wedding with Constance of Aragon, 1209——Death of Aragon knights——Revolt of island barons

I. FREDERICK'S CHILDHOOD

OF all the prophecies in verse foretelling a future Saviour to which the West has given birth, Vergil's Fourth Eclogue is the most famous. Before celebrating in his mighty epic the future of Imperial Rome, the poet painted in this relatively short poem his picture of the future ruler of the world. He lent him all the attributes of the Messiah : as befits a son of the Gods he shall greet Life with a smile, he shall bring peace on earth and the Age of Gold, and shall evoke once more the kingdom of Apollo. The Middle Ages never paused to reflect that Vergil's promises might seem to be fulfilled in Augustus, Emperor of Peace, the poet's patron. To that Christian age such prophetic verses could bear one interpretation only—a miraculous fore-telling of Christ's advent. That they foretold a " Ruler " was no deterrent, for men were wont to praise Christ as " King of the World " and " Emperor of All," and to represent him graphically, in a *mandorla*, throned on clouds, bearing the globe and law book in his hand and on his head the diadem : the stern Ruler of the Cosmos. To the pious mind it was but one miracle the more, that the heathen Vergil, like the prophets of the Ancient Covenant, had known and told the coming of the Redeemer. Thus this short poem, with its miraculous fore-knowledge, earned for Vergil the admiration and reverence of the medieval world. This Vergilian prophecy provided the inspiration both in manner and matter for the song in which the Campanian poet, Peter of Eboli, extravagantly hailed the birth of Henry VI's only son. It is by no means without significance that Vergil thus stands by the cradle of the last and greatest Christian Emperor of the German Roman Imperium.

The learned Peter of Eboli was not the only poet and sooth-sayer who offered his prophetic wares to the new-born child on the day following the Christmas of 1194. Godfrey of Viterbo, the tutor of Henry VI, hailed the boy as the future Saviour foretold of prophets, the time-fulfilling Caesar. Even before the birth Godfrey had in sibylline speech informed his master that the coming son was destined to prove the long-awaited King of all the World, who should unite East and West as the Tiburtine sibyl had foretold. And later the story ran that East and West had cried aloud with joy at the birth of the imperial heir. Meanwhile other and less flattering predictions gained currency which had likewise accompanied the birth of the youngest Hohenstaufen. The Breton wizard Merlin was said to have spoken of the child's " wondrous and unhoped for birth " and in dark mysterious words to have hinted at disaster. The child would be a lamb, to be torn in pieces, but not to be devoured ; he was to be a raging lion too amongst his own. The Calabrian Cistercian, the Abbot Joachim of Flora, the " Fore-runner " of St. Francis, was swift to recognise in the new-born child the future Scourge of the World, the Anti-Christ who was to bring confusion in his train. The Abbot, indeed, full of prophetic fire, was said to have informed the Emperor betimes that the Empress—overlain by a demon— was pregnant, without yet knowing of her pregnancy. The Empress too had had a dream and it had been revealed to her that she was to bear the fiery brand, the torch of Italy.

Constance obsessed the imagination of her contemporaries as few empresses have done. The strangely-secluded girlhood of the heiress of Sicily, posthumous daughter of the gifted Norman king and state-maker, Roger II, the great blond-bearded Viking : her belated marriage, when she was already over thirty, with Barbarossa's younger son, her junior by ten years : her nine years of childlessness : the unexpected con-ception by the ageing woman : all this was—or seemed— mysterious enough to the people of her time to furnish ample material for legend. According to current rumour Constance's mother, Beatrice, daughter of Count Gunther of Rethel, had been a prey to evil dreams when, after the death of King Roger, she was brought to bed of the future Empress. And the augurs of the half-oriental Norman court declared that Con-stance would bring dire ruin on her fatherland. To avert this evil fate, no doubt, Constance was at once doomed to be a nun. The fact that the princess actually spent long periods in various nunneries in Palermo may well have strengthened such a report. The story further ran that Constance had been most unwilling to marry at all, and this coloured Dante's conception of her : because she left her " pleasant cloister's pale " under pressure and against her will, he gave the Empress a place in Paradise. The tale that Constance had taken the veil was widely believed, and later deliberately circulated by the Guelfs out of malice towards her son. The similar super-stition of a later day foretold that a nun should be the mother of Anti-Christ. Meantime this first and only pregnancy of the forty-year old empress gave rise to another cycle of legend. It became the fashion to represent Constance as being consider-ably older than she was, in order to approximate the miracle of this belated conception to Bible precedent, and she is tradition-ally depicted as a wrinkled old woman. The rumour that the child was supposititious was bound to follow, and it was given out that he was in reality the son of a butcher. Shrewd woman that she was, Constance had taken measures to forestall such gossip : she had had a tent erected in the open market-place, and there in the sight of all she had borne her son and proudly displayed her well-filled breasts—so the counter-rumour ran.

Not in Palermo, but in Jesi, a small town dating from Roman times, in the March near Ancona, Constance brought her son to birth. After he was Emperor, Frederick sang the praises of his birthplace in a remarkable document. He called Jesi his Bethlehem, and the Divine Mother who bore him he placed on the same plane as the Mother of our Lord. Now the Ancona neighbourhood with its landscapes belongs to the most sacred regions of Renaissance Italy. As soon as the Italian people awoke to self-consciousness it recognised this as a *sancta regio* and consecrated it as such. From 1294—a hundred years after the birth of the Staufen boy—the Virgin's house from Nazareth stood in the Ancona Marches, and Loreto, where it eventually came to rest, became one of the most famous places of pilgrimage in Italy. So it need cause no surprise that the March—the home moreover of Raphael—supplies the actual landscape basis (so far as a mythical landscape has a real prototype) for innumerable pictures of the Madonna playing with the Holy Child.

These sunlit scenes played no part in the actual childhood of the boy. A few months after his birth Constance had the " blessed son "—to whom for the moment she gave the name of Constantine—removed to Foligno near Assisi and placed in the care of the Duchess of Spoleto, while the Empress herself hastened back to her Sicilian kingdom. She had only stayed in Jesi for her confinement, while the Emperor Henry travelled south to repress a Sicilian insurrection. This he accomplished with severity and bloodshed, and at last, after years of toil and fighting, he took possession of the hereditary country of his consort. All that Barbarossa had once dreamed, and had hoped to achieve through the Sicilian marriage of his son : to checkmate the exasperating Normans who always sided with the enemies of the Empire ; to secure in the extreme south a firm fulcrum for the Empire of the Hohenstaufen, corresponding to their stronghold north of the Alps, and from these two bases —independent of the favour or disfavour of the German princes—to supervise and hold in check the Patrimonium between, and the ever-restive Italy : all this had reached fulfilment one day before the heir to this imperial power was born. Escorted by Saracen trumpeters, Henry with unexampled pomp entered as victor into the conquered city of Palermo, the terrified populace falling on their knees as he rode by, and on Christmas Day 1194 he was crowned King of Sicily in the cathedral of the capital. He was soon able to announce in one and the same letter both the victorious outcome of his campaigns and the birth of his son and heir. The assurance of the succession gave full value to the conquest of the southern kingdom, a hereditary not an elective monarchy, and to the other great achievements of the indefatigable Emperor.

Henry's rule over the Roman Empire lasted but six years. But this short space sufficed him to crush the world into the dust before his throne. If, like his son, he had possessed the skill to read the stars, and had learned from them how short a span was accorded for the fulfilment of his gigantic task, he could scarcely have economised his time more drastically than he did without this foreknowledge. He recognised no values but the concrete and the practical ; he allowed no scruple to stem his progress ; when state policy was at stake all conventions were but will-o'-the-wisps. The sober statesmanlike genius that reveals itself in this he shared with the other Hohenstaufens, but he lacked many another quality of that favoured house : he had nothing of the genial *bonhomie* of his family, nothing of their gracious exterior. His body was gaunt and frail, his sombre countenance, dominated by the mighty brow, was unvaryingly stern. His face was pale, his beard was scant. No man saw him laugh. His personality completely lacked the amiability and compelling charm of Barbarossa. He had a gloomy autocratic way with him ; in later days he might almost have been of stone. His policy was ambitious and all-embracing, but hard and uninspired. Hardness was indeed the keynote of his being, a hardness as of granite, and with it a reserve rare in a German. Add to this a mighty will, a passion immensely strong but cold as ice, an amazing shrewdness and political acumen. There was a remarkable absence of youthfulness in all these qualities, and indeed it is easy to forget that with his thirty-second year Henry's career had run its course.

In addition to the Empire itself, Barbarossa had bequeathed to his son the sum total of imperial claims and demands which were his by Roman Law : the theory that the whole circuit of the world was by right under the tutelage of the Roman Imperator. And the task now fell to Henry to make good these claims. He had none of Barbarossa's devouring fire or infectious enthusiasm and none of his ingenuous naïveté—Barbarossa for instance had once commanded the Sultans to place their lands under his rule as heir of the Augusti, because these eastern territories had of old been conquered by the generals of his Caesar ancestors. Henry possessed, however, one quality most essentially Roman : a boundless, sober common sense. He was skilful in turning to account for his own success as a world-conqueror the enthusiasm kindled by his father. " As the sun outshines in greatness and in glory all the massed stars of Heaven, so the Roman Empire is lofty above the other kingdoms of the world. Sole overlordship belonged of yore to the Roman Empire, and as the stars receive their light from the

sun, so do the kings receive from the Emperor the right to rule."
Thus wrote not long afterwards the Rhenish Cistercian,
Caesarius of Heisterbach, and many non-Germans would have
agreed with him. The English John of Salisbury, writing in
an almost humanistic atmosphere, dubbed them " petty kings,"
and again Huguccio of Pisa, with his mental background of
Roman law, taught : " there be many provinces in the Roman
Empire, with many kings, but only one Emperor, their suzerain."
Such is the familiar conception of the imperial power held
by the house of Hohenstaufen. As Walther von der Vogelweide phrased it later, " the minor kings surround thee."
The imperial claim could not always be made good in the form
of an immediate, absolute autocracy, but with the aid of feudal
law it could be realised mediately. Within a few years the
West, and not the West alone, had in fact learned to recognise
in Henry VI the highest feudal lord. Even before the death of
Barbarossa Henry had laid claim to Denmark and the Polish
East ; England had become a tributary vassal state—the capture
of Richard Cœur de Lion was a master stroke of Henry's
calculating statesmanship. He claimed further, through
Cœur de Lion, to be acknowledged as overlord by Philip
Augustus of France : for the great English possessions, from
Normandy to the borders of Navarre, were French fiefs. France
was to be compelled to take the oath of fealty, and Richard of
England was commissioned, as any subordinate general might
have been, to make war on France in the Emperor's name, and
to conclude peace only with the Emperor's permission. The
Emperor's pretensions extended to the kingdom of Burgundy,
which, since Barbarossa's marriage to Beatrice, had once more
reverted to the Empire. He even claimed Castile and asserted
rights in Aragon which he looked to the Genoese to uphold for
him. Italy as a whole was in his hand. The Italian islands
belonged to the Empire, the Lombard states scarcely ventured to
resist, and the Pope—in no wise a match for the imperial power
—was restricted to a patch of the Campagna : " where none
the less men feared the Emperor rather than the Priest." The
entire Patrimonium, Spoleto, the March, Tuscany, were in his
possession. Rome accepted her Prefect from the Emperor's
hand, and the whole side of the city lying on the right bank of

the Tiber was incorporated in Tuscany. Once Sicily had been conquered, therefore—an undertaking that for many years taxed all the Emperor's strength—the whole of Italy was united under a single all-powerful monarch.

With the possession of Sicily a new world opened to Henry : from the pillars of Hercules to the Hellespont the whole basin of the Mediterranean lay within the radius of his power. He conceived himself the heir of the Normans, not alone of the royal citadel, of Palermo and of the royal dignities, but also of their rights and claims. Since the days of Roger II the Normans had styled themselves " Kings of Africa," and the Muslim princes, from Morocco to Tripoli, were now compelled to render to the German Emperor—the new Lord of Sicily— the tribute heretofore paid to their Norman masters. The Sultan of the Almohades did not hesitate long about paying tribute, for he saw his Balearic islands threatened after the fall of Sicily. Henry VI further considered himself the heir of the campaigns of Robert Guiscard and his followers against the Eastern Empire. The vivid German picture of one universal Roman World would have been far from realisation if Henry had tolerated the existence of the Greek Emperor by his side : the ring round the Mediterranean would not have been complete without Byzantium. Henry VI was able to back his claims by various legal titles, and where these failed the fear of his power was by itself enough to make the powerless Greeks speedily complacent. As heir of the Normans he demanded all the territory from Epidaurus to Thessalonica, and through his ambassador he inexorably exacted tribute, followers, and ships from the anaemic usurper, Alexius III. " As if he were Lord of Lords and King of Kings " he conducted his business with Byzantium. To raise the tribute-money Alexius was driven to institute a " German Tax," and he did not shrink even from opening up the imperial tombs— including that of the great Constantine—and plundering the dead of their ornaments. But all these things were only the preliminaries to the conquest of the East, to which the ambitious schemes of Henry's last years were almost exclusively directed. Some individual Christian princes in the East had voluntarily placed themselves under the protection of the only man who at that time could afford them any : the thirty-year-old Emperor. The king of one of the Crusader states, Bohemund of Antioch, had besought the Emperor to be his feudal lord ; ambassadors from the King of Cilicia had done homage to Henry and begged him to grant their master as his vassal the crown and title of " King of the Armenians," exchanging thus their old feudal allegiance to the Eastern Emperor for allegiance to the new world-ruler of the West. The messengers of King Amaury of Cyprus penetrated as far north as Worms to ask that their master should be feudally invested with his kingdom and his crown at Henry's hands. Meantime Henry was now planning a Crusade which was finally to unlock the East and make it subject to him. All preparations were made with the greatest care. The Pope, the octogenarian Celestine III, suspected no doubt the real intention of this Holy War, but as spiritual overlord of Western Christendom he could not, in those days at any rate, take up any but a benevolent and helpful attitude towards such an undertaking. Against his will he was harnessed to the imperial plans and was able successfully to oppose the Hohenstaufen will in one particular only.

Henry VI was well aware that his giant empire lacked organic unity, for each of the component countries stood in a different relation to the Emperor : Germany was an elective monarchy ; Sicily a hereditary one ; and the other countries were feudal dependencies, many of them mediate. He did his utmost to pull the whole together and give it a certain stamp of uniformity. When his son was born he thought the time had come. He sought to win over the German princes to his schemes by offering to the temporal princes the promise of a hereditary succession, and to the spiritual ones free testamentary powers. He hoped thus to transmute the German Elective Kingdom into a Hereditary Roman Empire. To achieve this end he was prepared to incorporate in the Empire his own personal hereditary kingdom of Sicily. The German princes declared themselves in favour of these proposals : all except the Archbishop of Cologne and a small following. In order to overcome the last remnants of opposition the Emperor betook himself to Rome. His idea probably was to induce the Pope, in defiance of any protest by the princes, to crown his infant son as Roman Emperor and Co-Caesar. The Pope declined, and Henry had no alternative but to do, as others before him had done : to get his son chosen by the German princes as their future king and thus to safeguard the Empire for the house of Hohenstaufen.

Henry had only twice, quite briefly, seen the heir of his immense empire : once in Foligno shortly after his birth, and once when he (probably) attended his son's belated baptism. The boy had been originally called Constantine by his mother (no doubt in allusion to her own name, Constance, for she liked to think of him as his mother's son and heir) and the German princes had chosen him in Frankfurt for their king under this foreign-sounding cognomen. When it came to the baptism, however, which ultimately took place in the presence of many cardinals and bishops—though not, as Henry had desired, of the Pope—the child was given the names of Frederick Roger after his two grandfathers : whom in truth he was to resemble rather than his parents. These names had been first suggested in a poem by Peter of Eboli, and it was not unnatural to prophesy a future of immense and almost god-like power for the grandson of these two mighty princes and the son of Henry VI. All the poets and wise men who had stood by the cradle of the boy had shown themselves at one in this anticipation : whether they were rejoicing, as friends of the Empire ; or, as partisans of the Pope, were trembling for the fate of the Roman Church. Before long, however, it looked as if all the prophets were at fault.

King Henry was spending the summer of 1197 in Sicily. That spring he had discovered a conspiracy of the Sicilian nobility directed against his life and he had escaped only by the skin of his teeth. People said that both Pope Celestine and the Empress Constance had had a hand in the plot, and there is nothing to render this improbable. The Emperor had the captured ringleaders done to death with the most cruel tortures, and he compelled his wife to be present at the ghastly execution of her guilty countrymen, while the court jesters played their grisly pranks with the still quivering bodies. Soon after this the Crusade was under weigh. The great majority of the Crusaders had sailed across to the Holy Land

from Sicily during the course of the summer, and it seemed
not impossible that the Emperor himself would bear a part in
the crusade, but he thought it wise to await developments, and
with a few companions he remained behind in Sicily. He did
not even see the Promised Land from afar as Barbarossa had
done. During a hunting expedition he fell ill of dysentery—
as northerners are apt to do in the dangerous summer climate
of Sicily. Within a few weeks, after an initial improvement,
he quite unexpectedly succumbed in Messina in September
1197. A chronicler announces with pride': " Henry showed
the world the superiority of the Germans, and they inspired
terror in all adjacent peoples by their valour." With Henry's
death all this was at once a thing of the past. German world-
rule and world-greatness, resting on the qualities of a single
man and not upon the people, was fated to crumble in a
moment.

Henry had been well aware of the danger threatening the
Empire : of that his last will and testament is overwhelming
proof. It recommends surrender on all sides and the renunciation of even valid claims. In the Empire itself it was all too
well known what Henry's death at this inopportune moment must
mean : his work was still incomplete, his successor a three-year
old child. The parties of reaction, which had hitherto been
prevented by the Emperor's power and rapidity of action, now
prepared for the inevitable counter-blow. It would have been
bound to come even if Henry had lived ; but now that the
only person competent to oppose them was dead, the forces
of opposition, Princes and Pope, hurled themselves into a
vacuum, in which they could unhindered work their devastating will. Some weeks before the Emperor's death, Philip of
Swabia and Otto of Brunswick, the one a Staufen and the other
a Welf,[1] had become kings in Germany, while at the same
moment Innocent III—in his own way the greatest and most
successful of all the Popes—mounted the throne of St. Peter,
as the true heir of world-wide empire. During these days some
people on the Moselle were terrified by an apparition : they had

---

[1] The German feud of Welf v. Waibling crossed the Alps and lay beneath
the Italian struggle of Guelf and Ghibelline, which Italianised forms are
more familiar to some.—Tr.

seen Dietrich of Bern, mounted on his immense black war-
horse, coming to foretell mourning and disaster to the Roman
empire.

While these events were happening the three-year old son
of the Emperor Henry was still in Foligno. Philip of Swabia,
the Emperor's brother, was to have fetched the boy thence and
escorted him to Germany for his coronation. But when Philip
had got as far as Montefiascone near Viterbo he received the
news of the emperor's death. The immediate revolt of all
Italy against imperial authority, and more particularly against
the hated Germans, compelled him to return at full speed
across the Alps, leaving his mission unfulfilled. He had
difficulty in hewing his way through to Germany. The few
days' delay which prevented the completion of the task that the
Emperor had entrusted to him was destined to be of fateful
consequence to the whole future of Frederick II. Firstly,
because he thus remained in Italy and grew up in the southern
kingdom of his mother, instead of in his father's Swabian home.
Secondly—and this was more serious—he thus forfeited,
through his absence from Germany, the German crown to
which he had already been elected. Quite apart from these
events in the north, and their consequences, Frederick's own
mother did her best to baulk her son of the German throne.

Soon after the death of the Emperor Henry, Constance had
the child fetched from Foligno by an Apulian count and
brought to Sicily. Dressed in widow's weeds she awaited
her son in Palermo. There were grave accusatory rumours
against the Empress current at the time : some said she had
poisoned her husband, and it was a matter of common knowledge that she had no love for Germans. The suspicion
of murder was unjust, but the hatred for Germans ascribed
to her was genuine enough ; she shared it with her Sicilian
fellow-countrymen and with the Italians oppressed by the
Roman Curia. The foundations of this hate were the same
then as they have always been : the arrogance " allied with
unwisdom " of the Germans alienated the Mediterranean
peoples, as did their " obstinacy and self-assertiveness."

Their physical strength and their savagery moreover terrified the Southerners, the discords prevailing amongst themselves brought them scorn and contempt. For rulers of the world they appeared " crude, coarse and uncivilised," while their yet unpolished language seemed to the Romans " like the barking of dogs and the croaking of frogs." But the main factor in this hate was fear : fear of the inrush " of the winter and the storm into the rose-gardens of Sicily." This fear was not allayed by the savagely cruel treatment meted out to the Sicilians by Henry VI. Perhaps Innocent with his biblical phraseology hit on the right description of the German visitation of those days when he wrote : " Because the people of Sicily and the other inhabitants of this kingdom have grown effeminate in sloth, and undisciplined through too much peace, and, boasting themselves of their wealth, have given themselves over to the unbridled lusts of the body, their stink has gone up to heaven and the multitude of their sins has delivered them into the hands of the oppressor."

Innocent spoke thus out of no friendliness to the Germans. The hate of Germans that flamed up throughout Italy on the death of the Emperor had been carefully nurtured beforehand by the Curia, had been given the air of a national pan-Italian movement and utilised as a means to shake off the imperial yoke in the south in favour of a papal Italy. In resonant periods Innocent III had taken pains to stir up and foster this hate : " The wrath of the North wind whistles through the mountains with a new quaking of the earth, it drives through the level plains of Apulia, whirling dust into the eyes of wanderers and country-dwellers." Thus he wrote about the German, Henry VI, whom Dante also designated " that loud blast which blew the second over Swabia's realm."

A reaction of this sort against the tyranny of Henry VI was of course inevitable. The importance of the movement in Sicily was enhanced by the fact that the Empress Constance took part in it. Her motives were probably personal, for Henry had made a terrific clearance amongst all related to the old Norman royal house and had banished the survivors to Germany. On his death Constance immediately resumed the sovereignty of her hereditary domain, in accordance both with the

Emperor's instructions and with the right she herself possessed
as Norman Queen. But the new ruler of Sicily was Norman
Queen only : not widowed Empress ; and the first act of her
reign was to banish from her kingdom the Emperor's interpreter, Markward of Anweiler, and with him all other German
notables, a considerable number of whom held fief and office
in the Norman territory. The pretext was that they might
prove dangerous to the peace and quiet of the kingdom,
especially Markward, who had not been slow to propose
himself as vicegerent. Her next step was to imprison the
Sicilian Chancellor, Walter of Palear, Bishop of Troia, who had
been from of old an opponent of the Norman dynasty and a
willing tool of the German Emperor. The intervention of the
Pope was necessary to effect the liberation of the Bishop-
Chancellor and his re-instatement in his former offices. Anti-
German feeling in the south was so acute that the first German
crusaders who were returning, all unsuspecting, from the Holy
Land were surprised and plundered by the excited Sicilians,
and after that the home-coming pilgrims had to avoid the harbours of this dangerously inhospitable kingdom. Curiously,
the German princes who were on the Crusade, when they
received in Acre the news of their Emperor's death, reconfirmed
the choice of Frederick as King of the Romans.

Constance, however, deliberately shut her eyes to all this.
Her hate of Germany reinforced the maternal anxiety which
heroes' mothers are wont to suffer from : in the German crown
she saw a never-ending series of future perils and struggles for
her son. She would as far as possible ward off such a danger
from him. Frederick should be king of the wealthy Sicily,
and in the southern Land of Dreams he would quietly forget the
imperial dignity of his fathers. A few months after the boy's
arrival in Palermo she had him crowned King of Sicily. The
solemn rite was celebrated on Whit Sunday 1198, with a pomp
and ceremony borrowed from the Byzantine court, while in
accordance with ancient custom the people greeted their newly-
crowned king with the cry—which may still be read on every
crucifix in southern Italy—" Christus vincit, Christus regnat,
Christus imperat." It is significant to note that this is also
the motto engraved on Frederick's early seals. From that day

Constance omitted from all official documents of the young king the title that had previously figured there : Rex Romanorum. From henceforth Frederick of Hohenstaufen was to content himself with the many titles borne by the *reges felices* of Norman stock. He was to be, body and soul, the son of the Sicilian Constance only, and to be kept aloof from all the fatal, unknown consequences in which the dangerous Hohenstaufen blood of his father might involve him. One is reminded of the childhood of Achilles or of Parzival.

The plans of the Roman Curia re-inforced in many points the wishes of the Empress. They shared a strong aversion from the Germans, they shared the desire to strengthen Frederick in his hereditary possessions, and to confine him strictly to them. Sicily was a fief of the Roman Church, and the Pope was unfeignedly delighted to see a four-year old king on the throne and the kingdom thrown open to papal influence for years to come. It was a matter of life and death to the Church that the imperial throne should be withheld from the boy. When the empire and Sicily were united in one hand the States of the Church were surrounded on every side by the imperial territories, and after its recent experiences under Henry VI the Papal Curia had no wish to be again exposed to this intolerable constriction. This was the only consideration that weighed with the Pope in formulating his imperial policy. Hence, in defiance of right and justice, Innocent III supported the Welf pretender against Philip of Swabia, so as to avoid the threatened union of the Empire and the Sicilian Kingdom under any Hohenstaufen.

Constance was in sore need of the Pope's support, so it was well that her wishes in regard to Frederick were in unison with his. Largely thanks to Constance's anti-German attitude, the Kingdom of Sicily had soon fallen into a state of chaos. Henry VI's partisans, more especially the Germans, who would in other circumstances have stood by her, were the most embittered and dangerous enemies of the Empress and her son. She was powerless to enforce her decree of banishment against them, and for ten years they successfully defied it and brought down endless wars upon the country. The Pope was the only friend whose alliance could help the Empress, and Innocent III sold his friendship dear enough. Constance was obliged to seek as a favour from the Curia what the Emperor Henry had always refused, and to implore the Pope to become the feudal overlord of Sicily. Before this feudal protection was accorded her she had to accept a Concordat which put an end to the unique independence of the Sicilian Church and most of the ecclesiastical privileges of the Sicilian kings. Constance did her best to stand out, but she found she had no option but to comply, and ere long a further step was necessary : a year after Henry's death she herself lay dying, and in her will she appointed the Pope regent of the kingdom and guardian of her son. Innocent was to be reimbursed for all expenses, and in addition to receive annually the sum of 30,000 tarens.[1] Constance thought she had thus put her son under good protection. She handed over the immediate care of Frederick and the kingdom to the royal party, the " Household Officers " of the old Norman officialdom, which at the time of her death consisted of four archbishops, with Walter of Palear, Bishop of Troia, at their head as Chancellor. On his mother's death in November 1198 Henry's son became therefore a ward of the Pope and of the Church, and the Sicilian kingdom fell into the care of bishops. For the time being Frederick's German crown was lost.

The Sicilian scion of the Hohenstaufen was soon forgotten in Germany in the midst of the rival pretensions of Welf and Staufen to the throne, of battles, disturbances and wild happenings. At first his name used to crop up occasionally when someone happened to remember that beside the two would-be kings, Philip the Swabian and Otto the Welf, there was a third pretender whose claim to the imperial crown might carry weight : the boy whose home was in the far-off south. On the whole, however, the friends of the Hohenstaufens, who might perhaps have espoused the cause of Frederick, simply drifted into the ranks of his uncle, Philip of Swabia. Philip was at first prepared, as " according to law and nature it was

---

[1] The taren was the gold coin current at the time in Sicily. 30 tarens = 1 gold ounce ; 1 taren = 20 grains. Tarens were minted in the royal mints of Messina, Brindisi and Naples.—*Tr.*

seemly," to undertake the direction of the Empire only as regent in the name and during the minority of his young nephew. But at such a critical moment the German princes wanted a man, not a child, on the throne, and they almost unanimously repudiated their choice of a short year before. The Archbishop, Adolf of Cologne, moreover, put himself at the head of an opposition hostile to the Staufens. In these circumstances Philip after some hesitation yielded to the pressure of his adherents and declared himself willing to wear the crown and thus secure it at least for his house. Walther von der Vogelweide was present at the coronation in Magdeburg, and records how he saw the " sweet young man," as that handsome and luckless prince proceeded " under the crown " to the Cathedral, accompanied by the no less beautiful and no less unfortunate Irene, his queen and well-beloved consort. The poet sings with what grace and dignity the prince wore the golden circlet :

> With measured step and kingly grace he came,
> Behind him moved his high-born dame :
> Rose without thorn, dove without gall was she. . . .

The many and varied endowments of the Hohenstaufen family had been divided in curiously contrasting fashion between the brothers Henry VI and Philip of Swabia. The former embodied all their stern severity and autocratic strength, the latter all their graciousness and generosity. In contrast to the rest of his house Philip united his attractive qualities to a perfectly genuine piety. He had indeed been originally destined for the Church, and might often be found sitting among the choir boys singing the Hours and the Responsories. No milder, gentler prince had ever swayed the sceptre of Germany's destinies ; he was too gentle and too mild for such a time. During Philip's joint rule of ten years he was never once able to lay down his arms. This man who was born for times of peace was fated to undertake campaign after campaign. Immediately after his election the Rhenish party of opposition, led by Otto of Brunswick, became active and secured the support of the Papal Curia, which most unjustly sided against Philip and excommunicated him.

This is not the place to pursue in detail the feuds of Welf and Waibling. After Innocent III, in his pettifogging *Deliberatio super facto imperii*, had declared himself against the Hohenstaufens in general and in particular against the Sicilian boy, not even the name of Frederick played any further part in the matter. In skilful special pleading the wily Pope weighs the pros and cons of Frederick's elevation to the Roman Kingship. In the first place, he points out, the claim seems specious enough, for Frederick had been duly elected, and almost all the princes had sworn loyalty to him and many had actually taken the oath of fealty. Nevertheless the election was in fact invalid, because it had taken place on the assumption that Frederick at the time of his accession would be of legal age : but this reasonable anticipation had not been fulfilled. Moreover, at the time when Frederick had been elected he was still unbaptised. He had even been chosen under the Greek name of Constantine. Secondly, the Pope continued, it might well appear unseemly that the Pope should rob his ward of his just dues, instead of being his helpful guardian. But he, Pope Innocent, had been appointed guardian, not to secure the Imperium for Frederick, but to defend his maternal inheritance of Sicily. Finally, he would remind his readers of the warning words of Scripture : " Woe to the land whose king is a child." Having thus disposed of these two possible objections to Frederick's deposition—his due election, and a guardian's duty—Innocent weighs the consequences that would follow the boy's recognition. With extraordinary clearsightedness the Pope foresees the whole trend of his ward's future career. " If once the boy reaches years of understanding and perceives that he has been robbed of his honours as Emperor by the Roman Church, he will assuredly refuse her reverence and will oppose her by every means in his power, he will free Sicily from feudal fetters and deny the wonted homage to Rome." Innocent foresaw precisely what was in fact in store for the Roman Church and yet he chose to act against his knowledge. His arguments were irrefutable, and when he was driven to speak against his own convictions he could only do so at the sacrifice of truth. He then proceeded to show that there was nothing to be feared from the boy's vengeance, for it was not

he, the Pope, but Philip of Swabia who had snatched from him
the Empire and the Dukedom of Swabia. Were King Philip
to presume to go further and send his vassals to take Sicily
the Church would stand by her ward with all her powers.

This decision of the Pope quashed all conceivable German
support of Frederick's claims : he had vanished from the
political and diplomatic horizon of Germany for many years to
come. For decades past, nay, longer, everything Sicilian had
worn a halo of romance in German eyes, and his German
contemporaries cherished a vision of a fairy prince living in
distant Sicily. Since the wanderings of the old Germanic
peoples Sicily had exercised on the imaginations of men a
peculiar fascination. The further the Northern invaders
penetrated south into regions of ever-increasing wealth and
luxuriance the nearer they seemed to approach the Garden of
Eden : a dream-fulfilment of an Earthly Paradise. The very
beginning of the Germanic epoch had seen the figure of the
lion-like young king, Alaric of the Western Goths, who with
scanty knowledge but the sure instinct of an animal had fought
his way towards the southern Paradise where he was to find his
grave. The end of the same Germanic age provided a fitting
parallel in that young Conrad of Hohenstaufen who lost his
life in Sicily. The fate of the Germans seemed bound up with
the south of Italy. In one way or another almost all the
medieval Emperors had sought to win it, until the luck turned
and Barbarossa's scheming obtained it for his son Henry as
his bride's dower.

The possession of the southern world wrought a fateful
change in Germany herself : for the Crusading Knight the Magic
Hoard had flitted southward from the Rhine to Sicily. And
around the Treasure played the heroic myths of Rome and
Greece—which now began to form a part of German culture—
driving out Burgundian kings and Hunnish warriors. Bishop
Conrad of Hildesheim, who accompanied the Emperor to Sicily
as his chancellor, brought back tales in plenty to tell the Provost
of his church at home about the marvels of Sicily. He had seen
the Fountain of Pegasus, the Home of the Muses, and Naples
was full of the wonders of the magician Vergil who had enclosed
the city in a glass flagon. The Bishop had sailed—not without

anxiety—between Scylla and Charybdis, and in Taormina he had gazed on the house of Daedalus, remembering the fate of Icarus, and the Minotaur born of Pasiphaë. He had seen the Well of Arethusa which first revealed to sorrowing Ceres the rape of Proserpine, he had seen the river Alpheus which rises in Arabia, and Etna he had seen—which he made the occasion of weaving into his narrative the myths of Vulcan, smith to Jupiter, and the legend of the Blessed Agatha. Granted that the learned Bishop saw in his travels nothing that he had not already read in the Roman poets, yet the journey had localised the myths for him and impressed them much more vividly on his mind, especially as he most reverently sought out all the places and marvels of which the poets sang. Proudly he wrote to the Provost : " You do not need to pass the boundaries of our own empire, you do not need to quit the realm of the German people to see all that the poets have spent so much time and art in describing."

Reports like these provided material and colour for German phantasy to paint pictures of the Sicilian kingdom which Wolfram of Eschenbach chose to be the site of his magic castle of Klingsor. And even in the North men could see much with their own eyes : in the year after Frederick's birth and Henry's conquest of Sicily a caravan of 150 mules appeared in Germany laden with gold and silks, gems and precious stones, on its way to the imperial castle of Trifels ; and people heard that this was only a fraction of the riches that the Emperor had plundered from the royal citadel of Palermo. The treasure was far from exhausted. For a messenger of the Empress overtook the Emperor after his return to Germany, announcing that the lost treasure of King Roger had been found. It had been concealed behind a secret door and a woman servant had betrayed the clue.

So the Sicilian kingdom had become to the German mind a distant land of wonders, and Frederick II was living his child-hood in the midst of it. Others had come to know that the wrath of the Sicilians against Henry VI was so fierce that a certain bishop had carried the child off and was bringing him up in secrecy for fear the inhabitants should find and slay him. The child indeed had persecutions and wonderful escapes

enough, and the actual happenings in Palermo in the ancient
royal fortress of Castellamare where Frederick passed his
childhood were more unreal and fantastic than all that legend
could invent.

When the Empress Constance died, the four-year-old boy
Frederick II was left alone in the world without a relation or
real friend of any kind. The few surviving relations on his
mother's side had been banished by Henry VI and were hostile
to the Staufen boy, and the only surviving Hohenstaufen, King
Philip, was so busy fighting in the north that he could do practically nothing for his nephew. Frederick had no lack of nominal
friends, men who without exception exploited the royal name
and dignity for their own ends, first among these Pope
Innocent III, guardian of the King. It cannot be denied that
during the ten years of fighting and confusion in and around
Sicily Innocent spared neither pains nor money to defend his
ward's kingdom. But the papal legates who always accompanied troops sent to Sicily were despatched to protect rather
the Papal feudal state than the interests of the boy king.
Innocent's decision in the matter of the German succession,
and his attitude to the French count Walter of Brienne, showed
clearly how much less the fate of his ward weighed with him
than his own far-reaching intrigues. This Count Walter was
the son-in-law of the illegitimate Tancred, the last of the
Norman kings, and he soon put in an appearance to claim
the provinces of Lecce and Taranto. A really conscientious
guardian would have considered it too risky to permit the return
to Sicily of any member of the exiled Norman dynasty, yet
Innocent, without any overwhelming necessity, decided the
feudal questions in the Frenchman's favour, though it is true
he exacted extensive guarantees from Walter for the personal
safety of Frederick. Pope Innocent badly wanted the French
count just then ; the fate of the boy prince was secondary. Not
of course that the Pope would dream of robbing him of his
rights ! But it mattered little whether Frederick II or a scion
of the Norman dynasty ruled in Sicily, provided the danger was
averted of a fusion of Sicily and the Empire, and provided that
Church influence in the kingdom was in no wise curtailed.
Pope Innocent III dealt only in practical politics. Therein

lay his greatness. We can well understand that Frederick II in later days thought of his papal guardian with wrath and bitterness, though in fact nothing but the Pope's regency had saved the kingdom for him. On the human side Innocent kept entirely aloof from his ward. He kept up an interest in the boy's affairs as far as he could, he sent legates to look after him, felt anxiety for his dangers, praised his progress and expressed unfeigned pleasure at his escape from enemy hands, but he saw him for the first and last time when the lad was seventeen, for he had never carried out, or never completely carried out, any of his many projected journeys to Sicily.

The other man to whom Constance had committed her child was the Sicilian chancellor, Walter of Palear. He remained for many years—though sometimes with interruptions of a year or so—in the immediate entourage of the King as head of the household officers and *de facto* Regent of Sicily. But what has been said of the Pope applies even more forcibly to the Chancellor : he also utilised his power for his own ends, with this difference that his ends were not of the same world-shaking quality as the Pope's. His chief preoccupation was to maintain as undisputed as possible his position as sole regent of the kingdom, to retain undivided control of the King's revenues and possessions, and to squander these freely for the benefit of himself, his family and his adherents. Politically he had been a supporter of the Emperor Henry and consequently an opponent of the Norman dynasty, hence the hostility which the Empress had felt for him. In spite of this she retained him as Chancellor from a natural reluctance to feel that so powerful a man was her son's enemy. Walter of Palear remained faithful to his Hohenstaufen allegiance, partly because it seemed useful and partly because any modification of his attitude might have lessened his independence as regent. There is nothing to show that he occupied himself much with the boy, and Frederick's later treatment of him makes this improbable. The most we can say is that he was apparently never actively unfriendly.

Though the Chancellor remained personally a defender of the dynasty of Henry VI, his external politics were extremely adaptable. He had first and foremost to protect the young

King's interests—and his own—against the Germans, whom
Constance had unfortunately banished and converted into
enemies of herself and her son. The Chancellor, as a partisan
of Henry's, might have come to terms with them, but their
leader, Markward of Anweiler, maintained that the Emperor
had appointed him to be Administrator of Sicily. There was,
no doubt, some truth in this contention. He certainly kept in
touch with Philip of Swabia and was presumably often acting
under his instructions. These relations with Philip were
enough to bring down on him the enmity of the Pope, while his
claims to the regency of Sicily earned him the hatred of Walter
of Palear. Pope and Chancellor were not long in taking measures together against Markward and the Germans. Markward
had no use for Frederick II. The " supposititious son " of
Constance—as Henry's former interpreter chose to designate
the boy, affecting to give credence to current rumour—stood
in the way of a union between Sicily and the German Imperium
of Philip of Swabia, and all Markward's efforts were directed
to the achievement of this union : as far as he was not merely
pursuing his own private interest. The papal party reported
that he had even attempted the child's life.

The general position of affairs in Sicily was further complicated by the appearance of the aforementioned Walter of
Brienne. The Pope had supported his claims to the duchies
of Lecce and Taranto and forthwith made use of him and his
French knights in the fight against the Germans. The Pope's
support of the son-in-law of the Norman Tancred alienated at
once the Sicilian Chancellor. As the sworn foe of the Norman
dynasty Walter of Palear looked with justifiable misgiving
on the arrival of the French count. On the first convenient
opportunity therefore he left the Pope in the lurch and went
over to the German side. The subterfuges of all parties,
differences of opinion amongst the officers of the household,
treacheries, and the force of arms ultimately resulted in delivering the capital of Palermo with the royal fortress and the royal
child into the hands of Markward of Anweiler, and on his death
into the hands of other faction leaders, his successors, such as
William Capparone and Diepold of Schweinspeunt. Many
years passed before Walter of Palear, having made friends

again with the Pope on the sudden death of the Count of Brienne, was able once more to re-enter Palermo.

It would be a waste of time to enter in detail into the squabbles, intrigues, hostilities and alliances of the ten years' Regency. The tangle is almost inextricable, for behind the four main actors—Pope, Chancellor, Markward and Walter of Brienne—there were innumerable subordinate characters who attached themselves now to this party and now to that, according as they hoped best to promote their own separate interests. First there were the Saracens from the inner highlands of Sicily. As Muslims they had nothing to hope from a papal rule and were therefore hostile to the papal ward. For the most part they leaned to the German side, though the Pope exerted himself to secure their armed assistance. The general anarchy offered a golden opportunity to the hill Saracens to plunder the whole country right up to the walls of the towns—the town Saracens in the main remained neutral—and even to occupy it from time to time. The Barons of the Sicilian mainland [1] formed another group whose alliance was much desired and sought after. Their policy was simple : they had nothing to gain from law and order, so they threw in their lot with whichever party appeared likely to promote the continuance of disorder. The people of Pisa were another factor. They held on principle with the Germans, for it was their established tradition to support the Empire, but on the other hand they had many trade interests in Sicily, and this again roused up the Genoese against them. Ultimately, after many and varied quarrels, the two sea states contrived to establish themselves in every nook and cranny of the Sicilian coast.

Though in his childhood the boy Frederick appeared the mere plaything of those forces which as a man he mastered and directed, he was even then being educated by destiny for the supreme power. In the small island of Sicily all the powers of East and West were represented ; on the island and in Apulia they tossed and tumbled and weltered, at the dictates of the most primitive impulses, surging through and over each other like the waves of primeval chaos : Henry VI's Germans,

---

[1] The non-specialist reader will remember the existence of Two Sicilies (see map inside back cover).—*Tr.*

Brienne's Frenchmen, Sicilians, Apulians, Saracens, Pisans, Genoese—with here and there a papal legate and Italian troops, and finally even Spanish knights superadded. These parties had only one thought in common : to pursue their own most obvious advantage, and to enrich themselves at the expense of the helpless King, who thus became the focus of all their struggles. The goal above all others to aim at was to get possession of the King's person, for this child denoted for the *de facto* victor and ruler the legal basis of his arbitrary power. Much like the royal seal of Sicily Frederick was therefore tossed from hand to hand, a valuable but indifferent piece of property, exploited by each in turn, persecuted by the majority, often in danger of death : " a lamb amongst ravening wolves," as the chronicler has it.

Such was the atmosphere in which Frederick grew up : amid the clash of weapons, sometimes in bodily danger, and for years in actual want. In the early days, as long as Walter of Palear was still at hand, things may have been comparatively bearable, but when Frederick at seven fell into the hands of Markward, with his companions and hangers-on, a wild and dreary time began. The circumstances that accompanied the conquest of the royal fortress and the change of regency were ominous enough. They are full also of significance, for Frederick on this occasion shows himself for the first time as a man— of seven—in action. Markward took possession of the capital in 1201. A treacherous chamberlain betrayed the King's castle, with the King, to the invaders. In this moment of danger the King, with his tutor, William Franciscus, withdrew to the innermost precincts of the palace. Again the guard betrayed the King and revealed his hiding-place. The treachery of the bodyguard and the boy King's helplessness precluded any attempt at defence : Frederick suddenly saw his pursuers enter the room. As they sought to seize him—to fetter him it might be—the young King, in spite of the hopelessness of the struggle, sprang at the intruders, full of loathing at the thought of being touched by dastard hands, and fiercely smote the hand that dared to lay a finger on the Anointed of the Lord. Seeing himself overpowered, he unlaced his royal tunic, rent his clothing wrathfully to ribbons, and with sharp nails tore his flesh : an outburst of childish but profound and savage wrath against the insulters of his royal dignity. Such at least is the interpretation put on this scene by the correspondent who describes it to the Pope ; the writer adds : " a worthy omen for the future ruler who cannot be false to his own nobility, who with royal instinct feels himself, like Mount Sinai, outraged by the touch of a beast of prey."

From this time forward no one in the fortress seems to have bothered his head about the boy. The royal property had been so shockingly squandered that the child was often literally in want of the barest necessaries till the compassionate citizens of Palermo took pity on him and found him food. One fed him for a week, another for a month, each according to his circumstances. He was a handsome boy whose clear bright glance already caused remark, and the people were probably glad to see him amongst them. At eight and nine years old the young King wandered about without let or hindrance, and strolled unchecked through the narrow streets and markets and gardens of the semi-African capital at the foot of the Pellegrino. An amazing variety of peoples, religions and customs jostled each other before his eyes : mosques with their minarets, synagogues with their cupolas stood cheek by jowl with Norman churches and cathedrals, which again had been adorned by Byzantine masters with gold mosaics, their rafters supported by Greek columns on which Saracen craftsmen had carved in Kufic script the name of Allah. Round the town lay the pleasure palaces and fountains of Norman Kings in the exotic gardens and animal preserves of the Conca d'Oro, the delights of which had inspired the Arab poets. In the market-places the people went about their business in many-coloured confusion : Normans and Italians, Saracens, Jews and Greeks. The lively boy was driven back on all these for company and soon learned the customs and the speech of all these tribes and races. Did any wise Imâm play the part of Chiron to the lonely child ? Did some unknown tutor teach the future ruler of men to observe, to know, to use, the forces of Earth and Nature ? We do not know. We are certain only that his education was

unique and radically different from any that ever fell to the lot
of a royal child. Later, men marvelled at his knowledge of
the habits of man and beast and plant as profoundly as they
trembled at his actual approach.

Frederick was not brought up, as his father for instance had
been, by a learned chaplain of the type of Godfrey of Viterbo,
nor reared like many another prince by world-shy monks in
the seclusion of a cloister. Amazed by his comprehensive
knowledge, his astounding exotic erudition, men have sought
diligently to trace the real teacher of this great Hohenstaufen—
research has not revealed his Aristotle. And with reason.
The teacher never existed whom he would not have surpassed
and disillusioned, and the school of a mere fencing-master
would not long have satisfied him. Frederick II is a typically
self-taught man : he had no one to thank for his education :
what he was, he was *suâ virtute*. Quite possibly he learnt the
elements from that Magister William Franciscus who has once
been mentioned in attendance on him as a seven-year-old child,
and is on record as still with him in 1208. Quite possibly one or
another of the papal legates may have taken an interest in him
and taught him the necessary amount of Scripture. Quite
possibly he received irregular instruction now and then in
other things, but he never enjoyed a systematic education. His
later learning bears all the marks of being not the product of
" school " but of life itself. He was compelled from his
tenderest years to absorb directly, without extraneous aid and
from every source, the strength he needed. This differentiated
his knowledge both in its content and in its application from
that of his contemporaries. Stern Necessity was his first tutor,
and she—to quote the Pope's expression—" taught him the
eloquence of grief and of complaint at an age when other
children scarcely lisp aright." His next instructors were the
market-places and streets of Palermo : Life itself. He laid the
foundations of his wisdom in those wanderings which made him
the friend of every man.

The vital importance of the fact that Frederick spent his
childhood in Sicily has never been ignored. The Romano-
Germanic mixture in his race inheritance, Swabian-Burgundian
on his father's side, Norman-Lorraine on his mother's, guaran-

teed a certain mental and spiritual universality of gifts. These
gifts Sicily fostered. Here in Palermo three great cultural
systems existed side by side, in tangible reality : Antiquity, the
East, the Church. Not merely the breath and spirit, but the
languages, rites and customs, and the human atmosphere of
those three worlds were familiar to the child from babyhood.
Pope Innocent once wrote : " His hereditary land, rich and
noble beyond the other kingdoms of the world is the port and
navel of them all." The phrase might be read almost in its
literal sense. Sicily was the navel of the new world that was
here to come to birth.

The rule of Markward of Anweiler and his successors lasted
five years, and five years lasted also the free unfettered vaga-
bondage of the young Sicilian king. When, at the beginning
of 1207, Walter of Palear resumed the charge of his protégé,
the Chancellor and his following must have been surprised at
the maturity of the twelve-year old prince. His conduct and
manners they found " awkward and unseemly," but this they
attributed to the " rude company " he had been accustomed to
and to no fault of his own nature, and they were only distressed
to think that " his too widespread intercourse with all and
sundry, and the public comment thereby provoked " might
diminish the due reverence of the Sicilians for their King. His
royal bearing and autocratic dignity were immediately remarked ;
his complete unreceptiveness to reproof was no less manifest.
" He will follow only the dictates of his own will," they said.
The boy possessed immense strength of will, which had been
left entirely untamed. Only Frederick himself, and Frederick's
own intelligence, and stern necessity at times, had ever curbed
it ; hence no doubt the unruliness of the boy, and the iron
determination of the later Emperor that brooked no opposition.
At twelve Frederick wanted to dispense with all regencies and
guardianships. It was " disgraceful " to his boyish pride to
be a ward, and to be treated as a boy and not a king. He
already compelled respect from those who saw him, and it
was clear that unconditional obedience would soon be the
order of the day. This self-confidence of his, not artificially
stimulated, but an entirely natural growth, made it possible for
him to take liberties which, people sometimes thought, often

overstepped the measure of what is allowed a king. On the other hand his entourage could not deny the complete assurance of his behaviour ; they had to admit that the young king had an unerring instinct for the true and the false, an opinion of his own, and an eagle eye to discern the nature of the men around him. His inborn kingliness and the nobility of his race enabled him, as Innocent once wrote, " to tread firmly on both feet." During the years of his unrestricted wanderings Frederick had thoroughly exercised his body. He was only of medium height, but even as a boy nimble and untiring. He had powerful limbs which gave him great natural endurance in every sort of physical exertion. He was skilful and efficient in handling any and every type of weapon. Even in the early days he was a good archer and a passionately keen horseman with a particular love of well-bred horses, as indeed we should naturally expect, remembering the famous huntsman he after-wards became. He was particularly skilful in fencing with the sword, and his opponents must sometimes have had a tough time of it, for with his fiery temper he easily worked himself into a passion during a fight. What struck people especially was that he " never passed a day quietly in continuous activity." If he had had exercise during the day the twelve-year-old boy would work late into the night to extend his knowledge. His favourite reading was history—probably Roman history—the tale of wars and deeds of arms. He thus showed already the unresting activity and zeal common to men of his quality which often made the Emperor seem more than human. He was able nevertheless to preserve the power of quiet reflection.

Pope Innocent was not to be troubled with the boy much longer. Like the other Hohenstaufens Frederick matured extremely early, but it was not that unhappy precocity (so often observed in Germans) which precedes a rapid exhaustion of strength after the prime. That old saying, which Pope Innocent once quoted of his ward, " the manhood of a Caesar sets in before its time " might apply to the whole house of Hohenstaufen. The country of his boyhood and the self-reliance which his severe youth imposed on Frederick as a child probably accentuated this natural tendency. The Pope at any rate reported that the boy was striding to the threshold of maturity with winged feet, and that day by day he grew in wisdom and efficiency. Men praised his clearheadedness and shrewdness and remarked that you must not judge Frederick by the tale of his years, for in knowledge he was already a man and in dignity already a ruler. In spite of his almost super-human ability Frederick was no artificially-reared phenomenon, but merely the best that can be hoped from youth. It was the thoroughness and completeness of his development, his absolute normality that was remarkable; he was *completus* they said. Similarly of his stature : " You must not picture the King as exactly small, but neither must you imagine him taller than befits his years." And another writes : " So completely has the King developed the knowledge and strength suited to his age that you will find in him only what would grace a perfect man." Thus the moment rapidly approached when Frederick could shake off the yoke of guardianship. In accordance with the feudal law of Sicily he came of age as King of Sicily with the completion of his fourteenth year.

Pope Innocent was anxious completely to fulfil his duties as guardian before finally releasing his ward. He married the boy. The Empress Constance had had in view a matrimonial alliance with the royal house of Aragon, and when Frederick at seven fell into the hands of Markward of Anweiler the Pope for practical reasons took up the scheme again. In 1202 he negotiated a betrothal between his ward and Sancha, the sister of King Peter of Aragon. The Pope's calculation in the matter was that King Peter would have to send a body of Spanish knights to Sicily to free Frederick from the power of Markward the German. He hoped, moreover, that the Spanish Queen-Mother would go to live in Sicily to bring the boy and girl together. For the Pope did not consider wholly suitable or desirable the exclusively male atmosphere in which Frederick was growing up. But the Pope's plans fell through and the betrothal was cancelled. During the following years, however, Innocent did not lose sight of an alliance that would spell no small advantage to the Church—Aragon, like Sicily, was a feudal fief of the Holy See. After lengthy criss-cross negotiations he brought about another betrothal—which irresistibly recalls the fables of the patriarchs and other fairy tales. Frederick is now to marry, not the young Sancha, to whom he was originally engaged, but her much older sister, Constance. Constance had been married to the King of Hungary, had just recently been widowed and was a full ten years older than the Hohenstaufen lad. The Pope had considerable difficulty in gaining the consent of the fourteen-year old Frederick to this match, but here for the first time he bowed to immediate State necessity. Constance of Aragon promised to bring him as her dowry five hundred Spanish knights to help him to reconquer his completely disintegrated Sicilian kingdom. And this troop of warriors—who ultimately were to prove a bitter disillusionment—seemed to the boy so invaluable that he was willing to accept the wife into the bargain. For, although he had made some most promising attempts, he could scarcely hope unaided to establish order in the whirlpool of anarchy that had been raging for so many years. Pope Innocent had, it is true, during the last years of his guardianship, seriously bestirred himself to establish a passable state of affairs in Sicily, though he hoped that the really essential work would be done by the Aragon contingent. He had, however, himself crossed the frontier into the kingdom and had assembled the Sicilian nobles in San Germano (near Monte Cassino on the border of the States of the Church) and had proclaimed a general peace throughout the land. To maintain this peace he appointed the two most powerful vassals of continental Sicily as Grand-Captains, hoping thus to neutralise their dangerous power. The papal efforts were not of any very decisive value, but, nevertheless, after the years of chaos the hand of authority began to be felt in the northern half of the kingdom, the Sicily that marched with the States of the Church. In the island itself, on the other hand, everything remained in a bad way until the young King, soon after attaining his majority, began to tackle matters himself with zeal and vigour. As soon as he was independent the boy—only just fourteen—displayed extreme daring. He issued challenges simultaneously in several directions against those who actually or apparently infringed his royal rights. On the 26th of December, 1208, the king's fifteenth birthday, the Pope for-

mally laid down his guardianship. From this moment
Frederick ruled alone. Two weeks later followed his first
brush with the Pope, the mighty Innocent—a beginning full of
promise. The point at issue was the appointment of a new
incumbent to the Archbishopric of Palermo. With the King's
approval the Cathedral Chapter proposed an election. Three
of the Chapter, however, objected, for reasons unknown, and
appealed to the Pope. The King considered this appeal a
direct infringement of his authority. He banished the appel-
lants from the kingdom, and wrote to the astonished Pope
that the moderation of his action was solely due to the respect
he felt for the Pope personally and for the Church in general.
Innocent III, one of the most powerful rulers the world has
known, was at that moment recognised by all the monarchs of
Europe as the *verus Imperator* of Christendom. He by no
means shared his ward's view of the situation. According to
the Concordat which Constance had signed with him the right
of the Sicilian king in episcopal elections was confined to one
single point : the Chapter elected the Bishop without royal
interference, but the King's consent was necessary before the
enthronement could take place. The final word, however,
remained with the Church, for even after his enthronement
the Bishop could officiate only after the Pope in final instance
had ratified the election. Thus, even if the King and Chapter
were at one in their choice of the future Bishop, the Pope
retained the right to reject a *persona ingrata*—and the *persona
grata* of the King was almost invariably *ingrata* to the Pope.
According to this Concordat, therefore, Frederick had only the
right of consent. He had not the shadow of a right to prevent
a direct appeal to the Pope, even if this would have been contrary to the older, now abrogated, privileges of the Norman
Kings. Pope Innocent was wise enough to dismiss this affair
with a long exhortation couched in paternal terms, the gist of
which was that Frederick had lent an ear to unwise counsellors. He must let secular business suffice him and not
stretch out a hand towards affairs of the spirit which were
reserved for the Pope alone. " It would have beseemed thee
to reflect, and to have been warned thereby," he wrote, " how by
the evil-doing of thy forefathers in seeking to arrogate to them-

selves spiritual authority, thy kingdom was plunged into the chaos and confusion that thou wottest of." A detailed exposition of the Empress's Concordat followed, and Innocent concluded his homily with the command that the banished members of the Cathedral Chapter should be forthwith summoned back to Palermo.

Frederick was unquestionably in the wrong and had no option but to obey. The interesting point is this : that in his very first act of government Frederick had put his finger with unerring instinct on the vital question of episcopal election which was for decades to provide the ostensible bone of contention in his quarrels with the Curia. In compensation for this setback Frederick had greater success in another direction. We cannot be quite sure what the first measures were which the young King took to restore order in his kingdom, but he must have accomplished much more in this way than it has till recently been the fashion to recognise. One thing is certain : in the spring of 1209 he undertook a royal progress " with great force " through Sicily, by way of Nicosia to Catania and on to Messina. We learn from his own words that this was no peaceful pilgrimage : he quelled " the sons of disturbance who hated peace, so that they bent their necks under his yoke." Within a few months the fourteen-year-old King had more than half subdued the North-East of the island and was evolving further plans of action. Individual proclamations, whose authoritative tone leaves nothing to be desired, indicate clearly that he was intending to cross to the mainland and re-establish there his royal authority. For that he wanted Aragon assistance.

While Frederick was still a minor his marriage with Constance had been celebrated in the cathedral of Saragossa, a Sicilian Bishop acting as the King's proxy. The Queen's arrival in Palermo was planned for March 1209, but she did not reach the Sicilian capital till August. She was accompanied by her brother, Count Alfonso of Provence, and the five hundred promised knights. Frederick, who was still in Messina, hastened to Palermo, where the wedding ceremonies were solemnised forthwith. Immediately after the festivities Frederick wanted to set out for Messina, to undertake without delay his projected campaign on the mainland. A year before, the

Pope, on the day of San Germano, had gathered together several hundred feudal knights, and these with the Spanish contingent would have constituted a very considerable force. All the hopes of the young King were doomed. The Spaniards, on whose help he had so eagerly counted, were struck down—either during their preparations for the start, or immediately after leaving Palermo—by an epidemic of plague, which slew the majority of them, including Count Alfonso the Queen's brother. This tragedy rendered the projected campaign impossible. Worse still, the discontented Sicilian barons seized the opportunity of their King's embarrassment to form a conspiracy to rid themselves of their inconvenient master : a prelude to many a similar occurrence. In the most amazing manner Frederick contrived to quell the revolt. The ring-leader was a Calabrian count. He was taken prisoner, and Frederick on his side seized the opportunity to wring from the conspirators a part of the *Demanium*, the royal demesne, which they had unjustly seized during the days of the Regency.

This success demonstrated the determination and forceful-ness of the young King, but also, alas, the full hopelessness of his position. He was irredeemably impoverished, and without foreign aid he could never succeed in accomplishing anything in Sicily. It had been decreed by his " two mothers," the Roman Church, his spiritual mother, and the Empress Con-stance, his mother in the flesh, that he was to wear out his life in his Sicilian inheritance and in Palermo, the " fortunate city " ; but the decree was theirs alone. Other tasks were to be laid on him. While he was still pluckily pitting himself against the Sicilian chaos, important events had been taking place in Germany. More than a year before, in June 1208, King Philip of Swabia had been treacherously murdered in Bamberg by the Count Palatine, Otto of Wittelsbach. Frederick, the Pope's ward, was now the last of the Hohenstaufen. A new vista opened before him : the mothers could no longer hold him down, the call had come to rise and join his fathers.

II. PUER APULIAE

II. PUER APULIAE

POPE INNOCENT III—by birth Lotario dei Conti—presided over the Christian world with a plenitude of actual power which many a bishop of Rome has claimed, but none other before or since has exercised. This learned priest, with his aristocratic Roman features, his majestic and distinguished air, was favoured in no common measure by the moment of his birth. He studied theology and law in Paris and Bologna and was completely master of the learning of the day. He was barely thirty-seven when in 1198 he mounted the papal throne, three months after the death of Henry VI.

The world which that great Hohenstaufen Emperor had welded into temporary unity immediately fell to pieces at his death, and no single power was competent seriously to challenge the papal claims still inspired by the spirit of Gregory VII. It was generally recognised as the particular business of the Roman Emperor to hold the balance of power against the Pope, but in the Imperium of that day there was no Caesar. It was rent asunder by the Welf-Waibling faction-fight, and so—since the world needs must look to an overlord—Pope Innocent held sway within the Empire as almost the *verus imperator* which he was called by his contemporary, Gervase of Tilbury.

The phrase was no idle curial flattery : Innocent's own figures of speech were more arrogant still, though it was reserved for Dante's pope, Boniface VIII, nearly a century later to coin the classic formula of papal-imperial majesty : " Ego sum Caesar, ego imperator," before with him there passed away the two centuries of papal claim to world dominion initiated by Gregory VII.

Innocent III, holding a place in time half way between Gregory and Boniface, was the actual fulfiller of the papal claim to universal rule. A chronicler writes : " The Church in his day, in the glory of her bloom and the zenith of her power, held sway over the Roman Empire and over all Kings and

Princes of the universe." As cardinal, Innocent had written
a book *On the Contempt of the World* ; in spite of this and of his
own Spartan mode of life—which he was fond of holding up
as an example to others—his whole being was permeated by
a profound belief in the sanctity and dignity of his priestly
office, a belief which dictated the display on occasion of
majestic and imperial pomp. Thus, for instance, contrary to
custom, he delayed his enthronement for many weeks after
his election in order to add to the glory of the ceremony by
taking his seat in the chair of St. Peter on the very festival of
St. Peter's Chair. No doubt he wanted to play the part of
Peter on that day—as at times he liked to take the rôle of Christ.
A witty story is told that he had once donned the " coat without
a seam," preserved in the Lateran, to see whether the Master
had not been a smaller man than he ; but, alas, it proved too
big. He felt himself to be completely the Emperor of Christendom, and in fact he was so in a quite peculiar way. As ruler and
statesman of the first water he was the first to make the Church,
in its narrower sense of the hierarchy of priests and bishops,
really an effective " State," an Absolute Monarchy in which he
himself as sole autocrat was sole fountain of power, justice and
mercy.

Innocent's life was immensely rich in events of magnitude :
he saw in turn all the kings of Europe kneel at his feet to receive
their countries from his hand in fee ; in the interests of the true
faith he conjured up all the horrors of the Albigensian war ;
he first banned the Crusaders who conquered Byzantium and
then founded a Latin Empire in the East under the aegis of the
Latin Church ; but this eventful life does not here concern us.
Our interest lies only with the statesman who proclaimed
himself the spiritual father of Frederick II, appointed by God
to replace the earthly father he had lost ; who in the line of
medieval monarchs filled the hiatus that fell between the son
and the grandson of Barbarossa, the aroma of whose spiritual
reign still filled the air when the last of the Hohenstaufens
mounted the imperial throne.

The royal High Priest of the Christian Church, the *verus
imperator* of the Christian Empire, the first judge of Christendom, these three are one and of one origin : they are the Pope.

That is roughly the underlying principle which first comes to the
fore with Innocent III, not as a claim but as an axiom, a rounded
whole, a " Summa." Innocent's point of departure was that the
Pope—though the successor of the prince of the apostles—was
not *his* representative on earth, not the representative of any
man, but the representative of Christ himself, and through him
the representative of God. Direct from God himself he held
the *plenitudo potestatis*, the sum total of all power, from which
derive all earthly powers : the priest's, the judge's and the
king's. Innocent in an unprecedentedly ambitious exposition
of the papal rôle of mediator inculcated this doctrine most
explicitly. All power is from God. The Pope, however, is
placed as " mediator between God and man ; nearer than
God, further than man ; less than God but more than man,"
and to complete the circle of transmitted power he further
states : " God is honoured in us when we are honoured, and in
us is God despised when we are despised." From this latter
postulate sprang the later dogma, probably first formulated by
Thomas Aquinas, " submission to the Pope is essential to every
man for the salvation of his soul."

This dual position of the Pope as mediator made possible
the transmission of power which is closely bound up with
Innocent's transmutation of the Church into a Priest-State.
The first conception of the hierarchy as a State was not his, but
by a fortunate concurrence of time and opportunity its realisation was his work. The priestly power was derived from God
through the papal mediator, and if this was to pass over
immediate and uninterrupted to the bishops, it was in the highest
degree important that every other influence should be ruled out
at their election, especially the influence of despised secular
authorities—whatever ancient privileges King or Emperor might
claim. Shrewdly, skilfully, unscrupulously, Pope Innocent
contrived to stage-manage in his own sense the bishops'
elections in all countries, exploiting for his own ends the political impotence that crippled Europe (with the sole exception of
France). Sometimes he made treaties, sometimes concordats,
and he contrived ere long to end the whole question of investi-
ture disputes, and make the bishops throughout the Christian
world his own immediate dependants, creatures whom he—

and in still wider measure his successors—began, like the veriest autocrat, to appoint, remove, transfer, according to papal caprice. This he had the right to do, for this Pope-god was mighty to bind or to loose the spiritual wedlock—otherwise indissoluble—of the bishop with his diocese, " not as man, for he was not the vicegerent of man, but as God, for he was the vicegerent of God."

With this " freedom of episcopal elections " the constitution of the Church achieved its complete independence of the temporal powers. On a plane above the profane world the Church became a peculiar state, in which the bishops played only the part of obedient civil servants, provincial governors and ambassadors of their papal Imperator. The divorce of the secular power from the Church patronage it had hitherto enjoyed was made final and complete by the papal Legates, who as plenipotentiaries of the Pope ranked above the archbishops themselves and supervised the activities of the bishops' officials, without the secular power being in a position to protest at finding itself deprived of all supervision over the Church.

Corresponding agreements, including the right of sending legates to the individual countries, were now usually added to treaties. A third stipulation commonly reserved to the priests the " right of direct appeal," the right that is to say of every priest to approach the Pope without the intermediary of the secular power. This first secured the real cohesion of the spiritual State whose head was the Pope. If the firmly dove-tailed fabric of the Church-state were not to be sprung, a further consequence inevitably followed : no " officials " of the Pope, with isolated exceptions, should in the future be amenable, as to a certain extent they had been heretofore, to secular courts. This necessitated a further development of the Canon law which Innocent made by a collection of Decretals, a work thus inaugurated by the Pope himself, though not completed till twenty years after his death. Like all the great Popes of the later Middle Ages, especially his predecessor Alexander III, Innocent was a first-class jurist, which in those days was almost synonymous with statesman. It is self-evident that if this great work of building up his state was to reach perfection he had no option but to proceed without scruple and without ruth.

The bishops and priests had hitherto been wont, not without advantage, to play off the papal against the royal power, and *vice versa*. The freedom that they lost, however, by the metamorphosis of the Church into a well-knit, monarchical, priest-state based on obedience, was made good in other ways. By Pope Innocent's lofty conception of his priestly office the prestige of the cleric *vis-à-vis* the layman was immensely enhanced. Every ancient edict which could serve to evoke increased respect for the priest was called anew into remembrance and given fresh emphasis. For instance, the layman was unconditionally dependent on the mediation of the priest ; the priest must be correctly ordained ; the sacramental power of the priest was independent of his personal unworthiness; simony was treason against king and state. This vital importance of simony from a political point of view is comprehensible, since it interferes with the transmission of grace, which instead of proceeding from God and the Pope has been bought for money.

This new aloofness of the priest and his severance from the lay world is clearly marked by certain pregnant innovations in ritual, provoked by acute reaction against the heretics—just now beginning to show their heads—one of whose expressed aims was to lessen the cleavage between the layman and the priest. Amongst these new ordinances may be cited, for instance, the rule that the priest henceforth completes the mysteries with his face turned towards the altar and the East, and with his back to the people, not facing the congregation as heretofore : " less than God, but more than man." The presence of the lay worshippers has become a matter of indifference in face of the magic metamorphosis of the elements which was wrought by the priestly benediction—the " Transubstantiation " as Pope Innocent first described the mystic miracle. In 1215 he elevated this doctrine into a dogma.

The reformed papacy of the eleventh century had under Gregory VII initiated the emancipation of the papal office and the papal elections from the power of the Emperor. Innocent III gradually extended this emancipation down to the bishops and sought to free their election and their office from temporal influences. This, however, was a very different matter, fraught with no little danger to the Church : might not a temporal ruler on his part create a wholly temporal state exempt from all allegiance to the Church ? It has too seldom been remarked that it was the Church who first craved complete severance, and achieved it by every means in her power, who first, by the creation of a unified self-sufficing priest-state, furnished a model for a wholly temporal empire. The most remarkable point is, however, that the Church herself laid down certain principles—in somewhat " unorthodox " fashion—for this imitation of the spiritual by the temporal empire.'

It was inevitable that the Pope should stress the unconditional and unique quality of his office as mediator with reference to priestly power. But it is notorious that he did not confine himself to this : the *plenitudo potestatis* conferred on him as God's vicegerent rendered him the mediator not only for all spiritual, but also for all worldly authority—the knightly as the kingly. The very words in which he celebrated his mediatorship, in what was practically a self-apotheosis, added a rider to the well-known doctrine : as mediator it was his mission " to judge all men, but to be judged of none." This priestly spirit which breathed fire into Innocent's judicial functions endowed the temporal power with new strength. This faith in the actual, uninterrupted working and overflowing of divine power, through the Mediator, into judges and kings as well as into priests, constituted the very essence of the medieval mediatorship. This conception had been till now foreign, in lay affairs at any rate, to the medieval mind. True, the ruler received his power always direct from God as a fief, a *beneficium*, but he, as a temporal sovereign, was no mediator in the priestly sense. Innocent, of course, was not concerned to distinguish a spiritual and a temporal mediatorship, since the totality of power, the *plenitudo potestatis*, dwelt in him alone, as High Priest. All the greater would be some day the portent when the temporal power would claim the temporal mediatorship in respect of royal and judicial functions, would sever this from the mediatorship of the high priest and, following the Pope's example, would perform its own apotheosis.

All unwitting, Innocent III had paved the road to a Kingship and a Judgeship that should challenge the rights of Priesthood. Eager to assert his limitless judicial powers he sought to break down all lines of demarcation. He liked to entitle Peter the *sacerdos sive judex*, " priest or judge," and to use the Levites as an illustration of the essential unity of the priestly and judicial functions. The Lord himself had recognised the fact that the highest judicial authority was to be found in Rome. Peter, flying from Rome, had asked the question : *Quo vadis, Domine ?* and did not Christ reply : *Romam venio iterum crucifigi* ! Rome therefore—that is, of course, the Pope—became the court of highest instance on earth, with jurisdiction in worldly matters also, wherever dubious or mysterious cases were in question. God himself had placed the Pope, as Innocent untiringly repeated, on the throne of Justice, so that he might pronounce judgment also on the princes of the earth. And thus the Pope, though for the most part not interfering in the secular admini- stration of justice, became the Over-Judge who could summon to his forum any quarrel in all the Christian world.

In precisely similar fashion Innocent sought to fuse priest- hood and kingship. The Old and New Testament were at one, he pointed out, in holding that kingship was a priestly, and priesthood a royal office, and thus it was that the Saviour who —like the Pope—had been the Mediator between God and man was, as scion of David's royal house, a King ; as a son of God, a Priest. Innocent lent new life to a Bible figure, hitherto unregarded, or insufficiently exploited, by the Curia : that remarkable foreshadowing of Christ, the Priest-King of Salem, Melchizedek. Christ, and, as his representative, the Pope also, was a priest " after the order of Melchizedek," such is the perpetually recurring formula in all the writings of Innocent the Great. With an inexhaustible variety of imagery he demon- strates that : " like as the soul is more than the body, so the priest is more than the king," and he applies to the Pope the words of Scripture : " By me kings reign and princes decree justice." He seeks ever fresh comparisons and metaphors to equate the vicegerent and mediator with the Lord himself, that he may appear as *verus imperator*, Emperor-Priest and Ruler of the world. There was nothing absolutely new in all this, save the Pope's unrelenting reiteration, which incessantly and particularly focussed the world's attention on the priestly empire and the imperial priesthood.

Pope Innocent achieved his end. The wearer of the papal tiara was enthroned henceforth on giddy heights. On the other hand, however, thanks to the great Pope's adoption of so many symbols and tokens of the Roman Emperors, the secular empire was saturated through and through with an atmosphere of hieratic sanctity. And the power of the Emperor, far from being weakened by this eloquence, received an undreamt-of accession of prestige. Thus Pope Innocent III, a spiritual father in very deed, must be reckoned, alongside Norman and Hohenstaufen, as amongst the immediate ancestors and predecessors of the young King Frederick.

Buoyed up by such conceptions Innocent III flung himself into the quarrel of the succession. Formerly he had favoured Otto the Welf against Philip the Hohenstaufen, first, because " no pope loves a Staufen " ; secondly, because a Hohenstaufen Emperor involved the danger, of which under a Welf there was no fear, of a fusion of Sicily with the Empire ; thirdly, because the Welf was poor and had few adherents and would therefore be wholly beholden to the Curia and likely to prove a useful and obedient creature of the Pope. Lastly, the Welf was uncultured and unintellectual, but possessed in compensation an exceptionally powerful physique which well qualified him to be " the secular sword of the Church." In spite of the Pope's assistance, however, Otto had not succeeded in making headway in Germany against the Hohenstaufen rival. He would inevitably have succumbed in the last campaign of the Swabian Philip which was to have taken place in the summer of 1208. The attitude of Rome is an infallible index to the hopelessness of his cause : Pope Innocent withdrew his support from the Welf, released the Hohenstaufen from the ban, recognised the latter as king, and promised him the imperial crown if he would but make a pilgrimage to Rome.

Just as the Hohenstaufen was on the threshold of victory his assassination by the Count Palatine, Otto of Wittelsbach, a purely personal revenge, and the first regicide since there had been a German Empire, decided the succession in favour of the Welf. For the German princes were weary of civil war and quickly united to choose Otto of Brunswick, who hoped to unite the claims of both parties in his own person by betrothing himself, with the Pope's approval, to Beatrice, the eleven-year-old daughter of the murdered man. Pope Innocent had conquered without effort : he hastened to declare himself ready to crown his protégé—whom he had so reluctantly thrown to the wolves—as Emperor in Rome.

It was not the wont of the Roman Curia, since she had come to power, to bestow the Emperor's crown without a *quid pro quo*, and it was natural to demand an extra large one from her creature Otto IV ; first, free episcopal election in Germany— which the Hohenstaufen had always refused to tolerate—then the recognition of Sicily as a papal fief, and an assurance of its absolute immunity from attack ; and, finally, the cession to the Pope of certain imperial territories in Central Italy : the March of Ancona, Spoleto, the so-called Matilda inheritance, and others. In the general confusion created by the death of Henry VI, Pope Innocent had hastily seized these territories from the Empire, rightly or wrongly, and under the name of " Recuperations " incorporated them in the Patrimonium Petri. The Patrimonium now—in this extent a creation of Innocent's—stretched right across Italy, a self-contained wedge driven between the papal fief of Sicily on the south and Lombardy, at all times hostile to the Empire. The dream of a united papal Italy seemed not too remote a possibility.

Otto was eager to reach his goal. He had already promised these concessions as long ago as 1201 ; he had no option but to cede what the Pope requested—without, however, securing the written confirmation of the German princes. He set out shortly to cross the Alps. As the boisterous march of his brilliant retinue broke the stillness of Rivotorto St. Francis is said to have sent one of his disciples to bid the future Emperor ponder on the evanescence of earthly greatness. Otto pursued his march. In the late autumn of 1209 he was crowned in Rome by Innocent himself as Roman Emperor. As for Innocent, he had, it seemed, accomplished all his desires. His protégé was Emperor ; the severance of the Hohenstaufen Sicily from the empire of the Welfs seemed final and complete.

Suddenly events took place which threatened to overturn

the whole nicely-balanced edifice of papal politics. The Welf,
no sooner crowned, repudiated his promises. He laughed
aloud when Innocent reminded him of his earlier agreements.
In the very first negotiations about the central Italian territories Otto showed himself anything but the Church's " docile
son." The barons of the Sicilian mainland gave the immediate
provocation for an incurable breach between Emperor and Pope.
The arrival in Italy of the German Otto was heralded by the
feudal nobility of Apulia as the signal to throw off for ever the
yoke of the impotent young King. The conspiracy of September 1209, directed against Frederick by the barons of Sicily
and Calabria, had fallen through, the Apulian barons had
recourse this time to treachery. Their ringleader was the
Count of Acerra, Diepold of Schweinspeunt, one of the young
Germans who had held sway during Frederick's boyhood in
the royal castle of Palermo as successor to Markward of
Anweiler. In addition to personal advantage and the hope of
power, Diepold, like Markward, held firmly to the conviction
that Sicily belonged unconditionally to the Roman Empire,
and that the Norman heir of the Hohenstaufen was simply an
obstacle in the way of union. After the lapse of over ten years
an Emperor had appeared again in Italy. Diepold, therefore,
immediately set himself to play into the hands of Otto IV as the
only legitimate ruler of the kingdom.

Soon after his coronation in November 1209 Kaiser Otto
visited Pisa, a town that had long been in alliance with Diepold
and the Germans. Here the Apulian magnates sought him
out, did him homage, and importuned him to seize the unpro-
tected kingdom, for " none but the wearer of the Empire's
crown may reign by right in Sicily." It is true that Otto had
given the Pope assurances of the inviolability of Sicily, but he
no longer held himself bound by the promise. It matters little
whether the Emperor had from the first contemplated the
reconquest of Sicily for the Empire—following the precedent
of Henry VI—or whether he was now lured into the enterprise
by the urgency of the Apulians, reinforced by the prayers of the
Pisans. He agreed. He soon created Diepold Duke of Spoleto
—an act of open hostility to the Pope—and in the following
months, while regulating the affairs of Middle and Northern

Italy, he began, as unobtrusively as possible, to make preparation for a campaign against Sicily. A further consideration may have weighed with him. The last of the Hohenstaufen, who was already a burden, might ere long be a danger. The imperial crown had been denied to Frederick after Philip's murder, but he might at least lodge a claim to his father's inheritance in Swabia, and there had in fact been negotiations between Pope and Emperor about some compromise with the young King. Many motives conspired to urge Otto forward to the fateful adventure, the Sicilian campaign.

It was a favourite boast of the Roman Curia to have " the ears and eyes of many " at its disposal. It was not long before the Pope was apprised of Otto's intentions. The Pope confessed : " the sword we fashioned for ourselves deals us dire blows." Now from the Welf side he saw arise the eternally recurrent nightmare of a German-Sicilian fusion, and well knowing that the bare possession of the Church's fief was at stake, he began at the first symptom of danger cautiously to lay his snares. From his base in the Lateran he put himself at once in touch with Otto's enemies. His first step was to send an encyclical to the German bishops, informing them of the Emperor's intentions. His letter began with the scriptural phrase : " it repenteth me to have created man, " and concluded with the exhortation immediately to release all vassals from their oaths of fealty in the event of the Emperor's being excommunicated. Innocent issued no direct command, but he gave the clearest instructions as to his wishes and their future line of conduct towards the Emperor. The bishops must have set to work at once to influence the secular princes, for it was easy to foster opposition to Otto, if it did not already exist, and there was only a question of working up a useful counter-party.

Innocent followed up his letter to the bishops by another to the King of France, the Capet, Philip II " Augustus ". He had always been the declared enemy of the Welf, for Otto, as nephew of his great foe, the English King, John Lackland, was always in alliance with England and had frequently threatened to make war on France. The King of France had therefore been hostile from the first to a Welf Empire, and the Pope had striven to mediate between the two rulers. Innocent now wrote in no

peace-making spirit. He regretted he had not been so quick
as Philip Augustus to see through the Welf, told him what he
had written to the German bishops, and skilfully wove into the
end of his letter a few remarks that Otto had made. He had
said—the Pope averred—that he could not sleep at night for
very shame while the French King was still in possession of
lands belonging to his uncle, John of England : and so forth.

In this case also Innocent refrained from making positive
suggestions, but he felt fairly sure of the ultimate effect of his
poison, temperately administered. Philip Augustus was not
slow to understand. With great precaution he proceeded to
get into touch with the German princes of the opposition party,
and by September 1210 Philip of France, Innocent III, and a
considerable number of Middle German princes were at one
on the vital issues.

Innocent could now take action. Kaiser Otto, having completed his preliminaries in the autumn of 1210, set out on the
march to Apulia. Just as he invaded the Tuscan Patrimonium
he was excommunicated by the Pope as agreed upon—after
the mockery of a fruitless negotiation—and his subjects were
released from their oath. For the moment this upset Otto
very little : within a few weeks he was in possession of considerable portions of Apulia, and the course of the following year
ought to have seen the southern half of the Italian peninsula
in his hands.

The most pressing and immediate danger now threatened
the young Sicilian King. The Pope had indeed warned him of
Otto's plans, but how was Frederick to withstand the powerful
emperor ? He was not even master of his internal enemies ;
almost the whole of the feudal nobility of Sicily had voluntarily sworn obedience to the invader. He could trust no one
in his ruined and neglected kingdom, not even, as it seemed, his
nearest entourage, for when the news came of the treachery of
the continental barons under the leadership of Diepold—whom
Frederick had himself nominated Lord Chief Justice of Apulia
—he was obliged to depose his Bishop-Chancellor, Walter of
Palear. Innocent promptly forbade such a step—the Chancellor was of course also a bishop—with the phrase " this is not
the time for boyish pranks," but Frederick did not revoke his

action. The Chancellor was related to the rebel barons and on terms of the closest intimacy with them, and in view of Walter's well-known adaptability in political matters—which Frederick was in a better position to assess than the Pope—his retention in so influential a post was certainly not without risk. The threatening danger was, however, not appreciably lessened by the Chancellor's fall.

During 1210, while Otto was still busy with his preparations, and even in the early months of the following year, while Aversa—encouraged to resistance by the Pope—stemmed Otto's advance for a time, Frederick still enjoyed some prestige in Catania and Messina, and when he passed through these towns he must have striven to secure, as a last relic of his realm, the north-east corner of the island, the first of his conquests. But the Welf continued almost unopposed his career of conquest in the Sicilian mainland ; towns like Barletta and Bari in Apulia surrendered to him, and thereupon the two provinces of Calabria and the Basilicata—the two nearest to the island— declared for the Emperor. Even the Saracens of the Sicilian highlands invited Otto to cross the sea, promising him their support : it looked as if Frederick might well give his whole kingdom up for lost except the city of Palermo.

Robbed of his towns, his castles, his lands, the *regulus non rex* seemed face to face with inevitable ruin. Frederick, however, had not lost his pride. In imitation of the Emperor he chose this juncture to insert in the royal seal of Sicily the figures of the sun and moon, symbols of world sovereignty. But even he could scarcely cherish a serious hope of salvation. In the spring Frederick had sought to enter into negotiations with Otto, had declared himself ready to renounce all Swabian claims, which he had just verified in the Swabian monastery records, and had finally offered the Emperor several thousand pounds of gold and silver—which it is unlikely that he possessed (for he had had to pledge the county of Sora to Innocent to reimburse him for the expenses of the regency). All had been in vain. The impetuous Welf hearkened to nothing ; he " spat upon " the tenders of Pope and King, who indeed offered only what he already held or proposed to seize. Now, in September 1211, he was in Calabria, about to cross the narrow river Faro. He

was merely awaiting the arrival of the Pisan fleet which had set
sail from the Arno that same month. Meanwhile Frederick
had fallen into such straits that he kept a galley ready at anchor
near the fort of Castellamare in Palermo to secure his flight to
Africa when the ultimate need should come.

At this very moment of maximum danger the incredible
happened. Otto relinquished his certain prey, abandoned the
entire campaign, and in sudden haste took his departure from
the kingdom : the incessant machinations of the Pope had begun
to take effect. Innocent had watched Otto's progress with
acute anxiety. Negotiations, in which the Pope was prepared
to offer up his " recuperations " in Central Italy in return
for the Emperor's recognition of Sicily as a papal domain, had
produced only a momentary wavering. Nothing had been
achieved ; the Welf could only be overthrown by indirect
methods. So Pope Innocent set once more in motion all the
intrigue and diplomatic art at his command, strongly reinforced
by edicts of excommunication ; he poured out letters to the
German princes, to the Italian clergy, to the King of France ;
threats of the papal ban against the adherents of Otto, words of
encouragement to Otto's enemies . . . all to one end—to undermine the Emperor's position in Italy and even more in Germany.
Now, at the eleventh hour, success attended the cumulative
effect of his exertions.

After lengthy secret negotiations the anti-Welf German
princes, not uninfluenced by the King of France, assembled in
September 1211 in Nuremberg, declared the excommunicated
Emperor deposed, and further—also at the instigation of Philip
Augustus, a pro-Staufen of earlier days—chose as rival King
Frederick of Sicily, the last of the Hohenstaufens. There was
in Germany no lack of wealthier and more powerful princes
than the Sicilian boy, but it was realised that for this anti-Welf
campaign there lay more might in the Hohenstaufen name than
in the wealth and weapons of other men. The glory of the
great Staufen emperors lingered yet, and a scion of this house
was secure of a far wider general support than any Thuringian
or other prince could at short notice hope to win. Nor was the
original choice of Henry's son without its weight. Thus it
came that the assembled princes unanimously despatched from

Nuremberg an express messenger to the Pope for his acquiescence in, and to Frederick for his acceptance of, their election.

Friends of the Welf sent likewise warning to their master : all Germany was in revolt, a rival king was chosen, Otto should return with speed, his rule in Germany was at stake. Kaiser Otto was still in Calabria when the German messenger arrived, accompanied by Milanese and men from other friendly Lombard towns. They urgently implored him to break off the Sicilian campaign at all costs and to return to save his Imperium. Their exaggerated reports did ill service to the emperor. A speedy conquest of the island would have been the shortest road to the possession of his royal rival's person, but the long-legged Welf was aghast at the shameful treachery of the German princes. He completely lost his head, and, " shaken to the marrow," he quitted Sicily and hastened north. Moreover, a dream had added to his panic : a young bear had mounted the imperial bed ; larger and larger it grew with every moment, till at last it filled the entire space and pushed him from his couch. In Lodi Otto IV held one last brilliant court on Italian soil, then crossed the Alps, in midwinter, and in March 1212 he was once more in Frankfurt.

Frederick of Sicily was saved. And more. Immediately after the stampede of the Welf the envoy from Nuremberg appeared, a Swabian nobleman, Anselm of Justingen, to announce to the boy his election as Roman Emperor and the summons of the princes. Beyond the bounds of possibility it seemed : just now prepared for flight, scarcely hoping to escape with his life . . . and now—without transition—offered the imperial diadem, the crown of all the Christian world. To his dying day Frederick held it to be a miracle. Later, when he spoke of his being directly singled out as an instrument of Divine Providence, he always quoted this as the first clear call from God, a sign from heaven " against all the probabilities or hopes of men." In Palermo every one sought to dissuade him from accepting the election, his wife Queen Constance above all. (She had just given birth to her first and only son, Henry.) The nobles of Sicily seconded her in seeking to restrain their barely seventeen-year-old king from the vague and unpromising adventure. They scented danger for him ; they mistrusted the *bona fides* of the Germans, one of whom, Diepold, had just betrayed him. These misgivings were assuredly not without excuse. Apart from the perilous journey and the impoverished impotence of the King, what assurance had Frederick that the German princes, faithless and capricious, might not have changed their minds before his arrival ? That conjecture struck home. For when Kaiser Otto reappeared in Germany a number of princes veered from Staufen to Welf again, playing the " princely game " of " hither and thither " as Walther phrased it. And—most vital question of all—what guarantee had Frederick that the Pope, now that Sicily was secured for St. Peter, would enter the lists to ensure the elevation of a Hohenstaufen, and the Sicilian Hohenstaufen at that ? For the Pope's ways were dark : he would first cut down a Staufen to exalt a Welf, and when successful would cast down his Welf again in favour of a Hohenstaufen. This procedure was far removed from papal immutability, and the best minds of the time were at a loss to reconcile themselves to the methods of the Curia. Walther von der Vogelweide writes bitterly of papal arrogance in his *Reichssprüche* :

> For God makes kings of whom he will . . .
> This word fills simple men with hope—
> But then again priests say it is the Pope.
> Tell us in sooth,
> Which is the truth ?
> Two voices in one mouth—it likes me ill.

The procedure least in accord with the whole trend of papal policy would be the elevation of the Sicilian King to the imperial throne. But Philip Augustus of France confronted Innocent practically with a *fait accompli*, and to hunt round for another pretender—especially as the princes had been unanimous in their choice of Frederick—would have been waste of time. Facts, for once, rode roughshod over papal politics. Or did Innocent dream that perchance the elevation of Frederick— his ward and vassal—might even be made to subserve his own omnipotence, for would not the Roman Emperor be in fact the vassal of the Holy See ?　Frederick II believed that the Pope acted under the direct compulsion of Providence, since " God, contrary to human knowledge, had miraculously preserved for the governance of the Roman Empire " the last of the Hohenstaufen.　So interpenetrated was Frederick by the fatefulness of this call to the " last survivor " that he turned a deaf ear to shrewd and prudent warnings.　He recognised his mission. He accepted his election.　A joyful pride in his own uniqueness informs the words in which he confirmed his acceptance : " since no other was to be found, who could have accepted the proffered dignity in opposition to us and to our right . . . since the princes summoned us and since from their own choice the crown is ours. . . ."　The miraculous call was followed by a not less miraculous fulfilment.

A rare and amazing luck—savouring of fairy tales and dreams —and his own peculiar charm of personality, enabled Frederick to reach his journey's end in safety despite unnumbered ambushes and pursuits.　Without men, without money, without an effective knowledge of German, at the mercy of the Pope's support, banking on the probable good faith of a few German princes and on the magic of his name, he set out, following the star, from Palermo to Messina, to conquer the Empire for himself.　With the long reddish-blond curls of his family, his boyish appearance, his " fair and gracious countenance : merry the brow and merrier yet the sparkle of the eyes," the sunburnt Sicilian boy looked less like the " chosen Roman Emperor " that he styled himself, than a fairy prince or an adventurer in tatters.　For " as torn and ragged as a beggar boy " he boarded a foreign vessel in the middle of March 1212 and with a handful of retainers quitted his hereditary home.

At the Pope's request Frederick's infant son, Henry, was crowned King of Sicily before his father's departure—for Innocent was again striving to forestall the new danger of the fusion of the two kingdoms—and the Regency was entrusted to the Queen.　Frederick had also been obliged to renew in writing his mother's Concordat with the Pope and was presently to reconfirm it in person.　Hence Rome was his immediate goal.　He was held up nearly a month in Gaeta, probably because the Pisan fleet, faithful to the Welfs, was lying in wait for him. He did not arrive in Rome till the middle of April. He was received with the utmost honour by Pope Innocent and the Cardinals, the Senate and the People of Rome, who, according to ancient Roman custom, recently revived, " colluded " him as Roman Emperor. For the first and only time Innocent and Frederick met face to face, but little has been put on record of this memorable interview between the rising and the setting suns.

As King " by the grace of God and of the Pope " Frederick presented his credentials to his erstwhile guardian, to whom, under God, he owed all power. Further he had, according to the custom of the Norman Kings of Sicily, to do homage and take the oath of fealty. This done the interests of Pope and Hohenstaufen were one. Innocent spoke words of encouragement and gave what help he could. He took on himself the expenses of Frederick's brief stay in Rome, and sent him on his way after a few days, equipped with a sum of money. In later years Frederick liked to recall his departure from the City of Cities, to celebrate it in a peculiar and symbolic way : " Not the Pope, not the German princes, but the Populus Romanus, yea glorious Rome herself, had sent him forth, as a mother sends her son, to scale the highest heights of Empire," and it may have been in that supreme moment that he felt " the august spirit of the Caesars take possession of the boy," as he triumphantly expressed it in a later document.

Little, however, of the ancient glory of the Caesars just then surrounded the Staufen prince. The land journey was too unsafe on account of Otto's garrisons, and so, on a hired Genoese ship, the " Son of the Church " (the Pope's phrase), the " Priestling-Emperor," to quote his opponents, continued his journey and arrived on the 1st of May at Genoa, a town that in rivalry with Welf-loving Pisa clung to the Staufen house. Here and everywhere he was received with honour and hailed with delight. But weeks passed and still the impatient lad was held up in Genoa because all the roads were unsafe. This proved, however, to be the last serious interruption to his journey. In exchange for a mass of promises that bore the quaint postscriptum " valid for the day when I am Emperor,"

Frederick extracted money from the Genoese for his maintenance, whilst Pavia shouldered the expenses for his journey
from Rome to Genoa. In the middle of July the King set out
for Pavia with a few friends and a Genoese escort. The direct
road was held by forces from the Welf towns, so Frederick
made a *détour* via Asti and thus at last arrived circuitously at
Pavia. Clergy, knights and populace received him as if he were
already the crowned Emperor, and carried over his head the
canopy " as the custom of imperial majesty demands."

The crucial test lay still ahead. To reach Cremona Frederick
must fight his way through hostile country. Piacenza lay
across his path. Any serious circuit would take him too near
Milan. Besides, the people of Milan and Piacenza had already
got news of his journey and of his plans, and had armed themselves in great wrath and excitement and had brought forth
their standard-bearing chariot for the fray. The loyal folk of
Pavia had publicly made oath to convey their future Emperor
to safety by force or guile, and to this end had made a compact
with the Cremonese to meet them half way at the river Lambro.
The Milanese, however, marched south to the same rendezvous,
while the Piacenzans held up every ship sailing down the Po and
searched it thoroughly to find the Staufen boy.

As the vesper bells were ringing one Saturday evening at the
end of July the Pavians set out at dusk and rode all night with
their guest till they reached the Lambro. Faithful to their
promise the Cremonese, under the Margrave of Este, had started
at the same time, and they also reached the river in the grey
dawn of the Sunday morning. While both parties were
enjoying a brief rest the Milanese suddenly appeared to seize
the King. At their approach he flung himself on a barebacked
horse—so the story goes—and swam the river, as little moved
by the taunts the Milanese hurled after him as by the bloody
massacre they made amongst his returning Pavians. Frederick
himself was saved. A few moments had been decisive. People
were amazed. They opined that " Christ sought to show forth
his wonders," and when Frederick finally arrived in the ever-
faithful Staufen town of Cremona they received the lucky
youth with loud rejoicing and welcomed him as if they saw in
him " the angel of the Lord." There was now no holding

him : from Cremona (which was not slow to secure considerable earthly benefits from the unearthly visitant, and see them duly put on record too), he hastened to Mantua ; from Mantua to Verona ; from Verona up the valley of the Adige to Trent. Further than this he could not use the Brenner road because the Dukes of Meran and Bavaria were supporters of Otto. Hence he had to leave the great Alp thoroughfare, and turning westwards seek himself a passage through the bleakest mountain tracts across into the Engadine. And thus in the beginning of September he reached Chur with a handful of followers.

The papal commands that the Hohenstaufen should everywhere be supported and received with honour began now to take effect in German territory. The Bishop of Chur received the traveller most hospitably and himself escorted him to St. Gall, where the Abbot of St. Gall and the Advocate of Pfäffers brought the strength of the King's forces up to some 300 horsemen. With this force Frederick hastened on to Constance. Once again his luck held ; a few hours decided his fate and the Empire's.

While he was riding full speed for Constance his enemy Kaiser Otto was already encamped at Überlingen on the northern shore of the lake. During the last few months Otto had to a very large extent re-established his power in Germany, and when he heard of Frederick's coming he hastened south to meet the Staufen on his first arrival. He was just about to cross over to Constance ; his servants had arrived there, his cooks were already busily preparing his imperial dinner, the town was arranging a reception for him. Suddenly, instead of the expected Otto, Frederick stood before their gates and demanded admission. The Bishop, who was prepared to welcome Otto, at first refused to receive Frederick. Everything was at stake. The papal legate, Archbishop Berard of Bari, who accompanied the King, rehearsed the Pope's excommunication of Kaiser Otto ; the Bishop gave way, not without misgiving, and accorded to the Hohenstaufen entrance into the town, already lavishly decorated in honour of his rival. Hastily they fortified the bridge over the Rhine on the Überlingen road. Three hours later the Emperor Otto stood without the closed gates of Constance. He had arrived with weak forces and scanty

retinue and could not risk a battle. " Had Frederick reached
Constance three hours later," so they say, " he would never
have been successful in Germany."

The news of the miraculous appearance of the Hohenstaufen
spread like wildfire. Frederick's success was manifestly a sign,
an act of God : his following grew hourly. Within a few
days all the nobles and princes of the Upper Rhine jubilantly
embraced his cause, castles and strongholds and towns were
illuminated. When he rode into Basel a week later it was with
a royal retinue. The Bishops of Chur and Constance, the
Abbots of Reichenau and St. Gall, the Counts Ulrich of Kiburg
and Rudolf of Hapsburg with many others joined the cortège
that had at the beginning been so modest, and in Basel the
Bishop of Strasburg brought him 500 troopers. The King of
Bohemia's ambassador petitioned the seventeen-year old monarch for the confirmation of his master's crown. Fortunate
and victorious, Frederick could now afford to forget the helplessness of his childhood and the Welf-persecutions of his
boyhood. He was in any case precociously mature, and now in
a night, not in a dream, like the heroes of romance, but in an
almost dream-like reality, he had won the security of a young
conqueror, though people still styled him " the child," " the
Child from Apulia."

The possession of Basel and Constance gave him a firm
footing. Kaiser Otto tried to bar the Rhine valley against him
by investing Breisach, but Frederick did not need to take up
arms against him in person. The Saxons had made themselves
unpopular in the south by many a deed of tyranny, and the
embittered Breisachers, hearing of Frederick's approach to their
relief, vigorously took up their own defence and frightened off
the Emperor and his troops. Otto was deserted by numbers of
his followers and fled to Hagenau, whence he was ejected by
Frederick's cousin, the Duke of Lorraine. The Welf was
unable to rally himself and his forces till he reached Cologne on
the lower Rhine, which had formerly acclaimed him. The
whole upper valley of the Rhine was thus in Staufen hands.
This valley had been the scene not long before of the Children's
Crusade, when hordes of boys and girls, seized with a blind
enthusiasm and passionate fanaticism had poured into Italy

from the countries by the Rhine. People had gazed in deep
depression at this hapless procession of ill-starred youngsters,
moving to inevitable destruction . . . the more gladly did they
now greet the festive progress of the Hohenstaufen boy.

He was hailed with matchless enthusiasm as German King
as he slowly moved downstream through the decorated
Rhenish towns. He traversed Alsace, " most well-beloved of
our hereditary lands " he called it, and was met everywhere by
cries of joy as the populace escorted him and his ever-swelling
multitudes in unbroken triumph through the valleys of the
Rhine. An Italian had said : " it is a joy merely to gaze on
the handsome Hohenstaufen boy," and the people of the upper
Rhine felt this still more strongly. In the driest and most
meagre chronicles you can read between the lines the sympathy
and joy of the writer in the young King's success, whose first
easy victory stood out like a miracle.

Even the outward circumstances of his surprising rise to
power seemed like the fulfilment of well-known legends and
fairy-tales : the Beggar Prince knocking at the gate of Constance,
finding the dinner laid for another, and winning the Empire in a
couple of hours—these were episodes familiar in story, which
yet in everyday life seemed strangely remote and far away. And
thus a touch of glamour lingered round the boy, and the Germans
seemed to feel a breath of Sicilian air and the dream atmosphere
of childhood enveloping him. His appearance too—so homely
in spite of its foreignness—marked him as one of their own
people. Just so must Duke Ernest of Swabia have looked long
ago, the songs of whose wonder journeys were now beginning
to be heard, set to the tune intended for Frederick. People
rarely called him by his name or title ; to all he was " the
Apulian Lad," " the Child of Pulle," or just " Our Boy," and
decades afterwards the chroniclers still added to the mighty
Emperor's name, as if it were a cognomen, the title *Puer Apuliae*.

As the chosen of the Pope a further peculiar glory surrounded
him, and the simple people who were accustomed to view
temporal events in the light of spiritual imagery, celebrated in
their Staufen hero the victory of the eternal CHILD, who with
invisible weapons overthrows the mighty. The Pope himself,
finding the Goliath story apt to existing circumstance, had sent

the boy forth as his " David " against the giant Welf.   And the people interpreted the victory in similar vein : one writer represents the Welf as a species of monster creeping off to its distant lair before the face of the Apulian child.   Another said : " The child has conquered the Welf with heavenly rather than with earthly might," and yet another speaks of the " wise child of Apulia."   " Behold the power of the child " sang one of the troubadours, and a rhymed chronicle in kindred mood summarises :

> Now comes the Pulian Child along—
> The Kaiser's sword is twice as strong,
> Whom yet the Child did overthrow
> Without a single swordsman's blow :
> The people's love towards him did flow . . .

About this time, or it may have been a few years later, the troubadour, Aimeric of Peguilain, at the court of the Margrave of Montferrat, maintained that till he had witnessed the deeds of Frederick he had never been able to believe in the exploits of Alexander : for the Staufen, the " Physician of Salerno," had raised Generosity from her sick bed.   The troubadours praised other qualities of Frederick's also—the freshness of his youth—his *joie de vivre*—his beauty—for he fulfilled the Minnesängers' ideal of a king—his medium height (for " moderation " was valued above all)—his golden hair ; but nothing was lauded so highly as his " graciousness," of which the Macedonian king had also been a pattern.   Openhandedness as a royal virtue was a relic of the heathen streak that coloured the ethics of the troubadours.   For the true medieval Christian—in the absence of a Bible parallel—knew nothing of *liberalitas*, whether as an expression of overflowing joy in life or of humane intent, but reverenced only *caritas* indulged for the soul's salvation.   Since Hohenstaufen days Generosity belonged once more to the make-up of the perfect king, and when Frederick in the very first document written on German soil thus expressed himself : " Kingly dignity is enhanced by openhandedness, and prestige loses nothing by the giving of gifts," this saying of his tallied word for word with many a verse of Minnesang.

Frederick II acted only, as he frequently asserted, "according to common royal custom on the one hand, and on the other according to a certain magnanimity peculiarly his own." Thus the poets praised especially his *innata liberalitas*, even when in later days for grave reasons of state he was least able to display it towards the troubadours. Just now, however, he had scarcely set foot in Germany than his " graciousness " bordered on prodigality. In the first intoxication of success the young prince gave with both hands ancestral estates and imperial property to all who crowded round him, and when resources failed him for the nonce he promised gifts for the day " when with God's help he would have wealth again." When money came his way he handed it over forthwith to his hangers-on. The ambassadors of the French King who in the first weeks brought him a very considerable sum of money must have been more than a little surprised when the Chancellor asked where the money was to be kept and received for answer : " Neither this nor any other money is to be kept at all ; it is to be distributed amongst the princes."

" When people heard of this high-hearted generosity of the King a universal shout of jubilation was raised in his favour " —" all were bound to him and he became dear to all by his liberality "—such is the unanimous verdict of the chroniclers. The *Puer Apuliae* knew exactly what he was doing, and the means by which he could secure the adherence of the ever-hungry counts and princes. The gesture of openhandedness perhaps came natural to him, but he was by no means unaware of the contrast it would point between him and the notoriously parsimonious Welf. He declared himself : " Wisdom counselled it, and it gives us advantage in men's minds over our foe who acts in other manner and thus brings down on his own head the hatred of men and the displeasure of heaven."

In a few weeks Frederick was master of the whole of the south of Germany from Burgundy to Bohemia without exertion and without a blow. His debt to Pope Innocent was immeasurable, and it has justly been pointed out that his progress had hitherto lain through lands predominantly belonging to the Church. Chur, Constance, Basel and Strasburg were all bishop's seats, as indeed was almost the whole plain of the upper Rhine. Next to the Pope's the French King's help had been of most value, and he was to get further assistance from the same quarter.

In November 1212 Frederick met the French heir to the
throne in Vaucouleurs near Toul and was reported to have had
a narrow escape from the daggers of Otto's assassins.   He
concluded an alliance with the French against England, binding
himself not to make peace with the foe without the consent of
France.   In these early years Frederick was wholly dependent
on the powers that had helped to raise him, and was particularly
bound to Philip Augustus who espoused his cause, a trifle too
warmly perhaps.   A certain arrogance was noticeable on the
French side, as for instance when a French vassal swore to his
king to support him and the Hohenstaufen Frederick, and, in
the case of the latter's death, the feudal oath ran on, " whomso-
ever the electors might, with the approval of the King of France,
choose for Roman Emperor."   As France supported the Hohenstaufen, England backed the Welf, and so the day was coming
when—sign of the appalling disintegration of Germany—the
imperial throne would be the stake in a war between England
and France.   French envoys were present when Frederick II
on the 5th of December, 1212, was once more formally elected
King at a great assembly of princes in Frankfurt, and four days
later at his coronation in Mainz.   He was crowned it is true
with imitation regalia, for the Welf had possession of the real
ones, and not in Aix la Chapelle which was for the moment held
by Kaiser Otto and his minions.

There was yet no open fighting between the two opponents.
Otto was busy with haphazard little feuds in his native Saxony
and Thuringia along the lower Rhine, and Frederick had not
yet mustered an army.   To gather forces, and at the same time
to show himself to his vassals in the various provinces and
receive their homage, Frederick held a series of royal courts :
one in Ratisbon for Bavaria and Bohemia, one in Constance
for Swabia.   Much as Frederick owed to the Pope and to the
King of France it was clear that in the south of Germany, and
above all in Swabia, other and mighty influences were at work
helping him to victory.   The populace hailed him as their
hereditary Lord, their Hohenstaufen.   His enemy had set ugly
tales in circulation : he was no son of Henry's but the bastard
of some papal official, just such a tale as had been circulated
at the time of his birth and was to crop up again not infrequently.

How the mere sight of him sufficed to quench all such gossip is best told in the words of the chronicler : " While now these fateful chatterings began to fly from lip to lip, lo, on a sudden, there appears amidst his Swabians, Bavarians and Bohemians, the young King as conqueror over his foes, and proves the nobility of his race by the courtesy and dignity of his behaviour." Here he was hailed therefore as the legitimate heir, entering the kingdom of his fathers, by birth the lord of Swabia, whose due succession as Duke had been recognised by the Swabian monasteries immediately on the murder of Philip. People recalled once more that long ago in the lifetime of Henry VI Frederick had been elected King, and that only his youth, his absence, and the wiles of others had kept him from his throne, and they maintained that the imperial crown was the prerogative of a Hohenstaufen. For, they told each other, there was only one imperial race, one *regia stirps* that begot Emperors, the race of the Waiblings which reckoned doubly royal blood, the Carolingian and the Salian, and through the latter traced its descent from Troy. The Staufen ancestor had, at God's express command, wedded a Waibling maid, and Barbarossa had been justified in his boast that he sprang from the *regia stirps Waiblingensium*. All this contributed not a little to the glorification of the last of the Hohenstaufens whom people had fetched home from Sicily.

Had not the Heruli of old—as with amazement the Byzantines related—sent out messengers to Ultima Thule to spy out the land and see whether a scion of their ancient royal house might there be found ? And had not the Heruli also—weary of waiting for their messengers' return—chosen themselves a new king whom, however, they stealthily forsook by night when the news came that their envoys were on the way bringing their hereditary prince. Not otherwise had it been in Swabia. Kaiser Otto had returned in haste from Italy and by his friends' advice had hastily married the Staufen heiress Beatrice, to whom he was long since betrothed, and had hoped thereby to secure the loyalty of Bavarian and Swabian warriors. But his young bride died shortly after, and almost simultaneously the news came that the last of the Hohenstaufens was coming home. By night his men of war crept off and returned to their homesteads, leaving bag and baggage in Otto's hands. For in these regions none loved " the Saxon " as they always called the Welf.

Frederick's life was to be rich in wars against almost all the powers. It is significant that his career begins with the renewal of a prehistoric racial feud. The boy had scarcely yet had time to make enemies of his own, but Otto the Welf, who from birth, as son of an Englishwoman, seemed destined for the most northern throne in Europe as King of the Scots, as the Staufen was born to a southern crown, seemed expressly created by fate to be the antithesis in every detail of his Waibling rival : even in his exterior. The Welf, heroic to foolhardiness, was a fearless dashing knight, unwontedly tall, with powerful frame and well-proportioned limbs. His strength lay in his mighty fist, trusting to which he bore himself with aggressive arrogance, " like a lion whose very voice inspires terror in all around." Not many years before Frederick's tour of his Swabian dukedom Kaiser Otto had visited the country in his royal progress. Swabia in those days centred round the Lake of Constance in the west and stretched far beyond the Rhine, embracing the whole of Alsace and reaching southward across the Alps almost to Lake Como. It was the oldest Roman settlement in Germany and as such tended to turn its gaze southward as of course. Throughout this Swabia then, Otto of Brunswick remained " the Stranger," " the Saxon." True, the Welfs were Swabian too by origin, and not until after the fall of Henry the Lion, Otto's great state-founding father, had they been restricted to Brunswick. Kaiser Otto in filial piety had made a pilgrimage to those spots of Swabia that were dear to his house : Augsburg for instance and the monastery of Weingarten, but he had spent his boyhood at the English court of his uncle, Richard Cœur de Lion, and had become estranged from the land of his forebears. He displays many an English trait : a frugality bordering on parsimony, which Walther held up to scorn—" If he had been as generous as he was long, he would have had many virtues " —an amazing lack of education, a poverty of intellect. How could such a boor hold his own in the delicate play of intrigue of the Roman Curia or prove a match for the great Pope

Innocent. He moves us almost to pity as we see him powerless
in the grip of forces which he did not even understand, ignorant
and unsuspecting in the toils of fate : not even rightly aware
what goal he sought or ought to seek. Not until the storm had
broken was he aware of its approach, and then he was bewildered
by it—*perplexus*, as the chronicler has it. The impact broke
him, instead of lending him fresh impetus.

By his own behaviour Otto wantonly squandered the attachment of people of all ranks, certainly in the South. Towards
the princes he showed himself inopportunely stern, arrogant,
unjust. He embittered the lower clergy by the favouritism
which awarded rich livings to Englishmen and Saxons instead
of to the Swabian candidates ; he irritated the higher ranks
by his lack of courtesy, addressing them all as shavelings or
priestlings. In short, by the multiplication of almost negligible
trifles he unnecessarily queered his own pitch. Even when his
edicts were wise and just, his unhappy touch prevented his
winning affection by his righteousness. His excommunication
was hailed with malicious delight by all who boasted "a different
standard of manners." " A burden to the Italians, a worse
burden to the Swabians, unpopular amongst his own," such was
the judgment of the South on the Welf Emperor whose brusquerie
was a symptom of self-distrust rather than of legitimate pride.
For this son of Anak lacked that genuinely royal dignity which
enabled Barbarossa without losing prestige to kneel before the
mightiest of his own vassals. Otto's feudal pride which only
force could bend turned all too easily into its opposite. A
cruel Nemesis awaited him. He was barely thirty-six when he
died a gruesome death at the Harzburg : deposed, dethroned, he
was flung full length on the ground by the Abbot, confessing his
sins, while the reluctant priests beat him bloodily to death with
rods. Such was the end of the first and last Welf Emperor.

The times were growing too intellectual and clearsighted for
a mere champion, however lion-hearted, to rule the Holy
Roman Empire. The ancient myth appointed to the two races
their two tasks with a merciless exactitude : the Welfs, though
mighty and great their Dukes, for ever vassals ; the Waiblings for
ever Emperors. For there was room in the Waibling state for
giants who preserved the might and prowess of ancient heroes,

but never in a Welf state would there be mental room for Waibling brains. The relationship had held since Carolingian times, even since the Wanderings of the Peoples. Again and yet again the Welfs had tried to break the evil spell, again and yet again had met the inexorable doom : the pride of the rebellious vassal had ended in ruin and a lonely death.

A breath of mystery and horror surrounds these luckless Welfs, like the atmosphere of northern myth : Ethico, one of the first of them, vanished full of sorrow into bleak mountain fastnesses when his son—unknown to the father—had fulfilled his fate and done homage to the Waibling emperor of the Franks . . . Henry the Proud after fighting long and vainly against his Staufen foe died suddenly as victory lay within his grasp. . . . Henry the Lion fell and was banished . . . Otto, the only Welf who reigned as Emperor—not by any means the greatest of his race—seemed to have belied the fateful prophecy, seemed about to found a Welf Empire of the North—which would assuredly have met a warm welcome from the Pope—and paid the penalty of his trespass into the Hohenstaufen empire with this shameful, grisly death. Perhaps we should add to the series that uncrowned founder of a northern kingdom, the lonely fallen vassal in the Saxon forest, Bismarck, the most sublime of all these giants, who stands in fate so near the Welfs. It is easy to understand why the Church took the Welfs under her wing—her short flirtation with the Sicilian boy was accidental—she wanted as her " Sword " a docile warrior-giant, not an intellectual Emperor. Danger lurked in the free, independent, unclerical mind of the Hohenstaufen.

It was the famous duel between Otto and Frederick—extreme types of the two races—that gave Italy the two party battle-cries that echo for centuries through her history : Welf and Waibling, Guelf and Ghibelline. It was no chance that allied Guelfdom and Popedom. For in the thirteenth century the Ghibelline spirit stood for that secular and intellectual light that often bordered on heresy, and which, even when it found room for itself within the Church, was yet able to take a detached view of the Church from outside and see it as a whole. Boccaccio said of Dante that he would have been ill able to create his work had he not been a Ghibelline. The first appearance of the two cries as party names would seem to have been in Florence on the occasion of the Amidei-Buondelmonti wedding in 1216 when the family feud developed into party strife. The Buondelmonti party called themselves Guelfs, as supporters of the Emperor, the Amidei dubbed themselves Ghibelline after the rival King. The papal and imperial element had not yet entered in (at that moment the papal would have been the Ghibelline). Later, under the empire of Frederick, Ghibelline became synonymous with the imperial, and Guelf with the papal party.

The struggle between Welf and Hohenstaufen was felt in all directions beyond the borders of Germany, not alone in Italy. England and France were intimately involved by the alliance of Kaiser Otto with King John and of Frederick with Philip Augustus. For these two western powers the German succession was only an episode in their everlasting weary quarrellings, but for Otto, who had little chance of winning the day against Frederick on German soil, the interference of these powers offered a hope of success. The Welf rightly reckoned that any English victory over France would at least seriously damage the Hohenstaufen's uncertain position in South Germany and might even completely undermine it. A simultaneous English-Welf attack on France was therefore planned. Philip Augustus's position was precarious. In the spring of 1214 the English king landed at La Rochelle, and simultaneously Otto, in alliance with the Duke of Brabant, invaded France from the north-east.

Frederick had waged an unsuccessful campaign against Quedlinburg in the preceding year, and at Easter in 1214 he availed himself of a Diet which he held at Coblenz to summon the South German army to a concerted attack on the lower Rhine, and thus, by diverting Kaiser Otto's attention, relieve the pressure on his French ally. But fate forestalled him. He had no need to take a hand in the French-English-Welf campaign, he had only to garner the fruits of a French victory. The French heir apparent inflicted a crushing defeat on King John in Poitou and Philip Augustus made short work of the hostile coalition. On the 27th of July, 1214, the memorable battle of Bouvines was fought which decided the fate of three countries.

Victorious France, whose oriflamme was the rallying point of the levies from the various towns, laid the foundation of her internal unity.   John's defeat furnished the opportunity for the English barons to rise against the King and wring from him

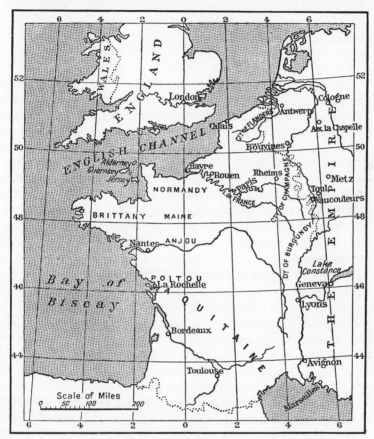

THE BATTLE OF BOUVINES, 1214

the great charter of liberty, the " Magna Charta " of 1215. And Germany displayed for the first time in the arena of European politics her complete internal disintegration.   The Empire, for one short brilliant moment, was to enjoy unity under this great Hohenstaufen, who received from the hand of France the golden eagle wrenched from the defeated Otto, but

the clear-sighted Philip Augustus had not failed to note—and
repair—its broken wings. " From this time forward the fame
of the Germans sank ever lower amongst foreigners " reports a
chronicler. Kaiser Otto never recovered from this defeat :
the trifling campaigns which Frederick undertook against him,
now here, now there, finally in alliance with the king of Denmark, are without interest or significance.

Philip Augustus and Frederick II were not the only victors
of Bouvines. Pope Innocent made a third. The promises
and assurances of his ward matured for him, now that Frederick
had the power to redeem them. Innocent had not lent his
potent aid gratis. Six months after Frederick's arrival in
Germany, as he celebrated Whitsuntide at Eger, he had surrendered, with the concurrence of the numerous princes there
assembled, valuable privileges and territories. He secured to
the Pope the internal Church powers he sought, he handed over
the disputed domains of Central Italy which Otto had conceded
before his coronation. For Frederick could ill refuse to his
" Benefactor and Protector "—as he now styled him—what his
rival predecessor had accorded. The weighty thing was that
the famous Golden Bull of Eger, which the German Church
delivered to the Pope, took the form—at the express wish of the
Curia—of an imperial grant, not of a personal promise. The
princes as a body, and each prince individually, had to counter-
sign and confirm it. For the personal promises of one—though
he were an Emperor—gave inadequate security, as the Pope had
learned from his experience with Kaiser Otto.

The papal power was slowing mounting by such successes to
its zenith. Like every great ruler Innocent III craved to give
himself and the world a visible sign of his greatness. No more
impressive demonstration could have been devised than the
great Church Council which he convened for 1215 at the
Lateran. It was to be the biggest Council that ever Pope had
held since the Church had come to birth. And Innocent saw
with satisfaction representatives of the whole of Christendom
pouring into Rome and rallying round him, the Vicegerent of
the one true God : 71 archbishops with the patriarchs of

Jerusalem and Constantinople, over 400 bishops, 800 abbots,
and the envoys of unnumbered princes and towns, with the
ambassadors of almost every western king.   Otto the Welf had
sent his messenger ; Frederick II was represented by the
Archbishop Berard of Palermo : the Council was to decide the
question of the German succession.   On the whole nothing
could be expected from its decision but the deposition of the
Welf Emperor—a decision immediately favourable to Frederick
II.   But a precedent fraught with omen : the deposition of a
Roman Emperor by a Church Council.

The remaining decisions of the Lateran Council concerned
matters of internal ecclesiastical discipline.   Pope Innocent did
not live to see them carried out.   Within a few months of this
triumph, in July 1216, he died, at the age of fifty-six, in Perugia.
And men remembered that he had opened the Council with the
prophetic scriptural words : " With desire I have desired to eat
this passover with you before I suffer."   Under the protection
of this mighty Pope the two greatest men of the immediate
future had been reared : Francis of Assisi and Frederick II.

Before the Council met in the palace of the Lateran the
cause of the Hohenstaufen had triumphed, and Frederick had
performed a most valuable service for the Church, which the
Pope, however, sedulously ignored.   The Pope had devoted
all his energies during the last year of his life to the promotion
of a new Crusade, which should be this time the work not of a
secular power but of the Church Militant.   Innocent had even
toyed with the idea of placing himself as the *verus imperator*
at its head.   Encyclicals had been despatched to the whole
Christian world, and preachers of the Cross had been appointed
for each diocese to fan to fresh flame the fire kindled in German
bosoms by St. Bernard.   Signs from heaven accompanied the
steps of the preachers and encouraged the waverers, as the
Pope's heralds journeyed to towns and villages and hamlets.
But enthusiasm flagged, fanaticism had faded to lukewarmness,
damped not a little by the fiasco of the Children's Crusade.
Still, a few of the princes, like the Duke of Bavaria, had taken
the Cross, when Frederick II in the spring of 1215 was preparing

for the campaign to Aix and to Cologne. For when he had marched along the lower Rhine after Bouvines he had not ventured to attack Cologne even with his considerable army, and he had made a fruitless attempt on Aix. His only success had been in winning over Otto's ally, the Duke of Brabant. So in May at Andernach he decided on a new Rhine campaign. But in July, just as he was about to quit Alsace, the situation on the lower Rhine suddenly cleared up. The citizens of Aix themselves drove out the governor, and they now invited the Hohenstaufen to come in peace and permit them to receive him as their lawful lord.

So in the last days of July 1215 Frederick made his triumphal entry into the sacred Roman town, not with the clash of weapons but with all the pomp of a Roman emperor coming to be crowned, escorted by princes and nobles in gorgeous array. Frederick called Aix " the capital and seat of the kingdom of Germany," and praised it beyond all other towns, " because in this town the Roman kings are sanctified and crowned and it shines out in glory second only to Rome herself." No German king in those days could claim his full rights or his title to the imperial crown of Rome till he had been anointed and crowned in Aix and had taken his seat on the throne of Charlemagne. Frederick, indeed, himself reckoned the years of his reign from the day of his coronation in Aix. Other solemnities took place during the coronation days. Fifty years before, in 1165, Barbarossa, though then under the ban of the Church, had disinterred the bones of Charlemagne, and in the presence of bishops and princes had had them consecrated by the—also banned—imperial Anti-Pope of the day " to the honour and glory of Christ and the strengthening of the Roman Empire." Barbarossa hoped by thus canonising the first Christian German Imperator to sanctify also the *sacrum imperium* (in Charlemagne's own phrase) of the said empire and the office of emperor itself, just as he had previously emphasised the biblical sanctity of kingship by transferring the relics of the Three Holy Kings from Milan to Cologne. In Barbarossa's time the solemn sequence had been composed in honour of Charles and his capital, whose words of praise rang, full alike of challenge and of promise, in the ears of Barbarossa's son :

Hic est Christi miles fortis,
Hic invictae dux cohortis,

as he entered the great cathedral to lay to rest the remains of
the first German Emperor.

The people of Aix had wrought a magnificent silver shrine
the sides of which were adorned with figures of the Emperors,
like images of the apostles.   The apostolic duty of converting
the heathen was part of the imperial office.   Frederick II was
represented on the shrine, which was to be closed in his presence.
The day after his coronation the young King flung off his heavy
robe, climbed the scaffolding which bore the shrine and with
his own hand drove the first nails into the lid.   No wonder that
Frederick's mind was filled in those days, as never before or
after, with visions of Charlemagne, Destroyer of the Heathen,
and of the aged Barbarossa, his grandfather, who lost his life
on a Crusade.   He solemnly declared that it appeared to him
" both reasonable and seemly to follow the example of the
Great and Holy Charles and of his other ancestors."   The deed
had in fact preceded these words, for immediately on receiving
the Diadem with which Sigfrid, Archbishop of Mainz, had
crowned him, Frederick had suddenly, to the amazement of
the onlookers, taken the Cross, and by fervent prayers and
exhortations, reinforced by promises and gifts, had eagerly
recruited the knights and princes for the new Crusade.   Many
of the princes followed the King's example.   Frederick spent
the whole of the next day from early morning till night listening
to Crusade sermons in the cathedral, and persuaded many to pin
the token of the Cross upon their shoulders.

Did people hope that the boy, so recently compared to King
David, would really lead the hosts to David's royal city of
Jerusalem ?   Frederick himself had every hope of it.   It was
an almost inspired masterstroke of diplomacy that prompted
the young King to set himself at the head of the crusading
movement.   Unwittingly he thus took the leadership and
direction of the Crusade out of the hands of the papal Imperator
and took up again the noblest task of an Emperor—by common
consent the imperial prerogative—to lead the knights of
Christendom to the Holy Land.   Pope Innocent was most
painfully disturbed by this inopportune zeal on the part of his

quondam ward and made no single allusion to Frederick's act. This wise political move was, however, only the inevitable outcome of the mental attitude of the man and the king, and it would be cynical to let its shrewdness blind us to the unique greatness of that moment. It is a scene that lives : the proud impetuous boy in the full flush of his amazing triumph and success, immediately after the Coronation Mass, when he has but just received the imperial diadem, dedicating himself in the noble enthusiasm of youth to the service of God and of the Empire with his crusader's vow. Frederick knew and felt the act as a sacrifice, a surrender of himself to his office and his calling : " With pure and spotless heart he had not only dedicated his body and his powers to God, but offered them up in the devouring flame, as it were a holocaust." Vow and consecration followed. The young Hohenstaufen is now twenty-one years old. With his coronation and his sacrifice the years of his boyhood had ended, the *Puer Apuliae* is no more.

III. EARLY STATESMANSHIP

Death of Otto——Dawn of national consciousness in Germany——Knight and Monk——The Cistercians—— The Templars——The Teutonic Order : Hermann of Salza——War with Denmark——The Golden Bull of Rimini, 1226——Pope Honorius III——King Henry elected King of the Romans——Diplomatic victory over the Papacy——Coronation in Rome ; ceremonial—— De resignandis privilegiis——The Sicilian barons——Diet of Capua——Count of Molise——Deportation of people of Celano——Remodelling of the Feudal System——Archi- tecture——Diet of Messina, 1221——Syracuse——Mea- sures against foreign trade——Creation of Sicilian fleet—— Saracen war——Lucera——University of Naples—— Crusading disasters ; San Germano——Death of Con- stance of Aragon, 1222——Marriage with Isabella of Jerusalem, 1225——Birth of Conrad——Berard of Palermo ——Lombard League——Feud of Cremona and Milan ——Franciscans and Dominicans——Diet of Cremona prevented by Lombards, 1226——Leonardo of Pisa—— St. Francis——Death of Honorius III——Gregory IX

III. EARLY STATESMANSHIP

A SERIES of uneventful, though not inactive, years followed in Germany the exuberance of Frederick's youthful début. He had solemnly dedicated himself to the Empire and indicated thereby the direction his future thought and activity would take. Anyone who was looking for spectacular effects, however, must have been disappointed in the new King's methods. It would be wearisome and purposeless to recount in detail the history of the next few years. Squabbles and differences with the Duke of Lorraine, with a certain Egeno of Urach about some questions of inheritance arising from the dying out of the Zähringen —these and similar trifles—are irrelevant to the tasks and duties of an Emperor, and have, as purely internal German affairs, no interest beyond their own narrow borders. Even the Welf struggle, which had at one point been a matter of European importance with world principles at stake, had sunk to the level of a casual feud, since Otto IV had abandoned Cologne and the lower Rhine and retreated into his Brunswick domains. Frederick attacked him again in the summer of 1217, but it was scarcely necessary, for no one now seriously questioned the Hohenstaufen rule. Nevertheless Otto's death at the Harzburg in May 1218 cleared up the general situation and brought a certain feeling of relief to Frederick. It was a remarkable coincidence that—so at least the legend runs—just a few days before the death of the Welf Goliath, the Hohenstaufen King stood godfather to a boy who was destined in Germany's darkest hour to rescue the remains of the shattered Empire and to restore some fraction of the old pomp and glory to his ancient house : Rudolf of Hapsburg.

The only events of these days were insignificant feuds whose origin and name are alike forgotten : more or less important diets accompanying the King's presence in various parts of his dominions, weddings, awards, gifts, confirmations of title, arbitrations—all the routine attaching to the daily duty of a king.

Frederick's favourite residence in those days was in Alsace, on the Rhine at Worms or Speyer. He had the body of the murdered Philip of Swabia brought from Bamberg and buried in the cathedral of Speyer beside the Hohenstaufen matron Beatrice, Barbarossa's consort. His other favourite German headquarters was Hagenau, where he could hunt in the extensive forests and yet slake his thirst for knowledge in the rich library of ancient manuscripts. He was also often to be found in Franconia and Swabia, in Würzburg and Nuremberg, in Augsburg and Ulm, and business took him now and then to Thuringia, Saxony and Lorraine, so that he acquired a wide knowledge of Germany.

These have been called his " Wanderjahre "; their importance lies less in what he achieved than in the goal he set himself. We know nothing of his personal self-education in those days. He was fortunate enough not to feel the need of an amateurish search for suitable mental food that drove Napoleon, for instance, at the corresponding age, to writing philosophical essays. He was perfectly clear in his own mind what he wanted —hesitation indeed never haunted him—and we can accept as correct his own later statement that from his earliest youth he had kept before him one lofty aim : to devote himself unreservedly, body and soul, to the exaltation of the Roman Empire. He therefore directed his policy solely with an eye to the Empire as a whole : a whole of which Germany was merely one important constituent. This is the key to his German policy : he took a passive line towards the German princes, interfered as little as possible, and surrendered one royal right after another, looking only to the good of the Empire. The princes, for the most part, were supremely indifferent to the wider imperial issues, and Frederick II sought at any cost to secure their loyalty and attach them to himself in order to divert at least a fraction of their vigour to his task.

Frederick's position towards the princes was a peculiarly delicate one. To maintain his rights, let alone seek to enlarge them, that is : to attempt to rule himself, without the mediation of the princes of the Empire, could only have been achieved in battle against them. Never would they have voluntarily consented to any curtailment of their independence or of the rights

they had won during the long wars of succession. But these
were the very men who had summoned Frederick to Germany,
by whose aid he had overcome the Welf. Moreover, the most
numerous amongst them, as well as the most powerful, were
spiritual princes who had given him their help as the protégé
of the Pope. Any step of Frederick against the princes would
infallibly embroil him with the Church, the other power to
which he owed his elevation. Such measures were not to be
thought of ; he who had come as a beggar to Germany was in
no position to exercise compulsion or persuasion on its princes.
His enfeebled Swabian dukedom did not of itself offer sufficient
resources to embark on a fight against the whole body of
German princes. Even if Frederick had wanted to confine his
activities to Germany, and to build up a strong, national German
kingdom, no opportunity for this was offered him. This particular ambition was in any case foreign to the philosophy of
his race with its leaning towards the universal. Moreover, he
was himself a Sicilian as well as a Hohenstaufen.

We have various indications that Frederick's one instinct was
to shelve for the moment the miscellaneous German problems
—which finally stirred him to unconcealed annoyance—even at
the cost of surrendering many a privilege. By the indirect
expedient of building up a powerful Roman empire, rather than
by civil war, Frederick hoped to strengthen the royal power in
Germany.

So during these German years Frederick systematically
sought out and turned to account whatever benefited the
Roman Empire, whatever he could find in Germany that would
be valid or valuable in a wider world and not only within the
frontiers of Germany. He exploited not German peculiarities
but German world forces, and these, in addition to serving the
Empire, brought advantage to the incoherent loosely-knit Germany herself. The only way to consolidate Germany was first
to extend it until it embraced enough material to weld into a
compact whole. As yet no German spirit existed, but only a
Roman spirit which was gradually civilising the Germanic. It
was not common German tradition which bound the Northerners together, but Roman form and culture. The German
races had nothing in common but their blood, and the call

of the blood was rarely vocal. Just now and then, on some auspicious occasion, in solemn moments of enthusiasm, when they assembled for crusade or pilgrimage, they felt with a thrill of pride that they—Saxons and Franks, Swabians and Bavarians —were one. But they did not even then feel " German." At most they felt that they stood together as heirs of the Empire of the Caesars, they prided themselves on being descendants of the Trojans, or styled themselves " Roman " citizens. The word " German " is reserved for our use to-day.

Frederick therefore in seeking out whatever struck him as most " Roman " in Empire and Church was also fostering whatever was most nearly " national." Awakening Germany offered scope enough in the dawn of the thirteenth century when she welcomed in her young king, the Child of Apulia, the personification of her own youth. For in that wonderful Hohenstaufen age, warmed through and through by southern light, Germany was experiencing within her borders for the first time (and for the only time in any such many-sidedness) a real blossoming of song and vision, of fairy tale and epic, of painting, building and sculpture. Despite world wars and political tension she was displaying that cheerful serenity, that emancipation and freedom which breathes from the creations of the time—almost incredible as German products. The existence of these works is the justification of Nietzsche's statement made at a time when freedom had reached its nadir : " There is a touch of something in them that might almost be Hellenic, which awakes in contact with the South." This fertilisation by the South did not necessarily entail a journey thither. The spirit can modify the climate, and by the spirit of the Roman Empire and the Roman Church Germany was southernised as far up as her Baltic coasts. Not that the essentially Germanic was surrendered or eliminated. These southern forces absorbed, without excluding, all that was most characteristic, as the thirteenth century, the most Roman century, abundantly proves. For all the Middle High German heroic epics took their final form in the Hohenstaufen period : the Nibelungen, Gudrun, the cycle of Dietrich of Bern, with the Rose Garden of Worms, Laurin, the Battle of Ravenna and Hugdietrich. Further, the epics of Duke Ernest and Ortnit, these and others belong to this period. Side by side with the great epic monuments—echoes of the Germanic heroic age— we find the stirring new lyrics of the courtly Minnesänger, Hartmann of Aue, Henry of Veldeke, Gottfried von Strassburg, Wolfram von Eschenbach, and Walther von der Vogelweide, whose voices blended with the solemn Latin hymns of the Christian ritual. The chivalrous epics of the Minnesänger, the Eneide, Poor Henry, Tristan, Parzival show the complete blending of heroic tale and Christian spirit. It was the Roman Imperium which imposed a sure, cultivated touch alike on German heroics and on Christian chivalry—the like of which Germany has never seen again.

We recall Bishop Conrad of Hildesheim writing of the marvels of South Italy : " We do not need to go beyond the borders of our own German Empire to see all that the Roman poets have been at such pains to describe."

Throughout the length and breadth of the Roman Empire the German felt at home, and on a sudden the Roman poets made a direct and personal appeal, and were no longer only the cultural and educational stock-in-trade of the Roman Church. The effective assimilation of such Roman spoils is shown by the now repeated attempt to translate a Roman poet into German—the first since Notker's Vergil in Carolingian times. Albert of Halberstadt translated Ovid—he did not find a successor till the days of the Humanists—and proved that at the time an interest in classical literature was beginning to be felt in circles not conversant with classical Latin, probably amongst those knightly laymen in the entourage of the Landgrave Hermann of Thuringia at whose instance the translation was undertaken. The Hohenstaufen were also responsible for the introduction of Roman Law, the most vital and permanent invasion of the Roman spirit into secular Germany.

The most remarkable manifestation of the German-Roman-Antique time—felt to be " most strange "—was the architecture of Bamberg, followed by Naumburg, in which for the first time a real German figure was portrayed. The surprising and stimulating thing about the plastic art which belongs to the later days of Frederick, the Sicilian-Italian Hohenstaufen, is

this, that in works like the " Horseman " of Bamberg or Magdeburg the possibility is for the first time revealed—not yet in
song or story, but to the eye in chiselled stone—of a work
showing a German subject and yet making a world-wide appeal.
This intermingling of the music and motion of Germany with
(imperial and papal) Rome has produced as by a miracle an
almost Mediterranean type, restrained, yet withal free and
unfettered, a type hitherto foreign to German art, for which
until then only the Italian had had an eye. The Bamberg
master worked of course under French influence and the
tradition of ancient Roman plastic art, but while this fact is
not without importance it does not alter the certain inference
that this nobly beautiful and chivalrous human type must have
existed in the Germany of the day.

Two figures of aristocratic life gave tone to the whole period
and gave Germany a share in the happenings of the world outside : knight and monk.   These were cosmopolitan figures and
German figures both.   The monk exercised so dangerous a
monopoly in Germany that no other characteristic type was
developed on at all an equal footing.   France on her side, since
the days of Erigena, Ivo and Abelard, in the schools of Paris,
Chartres and Orleans, produced the scholar ; Italy by the commerce of the coast towns, Pisa, Venice and Genoa, evolved the
merchant.   For Germany all paths into the distance lay open
before the knight and the monk, the two visible representatives
of the two great powers : Empire and Church.   Prince and
bishop were tied to their domains, but knight and monk, rejoicing in greater freedom of movement and more varied range
of activity, mirrored like them, on a smaller scale and a more
modest plane, the figures of Emperor and Pope.

This fact successfully solved a problem which had never
before been solved in German history : for the first time,
throughout all the many and diverse provinces of Germany, the
aristocratic youths who overflowed the monasteries and religious
foundations were offered a career which would be valid not only
within the narrow limits of their immediate homeland but in
the wider world beyond.   It was the only time in history that

the German became—in the best sense of the word—cosmopolitan.   This prepared the ground for a great period of plastic
art which was, alas, abruptly terminated when the fall of the
Empire severed German knighthood from the rest of the world
and condemned it to blunt itself in bourgeois stupidity or to
seek service outside Germany in foreign pay.

There were two powers which Frederick courted during
those German years, and courted not in vain : a monks' and
a knights' Order.   A few weeks after the coronation at Aix
his close association with the Cistercians was remarked.   The
Order to which St. Bernard of Clairvaux belonged, in which at
that time " the Church of Christ had broken into bloom," had
not in fact been founded by St. Bernard himself, but the community owed its importance to his zeal and fire.   Like almost
all orders of the Roman Church it had its roots in the need to
reform abuses, and Bernard had emphasised the stern asceticism
and discipline of the Order, but these were balanced in the
doctor mellifluus by the passion of a great love.   Hence Dante
chooses Bernard as his final guide to the Throne of God :

> The Queen of Heaven, enthroned above,
> Knowing my heart's devotion, will not fail,
> For am I not her Bernard, her true love . . .

He was the first to breathe into the Order a passionate devotion
to the Virgin, just at the time the outer world was singing the
earliest lyrics of the troubadours.   And he was the first also
who sanctified " the work of the chaste earth " and so gave a
new direction to monastic ambition, the combination of an
active with a contemplative life.   " Free from earthly disturbance and earthly broils the Order enjoys earthly peace," wrote
Frederick once, and so it was.   The Order sought out the remotest and quietest valleys for its settlements, and there set
up its monasteries and its extensive farm-steadings, its simple
churches, towerless and unadorned, bearing only, instead of
other decoration, the first rose blossoms of Burgundian Gothic.
Maulbronn and Ebrach are our witnesses for these early days
when the Grey Monks " lived amongst, but yet above, their
fellow-men."

The obligation to till the soil ensured the rapid geographical
extension of the Order.   The Cistercians became a quiet, steady

pioneer influence, cultivating the ancient tracts and opening up new ones, especially for Germany. It was they who first Christianised and colonised Prussia. The whole organisation of their monasteries anticipated growth. There was never to be more than one abbot and twelve brothers, with twelve lay brothers, in one cloister. If the numbers grew beyond this, the excess hived forth to seek a new abiding place. This self-sufficing restriction of their numbers to the number of the apostles was the origin of the innumerable daughter-establishments which were subordinate to the mother-cloisters, as they in turn were related—like the branches of a genealogical tree—to the parent settlement at Citeaux. Thus the cohesion of all the monasteries was secured, and the Cistercians gradually grew to form one single world-wide institution which never split asunder. This organisation was without parallel, for with the Benedictines each monastery was entirely independent of the others.

The unity and the monarchic graduation of the whole Cistercian Order were still further developed. Once a year the Abbots from each settlement from Syria to Sweden assembled in a General Chapter. This statesmanlike assembly, which put the resources of all at the disposition of each, breathed the same spirit from southern Burgundy to Pomerania and Prussia, as the Cistercian churches in the north-east of Germany (nearly all of which date from the thirteenth century) clearly testify. This centralisation was as much an innovation as the agriculture and horticulture which the monks introduced into the newly opened districts, in improving the tillage and domesticating wild crops.

These brothers, pushing ever forward, colonising the valleys with their Virgin-led hosts, spreading the teaching of Christ and ever planting daughter-settlements, evoked a late Christian reflex of the *ver sacrum* of earlier times.

The Cistercian Order, with its landed properties, its disciplined constitution, its immense extension, was the most patrician of the monkish orders under the Hohenstaufen Empire and the aristocratic medieval Church, contrasting with the plebeian Mendicant Orders who were just then emerging, and who were really at home only in the towns. The wide distribution and the monarchic constitution of the Cistercians had the result

that they were directly under the leaders of the Christian world ;
no territorial prince, no individual bishop appointed or influenced the governors of their monasteries ; they were ruled
directly, in spiritual matters by the Pope, in worldly affairs by
the Emperor alone.   Earlier Emperors had made generous gifts
to the Cistercians, but none to the same extent as Frederick II,
especially in those German years of his.   The tokens of favour
with which he honoured the Order and at times almost over-
whelmed it, are well-nigh innumerable.   The warmth of feeling,
the reverence, which the records show he felt for the Order,
" the shady grove of Christ," exceed all that any other community can boast, and till his dying day Frederick loved to
consider himself intimately bound to them.

After taking the Cross Frederick got himself received into a
prayer-community of Cistercians, and his curiously humble
petition addressed to the Abbot of this powerful Order is still
reminiscent of his crusading mood.   The pious and edifying
style of this letter—in which Frederick pictures himself as a
sinner in the weakness of the flesh—served its purpose.   He
was received into the community, a fact of which in later years
he did not fail to take advantage.   This sort of thing was
of course a regular custom of the Emperors, and Frederick II
followed in their footsteps the more readily that he was anxious
to secure adherents in the clerical camp.   The Cistercians were
to act as " Preservers of the harmony between Emperor and
Pope," a scheme which had often proved fruitful under Barbarossa and Otto IV.   But Frederick had yet another axe to
grind.   Their experience made the Cistercians masters of
agriculture.   Caesarius of Heisterbach, himself a Cistercian
monk, proudly records that the lay brothers of the grey brotherhood had been recommended to the Archbishop of Cologne
as the best household administrators.   Frederick could turn
such men as that to good account.   He loved to gather round
him Cistercian lay brothers trained in agriculture and cattle-
breeding and set them to organise and administer his imperial
estates in Apulia and the Capitanata.   He used others as archi-
tects and overseers for his castles and pleasure palaces, while
in his most important and handsome buildings in South Italy
Cistercian builders played a distinguished part.

We have written evidence of the Cistercians' activities as the Emperor's builders. It is clear from a statute of the General Chapter that lay brothers and monks were later told off in great numbers for the Emperor's service. The Pope even complained that Frederick was using too many of them for his building projects. The evidence of the Apulian castles and palaces themselves is plainer still. As far as can still be traced they all have in common the new Gothic style of the Cistercians which was supplanting more and more the native Norman-Byzantine architecture. Not of course the "broken forms" of later Gothic, but the principle of utilising piers and buttresses to denote strength and striving—just what makes the magic of the transition period. The late-Roman forms are touched and penetrated by the young Gothic strength, so that for a few decades of conflict and exuberant wealth the two—both fruit and blossom—are found side by side. It was in such a "fulness of time" that Frederick was destined to rule.

People have designated the whole Hohenstaufen culture of Germany as "knightly," and knightly too the crude early-Gothic of the Cistercian monasteries. There was something of the knight in these monks, and indeed in the days of the knightly orders the antithesis between monk and knight was almost obliterated. The epic poet—by a slight anachronism—makes the monk Ilsan, who in the suite of Dietrich of Bern burst so devastatingly into the Rose Garden of Worms, a Cistercian. The connection between the Grey Monks and the spiritual knights goes back in fact to very early times. People even say that the first knightly Order of the West was founded by Spanish Cistercians who courageously flew to arms when Calatrava was threatened by the Moors. And the interplay of the two types of Order can be easily explained, for the spiritual knight, like the monk, loved to trace his origin back to St. Bernard. It may not be strictly true that—as the legend will have it—Bernard himself dictated the Rule of the Templars to the knights Hugo of Payens and Godfrey of St. Omer, but the original spirit of the Templars was closely akin to the spirit of romantic devotion and stern sobriety which animated St. Bernard and his Order. It was Bernard who, in the time of the second Crusade, recruited with zeal and eloquence for the

Templars, and who wrote a tract, "In Praise of the New Chivalry of Christ": "These warriors are gentler than lambs and fiercer than lions, wedding the mildness of the monk to the valour of the knight, so that it is difficult to decide which to call them : men who adorn the Temple of Solomon with weapons instead of gems, with shields instead of crowns of gold, with saddles and bridles instead of candelabra ; eager for victory not for fame ; for battle not for pomp ; who abhor useless speech, unnecessary action, unmeasured laughter, gossip and chatter as they despise all vain things : who in spite of their being many live in one house according to one rule, with one soul and one heart."

St. Bernard, when he pointed the Templars to a spiritual life, as he had the Cistercians to an active life, had really the same, or a very similar picture of an ideal community in mind, but while he recommended to the monks the honourable and self-denying service of the Queen of Heaven, the Order of Templars was dedicated to the service of Christ himself, for whom the brothers bore in common their strife and suffering ; the Saviour himself was the spiritual head of their State.

People have often exalted St. Bernard because of his miracles. Not the least of these was the foundation of the first knightly Order. What a revolution was there ! The restless, vacillating secular knight errant, who flew from adventure to adventure, or sacrificed himself in the service of his lady-love, leading his own individual life and entirely destructive to the firm fabric of the State, was thus induced to fit himself into the strict bonds of the Order, to give a social value, instead of a personal value, to his battles, to seek the inspiration of his noblest deeds not from his mistress but from God himself, under whose law and in whose service the Order fought.

For the first time in post-Christian days warriors and men of the *vita activa*, not merely monks, banded themselves together for an idea, and for a spiritual Lord, and assimilated themselves to each other. *Uniformitas* was the principle, the final keynote of the German knightly orders, emphasised again and again, and extending far beyond the mere question of dress —the mantle with the cross. The Templar, serving like the monks a common master, evolved that virile, knightly, rigorous constitution which later statesmen inevitably took as their model, developing it each in his own way for his own material advantage and placing himself in the place of the transcendental Master. One of such earthly state knighthoods is the Teutonic Order, founded a bare century after the Templars, which devoted its powers solely to the terrestrial state.

The feeling for spiritual knighthood was almost extinct in the East, when at the turn of the twelfth-thirteenth century in Acre the nursing community of the German Knights of St. Mary bound themselves into a third spiritual Order beside the Templars. The Templars were mainly French, and the Knights of St. John were largely English and Italian. Pope Innocent III gave to the Teutonic Knights the Rule of the Templars, whom they were to emulate in everything spiritual and knightly as they were to emulate the Knights of St. John in care for the poor and the sick. The Order was to be strictly national; only knights of German birth were to enter it.

The story of the new Order is much tamer than that of the Templars. Its origin, lacking the blessing of St. Bernard, lacks fire and inevitability ; its battles lack the glamour of the distant East ; its end the mystery of early death which always over-takes the heroes of myth. The German Knights never enjoyed such lavish wealth, their temptations were not so great, they never sank into the same corruption, but never did they inspire tale or legend with the glory and mystery that surround the heroes of the Temple, the secret guardians of the Grail. The history of the Teutonic Order, however, is all the more real because it was neither born in myth nor buried in mystery, and because its battles were fought on familiar fields near home. When Frederick II came to Germany the Teutonic Order was still an insignificant body. Henry VI had turned his attention to them while he was planning the Crusade, but, in spite of many benefactions, the confusion that followed his death hampered this purely German movement in its development.

The Church and older rivals looked at it with no friendly eye, and its real prosperity began with Frederick II. After he had taken his crusading vow a definite opportunity presented itself for the employment of the Teutonic Knights, and Frederick at once got into touch with them. Numerous gifts in this and the ensuing years bear witness to Frederick's determination to strengthen the Order by every means in his power. He even granted its members privileges which encroached on his own imperial rights, or which robbed him of considerable royal revenues. He was here even more open-handed than towards the princes. He had at first primarily the Crusade in view, but beyond the needs of the moment Frederick sought to enlist their enthusiasm and their strength for other tasks. He created out of them a little *corps d'élite*, free from feudal fetters and extraneous influences whether of temporal or spiritual lords, independent, reliable, unconditionally loyal to himself—a small body, but one immediately at the service of the Empire as sword and weapon, and in spiritual matters subject to the Pope alone. To increase the authority of the Order in Church affairs Frederick applied personally to the Pope, with the result that the notaries in the papal Chancery were busy night and day preparing nothing but charters for the—hitherto sorely neglected— Order of Teutonic Knights.

In other ways, too, Frederick always showed a great affection for the Teutonic Knights. He encouraged and assisted young noblemen like the three Hohenlohe brothers who were seeking admission to the Order, just as later he did his best to dissuade young noblemen from joining the Mendicant Orders. In the early days especially, when he wanted probity and trustworthiness, he turned to the Teutonic Knights : whether to oversee the building of his ships or to carry important despatches. In the Holy Land he hardly employed any others, and in later years he entrusted the administration of Alsace to Berthold of Tannenrode, one of the brethren, and even placed the German regent for a while to a large extent under the influence of the Teutonic Knights, so that a chronicler was not unjustified in exclaiming that the whole Empire is ruled according to the counsels of the Order. He was overstating the case of course, but it is remarkable how much attention Frederick devoted to attaching the Order to himself. One of the first privileges accorded to them was that the Grand Master of the day, whoever he might be, when attending court, should form part of the royal household and belong to the *familia*, while his escort also should enjoy the hospitality of the court. Further, two brethren of the Order were to be in permanent attendance on the royal person. The Spanish king Alfonso VIII had shown similar favours to the Order of Calatrava, but this only goes to show that these knightly orders, in proportion as they became national institutions, tended to become " courtly." It is common knowledge that the knightly orders of the late Middle Ages, the fourteenth and fifteenth centuries, were purely court affairs, and preserved an aristocratic form of life that had perished elsewhere.

Frederick liked to attribute to the earlier Hohenstaufen, indeed to Barbarossa himself, the founding of the Teutonic Order, so as to lend age and dignity to the institution. He also liked to talk of it as his own creation. It was in fact the work of his own hands, his and the first great Grand Master's : Hermann of Salza. For over twenty years Hermann of Salza was always to be met in Frederick's court and camp, his most trusted counsellor, his most valued intimate, not in virtue of his office as Master, but on account of personal qualities which made him practically indispensable.

It seems probable that Hermann of Salza was a Thuringian and there is something Thuringian in his whole personality. He was dignified and thoughtful by nature, and he possessed in every department of life that manliness, righteousness and good faith which distinguished the Order that he ruled. His faithfulness had become proverbial ; it was with him no passive virtue but—as from the dawn of time you find it only in Germans—a positive driving force. There is something almost tragic in this great man's fate. For Hermann of Salza had two masters ; he had sworn an oath of fealty to both Pope and Emperor, and every conflict between them exposed him to an intolerable strain. So we see him, bent on keeping faith with both, flying hither and thither from court to Curia, and from Curia to court, again and again during those years of incessant quarrelling seeking to keep or to restore the peace. He once described his life work as " to strive for the honour of Church and Empire," and when the breach between the two powers became final and complete, life became for him impossible. On Palm Sunday 1239 Frederick II was excommunicated for ever, and on the same day the great Grand Master, Hermann of Salza, breathed his last.

Amongst Frederick's courtiers the distinctly older Master represented at all times the calm, practical wisdom which more than once deterred the hot-headed young monarch from wantonly provoking his foes. Hermann of Salza's long experience had made him acquainted with the state of affairs in the East no less than in Italy, in the papal Curia no less than in the German court, and this experience combined with most unusual diplomatic and political skill gave him a unique value in every branch of imperial policy. The collaboration of Frederick with the Grand Master, whom he met for the first time in the Nuremberg court of 1216, had most significance for north-east Germany.

Frederick had been—to quote a Livonian chronicler—" so deeply preoccupied with the varied and lofty duties of the Empire " that, truth to tell, he had felt scant interest in the affairs of north-east Germany. With Hermann of Salza it was different. The politics of his Order had a very lively concern with the north-east, and so it came about that all important matters concerning regions round the Baltic Sea from Denmark to Livonia passed through his hands or were confirmed by him.

Waldemar, King of the Danes, was a man of some importance ; he had extended his rule—at the expense of the Empire —along the Baltic towards Livonia and Esthonia, as far as the mouth of the Dvina. Finally he was taken prisoner by a vassal of the Empire, and the envoy whom Frederick sent to treat with him was Hermann of Salza. He concluded peace with the Danish king, and in 1226—probably at the Grand Master's instance—Frederick created Lübeck, the most important port on the Baltic, an imperial town, thus putting an end to all Danish rights over the Elbe country and to all claims of the Roman Curia which stood behind Denmark. Hermann of Salza called the Emperor's attention to Prussia also, where the Roman Curia with the aid of the Cistercians had been founding colonies and missions.

We may here anticipate the events of the ensuing year. In the winter of 1225-26 Conrad of Masovia, Duke of Poland, finding himself unable to repulse the Prussian heathen, applied to the Teutonic Knights for help, and provisionally gave a verbal promise—not yet confirmed in writing—to hand over his territories of Kulm to the Order in return for their services. This offer came at an opportune moment, for the Order had just been unsuccessful in a somewhat similar enterprise in the Burzen country of Hungary.

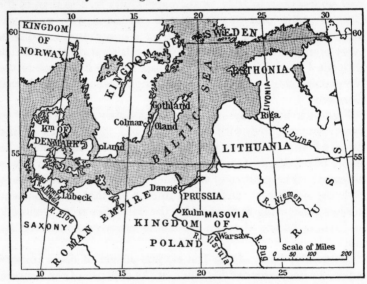

THE BIRTH OF PRUSSIA
1226

With wisdom and foresight and a fortunate appreciation of the whole situation the Grand Master took up the scheme, talked it over with Kaiser Frederick, who at once gave it firm and final shape by granting weighty privileges to the undertaking. So thoroughly had they thought matters out that the memorable Golden Bull of Rimini of 1226 lays down the future tasks and aims of the Teutonic Order, draws up the constitution of the future State in a scheme complete down to minutest details. All this is in order before negotiations have begun, before an agreement has been reached with the Polish Duke, before a single Teutonic knight has set foot or eye upon the land of Kulm. This great charter that founded the Prussian State under the Order of the Teutonic Knights has justly been called a " plan of campaign," for the territories granted by it to the Order had still to be won, and the Order therefore knew for years ahead just where its duty lay. This Charter indeed secured the future of the Teutonic Order : it was so comprehensive that whatever the Order did was done under the special aegis of the Emperor and was covered by imperial privilege. It is expressly laid down in this document that " all gifts and conquests are to be the free property of the Order, which is to exercise full territorial rights and be responsible to none. The Grand Master is to enjoy all the privileges that pertain to a prince of the Empire, including all royal privileges, and the Order shall be in Prussia free from all imperial taxes, burdens and services." Thus Frederick permitted the Order to found an autonomous State, owning no territorial master save the Order itself, " to be an integral part of the monarchy of the Empire " as the Charter says. This position of the Order was assured not only by earlier privileges granted under the immediate protection of the Empire, but by a most remarkable attitude taken up by Frederick.

Since the days of Charlemagne the warfare against the heathen had been one of the tasks of a Roman Emperor, and Charlemagne had demonstrated that it must be waged in two directions : first, against Islam, as in his Spanish campaign, and, secondly, against the heathen of eastern Europe as in his Saxon wars. The Crusades had concentrated attention on the war with Islam, but the other task had lost its full importance after the time of Barbarossa but was not yet quite forgotten. Frederick II revived this East European mission.

The Empire had been chosen by God to preach the gospel. This was Frederick's conviction, frequently reiterated ; he found room to incorporate it in the Charter of the Order : " For this end has God uplifted our Empire above the kingdoms of the earth, and extended the limits of our power beyond the various zones, that our care may be to glorify his name and diligently to spread his faith among the peoples, for he hath chosen the Roman Empire for the preaching of his gospel : let us therefore bend our minds to the conquest, no less than the conversion, of the heathen peoples. . . ."

These sentences contain an unmistakable challenge to the Pope. For the Church, with the help of the Cistercians, had already begun to christianise Prussia, and there was a very real danger that Prussia might become a feudal appanage of the Roman Curia as Sicily had done, though it was the Normans who had won it from the infidel. The Pope indeed had signalised his intentions, styling the conversion of the heathen as " emancipation," since the new converts were to " owe obedience to none save Christ and the Roman Church "—not, therefore, to the Empire. As a counter-move Frederick now came on the scene with his theory of an imperial mission and spoke expressly of " conquest " as the goal—indicating an intention of ruling the heathen peoples. He incorporated the land belonging to the Teutonic Order in the " monarchy of the Empire," and supported this line of action by reference to an old royal right. Heathen land was lordless land and thus belonged, not to the conqueror, but to the ruler, to the Emperor who, like the Pope, was here the vicegerent of Christ. Thus Frederick planned to save Prussia for the Empire.

The importance of this plantation of the Teutonic Knights in Prussia needs no emphasis. The spiritual Order had thereby acquired, as it were, a physical body ; it had exchanged landless ubiquity for territorial possession, and it quickly metamorphosed itself into a real state which preserved the standards and ideals of chivalry through days when these elsewhere were being degraded or urbanised. It is highly characteristic of Frederick that he thus founded the Prussian State more or less fortuitously. We shall observe again and again, what we here note for the first time, that his hand possessed some magic, as people later contended, that brought life into whatever he happened even accidentally to touch. Things forthwith assumed an importance he could not possibly have foreseen, out of all proportion to the slight effort he had expended. The Charter of the Order, the Golden Bull of Rimini, which was drawn up more or less casually in a busy moment when the Emperor was occupied with innumerable more important questions, is a proof of his happy touch. The godfather of the Hapsburg was the godfather also of Prussia.

The Order of the Cistercians and the Order of the Teutonic Knights were the two most weighty allies that Frederick won during his German years ; nothing else approaches them in importance. The power of the German towns was still slight; moreover, the princely towns and the episcopal towns were wholly outside his influence, and privileges which he granted now and then to one or another—Cambrai and Basel for instance—might have to be revoked if the imperial princes so decided. For the body of princes were swift to resent any encroachment and acted together as one man to resist any interference with their rights. Only the Swabian towns and those immediately under the Empire were under Frederick's care, and here he bestirred himself to improve communications, to secure safe convoy for the merchants throughout the Roman Empire, and to protect the highways against robbers, measures which were much appreciated.

Apart from what he actually did for them, Frederick contrived to inspire his towns with the faith that he had their interests peculiarly at heart, and he strengthened this belief by gifts and privileges. He turned villages into towns, presented towns with market-places, gathered scattered rights and privileges into one charter which formed a code of justice for the town. Later, when the days of tribulation came, it was the towns who rallied to the cause of the Hohenstaufen and of the Empire against the princes.

The laborious methods of natural cultivation practised in Germany made it an unsuitable sphere for the wonderful experiments in state agriculture which Frederick later made so brilliant a success in Sicily, and the German feudal system permitted no direct interference in administration. Frederick's strength was frittered away in handling all the various minor internal affairs of Germany without any visible advantage to the whole, and soon after his coronation at Aix he seems to have aimed at evolving some scheme for delegating minor German business to others, retaining the decision only in major matters. " Wherever the Roman Empire and some of the princes meet— there is Germany " became the dictum, showing that the whole

Imperium—not only the countries north of the Alps—could be German through the German Imperator.

Many adjustments were gradually made to organise a subsidiary government for internal German affairs so as to set the Emperor free for larger issues. Frederick never hustled. All his big undertakings can be traced back through years of quiet preparation, and he never sought to conceal what he was aiming at. What he did, he did *coram publico*, and he always announced beforehand what his intentions were. Yet his actions always contained an element of suddenness and surprise, either because no one had taken him seriously, or because he carried out his intention at a moment when people had ceased to expect it. His first great diplomatic victory over the Church exemplifies this.

Honorius III had been since 1216 the occupant of the papal throne. Whoever had succeeded Innocent III would necessarily have appeared something of a pigmy by comparison; certainly Honorius did. He was a jurist, primarily an administrative official. Cencio Savelli had been, before his elevation, the Pope's Chamberlain, and had edited the famous "*liber censuum*," the tax-book of the Roman Church. Later, when the battle between the Emperor and Pope had become an economic one, the fact that the Church could take the field as a first-class financial power was due in no small measure to Honorius. For the rest he was old and frail, and inclined therefore to be placable and gentle rather than bellicose, though he asserted on occasion the lofty claims which were nowadays part and parcel of the Papacy. If the peace of the world were to depend on a balance between these two great forces Honorius was the very best make-weight for Frederick, and for a good ten years the two held the balance fairly even. The most absorbing affair which in those days engrossed the two heads of Christendom was unquestionably the Crusade, and Honorius regarded the recapture of Jerusalem as the loftiest and most personal ambition of his pontificate.

Frederick's assumption of the Cross had at first awakened little enthusiasm in Rome. Innocent, who had been planning to march into the Holy Land at the head of the peoples, completely ignored Frederick's action, and without consulting his

youthful rival fixed the day of the start of the Crusaders for
1st July, 1217—a date which completely ruled Frederick out,
for Otto IV was still alive and the Hohenstaufen could not
possibly leave Germany.

Honorius III seemed at first oblivious of Frederick's existence
as a Crusader, and a legate of the Pope's directed the arrangements for the Crusade as an exclusively papal affair. The first
rendezvous of the warriors was not to be the Holy Land but
Egypt, by the conquest of which it was hoped to engineer the
fall of Jerusalem. The whole undertaking was badly organised
and sorely mismanaged. Damietta fell at the first onslaught,
but an ill-advised penetration into the interior brought the
entire crusading army into the greatest danger. When the
Crusaders began to feel the pinch they spontaneously turned
for help to Kaiser Frederick, and the Roman Curia suddenly
bethought itself that he too was a Crusader. Pope Honorius
took up the general cry and painted in the most glowing colours
the opportunity that now opened for Frederick to fulfil his vow,
and addressed him prophetically as " the victorious king before
whose countenance the heathen fly and who in fighting God's
battles wins his own eternal salvation."

Frederick, however, had not awaited the summons from the
Pope. He had already declared himself ready to promote the
cause of the Crusade in Germany, and to arrange the date of
departure at the Diet he was immediately about to hold. He
requested Honorius kindly to excommunicate dilatory Crusaders, for if any delay occurred it would be due to the Roman
Curia and not to him. Further, would the Pope be so good
as to take the Empire under his protection during Frederick's
absence, and with it the imperial regent whom he was about
to appoint.

In the days of Innocent, Frederick had almost always styled
himself " King by the Grace of God and of the Pope." He
dropped the phrase in writing to Honorius ; it no longer fitted
the facts. He adopted in other ways also an entirely new tone
towards the Curia ; the note though perfectly courteous had in
it a ring of decision that must have quickened many an ear in
Rome. The Pope's need, however, was great. In spite of
reinforcements the position of the Crusaders before Damietta

grew daily more critical, and Pope Honorius's one anxiety was
to send Frederick to their assistance with all speed. Francis of
Assisi had accompanied the forces to preach Christianity to the
Egyptian Sultan. Before finally setting out on the Crusade
the Staufen was to receive the imperial crown from the hands
of the Pope in Rome. And Honorius impatiently awaited the
moment. Though Frederick was no less eager, circumstances
compelled him to postpone his Roman journey and with it his
Crusade: from the Feast of St. John in 1219 the date was
changed to Michaelmas, and then to March 1220, then to May,
and finally adjourned *sine die*. The vow could not be wholly
cancelled without a dispensation from the Pope.

What was detaining Frederick in Germany ? Apart from
trifles he had much to arrange before he could leave Germany.
First, it was imperative to come to some understanding with the
Pope on the " Sicilian question " ; secondly, to arrange for the
administration during his absence ; thirdly, to secure the election of his son Henry as King of the Romans. In defiance of
the Pope's impatience Frederick made his Roman journey and
his Crusade contingent on these questions.

Pope Innocent III had strenuously sought to guard against
the danger of a union of the Empire and Sicily, and in pursuance
of this policy had demanded securities : Frederick's son Henry
had been crowned King of Sicily at the express request of
Innocent. In several documents Frederick had recognised the
Church's feudal rights over Sicily, had solemnly undertaken not
to unite the kingdom with the Empire, had promised, on the day
of his coronation as Emperor, to waive his rights over Sicily
in favour of his son. During King Henry's minority a regent
jointly appointed by Pope and Emperor would rule the south
Italian kingdom.

The day of the Crusade and of the imperial coronation was
drawing on, and therewith the day on which Frederick must
formally renounce all claims to the government of Sicily . . .
but the Emperor, who had very definite views about his hereditary kingdom, made no attempt to disguise from the Pope
that while recognising his own earlier renunciation of Sicily as
valid he intended to take over the regency himself. The Curia
was anything but satisfied. Frederick must renew all his earlier

promises—this he did willingly enough. But he did not give up his intention of ruling Sicily. His hereditary kingdom was going to mean for him the beginning and the end of his Imperium. He must achieve his goal by an indirect route, and the Curia in its excessive foresight had pointed out the way when it had demanded the coronation of his infant son as King of Sicily.

The other important matter that Frederick had to arrange was the administration of Germany during his absence. A complicated system was elaborated, but it was soon perfectly clear what Frederick had in mind and was determined to accomplish. Immediately after his coronation in Aix he had, most naturally, sent for his Queen, Constance, and his little son Henry to join him in Germany. In 1217 he installed the boy, who was already King of Sicily, as Duke of Swabia; in 1219 he entrusted to him the regency over the Kingdom of Burgundy, and since then he had been busily winning over the German princes to the idea of electing Henry King of the Romans. There was nothing unprecedented in all this, and the dangers of a Crusade to which he was now about to expose himself gave a sufficient colour to Frederick's desire. He wished during his own lifetime to secure the succession to his house, as many an Emperor before him had done. Technically, however, Frederick was not yet Emperor, and difficulties confronted him on every side. The important thing was first to get the princes to agree to his plan, and his immediate efforts were directed to that end.

Negotiations were being carried on at the turn of the year 1219-20 : first about the Crusade, then about the Roman journey, thirdly about the Sicilian question, fourthly about the German regency, fifthly about the election of the infant Staufen, negotiations that were all interdependent and ought all to be concluded in the shortest possible time. For matters were nearing a crisis; the Pope urged Frederick to hasten his departure and began to show ill-humour over his procrastinations, while the longer the negotiations were drawn out the more hopelessly the skein became entangled. All possibility of a solution seemed past when Frederick finally succeeded with one stroke in cutting all the knots. By weighty concessions and a

fresh abandonment of many royal prerogatives he purchased
the acquiescence of the princes, and at the farewell Diet which
he held in Frankfurt on his departure for Rome in the spring
of 1220 the Sicilian King Henry was elected King of the
Romans. Frederick had won the game. The Hohenstaufen
dynasty was established, the regency arranged for, and the
Sicilian question solved exactly as he had planned. Sicily had
of course not been legally incorporated in the Empire, the feudal
overlordship of the Church over Sicily still stood, but that personal union of the two crowns which Frederick had had to
renounce on his coronation as Emperor became suddenly an
accomplished fact, when Henry, long since the crowned King
of Sicily, was elected King of the Romans by the German
princes. The personal union had come to life again without
any breach of all the treaties with the Pope, for they were all
made in the name of Frederick II, and contained not a syllable
about Henry. All the rights and powers which Frederick was
debarred by treaty and agreement from claiming for himself he
had now passed on boldly to his son. The one flaw in the
treaties had been exploited. For even if the Curia had insisted
on Henry taking the reins himself—at eight years old—his
father's " advisership " could not be prevented, which meant
that Frederick was himself the *de facto* ruler of the two realms
of Sicily and Germany. In short, from the papal point of view,
there would have been a perfectly futile insistence on mere
appearances if they had attempted to exclude Frederick from
Sicily.

The Roman Curia, though gravely annoyed, at once recognised the real state of affairs, and finally had to accept the fact
that the cherished parchments which Frederick had so recently
confirmed, and even added to, had become so much waste
paper. Frederick meantime had won his first great victory over
curial diplomacy. He had succeeded in uniting Sicily and the
Empire—in however roundabout a way. That union, to avoid
which Pope Innocent had literally set the whole world in motion,
had exalted and had debased the Welf, was now restored;
the States of the Church were again shut in on north and south.
The only difference was that Henry VI had never acknowledged
Sicily's feudal dependence on Rome, which Frederick II for the

moment at least upheld, and once more confirmed in writing. Nothing now stood in Frederick's way, and a few months later he set out for Rome.

It was one of the most characteristic gifts of Frederick to win a whole series of positions with one skilful move. He raised it to a high art. His taking of the Cross at Aix was prophetic, he now gave his first serious demonstration of this typical procedure. Apart from the advantages already mentioned, King Henry's election gave Frederick just the opportunity he wanted to set up at the court of the young King of the Romans a subordinate government which could deal with all the minor questions of German internal administration. This was arranged provisionally with a view to the Crusade and was afterwards made permanent, so that henceforth Germany was ruled by King Henry while the Emperor himself had his headquarters in Italy, the centre of the world. All this followed from the one well-judged manoeuvre.

The taking of the Cross in Aix had had far-reaching consequences in many directions, but it had been the outcome of an almost delirious enthusiasm and it had nothing of the usual transparency of the air of Frederick II's court, in which men far superior to their spiritual opponents played a subtle game with gentle irony. The election of the Sicilian king was more typical and showed the unstudied ease with which Frederick met even the most complicated situations.

Frederick kept this light and happy touch in similar delicate situations for years to come, and in spite of occasional ruthlessness, of occasional severe violence, he succeeded on the whole with a minimum of actual force. To sever Gordian knots with the sword was not his way—nor did he think it his mission ; his great skill lay in allowing the loose threads to twist themselves into a seemingly inextricable tangle, and then at the decisive moment with firm hand and unerring eye to seize the whole and secure it in a knot which only Alexander could have cut in two. And in his day there was no Alexander.

In this connection Frederick's first victory over the Curia may serve as something more than a sample, though he had not yet reached the heights of later years. The Roman Curia had seen plainly enough what he was aiming at. He had made no secret

of the fact that he would have liked to retain Sicily. The Curia
knew that Frederick's son was to be chosen King in Germany
and had at once perceived all that this implied. None the less
they were entangled in Frederick's skilful web and were not
able to extricate themselves.

Frederick was able to preserve throughout an air of childlike
innocence, for it was not he but the princes who were responsible for this election of King Henry. The better to keep up
this convenient fiction the election was arranged to take place
in Frankfurt at a moment when Frederick happened to be
absent, so that he was able to maintain with perfect truth that
everything had taken place " without his knowledge and actually
during his absence." The Curia had probably foreseen the
issue, but had to confess that this German royal election was
none of her business. In the background Honorius had done
his best with the help of the spiritual princes to prevent the
election, and this accounted for the initial opposition Frederick
had met with. The Pope could not plausibly complain that
there had been any breach of previous agreements ; he could
only hope that the threatened fate might in some way be averted
after all.

Fate itself seemed to walk the earth incarnate in this Hohenstaufen, not sinister or menacing but smiling, innocently playful,
with buoyant dancing step. In later years this fateful quality
assumed terrifying proportions, the smile became a cynical
witticism, the dance a dance of death. An atmosphere of
magic played round this Hohenstaufen, some wholly-German
Germanic emanation which Napoleon for instance conspicuously lacked, an immeasurably dangerous emanation, as
of a Mephisto free of horn and cloven hoof, who moves among
men disguised as a golden-haired Apulian boy, winning his
bloodless victories with weapons stolen from the Gods. Already
without effort of his own the *Puer Apuliae* had played Nemesis
to a giant like Innocent III, till the most mighty opponent of a
Hohenstaufen dynasty became so mysteriously entangled in the
coils of fate that he had no option but to elevate to the throne
of the Roman Empire the Sicilian king whom he had failed
to crush.

It rounds off the picture of Frederick's German years that

he paid for his victory over the Curia and for his Sicilian inheritance with a number of royal prerogatives and rights which he
lightheartedly abandoned to the German princes.   The spiritual
princes had at first stood out against the election of Henry, but
when Frederick offered them the free testamentary disposal of
their wealth, rights of custom and coinage in the bishops' lands,
even the free disposal of the feudal fiefs in their domains; when,
finally, he limited in their favour his own freedom by promising
that henceforth the ban of the Empire should automatically
follow the ban of the Church, they could resist no longer.
For such a bait they were ready to throw over the Pope and his
Sicilian policy.   The royal rights were already subject to many
exceptional grants of privilege, so that Frederick's actual sur-
renders were not so very serious.   The gravity of the " Constitution in favour of the spiritual princes " was, that what had
been the exception now became the rule.   Frederick has often
been reproached on account of these concessions, but the possession of Sicily weighed more with him, and most rightly, than
sundry royal prerogatives.

It might with equal or greater justice be cast in the princes'
teeth that their support for any cause, however great, could only
be won by bribes, and that they for the sake of a brewing tax
would follow their Emperor or betray him.

Frederick II could not play the statesman amid such conditions ; he needed raw material to work with and great foes
to fight ; perhaps he was not equal to these hucksterings.   All
thought for princely greed and princely bickering he thankfully
handed over to the subordinate government which he set up,
and which during the minority of King Henry was in the first
place entrusted to Archbishop Engelbert of Cologne, who was
to be Germany's *Gubernator*.   To himself he drew all the virile
manhood of Germany.

A topical poem of Walther von der Vogelweide's sketches
the position of the day with bitter irony and acumen.   The
princes' delay in electing Henry was holding up Frederick's
departure for Rome and for the Holy Land.   To influence the
election in the direction of Frederick's wishes Walther offers

the princes a piece of advice ; they are at all times eager enough
"to be rid of the king"; he shows how, by merely electing
Henry, they will be able to despatch him " a thousand miles
and more away to Trani: "

> Ye foes !   Just let him have his way and go,
> Perhaps he thus will never vex you more !
> If he dies there—which Heaven forfend—you score ;
> If he return to us, his friends, the more
> We praise the fate that doth our lord restore.
> My plan will profit both the friend and foe.

Walther von der Vogelweide was in close touch with Frederick,
and the verses were intended to assist his plans.   The poet at
length received " his fief," for which he had so long and vainly
petitioned Kaiser Otto.   Thus Frederick attached the Minnesänger to his cause ; the best that Germany had was his.   On
the whole, however, it was time for him to quit the North.   The
same year found him in Sicily displaying his prowess and adding
a second more brilliant success to his first.

In August 1220 he started out with a smallish force from
the Lechfeld at Augsburg, the usual rallying point for armies
marching to Italy.   He was accompanied by Queen Constance
and a number of princes, chiefly those who like their King wore
the Crusaders' Cross.   Slowly he marched southwards, following the Brenner Road that had seen so many German Emperors
march to Rome, past Innsbruck, Bozen, Trent—where eight
years before as an adventurer he had turned aside into the
pathless mountain tracts—and on to Verona.

He did not enter the town, but camped outside in tents during
those September days, beside the Lake of Garda, with his court.
The first letter that he wrote on Italian soil was addressed to
Pope Honorius, thanking him for all his kindness, and informing
him that the writer had, for the good of his soul, submitted to
the penances prescribed by the Church and been freed from
the ban which might have fallen on him as a dilatory Crusader.
He had acted thus, he hastened to add, not because he felt himself at fault, but solely to testify his reverence for Pope and
Church.   He sent in advance his Court Chancellor and the
Archbishop Conrad of Metz as royal legates to see that all was
quiet in imperial Italy, a country always easily roused.

The towns of Lombardy had all recognised Frederick II, even his hereditary enemy Milan. Nevertheless, the country was seething with excitement, and people were just waiting in momentary quiet to see which of the parties in upper Italy Frederick would elect to join. A reputation for extraordinary vigour, courage and shrewdness had preceded the King, spread during the recent years by the songs of the troubadours, as they travelled from court to court of the north Italian nobility. They seem to have been a little disappointed when they saw their future Emperor, for in spite of his six and twenty years he still struck them as too boyish looking.

Frederick II most scrupulously avoided taking sides amongst the towns, and even carried this reserve so far that on the whole journey to Rome he never entered any town but always camped outside. The only exception he made was in favour of Bologna, famous for its Roman Law, and his retinue was presently increased by the addition of the famous lawyer Roffredo of Benevento, who had formerly been a teacher of law at Bologna and was now posted in Arezzo.

It was remarked that while Frederick, as was the Emperor's custom on entering Italy, confirmed in their rights all the Italian towns, he only confirmed such freedoms and privileges as they enjoyed *vis-à-vis* the Empire, and no allusion was made to Sicily. The Pope had not yet made an authoritative pronouncement about the crown of Sicily ; this served as a welcome and valid excuse for Frederick II's careful reservation. The truth was, however, that he was anxious not to part with any of the privileges pertaining to his hereditary kingdom. The Genoese were most bitterly disappointed over this, for their envoys had hastened with high hopes to the royal camp at Modena. Genoa, the town that had so warmly espoused Frederick's cause on his journey to Germany, and had boasted herself his " Gate of Empire " (Genoa—Janua), had been hoping for favoured treatment in respect of Sicily. Frederick, however, confirmed only her imperial rights, and announced that in no circumstances would Sicilian concessions be made prior to his arrival in the kingdom. What he was planning soon became apparent.

Frederick had announced his approach to the Pope in the

early days of October, sending as ambassador—for the first time
—the Grand Master of the Teutonic Order, Hermann of Salza.
Travelling by the Via Flaminia across the Apennines, the King
followed at his leisure, and a month later when he drew near
Rome he received a counter-embassy from the Pope, who on
the eve of Frederick's coronation as Emperor was anxious
to receive final assurances : that the Imperium as such had
no claims at all on Sicily, that Sicily was exclusively the
hereditary possession of the Empress-Mother Constance,
that Frederick must instal no foreign officials in Sicily and
must employ a separate royal seal. All this suited Frederick
admirably. So long as Sicily was his, he was supremely
indifferent as to the precise legal phraseology under which
he possessed it. A far weightier point was that the Curia by
this agreement showed itself officially reconciled to the personal union. A few other points in connection with the
Crusade were agreed on, and, finally, the date of the coronation was fixed for the 22nd of November, the last Sunday
before Advent.

The early days of his success were far behind, yet Frederick
constantly recalled them to the world's remembrance. Providence had preserved him through all the perils of his boyhood
that the tempests of the storm-tossed Empire might obey him.
He early conceived his personal fate to be under the immediate
law of a higher power, a point of view which later became of
immense importance. Earlier emperors had sought to base the
immediacy of their imperial office under God on theories and
doctrines of law—always disputed by the Popes from Gregory
VII onwards. Frederick seldom troubled to seek legal proofs.
With far greater effect he simply pointed to his own personal
good fortune, which marked him in the sight of all the world
as one chosen by the providence of God. It is true this did not
demonstrate the immediate derivation from God of the imperial
power in general, but all the more cogently that of the present
Emperor—which was vastly more to the point. For thus every
glorification of the Emperor's office became a glorification of
himself, and the general mission of the Empire became a personal
mission of just this particular Emperor, or, to use the phrase
which Frederick himself minted, " our unconquerable will

became fused in the imperial dignity." Person and office began to merge in one.

Frederick's assumption of the imperial dignity with all the ancient ceremonial pomp was to be the closing scene of the first act, the climax of these years of earliest successes. On the great day Frederick rode with the Queen Constance from the Monte Mario down into Rome along the ancient coronation way, the Via Triumphalis. Halting at a little bridge outside the town the future Emperor had to confirm the Roman people in their lawful rights, and thereupon he received at the Porta Collina, near the Baths of Diocletian, the homage of the clergy of the city, who escorted him in solemn procession with censers and crucifixes to the Church of St. Peter. Chamberlains scattering largesse paced ahead, and the *praefectus urbi* bearing the sword. In the space before St. Peter's the escort was changed: Roman Senators now strode on the King's right hand to take his horse at the steps of the church. Meanwhile the Pope had likewise issued in solemn procession from the Sacristy of St. Peter and on the topmost stair awaited in state the arrival of the King. On his right were the cardinals—bishops or priests —on his left the cardinal-deacons, the remaining clergy on a lower stair. The King with his retinue drew near. With reverence Frederick kissed the Holy Father's feet and brought him golden tribute as the vicegerent of Christ. Pope Honorius received him graciously with kiss and embrace; the King rose again, and the Pope, with the King on his right hand, moved towards the Chapel of Santa Maria in Turribus. Here Frederick was to take the oath: to be the defender and protector of Pope and Church in every hour of weal or woe. While the Pope proceeded to the altar to pray and then took his seat the King remained behind to be received into the brotherhood of the Canons of St. Peter.

In earlier days it had been the custom to receive the King at his coronation into Holy Orders, and dress him in a priest's robes. They made him a cleric of the Roman Church, for the standpoint was that in spiritual things the Emperor " could not be quite a layman." The course of history had found expression in a change in the coronation ceremonial; with the growing power of an imperial Papacy the priestly prerogatives of the Emperor were very considerably weakened though not quite eliminated.

The Emperor no longer received a bishop's ring, he was no longer anointed on the head but only on the arm and between the shoulder blades ; no longer was chrism used for his anointing, simple consecrated oil was considered good enough ; instead of the consecration as bishop there was substituted this reception into the brotherhood of the Canons of St. Peter. The ritual of prayer and litany remained nevertheless very similar to a bishop's. Clad in the imperial vestments Frederick now entered St. Peter's through the silver gate, where cardinals met him with blessing and prayer. He halted to do reverence at Peter's tomb and in front of the tomb of St. Maurice he was anointed by a cardinal. Not till this was accomplished did he advance to the altar of Peter to make confession and receive from the Pope the kiss of peace. Then with his retinue he sought his appointed place. The Pope rehearsed the prayer, adding a special intercession for the King, whereupon Frederick approached the Pope to receive the insignia. The Pope crowned him with mitre and with crown, and thereupon handed him the sword which Frederick was lustily to brandish three times to show that he was now a *miles Beati Petri*, after which he received sceptre and imperial orb. The choir now burst into song: " To Frederick ever glorious, of the Romans the unconquered Emperor, be Life and Victory ! " The coronation of Queen Constance was completed in corresponding style. High Mass followed, in which the Emperor, laying aside crown and mantle, ministered as subdeacon to the Pope. Then he and the Empress received the communion at the Pope's hands and finally the papal kiss of peace. The Pope then pronounced the blessing and with the Emperor quitted St. Peter's to mount his horse outside the cathedral. Frederick held the Pope's stirrup and led him a few paces forward before mounting his own white horse. At Santa Maria Transpadina Pope and Emperor parted after exchanging one more embrace, and Frederick returned to his camp at Monte Mario.

At his coronation Emperor Frederick had once more taken the Cross—from the hand of Cardinal Hugo of Ostia, later Pope Gregory IX—and had promised to proceed to the Holy

Land in August 1221. Further, he issued a number of new laws : first and foremost an edict against heretics, and another which laid down the indissoluble connection between the ban of the Church and the ban of the Empire. Bologna was the only one of the Italian towns which he had visited on his journey south ; he now commanded the doctors and students of the " Holy Laws " to enter his new coronation laws in the codices of Roman Law and to incorporate them for ever in their teaching. The coronation laws were in fact embodied in the Corpus, following immediately on the laws of Barbarossa ; Frederick and his grandfather being the only two German Emperors whose names are immortalised in Roman Law.

All the coronation solemnities and festivities went off without disturbance—a very rare phenomenon. For there was usually serious friction between the imperial troops and the citizens of Rome. Barbarossa had had to be crowned in secret, and pitched battles had accompanied the coronation of Otto IV, for both of them had refused the usual largesse to the Romans. A similar parsimony would have been wholly out of character in Frederick's case. Moreover, he considered himself as the chosen of the Romans despatched by them to Germany to seek his *imperium*. He had not less pride or independence than his predecessors, but he scorned to raise a protest against stirrup-ceremonies or coronation gifts or mere material costs. He reserved his fighting powers for larger issues.

Immediately after the coronation Frederick turned to Sicily. He felt the lure of Sicily partly because it was his home, but even more because it offered to his hand the raw material for his statesmanship. Here he could fashion what he would. Germany had denied him all opportunity. Every step he took in Germany had in one way or another to be accommodated to the princes' wishes ; he could not stir a finger in any direction without coming up against some constitutional obstacle. The feudal system excluded all immediacy of the overlord. These formalities and obstacles were deep-rooted in the customs of centuries ; they could not be altered without immense revolutions. So Frederick could draw on the strength of Germany

only in a very limited degree ; her constitution, though anything but perfected, was too set and well established. She
could serve him only to the same extent and in the same manner
as she had served innumerable Emperors before him, but it
would be far too great a risk to depend on her alone for support
in any far-reaching measure.

Conditions in Sicily were more favourable. The Norman
kings had only held Sicily for two or three generations.
Frederick's grandfather, King Roger II, had wrought indeed
with great intensity and a wisdom and statesmanship amount-
ing to genius, but all that he had built up had been shattered
beyond recognition in nearly thirty years of uninterrupted war
and strife. During Frederick's childhood it had been the scene
of anarchy and confusion. After his long absence Frederick
found now the same picture of woeful ruin and neglect that he
had left behind him. Chaos reigned in Sicily, but chaos pregnant with possibilities of every kind. Everything was in movement, and for decades all the various forces of the known world
had tossed and tumbled there. The real statesman can only
reach his full stature in fluid circumstances—all great men have
needed revolutions—and this very chaos offered the most
favourable possible conditions without the fear of organised
opposition. Another point: for an Emperor who wished
effectively to play the Roman Imperator, Sicily, from her
geographical position, offered the required basis of power.
The three great Hohenstaufen Emperors all turned persistently
to Sicily precisely because they knew exactly what Sicily had
to offer that Germany denied. In the time of the Crusaders
Sicily was in fact the " port and navel of all the kingdoms of
the world," just as Spain was to be in the age of discovery.
As Charles V was one day to take Holland for his northern base
and make Germany an Atlantic state, the Hohenstaufen was
now to create a Mediterranean state including Swabia and
south Germany.

Frederick's personal affection for Sicily is undeniable and in
the given conditions was pure advantage. But he loved it also
because he needed it. It is characteristic that this affection was
not chiefly directed to the luxuriant half-tropical Palermo,
which he never visited in the latest years at all, but Apulia,

Campania and the Capitanata, the provinces marching with the States of the Church, and the territories nearest to *Roma caput mundi*.

The data in North and South were radically different; so was Frederick's method of approach. In Germany Frederick had set free all the cosmopolitan forces he could, to fuse Germany into the Roman Empire. In Sicily, on the other hand, there was cosmopolitanism enough and to spare, and no fear of stagnation. Sicily was more likely to tear herself to pieces from over-vitality, and Frederick had to tame and bind those very forces which he had sought to loose in Germany. Thus ultimately the two kingdoms would be drawn together and each would in its own way be " romanised." The sensitive and educative statesmanship of Frederick was so successful that Germany in his day gave birth to a plastic art and—for the first time since the days of her tyrants—song was heard again in Sicily. In both cases these periods of artistic creation were the product of incomparably daring, almost foolhardy, experiments which none but a master, and he for a limited period, could have dared to try.

The Sicilians had been anticipating the Emperor's arrival with justifiable anxiety ; for almost all had at one time or another betrayed the boy king. A number of the Sicilian barons appeared already at the coronation in Rome to do homage to Frederick and draw, as far as possible, a veil over the past. Frederick had carefully and thoughtfully planned every step beforehand, and had even begun his preparations during his years in Germany. They well might have divined from one straw or another how the wind was blowing. One of the usurpers, Count Rainer of Manente, who was reputed to have on one occasion attempted Frederick's life, had rashly entered Germany and approached the King without a safe conduct. Frederick secured his person. It is true that, at the Pope's request, he ultimately released his prisoner, but the Count was made disgorge the entire crown property which he had appropriated and which his relations with the help of bandit allies sought to retain. The fact also that on his march through Upper Italy Frederick granted no privileges relating to Sicily, indicated well-defined plans. His first aim was to bring to-

gether again all the crown property which had been scattered
and squandered by each temporary wielder of power. His
second to eradicate all the little nests of secondary powers
dotted over his kingdom and so to establish a central government once more. With all his fiery lust for action (which Pope
Honorius mentions, more in blame than praise) Frederick II
set himself to his task.

The Roman Curia had seen Frederick's happy faculty for
solving many difficult issues by one well-judged move. This,
however, was in the diplomatic sphere and might have indicated
merely a skill in casuistry. Frederick was now in the thick of
real life. One single simple law, almost ludicrously simple,
brought in a moment to a standstill all the hurly-burly of strife
and disaffection in Sicily, precisely in the way most useful
to Frederick personally. The last legitimate Norman king,
William II, had died in 1189, and for the succeeding thirty years
sheer confusion had prevailed. Royal prerogatives and rights,
crown lands and fiefs had been recklessly squandered, abandoned, given away, some by Henry VI, with the full intention
of ultimately recovering them, some by the many fleeting
regents of Frederick's youth, till the Crown was completely
impoverished and had lost all power. The evil of these thirty
years must be undone. The strong position which the Norman
Kings had upheld was largely grounded on the extensive crown
domains ; the *Demanium* must be restored to the ruler. By
a law which he had long before excogitated " de resignandis
privilegiis " Frederick declared to be null and void all grants,
gifts, donations, privileges, confirmation of titles and the like
of the last thirty years. Every man must bring his documents,
except those relating to purely private property, within the
next few months and table them in the imperial chancery.
Here they would be examined and, if it seemed desirable,
renewed.

Every possessor therefore of crown lands, crown fiefs, royal
grants, tolls, privileges and what not, was suddenly reduced to
beggary, and at the Emperor's option would retain or forfeit
his possession. We cannot speak with certainty about the distribution of such property, as the vital Chancery records have
been destroyed ; but we know that nobles and monasteries and

towns, and even numerous simple citizens (as farmers of petty
taxes or holders of certain privileges perhaps), were hit by this
enactment.   The decisive consideration for the cancellation of
privileges was, broadly, whether the Emperor needed the castle,
the land, the tax or the special prerogative at the moment for
the construction of his state, or whether he did not.   If wanted
by the Emperor, the property whose titles had been submitted
to the inquisitorial eyes of the imperial court was simply confiscated, otherwise the holder received his diploma back again,
new-issued and with an added formula by which the Emperor
reserved the right to recall the new title at any time.

A further advantage had been secured by the imperial
Chancery—an exact knowledge of all grants of every kind and
their distribution, by which the Crown could at any moment
lay hands on anything it wanted.   Further, the Emperor could
at his own good pleasure cancel at least the special separate
privileges of any disaffected persons or powers.   Further yet,
the Crown—that is the King and State, for no separation of the
two was dreamt of—regained possession of its extremely extensive property, and, finally, the Emperor was provided with a
legal backing for the measures he directed against the various
petty powers.   This was a characteristic device of Frederick's.
He took the stage not as a conqueror, but as a fulfiller of the
law.   He was quick to point this out and warn all against
putting their trust in illegal evasions ; these would be valueless,
for he had come to place justice on her throne once more and
let her light shine again under his rule.

" Justice " for Frederick meant no rigid code, but the rights
of a living state determined by the ever-changing necessities of
the hour.   In defiance of well-known medieval theories justice
thus became a living thing, moving, progressive, capable of
development and change—as we shall expound more fully
later.   From this chameleon justice sprang the Emperor's legal
" Machiavellianism " in the service of the state (not of the
prince) which made its abrupt appearance in the first application of the Law of Privileges which in the manifold ramifications
of its operations was the basis on which the whole new order
in Sicily was founded.

A considerable number of the Sicilian barons had attended

the coronation in Rome. The most powerful of them all, Thomas of Celano, Count of Molise, who alone could put some 1400 knights and esquires in the field, had sent his son to meet Frederick to do him homage and to enlist his favour. Like most of the other nobles the Count of Molise had played the traitor, and his father had been one of the chief supporters of Kaiser Otto. In spite of the weighty advocacy of the Pope and of Cardinal Thomas of Capua, Frederick refused to accept the proffered submission. There is no reason to suppose that Frederick cherished any special ill-will towards this particular count. He was determined to subdue the entire body of continental nobles, and he was exactly obeying that first and simplest rule—which Machiavelli later preached as a doctrine—by boldly declaring war against the most powerful and playing off the lesser barons against him. When the big man was disposed of by their help he would find it an easy matter to rid himself of the small ones in their turn. Frederick accepted the homage of the minor nobles in Rome; at least he immediately found a means of utilising Counts Roger of Aquila, Jacob of San Severino, Richard of Ajello, Richard of Celano and many another. On the ground of the Law of Privileges which he was just about to promulgate, and other orders which he issued immediately after the coronation, he commanded them to hand over certain castles which they possessed. For it was all-important to be in control of fortified positions in the kingdom.

It was a happy chance that the barons had been witnesses of the coronation ceremonies and the entente between Emperor and Pope; overcome by all they had seen, they obeyed him without protest. The Emperor cared nothing for individuals, only for the cause. The Abbot of Monte Cassino, who had also come to the coronation in Rome, had always been loyal and submissive; nevertheless he had to surrender, under the same law, not only certain revenues, but also, most surely against his will, two important border fortresses, Rocca d'Evandro and Atina. These with three more castles, Suessa, Teano and Mondragone (which Count Roger of Aquila was compelled to hand over), covered Frederick's entrance into the kingdom and secured the road to Capua. Frederick crossed the border at Monte Cassino in December 1220.

These first castles were chosen for confiscation solely on account of their strategic importance. They were the same positions which the Romans had fortified of old against the Samnites. The same considerations applied to Sora and Cajazzo, which he next seized. These castles would strengthen his front towards the South-East. His first immediate goal was Capua.

Thus before he had entered his kingdom he had firm ground under his feet. There were a few entirely trustworthy families of the royal nobility on whose strength he could rely : the Cicali, the Eboli, above all the lords of Aquino. Immediately on entering Sicily Frederick created Landulf of Aquino Justiciar of the Terra Laboris, roughly the modern Campania ; while another, the elder Thomas of Aquino, he named Chief Justice of the same district and of Apulia and created him Count of Acerra. He had, further, at his disposal the fighting forces of the erstwhile traitor barons mentioned above, who had now done homage. Relying solely on the barons, Frederick set out to fight the barons. He had brought very few troops with him from Germany to Italy and most of these were crusaders, so he entered Sicily almost without an army, but, on the other hand, accompanied by Roffredo of Benevento, sometime professor of law in Bologna. Frederick was anxious to conquer his country with the forces of the country itself.

In December 1220 he held a great Diet in Capua and promulgated a number of laws. The most important was the Law of Privileges ; another, also directed against the barons, was closely allied : all castles and fortified places erected by vassals in the course of the last thirty years were to be surrendered to the crown or, alternatively, razed to the ground. The right of fortification was a royal prerogative, and from time immemorial vassals had therefore been forbidden to build castles even on their own land. So the new law was only the re-assertion of an ancient royal right. The Diet of Capua created the legal basis for Frederick's future procedure, for which the struggle with the barons, the resumption of crown lands and castles, formed only the *lever de rideau*. The Emperor did not even conduct these operations in person. If the surrender was peaceful the two *ad hoc* officials were sufficient; if resistance

was offered the submissive barons were delegated to break it.
Thomas of Aquino, for instance, was presently put in command
of the campaign against the Count of Molise. Frederick
thus kept his hands free for other work : for many things were
happening simultaneously.

We must now follow in detail the two years' campaign for
the reduction of the continental barons. Within a few months
the Emperor was in possession of quite a number of fortresses
in the north of the kingdom. The Count of Ajello surrendered
the castle from which he took his name. The Rocca d'Arce, a
border fortress against the States of the Church, was quickly
conquered by Roger of Aquila. Diepold of Schweinspeunt's
brother surrendered the castles of Cajazzo and Allifae, and
Diepold himself, whom Frederick had for years held prisoner
as hostage for these castles, was finally released and ostensibly
received into the Teutonic Order. The county of Sora with
its castle of Sorella was attached ; it had been at one time
pledged to Pope Innocent III and by him handed over to his
brother Richard. During the next few years a whole series of
further fortresses were conquered, destroyed or newly fortified,
amongst them Naples, Gaeta, Aversa, Foggia. The Alsatians
had coined a phrase about the Hohenstaufen, Duke Frederick,
" He always has a castle tied to his horse's tail," and this would
equally be applicable to his later namesake.

The spring of 1221 saw the beginning of the campaign
against the Count of Molise. He had entrenched himself in
two almost impregnable Abruzzi fortresses, Bojano and Roccamandolfi, and was beleaguered by the imperial generals. Bojano
was taken by assault. Roccamandolfi was forced to surrender ;
the count himself escaped to a third stronghold, Ovindoli,
whose resistance was not lightly overcome. After lasting the
better part of two years the campaign was finally ended by a
treaty under which Ovindoli was surrendered. The Count
went into banishment ; his personal possessions in Molise were
for the present secured to him, or rather to his countess.
Before long, however, a pretext was made that he had broken
the treaty ; he failed to obey the summons to appear before
the imperial court, and Frederick confiscated the entire Molise
property, as he had doubtless all along intended to do. Celano

vassals arose.   Moreover, any independence of the subject, such
as was implied by the sub-division of fiefs, was contrary to
Kaiser Frederick's principles of government.

The new feudal order in short laid down : that with reference
to fiefs and their distribution no alteration was to be made in
the *status quo* as existing at the death of the last Norman king
—no marriage, no inheritance, no sub-letting without express permission from the Emperor.   What had been an independent, living, moving, fluid form of life became in a moment
petrified by one single edict into rigid permanence.   Henceforth modifications could emanate from the Emperor alone, and
he was put in a position from which he could review the whole
detailed situation and exert his direct influence through the
most distant ramifications of the system.   Every independent,
natural development was checked and—what entirely suited
Frederick's whole conception—every impulse, every activity
must derive from him personally and have its source in his
imperial will.

The loosely-knit framework of a feudal kingdom, held together by land-tenure alone, was to be succeeded by the firm
architecture of a state : neither land nor fief would in future
bind the noble to his lord—these now imposed duties on him,
without entailing corresponding rights, nothing but personal
service.   Thus matters henceforth remained.   The possession
of a fief gave the nobleman no weight, only his personal service
rendered directly to the King, either as warrior or, what Frederick valued more, as official.   This paved the way to the
foundation of a " Court Nobility," such as developed later
under absolutism.

Another measure ran parallel with this state-organisation of
the nobles and the knights.   Frederick II was the first to place
castles and fortresses under the immediate administration of the
Crown and State, which was in effect to transform knightly
castles into national strongholds.   Over two hundred of these
national towers, castles and fortresses date back to Frederick's
time.   This entailed the creation of a new government department of " national defence," which was made responsible for
the administration, construction and upkeep of the fortresses,
for the supervision of the necessary staff, the payment of the

garrison and the like.   The castles carried naturally no garrison
in times of peace—a custom never known elsewhere—or at most
a châtelain and a couple of men-at-arms.   In time of war it was
the duty of the neighbouring fief-holders and districts, who
were also normally drawn on for construction and repair, to
man the forts at command and to bear the costs of so doing.
A type of national defence was thus organised, based on the old
but considerably simplified feudal substructure.   This was a
unique creation for the period, especially because it was the
unified product of systematic thought.

Attention should here be drawn to a very important implication of this transformation of knightly castles into state
fortresses : an entirely new style of architecture was evolved
for the new imperial castles that soon began to spring up.
These were no residential castles, as were otherwise the norm,
in which the knight lived with his wife and family ; these were
state strongholds which served as men's quarters only.   They
could therefore be built, as were the Roman castra, according
to one single uniform ground plan with slight variations—
representing the last word in simplicity, economy and rectangu-
larity : a stone square or rectangle with a tower at each of its
four corners similar to the well-known specimen in Naples.
Certain sportive variations, especially in the interior and in the
ornamentation and artistic accessories, are of course distinguish-
able ; many modifications also due to the site ; but the same
principle underlay them all and the pure form may be seen in
plains and on the coast.   People have justifiably seen in these
Sicilian castles of Frederick II the prototype of the Prussian
strongholds of the Teutonic Knights which show the same stark
simplicity of plan.   The conditions of the early Prussian state
under the Order corresponded in many particulars to the
Hohenstaufen state in Sicily.   The Prussian castles housed no
family life but served only as soldiers' barracks and arsenals.
Both entirely lacked any element of the " picturesque " ; they
are characterised by massiveness and stern straight lines, by
their utilitarian plan and the mathematically simple form.   In
the interior there might be groined vaults or cloisters with
pointed arches : Gothic windows and Gothic portals would also
not be lacking; but the outside, with flat roofs and squat towers,

showed nothing but right angles—gigantic stone blocks and cubes.

The arrival of the Emperor had been anticipated with some anxiety ; after a few months Frederick II was feared. " In the kingdom all bowed the neck before the Emperor," announces the chronicler. After the Diet of Capua, followed by a short stay in Apulia and Calabria, Frederick crossed in May 1221 to the island of Sicily, leaving his generals and the loyal barons to prosecute the Molise campaign. He held a new Diet in Messina and issued new laws, not in brief judicial form but in a style which later he made his own. The law was accompanied by a statement of the causes that led up to it and the needs it was designed to meet. The Assizes of Capua had sketched out the ground plan and the primary organisation of the Sicilian state, the edicts of Messina regulated the affairs of subjects who were outside the feudal framework. Frederick sharply divided them off from his own citizens. There were laws dealing with players and blasphemers, with Jews and whores and wandering min-strels. These constituted a potential danger, and Frederick II set limits to their activities. Players were wont to curse and blaspheme. It was most unsuitable for them to keep company with clerics, since it was the churchman's duty to " uphold the standard of right living in conduct and in speech." The Jews were to stitch the yellow patch on their clothing and to let their beards grow . . . in imitation of the Lateran edict of 1215 against Muslims. Without such distinctive marks " the duties and the practices of the Christian faith will be confused." Whores might not live in the town or frequent the bath with respectable women, " for one sick sheep infects the herd." Players and wandering minstrels should be outlaws " if they dare to disturb the Emperor's peace with ribald songs." So the Emperor strove to separate out his own, according to the precept of the Church.

The necessity to cleanse his land of foreign powers decided the next blow that Frederick struck on the island. On the ground of the Law of Privileges he withdrew their prerogatives from foreign sea-powers and hunted them from the ports of

Sicily. Amalfi and Pisa, Genoa and Venice had formerly acquired numerous trading rights in the fertile island. Sicily was not only as of old one of the great "granaries" from which the merchant could fetch his corn and perhaps sugar too, and dates, hemp and flax, silk and wool. The harbours of Sicily were also important as dockyards and ports of call for sailors of the Levant, who on their outward or homeward voyage could sell their Eastern wares or exchange them for Sicilian corn. Since being sacked by the Normans in 1135 Amalfi had lost her share of world trade. Venice made use of the harbour of Brindisi—the island of Sicily lay off her direct route to the East—so it was Genoa and Pisa who were chiefly interested in Sicilian commerce. The geographical contiguity of the two mighty north Italian republics destined them to be rivals, and rivals they were in every sphere; at home, in the Ligurian Sea, in Sardinia and Corsica, in Provence, in the Holy Land, and also in Sicily. In Sicily they enjoyed almost identical privileges; each had a special quarter in all important harbours, a consulate, a warehouse—the "fondaco" taken over from the Arabs—and the enjoyment of free trade, which exonerated their merchants from the payment of taxes, duties, dues, levies, etc.

In political matters the rivalry of the two towns had resulted in the Genoese allying themselves with their neighbours the Lombards as anti-Emperor, while the Pisans were correspondingly pro-Emperor. Pisa had always placed her fleet at the Emperor's disposal. In Frederick's youth, therefore, Pisa had supported Kaiser Otto, while Genoa had had leanings towards the young King of Sicily. By this connection with the Sicilian king the Genoese had gained ascendancy in the island, and in those early years had helped the young king against Pisa. When Otto IV came to grief, and Pisan politics with him, the predominance of Genoa in Sicily seemed assured.

An episode that took place during the fighting in Frederick's youth will illustrate the conduct of the sea-towns. Warlike Pisan merchants or seamen—corsairs at any rate—had taken advantage of the confusion prevailing in the kingdom to make themselves masters of Syracuse and had driven out bishop and people. Syracuse became a pirate fortress under the protection of Pisa, who used it as a base, at the same time that she officially disclaimed all responsibility for what happened there. In the summer of 1204 a body of homeward-bound Genoese chanced to meet in Crete others returning from Alexandria, so that a very considerable Genoese merchant fleet was accidentally assembled there. They took counsel together and decided to take Syracuse from the Pisans. The far-famed Genoese corsair, Alaman da Costa, who had just captured a Pisan ship laden with arms, was the originator of this scheme. He put himself at the head of the Genoese fleet. They sailed for Syracuse, via Malta, which was then a Genoese dependency, received the reinforcement of several war-galleys, attacked Syracuse, and in eight days were masters of the town. Alaman da Costa was their lord and signed all documents as " by the grace of God, of the king, and of the town of Genoa, Count of Syracuse and Officer of the King." He proceeded to enlarge his Syracuse domain and to assert his influence in Sicilian politics. This Sicilian Corsair-Tyrant was subject to the mother-city of Genoa, who could raise certain other claims to Syracuse, based on a grant of Barbarossa's. So Genoa held Malta, Syracuse and Crete, the most important bases on the route to the East.

Genoa had thus built her nest in Sicily. Frederick had the kindliest feelings towards the Genoese, and was not unmindful that they had stood by him on his march to Germany. But there was no place in his new state either for a Genoese dukedom of Syracuse, or for preferential treatment of foreign commerce, be it Genoese or Pisan. Pisa was now in many respects better off, for Frederick treated the two rival sea-towns exactly alike. Pisans and Genoese had done him homage on the death of Kaiser Otto, and he had confirmed both parties in their imperial, while cancelling their Sicilian, rights and privileges. The Pisans, having a much smaller stake in Sicily, were well content, and preserved their traditionally loyal attitude, remaining faithful to Frederick throughout his whole reign, as they had once been faithful to the Welf. The Genoese, however, once the most highly-favoured sea-power in Sicily, were extraordinarily hard hit.

Frederick II set at once to work. Count Alaman da Costa and his Genoese were driven out of Syracuse, a palace in Palermo which Genoa had used as a warehouse was confiscated under the Law of Privileges, and similar events took place in Messina, Trapani and elsewhere. The Sicilian admiral, William Porcus, was by birth a Genoese ; he prudently saved himself by flight. The Law of Privileges, which cancelled all advantages, bore heavily enough on the Genoese, but they were still more severely hit by a law of the Capua Assizes which forbade all favours to foreigners at the expense of the native population, such as freedom from taxes and dues. All this was most painful to Genoa, who naturally accused Frederick of crass ingratitude. Frederick, however, could not imperil the structure of his state at the dictates of private gratitude, and he had to resign himself to the ever-growing ill-humour of the Genoese, which ultimately, in spite of his repeated efforts to placate them, developed into open hostility. The needs of Sicily came first : the state revenues from duties and harbour dues necessarily sank to a minimum when the most important commercial towns were untaxed. How considerable these losses to the state had been in the past is best proved by a Genoese writer, who complains in his chronicle that the Sicilian taxes on goods amount now to 10 per cent. and over.

Frederick had broken the power of the feudal barons on the Italian continent, and set up a definite counter-force in his national defence ; he now took corresponding measures in maritime affairs. The banishment of the foreign sea-powers made some new creation absolutely imperative : he must himself create a Sicilian fleet. Here again he utilised his Law of Privileges : previous exemptions were cancelled and an old Norman ordinance again enforced, which laid on certain districts the obligation to furnish seamen, and on the barons the duty of supplying wood for shipbuilding. The Emperor erected state wharves and shipyards without delay ; but in any circumstances the building of ships takes time, so he created his first fleet chiefly by hire and by purchase. His methods were not a little inconsiderate : ship masters from the Italian coast-towns or other merchant seamen who happened to call at Sicilian ports were invited to hire or sell their vessels voluntarily ; failing this the ships were taken by force. The Venetians warned their captains who were touching in Apulia against such sales, and prosecuted those who sold. War galleys as well as merchant

ships were thus commandeered—since merchantmen need war-
ships for their protection—and the Emperor also set about
building galleys for himself.

Frederick must have strained every nerve over his shipbuilding, for by 1221 two considerable squadrons sailed to Egypt to
help the crusading army, and his intention was to have fifty
transports and one hundred galleys ready for sea by 1225.
Gradually he created a strong merchant fleet and a powerful
fleet of war, which did him valiant service in his Italian campaigns and brought him many a welcome victory.

It was of course at first a purely Sicilian fleet and was not to
become an imperial fleet for some time to come. From the
beginning it flew the banner of the Hohenstaufens—the imperial
Roman eagle on a golden field. In Frederick's day, for the
first time in history, a German-Roman imperial fleet sailed the
Tyrrhenian, Aegean and Ionian Seas, and for the first time merchants traded to Syria, Egypt and Tunis under imperial eagles.
One of these ships was styled Aquila, another went by the name
of " the half world," Nisfu'd Dunya. The like was not seen
again for three hundred years, till the time of Charles V.
Frederick gave his new fleet a new admiral, Count Henry of
Malta, like his runaway predecessor a Genoese by birth. He
had been a daring pirate and was likely to prove dangerous ; the
Emperor forestalled his possible hostility by this appointment.

Simultaneously with all this Frederick began to take over the
island castles and put them under the Crown, and to establish
a coastguard service both as a protection against hostile ships
and in preparation for the future war against the Saracens,
which he was not yet ready to attempt. The purging of Sicily
from the foreigner had increased the unity of that country ; the
re-creation of the fleet had extended its authority. The new
independence from foreign commerce and foreign shipping
secured through the fleet made possible a new economic policy.
With great versatility and clearsightedness Frederick immediately
began to foster an active Sicilian trade which had no longer to
compete against the crushing privileges of foreign powers. The
full development of Kaiser Frederick's much admired and
wonderfully organised policy is not attained till later, but
even in these early days it is possible to recognise in various

occurrences Frederick's passionate and indefatigable pursuit of unity and the uncompromising forcefulness and directness of his methods.

In spite of the rigid enforcement of the Law of Privileges, which took cognisance of the last thirty years, the Pisans and Genoese still enjoyed many privileges and prerogatives dating from earlier times, so that the Sicilians were still handicapped in trade competition with them. Frederick might have rectified this by conferring on his own subjects corresponding rights and favours, and thus putting them on an equal footing with the foreigner. This expedient, however, would have stultified his entire policy, which had suppressed most of the privileges of the harbour towns. Foreign commerce had suffered somewhat by Frederick's forcible purchase of ships belonging to the sea-powers—particularly because he thus withdrew for his own use tonnage from the foreign corn trade. He now drove them from the field without infringing their ancient Norman charters. The Emperor, at a later date, contrived to divert to his own coffers the enormous profits which accrued to the foreign sea-states from the purchase of relatively cheap Sicilian corn, by conveying the corn himself to the foreign markets in his state ships and selling it there himself at the high local prices. In these early years, however, while the imperial fleet was still in the making, and, moreover, subject to heavy claims on it in connection with the Crusade, the Emperor devised another scheme for preventing excessive gains by foreign profiteers.

In 1224 he for a time forbade all export of corn, foodstuffs and cattle. The commercial powers might only purchase their corn direct from the Crown, and Frederick took care to fix the price so high that the old privileges were of no avail, while the Crown benefited most handsomely. The immediate result in Sicily itself was such a fall in food prices that the producers scarcely recovered their costs. The Emperor immediately seized this opportunity of making large purchases for the Crown. This had been a bye-product—pleasant or unpleasant—of the em-bargo ; it had not been the motive of the imperial measure, which was directed in the first place against the ancient privi-leges. Private trade (which, however, recorded the very next year considerable shipments to Venice) was inevitably injured by this arbitrary interference, a fact which will not greatly have disturbed the Emperor. For his emergency measure was necessary at the time unless the greatest gains were to be lost to the country, and the individual was not, in any case, in a position to reap them.

The sea-powers were driven out, their warehouses abolished, and the supervision of the Sicilian harbours became possible. The Emperor did not fail to avail himself of the fact. In order to attract as large a supply of food into the island as possible during the Saracen war Frederick granted in 1222 complete freedom from import duties in Palermo. By the opening of this one port (together with the closing of the others, which we may assume) Frederick once more attracted trade and directed it to the very point which was most advantageous for his military operations. This proved most successful ; the feeding of the army was assured.

Similar autocratic measures are observable in other departments, though we have not always the clue to their interpretation. The export of the precious metals was sternly forbidden, and all payments to foreigners had to be made in the coarse newly-coined silver " imperials," which became legal tender. Frederick guaranteed that this currency would be maintained and he watched carefully over it. Numerous fairs were abolished, which indicates an attempt to centralise trade, for the local fair frittered it away and brought advantage only to a few great folk. For the first time in 1223 Frederick began to impose a direct tax which was repeated every three, two or one years according to need, but in his later days became a regular annual tax. These " collections," which were originally an extra-ordinary source of revenue, were thus conducted : the Emperor named the total sum required, and probably also dictated how it was to be distributed over the separate provinces ; the further sub-division was then left to the provincial governors, the *justiciars*, who with the tax-collectors were responsible for actually getting the money in. Only when taken in conjunction with the Emperor's later measures do these scattered individual ordinances give a complete picture of his economic policy. Even by themselves, however, they show a definite tendency : to seek a state unity even in commercial affairs, and to institute

as far as possible a state trading-monopoly with the outside
world.

The Saracen war has several times been mentioned.   Frederick began it in 1222, his second Sicilian year.   It was not
his task to combat an independent Muslim amirate dating from
the days of the Aghlabites, who had from Tunis conquered
Sicily in the ninth century as heirs, in the second degree, of the
Phoenicians.   That had already been done by the Normans.
He had to fight the scattered remnants of originally independent
Saracens who still maintained themselves in the inaccessible
highlands of the interior.   They were strengthened by
numerous fugitives from Palermo, who with a few of their big
men had escaped a bloody massacre which the Christians of the
capital had indulged in in 1190.   Runaway Saracen serfs joined
them, perhaps some clansmen also from Africa ; be that as it
may, they constituted a very considerable power, which for
decades had owned allegiance to none, and had gradually got
the whole centre of the island into their power.
    In the days of Pope Innocent's guardianship these Saracens,
like the continental knights and the corsairs of the coasts, had
been redoubtable foes and much-coveted allies.   They had
been uniformly hostile to Frederick, the Pope's ward, and in
various ways had more than once sought his life.   Just as the
Genoese had established themselves in Syracuse, the Saracens
had made themselves a base at Girgenti, probably in order to
maintain their communications with Africa.   They had also
taken the bishop prisoner and driven out a portion of the population, and had finally pursued their robber-raids northwards
almost to the coast as far as Monreale just south of Palermo.
A struggle with them was inevitable, for the Emperor's writ ran
only round a narrow strip of coast.
    The campaign developed into a weary and expensive petty
war against these enemies in their mountain fastnesses.   The
details are little known.   At the very outset, in the first summer,
the chief Saracen fortress Yato had been besieged and even
temporarily occupied.   The Amir, Ibn Abbad, had abandoned
all hope of victory and had set out with his sons to go to

Frederick and sue for peace. The Emperor was in the highest degree incensed against Ibn Abbad—who had maltreated some imperial messengers. So enraged was he that a scene followed which recalls the passionate outburst of the seven-year-old Frederick. Ibn Abbad entered the imperial tent and flung himself at the Emperor's feet ; on the instant Frederick plunged his spur into the Amir and tore his side open. Frederick had him removed from the tent and a week later hanged him and his sons as rebels. Two merchants from Marseilles who happened to be captured at the same time as the Amir shared his fate. Ten years before they had hawked boys and girls of the Children's Crusade in the slave markets of Tunis and Cairo, and had now been just in the act of betraying Frederick to the Amir.

After this initial success the Emperor spent the winter in continental Sicily. But the garrison he had sent to Yato was betrayed and massacred by the Muslims to the last man, and the Admiral, Henry of Malta, who had been left in charge of the island had been powerless to prevent another rally of the Saracens. The Admiral's excuse that his forces had been too small to risk an attack was rejected. He fell into disfavour and forfeited Malta. Later Frederick restored him again to favour and gave back his possessions—all but the fortress of Malta. Frederick had to re-open the Saracen war next summer, for its continuation was imperative. By a raid on the islands of North Africa, in which the fleet was employed for the first time as a fighting force, Frederick sought to sever communication with Africa and establish the imperial authority there. In spite of this and further successes the Emperor was compelled for many years to come to keep imperial troops in the island, and the war flared up again from time to time, but the outbreaks were always of short duration.

Such is, in brief, the tale of the subjugation of the Saracens of Sicily, of which all the chroniclers speak with admiration. The most amazing thing is Frederick's method of dealing with the situation. After the second campaign the Emperor decided to remove as many Saracens as possible from the island. They gave no peace in the mountains of Sicily ; he transplanted them to the plains of Apulia. Some 16,000 Muslims, in the beginning mostly agricultural serfs—all Muslims were in any case slaves of the king, *servi*, just as were the Jews—were gradually transferred to Lucera, which was transformed into a military colony. The town thus resumed its original function : for in the oldest Roman times Lucera had been a military colony. It lay in the Capitanata near Monte Gargano and Foggia, the favourite dwelling-place of Kaiser Frederick in later days. During Hohenstaufen times it had sunk into a half-depopulated town of the *demanium*. Frederick soon strengthened Lucera with a large imperial fortress, and here the Muslims lived entirely amongst their own kind. They had their own chief, the Qâ'id, with their own Shaikhs and Faqîhs. Thus there grew up in the heart of the oldest Christian country near the frontier of the papal *patrimonium* a genuine Muhammadan town with all its characteristic mosques and minarets, visible afar across the levels of Apulia. The duty of the new inhabitants was to cultivate the neglected land, and they proved remunerative citizens also through the special taxes imposed on Muslims : a poll-tax, *jizya*, for toleration of their faith, and the *terragium*, for enjoyment of the soil. Frederick transported to Lucera all the Saracen serfs on whom he could lay hands, whether they had fought against him or not, and the landowners of the island were thus robbed of labour. To replace this the Emperor sent them the exiled citizens of Celano, and later some people from Lombardy, but these probably did not suffice to make up the deficiency. The Emperor, however, needed labour for his extensive domains more than anyone else could. Moreover, he had another and far more important use for his Lucera colonists. These peaceful agriculturists could leap in a moment to their home-made arms, bows and arrows, and take the field as an ever-ready military force. They could serve as light infantry or, with no change of weapons, as light-armed cavalry, drawing their excellent horses from their own studs. It was an extra-ordinarily dangerous troop, obeying the Emperor alone, un-heeding the Pope or his ban, whom Frederick thus collected round him. He succeeded in an incredibly short time in changing the savage hate of the conquered into that fanatical devotion which the Oriental is ready to bestow on the master who protects him, the lord of whom he is the slave. In later years Frederick never felt so safe as among his Saracens, and it was a Saracen bodyguard who permanently watched over this German emperor or—as they called him in Lucera—this " Sultân." There were always numerous Saracen servants in Frederick's household, while in the imperial quarters in Lucera, the notorious " harem," the industrious Saracen maidens had to weave and work for their master.

It is impossible to withhold admiration from the wisdom with which Frederick—still scarcely thirty—knew how to tackle all the forces of opposition, and liberate their hidden strength for the benefit of the state. No material came amiss to his hand. He had in him more than a little of an Eastern despot, hence this idea of transplanting the Saracens, cutting them adrift from all connection with their past, demonstrating to them that they were wholly dependent on their master for weal or woe. Finally, taking advantage of their resignation, their natural joy in servitude, he cultivated in them systematically a fanatical devotion to his person. This is the constantly recurring principle in the East, which reached its culmination in the Janissaries of the Osmanli Sultans.

It can easily be surmised that this Muslim colony in the middle of a Christian country was a rock of offence to the Church—a matter of complete indifference to Frederick. For he had in his Saracens what no other western monarch of the day could boast : a standing army, a body of men ever ready for action, unreservedly devoted to him as the protector of their faith. This was the tie which bound the Saracens to Frederick II. Exiles as they were in a foreign land, they found protection for their faith in him alone. Frederick was careful not to loose the bond. The last thing he desired was their conversion to Christianity. Only for a very short time, at a moment of acute tension in his relations with the Pope, did he, most reluctantly, give permission to a few Dominicans to undertake a mission in Lucera. It was scarcely necessary, he added, for a few of them were already converts. The conversion of the Muslims had another disadvantage from his point of view—he lost the poll-tax. Muhammad's own hordes of Arabs had, for the same good reason, looked on it with no great enthusiasm when the conquered embraced Islam. The whole idea of a poll-tax on unbelievers was an inheritance which Sicily owed to the Saracens.

The deportation of the Saracens had as a consequence the purging of Sicily from " heathen and heathen households," as a chronicler expressly remarks. Frederick was the first who, by this weeding out of the Muhammadans, made the kingdom of Sicily almost uniformly Christian—with the exception of a few Jews. The Greeks counted only as schismatics. This cleared the way for a new development : the conceptions of purity of faith and purity of race, topics on which Frederick later found remarkable things to say. His Saracen war was the end of the struggle with Islam on Italian soil. The only spot in Europe in which the faith of Muhammad still flourished was Spain.

In less than three years Frederick II had thus converted the Sicilian chaos into some semblance of a state. His methods and his weapons had varied with the adversary ; more un- scrupulous than the shifty barons, politically more far-sighted than the coast towns, or at least fully their equal. The goal was always the same : the abolition of unjust privilege in favour of national unity. Here for the first time we note the uncom- promising directness of Frederick's action ; he always chose the shortest road through the jungle ; the immediate practical need of the state was his guide and over-rode all moral, senti- mental or other considerations whatsoever.

A highly important institution owed its foundations to state necessity. The rough work was hardly complete when Frederick issued, in the spring of 1224, the edict that called the University of Naples into being. At the Diet of Capua the Emperor had most sternly forbidden lay or clerical nobles to administer justice themselves or empower others to do so. It was the Emperor's business, and his alone, to set up justices and courts of law. The justices' business was to provide them- selves with such legal knowledge as was necessary for the ad- ministration of the law. The University of Naples was now created to supply them with such knowledge.

The Emperor stated most explicitly in the charter of the

university that its first function was to train shrewd and intelligent men for the imperial service ; men to whom the practice of the law could be entrusted throughout the kingdom. It was not Frederick's way to do things by halves ; he established not only a Law School in Naples but a *studium generale* which embraced every sort of intellectual training, including medicine, on the model of the adjacent Salerno. Naples thus became the first utilitarian State University, distinguished from all existing high schools and Church universities by the fact that teaching was to be carried out not for the sake of knowledge merely but for the advantage of the state, that it was to be a nursery for imperial officials and not for priests. There had hitherto been no demand for such a school : counts and bishops had sufficed to supervise the country, of whom we may state Barbarossa's two paladins to be characteristic types : Otto of Wittelsbach and Archbishop Reginald of Dassel. Frederick II's state was the first to feel the need of enlisting intellectual, well-educated laymen, skilled in the law, to undertake the administration. Alongside Church universities and town universities there now springs up this university whose teachers are appointed and paid by the state. Clearly the new university was founded with one fighting front towards the Church and one towards Bologna. Frederick had from of old great respect and affection for Bologna and had no wish to injure it by competition, but he was anxious to protect his budding officials from the rebellious, free-thinking atmosphere of the north Italian communes, for which he had less than no sympathy. So Naples was to educate and train men who would be not only intellectually equal to Church and commune, but who should embody the exactly opposite spirit to that animating the two powers who were ultimately to prove Frederick's deadly enemies, and who even thus early were causing him uneasiness.

Apart from these larger issues the foundation of this university was justified by domestic considerations. Frederick was determined forcibly to win control over men's minds and bring them within the unity of the state. The charter states that the courses of general study shall be so organised that those who hunger and thirst after wisdom may find what they seek within the kingdom itself, and need not be forced to leave the country to pursue their studies abroad. The scholars will be released from long journeyings and free to study under their parents' eyes. Frederick forthwith ordained—to make it clear to students that they had in no wise the option of accepting or rejecting the Emperor's benevolence—that in future no Sicilian subject might attend any university other than that of Naples, and those Sicilians at present studying elsewhere must transfer their work to Naples before a certain date. The first object of this ordinance was to ensure for the newly-founded university, which had behind it no long and gradual development, the greatest possible number of students. To the same end Frederick sought to entice foreigners to Naples by every means in his power. All inhabitants of the Roman Empire were permitted to study at the Emperor's university which he had founded in "pleasant Naples"; lodgings, security, money advances, cheap living conditions, everything had been provided for ; the country had abundant supplies of corn and wine, meat and fish. A highly-qualified teaching staff was assembled in Naples, for the Emperor had appointed his judge, Roffredo of Benevento, and several other eminent men, professors at the new university. All other universities being out of bounds for his subjects, Frederick's new creation at once enjoyed a monopoly; no one in the kingdom might undertake to teach any subject taught at the university. Any existing schools of this sort were closed.

A further consideration underlies all these arrangements. However much the Emperor rejoiced in the "joy of the road" that possessed the wandering scholars in the Empire, he had no sympathy or patience with it in his kingdom. Wandering knights, wandering scholars, and even wandering singers "who with ribald songs disturb the Emperor's peace" had no legitimate place in his concentrated, severely-organised society. As far therefore as lay in his power he cut their wanderings short, unless they were directly employed in his own service. Frederick's intention was, by his university, to retain in the country the best brains it possessed, to educate them in his own spirit, free from outside distractions, and to enlist their unlimited and undivided devotion in his service and the state's.

It was his task to see that Sicily herself offered to his subjects all that they had hitherto gone abroad to seek. Frederick was as thorough in this as in his other enterprises ; he is the first Emperor who consciously and deliberately set himself to establish an empire over the minds of men.

Frederick II had thus rapidly tackled every department of life in his state and had left his mark upon them all. There was to be practically no activity which did not emanate from him, and none which did not in its turn advantageously react upon the state. The feudal system had become static : the more important nobility were in the direct service of the Emperor ; the castles had become national fortresses ; trade had been to a large extent nationalised ; markets and fairs reduced in number and concentrated ; a stately fleet created, in comparison with which private merchant ships were almost negligible ; unity of faith had been approximately achieved ; the Saracens herded into one single colony ; a standing army established ; independent justice assured ; and now, finally, those halls of learning opened which would spread the imperial spirit and attract collaborators. It was no small achievement for a man of thirty, and all had been accomplished with joy and zest, almost in play, on the basis of one single law. All had been set in motion almost simultaneously ; indeed only the immediate successful interlocking of the various cogs made the wheels turn. Only one power, not a Sicilian but a world power, the Church, still resisted every onslaught of Frederick's.

For some years Frederick had worn the imperial crown, but his achievements had been confined to one relatively restricted sphere : he had been playing the king only, and though these kingly deeds would presently serve the Emperor they had not yet assumed any importance for Christendom at large. Frederick could already, as Roman emperor, hold the balance even against a world power like Church and Pope, but before he could seriously challenge it he must himself become a "world power" too. This position could not be achieved all in a moment, nor could Frederick in his progress have overleaped the king stage. Pope Honorius still wrote to him during these years that he was overlooking occasional trespasses as natural to " the fiery spirit of your youth," by which phrase he drew the sting from Frederick's attacks.   The political relation was parallel to the human.   Frederick had not yet got a unified, consolidated World Empire to oppose to the World Church. The Empire was still in the making.   Frederick had only mediate authority in Germany, and had not even shown himself there since his formal coronation in Rome.   He had indeed conquered Sicily, but the fruits of his new constitution had naturally not yet been harvested.   He had not even tackled imperial Italy.   So every attempt he made to exercise definite pressure on the Church was doomed as yet to failure, though he was able successfully to best her in diplomacy—no contemptible achievement.   He had not yet redeemed his crusader's vow and had been able, again and yet again, to postpone the date of his departure and gain time for his Sicilian reforms. Many circumstances had favoured him.

On the occasion of his coronation Frederick had promised to start on the Crusade in the late summer of 1221.   He had only sent two imperial squadrons to Damietta under Admiral Henry of Malta and the ex-Chancellor Walter of Palear, now Bishop of Catania ; he himself remained at home.   The imperial reinforcements arrived in Egypt too late, mistakes were made, the catastrophe of the Nile delta was not to be averted. Without waiting for the reinforcements, and with wholly inadequate means, the crusaders had advanced up the Nile from Damietta to conquer Cairo.   The Nile was just beginning to rise.   The Egyptians breached the dams, and finally the Christian army had to capitulate and surrender Damietta. The Emperor's presence would have been of no avail.

All Christendom was affected by the defeat of the crusading army ; most heavily of all Pope Honorius, who had himself initiated the Crusade.   Frederick II was not unaffected by the failure either.   His correspondence and some meetings with Pope Honorius had reference to the events in the East. New extensive preparations were agreed upon, arrangements for which made further postponement inevitable, and this in turn secured further respite for Frederick II's work in Sicily.

He pleaded, not without justification, that he was waging war against the infidel Saracen just as much in Sicily as in the Holy Land. Fresh recruiting for the Crusade must be begun (Hermann of Salza undertook it for Germany) and for three successive years laymen and clerics had to submit to extraordinary taxes for the new enterprise. Success was everywhere slight, Crusade-enthusiasm seemed to have evaporated for ever, protracted preparations were needed. The reports sent by the German Grand Master, and corroborated by others, at last convinced Honorius of the general apathy and discontent, and he decided to grant Frederick a further respite till 1227. This was agreed on at San Germano in 1225 and laid down in a treaty after earlier conferences on Eastern affairs between Pope and Emperor (in 1222 at Veroli, in 1223 at Ferentino). At each of these meetings Frederick had succeeded in winning a further delay, which, in the circumstances, the Pope was unable to refuse. Pope Honorius showed considerable annoyance, which was not to be wondered at, for the Crusade was the very breath of his nostrils to this ailing, aged man.

The San Germano agreement gave Honorius the necessary securities for the ultimate undertaking of the Crusade, but he had the vexation of seeing the whole organisation of it slip from the fingers of the papal Curia and pass into the Emperor's hands —where many people thought it should have rested all along. The conditions of the agreement were certainly not light, for Frederick shouldered sole and only responsibility. It is a testimony to the capacity of his kingdom that he swore on his soul to set out for the Holy Land in August 1227 with 1000 knights ; to maintain this force there for two years ; to hold ships in readiness for the transport of a further 2000, each knight with his following and three horses. He promised finally before crossing over to deposit in five instalments 100,000 ounces of gold (about quarter of a million sterling) to be forfeited for the cause of the Holy Land if for any reason the Emperor failed to go on the Crusade. Hermann of Salza was to be the trustee for this immense sum. Apart from the money penalty the Emperor declared himself ready to incur the papal ban as a dilatory crusader if he failed to start on the appointed date or in any other way played false, and he allowed the ban to be provisionally suspended over him.

In spite of these heavy commitments the Emperor was the gainer. He had again secured two years' respite for Sicily and could turn the Crusade to imperial advantage. Frederick's present complaisance obliterated for the moment the annoyances of the last five years. In his first meeting with the Pope in 1222 the Emperor seems to have sought to get back into his power by some means or other the old imperial territories of central Italy, the " Recuperations " which he had been compelled to renounce in favour of the Church. He coveted in particular Spoleto and the Ancona March. Pope and Cardinals incontinently refused what the Pope termed "these unseemly requests." This central Italian complex of territory cut Frederick's empire in half, and drove a wedge between Sicily and imperial Italy. It was an unendurable thorn in Frederick's side, and sooner or later the question would have to be thrashed out. Frederick absolutely needed at least the Adriatic coast districts, the March and Spoleto, as a corridor between Sicily and Lombardy. The time for forcible annexation had, however, not yet come and Frederick had prematurely disclosed his plans. The Roman Curia was on the *qui vive*. Not long after this the imperial governor, Gunzelin of Wolfenbüttel, committed certain encroachments, drove out papal officials and demanded that people should take the oath of allegiance to the Emperor. In vain the Emperor protested his innocence and declared that the Governor had exceeded his instructions ; his assurances fell on deaf ears. Nothing short of the disgrace of Gunzelin and the intercession of Hermann of Salza sufficed. With that the storm blew over.

The heavy obligations which Frederick had assumed at San Germano were in the spirit of his original vow : the Emperor was the Sword of the Church and the Leader of Christendom, and on him fell by right the conduct of the Crusade. Other reasons were operative as well. The Empress Constance had died in 1222 in Catania. Frederick acceded to a wish of the Pope and of the German Grand Master, and in order " the better to conduct the affairs of the Holy Land " declared himself ready to contract a fresh marriage with the daughter of King John of

Jerusalem. The intention of the Curia was to strengthen the Emperor's connection with Jerusalem, and the plan was successful. Isabella of Jerusalem was penniless, but she brought as her dowry the sceptre of the Holy Land, and the lustre this would lend the Empire was unique.

The hereditary succession of the Syrian kingdom was such that on the death of her mother Isabella became the heir ; while her father, Count John of Brienne, merely bore the honorary title of king. The marriage was celebrated in Brindisi in the beginning of November 1225, and the barest recitation of the events flashes a momentary light on the glamour and the glory of crusading times. The Emperor sent a squadron of ships with his notables to Acre, and there in the Church of the Holy Cross the princess was solemnly betrothed, to the wonderment of all, to the absent Emperor, whose ring was placed on her finger by a Sicilian bishop. In Tyre the bride received from the hands of the Patriarch the crown of the Holy Land, and the Knights of Jerusalem did homage to their Queen. The Franco-Syrian child of fourteen, escorted by a knight of the Teutonic Order, embarked on the imperial galley and sailed across the sea to wed the Emperor of the West. The poets of the day could not resist a theme so ready to their hand ; the German epic Ortnit makes this Syrian bridal—adorned with many a fable, worked up almost into a fairy tale—the centre of the plot, while other touches hint at Frederick's story. The hero after many adventures wins his Syrian bride—a worshipper of Apollo and Muhammad—but not without the help of Zacharias the King of the Sicilian Saracens, the " wise heathen of Apulia." A thread of chivalrous romance—hard to reconcile in appearance with the sober, statesmanlike sense of the Sicilian autocrat—runs through the whole life of this last Hohenstaufen, who must in person have lived through all the saga episodes of the medieval world of knights. If one sought out and wove together the marvellous adventures of the imperial story, as reported in history and in legend, the tale would be the typical biography of a crusading knight as recounted by current romances.

This magic spell for a moment hid political realities ; their recrudescence marred the marriage feast. On the wedding day

Frederick, as was his right, adopted the title, King of Jerusalem, which appears henceforth in all his documents after the title of Roman Emperor, and before that of Sicilian King. Immediately he demanded that John of Brienne, titular King of Jerusalem, should formally renounce his royal rights. King John was a personal friend of Frederick's, like him one of the earliest poets to write in the Italian tongue. He had been for months the Emperor's guest. He had reckoned on being at least the Viceroy of Jerusalem. He was deeply hurt, and after a wordy quarrel with the Emperor he fled to Rome. The Emperor received without delay the homage of the Syrian grandees. Little is known of Isabella's fate. The Emperor's quarrel with King John gave rise to many a tale. A Frenchman relates that Frederick spent his wedding night with a Syrian niece of King John's, beat Isabella, threw her into prison and never went near her. But facts give this tale the lie. Frederick assigned the castle of Terracina near Salerno to his consort, and took her with him to Sicily. The young girl certainly exercised no influence on Frederick, and she died in 1228 at the birth of her son Conrad. The crown of Jerusalem had suddenly lent a tangible political value to the Crusade in Frederick's eyes. He must win a new kingdom in the East. State and personal factors were thus combined ; when World Church, World Empire and World Politics were intermingled the Crusade gained in importance. Nothing further was needed but the opportune moment to achieve success.

Pope and Emperor, being in the matter interdependent, were in the main at one about the Crusade, though it was inevitable that misunderstandings and differences should arise from time to time in the intricate negotiations entailed. On both sides every effort was made to avoid friction, and for the moment they even steered clear of the rock of the " Recuperations." The first serious conflicts arose over Sicilian questions, for Frederick in the new organisation of his state began to regulate Church matters after his own fashion. At the Diet of Capua he had urged on his subjects the punctual payments of tithes to the Church. Soon after he revived a Norman edict which forbade the accumulation of lands under mortmain : churches and monasteries might purchase land and receive it as gifts—later the Emperor forbade this also—but they must part with it again within a year a month a week and a day, otherwise, as Frederick later expressed it, " the Church would ere long have bought up the entire kingdom." These laws were quite customary and roused no hostility against the Emperor.

Matters assumed a different complexion, however, when Frederick threw down the gauntlet to the Sicilian episcopacy. He was always ready to apply the surgeon's knife and cauterising iron to get rid of sores and ulcers—the metaphor was a favourite with him—and he embarked according to these principles on a purification of the Sicilian clergy. He suspended Bishop Arduin of Cefalù for his general conduct in squandering Church property—the records of the trial prove that the accusations were well founded—and soon after Archbishop Nicholas of Taranto on similar grounds. The ex-Chancellor Walter of Palear, Bishop of Catania, whom Frederick had mistrusted of old and whom he had sent out of the kingdom ostensibly with reinforcements for the crusading army, did not venture to show his face again in Sicily. He went from Damietta probably first to Rome and on to Venice, where he finally died, it was said, in utter poverty. The irregularities of the Sicilian clergy were probably extreme : Frederick was obliged to imprison a large number of the inferior clergy, and even the Pope had to remove individual bishops such as those of Carinola and Squillace. The bishops deposed by Frederick took refuge in Rome, which gradually became the asylum of exiled Sicilians. In addition to the three bishops, Count Thomas of Molise was there, Roger of Aquila, Jacob of San Severino and the other barons, presumably also the Count of Syracuse, Alaman da Costa and King John of Jerusalem. These episodes contributed to Honorius's irritation. He had acquiesced in the Emperor's proceedings against the bishops at the time, but they did not cease to rankle, and on occasion formed a subject of reproach. The thing that ultimately provoked a heated correspondence on both sides was the question of the episcopal elections in Sicily.

It has already been explained how vital was the so-called " freedom of episcopal elections." One further consideration should be added : at the same moment that the Curia set out to tighten up the relationship between itself and the bishops throughout the Christian world, and convert them into immediate dependants of the Pope and his direct representatives, a parallel movement was at work in the West, a development of strong national self-consciousness in the various countries. The Church's endeavour to subject episcopacy in each country to the direct and immediate control of Rome ran violently counter to this new tendency of the ancient Roman world to resolve itself into individual nations.

On the other hand it also stood in the way of each individual nation as it strove to consolidate itself into a unified state, for everywhere the Church was a " state within a state." The more because she was in no wise a purely spiritual force, but a very material one, endowed with land and possessions, and in the most important matters refusing allegiance to the state. This situation led sooner or later to serious friction in every country in Europe. Things came to a head in Sicily first, because Frederick II was not only King of Sicily but also Emperor. As Emperor he had a dual rôle to sustain. For the preservation of world unity the Church's aims were the Emperor's, for the Roman Emperor felt himself just as responsible for the oneness of the world as any Pope, but their views diverged in this, that the Emperor fully recognised national individuality—nay, was in the act of creating a new and well-knit nation. Frederick's dual attitude had been latent from the first ; its full extent began to be revealed when the evolution of the Sicilian state made the question a vital one for him. A permanent conflict that haunted Frederick all his days is here seen in its beginning : it may be summed up in the formula " an empire—and yet—nations." A tension which Dante felt in yet acuter form : " individuals and yet a Roman Empire."

It is interesting to note that in Germany, where national feeling was less developed, the time was not yet ripe for conflict with Rome, and Frederick was content to leave the Curia unmolested in its bishops' elections. But in Sicily, where he was not only Emperor but King, he fought the Pope most strenuously. As a mere boy he had crossed swords with Innocent III about the Palermo elections. Episodes of this sort were bound to multiply with time, and a glance at the constitution of the Sicilian Church will show what importance these elections

assumed in Sicily.   There was no other country where new
elections were so frequent, for this tiny land boasted 21 archbishops and 124 bishops.   The disproportion of this becomes
more manifest when we realise that at the Lateran Council of
1215, which was graced by all the spiritual dignitaries in Christendom, 105 out of 405 participants came from the Sicilian
kingdom.   The enormous number of archbishops is probably
rightly traced to the Byzantine influence in southern Italy.
The Greek archpriest develops into the Roman archbishop,
though the two are radically different, and "archpriest" connoted no more than a priest independent of the Patriarch of
Constantinople.   Vacancies occurred in Sicily with extraordinary frequency, and it was absolutely vital to the Emperor
to keep his bishoprics in trusty hands, that the bishops might
be as they had been in Norman days, organs of the king and
of the state.   The excessive number of the bishops made this
in one way easier to achieve.   The Sicilian bishop was not, like
his German brother, a mighty prince of the Empire, holding
extensive territories, but of humbler status, well suited to be a
Church or state official.

The episcopal type dear to Frederick's heart is well represented by the Primate of the Sicilian Church, Berard of
Castacca, Archbishop of Palermo.   To forestall an election
squabble with Frederick, over Palermo, Pope Innocent III had
entrusted the church of the capital to Berard, formerly Archbishop of Bari.   From Frederick's point of view no more
fortunate choice could have been made.   Archbishop Berard
of Palermo became quite indispensable to the Emperor, a second
Hermann of Salza.   He had not the statesmanship of the
German Grand Master, but he was his superior in learning and
culture.   He enjoyed the respect of the Roman Curia while
being whole-heartedly devoted to the Emperor.   Ultimately no
weighty negotiation with the Pope could be conceived in which
the shrewd and reverend prelate did not represent the Emperor.
There was indeed no weighty event of any kind in which
Berard had not his share, so completely did he command the
Emperor's confidence.   The services he rendered are innumerable.   Frederick himself wrote ". . . in danger of every sort
he stood by our side and many things hath he endured on our

behalf." Berard was one of the few churchmen who could breathe the intellectual atmosphere of Frederick's court and was able to hold his own in the literary activities of the courtiers. Indeed it was he who discovered Piero della Vigna and brought him to the imperial court. His greatest service, however—and it was no slight one—was that he lived through the whole of Frederick's life in closest proximity with him. As Bishop of Bari he had been one of the household officers of the boy king. He had accompanied him on his adventurous journey to Germany. It was on Berard's summons that the Bishop of Constance had opened the city gates ; it was Berard who represented Frederick at the Lateran Council. He lived almost continuously at the imperial court, and was destined to outlive his master and administer to him the final sacrament. We have no detailed knowledge of Berard's personality—he was the Emperor's instrument and clung to his master through ban and curse—but as the faithful and honourable priest who stood by the Emperor from his boyhood to his dying bed he is one of the most human of the secondary figures in the picture of Frederick's life. No astounding achievement immortalises his name ; it is enough that when great deeds were doing he was there.

Such will be roughly the type of prelate which Frederick II liked to have, and there always were a considerable number of such in Sicily, though none enjoyed the same intimacy as Berard of Palermo. The only right remaining to the Emperor under the Concordat was that of choosing such adherents for episcopal vacancies—or rather of giving his concurrence only to such candidates. The Concordat of the Empress Constance had reduced the King's right to simple concurrence in the choice made by the Chapter. The bishop thus chosen by the Chapter and confirmed by the King could only officiate after final approval by the Pope. Even this meagre privilege of the King's was further whittled away by the Pope's revival of an ancient " right of devolution." According to this a vacancy which lasted over six months entitled the Pope to fill it immediately himself, without reference to either King or Chapter. A favourite practice of the Roman Curia was therefore to postpone on the flimsiest pretexts the final confirmation of the bishop till the six months had elapsed, and then simply to appoint another man, whom neither King nor Chapter wanted, but who best suited Rome. The Emperor, conversely, sought to exceed his rights, and by promises or pressure to induce the Chapter to choose a candidate of his proposing, an imperial physician it might be, or notary—a procedure which the Curia did not fail to challenge.

Things gradually came to such a pass that the mere recommendation of the Emperor damned any candidate in the eyes of the Curia. In Capua, for instance, a certain dean, Hugo by name, had been unanimously chosen and was recommended to the Pope by Frederick—who did not apparently even know the man personally—as " an educated, suitable man and a native of the country." Thereupon the Pope rejected him.

In Nola Master Peronnus, a notary of the Emperor's, was chosen, but a minority dissented and his appointment was not confirmed. On the other hand the long vacancy in Salerno is to be thus explained : Archbishop Nicholas of Ajello had proposed his own successor. Now Nicholas was some relation of Count Richard of Ajello, no great friend of Frederick's, and had himself been an adherent of Kaiser Otto's and had rebelled against the Law of Privileges. He had therefore fallen into disfavour, sufficient grounds for Frederick on his part to reject the proposed successor.

In Brindisi matters reached a climax. The unanimous choice fell on a notary and household officer of the Emperor's, John of Trajetto, a man well known to the Roman Curia. Frederick had exerted himself most eagerly to secure this candidate's appointment by the Pope, had even sent a special deputation to Rome. It had, however, become almost a point of honour at Rome to reject the Emperor's candidate. Honorius made the excuse of a technical error in the election—it had taken place three months after the death of the previous incumbent—and refused John of Trajetto even when Frederick wrote again. A similar state of affairs prevailed in Aversa, Acerno, Sarno, Conza, Bari : as far as can be judged the Emperor never succeeded in carrying the day.

Bitterness increased on both sides. Honorius reproached Frederick with interference in the election in just such words as Innocent had used to the boy of years ago : he had better be warned to avoid the evil practices of his ancestors whose trespasses had brought it about that he, Frederick, was the last scion of his race. The Emperor replied that Honorius was seeking his destruction : this papal protection was not protection but extinction. With extreme incisiveness he declared that if the Pope would not confirm in office the bishops nominated by the Emperor he might save himself the trouble of sending other persons as bishops into the Sicilian kingdom, for the Emperor on his side would henceforth refuse to receive the men chosen by the Pope. He would give orders to close not only the churches but the towns against them. That had all the ring of an ultimatum, yet Honorius did not so interpret it, but turned it aside with the comment that the young Emperor was misled by evil counsellors, and swept off his feet by his own youth. Such procedure, however, was bound to cause unpleasantness. He requested the Emperor to apologise for the unseemly utterances of his messengers—by which was meant the unseemly tenor of the imperial letter itself. Whether the Pope received his apology or not we do not know.

The Pope, however, set about filling the vacant sees after a further warning to Frederick not to interfere with Church affairs—a dangerous thing for laymen. Witness the Bible example of Uzzah who put forth his hand to the Ark of the Covenant of the Lord when the oxen shook it and God smote him there for his error and there he died by the Ark of God. The Pope would henceforth appoint his own shepherds for his flocks. Even when the persons chosen were not in themselves unwelcome to Frederick—Marinus Filangieri, for instance, was a brother of the Emperor's marshal Richard Filangieri—he nevertheless forbade their admission. The correspondence between Pope and Emperor grew steadily more hostile, till last the hoarded wrath burst forth simultaneously on both sides, just at the moment least convenient to the Emperor when he was busy restoring order in Lombardy.

Frederick's early days were not to pass without his learning the bitterness of his other enemies, the Lombard towns, for whom he was as yet no match—largely because the Roman Curia of the time was behind the Lombards.

The Treaty of San Germano had granted Frederick two years' respite before the Crusade. He intended to utilise this interval to round off all Western affairs before tackling the problems of the Orient. The reorganisation of Sicily was already more or less complete, and German problems were to be regulated at a Diet which Frederick decided to hold in Lombardy, so as to give full weight to his imperial authority in those regions. He therefore invited the German princes and King Henry to Cremona for Easter 1226, " and if you come for no good reason but to see ourself, ourself will be well pleased by sight of you," so he concluded his letter of invitation. The Court agenda mentioned only very general topics : Restoration in Italy of Imperial Rights : Eradication of Heresy : Prosecution of the Crusade. Frederick particularly stressed the last two items, which concerned Church affairs. Backed by the united armed forces of Germany and Sicily he had good hope of finding the Lombards docile and complacent.

The Lombards, however, had unfortunately noted the recent re-assertion of royal rights in Sicily, and Frederick's " Restoration of Imperial Rights " rang ominously in their ears. The normal *status quo* for Lombardy was laid down in Barbarossa's Peace of Constance dating from 1183. For several decades no Emperor's eye had been upon the Lombard towns, and there was no question that they had quietly encroached on imperial properties and on imperial rights, quite as seriously as the minor powers had in Sicily usurped royal rights and property. The Lombards might well dread another Law of Privileges with more far-reaching effects than the Sicilian one. They had no wish to take risks. Exaggerated reports reached them of the mighty army that Frederick was gathering for his Lombard Diet. This was decisive. With quick distrust the Lombards, under the leadership of Milan, formed themselves into a League which was joined by the majority of north Italian communes.

It is most unlikely that Frederick had had any such Law of Privileges in mind, for he was well aware that the Lombard problem was very different from the Sicilian. He was here opposed, not by a multitude of disconnected, mutually warring, minor powers, but by a large number of homogeneous foes, territorial powers who, not unlike the German princes, would immediately rally to a common banner to repulse a common enemy, all their mutual jealousies and squabbles notwithstanding. The Peace of Constance did not forbid a union of the towns, but this revival of the ancient Lombard League was a manifest act of hostility, provoked it is true by Frederick's attitude, which in Lombard politics had gradually become more and more obviously that of a partisan. Lombardy was in fact split into two camps, and a non-party Emperor was scarcely possible. Traditional as well as personal bias determined his choice of party.

Cremona and Milan strove for the hegemony of Lombardy, just as Genoa and Pisa disputed the supremacy of the Mediterranean. Milan was of old the most powerful of the Lombard towns. The arrogance of the bishops who sat in the seat of St. Ambrose rose in the eleventh century to actual rivalry with Rome, as Frederick reminded the Romans, to spur them on to humble the pride of Milan. Milan, moreover, was an ancient coronation town. In quite recent times Henry VI had worn there the crown of the Italian King. The people of Milan, with justifiable pride, had been the first among the communes to fight for freedom. Here for the first time the burghers and the humbler aristocracy made common cause against the Great, and had in the *motta* [1] achieved municipal unity. Milan was the first town which quite early dared to defy imperial authority. Having once talked of freedom, Milan under its consuls strove for political independence and submitted only with extreme distaste to any law, spiritual or temporal, emanating from a higher power. This attitude on the part of its powerful citizens of dual rebellion—against Church and Empire—made Milan the focus of heresy and insurrection. Its territories were the size of a dukedom, and no other Lombard town could compete with it in wealth or power. The other towns also early developed a taste for freedom, for independence and for territorial aggrandisement. In spite of endless wars amongst themselves they all willingly acknowledged the primacy of " the central town " if outside aggression threatened their liberties and challenged them to common resistance. This did not preclude

[1] Motta is roughly : the revolutionary popular party.—*Tr.*

them from occasionally banding themselves together against the oppressive superiority of Milan, or even lending Barbarossa a helping hand when he destroyed the town in 1162. Such alliances between the towns did not denote any dream of a larger unity. The *polis* was all in all to the Lombards as to the Greeks, and this narrow-minded pre-occupation with solely municipal affairs militated against all serious political thought, and against any wish to subordinate their town to the overlordship of the Roman Empire.

Not all the towns, however, followed Milan ; a proportion held to Cremona. Tacitus's judgment seemed for many a long day to hang like a curse over this town : *bellis externis intacta, civilibus infelix*. But from the ninth century on Cremona became powerful and rich and her ships sailed down the Po to trade with Venice and even directly with Byzantium. The first Italian town to be granted a town charter, as far as is known, was Cremona, and since then the burghers whom Otto III protected had in the main stood by the Empire. A hundred years later, in 1098, the final seal was put for all time on Cremona's loyalty. The Margravine Matilda, who had in her lifetime witnessed the great Canossa struggle, threw down an apple of discord between Cremona and Milan when she amplified a gift to the Cremonese by including the land between the Adda and the Serio, the so-called " insula Fulcherii," and the town of Crema. " In this year the fight for Crema began," declares the chronicler, and from this time onwards Cremona was always on the side of the Emperors, for only they could secure to the Cremonese the possession of the bequest by protecting them against Milan who also laid claim to Crema. It was important therefore for the Emperors to strengthen the loyal communes, and those towns which from time to time for one reason or another were enemies of Milan or of Milan's satellites. The political groupings in Lombardy altered often, and altered suddenly. But however greatly the following of the two rival towns might change, one thing remained unchanged in Lombardy : the hate between Cremona and Milan.

Frederick II had to take up his position. Two ways were theoretically open : he could hold himself aloof and above the quarrels of the towns, if he could have found a formula to satisfy all rivals, and thus have won the Lombard towns for himself. This might in fact have been possible if Frederick instead of ever and again seeking reconciliation with the aristo-cratic Church had made common cause with the Lombards against the common enemy—the papacy. But an alliance of the Empire with the *tiers état* against the clergy—in other spheres the greatest of Frederick's great achievements—had for many reasons not yet risen above the Hohenstaufen's horizon in the sphere of world politics. So only the second path lay open : to take sides ; to espouse the cause of Cremona, and with her help and her allies, in addition to the resources of Sicily—which earlier emperors had not had at their disposal—and with Ger-man backing, to intimidate the opposite party, if possible with-out fighting, and so to restore imperial rights. The personal factor was not wanting. Frederick on his first journey to Ger-many at seventeen had been hunted by Milan, whereas Cremona had helped him in his need. He had pledged his faith to her, confirming her title to Crema and the Isola Fulcheria. Frederick apparently considered this old attachment to Cre-mona still of value ; at any rate he professed to feel himself still bound by his early promise—by no means always his case—and accepted now her friendly demonstration with a graciousness he rarely showed at any time to any town. " This faithful town, hereditarily loyal to the Empire," as he called it, was later even permitted to play the godmother to Frederick's son, Conrad.

Yet another factor carried weight. The Emperor nourished an instinctive constitutional hate against rebels in general, and an inherited hate against Milan in particular. " No sooner had we ascended against all the expectation of men, by the aid of Divine Providence alone, the highest peaks of the Roman Em-pire, in the years of our ripening adolescence, in the glowing power of mind and body . . . than all the acuteness of our mind was continually directed to one end . . . to avenge the injury offered (by the Milanese) to our Father and our Grandfather and to trample under foot the offshoots of abhorred freedom already carefully cultivated in other places also." Thus the Emperor, ten years later. Such abysmal hate, such lust for vengeance, admits no argument. It is simply a fact to be reckoned with. As early as 1219 in Germany Frederick had vowed to the Cremonese never to receive Milan into favour without their concurrence. He soon delegated to Cremona control over the affairs of Lombardy.

This was the major schism in northern Italy, and the Emperor's attitude to it was already laid down. The mere fact that he summoned his Diet to meet in Cremona showed the enemy his hand. But in the tangle of divisions and feuds the rivalry of the two groups of towns only represented one of many cleavages. From somewhere about the turn of the century the inhabitants of the towns had been divided by internal faction. In the eleventh century burgher and inferior noble had made common cause against margrave and count, and had wrung from the great landowners the territories of the town. And now the plebeians had risen against the inferior noble and the town knight. In most towns two factions had developed, the knightly party and the popular party, and in some cases the similar parties of different towns had formed alliances.

This quarrel divided Lombardy horizontally into two factions, between whom the Emperor must needs make his choice. His attitude could not be merely to support the knights, though in general of course they were pro-Emperor, while the plebeians as the revolutionary section seemed naturally the Emperor's foes. Matters were not however so straightforward and simple as that. The knights were frequently anti-Emperor and the plebeians the opposite. It even happened now and then—as later once in Siena—that one of the Emperor's men cleverly contrived to place himself at the head of the popular movement and that the victorious popular party was thus the Emperor's. In spite of the confusion, however, we can trace certain well-defined principles that guided Frederick's conduct : in the traditionally loyal towns like Cremona, Parma, Pavia he tried to smooth out differences and establish peace, so as to secure the support of these imperial cities as a whole. In the towns which he felt to be wavering, and whose population as a whole he could not hope to win, he sided with the knights. In Piacenza, for instance, he broke up the plebeian party, declared them rebels and outlawed them, while he recognised and protected the potentially loyal knightly party and issued orders to the neighbouring towns to support the knights of Piacenza. A

short-lived alliance even came to birth between the knights of
Piacenza and the imperial commune of Cremona. In the
actively hostile towns the Emperor set himself to fan the discord as far as possible. It was a complicated policy, since
Frederick had to treat each town individually and could never
bring his direct, wholesale straightforward methods into play,
unless he were prepared to fight.

A sample correspondence will illustrate the radically different
points of view of the pro- and anti-Kaiser towns. If it is a
fabrication it is all the more illustrative. Florence wrote during
these years to the imperial town of Siena : " It is true that the
Emperor's Majesty being bound by no law enjoys the fulness
of power. Yet it is dependent on the law for life and must not
hanker after what is alien, lest it break the law and be itself
accused of injustice at the very time that it enforces obedience
upon others." Whereupon Siena writes : " Whereas it is the
property of the Roman Princeps to tower above others in peace
or war as victor, it is not to be tolerated that his subjects should
crave equally to be his equals. For if the condition of all men
were equal the name of Princeps would be an empty sham ;
there can be no superior without inferiors. And the law of
nations would have accomplished nothing, whereas it has established inequality and arranged ranks and grades."

It would not be easy to formulate more sharply the contrasts
in which the question of the Church's attitude to the parties is
bound up. For the aristocratic Church of the Middle Ages
must of necessity be as hostile as the Emperor to the popular
movement, which was asserting the freedom of the individual
alike against temporal and against spiritual authority. And so
in fact it was. Just before this, when the populace of Milan
rose against the bishop, the papal legate in Lombardy, Cardinal
Hugo of Ostia, assisted the knightly party against the people.
Frederick II, like his predecessors, always strove to preserve,
as far as he could, the feeble remnants of episcopal power
in the Lombard towns. In these matters he was, to all
appearance, hand in glove with the Pope, who went so far as
to excommunicate Milan and stigmatised it as " saturated with
the poison of heresy." Frederick had demonstrated his unanimity with the Church on such matters by stiffening up, in

March 1224, the edict against heretics which he had already
issued on the occasion of his coronation. Those condemned
as heretics by the bishop were summoned before a secular
tribunal, and the punishment for heresy was death by burning
or the amputation of the tongue, that further blasphemy might
be forestalled. These edicts were no mere " courtesies " from
Emperor to Pope ; they represented, as will be seen later, the
innermost conviction of Frederick, for whom the heretic was
synonymous with the rebel, who blasphemed the divine majesty
of the Emperor. Being at one with the Church on questions
of rebels and heretics Frederick had counted on considerable
support from the Church for his Lombard Diet, the more so
as his agenda especially stressed the two items of heresy and
Crusade.

The Curia had to stand by him over the Crusade, but that
by no means implied taking an anti-Lombard line ; quite the
reverse ; politically the Church was driven into the Lombards'
arms. For if the Emperor were to succeed in establishing in
north Italy a power similar to that he had organised in Sicily,
the states of the Church would be hemmed in, north and south,
by imperial territories, and the Curia could foresee his next
move. The papal " Recuperations," the central Italian provinces of the Church, were menaced ; at a very minimum the
Adriatic strip, the March and Spoleto, but probably other sections of the Church's land as well, would be commandeered to
give Frederick a corridor from south to north. Frederick had
let it be seen how sorely he craved these lands.

As long as the Lombards, however, resisted the Emperor, and
stood out against any reproduction in northern Italy of the
Sicilian monarchy, the Church was safe. The Curia therefore
could not possibly take the risk of helping the Emperor to break
down the opposition of the Lombard towns. Politically the
Church found the Lombard Confederation a valuable ally, and
in Rome the fact was welcomed that the League was organising
itself into a semi-state. The Confederation was renewed for
twenty-five years. All the confederate towns had annually to
renew the oath ; none were to conclude independent peace ;
and resignation from the league was to be considered as
" rebellion " and dealt with accordingly. The Emperor saw

in the Confederation a rebel state within a state; the Church hailed it as a bulwark against imperial encirclement.

In questions relating to heresy and popular movements the views of Emperor and Curia were by no means identical. As regards the recalcitrant Roman plebeians they saw eye to eye on many points, but the Curia was in touch with the Roman populace in a way in which the Emperor was not. The Curia too was willing enough to use the Emperor's sword for the eradication of heresy, but felt by no means so exclusively dependent on his good offices in the matter as Frederick liked to think. Here quite a new factor enters in. The two new mendicant orders aimed at reaching these two classes, plebeian and heretic, and either luring them back into the Church or rendering them innocuous. The democratic Franciscans and the heresy-hunting Dominicans had recently sprung from the womb of the Church in her old age. These two Orders lent a significance, beyond the merely political, to the alliance between Lombards and Curia. Without here pursuing the very varied activities of the Orders in detail we may quote an episode which legend records, that illustrates the sympathy existing between a man like St. Francis and various strata of the populace. One day when the saint was preaching in Perugia before a large crowd the knights of the town invaded the piazza and began to joust and to manoeuvre their horses, doing their best to disturb the saint's discourse, whereupon the populace set upon them. For the message of St. Francis was directed to the humbler townsfolk who enthusiastically clung to the apostle of poverty.

Such was in rough outline the tangled state of affairs in northern Italy when Frederick set out to hold his diet in Lombardy. To add to existing difficulties Frederick's quarrel with the Curia over the episcopal elections in Sicily was just then at its height. And, finally, his march to the north provoked a quarrel with the Curia that nearly amounted to a final breach. Without asking permission Frederick marched his troops right through central Italy and, acting as if the Church only held these territories from the Empire in fee, he enlisted auxiliaries for his Lombard Diet. This procedure was no doubt a little brusque. Frederick II, however, had not acted without reflection. If the Pope had denied him permission the breach would have been even more inevitable, and he would have created a dangerous precedent for himself by appearing to acknowledge that the Emperor had no right to march his troops from Sicily into north Italy without papal sanction. Pope Honorius now taxed Frederick with this march, reproached him for ingratitude to the Church, and at last the long-repressed resentment on both sides burst forth. *Quousque tandem patientia mea abutetur pontifex !* Such was the gist of Frederick's answer, if we may anticipate an expression attributed to him later in a reply in which he likened the Pope to Catiline.

Frederick poured out in a violent letter all his grievances against the Curia : for his own part he owed the Church no thanks ; in any help she had at any time accorded him she had sought solely her own advantage. He on his side had met every wish the Pope expressed. The Pope had welcomed to Rome every enemy of the Emperor and every exile from Sicily ; he had curtailed the Emperor's rights in Sicily ; he had obstructed the Emperor's procedure against licentious priests ; he had " lifted no finger " to ease the burdens of the Crusade that rested on the Emperor's shoulders—and so forth.

Pope Honorius replied in a long document, refuting the imperial letter point by point, a document that was a masterpiece of style, beginning " strangely our letter smote upon thy mind —so writest thou— . . . more strangely yet thy letter smote on ours." Honorius omitted nothing, and when he came to speak of the treatment Frederick had meted out to those who were now refugees in Rome, especially the unfortunate King John of Jerusalem, " whose only crime has been that they are still alive," he took occasion to remind Frederick of his great prototype : " Thou wilt have read no parallel to these things in the deeds of Julius Caesar, who spared Domitius in his own despite and held Metellus to be unworthy of his wrath when Metellus offered his breast to the sword. . . ." For all the perfection of its form it was a spiteful document, into which the Pope poured the full measure of his anger. The ill-will of both reached its climax in these two letters—and its end. Frederick answered very briefly, though he could not refrain from a few sarcasms over the inordinate length of the epistle. The Pope's long-winded letter had disinterred from the papal storehouses so much material, old and new, that if a womb so teeming should, from fresh imperial replies, again conceive, it would bring forth another foetus like unto the first. Frederick cherished the feelings of a pious son to an angry father, and therefore preferred to let the matter drop, if only because the Pope had the advantage of him in the multitude of his scholars and his scribes.

The Emperor's thus " coming to heel " coincided with the complete failure of his Lombard adventure. A few words will suffice to narrate the events. Frederick first sought to counter the unexpectedly hostile attitude of the League by emphasising his peaceful intentions and placing in the foreground his anxiety about the Crusade. On the whole march he scrupulously avoided coming into contact with any of the towns. This self-restraint emboldened the Lombards ; they were no doubt also informed of the serious friction with the Curia and so were reassured that their worst foreboding was groundless—the Pope and the Emperor were not going to proceed as one man against them. They promptly exercised their sense of power. As the German army under King Henry, approaching along the Brenner road, had just reached Trent, the confederate towns—of which Verona was one—closed the narrow defile and denied passage to any person bearing arms. The German army, which was wholly composed of cavalry, was probably not strong enough to fight its way through, but in any case the use of force would have been contrary to the Emperor's intentions—he had no wish, nor indeed the means, to embark at the moment on a Lombard war—he preferred to lodge a complaint against the Lombards with the Pope. Meantime King Henry awaited events in Trent. Without his German knights the Emperor's forces were too weak to exercise even moral suasion, still less serious practical pressure. So Frederick opened negotiations with the Rectors of the Confederation, especially with reference to the passage of the German party. Before opening the road —the closing of which was an unprecedented arrogance—the Lombard towns proposed such inacceptable terms that the Emperor refused to negotiate further, in which he was unani-

mously backed by the big men about him and numerous bishops
from Germany, Italy, Sicily and Burgundy. As repeated summonses to give in were in vain, the Emperor induced the bishops
assembled with him to excommunicate all the confederate towns
for hindering the Crusade, and for his part exercised the imperial ban and declared the Lombards outlaws and traitors to
the Empire. By this he forbade all intercourse with them and
declared all schools and institutions closed—including the
University of Bologna. After months of delay that was the
only thing he was able to accomplish. He could only save his
face in the whole affair by consistently posing as the simple-
hearted crusader who had come to Lombardy not on his own
private business but on a mission for God and for the Church.
The Lombards' opposition had thus been directed not against
him but against the Church. By skilfully playing this rôle he
compelled the Church eventually to take his part. But for the
time being he had to let outlawry and excommunication suffice
him, and vengeance for many a deed of treachery—in Faënza
a knight had been murdered in mistake for Frederick—had to
be adjourned till another day. The Diet was never held at all.
A few German princes had joined him by way of Venice, but
King Henry and the bulk of the other German nobles had had
to return home from Trent after months of fruitless waiting.
The confusion in Lombardy was greater than ever and Frederick
had accomplished nothing. In July 1226 he began the return
journey to Sicily. His route was already threatened ; finally
Pisan troops came to fetch him and escorted him safely to their
town, where he halted a short time.

In spite of everything Frederick II found time during his
stay in Pisa to converse with a scholar whose writings were
already known to him. They discussed at length a number of
problems in Geometry and Algebra which were occupying
Frederick's mind. The scholar was Leonardo Fibonacci of
Pisa, the greatest mathematician of his time, indeed the greatest
mathematician of the Middle Ages, whom a Spanish scholar,
one Dominicus, introduced to the Emperor. Leonardo had
pursued his studies in Egypt and Syria, Greece and Spain, and

was trying to introduce a new style of reckoning into Europe
" after the manner of the Indians " : reckoning with the Arabic
numerals and the zero. The problems which Frederick laid
before him through his court philosopher, Master John of
Palermo, are so difficult and technical that even to-day only a
mathematician can follow them. To the Emperor's admiration and delight Leonardo was able to solve them. He wrote
them down in a book for the Emperor, and henceforth maintained contact with the scholars of the court—with Master
Theodore for instance, and, in particular, with Michael Scot,
who arrived shortly after at the imperial court.

These intellectual friendships were not the only outcome of
the stay in Lombardy. A number of German princes had come
round by Venice to join Frederick, and their presence had
brought the Emperor again into closer touch with German
affairs, with which, however, he did not attempt to interfere
except corroboratively. The year before, in 1225, Archbishop
Engelbert of Cologne, till then the *Gubernator* of Germany,
had been murdered, and Duke Lewis of Bavaria, one of the
guardians of young King Henry, had been appointed his
successor.

Further, without any connivance of the Emperor, the Danish
power had crumbled, and North Albingia as far as the Eider
had fallen to the Empire. This is the period, too, of the Golden
Bull of Rimini, which established the Order of Teutonic Knights
in Prussia to extend the power of the Empire in those regions.
For the moment, however, nothing was so vital to Frederick II
as to get the Lombard business disposed of, and for this he
needed the co-operation of the Roman Curia.

Many contemporaries contended that Pope and Curia were
solely responsible for the failure of the Lombard Diet. That
is to put the case too crudely. It is clear that Rome had watched
the progress of events not without malicious satisfaction, especially as she reaped direct advantage from Frederick's embarrassment. Frederick now acceded to every wish of the Pope's ;
acquiesced without a murmur in his choice of Sicilian bishops,
as if they had never had a difference of opinion on the subject, and when famine broke out in Rome eagerly came to his
assistance with Sicilian corn.

With his characteristic adaptability Frederick changed his tactics in a night, and leaped without transition from downright brusquerie to affectionate docility. Nevertheless the Pope's position was delicate. It seemed possible that the Emperor's whole Crusade would be wrecked by the intransigence of the Lombards if Frederick were to make the new developments a pretext for further delay. The Pope was anxious to clear even imaginary obstacles from the Emperor's path, so he bestirred himself to achieve some workable compromise in Lombardy by acting as go-between. It was no easy task. Honorius did not want to forfeit the Lombards' support against the Emperor ; on the other hand they were most manifestly in the wrong and had had no shadow of justification for the closure of the Brenner road. After lengthy negotiation a temporary accommodation was arrived at, thanks to Frederick's placability. The Pope would release the confederate towns from his ban, the Emperor would rescind his edict of outlawry, and the Lombard League would keep the peace with the imperial towns, Cremona and the rest. The *status quo ante* which the Emperor had before found unsatisfactory was thus in effect restored, and Frederick had received no reparation or apology for the insult offered him.

The Emperor shut his eyes for the moment to this flaw in the Pope's arbitration and declared himself—in the interests of the Crusade—willing to accept this provisional award. He could, however, no longer blind himself to the political alliance of Lombards and Pope, whose embrace drew closer and closer in proportion to the growth of the Emperor's power. From the imperial standpoint he justifiably regarded this alliance of the Pope with heretics and rebels, enemies alike of Church and Empire, as treason to the Church herself—treason that is to the aristocratic medieval Church. Frederick could not feel otherwise, and in his wrath at this betrayal he could justify to himself and to the world his fight against the papacy. Indeed his faith in his mission and in the justice of his cause was mainly based on the conviction that this " incestuous " coalition of Church and heretic undermined the God-ordained constitution of the world. This was a purely aristocratic constitution founded on the unity of the two Swords—the spiritual and the temporal— and the unity of the two monarchs : Emperor and Pope.

Frederick would have been unreservedly in the right in talking of treachery if nothing but papal aggrandisement had prompted this unnatural *rapprochement* between the Curia and the townsfolk of Lombardy, for which the Pope finally threw over the Emperor and therewith the unity of the spiritual and temporal worlds. Political advantage certainly held the foreground ; but behind the scenes, behind Lombards and papacy, a new world-power was at work, a power against whose visible warriors Frederick II consciously fought, against which itself he fought his life long all unknowing, and growing thereby in stature : Francis of Assisi and the new Christ image he had evoked.

Frederick grew in the conflict with Francis of Assisi, and the course of his imperial life will demonstrate the manner of his growth. Francis of Assisi, the greatest contemporary of this last Hohenstaufen, was the bearer of the strange, mysterious power which Frederick in his cradle was destined to rebel against, and in reaction against which he was to mobilise all the forces of the world. Abbot Joachim of Flora had years ago prophesied the coming of power and counter-power : the founder of an order should bring again the age of Christ and the Apostles. The Church should renew her youth and an Emperor should be the Church's scourge. Following the myth, Abbot Joachim had hailed the son of Henry VI as the future Castigator, and Confusion-bringer, the herald of Anti-Christ. The inference was clear—a renewal of Christ must necessarily beget the Anti-Christ.

Legend tells us of a meeting of the two great foes. Somewhere about 1222, as Frederick II held court in Bari, St. Francis had come thither with holy exhortation to warn the people of the dangers of sin, and to warn the nobility of the dangers of the court. The encounter between the young victorious king and the man who had taken Lady Poverty to wife is humanly akin to the meeting of Alexander the Great with the Cynic Diogenes. Legend assigns to Frederick the rôle of the tempter. He sought to undermine the celebrated continence of the holy man by the wiles of a lovely woman, but when this attempt was vain, and the Emperor saw that " his practice was even as his precept," he dismissed his imperial retinue and spent many hours in an earnest *tête-a-tête*, listening attentively to what the saint had to tell for the salvation of the soul.

Not long after, in 1223, the final Rule of the Brothers Minor was confirmed by the Pope, and when Francis of Assisi died three years later in 1226 the zeal that fired him had communicated itself to tens of thousands. What Francis of Assisi brought was heresy dressed in canonicals ; his first appearance was closely allied to that of the heretics, " The Poor Men of Lyons," and indeed to the Albigensians, with whom the Church for many years waged bloody war in Provence. The heretics had spread a dangerous doctrine summed up in the famous phrase " to obey God rather than men," maintaining the communion of the individual soul with God without the mediation of the Roman priest, without the need of sacrament. To combat this heretical doctrine Pope Innocent III had magnified the position of the priest, and reasserted the principle that the layman could not forego the priest's mediation. The only difference between St. Francis and the heretics was that he recognised the mediation of the priest as of right, though no man had less need of priest than he. He even brought " these heretical tendencies " into the service of the Church by himself bringing the supreme sacrifice of submitting to the church universal.

Francis of Assisi was canonised in 1228, a couple of years after his death. Uncounted were the miracles that he performed. The miracle with which we are here concerned seems to lack heavenly magic and seraphic glamour, but in compensation it reveals Francis to us as a man, a complete man, a figure which to-day is frequently forgotten in mawkish sentimentalizing over the tender, childlike saint. And this in spite of his " royally independent " attitude to the Pope—the word is Dante's—in spite of his manly opposition to the Church ; in spite of his forbidding the Brothers to read the Holy Scriptures for beauty—for the holy is above and beyond both the ugly and the beautiful ; in spite of his belonging to that company of the great whose holiness lies in spartan discipline against the " all too venal flesh."

The wounds of the Saviour, which he bore in the body, were less painful to him than the terrible oppression which weighed on him when he compelled his free soul, dwelling in free and

direct communion with God, into the rigid, ruthless formalism
of the Roman hierarchy.   This constriction which the heretics
escaped by forming independent groups outside the Church,
Francis voluntarily accepted—though he felt it more profoundly and suffered under it more severely than others.   He
knew that the personal immediate one-ness of the Soul with
God was the loftiest aim, but held that nevertheless the Papacy
was the necessary means.   None of his contemporaries was so
full as was St. Francis of high explosive forces to disrupt the
Church, but though at first he would hear nothing of the hierarchy and forbade his brothers to accept privilege from her or
exercise her offices, yet he recognised, in contrast to the heretics,
one universal Church, and forced his wide, nature-loving,
sublime spirit into the narrow, rigid legalism of the hierarchy.
This opposition corresponds to that which Frederick, his
worldly counterpart, had begun to conjure up in the worldly
sphere : the tension between the individual and the world-wide
Roman Empire.   With Dante the man is born who consciously
suffers in both conflicts.

Francis found a means of incorporating in the Church and
utilising for her service the hitherto decried egotistical tendencies of the heretics.   The founder of the Franciscans might not
easily have accomplished this single-handed.   He had a friend
at hand, a Cardinal of the Roman Church whom he placed as
Protector over the Order, Hugo of Ostia.   The Cardinal, a
priest almost overladen with scholastic wisdom and learned lore,
was poles asunder from the original, creative Francis.   What
drew him to the saint was his yearning for simplicity, for abandonment, for mystic rapture which the cares of this world and
the duties of a Cardinal's office put continually and ever further
beyond his reach.   The mystic vein was still alive in Hugo
of Ostia : in his youth he had been filled with admiration
for Abbot Joachim of Flora—the " John " of the Franciscan
gospel—and had founded two monasteries in Florence out of
his private means.   It was Hugo of Ostia who by his drafting
of the last Rule of the Order introduced the founder's spirit into
the Roman Church.   It was he who skilfully kept the Franciscan spirit that filled north Italy alive in the penitential
brotherhoods lest it should evaporate or—what was even more

probable—in that dangerous north Italian soil, degenerate into heresy, from which indeed it ultimately sprang. Hugo of Ostia arranged and organised, created centres for the brotherhoods in all the towns, and so turned to the Church's advantage that passion for individuality that was a feature of the time and affected by the heretics. The alliance between Papacy and Lombards on other sides than the merely political was therefore a product of Cardinal Hugo's labours : a man whose influence can often be traced in the later measures of the aged Pope Honorius.

The truce effected between Kaiser Frederick and the Lombards was destined to be the last act of Honorius III. He died shortly after, in March 1227, while the Emperor was about to start on the Crusade. Cardinal Hugo of Ostia, the friend of Francis of Assisi, sometime Legate in Lombardy, succeeded him. He was a Conti, a near relative of Innocent III, under whose influence he had grown up. As Pope he chose the suggestive name of Gregory IX. With the coming of this elderly opponent, who united in his person all the anti-imperial forces of his time, Frederick II's youth ended. He must prepare for the worst and strain every nerve to build up speedily an all-embracing imperial world, ready to face the foe.

IV. THE CRUSADE

Rendezvous in Brindisi, 1227——Plague——Frederick falls
ill and turns back——Hostility of Gregory IX——Excommunication——Gregory's entente with Lombards——
Loyalty of Rome to Frederick——Frederick's first manifesto——Frederick sails for East, June, 1228——Gregory
attacks Sicily——Frederick recovers Cyprus——Lands at
Acre——Treaty with al Kamil ; ten-year truce——Saracen
chivalry——Treachery of Templars——Influence of East
on Frederick——Entry into Jerusalem, March 17, 1229,
and Self-Coronation, March 18——Jerusalem manifesto
——Frederick lands at Brindisi, June, 1229——Last scenes
in Palestine——Exeunt papal troops from Sicily——Attitude
of Gregory IX ; truce——Peace of Ceperano

IV. THE CRUSADE

It has at all times been the case in Western history that none might reach the heights of world dominion save the Conqueror of the East, the man who brought the Orient into his Empire. It seems almost a natural law that each World Ruler must renew his youth in the land of the rising sun, and return thence crowned with glory to build up his Western power. World monarchs have been few, but all have brought from the East the authority and the halo of a God. From the moment that the Hohenstaufens began to dream of world power the Crusade became their proudest ambition.

Soon after the first Franco-Norman Crusade of Godfrey, Bohemund and Tancred, St. Bernard called men to the second. The leaders of the Christian host were the Hohenstaufen Conrad III with the King of France. Twenty years later Barbarossa deliberately treated Emperor and Crusader as synonymous terms. His first step was the canonisation of Charlemagne, and shortly afterwards he commissioned a monk of Aix to write the *Legenda Karoli Magni*, in which much space was given to Charles, the Crusader, and his Pilgrimage to the Holy Land. Charlemagne's wholly utilitarian campaign against the Moors of Spain had gradually been sublimated by legend into a Crusade. The legend was French in origin, but Barbarossa eagerly imported it, and with further Christian-imperial embellishments gave it currency in Germany. Many a dream of the time he thus fulfilled and many a dream he conjured up. The Western world was waiting, with bated breath, till an Emperor of the West should make his entry into Jerusalem. Ever new prophecies hinged on the great event : he who rides into Jerusalem as King will bring the long-awaited Reign of Peace before the Anti-Christ shall come. Toledo was the medieval capital of prophecy, and her astrologers announced that after plague and earthquake the days of Islam should be numbered ; while Sibylline sayings ran : " An Emperor of the

East shall in Jerusalem meet an Emperor of the West and the dry tree shall send forth green shoots when the Emperor of the West shall hang his shield upon it as the token of his law-giving." Such prophetic utterances gained in strength and pervasiveness, and men looked towards the Emperors' Crusades with hope. In spite of his age, Barbarossa had not hesitated to take on him the highest duty and proudest privilege of an Emperor when the Sultan Saladin conquered Jerusalem in 1187. At his departure men hailed the aged King as a " Second Moses " who was to lead the host of the chosen into the Promised Land : it was only granted him to see the land of promise from afar. His mighty son, Henry VI, was also destined not to enter the Royal City as Christian Emperor : no German Emperor yet had trodden the sacred soil.

Frederick II began where his ancestors left off. Not only did the Crusade represent his services to the Church, his duty as Roman Emperor—a new crown awaited him in Jerusalem. Moreover, the East was for him no magic land of wonders as it had been to his ancestors ; it was the spiritual home of a mind well versed in oriental lore. Frederick made most extensive preparations for his imperial crusade. He had sent on in advance Count Thomas of Aquino to act as Regent of his Syrian kingdom. He had succeeded by great efforts in kindling once more crusading enthusiasm in the West, not by inspired preaching : his agents numbered no St. Bernard, no Hermann of Salza in their ranks. The Emperor's promises, however, and the Emperor's gold, lavishly bestowed on all who enlisted, were not without their power to lure men to the Holy Land. Frederick not only promised free transport to princes, knights and esquires, but made them generous cash advances. He had thus attracted a number of German princes, most important of them all Landgrave Lewis of Thuringia, the husband of St. Elizabeth, who arrived in Frederick's Sicilian kingdom in August 1227 with an entire crusading army. Pilgrims of every German race crossed the Alps in numbers and travelled to Brindisi, the port of embarkation. The Frisians preferred the long sea route round Spain as did the English who, under several bishops, had responded to the call in thousands. By a generous issue of indulgences the Church had lent the necessary weight to

Frederick's recruiting campaign. Thus, enticed by the favourable offers, stream after stream of pilgrims poured ceaselessly
into Brindisi. A few turned back *en route*, but they did not
preceptibly reduce the masses who poured on. Many of the
pilgrims had travelled by way of Rome. A swindler, disguised
as Vicar of the Pope, took up his station at the gate of St. Peter
offering to release the pilgrims from their vows, without detriment to their indulgences, for the sum of four silver marks. The
Romans looked on this comedy with great amusement and did
not interfere. It was weeks before the Pope, who was in Anagni,
heard of the affair and hastily put the "vicar" out of action.

It would have been no bad thing if more pilgrims had bought
themselves off in Rome. We cannot attempt even an approximate estimate of actual numbers, but gradually an appalling
horde of crusaders had accumulated in the pilgrims' camp at
Brindisi—immensely more than the Emperor had calculated on
or provided for. In spite of all preparations the ships were
insufficient ; the pilgrims ran out of food—which, in any case,
had not been amongst the things Frederick had promised.
The ship room, however, was destined to prove in the end more
than sufficient—indeed ships remained empty behind—for in
the middle of August a terrible plague broke out to which the
Crusaders succumbed in shoals, while it was said that tens of
thousands fled from the plague-camp and scattered over Italy.
No one could be held responsible for this outbreak : many a
German army before had perished in the same way in the August
heat of southern Italy, and no modern observer needs to seek
any further cause than the herding together of thousands of
pilgrims, unaccustomed to the food, climate and conditions of
the south. Many of the German nobles also died of the disease,
and finally the Emperor himself caught it. In spite of illness
he superintended the embarkation of the first two squadrons
in person, and then just before the third division of the fleet was
to start, which was to take him and Count Lewis of Thuringia,
he betook himself with his friend to the small island of St.
Andrea outside Brindisi harbour to try to recover by escaping
the poisoned air. For the Landgrave, his chief assistant in the
undertaking, had also been attacked. In spite of everything
they both embarked on the 9th of September in the hopes that

the sea air and the sea journey would cure them. Two days
after Count Lewis died, and the Emperor took the advice of his
doctors and the German Grand Master, in which the Patriarch
Gerold of Jerusalem concurred, and landed again in Otranto,
postponing his Crusade till after his complete recovery. He
handed over the chief command to the Duke of Limburg and,
promising to follow in the Spring with fresh contingents, he
went off to the Baths of Pozzuoli to seek a cure. He immediately despatched two court judges to the Pope at Anagni to
announce what had happened and to excuse his defection.

The Emperor's relations with Pope Gregory IX during the
few months of the new pontificate had been friendly. Frederick
had, on several occasions, gone out of his way to gratify the
Pope, and there existed at the moment no grounds for irritation.
The Emperor had started on his Crusade according to agreement,
and Gregory IX, while a Cardinal, had always seemed particularly favourable to the erstwhile protégé of the Church.
Not so many years before he had even called the Hohenstaufen
" the Church's beloved sapling." The Pope's benevolent
attitude had, however, undergone a radical change. Perhaps
his intimacy with St. Francis had sharpened his senses to detect
potential foes, perhaps he had naturally a very delicate perception ; be that as it may, Pope Gregory IX was the first fully to
realise the immense danger latent in Frederick II which no
one else yet suspected. Gregory was not a real statesman
but an astute diplomat with an eye for all political cabals, and
he suddenly detected—perhaps during the days of the Lombard
Diet—the dawning of a new danger that immediately threatened
the States of the Church. For the Patrimony blocked the
Emperor's passage from south to north, and if the Emperor
attained sufficient power the papal territory would be in certain
danger. The Pope, judging from Frederick's early career,
could cherish no hope of making the Emperor a docile tool of
the Curia : he saw only one possible line of action, he must at
all costs strive to keep him down. From the first moment of
his power Pope Gregory's one aim was the humiliation—if not
the annihilation—of Frederick II.

Gregory IX was not the man to flinch from the struggle. Though an old man he was still strong and handsome ; he was a priest who knew the art, and loved to practise it, of enhancing the impressiveness of his person by pomp and ceremony : tiara-crowned, a papal Imperator. The wild fire of his youth still burned in the aged man and flamed up, now in the ecstatic mysticism of a Francis of Assisi, now in passionate unbridled hate towards Frederick II. This natural bent, reinforced by the recognition of threatening danger, make him ere long the aggressor. For Frederick had nothing to gain and much to lose by a conflict with the Church. Pope Gregory felt himself by stern necessity compelled to compass the destruction of the Hohenstaufen. He seized the first opportunity of compelling the foe to fight.

His weapons and methods were for the most part unattractive : slight untruths, imputations, calumnies : they were often too transparent and produced an ugly impression, robbing the Pope's procedure of every shadow of right, especially as no one but himself recognised the deeper necessity of the struggle. The obstinate old man, drunk with hate, pursued his end with singleness of aim to his last hour, indifferent to the fact that he was called a " heretic," that he was forsaken by those nearest him, until he became—for all his petty dishonesties—not only a dangerous enemy but a great one.

Here was his first big opportunity, and Gregory launched forthwith a savage attack on Frederick. It will have been the 12th or 13th September that the Emperor decided to halt in Otranto ; on the 18th the Pope nominated several new Lombard cardinals to strengthen his hand ; ten days later he excommunicated Frederick. He had not received the imperial messengers, still less given them a hearing. The Pope was entirely within his rights in excommunicating Frederick. In accordance with the agreement of San Germano the Emperor was declared unreservedly under the ban if for any reason whatsoever he failed to keep the appointed date, August 1227. In consideration of his illness Gregory could, of course, have given him dispensation, but he was fully entitled to exercise the ban, and Frederick II always recognised the right. There was no dispute as to the facts : the Emperor had not started—

the reason was irrelevant—he had therefore incurred the
penalty. Frederick was the very man to understand that facts
should weigh heavier with the Pope than reasons or motives.
Gregory, however, looked at neither the one nor the other.
He paid no heed to the fact of the Emperor's illness ; he would
neither see nor hear the numerous witnesses ; he immediately
pronounced it to be counterfeit. The simple truth might have
sufficed him. Frederick had failed to keep his engagement ;
Frederick was therefore excommunicate. The whole Christian
world would have understood. People were tired of the recurring postponements of the imperial Crusade and none too
greatly prejudiced in Frederick's favour, and " public opinion "
was, in those clearsighted days, a potent weapon, dear alike to
Pope and Emperor.

Actual events, however, played a small part, and baseless
accusations a large one, in the envenomed encyclicals of the
Pope. Pope Honorius shared the blame of specifying the
month of August as the date of starting. He and the Emperor
were calculating how to secure the whole autumn and winter
for the Syrian campaign, and they gave too little thought to the
dangers of the late summer heat in Southern Italy. The choice
of Brindisi as starting point was a perfectly natural one. It was
traditionally a favourite port for the Orient, and habitually used
by the Venetians before leaving the Adriatic for the Mediterranean. Ignoring these things Gregory IX represented matters
to the world as if Frederick's mismanagement of his Sicilian
kingdom—the papal fief—had been so gross that he was driven
to the choice of the most unhealthy of all Sicilian harbours ;
further, that he deliberately chose the most unhealthy month of
the year for setting out ; further, that he intentionally supplied
too few ships and intentionally detained the pilgrims, and was
therefore the guilty cause of the Great Death. In later years
Gregory went even further and accused Frederick not only of
intentionally slaying the pilgrims by the plague, but of having
poisoned Count Lewis of Thuringia. On this theory Frederick
himself was suffering from mental not bodily illness. The
Emperor had been unwilling to tear himself from the luxuries and
lusts of his kingdom and had sacrificed to them the Holy Land.
Gregory imparted still further information to the Christian

world : the Emperor was also to blame for the catastrophe of Damietta and the Nile (Frederick had in fact forewarned the Pope of the dangers incurred), he had allowed his followers to loot the town and then surrendered it to the Sultan. From the first he had failed to fulfil his undertakings about the new Crusade : he had not only been short of ship room—which was true—but had made no arrangements for the care of the pilgrims ; the thousand knights which he was to provide he had not provided ; the 100,000 ounces of gold which he was to pay he had not paid. The Sicilian bishops and the Sicilian Admiral Henry of Malta hastened to inform the Pope that their master had sent considerably more than a thousand knights to Syria ; that the gold had been paid ; that the Emperor had made himself responsible for the transport of the pilgrims, but not for their maintenance. They were also able to remind the Pope that the Lombards had failed to send the 400 knights which they had undertaken to do under the Pope's arbitration award —the only penalty they were to pay for blocking the mountain road. But the bishops' protests bore no fruit, the Pope simply reiterated his excommunication of the Emperor.

Meanwhile Frederick had stated that he was prepared to undergo any Church penances that might be assigned him as an *amende honorable*, and renewed his promise to sail the following May. He looked on the ban as the usual formal Church penalty incurred by dilatory Crusaders which was always rescinded on due penance being performed. Pope Gregory had no shadow of an excuse for refusing absolution to a penitent offender willing to make amends. But the Pope had other schemes brewing and was determined to continue the ban, so he took up an entirely new line of attack : there was soon no more talk of the abandoned Crusade save as a side issue; the front of the Emperor's offending was his administration of Sicily, the papal fief ; his enslavement of the Sicilian Church ; quarrels long since disposed of ; the banishment of the barons, and finally a mass of new, baseless accusations, some of which can be proved to have been entirely false. Pope Gregory had no wish to find a solution of the conflict ; he did his best to make the breach complete. Frederick II could have his absolution only on condition of accepting papal tutelage in Sicily. This he

could not conceivably submit to, and reconciliation was therefore for the time being impossible.

Pope Gregory's aim was probably to create so many difficulties for the Emperor in the West that an imperial Crusade
in the following May would be a sheer impossibility. If
Frederick again failed to sail, public opinion would be behind
the Pope if he should resume the Church's fief of Sicily, or
even depose the recreant Emperor, as Innocent had once deposed the Welf.   Lombardy was the place to make difficulties :
the Pope began to get into touch with the Lombards.   He had
completely overlooked their failure to provide a contingent for
the Crusade and had appointed some Lombard cardinals : the
entente now went still further.   Frederick proposed to summon the German princes to a Diet in Ravenna in March to
discuss the breach with the Pope.   The Lombards, at Gregory's
instigation, threatened again to bar the road, so the Emperor
was forced to abandon the project.   The understanding between Gregory IX and the Lombard League, which now embraced almost the whole of Lombardy except. Cremona and
three or four other towns, grew and flourished till it blossomed
into a formal alliance.   The Pope's one thought was how best
to hinder Frederick's enterprise ; he therefore prompted his
Lombard allies to seize and plunder any Crusaders who crossed
their territories on the way to join the Emperor.

Such were the Pope's first preparations.   It was not all plain
sailing for him, however.   Maundy Thursday was the usual
day for proclaiming excommunications ; when Pope Gregory
renewed the ban against Frederick II an unedifying scene followed.   The Roman town nobility, led by the Frangipani, a
family whose support Frederick had won, stirred up the Roman
populace against their Bishop ; on Easter Monday during mass
the people mobbed the Pope, and their attitude became so
threatening that Gregory had difficulty in extricating himself
and escaping to the Lateran.   But the mob were roused and
would not tolerate his presence in the city, so that he was forced
to accept a safe conduct and fly to Rieti.

For a long time Frederick II was silent under all the Pope's
attacks ; he hoped at first that the breach would soon be healed.
At last he decided that he must defend himself against the

accumulated accusations and reproaches, and now on his side
began to issue circular letters to the world—his first.   In contrast to the Pope's effusions the Emperor's were accurate and
calm : they rehearsed without betraying heat the actual facts
of the Brindisi happenings and the conduct of the Pope.
Frederick II had no wish to widen the breach which, as a
chronicler phrased it, " confused almost the whole Christian
world with new and unaccustomed miseries."   He kept himself well in hand.   Only towards the very end of his first letter
is there a trace of feeling and appeal, when he solemnly enters
a protest before " heaven and the circuit of the earth," and
begs the recipients of his letter, the kings and princes of Europe,
the bishops and nobles of Germany : " pray cause this our
present letter to be read aloud and listened to with honour and
respect, so that from its contents the certainty of our innocence
may be clear to all, and clear also the shame which is being
done to us and to our Empire."   A remarkable reception
awaited the imperial letter in Rome, his " capital city."   The
Senate and People of Rome insisted that the Court judge,
Roffredo of Benevento, should publicly read the Emperor's
letter from the Capitol.

The Emperor's aim in issuing his manifestos was to get back
to facts.   He did not plead that his excommunication was unjustified ; he emphasised that he had incurred it solely on
account of the non-fulfilment of his crusading vow.   For the
Pope was deliberately obscuring the issue, and Frederick was
bent on bringing it again to light.   To rob the Pope of his
weapons Frederick solemnly undertook before all the world to
sail early in the following year, " unless indeed it be—which
God forfend—that the new-awakened bitterness of this feud
should hold us back against our will from such a holy task."
The allusion here was, of course, to the papal intrigues which
Frederick exposed in detail in two subsequent letters : the
Pope, in the sight of the assembled people had taken the
Milanese, the Emperor's enemies, into favour ; the Pope had
issued orders to take up arms against the Emperor ; the Pope
had already begun to foment insurrection in Sicily against its
king.   It was indeed true that Gregory IX had forbidden the
Sicilian clergy to help the Emperor in any way with his new

preparations, and that he was now threatening to release
Frederick's subjects from their oaths of fealty unless the
Emperor would obey the Curia. The Emperor took care to
keep his friends informed of the facts : the Pope refused to
accord him the usual Crusader's blessing on his departure for
the Holy Land ; he refused to inform the venerable Archbishop
Albert of Magdeburg, the imperial envoy, what penance or
amends he would be prepared to accept. The gravest charge
against the Pope, and one to which Gregory could find no
answer, was reserved for the last. " With the moneys which he
has received to aid the Crusaders in Christ's work this Romish
Priest entertains mercenaries to molest us in every way."

Frederick was well aware that the best his writings could
accomplish was to place matters in a certain light, and that he
must show his intentions " not with words but with deeds."
Only thus could he ward off the Pope's attacks and perchance
even turn the papal weapons against the Pope himself : by his
action expose the Pope's machinations and give his words the lie.

Nothing should now detain him from the Crusade, not even
Gregory's " devilish inspiration " in forbidding him to set out
till he had been released from the ban. The Pope's tactics
were too obvious : the excommunicated Emperor must not
start, he refused to lift the ban, he refused to state what amends
would be acceptable. If Frederick stayed behind the Pope
had won : a new procrastination would justify the Pope's
procedure. It was in the circumstances a clever move of the
Emperor's to let nothing detain him. Only some visible act
could make him again master of the situation : in the spring
he sent on in advance his Marshal, Richard Filangieri, with
500 knights to the Holy Land, held himself a Diet in Barletta
at which he appointed Reginald of Urslingen, Titular Duke of
Spoleto, as Regent of Sicily. He then embarked on his galley
and at the end of June set sail from Brindisi, having just received
favourable news from Syria.

" We have just left Brindisi for Syria and are speeding along
before a favourable wind with Christ our Leader . . . , " so the
banned Emperor announced his journey to the world.

No one had been expecting the Emperor's departure, least of all Gregory IX. His stiffnecked implacability put him into a very painful position : " We do not know whose foolish counsel he hearkened to, or, better : what devilish cunning betrayed him into secretly quitting the harbour of Brindisi without penance and without absolution, without anyone's knowing for certain whither he has sailed." The fact that he saw himself placed in the wrong by no means inclined Gregory to give in, rather the reverse. Now that he knew the Emperor far away he had a free hand in the West. No sooner had he received tidings of Frederick's landing in Syria—whence a sudden return was not to be feared—than he opened the long-prepared war : in the Empire and in Sicily he released all subjects from their oath, and then sought to set up a rival king in Germany. He found himself another Welf, but his protégé quickly thought better of the offer and opined " he had no wish to die the death of his uncle, Kaiser Otto IV." In other ways, too, the Pope's German plans missed fire. The secular princes and the bishops remained faithful to their openhanded Emperor, especially as there was nothing particular to be done for him at the moment : they were completely indifferent to the papal ban which extended to their sixteen-year-old King Henry VII, and by the time the news of Syrian victories began to penetrate to Germany even the common people were criticising the Pope's intriguing ways : " The Pope would seem to be possessed by a devil," " his head is ailing, hence he is obstinate." Another characterises Gregory's conduct as an abhorred sign of the decay of the Church, a third exclaims : " Christian folk will suffer from it till the Judgment Day." What aroused the greatest indignation against Pope Gregory throughout Germany and everywhere else in the world was his behaviour in Sicily. The Emperor's regent, Reginald of Spoleto, took the Pope's release of Frederick's subjects from their oath to be a declaration of war and invaded the March and his own earlier dukedom of Spoleto with Sicilian and Saracen troops—perhaps exceeding his instructions in so doing. Whereupon the Pope, who had long since made full preparations, invaded the kingdom of Sicily with his own soldiers—the first army to fight as Soldiers of the Keys under the banner of Peter—supported by the Lombard rebels. A body of Franciscans under his orders worked through the country spreading the news that the Emperor was dead. The Sicilians did not know what to do, and in a short time a large part of continental Sicily was in his hands. People now began to believe what Frederick had said, that the Pope was using Crusade money to pay his soldiers, and indeed the Pope's vindictiveness against a Crusader was incredible. The Pope who must not carry out a death sentence was now maintaining a papal army and leading it to battle against a Christian prince, and a Crusader to boot, who was absent in the Holy Land fighting for the true religion, and whose land and property ought, according to time-honoured convention, to be held sacred under the protection of the Church. This brought the Pope into such bad odour that no one can have believed his final justifications—in which there was nevertheless a certain truth—" This war is necessary for the Christian faith that such a mighty Persecutor of the Church may be driven from his throne." Gregory saw the dire necessity. What the world saw was the reverse.

The Emperor's resolution to leave the West was an incomparably daring gamble in which his all was at stake. When he sailed Lombardy was already lost. He knew the Pope's intention to release his Sicilian subjects from their allegiance and resume the papal fief. He knew that the next step would be to dethrone him. He was sufficiently experienced to have no illusions. His whole western power was in the balance, and if defeat awaited him in the East—a visible judgment of God against the " hubris " of the excommunicated man who with his curse upon him had dared to set foot in the Holy Land— then his thrones were lost, and with them his dreams of Roman Empire. There was no alternative : he must at all costs succeed. There was heavy work ahead, and well Frederick knew it. But, as he said himself, he let none perceive his anxieties, but turned the same confident and smiling face upon the world. This crusade adventure of the excommunicated Emperor, pursued even into the Holy Land by the papal curse, is one of the most stirring episodes in his eventful life. For a brief space

Frederick II was cut off from all the confusion of the West, as free as any young adventurer, or as the " pirate " Gregory IX called him.

It was with a fleet of forty galleys under the chief command of Admiral Henry of Malta that Frederick II eventually sailed from Brindisi in June 1228. He was accompanied as usual by the faithful Archbishop Berard of Palermo and the imperial chamberlain Richard, a Sicilian who had never left the Emperor's side since he journeyed with the *Puer Apuliae* to Germany, and finally by Archbishop Jacob of Capua, who also belonged to the trusted courtiers of the Emperor. Frederick's other immediate friends, the German Grand Master, Count Thomas of Aquino and Marshal Richard Filangieri, were awaiting his arrival in Syria. There were many Germans too in the Emperor's suite, one of whom, Conrad of Hohenlohe, soon entered his personal service. Amongst the Saracen retainers who as usual accompanied him was Frederick II's teacher of Arab dialectic, a Sicilian Saracen. The gifted Frederick was to find his fluency in Arabic conversation of more value than warriors or weapons.

Pope Gregory was not wholly beside the mark when he stated that no one knew whither the Emperor sailed, for Frederick II was killing two birds with his one stone. Three weeks after leaving Brindisi, and sailing mainly close to the coast past Corfu, Cephalonia, Crete and Rhodes, the Emperor's galleys cast anchor in Limassol, the harbour of Cyprus. The prince of the island, Amaury of Lusignan, had at his own request done feudal homage to the Emperor Henry VI and received the crown at his hands, and since then Cyprus had been counted a fief of the Roman Empire. During the years of chaos in Germany the island had been lost to the Empire and Frederick had long intended to reconquer it. This necessitated an interruption of his journey. The Emperor looked on it as one of his duties to reassemble under one firm hand the scattered possessions of the Empire, but Cyprus had just now particular importance as a base for the Syrian campaign. This large island could easily support a thousand fighting men who could release the Emperor's own troops for other work. We need only mention here that Frederick without fighting, though not

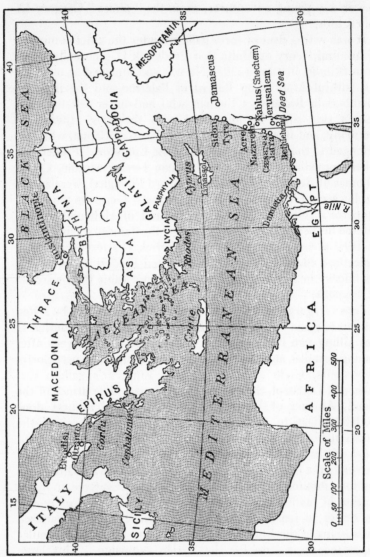

The Fifth Crusade

without a few adventures, achieved what he wanted. He concluded an agreement with John of Ibelin, the guardian of the twelve-year-old king, a Syrian nobleman who enjoyed a great reputation throughout the whole of the Christian East as a lawyer and a scholar, and was renowned for his shrewdness, eloquence and ingenuity. By this agreement the regency passed, in accordance with German feudal law, to the Emperor, who immediately nominated a Sicilian regent and installed Sicilian chatelains in all the fortresses, while he appointed finance officials to collect the revenues of the various districts. Ibelin and the Cypriot knights were carried off to fight in the Holy Land.

Such was the result of the halt in Cyprus, which lasted many weeks. Individual events on the island belong to the epic story of knightly deeds which constitutes the life of Frederick II. People loved to hear and tell how John of Ibelin, leader of the anti-imperial party, appeared before the Emperor in mourning for his dead brother. The Emperor immediately sent him the most costly scarlet robes and begged him to put them on : for his joy at welcoming the Emperor must surely triumph over his grief for a lost brother. A day or two later a brilliant banquet was held at which Ibelin sat on the Emperor's right hand while his sons served as pages. As the feast drew to a close the castle gradually filled with sailors and armed men from the Emperor's galleys, while Frederick in a stern tone demanded an account of Ibelin's guardianship. Confounded, Ibelin at first could make no reply. The Emperor wrathfully swore to arrest him, when the celebrated jurist was inspired to one of his famous speeches which held Frederick spellbound, as often before Ibelin had enthralled the feudal court. The episode, however, had alarmed Ibelin. A night or so later he took flight secretly with his knights, who had been instant in warning him, and were minded to avenge themselves for Frederick's autocratic behaviour. The Emperor heard the noise and fearing an ambush slept the night on board his ship, and next morning pursued the fugitive who had fled to the castle Dieu d'Amour, well known to be difficult to capture. The agreement closed the adventure. Ibelin followed the Emperor to the Holy Land and for the moment did him good service there, biding his time for revenge.

The news of Frederick's speedy triumph in Cyprus must have preceded him to Syria. On landing in Acre he was hailed with indescribable joy, and the pilgrims greeted the Pope's accursed as the " Saviour of Israel," mindful of the ancient, ever-living prophecy that an Emperor would come out of the West to fulfil the time, to unite East and West, and to free Jerusalem. Even the clergy appeared to welcome him; though they refused the kiss of homage, the Templars and the Knights of·St. John knelt before the excommunicate Emperor. The Muslims believed that the mighty Emperor of the West, the " King of the Amirs," had come with uncounted hosts, and they were afraid.

They soon found out that the fear was groundless. Frederick had assembled in Acre at most ten thousand pilgrims and some thousand knights, and he could not wholly trust even this exiguous force. A few days after his arrival two Franciscan emissaries of the Pope made their appearance, commanding that none should render obedience to the banned Emperor. Thus the quarrel between Pope and Emperor was carried even into the Holy Land, where Frederick's fulfilment of his vow might have been expected to effect his release from the ban. The Emperor's position as leader of Christendom was undermined, and the pilgrims split into two hostile camps. The Sicilians, the Germans with the Order of Teutonic Knights, the Pisans and Genoese remained faithful to the Emperor, but all the rest, the English and French with the Templars and the Knights of St. John, and above all the clergy, concentrated on one purpose : to hinder the Emperor in every way and to nullify his every action. For the sake of the cause Frederick exercised the greatest self-restraint and sought to obviate all grounds of discord. He went so far as to hand over the nominal leadership to the Grand Master, Hermann of Salza, Marshal Richard Filangieri and the Syrian Constable, Odo of Montbeliard, so that no one should need to obey an excommunicated leader. He even acquiesced in the Templars' demand that orders should no longer be issued over the imperial name but in the name of God and of Christendom. All moderation on the Emperor's part was fruitless as long as the Pope and his Legate, Gerold, Patriarch of Jerusalem, hounded his enemies on. Their hostile propaganda strengthened from day to day.

The situation was aggravated by the news that Pope Gregory had released the Emperor's subjects from their allegiance. Under such unhappy auspices Frederick began his difficult enterprise in the East. Circumstances forbade warlike action against the Saracens, even if that had formed, as it did not, part of Frederick's plan.

A short while before, the position in the East had been phenominally favourable for Frederick II. The Muslim princes were at strife with each other and the Emperor had hoped to take advantage of their rivalries. He had been carrying on negotiations for a long time back with al Kamil, the Sultan of Egypt. Al Kamil was a nephew of the chivalrous Saladin, the first of the Ayyubids whose immense Empire was divided up at his death ; he conceived himself threatened by his brother al Muazzam, Sultan of Damascus, and sought to win allies against him. The Sultan of Egypt therefore, as soon as he heard of the Emperor's projected Crusade into Syria—which would necessarily make Frederick a enemy of the Sultan of Damascus—immediately sent ambassadors to Sicily to invite an alliance, promising to give up to Frederick the whole of the Kingdom of Jerusalem, which they would conquer together, and begging only the Emperor's speedy arrival. Further embassies were interchanged, led on Frederick's side by Archbishop Berard of Palermo, and on the Sultan's by the Amir Fakhru'd Din ; presents were exchanged, one of the gifts to Frederick being an elephant, and negotiations had reached a fairly advanced stage when Frederick reached Acre—much later than originally intended—and at once announced his arrival to the Sultan through his Syrian regent Count Thomas of Aquino.

The story later ran that the Sultan had spread the streets with carpets to welcome Frederick II : even in a metaphorical sense this is far from true. Al Kamil was lying at Nablus with a great army. He received the Emperor's envoys with the greatest honour, held a review, and sent Fakhru'd Din on his behalf to the Emperor with costly gifts, fabrics and gems, riding camels and mules. All talk of handing over Jerusalem, however, suddenly ceased ; the general situation had greatly altered to Frederick's disadvantage. The feared al Muazzam, the Sultan of Damascus, their common foe, was dead, and his little son could scarcely rank as a serious enemy. So al Kamil, who had also concluded an alliance with the Sultan of Mesopotamia, had conquered a large part of the Damascus territory, including Jerusalem, without Frederick's help. His western ally, whom he had so urgently summoned and to whom he had promised so much, was for the moment an encumbrance, for the Emperor would want land which the Egyptian Sultan had just conquered on his own behalf. Al Kamil, therefore, had recourse to the time-honoured Oriental device of exercising lavish politeness, inexhaustible courtesy, the liveliest assurances of friendship, and maintaining the silence of the grave on the point at issue. The Sultan, moreover, was aware of the weakness of Frederick's actual forces, the quarrel in the Christian camp, and the breach between Emperor and Pope. So before long he completely " forgot " the Emperor's existence and quietly overlooked the notary, his new messenger.

The Emperor's position was desperate. He must have success, and everything was conspiring against him. He could not dream of attacking al Kamil's mighty army ; the pilgrims and the troops whom he had marched, by way of demonstration, a little nearer to Nablus as far as Jaffa, were on the point of starvation, for storms had detained their supply-ships ; the negotiations on which he had built so much had fallen through ; sensational news was arriving from Italy about the Pope's activities, and—worst of all—the disaffection in his own camp was on the increase. Intercepted letters proved that the Pope was conjuring the Sultan on no account to hand over Jerusalem to the Emperor. The Pope stooped to this because the success of the banned Emperor would mean the Judgment of God against himself. That his contemporaries were ready to believe in the Pope's treachery is shown both by spurious letters of the time and by the Crusade sagas which grew up round the events of the day. Later versions even relate the capture of Frederick, and tell how the Pope had a " counterfeit " of Frederick made, and sent the portrait to the Sultan so that he might make no mistake about the person of his victim.

Meanwhile Frederick had not gained a foot, and his presence was urgently needed in Sicily while he bootlessly wasted valuable time.   It is not hard to believe his own later account that at times he wept with rage and grief and thought of turning back, but " I began to treat of peace and of agreements and hastened preparations for my return, concealing my consuming pain behind a cheerful countenance so that the enemy might not triumph and rejoice."   It is true that in these cheerless days negotiations were resumed by help from the enemy himself.   The Sultan's ambassador, the Amir Fakhru'd Din, was attached to Frederick by profound admiration and personal friendship.   He gave the Emperor a hint that something might be accomplished by changing his envoy—the present one being none too acceptable to the Sultan.   So Count Thomas of Aquino was sent once more to the Sultan in place of the notary while Frederick treated with Fakhru'd Din, which all goes to indicate how important the personal factor was throughout. The Emperor was a past master in the art of discussion.   The charm of his personality, his astounding knowledge, his quickness of repartee made him the equal of any, though at times his passionate pride and his biting wit led him into danger.   In this case, however, where he was not upholding claims but seeking favours, this danger was absent, and it may well be that, after all the dissensions of his own camp, the conversations with the cultured and courteous Fakhru'd Din were restful and refreshing.   Frederick had complete command of Arabic, and was acquainted with the Arab poets ; his amazing knowledge of philosophy, logic, mathematics and medicine, and every other branch of learning enabled him to turn any conversation into the philosophical channels dear to the Oriental heart.   He had been completely successful in his handling of his Saracen colonists of Lucera, and now he moved amongst the Saracen princes with the perfect *savoir faire* of an accomplished man of the world.   So he conversed away with Fakhru'd Din about philosophy and the arts of government, and Fakhru'd Din must have had much to tell his master about the Emperor.

Al Kamil was the very man to appreciate such qualities.   He was an oriental edition of the Emperor, unless indeed it be more correct to call the Emperor an occidental edition of the Sultan.

Al Kamil loved to dispute with learned men about jurisprudence and grammar, beloved especially of the Arab ; he was himself a poet—some of his verses still survive—and in his mountain castle, as they tell, " fifty scholars reclined on divans round his throne to provide his evening conversation." He spent money willingly in the furtherance of learning ; founded a school in Cairo for the study of Islamic Tradition, and appointed salaries for jurists. People praised his courteous bearing as much as his stern and impressive dignity. In addition he was an admirable administrator, who checked his own revenues and even invented new varieties of tax. He had no more fancy than Frederick for aimless bloodshed if the end could be reached by friendly means, and so it came about that their negotiations presently bore fruit.

The little that we know suffices to make it clear that Frederick set himself to win the personal friendship of the Muslims. He had not come to seek conquests, but peaceably to take over the districts that had previously been offered him. " I should not have sought to win such terms from the Sultan had I not been fearful of losing my prestige amongst the Franks," he said quite frankly at the close, and probably the same tone had prevailed throughout. While the negotiations were in progress not a whisper of their political significance was audible outside. People have sorely reproached the Emperor for this secretiveness, which, however, was imposed on him by the papal intrigues and the dissensions in the Christian camp. It was revolting to Gregory's supporters that the Emperor should treat at all with unbelievers. Even the Swabian poet, the " Freidank," an admirer of the Hohenstaufen, himself a Crusader, thought it high time there should be " an end of whisperings," whose worth, in the absence of " high counsel," he gravely questioned. Neither the papal nor the German party could tolerate this autocratic method of imperial negotiations, centring round the person of the Emperor alone, divorced from the advice of the great. Yet this method suited al Kamil as well as it suited the Emperor. We know that he was wont to conduct the affairs of state singlehanded, without reference to his Wazir ; indeed, on the death of his Wazir he omitted to appoint a successor and contented himself with the services of a scribe. Frederick was shrewd enough to perceive how much might be achieved by mutual personal friendship and courtesy, that was unattainable by public discussion. A certain degree of give and take was possible in secret—and it was now a question of giving on both sides. The treaty which Frederick concluded on the 18th of February, 1229, is most obviously coloured by the personal desire to please on al Kamil's side. The Christians, however, felt it to be rather a weak point that there were no guarantees on either side save the personal good faith of Emperor and Sultan. According to this agreement Frederick was to receive back Jerusalem with the exception of the Haramu'sh Sharif, the sacred enclosure in which the mosque of 'Umar and the rock temple of Solomon were situate. The Christian pilgrims, however, were permitted to perform their prayers in this area, and the Muslims conversely theirs in Bethlehem, which was ceded to Frederick. The Emperor also acquired Nazareth and a strip of land running from Jerusalem to the coast, further Sidon and Caesarea, Jaffa and Acre, and some other places. All these might be fortified by the Christians, and, though the kingdom of Jerusalem was not to be militarised, a ten-year truce was concluded which Frederick hoped to renew with his friend al Kamil on its expiry.

The treaty was not without its weak points, but the papalists' attacks on it as a " patchwork " were unjust. Frederick II, the banned Emperor, had done what no other Emperor had succeeded in doing, what all Crusaders had failed to do since Saladin conquered Jerusalem—he had set free the Holy City. When Frederick assembled the German pilgrims and announced the news they broke out into shouts of uncontrolled rejoicing. On the advice of Hermann of Salza the Emperor decided himself to enter the liberated Jerusalem at the head of the pilgrims. The joy of his adherents was equalled only by the rage of his enemies. The Emperor's success was for the Pope the most unwelcome thing that could have happened. The Patriarch, unsuccessfully, forbade the pilgrims to enter Jerusalem with the Emperor. He was infuriated by Frederick's omission to consult him, and also by the rejoicing of the Germans, and wrote to the

Pope : " The Germans had only one thought, to be free to visit the Holy Sepulchre ; they were the only nation who raised paeans of praise and illuminated the town in festal wise ; all others considered the whole thing a folly."

Gerold's hatred of the Emperor finally exceeded all bounds. He informed the Pope at great length about the treaty, emphasising pharisaically its weak points—many of which were primarily attributable to his own multiple treachery—and painted the Emperor as a fool who had allowed himself to be hoodwinked by the Mussulmans. He was more particularly embittered because the treaty contained not a word about the restoration of Church and Monastery property. The Pope lost no time in further blackening this report and circulating it to the world, maliciously representing Frederick's conduct as disgraceful in treating at all with the Infidel and permitting the Heathen to worship in Jerusalem. He was skilful in glossing over the fact that Frederick had after all accomplished more than all the mighty Crusaders of recent times.

The loss of Jerusalem made so unhappy an impression on the Musulmans that it is quite clear that al Kamil had gone to the utmost limit of the possible. Saladin had written once to Cœur de Lion : " Jerusalem is to us as holy as to you, nay, more holy, for thence the Prophet made by night his flight to Heaven, and there the angels are wont to assemble." The Khalif of Baghdad called him to account, the other Sultans were wroth with him, and mourning for the loss of the Holy City, which was felt to be a most bitter blow to Islam, rose to open demonstrations against al Kamil. Finally, a service of protest was held, which the Sultan punished only by the confiscation of the treasures of the mosque—an expedient which probably impressed Frederick. The Muslims, however, conceded that al Kamil, who had himself called the Emperor to his help, had been in a dilemma, and they comforted themselves with thoughts of the future and of the Will of Allah. The Sultan's advantage in this pact was slight, and consisted mainly in having secured for himself the opportunity of pursuing his campaigns of conquest undisturbed by a new Crusade, which would certainly have followed his refusal to surrender Jerusalem. Al Kamil's relations with Kaiser Frederick grew more and more cordial, though partisans on both sides bitterly resented this friendship with one of an alien faith.

Frederick II owed his great success unquestionably to the Amir Fakhru'd Din, and tradition has it that the Emperor knighted him and gave him permission to wear the imperial eagle on his shield. There is nothing improbable in this ; similar tales are told of Cœur de Lion. For the world of East and West was then one great knightly comradeship, in which there reigned so much common chivalry that the barriers of religion were not insuperable. The aristocratic standards of chivalry were indeed earlier developed in the East, in Persia, than in Europe, as the epic of Firdausi and many another poem reveals to us. Both in East and West this feeling for knightly comradeship was a living thing, and the epic of the West always represents the Saracen knights as conspicuously noble and distinguished : think only of Feirefiss,[1] Parzival's black-and-white brother, of Ortnit's helper, of the wise heathen Zacharias, of Ariosto's Medor, and, above all, of Saladin, the pearl of oriental chivalry, to whom Dante accorded a place in Elysium, beside the great pagan heroes and poets, though it was he who had taken Jerusalem from the Christians.

The Emperor had still something to learn of Saracen chivalry. He was anxious to visit the place of Christ's baptism on the Jordan and set out from Jerusalem with a few followers. The Templars, who had allowed themselves to become the blind tools of the Patriarch, sent news of this expedition, apparently at the direct instigation of the Pope, to the Sultan al Kamil : here was his chance to take Frederick prisoner, and if he wished to make away with him. " Disgusted by this low treachery," and not sorry to put to shame the Pope's Christian knights, al Kamil sent the letter with a covering note to the Emperor, who from that time forward cherished an undying hatred of the Templars. He was grateful for the Sultan's friendship, which he cherished till al Kamil's death and then transferred to his son.

[1] Feirefis, Old French : *vaire fiz*, " the particoloured son," Wolfram von Eschenbach, i. 1705.—*Tr.*

The Arabs on their side preserved kindly memories of the Emperor. Partly from motives of expediency and partly from genuine inclination Frederick II liked to make himself one of the Saracens. He had a great admiration for their science, and he purposely paraded also his unfeigned respect for their religion and their customs. The Muslims related many anecdotes of the Emperor in this regard, which tally well with utterances of Frederick's. The Emperor, for instance, attended the Mosque of 'Umar with one of the Sultan's amirs. As he came forth he saw a Christian priest standing at the door of the sanctuary with the gospel in his hand begging from the pilgrims, and even from the Emperor himself. Enraged at this breach of the Saracen's hospitality Frederick smote him on the chest and knocked him down, shouting " Thou viper . . ., we are naught but the slaves of the Sultan who allows us so many privileges, and thou darest to transgress the bounds that he has set ! The next of you who so offends I shall most surely slay." The Emperor's violence when roused was well known, and many anecdotes of it are told.

In Jerusalem Frederick lodged in the house of the Qazi Shamsu'd Din. The Sultan had expressly given orders out of courtesy to his friend, whose religious feelings he did not wish to offend, that the muazzins must not chant the call to prayer during the Emperor's stay. One of them forgot, and at the time for morning prayer mounted the minaret and sang out the verses, expressly directed against the Christian faith, " He begetteth not, neither is he begotten, and there is none like unto him," and so forth. The Qazi reproved him and the next night he refrained. In the morning, however, the Emperor summoned the Qazi and asked him why the muazzin had not chanted the call to prayer. The Qazi quoted the Sultan's orders. " O Qazi "—Frederick is said to have replied—" you are doing wrong to alter your cult, your customs, your religion for my sake. You would not need to do so even if you were in my country." This was quite true. An Arabic scholar, who in later years visited King Manfred, was not a little surprised to hear the muazzins calling the faithful to prayer from the minarets of Lucera. The story about different religions and the three rings was told in relation to Frederick. The Arabs learnt on another occasion that the Emperor refused to be hedged within conventional boundaries and had an opinion of his own about religion, differing in many points from that current in his day. On the cupola of the Sakhrah mosque in Jerusalem Frederick read the golden inscription of the conqueror Saladin : " Saladin cleansed this temple of the polytheists." The Emperor pretended not to understand, and for the pleasure of seeing the Muslims' embarrassment insisted on their explaining to him who the polytheists could be. They told him that the Christians with their Trinity were meant. He then went on to ask " What is the point of the grill over the doors of the mosque ? " " To keep out the sparrows "; whereupon the Emperor—using the Arabic term of contempt for Christians as " unclean "—smiled and said, " Yet Allah has brought the swine amongst you after all."

With phrases like these Frederick II shocked even the Saracens themselves ; they thought he could scarcely be even a Christian, but must be some materialist who denied the immortality of the soul. They had no great opinion of his looks —he was beardless and of medium height—" If he were a slave," they said, " he would not be worth two hundred drachmas "; but his dignified bearing and his *bonhomie* were appreciated. The Muslims were amazed when at the time of midday prayer almost all the Emperor's servants and one of his teachers stood up and went through the orthodox Muhammadan ritual as true believers : they were the Sicilian Saracens of the Emperor's household.

So Frederick did not even maintain the pretence of a war for the faith : his Crusade was purely an affair of state, a matter concerning the Empire, not the Church, and this could not have been made clearer than by the existence of his Muslim retinue. It was perfectly natural for Frederick, from the political point of view, to pose as an Oriental here in Syria. Napoleon in Egypt was prepared to go considerable lengths and loved to be called Sultan al Kabir. Making due allowance for the difference of centuries great men on the human side are much alike. Each of these wanted in the East to be an Oriental. The same impulse made Frederick occasionally use pure oriental formulas. In concluding the Treaty he swore, for instance, " to eat the flesh of his left hand " if he should break the agreement. Once, when negotiations had come to a standstill, the Emperor advanced towards Jaffa, sending—in the symbolism of the Orient —his imperial weapons, armour and helmet, to the Sultan to indicate that he still had these resources behind him.

The Orient had different connotations for these two great men. Unstinted admiration of the Arab mind was the weightiest factor with the Hohenstaufen Emperor. For Frederick II lived in a day when the East was the source of all European knowledge and science, as Italy and Roman culture were to the barbarian North, as of old the art and philosophy of Hellas were to Italy. The spirit of the medieval Church was imprisoned in formula and dogma, the fetters could be loosened only by oriental hellenistic knowledge, chiefly knowledge of the laws of Nature. Frederick was more determined than any contemporary to unlock these stores of knowledge, and he was destined to be, in virtue of his mental receptiveness and his Sicilian birth, the great intermediary and reconciler of East and West. He may be seen in philosophic discourse with Fakhru'd Din, exchanging geometric and algebraic questions with al Kamil, mixing with the most celebrated Arab astronomers whom he had begged the Sultan to lend him. Architecture again claimed his attention, as so often. He studied the octagonal Mosque of 'Umar in Jerusalem, with the cupola of green and gold and the artistic pulpit, which he mounted with admiration. He even collected information for his hunting. " When we were in the Orient we observed that the Arabs themselves use a hood in hawking, for the Arab kings sent us their most skilful falconers with falcons of every kind."

It is self-evident that affairs of state naturally challenged his most serious attention ; a conversational fragment is instructive. He was discussing the Khalifate with Fakhru'd Din. The Amir explained to the Emperor how the Khalifate of the Abbasids could be traced back in unbroken line to al Abbas, the uncle of the Prophet, and thus still remained in the family of the Founder. " That is excellent," said Frederick, " far superior to the arrangement of those fools, the Christians. They choose as their spiritual head any fellow they will, without the smallest relationship to the Messiah, and they make him

the Messiah's representative. That Pope there has no claim
to such a position, whereas your Khalif is the descendant of
Muhammad's uncle." Here speaks the pride of race of one
who later loved to style himself " son and grandson of Emperors
and Kings "—in contrast to the Pope—and here we see too his
reverence for natural above spiritual law, for Frederick was
fully emancipated from the excessive mysticism of his time.

These things all gave a pretext for the papal reproach that
Frederick II had adopted Saracen customs. Legend, partly
friendly, partly malicious, strengthened this belief. The
Saracen dancing girls, whom the Sultan had sent for his entertainment became, in the Pope's letters, Christian women whom
Frederick had compelled to dance before the Infidel before
being outraged. An English pilgrim even wrote home that the
Emperor had married the Sultan's daughter and fifty Saracen
women. His marriage with Isabella of Jerusalem may have
lent colour to this story, perhaps also the fact that he had a
natural son, Frederick of Antioch, of whose mother nothing
was known and whose name suggested an oriental origin.
People later even explained the normal dress of the Muslim
women, the black " chadar," as mourning for Frederick which
the women had worn ever since his departure.

It is obvious that Frederick's stay in the Holy Land kindled
the imagination of his contemporaries in the very highest degree,
especially his relationship to the Assassins (Hashishin), with
one branch of whom, the Ismailites of Lebanon, he did in
fact exchange embassies. The Hashishin were, as Marco Polo
recorded a generation later, a fanatical sect who were trained
to the most unquestioning obedience by their leader, Hasan i
Sabbah, the so-called " Old Man of the Mountain," and committed every kind of murder for the service of Islam. Suitable
boys were selected and for years subjected to a most spartan
regime, the delights of Paradise recounted to them the while.
When the right moment came they were given a draught of
hashish with their usual frugal meal. When they awoke it was
to find themselves in a veritable garden of Paradise, which the
" Old Man of the Mountain " had contrived in a beautiful

valley. Here all the realistic promises of the Qur'an were fulfilled, streams flowed with honey, milk and wine, there were leaping fountains, *huris* and boys. After a few days of glorious enjoyment the disciples were given a second draught, from which they woke to find themselves again at the Old Man's table, filled with yearning for the Paradise they had tasted. They were promised a return to Paradise if they should find death in their master's service. The one ambition of the Hashishin was, therefore, speedy death.

The Emperor had had intercourse—though very transitory— with this terrible sect whose daggers had laid low innumerable distinguished crusaders, and people told tales of a visit he was alleged to have paid to the " Old Man of the Mountain." To demonstrate the obedience of his people the Old Man had signalled to two who were standing at the top of a high tower ; happy to attain Paradise so soon, they hurled themselves down at his bidding. A later version represents Frederick as rearing his own " obedient stabbers " on similar lines. He locked children in a cellar, it was said, showed himself very rarely, and had them taught that the Emperor was God Almighty. When the little prisoners learned this :

> They thought that this indeed was so,
> The Kaiser was Lord God below.

No prince was murdered during Frederick's lifetime whose death was not ascribed to Frederick's assassins, and even the Popes did not scorn to spread such rumours.

These tales, of course, lack all historic truth, but it is interesting to note how tales of horror and wonder tend to focus round one great name, partly in order to gain greater credence from its authority and partly out of a strange desire to see two incongruous elements brought together in one person's story—the real and the fantastic ; Muhammad and Christ ; Kaiser and Khalif. The oriental atmosphere that surrounds the figure of Frederick II was a necessary factor in the evolution of the autocratic mind, which loved to exercise the unchallenged caprice of a master. The *Puer Apuliae* has developed and revealed himself : he is no longer the fate and destiny of individuals ; but as the Emperor, imitating the Old Man of the Mountain and playing God to his little prisoners in the cellar, he becomes himself the fate or destiny of communities and peoples.

There is no doubt that the Emperor was deeply impressed by the unquestioning obedience that he saw and by the unlimited autocracy of the oriental despot and the aura of Fate that surrounded them. A few years later the Pope wrote bitterly to him : " In thy kingdom of Sicily no man dares move a hand or foot save at thy command."

In all the anecdotes and reported conversations that record Frederick's words and deeds during his Syrian stay, one recurring note is the immense admiration and reverence that he displayed for men and things. No doubt this had a political value—but the same is true throughout his life. When Frederick, in later days, was showing distinguished visitors his priceless planetarium, in which sun, moon and stars moved in mysterious harmony, he loved to tell that this was a gift of his Arab friend the Sultan, who was dearer to him than any living man save only King Conrad, his son and the heir of his body. Such a phrase indicates how boundless was the admiration felt by this greater Emperor for the Muslim princes—himself almost sole arbiter of the West. Constantly the proud boast recurs : " The Hohenstaufen Emperor, friend of the Muslim King "; when, for instance, he begs on occasion the loan of a small force from the Sultan of Egypt to intimidate the Lombard rebels, or when he opines that certain events in the East would not have taken place if he had had his way, sighing : "Ah . . . if my friend al Kamil were alive . . .!" Or, at a Diet of the German princes in Friuli, when the Emperor received with ostentatious favour a deputation from his Arab friends and celebrated with them—in sight of bishops and princes—in a great banquet the Muhammadan feast of the Hijrah, and then departed for Apulia in company with his Muslim guests ; or when for a long time he mourns and bitterly laments the death of his friend, al Kamil—whom he had scarcely ever met—the chronicler who reports this imperial grief suggests a remarkable cause : the Sultan had perished unbaptised. All indications point to the fact that for the only time in his life, now *vis-à-vis* the East, Kaiser Frederick felt himself to be the learner and the gainer. He is ever ready to acknowledge the debt and proclaim himself the disciple ; or, to use his own strong expression, " We are all naught but slaves of the Sultan." That sums up the situation. On every convenient occasion Frederick endeavours to imitate his Eastern models, to pose as one of themselves. He sends mathematical and philosophical questions to the Sultans, or begs the Khalif for his good offices to convey an imperial letter on such topics to one scholar or another. After his return to the West Frederick kept up his Eastern correspondence, and recounts to his Muslim friends his quarrels with the Pope and with the Lombards, quoting by the way the famous Arab poets and imitating Arab custom in the endless titles he gives himself : Frederick, son of Kaiser Henry, son of Kaiser Frederick, etc., etc. He does not omit the customary emulation in the giving of gifts : al Kamil had presented him with an elephant, Frederick sends him in return a polar bear, which to the amazement of the Arabs eats nothing but fish. It is easy to detect the Emperor's pride in being thus able to return the Sultan's costly gift. In his intercourse with Easterns Frederick displays the gratitude which the Pope used to demand from him in vain. Only from the East did Frederick in fact receive new ideas and intellectual stimulus.

The Emperor was naturally not indifferent to the impression he created ; he succeeded in exciting great admiration : no western prince has ever evoked so much affection and understanding as he. Not only did they admire the encyclopaedic learning of the Emperor, who maintained erudite correspondence with the learned men of Egypt and Syria, Iraq, Arabia, Yemen, as well as Morocco and Spain, but they followed all the more important events of his life with unflagging interest. They knew of his Lombard troubles, of the conspiracies engineered by the Pope, spoke familiarly of Tuscany and Lombardy, quoted admiringly the interminable titles of the Emperor in which all his kingdoms and provinces were rehearsed by name. " I wished to include this letter (with the titles)," writes an Arab historian, " to record what territories are united under the sceptre of this Emperor and King. In truth there has never been in Christendom since the days of

Alexander a monarch like to this, not only because of his power
but because he challenges the Pope to battle, their Khalif, and
drives him from the field." A hundred years later people still
quoted Frederick on the political constellations of Italy : whoever wished to rule in Italy—he had said—must be good friends
with the Pope, must have Milan in his power, and must possess
good astrologers.

It was a highly intellectual " Marriage Festival of Susa " that
Frederick celebrated when he surrendered to the East as all
great men have done since Alexander of Macedon, each after
his own kind. What intoxicated the Hohenstaufen was not the
space nor the sensual magic, which had been familiar to him as
a Sicilian from his boyhood, but the inspiring freedom of the
spirit, unfettered by scholastic philosophy and church dogma.
He was the first and only medieval Emperor who drank of the
spirit of the East and came home to fuse it with the Holy Roman
Empire, the Empire of the Salians and the Hohenstaufens.

It was the Eastern triumph, not merely Eastern travel that
won for Frederick the halo of the Caesars. On the 17th of
March, 1229, the Emperor Frederick II made his entry into the
royal city of Jerusalem. In defiance of Patriarch Gerold's
commands, the bulk of the pilgrims followed him, impelled
partly by the yearning to do reverence to the Holy Sepulchre,
partly by the desire to witness how the age-old prophecy would
be fulfilled, of the Messianic ruler of the West who should set
free Jerusalem. More than ten years before a widespread Arab
prophecy had named the Calabrian King as Saviour of the
Tomb, and many thought that King of the East was drawing
nigh who should attack Islam in the rear. It was true enough
that the Muslims had a hard fight to fight in the further East,
but no man knew in all its fulness what this meant. For the
distant thunder was the trampling of Chingiz Khan's mounted
hordes, while the Christians were still thinking of the Nestorian
Prester John, whom men compared to Alexander, and with
whom the Emperor was supposed to have exchanged remarkable embassies. There was no doubt at all in the minds of
" the Pious," as Frederick now began for the first time to style

his adherents, that the Hohenstaufen Frederick II whom the
pilgrims followed was the true Emperor of the Fulfilment who
as by a miracle had succeeded in freeing Jerusalem, " without
battle, without instrument of war, without bloodshed," as the
promise ran. To the papalists the Emperor now appeared to
assume the features of the impious Anti-Christ who should
take his seat like a God in the temple of the Almighty for the
confusion of the faithful.

On the day of his entry Frederick immediately betook himself
to the Church of the Sepulchre, " In order," as he wrote, " as
a Catholic Emperor, to worship reverently at the grave of our
Lord." The whole world assumed that since the Emperor had
now not only fulfilled his vow to make a Crusade, but had also
accomplished the liberation of Jerusalem, he would be forthwith released from the papal ban. . . . " For no ban can endure
longer in the eyes of God than a man's sin," so " Freidank "
declared, in almost heretic phrase, challenging thereby the papal
claim " to bind and to loose." Even more anti-papal was his
next clause : " Obedience is good as long as the Master worketh
righteousness. If the Master seek to compel the servant to do
what is wrong before God, then the servant must quit his
master and follow him who doeth right." Many another pilgrim shared Freidank's views, and in Germany the Pope was
often styled a " heretic." The Emperor, too, was hopeful that
his excommunication would now be ended. He wanted to
arrange for a Sunday Mass in the Church of the Sepulchre.
The wise and prudent Hermann of Salza, however, dissuaded
him from thus rashly forestalling the Pope and challenging his
further displeasure, for all the attempts at reconciliation that
Frederick had made before and after his arrival in the Holy
Land had been ignored, or had only provoked a renewal of the
ban. The Pope's unforgiving spirit was turned to good account.
Thanks to it, it came about that on the 18th of March, the
fourth Sunday before Easter, there took place in Jerusalem in
the Church of the Holy Sepulchre the most memorable self-
coronation of an Emperor that the world was to see till the days
of Napoleon. In full imperial State the banned and excommunicated Emperor—outside the congregation of the faithful—
accompanied by followers and friends, crossed the threshold of

the sacred edifice. Here, where the first king of Jerusalem, Godfrey of Bouillon, with humble emotion, refused to wear a golden circlet where his Lord had worn a crown of thorns ; here, without intermediary of the Church, without bishop, without coronation mass, Kaiser Frederick II, proud and unabashed, stretched forth his hand to take the royal crown of the Holy City. Striding towards the altar of the Sepulchre he lifted from it the crown, and himself placed it on his own head—an act, whether so intended, of far-reaching symbolism. For thus, on the holiest spot of all the Christian universe, he asserted a king's immediate vassalhood to God, and without the interposition of the Church approached his God direct as a triumphant conqueror.

Frederick II made no effort to derive from doctrines and theories a belief in the immediate relationship of God to Emperor—a doctrine fiercely denied by the Popes since the evolution of the Hierarchy—he based it on the miracles of his own career, obvious to all and far-renowned, which proved as nothing else could do that God's immediate choice rested on his imperial person, if not on his imperial office. This personal element could be reinforced by doctrine, such as the teaching of a certain supernatural character inherent in the imperial majesty. Before the great breach Pope Gregory had written that God had installed the Emperor as a Cherub ; he had been elevated " not as a Seraph but as a second Cherub, as a token of resemblance to the only-begotten son," so they wrote later. This angelic character, which Pope Innocent had claimed for himself—" less than God, but more than man "—was alluded to by Frederick in the words wherewith he announced the imperial triumph in Jerusalem to the world at large. Immediately after the coronation Frederick made a public speech to the assembled pilgrims, while Hermann of Salza repeated the Emperor's words in Latin and in German. The same speech, greatly expanded and enriched, formed the basis of a manifesto which was to announce the glory of this day to all the world : magniloquent pathos in which the Emperor's more than mortal voice should make itself heard throughout the entire *orbis terrarum*. " Let all that are of righteous heart rejoice and give thanks unto the Lord, who hath taken pleasure in his people as they praised the Emperor of Peace.   Let us praise him, whom the angels praise. . . ."   The very first phrases place Frederick in the due proximity to God amongst the angels, like them aloft above the people, and now through the Emperor's mouth is heard the very voice of God himself making known to the peoples the deeds of the Emperor as his own : " God he is the Lord, and it is he alone who worketh great wonders, it is he who mindful of his own mercy renews in our day the marvels that he wrought of old, as it is written.   For God when he would make known his might hath need neither of chariots nor of horses : he hath shewn his power by the small number of his instruments, that all peoples might see and know that he is terrible in his might and glorious in his majesty and marvellous in his planning beyond all the sons of men.   For in these few last days, more by the power of his wonders than by men's courage, he hath happily caused that work to be accomplished which for long times past many princes and many mighty of the earth with the multitude of their peoples have all essayed in vain."

Thus Frederick ascribes to God what he himself had done, and while the Emperor praises the triumph of the One God he skilfully (with God) praises himself.   Then, after an appeal to the nation, he bursts out :   " See ye, now is the day of that salvation . . .", and the manifesto proceeds to recount the wonderful proofs of God's counsel and help displayed from the beginning.   The pitiable plight of the pilgrims in Jaffa is pictured when suddenly the storms have cut off all supplies and when thereupon fear and murmuring waxed strong amongst them.   God commanded the winds and the sea and a great calm fell, and all men cried " How great is he that commandeth the winds and the waters and they obey him."   The Emperor then related other difficulties, all of which God and his Son had miraculously solved by the instrumentality of the Emperor. How the hostile Sultans had lain at the distance of but one day's journey, and how Christ himself, having witnessed from on high the Emperor's patience and long suffering, so directed the negotiations that the Holy City was yielded to the Emperor and the treaty was ready for confirmation on the very day of our Lord's resurrection.   Finally, the scene in Jerusalem was briefly painted

when the excommunicated Emperor donned the crown, " For
Almighty God from the throne of his majesty in the plentitude
of his grace hath exalted us above all the princes of the earth,
that all may know that the hand of the Lord hath done this.
And all who revere the True Faith shall proclaim far and wide
that 'the blessed of God hath visited us and hath wrought
salvation for his people and hath exalted a horn in the house
of his servant David.'"

Beneath the appearance of humble devotion all this ascription
of each success to God served but to exalt the Emperor himself.
This was, moreover, the first time that Frederick II had adopted
the words of Holy Scripture about the Son of God and applied
them to his own Majesty : through the God-Kingship of David
approaching the Saviour. There was nothing sensationally
new in this. All the Emperors since Charlemagne had held
themselves to be the heirs and successors of King David, the
Chosen of God, and this was an argument for the ancient claim
of the imperial immediacy. The coronation formula has this
in mind, " David thy son thou hast exalted to the summit of
Kingship." The claim, however, was one thing ; its actual
realisation was another. For Frederick II was not merely
claiming intellectually the inheritance of David, but claimed
miraculously to have entered into actual possession of his
inheritance, and showed himself to all the world as King of
Jerusalem. Men sang the praises of the Emperor, " David
wast thou in Jerusalem," and Frederick himself wrote " It fills
us with joy that our Saviour Jesus of Nazareth also sprang from
David's royal stock." Similar thoughts were in the mind of a
German poet who celebrated the Emperor's triumphs of these
days in pompous hexameters comparing Frederick to Jerusalem's other King :

> Jerusalem gaude nomen Domini venerare
> Magnifica laude : vis ut dicam tibi quare ?
> Rex quia magnificus Jesus olim, nunc Fridericus,
> Promptus uterque pati, sunt in te magnificati.
> Obtulit ille prior semet pro posteriori
> Et pro posterior sua seque prioris honore. . . .

Both Kings of Jerusalem, in Christian times Christ the first,
Frederick the last, the Saviour and the Emperor, both thought

of together as the successors of David, as the Son of God, the
spirits like unto angels that mediate between God and man.
Godfrey and his successors on the throne of Jerusalem had
rejoiced in no such connection, but then they had not been
Roman Emperors, Rulers of the World.

" Christus vincit, Christus regnat, Christus imperat," the
historic coronation cry of the Sicilian kings, dating from the
earliest days of Christianity, when still-surviving paganism
represented Christ in the figure of Apollo, was more than ever
the watchword of the triumphant world ruler.   Frederick II
was fain to compare himself wielding the swords of justice and
of power with the royal and victorious Christ, the hero of the
Germanic peoples, as the old Saxon poem of the Heliand
depicted him, the warrior Lord with his battle companions.
This was Kaiser Frederick's limit.   Quite expressly this Fulfiller of the Law had been called " a token of similarity to the
Only-Begotten Son as second Cherub not a Seraph. . . ."   But
the " Other " had become man once more : Francis of Assisi had
again incarnated the seraphic Christ, the Redeemer, the Sufferer.

While still a boy Frederick II had offered himself to God
after his first triumph in Aix.   Fifteen years later in the prime
of life, in his thirty-fifth year, he had in Jerusalem made good
his boyish vow, and in a second triumph united himself with
God.   The distant future held a third triumph in store.
Frederick's triumphs were always of the kind that opened to
him new spheres.   A critical change is to be noted : in the
Puer Apuliae the Church herself, and with her Pope Innocent
III, had triumphed ; in the godlike triumph of the excommunicate Emperor in Jerusalem the Church had neither part
nor lot—through the fault of the irreconcilable High Priest.
Not one word of Frederick's manifesto alludes to the Church
triumphant ; the Victor was God, was the Saviour and through
God the Emperor.   Their deeds are one and the relation of the
miracles bring thereof the clearest proof ; they display Frederick
in tune with God, much as Caesar's tale of portents on the
day of Pharsalia, showed Caesar in harmony with the Roman
Pantheon.   Not through the Church, but alongside and without the Church, Frederick II had consummated his triumph
as it were an *unio mystica*.   It is not irrelevant to note how

the Emperor's great antagonist, St. Francis, through deepest humiliation, achieved outside the Church his union with God. Neither the glorious triumph of the Emperor nor the unexampled humility of St. Francis could in fact find a place within the Church ; as Spirits, as Cherub, and as Seraph they might serve the Church with sword and palm in her strife against infidel and heretic, but both had outgrown the mediation of the Church, and as immediately in touch with God they both were driven to create : the one a following, an Order of his own, the other a State.

The Emperor Frederick's self-coronation at the Saviour's tomb serves as a tangible expression of this immediacy. He already shared the atmosphere of romance and fatefulness that surrounded the Khalifs ; he now wore the divine halo of an eastern potentate. As the sibylline saying had foretold—though in far other wise than the world had understood—the rulers of East and West were united in Jerusalem in the one person of Frederick II, and the Holy City was free. With Frederick, the only emperor who in Jerusalem wore the crown of Jerusalem, the epoch of a Christian Empire was ended. A new era was dawning. Out of the East Frederick brought back not the renewal of a Christian Empire, but the birth of Western " Monarchy." His was the last figure round which the double glory played : the old Christian majesty and sanctity and the new western secular monarchy. The Frankish-Germanic feudal kingship which sanctified blood and race, the Hohenstaufen-Roman Empire of Barbarossa, which sanctified the office, had been further exalted under Frederick II by the eastern conception of despotism which worshipped the actual wielder of power as such, the person of the ruler as the *Homo Dei*, a god-man, a son of God, himself divine. This fourth and last coronation marked the end of Frederick's personal " development," his purely individual rise to power : no further growth was possible to him as a man, save with and through his states. The question was whether he could awaken an echo in some nation, whether some people could comprehend him, as the divine power within him seemed to portend.

The eastern successes began to act with steadying force on the Emperor's tottering position in the West ; at first only in Germany, where the papal machinations had all along carried but little weight, while the reports of the Emperor's victories had carried much.   Duke Albert of Saxony immediately issued the joyous manifesto to the Germans in Reval, while Count Adolfus of Holstein dated his documents " in the year of the reconquest of the Holy Land by Frederick the unconquered Roman Emperor."

In Sicily, on the other hand, the prospect was blacker than ever.   In spite of the zeal of the Lords of Aquino, and the Chief Justice Henry of Morra and the Regent Reginald of Spoleto and the Saracens—showing for the first time their full worth—the kingdom was proving not nearly so invulnerable as Frederick had hoped, particularly in the absence of its king.   The imperial forces were divided ; one detachment lay in the Abruzzi, the other in Capua.   The Pope's Soldiers of the Keys, under the leadership of John, quondam King of Jerusalem, had succeeded in invading the kingdom and reducing the majority of the continental provinces.   The Church played her favourite rôle of " Liberator of the Oppressed."   The yoke of Frederick II had been no light one; the Pope spread rumours of the Emperor's death, and freed Sicilian subjects from their allegiance.   These combined causes hastened the downfall of the imperial rule in the peninsula.   Nevertheless, a faithful few retained their loyalty and looked for Frederick's return as eagerly as the Papalists feared it.   John of Brienne, the Pope's general, had secretly given orders to watch the ports of Apulia and take the Emperor prisoner in the moment of landing. Suddenly in early June 1229—in spite of all these precautions —the rumour arose that the Emperor was in Apulia.

Before quitting the Holy Land Frederick had had some further unpleasant experiences.   In his address to the assembled pilgrims after his coronation in Jerusalem he had been most scrupulous, in accordance with the line he had adopted from the first, to use only conciliatory phrases in speaking of the Pope.   Instead of raising complaints against Gregory, which would have been easy, he took pains to find excuses for him. It was no less in harmony with the whole conduct of the

Papalist party that they redoubled their hostile activities and intrigues as his success increased. The Pope had dubbed Frederick a " pirate " and refused to recognise his crusadership. The patriarch Gerold had, therefore, full assurance that none of his perfidious schemes would rouse the disapproval which Frederick had prophesied to the pilgrims. Thus it came about that Frederick's eventful stay in Jerusalem lasted only two days : he entered on a Saturday, crowned himself on Sunday, and quitted the town on Monday. For Gerold had not only ordered a Dominican to renew the Pope's excommunication, but had actually laid the Holy City under an interdict—to the inde-scribable wrath of the pilgrims. They could not offer their prayers in the holy places which the Emperor had restored to them and felt themselves befooled by Church and Pope. The Emperor forthwith left Jerusalem after a smart encounter with Templars and clergy—the Templars' plot to betray him falls chronologically here. For the rest, his advice to the pilgrims was to join him and embark with him from Acre.

There was nothing now to detain Frederick in the Holy Land. Bad news from Sicily had reached Acre. He looked impatiently forward to the return, and had ordered his admiral, Henry of Malta, to be ready by Easter with the galleys in Acre. The wildest and most shameful scene was to come before he left Palestine. In spite of Frederick's veto the Patriarch had en-listed troops in the Emperor's own kingdom of Jerusalem. This defiance of the imperial authority was the more flagrant that the troops could only be wanted to serve against the Emperor himself, since a truce existed with the Saracens. In retaliation the imperial troops shut up the Patriarch and the Templars in their own quarters in Acre, cut off their supplies, blockaded the town, tore from the pulpits and thoroughly thrashed a couple of mendicant monks who were preaching against Frederick and stirring up disorder. This was not all. As the Emperor on the early morning of the appointed day was preparing to embark, the populace, incited by the Papalists, pursued him, throwing filth at him and his followers. With a curse upon his lips Frederick left the Holy Land.

A few weeks later the unexpected happened in Apulia. Outdistancing the other Crusaders Frederick II landed on

June 10th in Brindisi—" God keep it," he wrote to the Amir
Fakhru'd Din. His arrival was so surprising that the towns-
people could not conceive what it meant when they saw the
imperial standard unfurled. They had long been mourning
their Emperor's death. Not till they had seen him with their
own eyes did they realise the papal treachery. Then they
hastened to welcome their master with joyful acclamation.
The news of Frederick's return spread like wildfire through
Sicily. The whole situation was changed. The Emperor went
immediately to Barletta and issued a stirring proclamation
announcing his unexpected return, exhorting the Capua detachment to hold out and preserve their loyalty. He despatched
Count Thomas of Aquino to their help and promised to follow
shortly in person. In the meantime he speedily assembled
troops, yet avoided undue haste. His adherents poured in from
all sides ; Reginald of Spoleto from the Abruzzi with his detachment, the Chief Justice with his Saracens and all other
Sicilians who had remained faithful. A fortunate coincidence
turned to Frederick's advantage. A severe storm had compelled a large body of Teutonic Knights to land in Brindisi on
their way back from the Holy Land. They forthwith declared
themselves willing to join Frederick. Some Pisans also made
their appearance. If the Emperor once more pointed to the
direct intervention of Divine Providence and God's active
miracles on his behalf he had every right to do so.

It was a remarkable army that assembled around Frederick II :
Sicilians, German Crusaders, imperial Saracens fighting side by
side against the Lombards and the soldiers of the Pope. Or,
rather, prepared to fight against them ; for matters did not
progress so far. The mere terror of the Emperor's name, the
realisation of the Pope's deceit in spreading false news of his
death, arrears of pay, bad leadership, and in the Lombards' case
a strong disinclination to be caught in open treachery and rebellion against their overlord : all this chased the Army of the
Keys in complete demoralisation back to the frontiers of the
Papal States. The appearance of the Emperor, his mere name,
had acted like a paralysing charm. Here and there the papal
soldiers succeeded in making a stand, but when the Emperor
set out for Capua at the end of August no stronghold could

retain the warriors of the Holy See : without waiting to be attacked they fled across the border. In vain the papal legate seized the Church treasures of Monte Cassino and San Germano to pay the troops. What indignation when one day Frederick II did the like !

Such was the famous rout of the Soldiers of the Keys and their expulsion from Sicily. That ended the campaign and left the world full of admiration for the Emperor, who once again had won a bloodless victory. The Muslims compared him to Alexander; the Greek Emperor of Nicaea sent an embassy, and, later, costly gifts and a large sum of money for his help. Simultaneously the Emperor's supporters in Northern Italy succeeded in conquering the Lombard League. Within four days two hundred towns had declared for the Emperor. Very few still held out. It had become important to make a deterrent example ; the town of Sora, which was still in rebellion, was besieged by the Emperor in person, conquered and reduced to ashes, and was to remain uninhabited for all time. The plough should furrow the site of the faithless city as of old the site of Carthage, so Frederick later phrased it. It may easily be conceived that the Emperor exercised extreme severity towards a few traitors and faithless officials. Any who had hoped for elevation through the Emperor's fall should now enjoy an extra lofty gallows—the chronicler tells us. As penalty for the treachery of the Templars in Palestine Frederick confiscated all the Sicilian goods and possessions of the Templars and the Knights of St. John.

What was the Pope's attitude to it all ? He was in a most difficult position : the hatred of the nobles kept him banished from Rome ; his supplies of cash and war material were exhausted ; the Lombards had left him in the lurch ; his cries to the western kings for help were unheeded. Yet not one of the Emperor's numerous embassies to Gregory IX met with the smallest success. It was not he, defeated though he might be, who was going to give in. The Emperor must yield. Frederick had a clear field ; there was nothing to prevent his conquering the entire papal territory and compelling the Pope to make peace—as he did on a later occasion. Yet, at the frontier he halted with his forces, most prudently still preserving the

unimpeachable tone of moderation and placability which he
had from the first maintained. He was well aware that in the
present state of affairs he did the Pope more harm by this submissive approach than by any show of violence. He made the
Pope from first to last the sole disturber of the peace of Europe,
and he reaped more advantage from that than from a temporary
occupation of Church lands, a continuation of the ban and the
martyrdom of the spiritual overlord of Christendom. Just now
the Empire sorely needed new òrganisation and settlement.
So the German Grand Master, who had already sued in vain
for peace, was sent again to Gregory. A section of the College
of Cardinals disapproved of the papal policy, and so a truce at
least was concluded. The Pope agreed most reluctantly, though
he was the sole gainer. As for Frederick, a beginning had been
made towards peace.

Negotiations dragged on for the best part of a year, and throw
a remarkable light on the overwhelmingly strong position of
the Church. The victorious Emperor was suppliant for peace,
while the defeated Pope refused every concession and sought to
dictate the terms of a peace which he did not desire. This
demonstrates how small an element in the Pope's power was
military strength, and how unassailable was the Head of the
Roman Church. It lay in Gregory's competence to release
Frederick from the ban, or not, and Frederick remained a disobedient child of the Church until he had surrendered in every
detail. Pope Gregory was entirely undisturbed by the fact that
the basis of the excommunication lay in the non-fulfilment of
the Crusader's vow, and that this had now become completely
meaningless. Gregory had sought to ruin the hated Emperor,
and, since he had failed in his main object, the Emperor must
purchase his release all the more dearly by concessions in Sicily.
Thus it was the Emperor, not the Pope, who needed peace.
Threats of war did not alarm the Pope : they gratified him
rather. During the whole course of the negotiations Frederick
displayed an incredible patience, an almost inconceivable sub-
missiveness, and it was not his fault that war almost broke out
afresh. At this point the Emperor summoned the German
princes to use their influence on the Pope, and they were so far
successful that they achieved an understanding, after themselves

guaranteeing the Emperor's good faith, which left Gregory no
conceivable pretext for refusing peace. He was loth to lift the
ban, if only because this stultified his whole previous procedure.
It undoubtedly created a remarkable impression when the Pope,
in the summer of 1230, again greeted as the " beloved son of
the Church " the Emperor whom he had so recently condemned
as a " disciple of Muhammad." The world was not blind to
the effect. One contemporary stigmatises the whole course of
events that opened with the Treaty of San Germano and terminated in the Peace of Ceperano as a "disgrace to the Church."
A troubadour expressed himself still more forcibly when he
cursed the Pope and breathed threats against the papal capital :
" It is my comfort, Rome, that you will plunge to ruin, when
the rightful Emperor comes to his own again and acts as he
ought."

It was with a view to restoring his fortune—that is : his power
—that Frederick was willing to accept the terms of this most
unfavourable peace. He granted an amnesty to the Pope's
partisans in Sicily, restored all Church property confiscated
during the war, including that of the Templars and of the
Knights of St. John, and these were the least of his concessions.
The chief place was taken, as of course, by the questions of the
Church's personnel in Sicily, for Pope Gregory was no longer
content with the Concordat of Queen Constance. It seemed
to contravene all Frederick's principles that, for the sake of
escaping from the excommunication he was prepared to make
the most sweeping concessions: the Sicilian clergy—with a
few exceptions—should no longer be amenable to secular law,
should no longer be subject to general taxation, and in the
matter of episcopal elections it would seem that the Emperor
went so far as to renounce the right of consent he had hitherto
exercised. Very different opinions have been held about this
treaty, so wholly at variance with Frederick's victories, but
historians have on the whole tended to overvalue the rights
surrendered. It is clear from the quarrel with Pope Honorius
III that the Emperor's right of consent had been in practice of
extremely little use ; the question of taxation and secular courts
for the clergy had always been points at issue. As long as the
Emperor was on good terms with the Pope such difficulties

could be got over. In case of war, which Frederick after his
recent experiences must have felt to be very imminent, all such
agreements fell to the ground. The most important thing for
the Emperor at the moment was to gain time to reorganise his
kingdoms, to concentrate his scattered powers, and then to subdue Lombardy. With a view to this it was vital to have even
a few years of peace, and it was even of greater importance to
have the Church, in spite of her collusion with the Lombard
League, as a neutral, or better still an ally, in this struggle
against rebels and heretics. The moment was favourable.
For in the Sicilian campaign the Lombards had not supported
the Pope to anything like the degree he had wished, and all
Frederick's relations to Gregory for the next few years were
intended to demonstrate how immensely more advantageous in
the three-party struggle was an alliance of Pope and Emperor
against Lombards, than one of Pope and Lombards against
Emperor. This unity of the two powers of Church and Empire
was always dear to Frederick's heart ; he was wholly sincere in
seeking it, and he had the world behind him : it represented
the God-ordained constitution. In this outlook Frederick was
completely reactionary ; he sought eagerly to secure the Curia
at any price, to wean her from the Lombard confederacy,
to re-awaken all the aristocratic elements in the Church in order
to re-establish the old traditional unity of the two powers. He
might be for a time successful, and for the moment the Pope
considered an alliance with Frederick useful on other grounds,
for his position between Emperor and Lombards was an uneasy
one. All three parties were in sore need of a breathing space,
yet the more all three recovered their strength the more ominous
and oppressive to the world at large was the thunderous atmosphere of threatening storm.

Thus ended Frederick II's first great fight with the Curia, and
for nearly ten years to come the strife was latent only. The
newly established accord between Emperor and Pope was osten-
tatiously manifested to the world. Frederick paid a visit to
Pope Gregory in his paternal home in Anagni, where they
sealed their pact " with holy kisses " as Frederick reported.
The Pope and the Emperor dined *tête-à-tête* in the presence of
one man only, whose mission in life it was to strive for the

honour of Church and Empire, and to whose efforts the conclusion of peace was in no small measure due : Hermann of
Salza, the German Grand Master.

Now the Emperor set to work to build up his power : first
in Sicily, later in Germany.

V. TYRANT OF SICILY

Influence of Eastern success——Affection for Sicily——
Three emperor models——Constitutions of Melfi, 1231
——Expectation of Golden Age and End of World——
Augustales minted —— Frederick's birthday a public
holiday.

I.

Liber Augustalis——Cult of Justitia——Invocation of
imperial name——" Crown Prosecution "——Theory of
the " Fall "——Necessitas——Dante's *de Monarchia*——
The Divine Comedy.

II.

Pope Gregory and the Liber Augustalis——Relation of
Church and State——Zeal against heretics——Muslims
and Jews——State organisation : justiciars, notaries——
Conditions of service——Treatment of suspects——
Rebellious towns——Augusta——Uniformity and simplification of government——Town creation ; frontier protection——Monopolies——Customs and revenue——
Weights and measures——Fairs and markets——The
Emperor as trader——Taxation——Commercial agreements——Overseas consuls and embassies——A Sicilian
nation——Marriage ordinances.

III.

Triumph of lay culture——Petrus de Vinea (Piero della
Vigna)——Frederick's public speaking——Frederick
amongst intimates——Youthfulness of Sicilian court——
Frederick's retainers ; menagerie——Famous families in
his service——Thomas Aquinas——Valetti imperatoris
——Frederick's sons——Chivalry at court——Foggia :
banquets, revelry——Michael Scot——Sicilian poetry ;
use of vernacular——Intellectual thought at court——
Learning at court——Astronomy and Astrology——
Hebrew scholars——Spirit of Enquiry ; Ibn Sabin of
Ceuta——Research and experiment——De arte venandi
cum avibus——The art of seeing " things that are, as they
are "——Frederick's personal appearance.

V. TYRANT OF SICILY

It was no accident that Frederick II's founding of the first absolute monarchy of the West followed his triumph in the East. This event had brought about a metamorphosis, as when a mythic hero becomes suddenly aware of his divine origin and the god in him springs visibly to life. Proclaiming himself the son of Jupiter Ammon, grandson of Venus Genetrix, or some other emanation of a Godhead, he gradually achieves his own apotheosis. From the moment that the divine sonship is proclaimed the career of the monarch takes a new direction: from the phase of mere personal activity and self-assertion he grows in stature, obeying the eternal law of his being by creative activity in empire and in state.

The Jerusalem coronation obviously marked such a turning point in Frederick's career. The *Puer Apuliae* had circled round Palermo, Aix and Rome, and now as German-Roman Emperor, embraced the Orient. The whole was in his grasp. This last and outermost circle bordered on the dreamlike and the infinite and set bounds to all further personal ambition. No higher office lay ahead, no new crown was waiting, nothing could now exalt him further. For the first time the Hohenstaufen Emperor had focussed the eyes of the whole world—the Christian West and the Muslim East—on the Imperator of Christendom. For the first time he had proved his mettle in a world enterprise, as leader of a crusading army. For the first time God himself—in the great Jerusalem manifesto—had spoken to the peoples of the earth, and through the Emperor's mouth proclaimed the Emperor his instrument. In the East Frederick had caught a glimpse of wider horizons; he returned to the narrower spaces of the West, and transplanting thither the conception of oriental autocracy he proceeded to grow anew—with his states.

Piling the eastern David-kingship on the Germanic feudal overlordship, and both on the authority of the Roman Princeps, the Hohenstaufens had succeeded in raising the medieval Christian Empire of the Caesars to a unique pinnacle. It was Frederick's unexampled good fortune to find at this point a willing and receptive people in whom he could confide—despite his greatness—and who were able to comprehend him, the dangers of his majesty notwithstanding. It was his luck to have a people of his own with whom he could feel at one. The medieval Emperor had hitherto held a remarkably detached position ; though he held the torch for all the Western peoples as lord of the Holy Roman Empire, he had possessed no land or people of his own, in whom his being and personality could be merged, as theirs in him, who would devote themselves to him with all their strength of mind and body and lend him the poise and weight that the " provincial kings " possessed as lords of the soil. The Emperor was of course the leader of Christendom, alongside the Pope, but only in certain circumstances, during a Crusade for instance, did Christianity as a whole centre in him. There was no one " Christian people," and if folk used the phrase it was a mere expression of faith.

The Imperator was Roman Emperor and Roman King, but the ancient *Populus Romanus*, that once had ruled the world, was dead, and only its empty shell still supplied the mould for imperial feasts and formulas. And what of the Imperator as ruler of the Germans ? A unity of German people was never more than a momentary flash: no conception existed of a German nation, no common German activity was possible save in the service of Empire or of Church. The Saxon, Frank and Swabian Emperors had found their support, not in a German nation, but each in his individual race. The Emperor knew no one land, no one nation in which he could rule untrammelled as a God. Many an Emperor had craved for it and sought it, always in Italy, especially that imperial boy who was the first before Frederick to catch a glimpse of the uttermost heights of priestly-imperial power : Otto III. But he found no popular support in the degenerate citizens of Rome, and the inspired vision faded while the lad himself, only a " Wonder of the World," died an early death—a kindred figure to the poet-boy Conradin, who sought a kingdom and found a scaffold : the last-born of the house of Hohenstaufen.

Frederick II alone, the last Germanic prince to found a state on Italian soil, was granted the fulfilment of German dreams. His success was based not on his Sicilian people alone, but also on the Empire, and on Divine Providence—as he habitually stated—and finally, and chiefly, on himself. He also might have faded out as a mere visionary, a sublime imperial ghost, had he not had his roots in reality and his feet firmly planted on mother earth, had he not wisely understood the art of drawing more and more on her reserves of strength, while he reached up to steal the fire from Heaven. Frederick II found a land of people that believed in him and understood him, though his majesty might frown threateningly down on them from distant regions, a people prepared to follow him blindly—whether from love or fear.

Every great ruler needs such a basis, a land in which his life is rooted, a land which, be it never so limited and small, yet begets men of his own stamp whom he can make lords of the world. Thus the Macedonian nobles held sway in Asia, the Spanish Grandees throughout the wide Hapsburg lands of Charles, and under Napoleon the Marshals of France rode Europe on a curb. Earlier Emperors lacked a nation, but they had their race, later Emperors had their households. The strength of the Germanic races—Saxons, Franks and Swabians —was flickering out ; they had let it stream from them into the outer world, into the Empire ; they had no impulse or desire, perhaps no power, for further wanderings to follow the Emperor as a whole clan wherever he might journey. As mercenaries they hired themselves to the Emperors in growing numbers, but mercenaries are not a people, and their obedience is radically different from the devotion of deeply-rooted racial loyalty.

Obedience, unquestioning devotion, and the mass-strength of a people was a prime necessity for Frederick if he was to get new blood into the Empire. A people and a state were peculiarly necessary to him personally. An Englishman has recently said of him that this Hohenstaufen was a man of such a personality that " a whole community of men, a sect, a party, or a nation, could look back to him as their prophet, founder or liberator." Frederick II, indeed, seemed by nature specially destined to be the founder of his own state. Only such a creation of his own could impose that restraint and moderation that was needed by a man who had grown up an orphan in a strange land, without the discipline of home or family or clan. This freedom from repression, this personal liberty—such as no predecessor had ever known—was precisely what gave Frederick such an immense advantage over the intellectually-fettered age in which he lived.   To it he owed his clearness and breadth of vision, his mental alertness and flexibility, his knowledge of tongues and absence of prejudice, and that immediate personal relation to God which enabled him to outgrow the bonds of the Church and left him free to stride along the shortest path, heedless of everything save state necessity.   The unique endowments of this Emperor, if they were not to be frittered away in dangerous versatilities, needed some firm framework within which to ply their creative tasks, needed a firmly organised state of his own devising, whose laws were his laws, and whose laws, for the sake of this state he had begotten, he himself must willingly obey.   A ruler of this type could submit to no fetters but those of his own forging.   His beloved Sicilian inheritance, the ancient kingdom of his Norman ancestors, offered him the opportunity to make what laws he would.

" Sicily is the Mother of Tyrants."   Almost cynically—for in Christian eyes the " tyrant " was the embodiment of Satan —Frederick II wrote this phrase of Orosius at the head of one of his later edicts.   With sound instinct for the practical, rather than from conscious wisdom, first the followers of Guiscard and now the Hohenstaufens harked back in many points to the statecraft of the old Greek tyrants of Sicily.   Now was the moment when a wise despot was more sorely needed than ever before in history.

The geographical unity of the Sicilian peninsula, bounded on three sides by the sea and bolted and barred on the North by Frederick's chain of fortresses, was the only unity he found to hand.   Corresponding to this we may reckon the unity of will and power in her ruler, the Emperor himself.   The most important link between the Ruler and the Land was missing still —the unity of the nation : which demanded as a condition precedent a unity of blood and speech, of faith and feast, of history and of law. The most wonderful task that can be set to a creator here awaited the Hohenstaufen Emperor : the Creation of a People—that is the creation of people—a task impossible to any but a tyrant, and a tyrant who believes himself divine, and who, more important still, can make other men believe him to be God. For every command and every utterance of the godlike majesty must be sacred and the populace must sink into the dust before his " oracles," a word Frederick II himself employed at times.

Such a state of affairs was only possible in Sicily, for Sicily was accustomed to it, and this rich, fertile soil peaked and pined without her tyrants. The Sicilians—half oriental in origin—worshipped their ruler as a God, and rightly so, for in a land, as indolent by nature as luxuriant, the tyrant was in fact the Saviour too.

When the Emperor Henry VI entered Palermo in solemn state with his victorious army the people flung themselves down with their faces to the ground, shunning the sight of their Lord's majesty. Under the *reges fortunati*, the Norman kings, prostration had been the custom, and it may have persisted, strengthened under Arab rule, since Narses, the Conqueror of the Goths, had brought the country under Byzantium. Sicily then was well accustomed to fall on her knees to any wielder of power ; it is easy to imagine how this ruler-worship would gain in intensity when, instead of a Norman Count or ordinary prince, these glorious days brought her the Roman Emperor for her King. According to Roman Law the Emperor was *Divus*, in whose person the whole Empire, from of old, worshipped the symbol of the Godhead, and before whom even the Christian knights, the Templars and their brothers of St. John were wont to bow the knee. In Sicily, therefore, Frederick II could count on finding the willing self-surrender that he needed.

Sicily had been the dream-paradise of the Germanic tribes, Goethe still terms it " the key to everything." Sicily, therefore, with Apulia, was the Land of Promise to an Emperor who sought to realise his dreams. When Frederick II crossed the sea on his crusade and saw Palestine and Syria, the " promised land " of Holy Scripture, he remarked—with his characteristically blasphemous wit—that Jehovah could not have seen his own hereditary Sicily, Apulia, and the Terra Laboris. If he had he could not so greatly have overrated this land that he was giving to the Jews. The south Italian kingdom where Frederick had spent his childhood, which he had known from infancy, remained through life his one true love. He would converse with " his Apulia " as with a living person, a beloved woman, and only in the lap of his hereditary land could he feel himself at home. When Napoleon said " I have only one passion and one love : France. I sleep with her, never has she forsaken me, she pours forth blood and treasure on my behalf . . ." he was expressing kindred feelings. Frederick II addressed to the land he loved, who gave herself to him, words of affection and of imagery from the Bible, and the poetry of his time and from the lyrics of the Orient. His southern kingdom is the " apple of his eye "; " the loveliness of his land exceeds all earthly sweetness "; " it is a haven amidst the floods and a pleasure-garden amidst a waste of thorns "; to it he turns " full of yearning, when he sails to and fro upon the Empire's seas." " Yet a little while to assure the highest victory to our titles and an end to your burdens and we promise our assured return ; then rejoicing in our mutual love we shall gratify you with our constant presence whom now we can only caress intermittently with letters." Thus he once wrote from Upper Italy. And again : " Though the multitude of peoples who happily breathe an atmosphere of peace under our rule, preoccupy our thoughts without intermission, yet impelled by a certain privilege of love we shall vigilantly devote constant thought to our own beloved people of Sicily, whose inheritance is more glorious in our eyes than all our other possessions, that she may be graced with peace and may flourish in the days of Caesar Augustus."

Such was Frederick's attitude to Sicily. " Sicily," in his mouth, always embraces the " two Sicilies "; not island Sicily alone, but also Apulia and the southern half of the Italian peninsula. With the Sicilians he feels himself completely at one. As the Jewish God out of the multitude of peoples on the earth chose himself one—it is not possible to exaggerate the exactness with which Frederick pressed home the analogy—so

the Emperor, King of Kings, Lord of the Imperium, chose him
the Apulian-Sicilian people. Sicily is his promised land, her
people are his chosen people, on whom he leans " as the head
on a cushion for repose "; " the radiance of their faithfulness
surrounds us like a star whose light grows brighter still as time
flows by." He professes that sympathy with the Sicilians
" which springs from the graciousness of tender love which a
father bears his sons "—the word is worth noting ; the hack-
neyed phrase " Father of his people " dates from Frederick.
A later writing expresses more completely the living unity of
ruler and ruled : " We have chosen our domain of Sicily for
our own amongst all other lands, and taken the whole kingdom
as the place of our abiding, for we—radiant with the glory of
the title of the Caesars—yet feel it no ignoble thing to be called
' a man of Apulia.' Borne hither and thither as we are on
imperial floods far from the havens and harbours of Sicily, we
feel ourselves a pilgrim and a wanderer from home. . . . Ever
have we found your wishes one with ours ; your willing and
not-willing ever like unto our own." These were no light
words. The assurances of love for Sicily, however, of identity
with her people would have remained words had Frederick not
cemented them with deeds.

His early years as king had betrayed little of all this, and no
such expressions then fell from him. As befitted his youth he
had then faced the task of purging his kingdom of the vampires
and parasites who were draining it of blood and marrow. By
force and guile he had combated many, if scattered, forces and
brought a preliminary order out of chaos. He had provided a
scaffolding and framework for the state, prescribed the lines of
future development, outlined the external unity of the state and
laid the foundation of much else. But all this was, as it were,
the preparation of the soil in which ten years later he was to
sow the seed. The second state was the work of the mature
philosopher and lawgiver, who " wove of the whole the warp
and weft," who impregnated the living state with his spirit and
his law and called his creature into life—" as the soul creates a
body for itself," to quote from a *Mirror of Princes*. Having
created a space in which to work, Frederick's scheme was to
fill it with himself as the law-giving Caesar, who followed the

deed of force by the deed of love . . . the " prime love," as
Dante extols it in the Law-Giver Justinian.

Here was the opportunity for the Hohenstaufen Emperor to
equate himself for the first time, not in dignity and office alone,
as Law Giver with the Roman Caesars. He could frankly not
compete in deeds of war. But the Caesars had excelled also in
intellectual deeds and acts—their activity is summed up in the
formula *arma et leges*—and in this he could approach them as
no western Christian potentate had done.

From the beginning Frederick's position had been unique
in linking the Roman Empire with Sicily. Both the Hohenstaufens and the Norman Kings were far in advance of other
European princes in emulating the Roman and Byzantine
Emperors. But however much Guiscard's heirs, as kings and
despots of Sicily, might deck themselves with Justinian's
imperial formulas, the plumes were obviously borrowed, the
splendid mantle was a size too large ; till the day came when
no mere Norman kinglet but a Roman Emperor sat upon the
throne of Sicily. On the other hand : however vigorously
Barbarossa might assert the absolute validity of Roman Law,
however effectively Henry VI might impose the feudal system
throughout the Roman world, however these two Emperors
might reach the highest summits, upborne by the glamour of
the imperial name, neither had its root in earth. In all their
gigantic Imperium there was not the tiniest province in which
they could rule with the unconditional authority of a Norman
King. Barbarossa deduced the theory of unconditional imperial authority from Roman law and no one questioned his
abstract idea—but in the length and breadth of Germany there
was no single village in which he could have put his theory
into practice.

Frederick II had never laid such emphasis on the pronouncements of Roman law and their recognition. The Normans had
made their validity in Sicily a matter of course, and the Emperor's availing himself of them attracted no comment. The
unique and fortunate coincidence that the heir of Norman
despots was at the same time Roman Emperor, and that a

medieval Christian Imperator not only claimed but exercised
the intimate despotic power of an absolute monarch over a real
land and real people, enabled Frederick II to employ Roman
imperial titles, formulas and gestures with unaffected freedom
and sangfroid.   He differed from his predecessors not so much
by a greater mass of knowledge or a more exact acquaintance
with the writers of antiquity, as by the fact that in his case the
premisses fitted the facts.   It is by no means accidental that
Frederick's first really close approximation to the Caesars
occurred in Sicily.   There were three Roman Emperors whom
he explicitly took as his models : Justinian, Augustus, and
Julius Caesar.

The Middle Ages took Justinian—with Scipio perhaps, and
Cato and Trajan—as the symbol of Justice, the *minister Domini*
who codified Roman Law ; Dante treats him as a sacred figure,
and he was the inevitable pattern for Frederick the Law-Giver.
Immediately after concluding peace with the Pope the Emperor
set himself to unify the laws of Sicily.   In August 1231, at
Melfi, he published his famous Constitutions—the fruit of
strenuous and prolonged activity on the part of the Imperial
High Courts.   This collection, representing a sort of State Law
and Constitutional Law, was based first on ancient Norman
ordinances, some of which had been collected orally from the
lips of aged inhabitants, secondly on earlier legislation of
Frederick's, and finally on a large body of new laws (further
increased at a later date), all blended into one coherent whole
by the Emperor and his colleagues.   The great codification of
a state's constitutional law—the first of the Middle Ages ; indeed, the first since Justinian—was deservedly admired by the
world, and annotated by scholars as a work that would be
authoritative for centuries.   Its influence on the later legislation
of the absolute monarchies of Europe can by no means be
ignored.   The emulation of Justinian was of course obvious in
the mere fact of collecting laws, but it was even more potent
in the whole conception and arrangement of this amazing work.
The spirit of Justinian informed the whole and communicated
itself to his Hohenstaufen successor.   The Late-Roman had
still a vivid feeling for firm construction and chastened form,
side by side with an intensified Byzantine-Christian pomp,

which betrayed itself in the details as well as in the whole. Justinian opened his digest with a rehearsal of his titles as Triumphator, " Alanicus, Goticus, Vandalicus "—which the Middle Ages speciously took to mean a recounting of conquered races. Similarly the Frederick's Book of Laws bore the magnificent and haughty title :

IMPERATOR FRIDERICUS SECUNDUS.
ROMANORUM CAESAR SEMPER AUGUSTUS.
ITALICUS SICULUS HIEROSOLYMITANUS ARELATENSIS.
FELIX VICTOR AC TRIUMPHATOR.

This had weight as well as style. It indicated not alone a claim to equality with Justinian but also the immense importance which Frederick attached to his work and to himself, though his Lawbook was to serve the Sicilian kingdom only, not the Empire. The imitation of Justinian was evident too in the solemn Proœmium with which the book was prefaced ; in the rehearsal of the origin of rulers' and judges' powers ; in the dedication of it as a sacrifice to the God of the State ; in the devotion of the first laws to heretics and Church protection ; and in many other details on the Justinian model.

After Justinian, the Emperor of Law, Frederick II's next hero was Augustus, renowned as Emperor of Peace. The Augustan age was the scriptural " fulness of time " and the only *aurea aetas* of peace since Paradise. For the Son of God had desired to be born under the rule of Augustus, Prince of Peace, to live as man under his laws, to die under his decree as Roman Emperor. In the days of this great Emperor, the contemporary of Christ, himself celebrated as the Saviour, the Redeemer, the SOTER, the constitution of the world had been perfect, because Augustus had rendered to every man his own, and Peace had therefore reigned.

Frederick II conceived it his peculiar mission to bring again this Augustan peace-epoch and the divine organisation of the world. If this order could once more be restored his own day would again be the " fulness of time," in which *pax et justitia*, the only end of earthly rule, would reign over the whole earth as in the days of Augustus. This faith was not unnatural.

The thirteenth century awaited daily, as no other had ever done, the end of the world, and the prophecies foretold : the end of the world should be middle and beginning, should be alike redemption and creation. People hoped therefore that the Golden Age was at hand and the peace-era of Augustus, and Frederick II exerted himself therefore that his hereditary kingdom " might be graced with peace and might flourish in the days of Caesar Augustus."

Frederick felt another bond with Augustus apart from world peace. Once, and once only, the Saviour himself had recognised the Roman Empire as rightfully existing, when he said " Render to Caesar the things that are Caesar's." Solemnly Frederick pointed therefore to that moment as the justification of his imperial office, when our Lord " looking on the portrait of the coin for the payment of tribute indicated in sight of all other kings the lofty height of the imperial destiny." According to the interpretation of the day the coin most probably bore the image of Caesar Augustus, the Saviour Emperor. Augustus coins were also in fact struck under Tiberius, bearing the Roman eagle on the reverse. When Frederick II, therefore, now reorganised the Sicilian currency he minted gold coins which he not only termed " Augustales," but in which he deliberately imitated the coins of Augustus. The obverse shows Frederick's head and shoulders, wearing the imperial mantle, a diadem of laurel or of rays crowning his head, and the circular legend IMP / ROM / CESAR / AUG. On the reverse the Roman Eagle, a perfect replica it seems of that on the Augustan coins, and round it the name : FRIDERICUS. Frederick was following Augustus in the smallest details, and the name Augustus was repeated on the eagle-side. Frederick's love of form no doubt prompted him for purely aesthetic reasons to revert to the antique, but a far stronger motive was his sober practical sense, so strangely wedded to his love of speculative thought : if his was the " fulness of time " then everything must be as far as possible identically as it was at the time of the redemption. This renewal of the antique was for Frederick, as also for the Renaissance, the practical expression of a sincere conviction : namely, that the age of Christ, and with it the age of Augustus, had come again.

That Frederick, with all this, possessed the independence to
substitute his own portrait for that of the Soter-Emperor, while
otherwise exactly copying the coins of Augustus, is the most
amazing phenomenon of all. And from one coinage to the next
it is clear and clearer that he did so, and that he modified the
eagle with the retracted claws to express something of the
greater restraint and tension of his own day. He dared in fact
to be Roman, simply and naturally, after his own fashion. It
will be a question to be answered later what significance underlay this " portrait "-likeness, and why it was indispensable.
One point is obvious already : these beautifully stamped coins
with their exquisite high relief—the most lovely mintage of the
Middle Ages till far on into Renaissance times—instead of a
symbolic impersonal head, instead of a Christ, or a Lamb, or a
Cross, such as are usual on other coins of the period, bear in
unmistakable lines the likeness of the reigning Caesar Augustus
and the whole eagle skilfully wrought in gold (a metal which had
almost ceased to be used for specie). In all ages of faith the
value of a coin has been guaranteed in one way or another by
the State God in whom people believed : amongst primitive
folk the money bore the Totem-animal ; amongst the Greeks
the God of the Polis ; correspondingly in Rome the Divine
Emperors, and in the Middle Ages the Saviour himself, under
one of many signs and symbols, stood surety for the value of
the coin. On these golden Augustales of Frederick II is not
the smallest Christian sign, not the tiniest of crosses on sceptre,
orb, or crown ; independent of the Christian God there reigns
here a Divus who summons men to faith in him, like a new
Caesar Augustus.

Justinian, Emperor of Law; Augustus, Emperor of Peace,
were Frederick's models ; peace and law ; " two sisters in
close embrace "; *pax et justitia*, a formula which in endless
variation eternally recurs, defining the purpose of a State.
This Two-in-one-ness permeates the whole Sicilian Book
of Laws : after the preliminary introduction the first and
weightiest section is divided into two distinct parts, the first
concerns internal peace : *Pax*; the second legal jurisdiction :
Justitia. The Lawbook itself Frederick called the "*Liber
Augustalis*" in honour of Augustan majesty ; and the book,

which was published in September 1231, bears on it the date of August.

Justinian and Augustus were for Frederick embodiments and symbols of certain features and organisations of the State, but another figure hovered before him, more human than *Pax* or *Justitia*, a man and a ruler of men : Julius Caesar. In later years Frederick apostrophises " yon glorious Julius, first of Caesars." Whether intentionally or by accident Frederick was following the example of the genial, open-hearted Julius, when he commanded that his birthday, which immediately followed the Saviour's, should be observed as a public holiday throughout the length and breadth of the Sicilian kingdom. Julius Caesar had been the first to make his birthday a festival—the omission to observe which is said to have been punishable with death. Perhaps this was in the Hohenstaufen's mind, perhaps he also had visions of Caesar's legendary hospitality. Be that as it may, the Emperor will have fed tens of thousands on his birthday, for at the festivities in the little town of San Germano alone, over 500 had been entertained with bread and wine and meat in the open market-place. Bible precedents may have influenced him also. In any case the Emperor's birthday was the first feast day common to the whole Sicilian people : to Greek and Saracen, to Christian and to Jew.

Law—Order—Humanity—typified in the three Caesar-figures, a trinity that embraces every function of a State. The Emperor's Sicilian Lawbook, the *Liber Augustalis*, teaches what forces, the *virtutes*, are potent to produce these three. True, they are obscured by scholastic-juristic conventions of expression, but they are nevertheless undoubtedly forceful. For these basic influences went to create the first purely secular state, freed from the bonds of the Church. This was the beginning of State-making and its influence, though blunted and obscured, has come down to us to-day through autocracy and bureaucracy. Dante immortalises the picture of the Sicilian imperial State in his lofty doctrine of the monarchic unity of the world and the divine kingdom upon earth which this most spiritual of poets fought for, with a passion as great as that which inspired this most gifted of Emperors, his forerunner.

I

In the case of a document so important as the Lawbook of Melfi, which has even been styled " The Birth Certificate of Modern Bureaucracy," the moment of birth must challenge attention.   The function of all secular rule in the Middle Ages was defined in the recurrent formula *Pax et Justitia*.   If Justice reigned there was Peace ; if Peace existed it was the sign that Justice reigned.   All rule was directed to the securing of justice; justice was an absolute thing, a gift of God, an end in itself. The earthly State—a product of the Fall—existed with one task before it : to preserve this gift of God.   This vitally distinguishes the medieval from the later commonwealth ; justice did not exist to preserve the State, but the State existed to preserve justice.   To quote St. Augustine " true justice reigns only in that State whose founder and ruler is the Christ."   Such a State, whose *raison d'être* was justice, was now completely transcended.

It is necessary to bear in mind that the Hohenstaufen Emperor lived at the end of the millennium which conceived justice to be the sole object of a State—an object to which Renaissance statesmen were notoriously somewhat indifferent—in the zenith of the " century of jurisprudence," which marked the close of that millennium, and which left its mark on Frederick, as surely as he left his on jurisprudence.   We must bear in mind his visit to Bologna ; Roffredo of Benevento ; the foundation of the University of Naples.   The designation of the hundred years that ended the Middle Ages, 1150-1250, as the " age of law " is amply justified.   Since the days of Gratian and Irnerius and the memorable resumption of Roman Law by Barbarossa which was symbolic of the spirit of the time, the world has never shown such genuine interest in any intellectual sphere as then in the science of jurisprudence.   It is true that this passion ultimately merged in madness.   In the late thirteenth century men began to versify Justinian's Institutes, as in our day they have rhymed Kant's *Critique of Pure Reason*. Such follies at least indicate that there was little left for serious study to do.   Jurisprudence by no means ceased with the

century, but the material was diligently sifted by the industry
of commentators who became progressively more sterile.   The
dawning Renaissance opened up spheres of knowledge so
infinitely varied and so urgently important that secular learning
was no longer almost synonymous with legal learning, as it was
in Frederick's day.   Jurisprudence, the study of law, indicates
the beginning of secular, non-theological, education.

The Church, on the other hand, maintained her lead even in
the pursuit of jurisprudence : all the important Popes of this
century—Alexander III, Honorius III, Gregory IX, Innocent
IV—were jurists ; a knowledge of canon law came to absorb
theology, or rather : theology and law-mongering came to be
dangerous rivals within the Church, and jurisprudence even became seriously harmful.   Hence Dante wrathfully calls curses
on the collection of Decretals, because from poring eternally
over the thumbmarked manuscripts Pope and Cardinals
had forgotten Nazareth.   Numbers of law-collections now
began to appear.   A beginning had long ago been made with
the small but important Assize Collection of the Norman
King, Roger II.   The great papal collection of Decretals which
Innocent III had begun and which was published by Gregory
IX in 1234—" following the example of Justinian " and " omit-
ting the superfluous "—was almost contemporaneous with
Frederick's great codification of his first state and constitutional
law.

It is a curious fact that an age which hourly expected the end
of the world should have seen legal erudition the fashion everywhere, as if a knowledge of law could avert the Last Judgment.
In all the welter of law-study there was only one work really
outstanding and pre-eminent : Frederick's *Liber Augustalis*.
Certain hypotheses were here so fused that *Justitia* herself
celebrated her apotheosis in the Sicilian Book of Laws.   In
virtue of his office as Emperor and Supreme Judge, Frederick II
placed himself at the head of the whole *Justitia* movement,
creating by this means a purely secular State, which, while free
from the spiritual authority of the Church, should present a
complete whole vitalised by spiritual forces.

Corresponding to the duality of Temporal and Eternal that
dominated the Middle Ages, people recognised as a matter of

course two irreconcilable types of law : an eternal law of God
and Nature and a positive or human law, always at variance
with the former.   This human law valid in earthly states, imperfect as are all earthly things, was based in part on the
traditional, customary and popular law ; in part on the precepts
of Holy Writ, which as revelations from God approximated
more nearly to Divine law ; thirdly, in more recent times on
Roman law which was sanctified and recognised because the
Saviour had submitted to it.   The princes' business was
primarily to maintain peace, and since any alteration in the law
inevitably injured somebody and brought disorder, the princes
as guardians of the peace had the secondary task of upholding
the law.   Necessary alterations of the law were therefore pre-
ferably based on a renewal of old laws that had been forgotten
or misused, and princely edicts were represented rather as the
restoration or enforcement of old forgotten laws ; no one would
have dared to claim that he himself evolved a " new law."   The
medieval state was therefore " law maintaining, law-conserving,
but scarcely law-creating," and this substantially describes the
ruler's duties : above all things to maintain and conserve the
laws.

According to the graduated constitution of the medieval
world, the Emperor was quite particularly called to exercise this
preservative function.   The correct phrase was " What God is
in Heaven that is the Emperor on Earth."   From the days of
Charlemagne the Roman Emperors were the image of God the
Father ; the summit of earthly authority, an image of the Ruler
of the Hierarchy of Heaven, and as protectors and preservers
of earthly law an image of the God who sustains the eternal,
immutable Law of Nature.

The Christian Emperor of the Middle Ages appeared therefore as the image of God the Father, Ruler and Preserver of the
World.   What was to be done when suddenly into this serene
and image-like repose, there burst a new, young, stirring force ?
When a spark from Heaven suddenly leaped out upon the
Emperor enthroned in clouds, and he who had been an image
of God the Father suddenly became an image also of the
Divine Son, the Mediator and Judge, yea the Redeemer !   No
longer guardian and preserver only, but bringer and inter-

mediary, source of divine and natural law, the Emperor brought
God's Law into his State, brought Heaven down to earth as
Holy Law, as *Justitia*. It remained the Church's service to
dispense the Holy Spirit.

An old Germanic proverb had it that God is the beginning
of all law, and St. Augustine taught that " God is the fount of
Justice." If the theorists of the days that followed the last
Hohenstaufen had substituted the " Emperor " in these two
sayings that would exactly describe the actual teaching of
Frederick's *Liber Augustalis*. The Ruler, in virtue of *Justitia*,
as the Priest in virtue of Grace, is mediator between God and
Man. Or, to express it differently, *Justitia* is the link between
God and the Emperor as between Emperor and people, for
" earthly law lies below the ruler, as divine law lies above him."
This expresses more cumbrously what is concisely implied in
the illuminating phrases of the " Constitutions " with which
Kaiser Frederick introduced some seventy laws concerning the
new order of things : " The Emperor must therefore be at
once FATHER AND SON, LORD AND SERVANT of *Justitia*." This
can bear no other interpretation—in the light of the whole
doctrine of the Logos—than that the Emperor had comprehended and represented the living God as Right and Law, as
Justitia. According to the revived Roman Law the Emperor
was indubitably the " *lex animata in terris*." Nothing less than
this mystic identity of the Emperor with the living God, the
Fountain of *Justitia*, qualifies him to propound law and so
expound right. The learned Roffredo of Benevento, Frederick
II's legal authority, formulated it thus : " the Emperor bases his
right on a gift of grace bestowed by heaven," and the Emperor
himself, following the Codices of Justinian, frequently proclaims
that he " receives his impulse (*motus*) from heavenly reflection."
The Emperor thus becomes himself the fountain of *Justitia* in
the State : through God and like unto God ; he is the creator
of law, not only the preserver of law ; he is the " Founder of
a new Law," for he declares that new law is begotten of him
daily, and requires that in all directions throughout the kingdom
the standard of law shall flow from the Emperor's court as
streams flow from a spring. He is the proclaimer of laws,
whose tongue is unloosed. The concluding words of the whole

collection run : " Posterity must believe of us in centuries to come that we collected this Book of Laws not merely to serve our own renown, but rather to wipe out in our day, the injustice of earlier times during which the voice of justice has been silent." Frederick here referred not merely to the injustice of earlier times but to the actual "dumbness" of justice, the lack of law-creation, as is clear from the introductory words which, as in other works of art, constitute a dedication to God and an appeal : " We hope therefore to render to God from whom we hold all that we possess, the talent he hath entrusted to us increased an hundredfold, and finally we render homage to Jesus Christ and we bring him a sacrifice of our lips by the statutes of law and the cult of justice."

That Frederick II felt his life and tongue set free to proclaim the law is thus almost an act of personal grace. Frederick certainly possessed a peculiar personal aptitude for law-giving. His enormous knowledge and his untiring research into the eternal laws of nature lent him a unique qualification for taking the mean position between the divine law, the law of nature, and the positive law, the law of man. The Emperor frequently boasts that he—in contrast to those who judge " without glancing at the facts of Nature "—has himself " studied the true science of Nature's laws." His knowledge of natural law now reinforces his unity with God and further established his infallibility ; for he goes on to say " therefore we scorn to err." The Pope under the inspiration of the Holy Ghost may be infallible in matters of faith, similarly the Emperor " overfilled by *Justitia* " is infallible in matters of law. In accordance with this imperial infallibility, Frederick adopted, as the Norman Kings before him had done, the sentence of Roman Law : " to discuss the Emperor's judgments, decrees, and statutes is sacrilege," a sentence that was so vital to the constitution of the whole state that Frederick boldly quoted it to the Pope when he ventured to criticise some measure of the Emperor's.

The Emperor was the pinnacle of the world's structure, who received directly unto himself the rays of " *Justitia* looking down from Heaven " and radiated them forth again on judges and jurists

—hence he issued Sicilian laws as Emperor, not as Sicilian king
—and by his knowledge of Nature's laws he was able to interpret
the divine and natural law : yet, the relation of God to Emperor
created no circuit. In the electric relation of creditor and
debtor the surety is a necessary third if power is to be transmitted. Frederick II now sought his third source—beside God
and Nature—in the earth-born right of the people, which he
focussed in his own person by the Roman *lex regia*. In such
majestic Latin as had not for centuries been heard, in which the
deep Christian rhythm blended with the lofty dignity of
the Roman Caesar he wrote the almost untranslatable words :
" *Non sine grandi consilio et deliberatione perpensa condendae
legis jus et imperium in Romanum Principem lege regia transtulere
Quirites.*"

Contemporaries and commentators did not fail to be impressed by the grandiose diction of these words in which the
Emperor recalled that according to Roman royal law the Roman
people, the *Quirites*, handed over to the *Princeps* the entire
power and the right of making laws. Reverting thus to the
critical procedure at the establishment of the Roman empire,
Frederick II—the last Caesar in this akin to the first—obliterates
the people's own authority and lawgiving power or, more
exactly, absorbs it into himself ; himself the divine source of
Justitia. All dignities and powers and mights : God's, Nature's
and the People's, Frederick thus accumulated in his own person
and united in himself. God, People, and Emperor were the
origins of Law which united in Frederick and informed him.

God ; the Emperor as emanation, as Son of God ; *Justitia* ;
this was the new secular trinity which dominated the state of
Frederick, without prejudice to the Church—and which found
in the Emperor its living representative, " Law incarnate upon
earth." The whole juristic official-state of Frederick II was
based on the cult of this trinity and here we begin to gain a
preliminary glimpse of the Hohenstaufen's great achievement.
God, who for over ten centuries had manifested himself only
in miracles, and as spirit had permeated space, was now captive
to this Emperor, and as far as the state was concerned was
converted from an intangible omnipotent Benevolence into a
tangible, comprehensible state law, *Justitia* . . . had become a

" State God," much as, in the time of Constantine Christ had been elevated into the State God in succession to Mithra. Frederick II had wedded the God of the other world to the *Justitia* of this : *Deus et Justitia* is the recurrent formula ; and thus, and thus alone, was it possible to comprehend the one universal God as a particular God of the state—to represent him, appeal to him, worship him—without the Church's aid. God had been forcefully brought down into the state, not merely the state exalted to a world-shunning universal Deity.

Now that God as Justice had become a state Godhead in the narrowest sense, it behoved the Emperor to transform the state judicial service into worship. Pope Innocent had averred : " God is honoured in us, when we are honoured " ; Kaiser Frederick countered this with : " our subjects serve and please God and the Emperor when they serve Justice " ; almost exactly as Roman law had formulated it : " He who honours *Justitia*, does homage to the holy things of God." This dictated certain observances of outward service. The law entitled *Cultus Justitiae* begins : " The Cult of Justice demands Silence." While popes and priests dispensed God as Grace to the people in wonder and magic, the Emperor and his judges were to the faithful the channels of God as Law, as Rule, thus actualising the theory quoted by the Normans from the Roman digests that judges and jurists were " Priests of Justice." It was completely justified therefore when people not only spoke of the Empire as the " Temple of Justice," but went so far as to talk of the Imperial Church, *imperialis ecclesia*. Down to the smallest details this imperial Justice-State mirrors the clerical God-State which Innocent III had erected with his elaborate hierarchy. Out of the Pope's *plenitudo potestatis* God's Grace is conveyed to the people through bishops and priests ; even so from the Emperor God's Justice through judges and officials. A living power of immediately divine origin thus coursed through the veins of the State.

All the metaphors of the Book of Laws point in the same direction. The Emperor was the sole source of Justice, and on the throne of Justice he who weaves the web of Justice takes the highest seat. His Justice flows as in a flood ; with the scales of Justice he weighs to each his right ; he interprets the

law and resolves the problems of the jurists and issues laws to
end their differences.   He must find new remedies daily for
new vices, for amid the changes of time and circumstance the
ancient laws do not suffice to pulverise the vicious with untiring
hammer blows.   From him Justice flows through the kingdom
in rivulets and those who distribute his rule throughout the
State are the imperial officials who take the helm in the Emperor's
stead, and are themselves the Emperor's image, even as he himself is the image of God.

These officials were no longer feudal retainers of varying
degree, but men selected by the Emperor's favour from every
rank, who held their posts not as a *beneficium*, a fief to possess,
but as an *officium*, a service to fulfil ; in Church phraseology :
they discharged the service of God.   Since these law-learned
officials were appointed by a special act of the Emperor's grace,
which only the Emperor could exercise—the " co-knowers of
our knowledge "—he called them—the purchase of office in
the State was forbidden as simony.   The official remains an
official, as long as the Emperor considers him worthy and the
charisma rests on him, irrespective of his personal worthiness
or unworthiness.   " It is sacrilege to debate whether that man
is worthy whom the Emperor has chosen and appointed."

The choice of officials appertains to the Emperor alone and
their offices are not transferable to others.   There exist no
hereditary offices.   None may dare, without the Emperor's
permission, to appoint an official, and the severest penalties
wait on any attempt to do so : the town in which such a deed
occurs is destroyed for ever, the inhabitants are reduced to
servitude and the office holder is beheaded.   The Emperor,
however, will see to it that there shall be officials enough and
to spare that justice may be freely available to all and that the
Emperor's " sacred wishes " may be made known.   The
officials were to celebrate divine service, the cult of Justice by
which they rendered service to God.   The service of the Courts
which officials held daily, and the Emperor himself three times
a week was a sacred act and therefore commands silence, while
the officials worship Justice and sacred justice is meted to
petitioners.   This service is rendered free of cost, as the
Church renders her services of grace, for the Emperor's

generosity and graciousness supplies salaries for the officials who conduct the *justitiae mysterium*.

There is absolutely no justification for taking at less than its face value the awed solemnity which breathes from every line of the Book of Laws. There are ample witnesses who describe the Emperor himself when he celebrated the *sacratissimum ministerium*, as was his custom in later years. Every new cult evolves new rites, and so we find here forms and ceremonies and customs which have never before been seen in the West, and have never prevailed anywhere in this combination. The *Sacra Majestas* of the Emperor was enthroned on inaccessible heights, over his head was suspended a gigantic crown ; all who approached must prostrate themselves ; the whole public remained prostrate for a time before the *Divus Augustus*, who remained in the background like the very Godhead. His voice was seldom heard ; before him stood the *Logothetes*, who announced the order which the Emperor confirmed by a gesture of his hand. This spokesman played the oracle to the Emperor's sacred and inspired decision, which was, in certain circumstances, accompanied by the tinkling of a bell. Such was the " most sacred service " and mystery : the High Court —like the High Mass—of the Justice-God-Emperor.

This is a suitable moment to recall the fore-runners of Frederick II and his remarkable Cult of Justice. King Roger II and Barbarossa contributed both to the ritual and to the conception : the Norman by the retention of Byzantine ceremonies and by his creative achievements as lawgiver in a newly-conquered country : the Hohenstaufen by his sanctification both of the Emperor and his office, deduced from Roman Law. After Barbarossa it became usual to designate the Empire as " Holy," and " Holy " too the palaces, documents, and edicts of the Emperor ; the Emperor became *Sacra Majestas*, *Perennitas*, *Numen* ; his predecessors *Divi*. Frederick owed most, however, in this respect, to Pope Innocent III. For Innocent had dinned into the ears of the world that judge and priest are one ; priesthood is royal, and kingship is priestly. Innocent was the first to imbue judgeship and kingship with the spirit of the High Priest, which Frederick now turned to secular account. This Pope who was himself a *verus imperator* had reduced the Emperor to a priestly go-between, and had obliterated the idea of the Emperor's figure as image of God which had prevailed till Barbarossa. Finally Innocent's emancipation of the Priest State from all secular tutelage showed the way in which a secular Law State might be erected, spiritually emancipated and independent of the Church—whereby the gulf between yawned deeper than before. The domain of the non-material, which hitherto had belonged wholly to the Church, had now been rent asunder by Frederick, and while the domain of the soul remained finally with the Church, the New State claimed the mind. Over against the Church's Hierarchy of Grace was set the State's Hierarchy of Law.

Another interesting possibility suggests itself. Roman law, it is true, called the judge also a priest ; but with Frederick's most unusual knowledge of Muslim customs, in all his lengthy conversations with Fakhru'd Din, it cannot have escaped his notice, that amongst Mussulmans the holy men, the ʿulamā, were jurists and priests in one. An innovation in Western speech also contributed. Since about the beginning of the " juristic century " the word " layman " had come to be used not only as the opposite of priest (*sacerdos*) ; it began to mean the man who is not learned in the law and to indicate the opposite also of clerk (*clericus*). It was as a nursery for such law-clerks that the Emperor Frederick had founded the University of Naples.

Frederick thus gathered together in a fortunate moment many existing tendencies and evolved the triumphant solemn cult of Justice, God of the Secular State. Justice was of course not the " whole God," but she was one emanation of God, the state manifestation of the Deity. The full importance of this is obvious if we reflect on the scholastic problem of the day—the antithesis between Faith and Knowledge. Justice becomes that manifestation of God which is comprehended by reason and by knowledge, and which is operative within the state as Living Law. Grace, on the other hand, comprehensible by faith alone, remains the Church's manifestation of the same God. The mental revolution effected by Frederick II is self-evident. There are two possible spiritual cults of the Deity—Law or

Magic. After the reign for over one thousand years of a God
manifesting himself mainly in wonders and miracles, a God
begins to appear in full daylight, outside and alongside the
Church, a God who can only be recognised by wide-awake
intelligence, as Law. Here the whole tension is expressed
between Church and Empire, both immediately related to God,
a tension which reaches its culmination in Dante.

The Deity was no longer solely dependent on the priest-
wrought miracle for his appearance in the flesh in the *Civitas
Dei*, the Church ; he was also summoned into the State, and
there by the Emperor rendered incarnate in the Law. The
radically new element in this conception was the fact that the
operation of Justice was conceived not as a rigid, written, unalterable law, but as a living, omnipresent power. " Since we
cannot be present in all corners of the world to execute justice
in person—though our power is present everywhere—we have
chosen some from the trusty ones of our kingdom . . . in order
that what we effectively perform through their agency may
suffice for the consummation of Justice." These are the words
in which contemporaries record Frederick's conception of the
inner meaning of the State and its officials and his conception
of Justice as a power to be received and handed on. They
confirm what Frederick himself says elsewhere : he receives
his impulse, his *motus* from divine reflection and passes it on
as instruction and command by which he evokes in the recipient " a stirring of the inner man (*motum interioris hominis*)
whereby the commands of the original motive-force are carried
into execution."

This unmistakeable Aristotelian doctrine : the Emperor conceived as the thought-centre and power-centre of the State
was implied in the wording of every law. This penetration of
the *civitas terrena* by an independent force immediately of God,
demonstrates at once the distinction between " state " and
" empire "—for the Empire was an inactive abstraction based
on an idea, and received its spiritual force through the Church.
The State with its finite boundaries is no abstraction based on
an idea but a living principle, active and potent to its uttermost
boundary. The Justice-God, conceived by the Emperor as a
power working in accordance with law, is the characteristic

symbol of the Sicilian State. Herein is the answer to a riddle :
Kaiser Frederick, in relation to the Empire, where his rôle like
that of his predecessors remained pre-eminently that of the
guardian and conserver of *Pax et Justitia*, appears " medieval,"
while in relation to his Sicilian State he is felt to be " modern,"
because he is a power at work. Caution, however, is necessary
here. The true " modern " has nothing in his make-up of the
image of God which Frederick II knew himself to be in Sicily.
This dual rôle—to be, at one and the same time, the image of
God and a living force—this is what makes the whole Sicilian
rulership of Frederick II unique.

This new alertness, this conception of God as a constant
force independent of the Church, links the new State with the
Renaissance. Here we are again compelled to think of St.
Francis—at every turn the Emperor's counterpart—who in
exactly similar fashion, without the Church's aid, proclaimed
God as power. The simple-minded saint saw this power as
ever-active Love, a divine *pneuma* which breathed in man and
beast and herb ; the learned, almost over-intellectual, monarch
recognised the divine power in the laws of nature and of science ;
the one perceiving the earthly manifestations of the Deity by
the mind, the other by the soul—each after his kind.

Two important innovations of the Emperor's will show the
practical application of all this to statecraft. A remarkable law
which the commentators term " a new law " expounds the
Emperor's omnipresence in the State : the Emperor is present
everywhere to help the weak, who is often unjustly oppressed
by the stronger. By a protective law, the Emperor empowered
every innocent subject if attacked to " defend himself against
the aggressor by the INVOCATION of our name " and in the
Emperor's name forbids the aggressor to continue his attack.
Any man who fails to respect this invocation of the imperial
name will be summoned direct before the highest court, from
which there is no appeal. The command was valid : thou
shalt not take the name of God in vain ; anyone who abused
the invocation of the Emperor's name, using it perhaps solely
to his own advantage, was most severely punished. What a

mentality is thus revealed! In the last extremity a man must call, not on God, but on the more direct and potent power of the Emperor, the incarnate Justice, the Helper and Avenger. No precedent for this law is known.

An innovation which Frederick II was the first to introduce into secular law revolutionised the whole legal procedure of the West and shows the active, nay the aggressive nature of the imperial Justice : the Inquisition-prosecution. The general view prevailed in the Middle Ages that a criminal prosecution implied a plaintiff : where none accused, none judged. For certain capital offences Frederick II definitely abolished this principle. Where the crime in question was the gravest one, high treason, an investigation could be set in motion on behalf of the State, without any plaintiff, without delay, without special imperial authorisation, simply by the proper authorities on the spot. For other serious crimes an official prosecution without plaintiff required the Emperor's authorisation. In the case of capital crimes therefore it no longer depended on the caprice of a potential plaintiff to drop the accusation or come to terms : serious crime was taken out of the hands of the accuser and—it might be against his will—investigated and pursued officially by the State. Here is the first embryonic appearance of a " Crown Prosecution," a thing at variance with all medieval modes of thought, so that the commentator remarks on the edicts in question : " this provision may be said to embody a new law." He styles the Emperor a " tyrant," and it must have borne an appearance of tyranny : imperial justice put into action not in order to secure his rights to an injured party, but as vengeance, as an end in itself—to propitiate the State-God, to secure satisfaction for the transgression of state ordinances. It is worthy of remark that Pope Innocent III, not Frederick II, was the inventor of this procedure. It was he who first, with his Inquisition, introduced spiritual disciplinary courts, independent of plaintiffs, to avenge every insult or injury offered by heresy to the sacred mysteries. The matter, however, assumed a totally different complexion when this extra-ordinary procedure, designed to protect the sacred mysteries against blasphemers and unbelievers, was unreservedly applied to the secular law of the secular State. We are

entitled to consider this either as a mere secularisation of a
spiritual procedure or as the recognition of the existence of
State mysteries no less sacred than the spiritual ones, and
demanding similar protection. Quite logically, the State-
Inquisition was primarily directed against traitors who were
the " unbelievers " of the state, exactly corresponding to the
" heretics " of the Church. The " High Court " prosecution
was carried through with a special, solemn ceremonial. This
" Crown-Prosecution " indicates a feeling that the worldly
state upheld a sacred, spiritual order, not less divine than the
Civitas Dei, the Church.

This self-sufficiency of the State is implicit in another pregnant act of Frederick II. If God is present on earth, not only
within the Church's realm of grace, but has condescended to
reveal himself as Justice in unconsecrated precincts, the State
can no longer be conceived as " sinful " ; a relative good amid
the total evil of the world ; but becomes forthwith an absolute
good in its own right, for God has entered in. The need for
redemption is not at an end, for redemption deals with the
future life of the individual soul in another world : a matter of
little moment to the Emperor. His sphere of action was the
Here and Now, and so large bulked the present in his eyes that
men whispered—not perhaps without good cause—that he
completely denied a future life. His new Divine State raised
another question to at least equal importance with redemption :
salvation after death was a divine and holy thing—not less
divine and holy; the fulfilling of God's will in this life here
on earth.

Frederick evolves the importance of the State as an end in
itself, attributes to the State a divine power of healing fully
equal to the healing power of the Church. In the Preface to
the *Liber Augustalis*, Frederick relates the story of the creation
beginning with his own cosmology (which we shall expound
later) and repeats it again later in certain warrant-diplomas of
his officers. For the most part he sums up the current belief
of the day in a few sentences, till he comes to the most important
point—the Fall. In the days of innocence and immortality
when natural law prevailed and man rejoiced in perfect freedom,
in the golden age of Paradise, Kings and States were superfluous.

Only the Fall imposed the " yoke " of government on man. The Middle Ages derived the whole theory of the State from the Fall. Perhaps that is why Dante symbolised the Roman Empire as the Tree of Knowledge in the Earthly Paradise. That is highly suggestive : for Dante held it to be the Emperor's noblest task to lead man back to the highest wisdom, to the Tree of Knowledge growing at the entrance to Paradise, back to the moment when man still was innocent. After this point the Church took up the task, reintroduced man into Paradise, into eternal bliss, and redeemed him from the curse of mortality. From the Fall onwards Frederick slightly modified myth, legend and dogma for his own purposes. From the Fall the Church deduced Original Sin which imposed on men the yoke of princes and kings as a penalty for the sin of their primeval ancestor. The Emperor brushed these moralisings aside. For him the first men were simply transgressors of a law, of a commandment, according to the Bible ; as a punishment for which they were driven from Paradise and forfeited their immortality. That was the Fall. Mortal man retained the tendency to lawbreaking of his God-created first father, and mutual hate had sprung up amongst the people who in such great numbers now populated the earth. For this there was one remedy—the Ruler, the State, Justice. Following classical lines of thought, Frederick deduced from the Fall, a perfectly practical, non-moralising, conclusion, which took cognisance of actual human nature and of " things which are, as they are," namely that Paradise being a thing of the past, and men being now inclined to crime and hate, they would destroy and annihilate each other but for the restraining hand of a Ruler.

Princes are therefore established, we observe, not as a moral punishment for sin, but as a practical expedient to prevent mutual annihilation. The Emperor's deduction continues . . . if the human race had perished, then, the subordinate lacking the superior to which it was subordinated, " everything else would have perished also, for it would have served no further need of anyone." Nature having been designed to serve man, would have had no further *raison d'être* and would have passed away—a current conception that may perhaps be traced back to Aristotle—a truly imperial picture of the world. For logically pursued the implication is, that without the Emperor, the highest superior, the whole human race and the whole realm of Nature would perish. This gives some conception of the almost inconceivably dizzy heights of responsibility on which an Emperor was enthroned. Hence the stern punishment of treason : the Emperor was frequently heard to say " the bodies of others were dependent on his life—the traitor imperilled the fabric of the world."

Without rulers men would have destroyed themselves, and therefore : to rescue the human race and to avert the danger of world catastrophe, " compelling Necessity, no less than the inspiration of Divine Providence, created the rulers of the peoples," or as it is later more briefly expressed : " Necessity created kings " ; that is : they were evolved to meet a natural need, not imposed as a punishment for sin. Frederick's great art, of turning negatives into affirmatives is manifest here : rulers and states are not a disciplinary scourge for sinful men, but the upholders of a world-preserving principle, they have become " an article of salvation as were Church and priests for the salvation of souls." Christ himself had, of course, redeemed souls, but " neither the waters of the Flood nor the waters of baptism have washed away the practical effects of our first father's imprudent transgression of the Law," said Frederick once, not denying the scheme of salvation but relegating it to its proper sphere of souls in a future world. Man on earth was still unsaved and could only be redeemed by the ruler and the state, and brought back to a condition of innocence, or more exactly of " correctiveness " by the power of Justice, " the regulator of human life." Justice thus becomes a world-saving force.

Thus the Emperor, the *Divus Augustus*, the visible bearer of healing power, becomes like the Roman Augustus the *Soter*, the World Redeemer, the World Saviour. What had been the teaching of St. Augustine ? " True Justice exists only in the state whose founder and leader is Christ." When the time came Frederick did not blench but boldly accepted the conclusion : he would appear, like unto the Son of God, not only as Judge and Mediator but also as Saviour and Fulfiller of the Law. His Empire aspired to the Justice of Heaven, nay more was founded by her, " Justice looking down from Heaven hath set up her throne amongst the peoples," the throne of the Roman Emperor, recalling the divine saying : " Render unto Caesar the things that are Caesar's."

Frederick II issued his new Book of Laws like new tidings of great joy in which the long-silent tongue of Justice again found voice. He wished these statutes to be read as a new code of ethics and behaviour, and at the close he apostrophised the faithful : " May our people welcome, to the glory and honour of God, this work begun in the hope of Divine Favour and completed under the guidance of Divine Grace. It is adorned with the superscription and name of Augustus in reverence for the Sublime Augustus and for the honour of the Royal Dignity. Receive these laws with thankfulness, O ye peoples, make them your own both within the law courts and without . . . that with the victory of your new King a new rod of Justice may bourgeon and grow."   And it was in very truth tidings of joy that Frederick brought.   Predecessors and con- temporaries conceived state order as consisting partly in punishment, partly in unfulfilled striving towards an eternal far-off Law of God and Nature, a perfection unattainable on earth. The Emperor taught that the State herself daily begets afresh the only true and valid Law of God ; that the living law of the temporal world is the Living God himself. That the Eternal and the Absolute must themselves adapt and change with time if they are to remain living. This was a decisive break with the past.

" In no wise do we detract from the reverence due to earlier Rulers, when we beget new laws to meet the peculiar needs of the new time, and find new medicines for new ills. The im- perial dignity carries this illustrious privilege as an inevitable condition of rendering service : daily to conceive new methods to reward the virtuous and to pulverise the vicious under repeated blows of punishment, when the old human laws under the changes wrought by time and circumstance no longer suffice to eradicate vice and to implant virtue."   Justice is here revealed in new activity ; no longer merely a radiation of living

power flowing from God over the State, but herself informed
by another force and varying from day to day in accordance
with the ever-changing needs of the State.   As the Emperor
was, at one and the same time, both " father and son of Justice,"
so Justice was the founder of, and founded in, the State.   The
State was in itself an end, a means of salvation, the needs of the
State were therefore divine and necessary to salvation.   Wherewith the circuit of power was complete in the reverse direction :
divine Justice begot earthly law and earthly necessity begot the
divine Justice.   The old far-off immutable *Justitia* lost her
immobility ;   filled with life, linked with time's changes, she
could in truth represent the " Living God " of the State, and
by her means the Emperor became indeed " Incarnate Law
upon the earth."   The second active force, the force of Life
itself, is here revealed—*Necessitas*.

The " necessity of service " gave the Emperor the right to
alter law and statute.   The legal Machiavellianism of Frederick
II rested on the fact that the form of divine Justice could be
modified by the Emperor to meet the varying needs of men.
He represented and he proclaimed " State Law."   Relying on
the phrase of Caesar's :   " *si violandum est jus, regnandi gratia
violandum est. . . .*"   King Manfred came to speak of a " Viola-
tion of Law," and finally Machiavelli defended the thesis : the
needs and the necessities of the State and of the Prince over-ride
every moral law (*i.e.* every divine and natural law).   Not so
Frederick.   Unscrupulous as he was in his choice of means,
his ruling principle was : the need of the State is the divine and
natural law.   For Frederick II this was true—though no longer
true for the Renaissance princes.   The fate of all " imperial
Europe " hung on the heeding or non-heeding of the tiniest
State necessity ;   hence each present need of the state rightly
assumed an immense importance in the Emperor's eyes till it
became a cosmic need, a part of the world-plan of God and of
divine Providence.   The needs of the State were absolute ; not
opposed to the divine, but themselves divine, and hence potent
to determine law and modify divine Justice.

" Machiavellianism was born of Aristotelianism " declared
Campanella later, and in so saying he does, as a matter of fact,
reveal vital relationships.   For it is clear that some outside

influence was bound to enter into and disturb the medieval conception of the world and cause a radical revision of medieval thought. The vision of the imperial lawgiver is a vision of a philosopher formed by Arabic and Hellenistic wisdom. It is amazing to see how, with one single word, Frederick II transformed the whole medieval conception of a State and filled it with active life. While the times were discussing whether the earthly State was of God or of Satan, of Good or· of Evil, Frederick II soberly announced : the Ruler's office was born of natural necessity. *Necessitas* as an independent active force, as a living law of Nature belongs to Aristotle's thought, and to the Arab disciples of Aristotle. It is the new axiom which the Emperor flung into the medieval State philosophy of the West to revolutionise the State. In the introduction to the Sicilian Book of Laws he writes : the people's princes are created " by the imperative necessity of things, not less than by the inspiration of the Divine Providence." In later documents even more briefly : *Justitia* has erected the rulers' thrones *necessitate*— of necessity. In interpreting the evolution of the imperial office the Emperor, in this passage, renounces all supernatural unfathomable designs of divine Providence and points simply to the Master's words at sight of the coin. The Emperor frequently employed " natural necessity " to make dogmas and sacred institutions intelligible to reason. As in the case of the State, so the sacrament of marriage for instance—without disparagement of its God-given sanctity—is a " necessity of nature " for the preservation of the human race. He made it clear that he rated the natural necessity of marriage higher than its sacramental sanctity, when in defiance of dogma he introduced the most thorough-going and revolutionary changes into Sicilian marriage, with the intention of improving the breed. These precedents were pregnant with consequences. By narrowing down scriptural and ecclesiastical conceptions and theories and giving scope to natural ones, the State was not driven back on mere force and the power of the sword, but was led forward to another spiritual conception, with which the Church had no concern, Nature recognised as spiritual and law-abiding. Metaphysics, one might say, was supplanting Transcendentalism.

Necessitas was indispensable to the Emperor's new gospel, as a basis for the secular state which appealed to reason and not to faith. The emotional assertion of earlier rulers that the state was an institution of God's, might indeed be believed, but could not compel belief. The *need* of the ruler could be grasped by reason—without him the human race would have destroyed itself. When Dante wished to prove that a world monarchy was indispensable he took up the Emperor Frederick's argument in the same sense, preaching belief in the saving mission of the State. Pope Boniface taught that for his soul's salvation every human creature must subordinate himself to the Pope. Dante—speaking almost as representative of the Hohenstaufen Caesars, in the absence of an existing Emperor—retorted with the great imperial gospel : that for the salvation of the world each human creature must subordinate himself to the Roman Emperor. Dante's whole-hearted endorsement of the earthly State is frequently, even in its methods, a continuation of Frederick's imperial outlook and teaching. The first book of the *de Monarchia*, in which he develops the peculiar divinity of the State and its divine mission of salvation, bears the title *de Necessitate monarchiae*. He expounded the natural necessity of monarchy for the preservation of life, and almost every chapter of the first part closes with the recurrent exclamation : " Thus Monarchy is necessary for the safety, for the advantage of the world." Emperor and poet were in this at one : in defiance of Church and Scholasticism, they attached so much importance to the earthly State, that they declared it part of the scheme of salvation, necessary to the realisation of the " better nature " of man and of the world at large which God designed.

What was there so significant in this doctrine of Necessity, which contemporaries labelled as a peculiar Ghibelline invention, and took to be a slogan of the Hohenstaufen's court, so characteristic that forged letters and exercises in style which sought to catch the note of the Hohenstaufen chancery rarely forgot to drag in the *necessitas rerum?* People have often dubbed Frederick II an Apostle of Enlightenment. He was the most many-sided man of his age and unquestionably also the most learned, a philosopher and dialectician trained not only in scholastic and classical learning but also in the learning of

Aristotle, Avicenna, and Averroes. In Frederick's scheme of
State-Wisdom, *Necessitas* represents the essential watchword
necessary to every movement of enlightenment, to every effort,
that is, to break asunder mental bonds felt to be repressive and
against nature—*Necessitas*, the implicit inevitability of things,
which weaves the threads of Fate in accordance with the law
of cause and effect ; the Law of God, the Law of Man, the Law
of Nature, in sum the fitness of things. How revolutionary this
doctrine was, needs no emphasis. As long as Miracle held
the field, world-creative, world-preserving, all causation could
be abrogated in favour of the providential ; natural consequences explained as divine intervention. No one wished to
think it otherwise—even if he had had the power—for no
importance attached to other things ; the God he sought, the
God in whom he believed, revealed himself not in the law of
cause and effect but in the marvels of divine grace. As long as
the causal relationships of phenomena sheltered behind the
miraculous, man had no perception of human fate : the most
eventful life was full of magic and fairy tale—never fateful,
never ruled by its own laws, never " demonic."

The doctrine of Necessity made for enlightenment in so far
as the recognition of natural laws inherent in things themselves,
broke the spell of magic. In this sense Frederick II, the *vir
inquisitor*, as his own son terms him, may be called an Apostle
of Enlightenment, or to be more accurate : he helped the cause
by raising knowledge to the same plane as magic. For although
he began by dissolving magic and myth and miracle, he utilised
and realised them too, and even created more ; he did not
destroy the miraculous, but he placed the scientific alongside it,
and thus called into existence one of those rare and priceless
transition moments in which all and everything is valid simultaneously : myth and insight, faith and knowledge, miracle and
law, corroborating yet belying each other, co-operating yet con-
flicting. Such was the atmosphere in which Frederick moved
and had his being—astoundingly learned yet childishly naïve,
clearsighted yet credulous : at once stark and hard and passionate. Such too was the air which Dante breathed.

The knowledge of the inevitability of Law throughout the
whole realm of Nature, subjected life to these same laws

which governed the rest. When Frederick breathed *Necessitas*, the unalterable laws of Nature, as a power unto the structure of his State, he evaded, as he had also done in the case of *Justitia*, the medieval conception of Nature as a Duality—a state on the one hand of mortality and sin, as far as mankind was concerned, and on the other of immortality and sanctity as far as God was concerned. Frederick II never attacked this conception. He demonstrated the same natural force and natural law operative in the higher and the lower spheres, potent throughout the entire Cosmos—*Necessitas*. Where this law held sway there existed also human fate, primarily revealed in the Emperor himself as he expounded and explained the meaning of the present need.

Frederick II treated the inevitability of himself and of his state as a matter of immense importance, an affair of World Necessity, he himself becoming the Fate Incarnate of his subjects. The imperial doctrine, that without an Emperor the world would perish of self-annihilation, showed to what degree the Emperor was Fate; and Frederick states unambiguously in his laws, " the subjects, under God, draw breath only by the force of the illustrious Caesar." The *fideles*, the faithful and the true, had no destiny of their own ; the *lex regia* had committed them into the Emperor's hand and their fate fulfilled itself in his, whose " life was the life of all." As is inevitable in this type of autocracy he was the sole and only individual in his State, because he and he only is a " One, that is not a fraction of another "—to quote Dante's phrase—he and he alone had direct access to God. On his dangerous, threatening, icy heights he alone perceived the free towering summit of the world, earthly need and earthly development, the rarefied air of World-Necessity, the inexorable operation of the forces of the upper and lower spheres comprised within himself. None has ever experienced so directly in his own person as this star-reading Hohenstaufen, the fates of Heaven and of Earth ; he felt himself bound with God and with the stars in their courses in the march of inalterable law. He is the mediator, the expositor, the interpreter who observed the paths of the heavenly bodies to ascertain the future of himself and of the world, and conversely to approximate the course of finite things to the courses of the stars. Such interplay between the individual man and the universal law makes possible the beginning of Doom and Fate. All great men who have grasped the cosmos as one gigantic whole have been, each after his kind, of the same opinion as Frederick II, that " by the indication of the heavenly will the position of the planets affects the welfare of the lower bodies." It was natural that this blending of heavenly and earthly nature was accomplished in the Emperor as the peak of the universal edifice, in the person who because of his dual nature was accorded the character of a kind of angel or genius, whom men called a " cherub " and even compared to the Saviour. In this blending of the eternal nature, the "better nature" as Frederick II styled it, with the temporal nature of man, degenerate from the original model, lies the purpose and aim of the earthly state. The unity which Frederick II strove to create, of Human Law, Divine Law, and Natural Law, which he at first himself lived, is clearly expressed in the words of a chronicler : " This Emperor, the true Ruler of the World, whose fame extends through the whole circuit of the earth, was convinced that he could approximate his own nature to the heavenly nature, perhaps by his experience in Mathematics."

It is unquestionable that Frederick did hold this belief : that he even strove to reverse the process and to approximate the nature of God to his own imperial nature. He took a much more anthropomorphic view of the Deity in action than earlier times had done. In the Book of Laws he unhesitatingly takes up his position to the philosophical query of the day : Did God create the World or did God only mould existing primeval matter ? God fashioned existing matter, he says—that is : just like the Emperor ! In another way he strives to set God his limits. The preface to the *Liber Augustalis* places in tense proximity the two powers who founded the ruler's office, " the imperative necessity of things and not less the inspiration of the divine foresight." No opposition was intended. The inherent law of Nature was not distinct in action from the divine foresight. Nature obeyed her own law, the imperative necessity of things, and if God were not to destroy his own creation he could not act against the laws of Nature : God is thus a slave to the law of his own creation. This was no denial of the divine Freewill : for God obeyed no other law than that which he had himself wished and foreseen, his own divine law. Here was the same mystery of obedience and freedom that was valid for the Emperor who was also " father and son, lord and servant of his own laws." He would not have submitted to the position if he had thereby ceased to be a symbol of the Deity. The Emperor's laws corresponded to the *Necessitas* of his creature the State, as God's law resembled the *Necessitas* of the divine creation—Nature. There is here no echo of the classical thought : that even the Gods cannot fight against *Necessitas*. The mystery of freedom and law is to be here understood wholly in the Christian sense. A later contemporary of the Emperor's thus sets it forth : The king—he says—is obedient to no man, but to God and to the Law. The king ascribes to the Law only what the Law ascribes to the king. " And that the king must be beneath the Law, though he stand in the place of God, is clearly demonstrated by Jesus Christ in whose room the king rules on earth, since the Son of God himself . . . was willing to be under the Law."

The mystery of salvation and redemption for the Emperor and for the earthly State lies, therefore, in the fulfilling of the Law. A capricious God—however merciful—working miracles and not amenable to Law, would be intolerable ; an arbitrary Providence, acting without regard to reason or the laws of Nature, would rend a state asunder. That was perfectly clear to Frederick. Though the Emperor would have been loath to forego the personal attentions of a wonder-working Providence which had been ceaselessly manifest in his own life, he firmly denied the possibility of any supernatural power intervening directly in the State and not through its head, an irresponsible miraculous Providence acting in defiance of the laws of reason and of nature. Frederick abolished trials by ordeal—not because they " tempted God," as Pope Innocent III expressed it, but because they defied nature and reason. " How could a man believe that the natural heat of glowing iron will become cool or cold without an adequate cause . . . or that, because of a seared conscience, the element of cold water will refuse to accept the accused." Mockingly the Emperor continues:

" These judgments of God by ordeal which men call ' truth-revealing ' might better be styled ' truth-concealing.' "   Similarly, he did away with the legal duel, another type of ordeal, in future only permitted in case of treason.   This was only logical and, moreover, characteristic, for this duel was a *Divinatio* and concerned the sacred and divine person of the Emperor himself, in which case human knowledge did not come in question, and only God could intervene.

On purely rational grounds love-potions were forbidden, and many other ordinances were issued : no miracle was tolerated in the State.   It would have undermined the regularity of the State if God's Providence, instead of being itself Law, had by miracles disturbed the operation of Justice, the State God.

God's Foresight as Law—that is : a Providence continuously and actively aiming at a state and world order obedient to law ; a Providence therefore indistinguishable from the Law of Nature because the natural order was also the completely divine order—such a Providence is called Reason.   Scholastic learning defined it : " Providence is the Reason of a purposeful order of things."   The Hohenstaufen Court disputed eagerly about the " Aim in Nature."   If, however, Providence in its working was indistinguishable from the Law of Necessity, we must not be surprised occasionally in Manfred's writings to meet with *Ratio*, where in the imperial formularies of his father—at once more comprehensive, more practical and more profound—*Necessitas* still reigned.

Familiar circumstances repeat themselves in the question of *Providentia*, who, with *Justitia* and *Necessitas*, form the trinity of state-creating forces.   On the one hand the image was retained : the *Provisio*, the world plan of God, was mirrored on earth in the *Provisio*, the state plan of the Emperor.   Whereas, however, scholastic philosophy rigorously distinguished the two and expressly designated the one temporal and the other eternal, the Emperor set all this aside and emphasised the practical extension of *Provisio* : " as executors of Divine Providence the rulers assigned fate, share and rank to the peoples, as befitted each."   In this also the Emperor was the mediator and inter-preter of the divine plan who, as well as *Justitia* and *Necessitas*, embodied in himself the Divine Providence as far as this aimed at the ordering of the State. Providence was here conceived in her specifically state-creating capacity, as a continuously-active force, and correlated with the Emperor. Yet Frederick II had assuredly not eliminated the Providence of God, active in beneficent miracle ; he claimed to rule " by the Grace of God " like every other medieval prince. Divine Providence had singled him out, him only, and elevated him directly to the throne, and the marvel of her grace had enveloped the last of the Hohenstaufens in a mist of magic glory far beyond that of any other prince, far from the ken of the profane. The purposeful active Foresight of God did not enshroud the Emperor but revealed herself in him as the highest Reason : " Leader in Reason's path " he has been called.

It is almost superfluous to distinguish between this and the later rationalism. Reason is here conceived as the highest illumination of the specially favoured ones, the Emperor in particular, and this is her first appearance ; she is still a shy, remote, ultimate goal for man into whom God might enter in this guise. Reason was in no wise merely a means ; the goal by no means merely welfare and advantage. The " means " in Frederick's State was *Justitia*, which also was once " Goal." *Ratio* therefore had value only in relation to Law and Right. " Justly and reasonably " (*juste et rationabiliter*) is an age-old juxtaposition, and the new thing is this, that Justice and Reason are now linked with the Law of living Nature, with Necessity. It is Law that first yields these juxtapositions : the strong emphasis on *Ratio* emanates from the jurists of Bologna and the blending in Justice of Nature, Reason, Foresight, was a product of Roman law. All these equal forces frequently merged in each other : " the Emperor receives his impulse from Providence " is a frequent assertion ; another time " the Emperor is impelled to action by Reason, not distinguished from Nature." Ultimately it all points to this : Justice was the living Deity. She varied with the varying need of the State and was thus linked with mortal life. Justice again was subservient to divine Reason which linked her to the immortal—a reflection of the Emperor himself : " Although our illustriousness is free of every law, yet it is not exalted above the dictates of Reason, herself the Mother of all Law." The Emperor was thus the image of God by his bondage to Reason, above which God does not soar, for God and Reason are one. With the new Justice, incarnate in the Emperor, and placed like him between the Law of God and the Law of Nature, the gulf was bridged that had yawned between positive or human law and the eternal divine or natural law : an emancipating achievement of Frederick II.

Before passing to the goal of the imperial doctrine of salvation we must review the whole magnificent structure of his State—like every work of art, a unity. The postulates were a *Tyrannis* which was part of an Empire, a transition period between two epochs, a philosopher as king. It is vain to question whether Frederick's Sicilian State belongs to the Middle Ages or to the Renaissance : founded in the fulness of time it belongs to neither—and to both. Sundered from the Middle Ages in this : that the State bore in its own bosom its own goal and spiritual meaning, and that the prince instead of steering his kingdom with a view to salvation in the next world, drew God down into the earthly State and represented him therein. Another innovation : this State throbbing with living forces, associated with a third strange power, the Law of Nature, with the medieval duality of the Law of God and the Law of Man. The State thus acquired depth, and the embodied trinity made possible a living circulation of forces. All this smacks of the Renaissance. The Renaissance State, however, completely lacked the hieratic element of the priestly-imperial Sicily, and lacked too the actual or imaginary breath and universality conferred by the Imperium. The Renaissance State was a means and embraced no world : the prince, the individual of the Renaissance, might be cosmopolitan and of cosmic importance —but not the State.

It is a matter of indifference whether we consider the chief importance to lie in Frederick's adaptation of the conceptions of Roman law, or the Arab influx of Aristotelian and Neo-Platonic ideas, or the adoption of the Christian priestly elements : for all these are welded into a new unity ; firm and stern and clear is the imperial Law-State based on the three world forces : *Necessitas, Justitia, Providentia.* This trinity of power pulses through the state in indistinguishable rhythm, recurs in every part as the Three-in-One of Natural Law, Divine Law, Human Law. The absolute symmetry of this construction, in which the upper and the lower spheres are related like reflections in a mirror and yet together form a whole, would, if graphically rendered, recall the architectural symmetries of the Renaissance. For these three forces rule in the Universe as in the State, stand above the Emperor and below, flow as power through the mediator from the heavenly into the earthly kingdom and back again, fed upon by land and people : each acting on the other and acted upon by the other.

This State was a " work of art " not because of its skilful administrative methods, but because the union of the laws of God, Man, and Nature made it an approximation to an ideal original. Consciously or unconsciously this new monarchy served as a model and a standard for centuries. This Justice-State of the Hohenstaufen Emperor almost seemed to be a late realisation of the picture that Plato had once borne to Sicily in his search for *Dikaiosyne*, and which Plotinus centuries later sought to realise in Campania on the Platonic model. The ground was strangely well prepared, and Frederick II may well have felt that he had created something approaching the " ideal state " when he had the entry made in his Book of Laws : " Sicily shall be a mirror of likeness for all who marvel at it, the envy of princes, the pattern of kingdoms."

Frederick II remodelled Italy on the Sicilian pattern. The dream which was assuredly present in the mind of the Hohenstaufen—to enforce these same proportions on the whole earth " throughout the Roman Empire stretching from sea to sea " —was not advanced till Dante painted his immeasurably powerful picture of the one Roman World-monarchy : not by a long way so Utopian a dream as is sometimes supposed. For the poet's model State had its prototype in reality, had been lived, no less than the platonic State of Plato. His work is called *de Monarchia* not *de Imperio*, and in its treble sub-division we see the reflection of the triple power of the Hohenstaufen monarchy. In the first book of this State Gospel Dante treats of " The Necessity of Monarchy " ; in the second he seeks to prove that Justice has been from the beginning

inherent in the Roman Empire ; and in the third that the
Emperor has been immediately appointed by God as the exe-
cutor of the world—directing Divine Foresight and the guide
to the highest reason. Dante seeks proofs, justification for
monarchy. Frederick had created monarchy, albeit on a
smaller scale. The three essential forces *Necessitas*, *Justitia*,
Providentia, are identical in Dante's vision and in Frederick's
State. True, the poet's writing exhibits not only the extension
of this complex of power to the whole world, but at the same
time its concentration in one single person, the Individual.
That is the culmination : the world as one unified State of
immense extent and therewith the unity and harmony of the
whole in each unit. Since the days of Plato and of Dante the
Cosmos has never again been so envisaged and so expounded
as a living State and the State as Cosmos. Frederick II, the
Man of Action, only outlined this extension, this concentration :
on the one hand he founded the colossal pan-Italian Signoria,
on the other he scarcely wished and certainly did not achieve
the concentration of the whole in any individual—except himself. He himself was the first whose soul was saved by the
Sacrament of the State.

Of what nature was this Salvation which the earthly monarchy
of the Emperor promised ? Which Dante with such fire
revealed anew, deepened, extended ? In the early days of
Frederick II, Francis of Assisi in wandering and in word
renewed the sacred gospel of the Crucified : that Poverty and
Love lead to salvation—love to every creature into whom God
had breathed the breath of life. With equal insistence
Frederick II preached the gospel of the Glorified, who—himself a king and of kingly race—pointed the path to salvation
when, in spite of his divine Sonship, he submitted to the Law
and as man fulfilled the Law. Such was the Gospel of the
Emperor : the fulfilment of Law is Salvation ; the service of
Law is freedom ; and obedience to Law leads to the righteousness and uprightness of man. For Justice implied not only
the penalising, avenging power which guarded mankind from
destruction, but was also the corrective of degenerate human
nature which in the beginning God had willed " upright and
simple "; Justice was the power which led to the highest goal ;

to the realisation of that better "nature" possessed by godlike man before the Fall.

Hence, the Emperor sets up for "man incorporating the divine idea" the dogma : that "of necessity man's nature is subject to Justice, and freedom is the handmaid of the Law." Only by homage to the law of Justice can man attain to freedom or, in Christian phrase, to the sinlessness of Heaven. For Sin is slavery.

Justice, therefore, shall create again the naturally simple and upright man, the image of God. The Justice to which it behoved man to submit was no abstraction (as, for instance, "conscience" later became) for—so said the Emperor—it was not seemly that the Divine Idea incarnate in man should bow to another order of beings from elsewhere ; rather had Man been exalted over men. According to the word of the Lord the Emperor reigned over all men. He was incarnate Justice, to which mankind was subject, and that man achieved freedom who fulfilled the Law of the Emperor, who alone was responsible to God for the righteousness of that law. The judgment of God on the Emperor corresponded to the judgment of the Emperor on the subject. Since, however, Reason was inherent in Justice, the Emperor was the guide to Reason also. Piero della Vigna wrote in admiration of his adored Emperor, the first who attained salvation through Justice and restored the divine image: "The path of reason required him for Guide." The Emperors had, of course, been long since styled the *imago Dei*, but Frederick was God's image in a special sense, for he was the first to whom was granted that salvation through Justice which he proclaimed. Though "whatever the Emperor decrees has the force of Law," he was above all others the servant, the debtor, the son of Justice ; more than any other he was bound by and subject to Law ; and in him therefore was again incarnate that originally God-like human form which the Saviour also wore : "From the likeness of Jesus Christ, in whose stead the King rules on earth, it is evident . . . that the King must be subject to the Law . . . since the Son of God also of his own will was subject to the Law," thus declared the Emperor's later contemporary, and we may here recall Goethe's phrase that there is no freedom on the highest rung.

Since Justice led back to true freedom, to the state of innocence, a further inference follows : the Emperor corresponds
to the First Man in Paradise whom God created after his own
image, the still sinless Adam whose better nature was once
scarce inferior to the nature of the angels. The Cosmology in
the Preface to the *Liber Augustalis* points out : " After the
Universe and its motion had been created by Divine Providence, and primeval matter, which was to realise the better
nature, had been distributed among the primeval forms, He
who had foreseen all that was to be accomplished . . . seeing
Man as the noblest of all creatures from the sphere of the moon
downwards (*i.e.* on earth), formed after His own image and
likeness, whom He created a little lower than the angels, placed
Man above all other created beings on the earth according to
His well-considered plan. Taking Man from a clod of earth
He breathed life into him and Spirit and crowned him with
the diadem of honour and fame. . . ." Adam, the first man,
created by God himself, free as yet from sin, is here taken by
the Emperor as a symbol of the first World-Ruler ; he is ruler
over all the creatures of the earth and crowned with the diadem
of honour and of fame, is symbol also of the first stainless man,
immediately dependent on God, who was free so long as he did
not transgress the " precept of God's Law." The World-King
was like unto the First Man whom God created : Frederick's
office therefore and his first predecessor were created when
God created man, and existed therefore BEFORE the Fall, and
were therefore not the consequence of the Fall. The Saviour
on earth had revived the first stainless world king, Adam, was
himself the " new Adam," begotten of God himself, so that he,
like our first father Adam, was free from original sin : he also
was a World King and subject to Law. The Emperor's words
echo a text of Scripture : " Thou hast made him a little lower
than the angels ; thou hast crowned him with glory and
honour." Frederick added to the text (which in the Psalm
applied to Adam and in the Epistle to the Hebrews to Christ)
one single weighty word : " diadem of glory and honour " is
Frederick's phrase—the diadem of the World King which
Frederick wore himself as Roman Emperor ! Almost as if to
banish any doubt that might exist of Frederick's intention to

liken himself to the only two men directly created free from sin by God—as Innocent III had likened himself to the Priest-King Melchizedek—his most intimate friend in a written eulogy directly styles his imperial master " the stainless prince . . . whom the Great Artificer's hand created man."

Free and stainless and innocent of sin are the three World Kings, because as men they sought their own fulfilment in the Law. Another speculative thought arises which equates the Emperor with Adam in Paradise and with the Saviour : the belief that the " Golden Age " is near at hand. It was a commonplace that the Creation (Adam in Paradise) and the Redemption (the Birth of Christ) were the beginning and the middle of an epoch, to which the end should be like. This fulness of time had now come, under the sceptre of the Emperor of Justice, Frederick II, the expected Messianic ruler whom the Sibyls had foretold. That this World King should resemble the Saviour is no matter for surprise, and the essential resemblance between Adam and the Messiah was set forth at length to the Emperor by an Arab philosopher. This completes the circle of the Imperial Gospel : subjection to the Emperor's *Justitia* leads man on earth to innocence of sin, to the better nature of unfallen man. If the rest of the world, taking example by the Emperor, the first human being to live in a state of freedom, would obey the Laws of Justice, then Paradise would be realised on earth and the Golden Age would dawn, whose Deity according to the oldest myths was named Justitia.

Let us here recall Dante—for all these conceptions are deep imbedded in the *Divina Commedia*, in which the poet points the way from a state of sin back to the earthly and then to the heavenly Paradise, and to the original God-like man, beholding God. In his eyes, too, the Empire is potent to lead to purity from sin. Vergil, the poet of the Caesars, the representative of the Roman Empire, and of the highest Reason was the Guide to the earthly Paradise, till Dante, freed from all sin, with spotless brow, was permitted as a stainless one to enter the Garden with the Tree of Knowledge. Here Vergil left him, but not before he had crowned him—now like unto the Emperor in sinlessness—with mitre and with crown.

The Guide's duty ended here for the mythical Dante-king. The actual Frederick reckoned only with the earthly Paradise ; and because of his indifference to eternal life Dante assigned him a place in the fiery sepulchres of those who despise immortality, the " Epicureans." Yet Dante had the most profound respect and admiration for the Hohenstaufen. All his life Frederick II was the model of the Ruler, and Judge, the Scholar and Poet, the perfect Prince, the " illustrious Hero " who—" so long as his good fortune lasted "—sought after the humane, the *humanum*, and who as a crowned monarch gathered round him the noblest and most brilliant spirits of the earth. Frederick II figures in the poet's works, not so much as an historic character but as an ideal of the *Justitia* Emperor. The Emperor's earthly goal : to attain once more the divine image by the fulfilment of the Law on earth and in the State, was the exact premiss of Dante's formula of faith, that in every man the contemplative element needs salvation through the Church, the active element needs a no less sacred fulfilment on earth in Law and in the State : " For the ineffable Divine Foresight has set two goals before man to enkindle him : the happiness of this life which consists in works of his own strength and is represented in the earthly paradise . . . and the bliss of eternal life which is the enjoyment of the sight of God which man cannot attain to by his own strength without help from the divine light, and the understanding of this is offered in the heavenly paradise."

In contrast to the Hohenstaufen, Dante conceived the heavenly paradise as accessible already on earth to living men. For man's powers are not exhausted in the accomplishment of works of his own strength and of the highest Reason : the pastures of the Blessed, yea even the Deity himself, may be perceived by the enraptured Love which animates the man who prays : St. Francis and above all St. Bernard, the last Guide to the Throne of God. The loftiest insight and the loftiest deed were necessary if a man was to recognise in himself the reflection of God ; to see a man's self in God needed yet something more, illuminated by the grace of the divine light. Thus, from the first canto to the last, the poet's path was the path of the living man. The man who, like the

Emperor, was the *imago Dei*, and then, in spite of highest
knowledge, remained capable of the simple faith of the man
who prays : to him the Deity reveals himself in the vision in
which the sin-freed man, the image of God, sees shimmering
the features *della nostra effige*.

II

The Emperor's law-giving aroused the most profound mistrust in Gregory IX. Even before the publication of the
Constitutions the Pope addressed himself to the Emperor in a
letter which clearly shows how accurately he appraised the
danger of the work. " It has reached our ears that thou hast
it in mind to promulgate new laws, either of thine own impulse,
or led astray by the pernicious counsels of abandoned men.
From this it follows that men call thee a persecutor of the
Church, an overthrower of the freedom of the State : thus dost
thou with thy own forces rage against thyself. . . . If thou,
of thine own motion, hast contemplated this, then must we
gravely fear that God hath withdrawn from thee his grace,
since thou so openly underminest thine own good name and
thine own salvation. If thou art egged on thereto by others,
then we must marvel that thou canst tolerate such counsellors
who, inspired by the spirit of destruction, are bent on making
thee the enemy of God and Man." Gregory expressed himself not less sharply in writing to the Archbishop Jacob of
Capua who had co-operated in collecting the laws. He reproved the Archbishop sternly because instead of publicly
protesting he had allowed himself to be used as the Emperor's
" writing reed " for these laws " which have renounced salvation and conjured up immeasurable ill," and which the Pope
" will by no means calmly tolerate." The Pope's anxieties
were well-founded enough, but the Emperor was in so strong
a position that Gregory was presently compelled to placate him,
for he had been stirred to profound anger by the papal letter :
it had been no public reproof but a confidential remonstrance
such as no son could take amiss on a father's part. Pope
Gregory had no illusions, however, about the *Liber Augustalis*.

It might well seem as if the new secular state, based on Law, Nature and Reason, and entirely self-contained, formed so independent and complete a whole that it had neither need nor room for the Church. Wherever Frederick II held sway, however, his motto was : a secular state plus the Church. One reason—apart from a thousand others—was the simple and personal ; the authority of the Church was well-nigh indispensable to him. Reason made clear the necessity for a Ruler, but Reason in no wise proved the necessity of this particular Hohenstaufen's being that Ruler. The belief in Frederick's person was certainly at that moment still bound up in the authority of the Church. The Emperor had it is true to a large extent emancipated himself from unconditional dependence on the Church, by calling to witness the wonders done on his behalf, which proved his immediate call by God to his high office, the amazing rise to power for instance of the *Puer Apuliae*, which he once more recalled in the Preface to the Book of Laws. It was impossible, however, to sever faith in his providential call from the credulity demanded by the Church, for the age was not ripe to grasp the Hero as such, and the Emperor's power singlehanded to evoke faith in his own person was strictly limited. To enhance his unconditional claim, especially for more distant regions where people rarely saw his face, the consecration and endorsement of the Church were necessary. It was a sufficient miracle, and a proof of the personal magic of this Frederick that after the second excommunication, when the Curia sought by every means in her power to shake the faith in the mysterious person of the Hohenstaufen, one half the world still clung—in defiance of the Church—to its faith in Frederick II as the Chosen. But in those later days, when he strained to the uttermost the powers at his command to outweigh the lack of the Church's consecration and support, and when in public he had to minimise the importance thereof, his whole conduct proclaims how grievously he missed the Church's backing. The fact that, sorely against his will, Frederick II provided the proof that the Church's blessing was not in fact indispensable, was a staggering blow to the Papacy.

The Church was to strengthen faith in the Emperor's person. More : the bulk of Frederick's laws, the whole cult of *Justitia*, presupposed the subjects' religious faith ; however much the Emperor might appeal to Nature and Reason as non-dogmatic axioms, these yet were one with the God of the Church's worship. Thus it came about that in a certain sense the Emperor felt a heretic to be more dangerous than a rebel. The rebel in his folly offended against a law of Reason and of Nature by revolting against the imperial government, which every wise man must acknowledge to be necessary. The heretic, in shaking the foundation of the Catholic Faith, shook also the faith in the Emperor's person and the basis of the Emperor's laws. The Emperor's rôle of Defender of the Faith, Protector and Guardian of the Church, was dictated by immediate state necessity.

Frederick II felt himself at one with the Church in virtue of this office of Defender of the Faith. In the Preface he writes : " The King of Kings and Lord of Lords demands this above all at the hand of a Ruler, that he should not permit the most holy Roman Church, the Mother of the Christian covenant, to be bespattered by the secret faithlessness of those who distort the faith, and should protect her by the might of the secular sword against the attacks of the enemies of the State." Following the example of Justinian, Frederick II opened his work by an edict against the heretics, the enemies of the state. At the first glance it would be easy to overlook the skill and thought which introduced this sole and only allusion in the whole *Liber Augustalis* to the relation between Church and State. Otherwise it contains only casual instructions about the Sicilian clergy. It has been held that the heresy edict was a courteous gesture toward the Pope : it was in fact almost the exact opposite. It was intended to demonstrate to the Church that she could not dispense with the protection of the State. This reminder of the princely protectorship brought into relief the one and only relation in which the Church showed dependence on the State. The Emperor studiously avoided mention of any other relationship, for every other would have impaired the self-contained integrity of the State. There could be no graver misconception than to read into the frequent emphasising of the imperial protectorship a weak amiability towards the Pope, or, worse, to interpret as hypocritical zeal Frederick II's campaign of fire and sword against the "plague of heresy." Other things were here decisive. The Catholic Faith was conceived by Frederick as a State Religion in an almost classical sense : it might be in a wider sense a universal faith, immediately, however, it was the religion of the State. Frederick followed Justinian in opening his Lawbook with an edict against heretics ; in each case Hohenstaufen and Byzantine meant no more than to set a seal on the religion whereon State and Laws alike were founded. The strictly state-conception of religion is brought out much more strongly in the phrasing of the edicts designed for Sicily than in those relating to the Empire. Frederick II always emphasised the co-existence of *Imperium* and *Sacerdotium* in the Roman Empire—for here the Church was primarily the tie that bound in spiritual unity the many-peopled Empire—while for self-contained Sicily the State was not dependent on the universal Church, nor was the Church even co-ordinate with the State, but the State embraced the Church as a protegée and absorbed her. In the Sicilian edict, therefore, the Papacy is not even alluded to, and the Roman Church is only casually mentioned as the orthodox one, which is to be considered the head of all other churches. For heresy was for Frederick II not a crime against the Church, but a blasphemy against God and therefore treason against the King's Majesty, and a crime against the State.

Frederick's great predecessor as *verus imperator*, Pope Innocent III, who was to the marrow an imperial statesman, equated heresy and treason when he said it was a graver thing to offend against heavenly than earthly majesty. There is an echo of the Pope's words in Frederick's Coronation edicts of 1220, but this is the first occasion of his translating the doctrine into state action. In the Sicilian edict it runs : " We condemn most severely the increase of heretics in Sicily and we command for the present : that the crime of heresy, the heresy of any and every accursed sect—under whatever name the sectaries are known—shall be accounted a crime against the State, as it is in the ancient Roman laws. It must be condemned as a yet more heinous offence than a crime against our own Majesty, because it is a manifest attack on the matter of the Divine

Majesty, though when the sentence is pronounced the one punishment does not exceed the other." In the whole edict there is no question of the identity of the two powers. Heresy is a direct crime against the State, against God, against the injured Majesty of the Emperor. The boundary lines between God and Emperor are indeed even more fluid than usual ; even the slight rise from the imperial to the divine majesty is neutralised by the anti-climax that in each case the penalty is the same, and, finally, the imperial majesty is not even directly balanced against the Majesty of God. For the phrase is the " matter of the Divine Majesty " ! Was God to be understood by this ?—or the Emperor himself ? The suggestion that the Emperor was meant must have been possible, for Pope Innocent IV when he revived the imperial heresy-edict in 1254 changed the word " *materiam* " into " *injuriam*," whereby the whole point was lost. The clause now read " an attack to the injury of the Divine Majesty " instead of " against the matter of the Divine Majesty." It is very clear that the one-sided relation of the State to God was now counterbalanced by the Deity's being imported into the State : the heretic injures God and thereby the Emperor, the rebel in injuring the Emperor commits, at the same time, a crime directly against God.

This position is not nearly so clear when set forth in the imperial laws against heretics ; the corresponding passage simply runs : " When our Illustriousness is incensed against contemners of our name, when we condemn in their own person and by the disinheritance of their children those accused of treason, it is both just and seemly that we should be the more incensed against those who blaspheme the Divine Name and those who lower the Catholic Faith. . . ." And even when the Emperor poses as the God of Vengeance who punishes the guilt of the heretic unto the second generation, " . . . so that the children, in memory of their father's crime may pine in misery and know in truth that God is a Jealous God, powerful to visit the sins of the father upon the children . . .," he is here an image only of the *Deus zelotes*, not " the matter of the Divine Majesty." The method of heretic hunting demonstrates more clearly than words that it was only in Sicily that heresy was directly treated and pursued as a crime against the State ; for

the Sicilian Inquisitors were not agents of the Church but
imperial officials, who interpreting Frederick's wishes did not
split hairs over the distinction between heretics, who through
God injured the Emperor, and rebels who through the Emperor
blasphemed God, but consigned both alike to the flames till
Pope Gregory himself was horrified, and intervened to mitigate
Frederick's zeal.   There is no basis for the supposition that
the "liberal-minded and freethinking" Hohenstaufen persecuted the luckless heretics only at the instigation of the Church :
the "accursed sectaries whatever they like to call themselves"
had nothing to hope for but a fiery death.   It happened that
this was one of the few laws of Frederick's that really pleased
the Church, and Frederick II had no hesitation in gratifying
the Church in the matter on all occasions.   In 1238 the severer
Sicilian edict was extended to the whole Empire, and in 1254
incorporated at the Pope's command in the Statute Books and
Town Laws.

As the Emperor himself pointed out, his whole heresy
legislation was closely modelled on Roman law.   Heresy was
treason, for God and Emperor were one.   In imperial Rome
there was no *crimen laesae Romanae religionis* (Tertullian first
evolved this conception) ; under the Emperors religious crime
is treason.   In accordance with this idea Frederick II described
heresy as "*perduellio*," high treason against the State—in Sicily
only.   The word is used here only, and the imperial Chancery
was well skilled, as has always been acknowledged, in its choice
of words.

The heretics were guilty of high treason, plague-carriers,
enemies of the State, as their interpretation of Scripture proved :
for they held that God was to be obeyed, rather than man ; a
doctrine ill adapted to Frederick's state, whose dogma ran
"over men a MAN is set."

People have detected in this an inner contradiction, "the
Freethinker legislates against heresy."   Even if there is something in common between the free mind of the Emperor and
the mind of the heretic, in that both release certain vital forces,
the Emperor was lord over these forces, and in his hands under

well-defined conditions subject to well-defined laws they could prove potent and beneficent. The same forces released by unauthorised persons were dangerous and destructive. For the Emperor personally the dictum might be valid : the Emperor must obey God and not man, but no lesser individual had the right to arrogate to himself this, or any other, imperial privilege. His whole life long, therefore, even in his last and bitterest struggle with the Church, Frederick strenuously repudiated any and every sympathy with heretics. When he was besieged on one occasion they approached and offered help, but were spurned on the instant. They were destroyers in his eyes of that world unity which he represented, though in order to preserve it he often had recourse to anti-dogmatic allies. Dante assigns to Frederick therefore a place, not among the sectaries, but among the Epicureans, those who despise a future life.

Another contradiction of Frederick's has been detected in his persecuting heresy at the same time that he ' tolerated ' Muhammadans, Jews, and orthodox Greeks. Frederick's relation to the non-Christian elements in his State is one of the most instructive items in his statesmanship, more especially when we study the limits of his complaisance. Compared with the mixture of races and religions and the peaceful co-existence in Norman times of Christians, Saracens, and Jews, living side by side in harmony, the freedom of the non-Christians had been very considerably curtailed under Frederick—not for the sake of religion, or of the Pope or of the Church, but for the sake of the State. Frederick's sympathy for professors of another faith, in which he displayed a broadmindedness shared by very few of his contemporaries, extended only so far as they were serviceable to the State and laid no hand upon its sanctities. To avoid any penetration by non-Christians he had, as we have seen, segregated them completely from the very first. He removed the Saracens from the island of Sicily and planted them in Lucera. After he had thus neutralised the Muslim poisons that threatened hostility and confusion to the State, he could afford to be tolerant of their religious observances, as he always showed himself tolerant of any good customs of conquered rebels.

The same principle governed his conduct towards the Jews. In one of his first ordinances, issued after his return from Germany, Frederick laid down that Jews must be distinguished from Christians by their dress and must grow their beards " so that the rites of the Christian faith may not be confused." Any offender was punished by the confiscation of his goods, or, if he was poor, by branding on the forehead—not from religious intolerance but to preserve order in the State. For the rest the Jews were permitted, nay obliged, to live according to their own religious laws unless these were harmful to the State. Many of their religious practices were even advantageous and some were therefore specified in the *Liber Augustalis*: " We exempt the Jews from obedience to our usury laws. They are not to be accused of usury forbidden by God, since—as is well known—they are not subject to the laws of the blessed Fathers of the Church." The moment injury accrued to the State the Emperor's toleration was at an end. An alleged ritual murder by Jews was brought up before the Emperor. Thanks to his astounding knowledge of foreign rites he immediately saw the baselessness of the accusation, but he declared that if it had proved that the Hebrew ritual demanded such human sacrifice he would be prepared immediately to massacre every Jew in the Empire. On the other hand, he constantly intervened against the Church on behalf of the Jews, but there was a special reason for that. In the age-old dispute whether the Jews as foreigners came under the jurisdiction of the State, or as infidels under the jurisdiction of the Church, Frederick II naturally decided for the former—to the intense annoyance of Pope Gregory. On the same principle he brought the Jews into the scheme of the State. In Norman days they had been mainly attached as serfs to churches and monasteries. Frederick II emancipated them almost entirely from this relationship, and rarely or never again farmed out his rights over the Jews any more than his other crown rights ; he insisted all the more strongly on their direct private bond to his own person. Even in the Empire the elected bishop of the Jews was replaced by an appointed Jewish master, who was practically a state official. In order that the State might gain the maximum advantage from its Jewish subjects, Frederick II, with unerring instinct contrived to link the Jew-monopoly with the renewed trade-monopolies, particularly the dye and silk works. To his private Jewish serfs the Emperor entrusted the state dyeworks, the manufacture of silk and the commerce in silk—matters in which the Jews had traditional skill and experience—with advantage to both parties, Emperor and Jew. This had nothing whatever to do with tolerance ; it was simply part of Frederick's usual policy to turn even the smallest force to the advantage of the State and to let nothing be wasted.

This solution meant, in fine, that the servitude of the Jews should be so organised and utilised, that their own industrial life might directly benefit the State. The non-Christians, on the other hand, being thus incorporated in the State, enjoyed in Sicily and in the other imperial territories, a State protection, such as rarely fell to their lot elsewhere. It was clearly stated " the master shall be honoured in his servants," and again " no innocent man shall be oppressed because he is a Jew or a Saracen." There was no suggestion of equal citizenship. An assassination cost the guilty community 100 Augustales if the victim was a Christian and 50 if he were a Saracen or a Jew. Conversion from Catholicism to Islam or to Judaism was severely punished according to existing laws. It was of course permissible for Jews or Muslims to seek baptism. We may be permitted to doubt whether Frederick II encouraged the step, for he lost his serf tax and his poll tax and the birth and marriage tax and many another imposition. Whatever the underlying reasons, the fact is incontestable : the Emperor was, on the whole, averse to changes of faith. Frederick's whole policy in the Jew and Saracen questions may be summed up by saying that the true statesman finds no material without its uses.

Frederick II persecuted no man for his belief. He had his hands full persecuting rebels and heretics for their unbelief. It is illogical to argue that toleration of other *genera* should involve a toleration of *degenerates*—for heretics were degenerates in Frederick's eyes—who rent the " coat without seam " and tore asunder the unity of the State. The contradiction lies not with the Emperor, but in the failure to recognise that heretics were for Frederick enemies of the State, much more than enemies of religion. The misunderstanding is based secondly on a false and arbitrary application of post-Reformation ideas of toleration originating in the days when Protestantism was an independent religion and included sectaries. The misapplication of these ideas to Frederick in his relations with sectaries and non-Christians, is all the more dangerous as it tempts to false generalisations about Frederick's character, representing him as an enlightened and tolerant potentate—an artificial picture that does not fit the facts.

In regard to his personal inclinations—especially wherever the sanctities of the State were at stake—Frederick II was in fact probably the most intolerant Emperor that ever the West begot. No Emperor was ever, both in claim and in act, so uncompromisingly the JUDGE as Frederick II. As judge he lived for centuries in the memories of men, as judge they awaited his second coming as the avenger of human degeneracy. A tolerant judge is like luke-warm fire.

The Emperor, who felt no hate to the non-Christian, showed himself in very deed a " Jealous God " towards rebels and heretics, offenders against the Deity *Justitia* and the sanctified order of the State ; a very fanatic, obsessed by a primeval hate that pursued its victim remorselessly to the second and third generation. The most appalling punishments seemed too mild for such offenders. The edict against those heretics who—to quote the Emperor—called themselves " Sufferers" Patarenes, after the " passion " of the heroic martyrs, closes with a blood-curdling taunt : " We therefore command by this our law that these accursed ' Sufferers ' shall in fact suffer the passion of that death they lust for : that they be condemned to the flames and burnt alive in the sight of all men ; nor shall we regret that we thus fulfil their own desire."

The Emperor's mission as Protector of the Church gave him his only opportunity to draw the universal Roman Church into his State, even to subordinate her to the State as in need of protection. On the other hand, the Church was indispensable to him, for his whole State with its laws was founded on the Catholic faith. This relationship of mutual dependence was quite in harmony with Frederick II's conception of all human and divine relationships, and however greatly he might magnify his protective office till he even filled the rôle of the Avenging

God, he never hesitated freely to admit that the Pope stood to
the Emperor as the father to a child, or as the Sun to the Moon.
Even in the heat of battle Frederick always conceded the
position, though reiterating that the moon was none the less
an independent heavenly body.   This was no sign of weakness.
It testifies to a higher degree of inner freedom, security and
highmindedness, calmly to acknowledge a superior than to deny
him.   Dante devotes a special book to depicting a World-
monarch whose independence of the Pope and immediate
relationship to God the poet seeks to prove.   It might be a
portrait of Frederick.   He concludes with words that might
easily be Frederick's own : " Let Caesar evince that respect
for Peter which the first born son must display towards his
father, that he, in the light of the paternal favour, may more
radiantly illumine the earth, over which he is set by Him alone
who is the Director of all that is spiritual and of all that is
worldly."

The " once and for all " factor in Frederick's imperial metaphysics has already been pointed out.   They were centred in
the person of just this one Emperor and were valid only in just
this one moment of time.   What the world, however, seized
upon, and what each of the European states sooner or later,
directly or indirectly, adopted was the technique of statecraft
which Frederick had deduced from his metaphysics : the
administrative body of jurists ; the bureaucracy of paid officials ;
the financial and economic policy.

This is not the place to pursue the development of all this
nor its gradual modification.   The maxims of State in time
asserted themselves everywhere ; first, of course, in the neighbouring Romance kingdoms, in France and Aragon as well as
in divided Italy, perhaps in Castile too, even before the end
of the century.   The new system of administration with its
officials in the king's pay was inevitable in time to come.   Such
a scheme, immeasurably more amenable to the ruler than
the feudal degrees, gave a security hitherto undreamt of and
the possibility of developing a comprehensive well-planned
organisation deriving from one central authority.   The feeling

was never wholly absent that the Jurist State had had its origin
in reaction against the Church while utilising Church methods
throughout. What unholy danger threatened the Church in
this spiritually independent bureaucracy was acutely expressed
by Napoleon during his own struggle against Pope and Church :
" Il faut faire agir les tribunaux, opposer robe à robe, esprit de
corps à esprit de corps. Les juges sont, dans leur genre, une
espèce de théologiens comme les prêtres ; ils ont aussi leurs
maximes, leurs règles, leur droit canon. On a toujours vu
l'administration échouer dans ses luttes contre les prêtres ; la
monarchie n'a pu résister au clergé qu'en lui opposant les
parlements." This mighty soldier with his eye for the essential,
got to the root of things when he called on the judges for help
against the clergy, as the only group of state officials in his day
bound together by a common spirit.

This gives us a measure of Frederick's genius. He was the
first to create this intellectual order within the state and to make
it an effective weapon in his fight with the Church—bound
together from its birth by sacred ties in the priestly-Christian
spirit of the age, and uplifted to the triumphant cult of the
Deity *Justitia*.

The organisation of this first western bureaucracy, this
priesthood of *Justitia*, is necessarily hieratic. Frederick himself styles the body of officials the " Order of *Justitia* " or the
" Order of Officials." Rigid precedence is clearly marked in
the most important department, that of the Justiciaries, as is
indicated by the Latin nomenclature of the highest grades
which are traditionally called the *Magister Justitiarius* and the
Magnae Curiae Magister Justitiarius. According to the new
orders of 1239, three grades are recognised ; the Justiciars,
governors of the ten provinces ; Master-Justiciars, governors
of the two halves of the kingdom—peninsula and island—and
the Grand Master Justiciar, the head of the whole judicial
administration who acted in place of the divine Emperor as
Grand Master of the Order, much as the German Grand Master
of the Teutonic Order in place of Christ. There is no question
of Sicily's having " copied " the Order-organisation. In those
days it was inevitable that any intellectual body of men of the
vita activa must approximate their organisation to that of the

knightly orders. It was in fact the case that the Prussian State under the Teutonic Order was more akin than any other to imperial Sicily, because Sicily and Prussia were the only two States whose constitution was based on a rational system. It is not irrelevant to compare the far-off State of the Teutonic Order ; if the Sicilian bureaucracy was modelled on similar lines to the Order, the office-holders amongst the Teutonic Knights were speedily officialised under the influence of the Sicilian model, with which the German Grand Master, Hermann of Salza, was of course intimately conversant. In complete contrast to the Templars and the Knights of St. John, the bearers of high office amongst the Teutonic Knights—Marshals and Commanders for instance—soon became " officials " whose functions were quite obviously in certain things under Sicilian influence. The Sicilian bureaucracy, itself the earliest intellectual state corporation of the Middle Ages, is at least as closely related to the knightly orders as to the modern state services to which people have retrospectively compared it.

Frederick II endeavoured to inspire the new body of officials with something akin to the *esprit de corps* of the Orders. The Justiciars were to know no other ties than those that bound them to the Emperor and the service of Justitia, they must have no private interests in their own province. They were most sternly forbidden therefore to possess money or land within their official district, to take part in any sale or purchase, exchange or presentation. Even a son might not possess property in his father's province. The justiciars must be " clean handed," they must not seek to enrich themselves, by venality or bribery, oppression or any other variety of corruption, but must be content with the salary allotted to them by the Emperor's grace. When they were holding courts in remote corners of their province they must accept no hospitality except purely official hospitality. For the duration of their office they must enter into no contract in their province, nor betrothal, nor marriage, nor any other. Inasmuch as most of the Justiciars were also fief-holders they could not, in any case, marry without the Emperor's permission. They were not even permitted—

certainly not in later times—to bring their wives with them into their official districts.

The principle that the official must be free from all private obligations is emphatically stressed. The justiciar must not be a native of the province under his jurisdiction, after his appointment he must draw no servant from his province, and, in order to prevent any kind of settling down, the offices must be yearly interchanged. Later it was generally laid down—in accordance with ancient Roman custom and the practice of the Lombard towns—that all officials held office for one year only, at the end of which they had to render an account, after which it was in the Emperor's competence to reappoint these proconsuls and propraetors for a further term of office.

This had many advantages : on the one hand the authority of the official was enhanced and his position magnified by this aloofness. He became the reflection of the Emperor. On the other hand every possibility of treachery or venality was eliminated by the " wholesome forethought " of the Emperor. Arrangements were made in such a way that the officials constituted a mutual check on each other, and this reciprocal vigilance extended down to the humblest grades. Frederick II almost always took further guarantees of various kinds for the good faith of his officials—who were in their degree omnipotent. They almost all had landed possessions or relations in other provinces, whom the Emperor could lay hands on if they played him false.

Except on Sundays and holidays, the justiciars had to sit daily—courts had previously been held only once a month. They had no permanent headquarters, for their main duty was continuously to tour their provinces, to hold courts, to oversee the land, to keep a lookout for suspicious characters, to pursue traitors or secret rebels. It was no light task to be an imperial official. All private life ceased for the duration of the office. In addition to the current work of their circuits, the speedy despatch of which was their first duty—no case was allowed to extend over more than two months—almost every justiciar constantly, at times almost daily, received a mass of special orders and special instructions from the Emperor relating to every department of life : law, finance, army, administration, university, agriculture, building, punishment, investigation, feudal affairs, marriage negotiations, and finally purely personal affairs of the Emperor's, to do with his hunting, his falcons, his horses, the game, the extermination of wolves and vermin, and the like. There were no sinecures in Frederick's service : Frederick II kept the whole State breathlessly on the run even when he himself was at a distance. The omnipotence of the officials and their very considerable independence was to a certain extent limited and bridled by these direct interventions of the Emperor ; they were responsible moreover with life and property for any injury to the State. In addition to the check exercised by the one official on the other, the subjects had, twice a year, the right to present complaints and each official was under the supervision of his superior. The functions of each were clearly defined and strict subordination enforced.

The Emperor strove in every conceivable manner to forestall any official arrogance. It is doubtful whether he was always successful, especially in the later times, and people have sought to make despotism responsible for the corruptness of the officials. The critics forget that the existence of a depotism and the need of it presuppose a corrupt and undisciplined people. If dishonesty and bribery took place in spite of all Frederick II's precautions, that proves nothing in a country that had been for thirty years without any ruler or any government. This exacting service was no longer the *quid pro quo* of the vassal in enjoyment of his fief (feudal duties and even direct taxes rested on the officials' shoulders in addition) and the salaries were extremely modest. Some other attraction than gain must have been offered to these Sicilian officials to tempt them to take service : the honour it may be of serving the King ; the opportunity of exercising power ; the prospect of fame and the special favour of the Emperor expressed in praise and at times no doubt in rewards : above all the privilege of belonging to the entourage of the Ruler : for the most part immaterial benefits. And this in a country where the aristocracy was radically corrupt and the populace of unreliable hybrid stock ! Frederick had first to awaken an appreciation of such imponderable advantages and create the conditions essential to every Service : official honour and official disci-

pline.   It is remarkable how all the well-known phenomena of
bureaucracy suddenly make their appearance here though still
rooted in primitive conditions and sanctities.   " Contempt of
court " was based on the theory that the official was the mirror
of the Emperor, consequently any insult to an official was an
insult to the Emperor and punishable as such.   The general
theory held that any crime against a person in the Emperor's
employment—whether serving as soldier or official or in whatever capacity—was to be twice as severely punished as the same
crime against a private individual.   Underlying this was the
principle of Roman law, that an officer of the Emperor was
more worthy than a private person.   The official was further
protected by the edict which affirmed : " It is sacrilege to
debate whether that man is worthy whom the Emperor has
chosen."   An intangible something was incorporate in the
official, with which he was endowed by the Emperor.

This carried the converse obligation on the officials' side to
protect his special endowment by worthy behaviour.   No
gambler might hold office.   No one might permit another to
officiate for him : the penalty for both was death.   The protection of the official against injury was only extended to him
by the Emperor while he was in discharge of his duties, it was
not valid in private quarrels.   On the other hand if an official
" under cloak of his office commits injustice " he is to be driven
from it *cum perpetuâ infamiâ*, because he has placed the Emperor's person in a false light in order to mask his own wrong
doing.   The idea of *perpetua infamia* was borrowed from
Roman Law : it was the regular Roman penalty for unfaithful-
ness in office and carried with it confiscation of property.
Here official honour is clearly outlined.   Each official is instructed by the Emperor in the duties of his office.

" The justiciar's name and title are compounded of *Jus* and
Justitia, and the closer the justiciar's relation to these the more
truly and zealously he will honour them."   Similarly with
respect to the highest officer of all, the Grand Master Justiciar :
let him be the " mirror of Justice " and let him be not merely
in name the Master of the other justiciars, but also their model

" that the lower ranks may see in him what standards they should themselves observe." Here is a hint of the importance of official precedence which is expounded elsewhere in terms of the stars : " To preserve the special honour due to our High Court we have commanded : ' when at any time the Grand Master Justiciar visits any town there to sit with our Court Judges, the justiciars of the provinces who may happen at the same time to be there, shall maintain silence as the lesser light is dimmed when it is overtaken by the greater.' " This was indeed a new departure and the commentator remarks of this law that it offends against common law, because a lower officer is by no means bound to silence by the presence of a higher.

The justiciars, as the King's commissioners and plenipotentiaries, and indeed his viceroys, in the provinces, united not only the administrative and judicial functions, but also the military : they had to summon the feudal knights, to recruit the mercenary knights, and in Frederick II's last decade when a permanent state of siege had resulted from the great war, they were army commanders in their own province. It is no cause for surprise that these branches of the service were not differentiated ; that the justiciars even on occasion led troops to battle. Apart from the fact that in those days there was no recognised " art of war," provincial governors must always be in supreme command. It was so in ancient Rome and with Napoleon's Marshals, and is always found where State discipline is highly developed. The *merum imperium*, power to command, cannot be separated from the *gladii potestas*, the executive power, or can only so be separated in peaceful bourgeois times.

The justiciars had also to exercise the highest powers of police. Their police subordinates were presumably the *comestabuli*. Special attention to political police, such as Frederick displayed, is a phenomenon observable under every dictatorship. The detective service was, of course, developed to the minutest detail, so that even when Frederick was far from Sicily on a campaign, he was often better informed about events in the provinces than the justiciars themselves. He required the aura of omniscience as urgently as that of omnipresence. In order to keep political suspects under constant state surveillance, the Emperor introduced a unique system which had the merit of publicity, but for that very reason was unquestionably far more cruel than the most suspicious secret surveillance. Every person on whom suspicion fell—of intrigues with the Roman curia, with exiles, with heretics, or with rebels —received from the authorities, a small notebook in which the details of the accusation were entered, and also the name of the denouncer. This procedure no doubt simplified the supervision of suspects, the accused was left in the dark about nothing ; but we can well believe the chronicler who tells us that this publicity led to acute discord and mutual hate between accuser and accused.

As regards legal matters, the justiciars represented the royal jurisdiction and were presidents of the law courts. There was no room left for feudal courts—except for a few insignificant survivals. Now though the justiciars must frequently have acquired considerable legal knowledge, it was rare that they were jurists by education—any more than a military governor to be the highest legal authority, needs to be a professional lawyer. They were empowered to maintain order and preside in the courts. Legal experts, professional lawyers, were associated with them who formed the curia of the justiciar, the real law court. There thus existed a second service side by side with the justiciar service, composed of a very large number of judges and counsel, as well as notaries and chancery clerks. In this the lower courts were small-scale models of the High Court. The Emperor himself was always surrounded by a large number of law scholars who acted as his permanent chancellors, his *consiliarii* and were employed in all kinds of State work : professional lawyers instead of feudal retainers !

The Grand Master Justiciar as President of the High Court had four High Court judges assigned to him, the Master Justiciars had two judges, each justiciar had one judge. Other assistant judges were to be found wherever there was a court, since every town had three town judges and six notaries : big towns like Messina, Naples, Capua had more. Notaries existed in great numbers down to the humblest posts in the departments of finance, army, fortifications, domains, forestry and harbours, and had to perform all the clerical work of an administration entirely based on written documents. Each official had to keep a considerable number of account books, registers, diaries, many of them in duplicate, for they had to be submitted at stated intervals for examination by the later-instituted Chief Auditor's Department. Every judgment had to be recorded in clear legible handwriting, not in signs or symbols of any special script which were most explicitly forbidden. As the judgments were filed, only parchment was used for them, though paper was permitted for everyday vouchers.

There were corresponding ranks and degrees in the legal profession, from the High Court Judges and Counsellors of the King down to the humblest local judges, but all were appointed and sworn in directly by the Emperor or his representative. No one might independently set up as a judge, notary or advocate. The judges had to be men of culture and education, and the Emperor kept careful watch that no unsuitable person was entrusted with the post of judge.

Lists of personnel were kept in every department, and the Emperor kept himself informed at all times of the personalities of his staffs and could usually avoid unfortunate appointments. He wrote to Sicily, for instance, from his camp before Lodi :

" To Thomas of Montenero
    Justiciar of the Principato and of Benevento—

An amazing rumour has recently reached our illustrious ears which makes a severe accusation of slackness against you and justly challenges our attention. We learn namely that our last edict about the appointment of the annual judges has not borne fruit in our town of Salerno, where thou hast permitted the appointment of one, Matthew Curialis, as judge, who is an illiterate merchant and wholly unsuited to the position. And this though amongst the population of such a town which chiefly produces cultured people there must assuredly be, we are certain, an educated man to be found to exercise the office. This displeases us all the more because firstly mischief to the town may arise therefrom, and further our command has not been obeyed as it was fitting that it should be. As we do not

wish that the legal affairs of our faithful subjects should be
bought and sold for a price by any of thy merchants, whose
fingers are deft for money making, we hereby command thee
to remove the above named Matthew from his office and to
instal in his place another man competent, trusty, sufficiently
educated. . . ."

In the whole Sicilian State, there was no department of life
in which the Government did not directly intervene to establish
order. Minor authorities lost all their independence, not only
the feudal ranks but the towns and—after the second breach
with the Pope—also the churches and monasteries. The head-
men of the towns were appointed annually by the Emperor,
and since Frederick II had a hard fight against the independence of the Lombard towns, it was most natural that he
strictly forbade the Sicilian towns to appoint their own heads :
the penalty was the destruction of the offending town. He did
not hesitate to give effect to this law, as he shortly proved. A
year after the publication of the Constitutions some Sicilian
towns rebelled ; the Emperor suppressed the rebellion with
the utmost rigour. The ringleaders whom he captured—having promised them immunity—were hanged or burned as
heretic rebels. This took place in Messina, Syracuse, and
Nicosia, while the smaller towns which had taken part in the
insurrection, Centorbi, Traina, Capizzi, and Monte Albona,
were completely destroyed. The inhabitants were reduced to
slavery and deported to a newly-founded town, which the
Emperor called Augusta, for the site of which rebellious
Syracuse was compelled to cede some of her territory. This
method was so successful that during the lifetime of Kaiser
Frederick the Sicilian towns made no second attempt to
achieve municipal independence.

The entire kingdom was to be uniformly administered by
imperial officials. The necessity for this ruthless clearing up
can only be appreciated by the student who bears in mind the
usual type of government prevailing in the Middle Ages : the
confused tangle of legal and economic relations ; the innumerable petty and pettiest authorities ; feudal lords, bishops,

monasteries, towns whose rights and claims endlessly criss-crossed each other and in every department of life cut in between the ruler and his people, and who remembers further the kaleidoscopic welter of privileges, immunities, special rights peculiar to each grade of society, to each calling, to each town, to each hamlet, causing obstruction and hesitation a thousand-fold on every side.

The measures by which Frederick II extended one unified system of administration throughout his whole kingdom, ulti-mately throughout the whole of Italy, making Sicily in very truth, the " pattern of states," were often cruel enough, but they brought in their train a most admirable simplification of the whole machinery of government. His influence on the legal situation was exerted externally. He embraced the whole tangle in one uniform system of law, but he left unmolested the private and civil rights of his subjects in their mutual relations. He was supremely indifferent whether their private affairs were to be decided according to Frankish, Lombard, Roman, Jewish, or Saracen codes, provided these did not run counter to the state laws.

This imperial administration was the first that had ever achieved *uniformitas* over an area so large, hitherto it had been possible only in the tiniest territories. The geographical con-formation of his hereditary kingdom was a factor highly favour-able to Frederick. Nature had provided the kingdom with a defined outline, with only one land boundary which he had strengthened by every known device. He had got possession of almost all border fortresses—often by very shady means. A certain abbot, for instance, owned a fort ; he was hospitably invited and then detained while his castle was annexed. Frederick next founded several towns himself in the North, Flagella for instance, and Aquila, which he equipped as arsenals. The method of foundation was simplicity itself : a certain piece of land was marked out ; the scattered inhabitants of this area were gathered into the new arsenal, they were released from all obligations to their previous lords, and in return for their freedom were compelled to work on building the fortifications.

The fortified zone of the northern land boundary prevented

egress as effectively as ingress.   All boundaries of the kingdom could now be watched.   Thanks to an ingenious and skilful harbour administration, Frederick was able to bolt and bar all the ports of Sicily, so that all communication—economic, political or intellectual—with the outer world could at will be completely cut off.   The Emperor controlled, as it were, a gigantic dam, or a castle with a hundred well-guarded gates, and could regulate all external relations.   With a word he could transform the whole kingdom into a fortress, or economically into one " closed trading centre."   Sicily thus approximated to a walled-in medieval town, and Frederick II's much admired economic policy is most easily understood if it is conceived as a medieval town-administration extended to a whole kingdom.   The Italian communes had been before Frederick, in fiscal matters, monopolies, currency and finance, and in many administrative details too : the yearly tenure of office, the justiciar a stranger in his own district, the initiation of the successor by his predecessor in office ; all these things they had introduced in various forms.   It must, moreover, be remembered that the communes had long since ceased to be simple towns surrounded by a wall.   Cities like Milan, Cremona, Piacenza, Ravenna, embraced landed property as large as a dukedom.   The Lombard cities taught Frederick much of his municipal technique, as in other spheres the Church had taught him.   He learned eagerly, not least eagerly from his foes.

We need here only dwell on the principles underlying the Sicilian constitution.   Its prime characteristic is the overriding of all private interests by the interest of the State.   The Emperor's phrase : " Sicily is the mother of tyrants " recalls the history of Dionysius of Syracuse, whose procedure in his day evoked not less amazement than Frederick II's.   The complete fiscal independence of the one was as great as that of the other, and the principle of centralisation grew more and more marked in the course of Frederick's reign.   One of the first measures to attract attention was the Emperor's creation in 1231 of State Monopolies.   Norman and Byzantine pre-

cedents may have had weight with him, but the idea was not
foreign to his own policy of utilising to the utmost all crown
rights and royal prerogatives. A monopoly of salt, steel, and
iron is readily deducible from royal mountain-rights. Hemp
and tar monopolies had no doubt some other pretext—the
needs of the imperial fleet were here decisive. The right of
dyeing was of old a crown prerogative and was now converted
into a monopoly ; only the silk monopoly is a clear case of
borrowing from Byzantine models. The working of the monopoly is most clearly seen in the case of salt—which remains a
state monopoly to this day. Some of the salt mines were
under state management, some were in the hands of private
people who had to deliver the salt to the revenue department.
On a certain day the entire trade in salt was transferred to the
State. In every centre suitable people were entrusted with the
selling of it, a uniform price was fixed for the whole kingdom :
wholesale four times, retail six times the purchase price. The
same method was applied to iron and steel, while the silk and
dye monopolies were handed over to the Jews. The manufacture of silk had originally been a prerogative of the Byzantine
emperors : King Roger having taken a number of silk weavers
prisoners—among them many Jews—in Thebes, Corinth, and
Athens, brought them to Palermo and introduced it into Sicily.
Here the royal " *tiráz* " (silk manufacture) won world-wide
fame. Frederick entrusted the trade in raw silk to the Jews
of Trani. No one else was allowed to purchase silk, and they
were obliged to make a profit of at least one-third on the re-sale,
for that was the tax they had to pay the exchequer. The manufacture of the silk was also in their hands, and the existing state
dyeworks, together with many new ones which Frederick built,
were handed over to them.

In the domain of economics, Frederick's greatest organising
triumph was his magnificent customs system. The name of
his customs officials, " *doana*," points to the Arab origin (*diwan*)
of the system. The state warehouses, " fondachi," which were
particularly important for the levy of frontier customs were also
of Arab origin. Frederick had reduced to a minimum internal
customs and tolls, which only benefited individual nobles or
towns, and in their stead had increased the frontier customs

and manipulated them in a way that created a standard for the whole western world. The customs revenues no longer enriched the insignificant middleman, the seaport or trading town ; they flowed into the coffers of the State. In all seaports and on all highroads of the northern frontier, Frederick II established state warehouses. Everyone, whether native or foreign, who wanted to import goods by sea or land into this closed kingdom, had to store them in the State magazine, where they were sold under the supervision of imperial officials.

The import duty which, apart from some special trade contracts with foreign powers, amounted to 3 per cent. of the value, fell on the seller, the slightly higher warehouse fee on the buyer. When customs duty and storage fees had once been paid the goods could, on production of the voucher, be transferred by sea or land to any other place in Sicily without further payment.

The export procedure was similar. The warehouse charges were the same, but the export duty varied for the different products and the tariff sometimes fluctuated. For exports were regulated according to the needs of the country itself and in war time all export of weapons, horses, mules, and cattle might be forbidden.

Warehouses, which also served as inns for the merchants, had long been traditional in the East. Venetians, Pisans, Genoese, and later Florentines also had all, for instance, their own *fondachi* in Alexandria. Before Frederick's day these were common in all Italian seaports ; the famous Fondaco dei Tedeschi in the Rialto was first recorded in a document of 1228. In inland Italy they were still almost unknown at the end of the thirteenth century. It almost seems as if these *fondachi* reappeared in the merchants' quarters of the German Hansa, which began to spread in the second half of the century in close connection with the Order of Teutonic Knights. At first these warehouses were the private property of foreign traders. Frederick made them state property throughout the kingdom, and compelled all merchants to use the state magazines by forbidding all sale of goods outside them. The merchants, moreover, were practically compelled to put up in these state inns, for the charge for bed, light and fuel, was included in the heavy warehouse fee. When this system was first introduced, the existing warehouses were insufficient and the merchants had to seek lodgings elsewhere. They were nevertheless compelled to pay the full fee, and their lodging bill was paid by the State. The system had the advantage of permitting the supervision of all imports and exports. Everything was exactly registered and had to be accounted for at regular intervals, the lower officials reporting to the provincial treasurer and he to the Court of Exchequer. Several copies of all customs-ledgers and warehouse-ledgers had to be kept. The customs officer, the *magister doanae*, was a different person from the warehouse master, the *fundicarius*, and so one constituted a check on the other. Further, all wares had to be weighed on the state balances at a considerable fee, or measured, in the case of cloth, etc., by the state measure. After anchor dues, landing dues, and harbour dues there were many other minor fees to pay.

The exchange, the baths, the slaughter-houses, the weights and measures, all belonged to the State. As Frederick had unified the coinage by his golden Augustales, he also established units of weight and measure, thus bringing order out of confusion. His aim in everything was simplification and practical convenience, as is obvious from his new regulation of markets and fairs. He decided to get rid of the distraction, overlapping and confusion, created by the clashing of dates and the like. Fairs were held each month in a different province. They began in the Abruzzi in the north ; they proceeded to Campania, the Principato, the Capitanata, Apulia, the Basilicata, they ended in Calabria. No fairs were held for a couple of months in the winter, during which time the merchants could replenish their stocks and travel north again to begin the year's circuit once more in the Spring.

The rigorous customs system admitted practically no privileges or exceptions ; only the Emperor himself and the Revenue Department were exempt. This had most practical importance in relation to the export of food stuffs, of which Sicily produced a superfluity. The Emperor was not only free from export duties, he was also the largest landed proprietor in the kingdom,

and consequently the greatest corn producer. He had first the
Crown lands, farmed by himself, which were frequently
organised by Cistercian monks, who no doubt also worked them,
the final supervision only being in the hands of imperial procurators.   In less fertile districts sheep-farming was extensively
carried on.   The harvests both of wool and corn under this
skilled administration must have yielded immense profits.   The
Emperor was himself an agricultural expert.   He once amazed
the Italians in Lombardy by investigating the type of soil and
then advising them whether to sow corn or beans or some other
crop.   He tried every sort of experiment with new crops : he
made plantations of henna and indigo, improved date groves,
or encouraged the use of sugar cane in Palermo by establishing
sugar refineries.   He gave instructions for the prevention of
pests.   When a plague of caterpillars threatened the harvest
he gave orders that every inhabitant should furnish daily a
certain measure of caterpillars.   He had more faith in this
method, he said, than in the efficacy of the prayers of the priests
as they perambulated the stricken fields.   He admitted that
harvests might suffer from the weather, but he saw the major
danger in the laziness of the population.   He therefore gave
orders that any landless person who was willing to work should
be given land at the expense of any who had land lying idle.

Such measures must greatly have increased the productive-
ness of his own estates, but he did not draw corn solely from
his crown lands.   He also received a twelfth of the products
of the Demanium and a tax in kind on all corn destined for
export was paid to the Treasury unless a money payment was
made instead.   No private person could compete with the
quantity of State corn, especially as the Crown with its immense
money resources could buy up private supplies. And the
Emperor was not only able to export his corn free of tax, but
to load it up on his own ships of the imperial fleet.   Hence
arose a virtual, though veiled, monopoly in corn, for the State
possessed every means of crippling competition.   One example
may be quoted to show how Frederick exploited these possibilities.   He was waging war in Northern Italy when the news
came that there was a famine in Tunis and that Genoese
merchants were buying corn with Tunisian money in the

Sicilian ports. The Emperor forthwith despatched his Arabic-speaking court philosopher, Master Theodore, from Pisa, as ambassador to Tunis, and at the same time gave orders to close all Sicilian ports, to let no private vessel sail, and to load with the utmost haste 50,000 loads of corn on the imperial fleet. The corn was to come from the imperial granaries or to be bought from private owners and immediately shipped to Tunis. Not till after the imperial fleet had sailed was any private boat free to proceed with her lading and quit Sicilian harbours. The imperial fleet reached Africa safely. The State made about £75,000. The record of this transaction happens to have come down to us.

Such dealings as these recall the mercantile theories of Colbert, but there lies a world of difference between the calm, state-rationalism of the later capitalistic centuries, and the passionate adventures of the Hohenstaufen, whose measures were always the immediate product of some actual State necessity. In this matter of the Tunisian corn, the Emperor had at first refused to interfere ; but his coffers were empty, he was himself deeply in debt to the Romans and his war with the Pope was at its height ; so he had no option but to seize the opportunity.

Frederick's collection of direct revenue was always by extra-ordinary taxes. Though in later years he raised them annually, they were always explained afresh as due to the present *imminens necessitas* of the State. Imperial finance operations were always dictated by a present need, they never served for the mere accumulation of wealth. The moment his position improved, the Emperor reduced the taxes or pretermitted the collection of them altogether. Frederick had no lack of shrewd commercial instinct, but he did not use it systematically to amass riches.

The Emperor busied himself in these years in opening foreign markets by means of commercial treaties. We have already noticed the commercial link with Tunis. Abu Zakaria Yahya, hitherto the representative of the Sultan of the Almohades, established a kingdom of his own in 1228 which embraced

Tunis, Tripoli and a part of Morocco, and founded the dynasty of the Hafsids. Three years later, in 1231, Frederick II concluded a commercial treaty with Abu Zakaria for ten years, which fixed their reciprocal customs duties at 10 per cent. and guaranteed protection to each other's merchants. Following the precedent set by the sea towns, the Emperor appointed his own Sicilian consuls for Tunis : this was the first time in history that a Western monarchy maintained a permanent representative overseas. The first imperial consul in Tunis was a Saracen, Henricus Abbas, after him a Christian, Peter Capuanus from Amalfi. Embassies to Tunis were frequent. Each side endeavoured to gratify the other, and the Emperor drew supplies for himself from Tunis, not only of Barbary horses, hunting leopards and baggage camels, but also at times of Tunisian warriors to supplement his Saracen body-guard. In return the imperial ships undertook, on occasion, to carry Tunisian envoys to Spain. Sicilian officials were sent as the Emperor's messengers to the Khalif of Granada, the " Commandet of the Faithful." No doubt Muhammadan Spain proved at times a valuable market for Sicilian corn.

While still in Syria, Frederick had concluded a commercial agreement with his friend al Kamil, Sultan of Egypt. He did not succeed in negotiating complete freedom from customs dues for Sicilian merchants in the harbours of Alexandria and Rosetta—which he appears to have aimed at—but trade with Egypt remained vigorous. An imperial ship, the " Half World," aroused the greatest excitement amongst the Egyptians by its enormous size when it sailed into the port of Alexandria with a crew of three hundred men. It is said that Frederick II stood in direct communication with India through his agents travelling by way of Egypt. We have no means of verifying the assertion, but it transpires in another connection that Frederick was extremely well-informed about India. The fascination which the word East Indies was later to exercise on the explorers is here foreshadowed. It was only a few decades after the end of the Hohenstaufen period that Marco Polo heralded the joyous age of discovery which shattered to fragments the Roman-Mediterranean world.

Meanwhile the revenue department of Sicily fulfilled its

purpose. Whatever was to be extracted from the rich country was appropriated by the imperial official. Before the outbreak of the great war, Frederick II was reckoned the wealthiest monarch of Europe since the days of Charlemagne. The Emperor's principle was well understood : Germany's business was to keep him supplied with fighters and Sicily's to find the funds. The war was being waged against the financially most prosperous powers of the known world : the Church and the Italian towns. It has been the fashion to admire Frederick's economic system, but at the same time to reproach him with having been guilty of exploitation by unduly increasing his demands during the war years. But every ruler of Frederick's stature has exploited the resources of the world, and the Sicilian kingdom, which, in return, enjoyed uninterrupted peace, could not expect to be immune. Without such exploitation—to the very limit of exhaustion—nothing really great has ever been accomplished. Consider France during, and after, the Napoleonic Wars.

Frederick II's new constitution, opening with the imperial Prœmium, had gently descended from the sublimest spiritual heights and settled on the land of Sicily, seizing the country in its iron grasp. Uniform administration, uniform law, uniform finance : the constitution of the State was complete. The way was paved for the Sicilians to feel themselves one unified people, to realise their cohesion as a nation ; but the goal was not yet reached. Except in a very few points the laws scarcely touched the elementary unities which make the inhabitants of a country feel themselves one and bind them into a nation : the essentials are : community of speech, of blood, of history and of festivals. These common elements were lacking in the Sicilian welter of peoples more than in most other countries. Happily for the Emperor, the other countries of Europe had scarcely yet begun to be conscious of the existence of these natural ties. For centuries it had been the Church's aim to stifle these natural forces, to displace folk-customs by the rites of the Church, local history by Holy Scripture, native festivals by the Church's feasts, while for every intellectual utterance the sacred Latin was preferred to the vernacular, and the blood of the race was of less account than the Blood of the Redeemer. The awakening of national consciousness in the twelfth and thirteenth centuries was the emancipation of the people's natural instincts from the spiritual bonds of the Church.

Frederick II in his capacity as Emperor dared not sever the ecclesiastical fetters that held the people in bondage, for the Church was the guarantor of his position and of the existence of the Roman Empire. On the other hand, he awakened and stimulated the " national " impulses more than anyone before him, and in Sicily he not only called out latent forces and feelings, but set about creating them in his chosen people and welding that people into a nation.

With his coming a new epoch began for Sicily. Frederick continually emphasised the fact : again and again in his Book of Laws he calls himself (with deliberate intent) " the New King." With him the Sicilian race-mixture begins to be a people with a history of its own. In a remarkable document of this time Frederick summarises the History of Sicily for his faithful subjects and conjures up the past, with the present intention of making the Sicilians conscious of their common history. Under the Greeks and Romans, Sicily had suffered great injustice, because the country was divided up and rent asunder. The Normans were the first to create a unity : " Since when this noble country . . . under the firm and heroic settlement of our ancestors rose to be called a KINGDOM and the inhabitants learned to love their kingdom and their throne of royal dignity." The zenith of Sicilian history came when " Divine Providence, in its wisdom, granted in our day this great happiness to your king, whom you had nourished with the milk of your love and weaned at your breast, that he should scale the heights of the Roman Empire." They were now living under the rule of the Sicilian Hohenstaufen, " this off-shoot of a new stem," who had grown up amongst the native born of the kingdom. . . . The valour of the Sicilians would grow ever greater under their Emperor, " for already in the early days of that heroic age our ancestors' noble plantations bore ample fruit." In such terms the Emperor spurred on his faithful to fight against the Lombard faithlessness : they should follow the example of their ancestors who conquered distant peoples and " feared not to face the dangers of the sea nor the buffetings of fate on land."

Such appeals presupposed a people for the Emperor to address, a people on whom such words would act. The Normans had certainly made the first " firm settlement," but Guiscard's successors could not have spoken in such terms to the mixture of Arabs, Greeks, Latins and Jews, nor by such words have hoped to fire any but the few noble Norman kinsmen who were round them. Frederick treated the Sicilians as a nation with its own glorious history, and he was the first to attempt to point the Sicilians to their common traditions, to address to them a common appeal. He was able to do so because he was no usurper, but " an off-shoot from the new Sicilian planting," who felt a bond with the new people amongst whom he had grown to manhood, a community of race between the ruler and the ruled, which had hitherto been lacking. The Emperor's allusions to race and nurture were no accident. We quote another pronouncement

The Emperor had once explained the sacrament of marriage as a natural necessity for the maintenance of the human race. Not every marriage, however, was calculated to secure the " better nature " of mankind. The Emperor therefore published a law which paid more heed to breed than to sacramental considerations, so that a commentator, long after, was moved to indignation, remarking " this discloses the whole spiritual degeneracy of this Emperor Frederick who would hinder the just and free marriage instituted by God in Paradise. Such a a law is not binding before the judgment-seat of God." Frederick II had forbidden, on pain of confiscation of property, any Sicilian man or maid to contract a marriage with a foreigner (that is anyone born outside Sicily) without special permission from the Emperor. He explains the reasons with profound wisdom : " It has often grieved us to see how the righteousness of our kingdom has suffered corruption from foreign manners by the mixture of different peoples. When the men of Sicily ally themselves with the daughters of foreigners, the purity of the race becomes besmirched, while evil and sensual weakness increases, the purity of the people is contaminated by the speech and by the habits of the others, and the seed of the stranger defiles the hearth of our faithful subjects." Hence, as a remedy against " degeneracy of race," against " racial confusion in the kingdom," the law forbids marriage with foreigners.

Nothing could demonstrate more clearly than this law the intention of the Emperor to create, even from the racial standpoint, a unified nation out of the Sicilian people. It was a measure which, aiming with wholesome severity at something higher, frankly ran counter to every custom of the Church and was always felt as a monstrosity, as the commentator shows. Though the same writer adds, not without admiration, " This Emperor, however, strove most diligently to preserve his people pure from corruption by the customs and conversation of strangers." Everything in this stern State aimed at unity, not only in theory but in practice, based on the *necessitas rerum*. For unity was of God and multiplicity was of the Devil.

History proves that Frederick II achieved his aim, and succeeded in awakening amongst the Sicilians respect for the dignity of their own race. Some sixty years after the death of their only Emperor the Sicilians rose (the most mongrel population of Palermo first of all) against the Anjous at the Vespers and slaughtered the French garrison in an unexampled massacre. They fought under the unfurled eagles with the cry " Death to the Gauls ! ", and when they found Sicilian women pregnant by the French they ripped open their wombs with the sword to trample under foot the foreign brood.

The history of Frederick II demonstrates how much a lawgiver can accomplish by force and compulsion, so long as he knows what his aims are, and so long as those aims are just. Nevertheless, certain limits are set to the direct spiritual influence of a ruler on the masses of his people, and his wishes, thoughts and opinions are for the most part handed on with necessary and inevitable dilution through intermediaries, those intimates who stand under the ruler's personal influence, the court, the entourage, the hierarchy of imperial employees. A picture of the Emperor himself can best be formed by studying his human influence on those most closely associated with him.

III

From the intellectual point of view Frederick's new secular State was a triumph of that lay culture which, for the last century, had been spreading in wider and wider circles. This was the first time that profane learning had been concentrated and organised. The pillars of the state were now educated laymen, no longer clerics, and it is only natural that the Founder of the State was himself the most highly cultured layman of them all. By his organisation of the emancipated "secular" spirit Frederick II broke once and for all the spell which the Church had laid on the whole domain of the non-material as an intellectual and spiritual unity. Even more clearly than by the state philosophy, the complete mental independence of the new State was demonstrated by the fact that the clergy ceased to play a part in the administration of Sicily, and their spiritual influence on it gradually ceased.

The Sicilian state itself is the proof that lay education had made great strides in Frederick's century, for the Emperor was able to risk basing his whole new kingdom on it. On the other hand the existing supply of educated laymen was not sufficient, and in order to be able to draw on larger numbers Frederick founded the University of Naples. In the Charter of the University Frederick stated : " We propose to rear many clever and clearsighted men, by the draught of knowledge and the seed of learning ; men made eloquent by study and by the observation of just law, who will serve the God of all and will please us by the cult of Justice. . . . We invite learned men to our service, men full of zeal for the study of *Jus* and *Justitia*, to whom we can entrust our administration without fear." The Emperor thus made clear what spirit was to govern his state—the legal spirit. This need not surprise us. For, since Justice was the Emperor's mediator with God the same must apply to his followers and servants.

The whole state was thick-sown with lawyers. Ousting the clergy, hitherto the only representatives of education and culture, the jurists now had the entry to the Emperor's court, and the replacing of a clerical atmosphere by an emancipated secular atmosphere was pregnant with momentous change even in the highest politics. The Church had long been striving to enlist to her side the newly-awakened town-dweller. Frederick II now entered the lists, and while the Church, with the support of the mendicant orders, was successful in capturing the masses the Emperor won over the educated classes, the new intellectual aristocracy. These were usually inclined to support the Government. It was, therefore, of the greatest importance that Frederick II, recognising their vigour and their potentialities, enlisted the town lawyers in his service, gave them the widest possible scope, in administration, in his chancery work, and in his court circles, and by this means within a few years revolutionised the whole central government of Sicily and even of the Empire. The two administrations of Sicily and of the Empire were originally to be kept apart, in accordance with the agreement with Rome, but they were afterwards amalgamated.

The University of Naples was to rear professional jurists, judges, and notaries with legal training. Hard and fast "careers" were unknown in Frederick's state, as was any systematic promotion by seniority which the one-year tenure of office made impossible. The factors making for success were the personal qualities of the individual, an opportunity of distinguishing himself, and luck in happening to attract the attention of the Emperor and the court. The number of officials was relatively small, and it was possible to keep them all under observation. It was probably rare for a really able man to be passed over, for the Emperor was quick to seize a suitable man for a given post, whether a precedent was thereby followed or created. Certain general tendencies can, however, be traced : the judge's career, for instance, was usually distinct from the notary's, though occasional interchanges took place.

Having completed his studies at the University of Naples (we have no clue to the length of the course ; in Northern Italy three to six years was prescribed) the new judge was selected by some town to act as town-judge. On this the candidate betook himself to court with a certificate, to receive his appointment from the Emperor or his representative, to take the oath and, if necessary, to be tested by the High Court

in his literary and legal attainments.   In this way the Emperor
and the Court Judges kept in touch with the rising generation
of lawyers, except so far as during the Emperor's absence
appointments were made by his provincial representatives, the
justiciars.   The young judge next had an opportunity of
entering the narrower State service as *judex* to one of the justiciars, or, later, in Northern Italy, to one of the numerous
vicars, vicars general or podestas.   With good fortune he might
ultimately reach the office of High Court Judge.   This was not
the only avenue to the High Court bench, for we know of High
Court Judges who had never officiated as ordinary judges : the
famous Thaddeus of Suessa, for example, a courtier and one of
Frederick's intimates.   It is worth noting that quite a number
held the title of High Court Judge without having officiated at
all.   These were the *consiliarii*, the counsellors who were
employed in the imperial Chancery and on diplomatic missions
and formed part of the Emperor's immediate following.
This is the first time that professional lawyers figure in
the permanent personnel of an Emperor's court, not merely as
occasional experts.   The judges of lower degree could find
many niches for themselves in the service ; we find them as
chamberlains, as tax collectors, as overseers of the accounts
departments, as keepers of the King's treasury and in other
capacities ; in offices which might perfectly well have been
filled by non-legal nobles or burgesses.   It is important to note
how the lawyers were thrusting into posts of every sort.

The second important group of educated lawyers were the
notaries.   They had to pursue a course of study, and probably
to win the degree of master, before seeking further training as
registrar of some chancery.   After examination by the High
Court the notary received the imperial nomination and
appointment.   For a notary as for a judge service at court was
the desirable goal.   A man might begin at the court of a
provincial justiciar or in some branch of the finance department, and then get an opening at court and become Court
Notary at the High Court, or President of some section of the
imperial Chancery : Current Business or Feudal Affairs, for
instance.   As a general rule the supply of court notaries and
chancery clerks was supplemented in other ways with which we

shall deal later. The state, as we have already seen, was full of notaries who had to deal with the ever increasing mass of written documents which gave the administration so modern an air. The immense number of orders issued by the Court, most of them required in several copies, demanded in every grade of the services a highly skilled staff of clerks not subject to annual displacement. Other departments, notably Finance, also required the services of notaries.

This penetration of the secular state by the legal spirit was only a reflection of what had already taken place within the bosom of the Church. A knowledge of Canon Law was indispensable for every cleric of any position. The carefully cultivated style of the notaries was also originally a product of the Church. It followed that a course of study at Naples and employment in the imperial Chancery might be the opening of a clerical career. There was the possibility of Church promotion for anyone who had mastered both laws, and if this did not offer the Chancery was a safe refuge. We have already alluded to the Emperor's efforts to secure the appointment of his notaries to vacant bishoprics. In the early days these efforts always failed, but after the second excommunication the Emperor flung aside all restraint and began to appoint Sicilian bishops of his own choice, or allow Archbishop Berard of Palermo to do so, except in cases where he preferred to keep a vacancy. The Ottos and the Salians long ago in Germany used to rear up their private chaplains to be their future bishops, and the Chancery of the Imperial Court now served the same purpose as of old the private chapel of the Emperor. The radical innovation was that these clerical Chancery officials, never very numerous, were appointed not because they were clerics but because they were jurists, and in spite of their being clerics. The Emperor found them in no way indispensable, and their priestly character was a matter of indifference to him, fraught with no danger. Walter of Ocra, notary and chaplain of the Emperor, and one of his busiest officials, rose to be Sicilian Chancellor, but he was on an entirely different footing from the bishop-chancellors of earlier days: he was simply an imperial official who happened to be a cleric. The higher clergy were still represented at Court, especially by prelates who were able to adapt themselves to the new spirit of the times.   The Archbishops Berard of Palermo, and Jacob of Capua, belonged to the most intimate circle of the Emperor. Frederick had utilised the latter as collaborator in the Constitutions of Melfi, especially in those sections which dealt with the Church and the Sicilian clergy.   A few other bishops were intimate with the Emperor, Archbishop Berard of Messina and Bishop Peter of Ravello.   These prelates had weight in the intellectual life of the court only in so far as they accommodated themselves to the literary and mental pursuits around them.   They were no longer themselves the independent purveyors of spiritual life as bishops had been wont to be. Still we must not undervalue the fact that the mental atmosphere of the Court was sufficiently catholic to give scope even to canonistic culture.   It was inevitable that the University of Naples should have a number of clerical students, since all Sicilian subjects were· compelled to attend it.   One of the greatest of all churchmen was a product of Naples : Thomas Aquinas, the *doctor angelicus* of the Roman Church.

Two years after founding the University of Naples Frederick II had closed the University of Bologna on account of the fiasco of the Cremona Diet in 1226.   In so doing he had a special intention of his own.   He wrote to the professors as well as to the scholars of Bologna : the last thing he wished was that learned men should suffer through the recalcitrance of the rebellious Bolognese who had joined the Lombard League.   He invited them, therefore, to quit Bologna and come to Naples, " where instituted by us with much care, study flourishes . . . the beauty of the neighbourhood attracts, no less than the lavish supplies of everything, and the reverend community of doctors."   This great plan of transferring to Naples the famous Law School of Bologna fell through.   The Pope's intervention secured a truce with the Lombard League, and the Emperor had to retract his outlawry of Bologna and permit the reopening of the University.   The scholars of Bologna made merry over the imperial University of Naples : this ambitious home of all sciences was at best an embryo, and one not likely to thrive.   For it depended on the caprice of its founder, who had no obligations and whose mood might easily change.   The

Bolognese were not far wide of the mark. For better or worse
the fate of this suddenly-founded University was linked with
the fate of the Emperor and his State. When the Papal troops
invaded the kingdom all study ceased in Naples, though only
for a few years. In 1234 Frederick re-established the University and attracted a really excellent teaching staff. At first
Roffredo of Benevento taught Civil Law ; the Canon Law
scholar, Bartholomew Pignatellus, the Decretals ; Master
Terrisius of Atina gave instruction in Arts ; a Catalonian,
Master Arnaldus, lectured on Aristotle's natural philosophy.
The grammarian, Walter of Ascoli, was secured, and completed in Naples his great Etymological Encyclopaedia, begun
in Bologna. Finally, Peter of Ireland, the teacher of Thomas
Aquinas, whom his contemporaries called *gemma magistrorum
et laurea morum*, represented natural science.

Frederick II's severe struggles with the Church compelled
certain retrenchments of study to be made at a later date, but
the university was never again dissolved. After its re-establish-
ment in 1234 its administration was in the hands of a Justiciar
of Students, so that the University enjoyed a certain independence, though it remained immediately connected with the High
Court and with the imperial Chancery. Students and professors were well aware who was the determining personality ;
when they begged, in 1234, for the opportunity of resuming
their studies, they did not appeal direct to the Emperor but to
the " Master," who was even then considered as " the ex-
pounder of the sole truth for the ears of the Emperor," the High
Court Judge, Piero della Vigna.

We know all too little about this famous scholar and writer,
who, like a second St. Peter, " held both keys to Frederick's
heart," and who even in Dante's Hell, in the ghostly wood of
the Suicides, maintained that his fall was solely due to " envy's
cruel blow," that " harlot of courts." He is sometimes
supposed to represent a frequently recurrent type, so much so
that Conrad Ferdinand Meyer had no difficulty in painting
from him his picture of the English Thomas à Becket. Yet
Piero della Vigna is radically different, by his whole position,

and his human relation to his master, from Chancellors like Cassiodorus or Reginald of Dassel. He was not the complementary brain of a warrior king, but an instrument which a most intellectual Emperor had consciously fashioned for himhimself : the spokesman and the mouthpiece of his master.

As Logothetes, " one who places words," this greatest Latin stylist of the Middle Ages was, both in writing and speaking, the mouthpiece of imperial thought and act, the creator of the imperial diction and the majestic utterance ; as jurist, probably the author of all the Emperor's laws ; as scholar and humanist of the first water, the counsellor and intimate, nay the friend of the Emperor. He was quite indispensable to Frederick, this master of expression, who had at his command the most telling phrase for each phase of the versatile Emperor's activity, who supplied the most convincing explanation of his master's acts, and often in so doing helped to determine the next step, whose duty it was to announce and make plausible Frederick's constant changes of front. Frederick had raised him up from nothing to the first position in the state, and made him the confidant of all his schemes, and was finally compelled to destroy him when the servant began, unaccountably, to stumble. With another man, reproof or banishment would have sufficed ; a blunder of della Vigna's merited extinction. His was a life which Fate entangled in the tragedy of the House of Hohenstaufen.

Legend ascribed the basest origin to Piero della Vigna, son of an unknown father, and an abandoned mother, who miserably supported herself and her infant by beggary. He was, in fact, of reputable family, his father probably a town judge in Capua, where Piero was certainly born. The boy seems to have gone to Bologna without the family approval, and to have carried on his studies in canon law and civil law amid considerable hardships. At last he addressed a petition to Archbishop Berard of Palermo. It is a testimony to both that on the strength of this one letter, so the story goes, Berard of Palermo immediately commended the petitioner to the Emperor's attention. When Frederick returned in 1221 he installed the young man as notary in his Chancery, and, recognising his outstanding ability, speedily promoted him to be High Court

Judge, then Chief Notary of the Sicilian kingdom, till he finally created for him the post of Logothetes, who should actually speak for the Emperor in the High Court, as well as write for him. As High Court Judge Piero della Vigna was one of the legal Counsellors in the closest attendance on the Emperor. In this capacity he formulated the whole body of Laws that comprised the Constitutions of 1231. So amply did he play " Tribonian to the Justinian of Sicily " that posterity inserted his name at the end of the *Liber Augustalis.* Later, della Vigna took over the sole direction of the imperial Chancery, and his fame rested more especially on his stylistic accomplishment. His art, however, was rooted in human things, and his facility of expression grew with the Emperor's growth. When the Crusades had given the Emperor new horizons the manifestos of the Capuan began to expand and to swell into a rhythmic emotion which, year by year, surrounded the majesty of Frederick II with more magnificent and more awe-inspiring eloquence.

His Latin was an artificial language, highly perfected in form, often difficult to understand, so that contemporaries complained of his highest style as " intentionally obscure." Only by a measure of obscurity was it possible, without sacrificing its living vigour, to extort from Latin, for centuries traditionally mishandled, the notes of height and depth required. When the humanists a little later revivified the classical Latin of Cicero they discovered—alas—a dead language, and brought it again to birth. Piero della Vigna is the last creative writer of living Latin. It was a living language that spoke with pomp and pride and smooth-flowing magnificence from his obscure periods. Its comprehensiveness and joy in style bore within them the seeds of classic humanistic Latin. Della Vigna's speech, a *Summa* in its own domain, exhausted every possibility of Latin-Christian linguistics in the realms of Church and Empire.

For centuries to come, long after the Christian Roman world that had begotten them was dead, his collected letters lived on in the Chanceries of Europe as masterpieces of style, and preserved the image of that Emperor who had imposed it on his spokesman. How much in these letters is Piero della

Vigna, and how much Frederick, will never be known, but the composite result dictated the style of all the other imperial secretaries. The Capuan's elaborate and emotional forms of expression would have rung false and hollow without the living reality that underlay them, without the wide circle of the Roman Empire, and in the background the Emperor holding the pen. King Manfred's letters in della Vigna's style disclose a painful discrepancy.

The information we crave about Piero della Vigna's personal and private life is not forthcoming, but his poems, letters and manifestos betray him as one of those highly-cultured literati whom humanism, awaking with Petrarch, later produced in numbers. Piero della Vigna was the most eminent amongst the few existing in the early thirteenth century. On the one hand he was master of the old : the formalism of the time, canon and civil law, scholastic and ancient philosophy, ancient authors and church divines, rhetoric, versifying, letter-writing. On the other hand he was zealous to face the new with an ele- mental fire and passion that flash from his writings. He was ready to turn his hand to anything : scholar and judge, philo- sopher and artist, stylist, diplomat and courtier, ambassador and go-between, even warrior when occasion demands, drawing up the lines of battle, perhaps even taking part in the fight. He wore himself out in service. He says himself that he had grown very old—in contrast to the ever-youthful Emperor. Little is known about his appearance. The so-called della Vigna bust of the bridge gate at Capua cannot represent the celebrated High Court Judge of Frederick II, but more likely portrays a late classical philosopher. Nevertheless, the con- temporary identification of this bust with a judge of the Hohenstaufen Court indicates that this human type, was not unfamiliar amongst the law scholars of the Court ; a heavy, serious, learned face it is, with supercilious, even mocking expression ; vigorous and strong, however, and massive, with the mighty beard which lends added dignity to the head—the very antithesis of the picture we form of the Emperor himself.

Piero della Vigna's duties to the Naples University and to the imperial Chancery and High Court were not confined to the administration, but extended also to the personnel. For one thing, Court officials gave lectures at the University ; amongst them the High Court Judge, Roffredo of Benevento, and later an imperial Court Notary, Nicolas of Rocca, who started rhetorical courses in Naples. The relation of the Chancery to the students was even more important, for the budding jurist, especially the young notary, received the groundwork of his training at the University, but the final polish at the Emperor's court. The literary education of the favoured few was more or less directly in the hands of Piero della Vigna, in whose Chancery they acquired the *stilum supremum*. Piero della Vigna was in this the upholder of a tradition which lingered, not in the Court, but in his native town of Capua. For the art of style, the *ars dictandi*, had been so specially cultivated in this town that one may fairly talk of a Capuan School, the peculiar character of which was its direct reversion to late classical prose. Piero della Vigna very possibly learnt his own skill in Capua, whereas the stylists of preceding generations had adopted the famous epistolary manner of the Roman Curia under the great Innocent. Piero della Vigna quite probably owed the Archbishop of Palermo's recommendation to the fact that the Emperor was anxious for his Chancery to attain the same distinction of style as the Curia. Della Vigna's first petition must have displayed remarkable skill to lead to his reception in the High Court. The value which Frederick II attached to the style of his letters, and his ambition to compete in this with the Curia, would have combined with his own artistic appreciation to perceive the political significance of such unusual ability. The Emperor had to win public opinion by his manifestos, which supplied in the Christian world the place of the ancient Forum. Epistolary art replaced the forensic eloquence of Rome and the Greek cities. People justly compared Piero della Vigna, the orator of Capua, to Cicero.

There was at the beginning of the thirteenth century in Capua a flourishing school of written rhetoric, of which Piero della Vigna himself was a product. It was extremely significant that he established a close connection between it and the High Court and even transplanted it to the imperial Chancery. The Chancery itself thus became a school of rhetoric, the focus of the literary life of the Court. Everything about the Emperor's Court which seems a foretaste of Humanism : the reversion to classic models ; the Emperor's cult of Rome ; his echo of the Caesars in formula and title, simile and metaphor, all this had its roots in the learned circles of Piero della Vigna, who were inspired on their side by the presence of a living Caesar. The two reinforced each other : Frederick II could pose as Caesar because his entourage could accept him in such a rôle, and he was driven to pose as Caesar because rhetorical and literary style proclaimed him such. The same applied to his Christian attitude : for the imperial art of letter-writing sprang from the curial style which provided all the Biblical comparisons, including the comparisons with Christ. This blend of the Christian and the ancient Roman which prevails in Frederick's writing and smacks of the Renaissance, is the product of this group of stylists to whom a knowledge of the Bible was as necessary as a knowledge of the classics. This does not explain their vigour. The many private letters of these imperial chancery officials that have come down to us are convincing proof of the passion for knowledge that possessed these men, when once they had breathed the strong intellectual atmosphere of the imperial court. A wretched notary writes from prison to his friends to send him a Livy or some other historian, feeling convinced that he was " not worthy to un-loose the latchet of their shoes." These officials shared the view the Emperor loved to inculcate : that " fame comes through knowledge, honour comes through fame, and riches come through honour."

The High Court and the Chancery itself distributed to the widest possible circles this knowledge which the Emperor so highly prized and his courtiers coveted. " The breasts of rhetoric have suckled many eminent minds at the imperial court," writes Piero della Vigna to a younger friend, whom he later brought to court and with whom, as with others, he kept up a correspondence that served the purpose also of exercises in style. This may have been a usual way of giving lessons in letter-writing, so that the letter served a double purpose. It is no matter for surprise that the later stylists were, for the most part, della Vigna's compatriots : Campanians if not Capuans. A number of his pupils are known, who themselves became the instructors of literary youth. John of Capua calls himself the pupil of Piero della Vigna. In a letter of consolation addressed to two of the Emperor's secretaries about the death of a third (all three having also been disciples of the great High Court Judge) he paints a very vivid picture of della Vigna's human methods : " Well I know how our master and only benefactor Piero della Vigna is shocked by the death of such a friend. For he had, with good reason, cherished the greatest hopes that his vineyard (vinea) would have brought forth three shoots from a fruitful vine and that he might have presented to the Emperor from the womb of his beloved, three worthy disciples, three wooers of his own worth, three followers of his own life. The unknowing would have sought to ascertain, the knowing would have marvelled, how all three had received the same teaching in the same manner from such a teacher, and how one affection had united all the three. Happy indeed this community of three in one, where domestic love unites teacher and pupils." This indicates the school-like character of the Capuan tradition. The inevitable jealousy of the courtiers is hinted at when we read that Piero della Vigna wins fame and praise, and envy too, when his pupils " find grace in the eyes of the Prince " and receive posts from him " who loveth the tribe of the young." Della Vigna is constantly alluded to in court circles with a pun on his name as the " fruitful vineyard." He was the centre and soul of all this courtly activity, and they turned to him for enlightenment when the courtiers " fell to merry quarrelling " over one problem or another, as intellectual men are wont to do in company.

Della Vigna enjoyed the Emperor's complete confidence. There was no lack of sycophants who flattered " the Master's Vineyard." One prelate wrote : " Vinea was the *Petrus* on whose rock the Emperor's Church was founded when the Emperor refreshed his spirit by a meal with his disciples." They called him " the Emperor's Vicar," corresponding to the Prince of the Apostles, Peter, Vicar of Christ, and as such the " Bearer of the Keys " of this world's empire, of the Emperor's heart, a simile of which Dante later made use. Della Vigna's indirect influence on Court society was no less great. Men hummed round him as Frederick's favourite ; the highest dignitaries of Church and State inquired of him the general temper of the Court, the mood of the "Dominus" or the "Caesar." They reproached him for his long silence, or forwarded requests and recommendations for the Emperor, begging his support. All these letters seek to attain the lofty style of the master, and his answers often show a touch of delicate irony as he couches them in even more pompous phrase and metaphor. Piero della Vigna maintained intercourse with the law professors of Bologna for some time. But whereas in earlier days Roman Emperors turned to Bologna to enquire the interpretation or application of a law, the doctors of Bologna now betook themselves to Frederick II to enquire from him about some enactment peculiar to Sicily, and right gladly Frederick answered them. Piero della Vigna's Constitutions of Melfi represent one of the greatest legal achievements of the century. Commentaries on the *Liber Augustalis* began to appear almost at once, and many of the commentators were alumni of the University of Naples. Thus one creation reacted on the other.

The art of writing Latin verse was part of the school routine for students of style and rhetoric ; it was practised almost exclusively in legal stylistic circles. Secular Latin literature was a relatively late growth in Italy, and one of the earliest goliard compositions in Italy is ascribed to Piero della Vigna. It is a long satirical poem, directed against the greed of prelates and mendicant monks, and differs from the other songs of vagrant poets by its positive political importance. Piero's pupils also wrote Latin verse : Master Terrisius of Atina, author of a lengthy poem, was counted among his friends. The Chronicler, Richard of San Germano, who interwove a number of poems with the text of his chronicle, was also a notary, but he did not belong to the actual della Vigna circle. Nor did the judge, Richard of Venusia, who composed a comedy in distichs full of topical allusions to imperial officials. He dedicated his comedy to the Emperor. It was the first effort of its kind.

Works in Greek verse were not unheard of in official circles. Calabria was still largely Greek in speech, and is said to have been the means of introducing a knowledge of ancient Greek to Renaissance scholars. Barlaam, who is the reputed Greek

teacher of both Petrarch and Boccaccio, was a Calabrian. The
Constitutions of Melfi were soon translated into Greek, and we
possess a number of Greek letters from Frederick (who was a
master also of that language) to his son-in-law John Vatatzes,
Emperor of Nicaea. They were probably drafted by the same
Greek-speaking notary as was usually employed to translate
Greek documents into Latin, John of Otranto. An iambic
poem of his on the Siege of Parma has been preserved. This
episode also formed the subject of a long poem by the Chartophylax, Georgios of Gallipoli in Calabria, together with an
enthusiastic encomium on Frederick II in which the Emperor
figures as Zeus, the Thunder God and Lightning-Wielder of
Greek mythology   A supernatural atmosphere thus surrounded
the Hohenstaufen, which was revealed in a remarkable manner
to the later humanists. The story goes that in 1497 a carp was
caught in a pond at Heilbronn, in whose gills, under the skin, a
copper ring was fastened, with a Greek inscription which stated
that Frederick II, with his own hand, had released this fish.
The humanists were much struck by " the remarkably life-
giving quality of the hand *Friderici Secundi* " and particularly
stirred by the inscription's being in Greek, and they decided that
Frederick's intention must have been to quicken to new life
the study of Greek in Germany by this message of a dumb fish.

The intellectual influence exercised in foreign countries by
the Hohenstaufen's court is revealed in a Latin poem of the
Englishman, Henry of Avranches, who offered his services to
the Emperor about this time. The poet shows himself a man
well skilled in every branch of stylistic art, master of all the
early humanistic culture of his day like John of Salisbury. He
writes at great length on the origin of Latin poetry, which came
from the Hebrews to the Greeks, through Adonis and Sappho,
and from the Greeks passed to the Latins, and which he himself venerates and practises. Verse is the divine form of speech,
and the man who can convert prose into verse can also transform the caves of a savage country into dwelling-houses. He,
therefore, the Englishman, would fain live at the Emperor's
court and be his comrade in the art of poetry or renounce his
honour as the king of song.

The Emperor himself did not write Latin verse—if we

except the verse inscriptions on imperial castles and forts, and a few occasional couplets which tradition ascribes to him. Nevertheless, he was in close touch with the stylists and their work. He shared their scholarship to a very large extent, and we are told in many places that he was able himself to speak with great eloquence and skill, though he later preferred to allow Piero della Vigna to make his speeches for him, taking a verse of Ovid for a text as readily as a messianic saying from the Bible. The Emperor had no craving for displaying his skill, and shrewdly refrained from over-much public speaking. Popular opinion averred: " He speaks little, knows much and can do much." It must have had all the more immense effect when, on really important occasions, the Emperor himself spoke after Piero della Vigna. A report informs us what a shudder of amazement seized the people on one occasion, when, from his throne, raised high above the heads of the multitude, the Sacred Majesty of the Emperor solemnly spoke down and defended itself against the Bishop of Rome. Perhaps the custom of princely ceremonial speeches dates from Frederick II, who has been called the " mirror of the world in speech and custom." With the great Hohenstaufen such speeches were provoked only by stern necessity ; no prince of the Renaissance will have been able to evoke the magic shudder that greeted Frederick's voice.

The magnificent gestures of a world-monarch came naturally to Frederick. Not less natural was his readiness to relax in the company of his intimate friends, when he could feel sure that none of his words would be misunderstood. Above all other things he loved good conversation ; witty and intellectual talk, in which he joined with an indescribable charm of his own, was an absolute necessity to him. He had no need to summon a Voltaire from abroad to provide the *dilicato parlare* that he loved. There were, it is true, many foreign scholars at his court, but their business was to conduct research in definite philosophic or scientific subjects and to expound these afresh, communicating their results to the court, most frequently through the medium of Frederick himself.

The whole court shared his spirit. There was none who did not, to the measure of his ability, respond to the intellectual stimulus of the Emperor's personality, and a very considerable proportion of his knowledge and modes of thought communicated itself to the court officials, notaries, and stylists of his entourage. Years after his death it is still possible to tell with almost absolute certainty whether the writer of a given letter had been in touch with one of those sucklings " of the milk of rhetoric at the imperial court."

Certain philosophical lines of thought which were simply dubbed " Ghibelline ideas " in later times were a product of the spirit that flowed from Frederick II and his circle : The recurrence of Nature, Reason, Necessity in certain connections, the belief in Fortune instead of Providence, the disappearance of threadbare Bible tags in favour of quotations from the classics. Frederick's contemporaries were ripe for these things. Della Vigna's activity has shown, however, how conscious, intentional and well-thought-out was the intellectual preparation of the ground.

It was something like a new gospel that emanated from the court, and one of the tokens of it was the inrush of a youthful spirit into an age of decadence and decay—a living something that drew into itself all that was actively alive. Outworn mental attitudes had no place in this State. The whole imperial group was young, not only in spirit but in years, incomparably young, full-blooded and alive. Aged, aged Pope Gregory had good reason to feel afraid ; he even lodged a complaint against the excessive youthfulness of the imperial officials. The Emperor curtly retorted that it was none of the Pope's business, and begged to call the Pope's attention to the fact that, according to the Sicilian Book of Laws, to debate about the suitability of imperial officers was sacrilege. That was fairly cynical. Indeed an immeasurable cynicism, a sign of vigorous life, prevailed in the circle of Frederick and his friends, especially in reference to their opponents. Not towards opponents only. Frederick always found it hard to repress his acid wit and probably gave it free rein amongst his intimates, pouring scorn not only on the Pope but on friends and contemporaries. He made merry over the envoys of his faithful Cremona and mimicked their absurd way of speaking, how they must first indulge in reciprocal flatteries before one of them would open his business. He said of his friend, the Margrave of Montferrat, that you would need a pickaxe to hew money out of him —a saying that a troubadour swiftly seized on and wove into his *sirventes*. He even indulged in mockery of Chingiz Khan, who had proposed (what would scarcely have been conceivable save for the Asiatic perspective) that Frederick II should do him homage and accept appointment at the Court of the Great Khan. The Emperor's prompt repartee was that he would apply for the post of falconer. On the other hand, the Emperor was only amused when one of his friends aimed a shaft at him. The chronicler remarks that Eccelino of Romano would have visited such a jest with instant death.

These are all signs of the intellectual freedom and detachment of the Emperor himself and his court. It was freedom on a large scale. Each of the imperial jests, each of the blasphemies which frequently leaked out, was a challenge to an entire world. These cynicisms would have been wholly unjustified had not Frederick himself been able to build up a new world with its own new sanctities. If anyone dared to breathe against the holy things of the State, Frederick took umbrage immediately: " He who provokes the Emperor with words is punished with deeds." The officials were not slow to catch their master's tone. One of his underlings speaks words that might be Frederick's own : some Guelf prisoners were to be executed, and confession was refused them with the taunt that it was quite supererogatory for them ; as friends of the Pope they were all holy together and would alight forthwith in Paradise. Before the days of Frederick II no one would have ventured such a jest. It presupposes an inexpressible contempt for the accepted dogmas of a future life and a complete fearlessness of death. This effect of Frederick's influence was inevitable and would certainly have been fraught with extreme danger had it not been for the restraints of the State. On Frederick's own lips such remarks, provoked by sheer defiance, are merely a by-product of his free-ranging mind that shrank from no breadth or depth or height.

People have often praised Frederick for his disregard of position and parentage in his choice of officials. His appointment of town-bred lawyers and his reinforcement of official cadres by outsiders seem to support this view. He was actuated not so much by freedom from snobbery as by a love of playing the oriental despot, who can take his scullion of to-day for his Grand Wazir of to-morrow—a trait which is quite in character. A whole army of slaves, male and female, were attached to the imperial establishment, many of them Moors—who were mainly employed in divers duties in the imperial residences. Frederick had quarters in a number of places : Lucera, Melfi, Canosa, Messina, to which special interest attaches. Until recently it was the fashion to consider these arsenals and clothing stores as imperial harems, and this belief was strengthened by some instructions of the Emperor, that the girls employed there should be provided with clothing and should be kept at their spinning when not otherwise occupied. People affected to consider this a humane and domestic trait of the Emperor in relation to his concubines. It is clear from the wording of his orders that the Saracen girls were in charge of eunuchs, but this would have been necessary for the discipline of Saracen slave women, employed at the looms and in the workshops which supplied the needs of the court, the clothing for the army, woollen coverlets and costly saddlecloths and trappings for horses, camels and hunting leopards ; we have no ground for assuming that the women were the odalisques of their lord. In these same quarters weapons and armour were manufactured, machines of war, riding and pack saddles. Frederick frequently fetched craftsmen from a distance to teach his slaves : a Syrian master perhaps for cross-bows, or a Pisan for chain mail.

Apart from the staffs of these provincial quarters there was a personal retinue which accompanied the Emperor on all his campaigns, baggage train and staff and everything appertaining, an immense following which was permanently in attendance. A most amazing cavalcade—such as the West had never seen— like the state of an oriental monarch, always followed Frederick on his journeys after his return from the East. Apart from administrative officials, High Court Judges and the Saracen bodyguard, a complete menagerie was in his train, that brought people crowding in from miles around : strange beasts, unseen before, some of which were useful in hunting, but whose chief function was to add to the glamour and mystery of imperial majesty. Costly four-in-hand teams drew mighty wagons laden with treasure, richly caparisoned camels bearing burdens were escorted by uncounted slaves, gaudily arrayed in silken tunics and linen gear. Leopards and lynxes, apes and bears, panthers and lions, were led on the chain by Saracen slaves. The Emperor even possessed a giraffe. Add to these countless dogs, hawks, barn owls, horned owls, eagles and buzzards, every type of falcon, white and coloured peacocks, rare Syrian doves, white Indian parakeets crowned with yellow tufts of feathers, African ostriches, and, finally, the elephant with his wooden tower on his back, in which were seated Saracen marksmen and trumpeters. On triumphal occasions, once in Cremona for instance, the Emperor himself rode at the head of this procession : the God-man visibly elevated above all the creatures of the world.

The number of animals alone, many of which people scarcely knew by name, let alone by sight, thrilled the world with excitement. All chroniclers give complete details about the imperial procession. Brunetto Latini, Dante's teacher, lets himself go about the elephant in Cremona which had dashed a donkey to the ground with its trunk ; apart from what he had actually seen he retails all sorts of marvellous tales : that the elephant, which was a present to the Emperor from King John of Jerusalem, would never step on to a ship until it had been promised a safe return, and that before copulation it must eat a mandragora root which grows only in the neighbourhood of the earthly paradise. When the elephant entered at last, the spectators waited breathlessly to see its bones turn into ivory. Others gave their attention to other animals ; the Frenchman, Villard de Honnecourt, who once saw this zoological collection on his travels, sketched the lion and wrote underneath : " Ci lions fu contrefais al vif."

The rest of the Emperor's escort aroused nearly as much speculation as the exotic animals. For the court retinue included Saracen women and eunuchs, as people never failed to

note when the train passed through the Italian towns.   Nothing
was more obvious—even without the hints of the Pope's letter
—than to see in these veiled women the favourite concubines
of the already legendary harem.   The very uncertainty was
stimulating.   Whether these girls, like the acrobats, conjurors
and rope dancers who were often in attendance, were kept by
the Emperor merely for the entertainment their skill provided
(as Kaiser Frederick protested in innocent surprise to the
reproaches of the Pope) or whether Frederick made use of them
on occasion in other ways (" swept away by their charms,"
as the Pope preferred to imagine) could not be ascertained.
' Who could testify in the matter ? " as the Emperor's ambassador later said to the Council of Lyon.   They were simply
part of the court staff, maidservants and slave-girls, perhaps also
dancers and singing-girls, which fitted in with the oriental
arrangements of the Emperor's court.

The Emperor's staff included also numerous male slaves,
whose duties were very various, and ranged from personal
attendance on the monarch to the most menial tasks.   The
Emperor provided suitable education and training on the most
varied lines for the abler ones.   Many were taught to read and
write Arabic.   Another time he selected negro boys between
sixteen and twenty to form a musical corps ; they were
magnificently clad and taught to blow large and small silver
trumpets.   We may assume that the duty of this imperial band
was to play at meal times, since the courts of Anjou and
Aragon, whom Frederick copied in every way, indulged this
custom.   Black page boys are frequently mentioned ; one pair
of these *servitelli nigri* [1] were called Muska and Marzukh, and
they brought down on the Emperor from the Pope the reproach of " scarcely veiled sodomy."   When Frederick's wrath
fluttered his accusers they later tried to take the sting out of
this by returning to the innuendoes about the Saracen girls and
the harem of Gomorra.   One of these boys will probably be
the slave who grew up at the imperial court and rose to
hold the highest offices of state, Johannes Maurus.[1]   The
slave-woman's son attracted the Emperor's attention ; he

[1] The Middle Ages were little interested in ethnology : Moors, Arabs,
Negroes were indiscriminately *nigri*.—*Tr*.

became guardian of the Emperor's chamber, rose to still more important positions, received a barony, and later, under King Conrad, became Chief Chamberlain, Commandant of the fortress of Lucera, and finally Lord Treasurer of the Sicilian kingdom. Ultimately he was overtaken by the usual fate of the slave who attains great office : he turned traitor and paid the penalty. The Pope took him into favour, but he was murdered by the Saracens who had remained faithful to Manfred. This was another of the types represented at the Court of Frederick II. There were isolated Saracen officials under Frederick, as under the Normans, especially in the departments of Customs and Finance, but they tended to disappear and no other had so brilliant a career as Johannes Maurus.

Beside the town-bred literati who grouped themselves round Piero della Vigna and the foreigners, there was a third group of officials, the aristocratic knights. Though Frederick looked more to the efficiency than to the origin of his officers, yet the posts of Justiciar, or, as they were later called in Northern Italy, the posts of Vicar and Vicar-General, were reserved almost exclusively for the lower, less wealthy nobility. The mere possession of a fief was not as in Norman times a qualification for office ; the decisive factor was the person. The nobleman could achieve distinction only by his personal service and according to his individual ability. It is the more remarkable that not only the circle of stylists who surrounded della Vigna, but the overwhelming majority of knightly aristocratic officials were drawn from Beneventan or Campanian stocks, were supplemented to a certain extent from Apulia. The Morra family to which the Grand Master Justiciar belonged came from Benevento. They liked to trace their descent, which, however, shared the uncertainty common to all Italian genealogies, back to a certain Gothic Chieftain, King Totila. The Lords of Aquino, who boasted a Lombard descent, came from Campania. They espoused the Emperor's cause more warmly than any of his other supporters, and Frederick even took a wife from among them. The only untypical scion of the house was the saint, Thomas Aquinas. A third famous family, the Filan-

gieri, claimed to be of Breton lineage and to have come to
Sicily with the Normans ; they had their seat in the ancient
principality of Benevento. The house of Eboli were also
reputed to be Lombards. The Montefusculi and the Monteneri came from Benevento, and also the Counts of Caserta, into
whose family also Frederick married. Other celebrated servants of the Emperor were the Cicala, probably originally from
Genoa, the Acquaviva, settlers in the Abruzzi, the Caraccioli
from Naples, the Ruffi from Calabria. The kernel of the
kingdom was undoubtedly the Campanian-Beneventan strip,
which was full of Lombard blood and had been early conquered by the Normans. It had been less exhausted by racial
admixtures than other regions : one is reminded of the similar
importance of the Lombard factor in the culture of Tuscany.
What influenced the Emperor was the fact not of their Germanic descent but of their undegenerate quality. Frederick
liked to boast himself " the offshoot of a new breed " and
never counted in the South as a northern foreigner. Nothing,
therefore, was further from Frederick's intention than to
create antagonisms where none existed, by re-awakening half-
forgotten Germanic memories.

Frederick had, at first, to make use of the Sicilian-Italian
nobility as he found them. Gradually, as time went on, this
aristocracy, having breathed the air of the court, began to
mould itself to a given model, as new generations arose both
under Frederick and after him. We gain a vivid insight into all
the chivalrous activities of the court—for the court was still
strong in knightly tradition—by following out the education
and evolution of the nobly born official. The men who were
later to attain the highest posts had nearly all served in their
boyhood as pages in the Emperor's immediate circle, and enjoyed that knightly education which is familiar from the court
poetry of the time. This education now had a new direction,
for it combined knightly culture with the hope of future
official employment.

In Frederick's vicinity we meet at every turn the noble
pages, or, to use the French phrase inherited from Norman days,
the *valetti imperatoris*. No nobleman could become a knight
unless he had served as page to some great man, Emperor or

Pope, or to some spiritual or secular prince. It was customary
for the Sicilian nobility to pass the years of boyhood at the
imperial court. Service began at the age of fourteen. Prior
to this boys of noble birth will have been taught in one of the
monasteries. We know of Thomas Aquinas that " as a small
boy he had to share the lot of the other noble youths who received instruction in Monte Cassino, as was customary in the
country of the saint." Having once come to court the pages
belonged to the Emperor's *familia*, received from him a salary
of six ounces of gold a month, were entitled to two shield-
bearers and three horses (which, like themselves, were maintained by the court), and for the rest formed the lowest rung of
the ladder of chivalry, as they are styled in the Sicilian Book of
Laws. If a page insults a knight who is of higher rank than
himself his hand is cut off. The pages, while at court and not
employed on special service, were under the orders of the
Seneschal. They fought under his flag, and they had to keep
him informed of their comings and goings, even though the
Emperor might be already aware of them.

The Emperor took a personal interest in the pages : one who
was sick was sent to Apulia for change of air ; another at court
expense to the baths of Pozzuoli and Salerno. The pages'
duties were very various. Some were told off for personal
attendance on the Emperor ; one was despatched for the honourable duty of meeting the messenger of Michael Comnenus,
another for the reception of the Duke of Carinthia. Their
more particular duties concerned all matters of chivalry. We
find imperial pages employed in the royal stables, others in the
kennels, another in attendance on the hunting leopard, a large
number busied about Frederick's favourite pastime : falconry.
Frederick's passion for hawking is well known. People were
so well accustomed to see the Emperor in hunting dress that
green became the fashionable colour amongst the Ghibelline
partisans in Northern Italy. A papal chronicler writes mockingly
that : " Frederick degrades his majestic title to huntsman's
work, and instead of adorning himself with laws and weapons,
he surrounds himself with panthers, hounds and screeching
birds, and converts the Emperor into a follower of the chase.
He exchanges his illustrious sceptre for a spear and disputes

with eagles their triumph in bird-slaying." The imperial hunstman needed numerous pages at hand, and kept them fully employed. There were hawks to be conveyed to the Apulian barons, to be cared for during their mewing ; there were the Emperor's *sacri falcones* to be fetched from Apulia ; other pages were sent to Malta, others again as far as Lübeck, to bring back certain types of falcon. It was probably exceptional for the lads to be permitted to take any actual part in the hawking. The Emperor's standard for an " ideal falconer " was high. He draws a picture of one in his book on falconry : quick wit, sharp sight, good memory, acute hearing, courage and endurance are essential, and the perfect falconer must be of medium height—long-legged ones are useless. Folk who were only half or quarter-qualified were not allowed near the birds, and the over-young must first grow useful in the Emperor's service. It is expressly stipulated : " The falconer must not be too boyish in behaviour, lest his boyishness lead him to transgress against the art ; for boys are wont to be impatient, and delight chiefly in seeing beautiful flights and many of them. But we do not banish boys completely, for even they will grow wiser. . . ."

The pages remained at court till they won their knightly girdle, often with the Emperor's direct assistance. Some of them then left the court and returned to live in their own baronies, or enlisted as mercenary knights in the imperial armies and are thus lost to sight. Others entered the state service, and this possibility may well have been one of the main attractions of coming as a page to court. The Apulian families sent nearly all their sons. Two lords of Aquino, several Morras, one Caraccioli, one Count Caserta, one Filangieri, one Acquaviva ; the sons of captains of fortresses, of non-official feudal barons, and many others served as pages. Sometimes the Emperor commanded the attendance of a boy at court, and he often sought out those who would be " responsive to the imperial discipline " in order to " receive them into the arms of his education " and interest himself like a father in their fortunes, though they had been begotten by another. He writes once to the father of one of his pages : " We have heaped on him the beginnings of all the virtues, so that he may grow

worthy of himself, useful to others and may bear fruit for us,"
and, further, that these young men " who live in our service with
honour and die in joy of great deeds may not pine away in
feeble vices or anaemic anxieties." Sicily was not the only
country represented by pages at the imperial court ; Northern
Italians came also, and when Frederick II was in Cyprus he
took a son of John of Ibelin into his service as a page. Similarly, during a short stay in Vienna at a later date, he brought
back Berthold and Godfrey, two sons of the Margravine of
Hohenburg, as pages to Italy, for whom a brilliant career was
in store, almost the only Germans in the Sicilian State.

We hear nothing of any special instruction of the pages
in administrative work, and probably there was none. The
Emperor might well reflect that these young noblemen would
see and hear enough during their years in his immediate entourage to be ready to take over even the highest office. A lad
of twenty who had served for years at court, even though
nominally in charge merely of falcons and leopards, must have
acquired as much *savoir vivre* as many an aged bishop. What
they lacked in experience was richly compensated for by
complete loyalty and eagerness to serve. In this connection
we may recall Goethe's dictum : " If I were a prince, I should
never give the first places to people who had come gradually
into prominence merely on account of birth and seniority. . . .
I should have YOUNG MEN . . . then it would be a joy to reign."
Under Frederick II we often find, in fact, quite young noblemen who had been pages holding the highest posts as his
representatives. The Hohenburg brothers can scarcely have
reached the middle twenties when they were Captains General
in Northern Italy. Count Richard of Caserta and Thomas of
Aquino junior were younger still when the Emperor entrusted
similar posts to them. We know with considerable certainty
that Landolfo Caraccioli, who afterwards became Justiciar of
the students at Naples, was in 1239 a sixteen-year-old page,
yet before Frederick's death he was officiating as Vicar in a
most difficult post in Tuscany in the upper valley of the Arno.

Other nobles who appear as pages of the Emperor at a later
date reappear in responsible posts under King Manfred :
Berard of Acquaviva, as Justiciar of the island of Sicily, the

younger Richard Filangieri as Captain of the Mainland, and many others. We cannot be sure whether noble pages attended the University of Naples, but the imperial page Nicholas of Trani, for instance, later entered the judicial service and was High Court Judge in Manfred's time. This is the first example of the infusion of the spirit of the town-bred jurist into the knightly nobility ; later jurists were sometimes raised to knightly rank, and their sons were received as pages by the Angevin kings.

The Emperor's own sons, whether legitimate or not, mostly grew up among the young nobles at court, and the sons of foreign princes were frequently educated with them. There appears to be no record of what became of the two orphaned sons of King John of Jerusalem, the young brothers-in-law of the Emperor, whom he invited to his court. His cousin Frederick, son of the King of Castile, was sent to grow up under Frederick's tutelage. The offspring of the Staufen-Castilian breed [1] were, however, neither to hold nor to bind. Frederick of Castile ran away from the Emperor after a few years : so did his brother, Henry of Castile, a wilder dare-devil still, who, after an adventurous life, was to exert a potent influence in Italian politics in late Hohenstaufen times. King Enzio must have spent some of his boyhood at the Sicilian court, and Frederick of Antioch, too, another natural son of the Emperor. We have considerable detail about Manfred's education at this intellectual court. He was eighteen when his father died, and Kaiser Frederick, in his later years, loved him more than any of his other sons. " A host of learned doctors " gave him lessons and taught him " about the nature of the world, the origin and development of the body, the creation of souls, their immortality and the methods of perfecting them, the transitory nature of matter, the security of eternal things." From his childhood Manfred clung to the ways of thought of his father, who was both nurse and mother to him. It was in

[1] Beatrice, daughter of Philip of Swabia was Frederick II's first cousin, she married Ferdinand of Castile : this Frederick and Henry are her sons. —Tr.

response to Manfred's urgent entreaties that Frederick II composed his Falcon Book.

Manfred is said to have later been put under the special care of Berthold of Hohenburg, the sometime page. The heir of the Empire, on the other hand, King Conrad, left his father's court at the age of seven, nominally to take over the Government of Germany. His tutor was a Neapolitan knight, "to whom Conrad's education was entrusted on account of his noble race, his great wisdom and eloquence, and his high character, in order that the lad by the elevating example of such a master might be thoroughly educated in every type of virtue, wisdom and self-control." This Neapolitan was presumably a Caraccioli, since Landolfo Caraccioli, himself then sixteen, accompanied the young king to Germany as a page. We also learn that Conrad was taught with a large number of other boys of noble birth, and the story goes that whenever the young king was at fault his teacher used to thrash one of the other boys, for if the young king had a generous heart it would be particularly painful to him to see others, who were innocent, punished for his guilt.

Some didactic letters of the Emperor to this son are preserved in which Frederick II strives to explain the true dignity of a king. Although Conrad is addressed as a "divine scion of the race of the Caesars," the letters show how soberly and clearly people at the imperial court thought about the Ruler's office, for all their hero-worship of the Ruler. "Famous extraction alone is not sufficient for kings nor for the great men of the earth, unless noble personal character is wedded to illustrious race, unless outstanding zeal reflects glory on the prince's rank. People do not distinguish Kings and Caesars above other men because they are more highly placed, but because they see farther and act better. As men they stand equal to other men by their humanity, they are associated with them in life, and have nothing to pride themselves on, unless by virtue and by wisdom they outshine other men. They are born as men, and as men they die." Only by wisdom of the spirit—Frederick writes again—are kings distinguished from other men, and it is incomparably more vicious for a prince to fail in serving wisdom and to remain in ignorance than for a

private individual, " for the nobility of his royal blood has made
a king more susceptible to the teachings of wisdom by inspiring
him with a noble and fastidious soul . . . hence it is necessary
and seemly that thou shouldest love wisdom, and for her sake
it is fitting that thou lay aside the Caesars' dignity, and under
the master's rod and the ferule of the teacher be neither king
nor emperor but pupil." And again : "We do not forbid thee
to practise with skilful people in due time and place the wonted
royal pastime of hawking and the chase. But we adjure thee
and wish to warn thee that in hunting and hawking thou do not
indulge in too familiar converse with beaters and keepers and
huntsmen, that they with presumptuous words impair the
royal dignity, or with chatter demean it and corrupt good
morals."

It is easy to forget that for all its learning and law-plying
Frederick's court was none the less a knightly medieval court,
which for many decades was a focus of chivalry. This was of
prime importance for Italy and enabled her to develop the life
of courts and kings. Frederick II and his court belonged far
more to Italy than the remote Norman Court had done. For
years the Emperor's headquarters camp wandered round
central and northern Italy, and even when the Emperor returned to his southern home he still remained in full view of
Italy, since he resided wholly in the north of his peninsular
territory. It may cause surprise that the Emperor so rarely
sought in Palermo, the old Norman capital, the joys and delights
of Sicily which he loved to extol.

The tales of a brilliant Hohenstaufen court at Palermo belong
to the realm of myth. During the last ten years of his reign
Frederick II only once set foot on the island, to suppress the
insurrection of 1233 in Messina. Palermo was still the capital
of the kingdom, but only in name ; with Frederick II it had
lost for practical reasons the privileged position of a royal
residence. It could only be reached direct by a long sea
journey or by a wearisome land march from the Straits, and was
much too far out of the world for the Ruler of an Empire.
Frederick had to shift the focus of his State to the spot where

its main strength was to be found : his most northern provinces.

Frederick had praised Apulia (the Adriatic coast provinces) and the Terra Laboris (the Campania of our day) above the Land of Promise, had boasted himself a " man of Apulia," and his actual home was now the land lying between these two— the Capitanata surrounding the Gulf of Manfredonia. Up to Frederick's day the Capitanata had possessed no particular importance, and the fact that for close on a century the threads of world politics met here in this god-forsaken Tavoliere di Puglia, and that the town of Foggia became renowned throughout the lands of East and West, was solely due to the Emperor's personal preference for this province. The political factor was undoubtedly the decisive one in Frederick's choice of these northern regions. He was close to the scene of his northern and central Italian battles and ready at any moment to take a hand personally, to set out for the north, to keep an eye on Rome. Other considerations, however, also carried weight in in choice of this sterile region. To-day's stony desert, serving at best for sheep runs, must in Hohenstaufen times, when all was more fruitful and better wooded, have possessed some *amoenitas* such as the ancient world had an eye for : that pleasant alternation of mountain and hill, of forest and plain and the neighbourhood of the sea. At no period of history, however, can the Capitanata have been able to compete with the colourful Palermo in its exotic almost tropical luxuriance, or with the marvels of the Bay of Naples. Possibly the hunting possibilities attracted Frederick and compensated for other shortcomings ; there will be at least a grain of truth in that hypothesis. Italy certainly had the impression that Frederick lingered for the winter in Foggia and spent the summer in the adjacent hills for the sake of hawking. The very barrenness of the region, so obviously unexhausted, probably had more charm for him than the thousandfold fertility of ever-pregnant Sicily, and offered him, moreover, more raw material for creative effort. And what a transformation Frederick succeeded in producing in these northern provinces of his !

He visited the Capitanata oftener than his other provinces, he wrote, because of his castles. He had found no castles

there.   In 1221 he saw the Capitanata for the first time,
and he must have forthwith resolved to make this part of his
kingdom his imperial headquarters.   As early as 1223 he began
the construction of his big castle of Foggia, the inscription on
which stated that Frederick had elevated the royal town into a
far-famed imperial residence.   Soon there arose at reasonable
distances pleasure palaces, hunting lodges, and rural hamlets to
which there was usually attached a farm or dairy farm.   These
solatia of the Emperor seemed to grow as simply and naturally
out of the soil of the Great Capitanata—to use Enzio's phrase—
as the neighbouring holy places of ancient days.   The Castel
del Monte, on its lofty site near Barletta, is the best preserved
and the best known of these Hohenstaufen castles.   Its ground-
plan is unique, and like many other of the Emperor's buildings it was probably sketched by Frederick himself : a regular
octagon of yellowish limestone ; its smooth perfectly-fitting
blocks showing no joins and producing the effect of a mono-
lith : at each of the eight corners a squat octagonal tower the
height of the wall ; two storeys identical in height, each containing eight large equal rooms, trapezium-shaped ; an octagonal central courtyard adorned with antique sculptures and
imitations of the antique, in the centre of which a large octagonal
basin served as bath.   Every fraction of the structure displays
the mental catholicity of the Hohenstaufen court : oriental
massiveness of the whole, a portal foreshadowing the Renaissance, Gothic windows and rooms with groined and vaulted
roofs.   The defiant gloom of the tiny-windowed rooms was
mitigated by the furnishings ; the floors were of mosaic, the
walls covered with sheets of reddish breccia or white marble,
the groined vaults supported on pilasters with Corinthian
capitals, or by delicate clustered columns of white marble.
Majesty and grace were fused in one.

Frederick II never stinted well-chosen splendour, and the
exotic luxury and magnificence probably produced a more
powerful effect in these sterner northern regions than in the
half-African half-Saracen Palermo.   What mysteries, what
unimagined revelries contemporaries pictured taking place
behind the mute walls of these castles !   What amazing brilliance they caught a glimpse of now and then !   In the rambling

castle of Foggia, which is described as a palace rich in marble, with statues and pillars of verd-antique, with marble lions and basins, those legendary banquets will have taken place amid riot and revelry the glamour of which still clings round the memory of the Hohenstaufen Court.

" Every sort of festive joy was there united. The alternation of choirs, the purple garments of the musicians evoked a festal mood. A number of guests were knighted, others adorned with signs of special honour. The whole day was spent in merriment, and as the darkness fell, flaming torches were kindled here and there and turned night into day for the contests of the players." So tells the chronicler, and yet another reports the wonders of the inner courts which the English prince Richard, Earl of Cornwall, was privileged to see. The English noble was returning home from the crusade in summer heat : they first with baths and blood-lettings and strengthening draughts made him forget the toils and hardships of the journey and the war, and then entertained him with every type of sport. He listened in amazement to strange airs on strange instruments, saw the jugglers display their skill, was ravished by the sight of lovely Saracen maidens, who to the rhythm of cymbals and castanets came dancing in, balanced on great balls that rolled across the many-coloured polished floor. Tales and romances tell of the feasts of Frederick and the glories of his court : how hundreds of knights from all nations were entertained in silken tents, how minstrels streamed in from every corner of the earth and foreign embassies displayed the rarest jewels. The messengers of Prester John brought an asbestos garment, an elixir of youth, a ring of invisibility, and, lastly, the philosopher's stone. Further, people told how the Emperor's court astrologer, Michael Scot, whose name was named with shuddering curiosity, on a hot day at a feast assembled thunderclouds at the Emperor's command and performed other miracles.

Apulia was never to see again such chivalrous display as flourished under Frederick II and Manfred. Chivalry itself, bound up as it was with crusade and Minnesang, was already growing dim in the later Staufen days. Moreover, the Anjous who followed the Hohenstaufen in Sicily were joyless bigots, and, although themselves Provençal, were far less in sympathy than the Swabian dynasty with the lighthearted, almost pagan spirit and the *joie de vivre* of the southern troubadours.

New love poetry came to birth in the chivalrous, not in the learned, atmosphere of Frederick's court. The much-debated question how, and through whom, Frederick learned to know the lyrics of Provence, and how their " transference " to the Sicilian court is to be explained, is otiose. It would have been inexplicable if Frederick had remained in ignorance of such poetry. He was quite as fully in touch with the whole world of French and Provençal culture as with the culture of the East. He knew both languages from boyhood, was acquainted with their literature, and will most assuredly have read the novels which were familiar to his court : Tristan, Lancelot and the rest. We have evidence that he knew *Merlin* and the *Palamedes* of Guiron de Courtois. The troubadours sang the praise of the *Puer Apuliae*, and legend located at the court of the fifteen-year-old king the first poet-coronation of the Middle Ages, the travelling singer crowned *rex versuum* who later became the Franciscan, Fra Pacifico.

The poetry of the imperial court was imitated from the Provençal, both in form and content. The foreign language was not used, however, as was customary at the courts of North Italian nobles, such as Saluzzo and Montferrat. Here, for the first time, poetry was written in an Italian vernacular, the popular speech of Sicilian Apulia. There must have been isolated forerunners writing in Sicilian—the legendary Alkamo perhaps—but every history of Italian literature begins with the songs of the Sicilian court. The concentration of the " Sicilian School of Poets " which here sprang up helped immensely to increase the influence and spread the popularity of the new vernacular poetry, as Petrarch recalls, " in a very short time this type of poetry, which had been born amongst the Sicilians, spread throughout all Italy and beyond." As late as Dante all non-Latin poetry in Italian was dubbed " Sicilian," which Dante in his book *De Vulgari Eloquentiâ* explains by saying " because, as is well known the royal throne was in Sicily."

The times were ripe for Frederick's experiment. Starting in Provence, the popular love poetry had spread to the other European communities, especially the French and German, and had been warmly welcomed. Only when its zenith was almost overpast did it find its way to Italy, for Italy had lagged far behind the other European countries in evolving a native language of its own, probably because no other country had remained so closely in touch with Latin. The realisation that the spoken tongue had ceased to be the speech of Rome, and had become an independent idiom, scarcely came before the thirteenth century. A feeling of Italian nationality, whose prophet Dante was to be, began to dawn about the same time—later than in other countries, delayed by the same misconception that Italian and Latin were one. Since the rise of a national self-consciousness and a national language are closely related we need not wonder that an Italian dialect first attained the dignity of a popular language in the South Italian State of Frederick II, that is, in that section of Italy in which national feeling had been first and most strongly awakened.

The question what " put it into Frederick's head " to utilise the native Sicilian dialect of Apulia for his poems in the Provençal style is childish. The sufficient explanation is that he was a statesman, and the founder of a nation. It is reported of the Normans, those highly gifted statesmen, that they had made the attempt, albeit prematurely and unsuccessfully, to unify the Sicilian people by introducing French : *gens efficiatur ut una*. Their hope was to introduce uniformity of speech by popularising the language of the court, for in the middle of the twelfth century French was the language of the royal capital of Palermo. Frederick had transferred the focus of his kingdom from the polyglot island with its confusion of tongues to the mainland of one speech, and it was characteristic of him that he did not seek to import a foreign language for courtly poetry and festivity, but seized for his experiment the raw material that lay to hand, and moulded it to his purpose. Dante is the witness for his success : " For although the native born Apulians in general speak coarsely, some of their distinguished people spoke in a refined manner, blending courtly turns of speech into their songs." By the refinement and cultivation of the common speech Frederick and his school elevated the local dialect to that *volgare illustre* of court and literature. He thus recognised Sicilian as an independent tongue, and established a common tie between the people and their ruler " of the new breed." How far Frederick acted with the conscious intention of establishing a unity of speech and race is unimportant beside the fact itself that he was the most important pioneer, as Dante was the actual creator, of modern Italian. Such an achievement by an Emperor is unique.

The problems created by the existence of two languages, which was, of course, a commonplace in other countries (Frederick was the first to issue an imperial decree in German as well as Latin) still remained in the southern Hohenstaufen State. The sacred Latin was indispensable to the Roman Imperator on account of its universal validity; and Frederick did not dream of using for his " Holy Constitution," his " Revelations," his imperial decrees, any but the language of the Caesars, which his Chancery handled with such consummate skill. The vernacular was not stately enough for the eternal verities ; even Dante still distinguishes between the immutable Latin, the master, and the changeable, ephemeral vernacular, the servant. The imperial sanctities were meant for immortality, but attempts were already being made in Italy to lend a consecration to the vulgar tongue which Dante's *poema sacro* finally achieved. Almost simultaneously with the first songs of Frederick, Francis of Assisi, the " minstrel of the Lord " had begun to sing. His was a rude vernacular, still strongly Latin-ridden, but he was writing from an inner compulsion which the Sicilians lacked. Frederick II used Sicilian as a light and living speech for secular and courtly merriment, he did not ask of it seriousness or solemnity. His songs are nothing more than an expression of *joie de vivre* and courtly life, born of the moment and serving the moment. In comparison with Provençal there is scarcely a new thought or feeling in the Sicilian songs : their sole aim was to sound merry at the festive gathering ; the important thing was not *what* was sung, but that there should be singing in the speech of the people and the language of one's neighbours. Frederick borrowed from the singers of Auvergne, Limousin and Provence not only metre and content, but—what was even more vital—their joy in life, which awakened a response in people, court and Emperor.

Nothing gives Frederick such unique distinction in the gallery of famous monarchs as the unruffled cheerfulness which he maintained through all vicissitudes : that intellectual cheerfulness of the man who feels himself equal to every emergency, whose glance scans the earth from Olympian heights and shrinks not from contemplation of himself.   This quality derives its name from Jupiter. It is called "*jovialitas*" or "serenity" in the official language of the court.   This cheerful serenity demands, beside a princely spirit, a certain maturity, and a complete, established, measurable world.   It is rare amongst rulers : amongst monarchs of this stature perhaps only to be met with in Julius Caesar.   After Frederick II none of the great men of action have displayed it to the same degree.   Clever and witty kings are not uncommon ; lighthearted merry ones are found in France ; Henry IV, drawing with his first breath the bouquet of the wines of Gascony.   They are far removed from the lofty, imperial cheerfulness of Frederick.   Cheerfulness, and joy in living, a sense of song and ryhthm in spite of the burdens of responsibility.   No other German stock achieved this lighthearted freedom of spirit so fully as the Hohenstaufen, and no other Hohenstaufen in the same measure as Frederick II, who even retained it in the midst of Empire.   Frederick handed on this quality to his handsome sons, none destined to be Emperors. They also sang, even when tragic fate was overtaking them. Henry, the first born, the rebel who ended his life in his father's dungeon, did not cease his singing even as the chamberlain stripped him of the royal insignia he had wantonly forfeited— "In the morning he sang, and in the evening wept."   Manfred, with irresponsible folly, forgot his kingdom for his song.   The old Occursius, who had served both the imperial father and the son, turned to Manfred shortly before they both were slain in the battle of Benevento, reproachful yet moved : "Where now are your fiddlers, where your poets, whom you loved more than knights and esquires, who hoped the foe would dance to their sweet tones!"   Enzio, in the Bologna dungeon, touched and cheered his very gaolers with his cheerful songs. And the amiable and knightly Frederick of Antioch, whom men called the King of Tuscany, sang like his brothers ; and, lastly, Conradin sang his own death and the death of his house in a sweet song of mourning. Not frivolity nor royal fashion is here, but an incomparable vigour of the blood, which even in ruin demands glory and fame. Their very beauty betrayed Manfred and Enzio to the foe. The whole of Hohenstaufen art and all Frederick's own compositions are steeped in this joy of living : a happy harvest of the world he ruled and represented, a poetry of love springing from the joy of the happy man " who understood the art of making and of singing songs."

The new poetry was not confined to the Hohenstaufen family, though without them it would have been unthinkable. The art exercised wide influence because Frederick the poet was Frederick the Emperor, and the court provided a responsive audience on festive occasions. The personality of Frederick II and of Manfred counted for much, and cannot better be explained than by Dante's praise when he breaks forth in wrath against his contemporary nobles, especially the successor of the Sicilian Hohenstaufen, Frederick II of Aragon and Charles II of Anjou. " The (literary) fame of Trinacria, if we read the signs aright, remains only to the shame of the Italian princes who, unlike heroes but like plebeians, follow their own conceit. The illustrious heroes Kaiser Frederick, and Manfred his not unworthy son, revealed the nobility and rightness of their mind, and as long as fortune favoured them they pursued the truly humane and despised the bestial. Hence all such princes as were of noble heart and lofty spirit clung to them, and in their time all the distinguished minds of the day amongst the Latins first blossomed forth at the court of such kings. And since Sicily was the royal seat everything which our predecessors produced in the vulgar tongue has been called Sicilian ; and we continue to say Sicilian, and our successors will not be able to alter this. But alas! alas! what poetry do we hear from this later Frederick ? What tinkle of bells from this second Charles ? What sound of horns from John and Azzo the mighty margraves? save ' Come, ye oppressors ! Come, ye double-dealers ! Come, ye disciples of greed ! ' "

When a poet of Dante's rank and courage celebrates in such language the humanity of the " illustrious heroes " this must have been an unusual phenomenon, as indeed it was. Not the least remarkable thing was the school of poets itself. Princes of taste have frequently " patronised poetry " at their courts, attracting players and travelling singers by largesse. This was not Frederick's way. Rather the reverse. Frederick distrusted the nomad minstrel, did not encourage him in his kingdom, and at a feast in Germany actually commanded that not so much money should be wasted on the wandering folk. The amazing thing was that Frederick produced all these early poets without exception at his own imperial court. Following the Emperor's example, the officials suddenly burst into rhyme. The Renaissance Princes bestowed office on poets, painters and sculptors, so also Karl August on Goethe. This was the exact opposite of Frederick's procedure : Frederick made no man a state official because he happened to be a poet, but the " compelling necessity of things " evoked poetic skill from the officials of this Emperor. Surely a phenomenon unique in history : one of the greatest statesmen and lawgivers creates the literary language of a whole people, and not that alone, but during two or three generations evoked the poets of a century. This reinforces the essential truth of Damon's saying that the laws of a State cannot be altered without altering those also of the Muses.

It was natural that although the impetus of the new poetry was given by the Emperor it was primarily the younger generation, not Frederick's own contemporaries, who practised the new art. None of the officials seem to have written verse before 1231, and the heyday of the movement was a full ten years later. The Emperor's own songs, which were more important in influence than in number, must have dated from before the Crusade. The King of Jerusalem, John of Brienne, Re Giovanni, was then at Frederick's court, and a poem of his in the Sicilian vernacular is preserved, which cannot well be of later date. The chronology is best established by considering who the poets were. And since it is not a question of learned art, but of courtly and knightly verse, we must seek the authors amongst the aristocratic officials, especially those who, during their impressionable years, had come most strongly under the influence of the Court.

No less than three members of the noble family of Aquino are amongst the poets : Reginald, Jacob and Monaldo. Reginald was page and falconer of the Emperor in 1240 and a few years later held a certain post at Court. He wrote numerous poems, a line of which Dante once quoted. We have no record of his cousin Jacob's having been a page, but Jacob's elder brother certainly was. When the father was killed in the Emperor's service Frederick expressly wrote that he proposed to make himself specially responsible for the two boys, so we may safely assume that Jacob of Aquino also belonged to the group of noble boys educated at Court. We know nothing of Monaldo beyond the fact that he belonged to the school of poets. Reginald of Aquino vainly sought to lure to court his younger brother Thomas—by far the most gifted of the family. Piero della Vigna seconded his efforts, but the young Dominican, Thomas Aquinas, was not to be enticed. Even Frederick himself secretly supplemented their attempts, for he liked to dissuade gifted young noblemen from joining the mendicant orders, which were attracting them in scores. We know that he similarly sought to influence a young noble of Parma.

The name of Jacob of Aquino is linked by an interchange of canzones with that of Jacopo Mostacci, one of the younger poets, who with his brother is recorded as a page of Frederick's, about 1240. He was later in Manfred's service as ambassador at the Court of Aragon. A Morra, son of the Grand Justiciar, and elder brother of one of the pages of 1240, also appears among the court poets. Jacob of Morra was already, at this date, Captain of the duchy of Spoleto, and on account of his father's high position was one of the most trusted intimates of Frederick II, one of those whom the Emperor had " brought up as sons and from whom nothing was concealed." Jacob of Morra had made a thorough-going study of Provençal. One of the troubadours, probably Hugh of St. Circq, wrote for him the earliest Provençal grammar that we possess, and some of the loveliest lyrics of the Sicilian School bear the name of " Giacomino Pugliese." He was entrusted with one of the highest posts in Frederick's gift, reserved for his special favourites, and made Vicar General of the Ancona March. In this position he betrayed his master and allowed himself to be entangled in a conspiracy.

Another poet, Roger de Amicis, met a similar fate. He also was amongst the highest officials, Grand Justiciar or Captain of Sicily, and amongst other verses of his we know an interchange of poems between him and his younger friend, Reginald of Aquino. Roger de Amicis, one of the Emperor's intimates, was a nobleman of Calabria. He was sent on one occasion as ambassador to Cairo to the Egyptian court. Folco Ruffo, also a poet, came from the same neighbourhood. He is frequently mentioned in the later days as in Frederick's train, and must still have been quite a young man when he witnessed the dying Emperor's last will and testament. He belonged to the famous family of the Ruffi, one of whom was head of the imperial stables, and another of whom wrote, at the Emperor's request, a book on veterinary science. Lastly, we meet Reginald of Palermo, also a page in 1240, a Sicilian feudal baron, and perhaps he is the author of the poems preserved under the name of Rainer of Palermo of whom nothing is known.

Numerous members of the Beneventan family of the Monteneri were amongst Frederick's higher officials. Reginald of Montenero was one of the poets, and is described in a novel which relates his adventures as a minstrel in Sardinia as " kavaliere di corte." The kingdom of Sardinia belonged to Enzio, and so this Montenero must, in some capacity or other, have been his subordinate. As the imperial administration gradually extended to the whole of Italy, and Sicilian officials were in charge everywhere, the northward spread of vernacular poetry is no matter for surprise. It is noteworthy that at first only the imperial, that is Ghibelline towns, like Pisa, Arezzo, Siena, Lucca and Florence, produced poets.

The story goes that the cultured youth of Bologna used frequently to visit King Enzio when he was imprisoned there. It is unlikely that Enzio made any secret of his poems, which he valued enough to mention in his will. Guido Guinizelli may well have been one of the visitors who will have heard them read.

Enzio's name is often quoted in relation to the poems of the
notary, Semprebene of Bologna, one of the earliest vernacular
poets of northern Italy, and who is also counted of the Sicilian
school.   A few other North Italians belong to the same school,
aristocratic officials of the Emperor, who were closely in touch
with the court.   Arrigo Testa is one, a knight of Arezzo, who
was frequently posted as podesta in imperial towns. and then
spent some time in prison in Florençe, where Frederick of
Antioch lived when officiating as Vicar General of Tuscany.
Frederick of Antioch was most exceptionally gifted, and his
poems signed " Re Federigo " have often been confused with
his father's.   Percival Doria, podesta in Avignon, and later in
Parma under Frederick, was a Genoese.   He was Captain of
the March under Manfred till he was drowned on active service
in one of Manfred's campaigns.   None of King Manfred's
songs have been preserved, though he was always surrounded
by a horde of German " fiddlers " (in Tuscany they used to
sing a song that ran : " Horses we get from Spain, and clothes
from France, and here we sing and dance in Provençal style to
new instruments from Germany ").   The songs of his High
Chamberlain have fared no better, Count Manfred Maletta,
" who was great and powerful at the court of the king, rich and
beloved of Manfred . . . who was the best (poet) and perfect
in inventing canzones and melodies and had not his like in the
world for playing of stringed instruments."

The town-bred jurists took a hand with the princely and
knightly singers in this vernacular verse-making, the first
courtly art which really united royalty, aristocracy and citizens.
These lawyer poets were fewer in number than their princely
rivals, but carried the more weight, for Piero della Vigna was
one of the first to write songs in Sicilian.   He may even have
been the rallying point of the poetical school, and numbers of
the younger poets exchanged poems with him.   As he had
not come into prominence much before the Crusade, and this
verse-mongering belongs to his later period, it is not unlikely
that he too owed his inspiration to the Emperor.   Whether or
not, he is one of the rare poets of Frederick's own generation.
In this, as in other matters, Frederick and della Vigna are
closely bound together.

Through Piero della Vigna the new art spread to the jurists. They were intellectually the most highly trained, and linguistically the most expert men of their time, and the most qualified to make this new art their own and to carry it on, when after a time the knightly poets found no disciples in their own ranks.   Thus poetry began in Italy to find its home in the towns, just as it had in Germany, where knightly Minnesang was succeeded by the burghers' Meistersang, until at last it became wholly wooden and mechanical. The same danger existed in Italy. We have probably to thank the lawyers' cultivated sense of style for the discovery of new strophe forms —Piero della Vigna is said to have constructed the first sonnet— but the increasing ossification and emaciation of poetry were due no less to their excessive learning.   At last the barren waste of legal and philosophical versification that flooded northern and central Italy was forgotten in the " sweet new style " of Dante.

Next to Piero della Vigna, one of the best-known representatives of the Sicilian school, was another lawyer of the imperial court, Notary Giacomo da Lentini. He also stood in close relation with most of the young aristocrats, and in quantity his output exceeds that of any other poet of the time. He is so typical of the school that Dante in the important conversation with Bonagiunta di Lucca picks out " the Notary " as a sample of the old tendencies. Lastly, we should mention the later judge Guido Colonna whose poems, like Reginald of Aquino's, Dante quotes on occasion.

Thus in the famous, and infamous, State of Frederick II (the " first modern bureaucracy " !) we find amongst the officials an inner circle of scholars, poets and artists round the Emperor, all men of greater or lesser intellectual gifts, living in considerable intimacy, sharing each other's many-sided knowledge, and each stimulated by the rest. How widely the Sicilian poets differ from the troubadours in being neither wandering nor professional minstrels ! The Sicilian poets, as later the Sicilian sculptors, were bound to the State, were one with it. The pillars of the new poetry were pillars of the State, which claimed the whole of each official, his private gifts as well as his public service. Frederick II had the great art of enlisting everything in his service and letting nothing waste itself in space : but this imposed on the individual an unrelaxing tension, not easy to be borne, from which the wandering minstrel was entirely free. There was no lack of poetic rivalry in Sicily, but it was on a higher plane than the troubadours' bread-and-butter competition, for the Sicilian poets had no anxiety about their livelihood ; they were one and all imperial officials.

The imperial school of poetry differed in another point from the poetry of other courts : at Frederick's court the Lady was not the centre of chivalrous devotion. According to oriental custom the Empress, with her own court pomp, lived apart from the Emperor in the " harem," and even Frederick's many lady-loves played no rôle in the life of his court ; we scarcely even know their names. There was only one centre—the Emperor. In this matter Frederick's court more nearly resembles the papal court than any other of the time. The Emperor's life amongst his cultured courtiers and officials, in spite of its intellectual recklessness, begot a tensely stimulating mental atmosphere that had not its like in the West, a new virile spirit which would have split everything asunder if it had not been held in the iron grip of the State. This intellectual stimulus was further quickened by the new knowledge of the natural sciences which Frederick himself, supported by many foreign scholars, introduced into his court.

The appearance of the doctrine of *Necessitas*, the doctrine of natural laws inherent in things themselves, shows how daringly advanced thought was in those days, how closely in touch with the living and the actual. We can determine this in yet another way. The ancients, starting from the primitive natural world of their Gods and Heroes, rose by a study of natural laws and of " Anankê " to a recognition of " Nous " ; then higher and ever higher till at last only one single World-" Nous " ruled the universe. After many hundred years the human mind was now descending from the repose of these spiritual heights in which all form was dissolved, retracing again in a downward direction the path by which it had climbed up. Once again a recognition of the living laws of nature, more especially those which were valid throughout the universe, a further descent of the mind to concern itself with earth and the creatures of earth, till Nature, Soul and Spirit, interpenetrated each other on earth in the age of the Medicis in Florence.   Each epoch of the Middle Ages found its own time already lived through in the past.   Otto III sought to renew the days of Constantine, and his teacher Gerbert, when he became Pope, took the name of Sylvester II to correspond with the bishop of Rome under Constantine.   The whole thirteenth century was conscious of a most intimate kinship with the first century of the Christian era, introduced by the prophecy of Abbot Joachim of Flora : the new era which was dawning would resemble that of the first Christians under the apostles.   St. Francis as a direct disciple of the Lord seemed to fulfil the prophecy.

Frederick II sought to bring in again the age of Augustus, and the sum of his speculation ultimately reduced itself to a belief that just before the end of the world everything must exactly correspond with the fulness of time of the first century. True, the actual moment, the Day of Redemption, was in a new sense not experienced till Good Friday of the *anno santo*, the jubilee year 1300, when Dante led by Vergil entered on the path to Paradise.

The philosophico-scientific impulses of the time revert to the early Christian or late classical epochs.   The same ancient authors who formerly lured men up into a spiritual world of intellectual abstractions now enabled men gropingly to feel their way down again into the corporeal world.   The whole phantom world of late classical philosophy was rediscovered on the way.   The normal course of organic growth, to arrive at the general law by abstraction from the individual, was reversed in the Scholastic age.   The Scholastic mind, always focussed on the Universal as the first given premiss, the thought accustomed to daily converse with the " Universal," was able more readily to grasp a general law about the collective Cosmos than the simplest single thing on Earth, and people learned to know Nature in her individual manifestations through intellectual speculation about Law and Species.   Anything related to Eternity and the Universal was quickly grasped by the trained mind : Astronomy and Mathematics were, therefore, more immediately understood than Botany and Zoology, and these in their turn more rapidly than the science of men. Plastic art shows every step of the road.

The recent fashion of ascribing to the Middle Ages a feeling for or observation of Nature is simply playing with words. The Middle Ages certainly considered Nature holy as the eternal order of the world, but no one before at earliest 1200 conceived it speculatively and yet intellectually as a live thing, moved by its own forces, throbbing with its own life. No importance attached to it in itself ; men preferred to grasp natural phenomena abstractly as allegory and to interpret them transcendentally. A late Alexandrine work, the *Physiologus*, which was translated into all the vernaculars, reinforced this tendency. It was almost the only source of natural science which the Middle Ages possessed except Pliny and the Encyclopaedia of Isidore of Seville, and it was by far the most popular. The *Physiologus* was a natural history which gave little anecdotes about the various animals and their habits, and recorded, at great length, their allegorical significance. What the Lion, the Bull and the Unicorn denoted from the moral, astral or cosmic point of view, awakened much more interest than what they, in fact, were.

Bishop Liutprand of Cremona, who was sent in the days of the Ottos as ambassador to Byzantium, exemplifies this type of nature study. He was shown an imperial zoological park in which there was a herd of wild asses. The bishop immediately began to excogitate what significance these wild donkeys might have for the universe. A sibylline saying occurred to him : " Lion and Cat shall conquer the Wild Ass." Liutprand first thought that this indicated a joint victory of his master Otto I and the Byzantine Emperor Nicephorus, over the Saracens. Then it seemed, however, that the two equally potent monarchs could not well be represented by the mighty lion and the little cat, where upon a little further reflection the true interpretation flashed on him : Lion and Cat were his masters Otto the Great and his young son Otto II, while the wild ass whom they should overcome, as was proved by the zoological garden, was no other than the Emperor Nicephorus himself ! Thus Bishop

Liutprand, one of the most learned of clerics, envisaged Nature.
And yet he was familiar with an immense number of ancient
authors : Cicero, Terence, Vegetius, Pliny, Lucretius, Boethius,
to name only a few, and to mention Ovid, Vergil, Horace not at
all.   In these things the classics carried no weight ; people
got from them what they brought to them—a moral or an
adventure.   Even the adventures that you experienced your-
self you interpreted intellectually if you were sufficiently
learned.   The letter of the Chancellor Conrad who describes
his Sicilian journey in which he had seen Scylla and Charybdis,
and the wonders of the Magician Vergil and the like, shows this
projection of the already-known on to the world of fact.   In
the age of the Crusaders men's fantasy took colour from the
fabled animals and mythical beings of Ovid and Apuleius, the
tales of Alexander, the wanderings of Aeneas and Odysseus.
Gradually, however, from using their fancy men learned to
use their eyes.

   It is remarkable what the ancients, who give to each age
according to its need, provided for the Middle Ages.   It is
probably the only time they have been called on to waken men's
senses to magic and formlessness.   The Middle Ages, fast
bound in forms and formulas, had enough and more than enough
of these.   Men who received their real life from another world,
a life that revealed itself in unalterable forms which were holy,
and beautiful and eternal, had naught to do with transitory life
that expressed itself in its own forms.   For them the ancients
needed to bring no new forms—they often produced effects
actually hostile to form—their mission was rather to awaken
and set free the hidden smouldering forces.   The authors who,
among the ancients, had a message for those times were a
motley crew, to many of whom access nowadays is almost
barred.   The favourite works were those innumerable pseudo-
Aristotelian writings which seek to make Aristotle " more
comprehensible " by neo-platonic speculations.   Men, unaccustomed to use their eyes, who were seeking the inner
meaning of things from the starting point not of life and man,
but of universal thought, could only find an approach to the

ancients through such authors as made most appeal to the
mind and least to the eye, and for them the Arabs were the best
interpreters.   The Arabs had sifted ancient literature with
but one end in view, and had transplanted everything purely
intellectual that would bear transplanting, but their minds
were entirely closed to anything that bore the special imprint
of Greek and Roman life.   Not one single historian did they
take over, not one single poet !   What were the tragic drama-
tists to them, the great lyricists !   What was Homer to them !
They only recognised one line of his as of any value :

$$\epsilon \hat{\iota} s \ \kappa o \acute{\iota} \rho a \nu o s \ \check{\epsilon} \sigma \tau \omega \cdot \ \epsilon \hat{\iota} s \ \beta a \sigma \iota \lambda \epsilon \acute{\upsilon} s.$$

On the other hand they had borrowed all the writings about
Natural Science and Medicine, and all the philosophers since
Alexander, and of the early philosophers only Plato's *Timaeus*,
Phaedo and the *Republic*.

After the natural history writers the Neo-Platonists appealed most to them, and in the neo-platonist version they
learned to know the great systematist Aristotle.   Even to the
great Arab philosophers of the tenth and eleventh centuries,
al Kindi, al Farabi and Avicenna, Aristotle was only accessible
in the garbled neo-platonist disguise.   The great interpreter
of the real Aristotle, the Spaniard Averroes, did not appear till
the twelfth century.   One of the greatest achievements of this
great scholar was to reveal to the West in translation and with
commentaries a purer Aristotle, and to retranslate other ancient
authors from Arabic into western tongues.   Averroes died in
the year which saw the four-year-old Frederick crowned King
of Naples in Palermo, though legend relates that he lived at the
court of Frederick.

Translations from the Arabic on an extensive scale began to
be made in the twelfth century principally, indeed almost
exclusively, in Spain in the school of Toledo, which in the
Middle Ages was accounted the headquarters of the magic
arts : astrology, necromancy, chiromancy, pyromancy and every
other sort of divination.   North Italians like Gerard of Cremona
worked here alongside Spaniards like Dominicus Gundissali-
nus.   About the turn of the century the first translations of
Averroes' works must have begun to issue from Toledo, and

along with them the physics and metaphysics of Aristotle.   As
early as 1209 these works were forbidden by Pope Innocent
III.   A second, but less important, collecting place for such
works was the Norman court of Palermo, the second entrance
gate of Eastern culture.   Here men like Eugene of Palermo and
Admiral Henry Aristippus were at work, but, as far as is known,
the sole translation from the Arabic that here appeared was the
Optics of Ptolemy.   Palermo was already far more important
as a link with Byzantium, and it was chiefly Greek works which
were there translated even into Latin : sayings of the Ery-
thraean Sibyl, the *Syntax* of Ptolemy, the *Optics* as well as the
Elements of Euclid, the writings of Proclus, the *Pneumatica* of
Hero of Alexandria, the logical and meteorological works of
Aristotle, Plato's *Meno* and *Phaedo*, etc.   Chalcidius' Latin
translation of the *Timaeus* and the never-lost translations by
Boethius of the Aristotelian *Topica*, *Analytica* and *Categorica*.
   We may assume that Frederick was acquainted with the
majority of these works.   It is also probable that through
his intimacy with the Saracens in Palermo he had learned in his
boyhood to know the scientific-philosophic writings of the
Arabs ; he certainly learned to know the Arab mind.   In the
thirty years of Sicilian chaos which followed on the death of
the last Norman king the scholarly activities of the court came
to a standstill.   Frederick II on every occasion renewed old
traditions, and on his return from Germany to his Sicilian
kingdom, still more on his return from the East, a period of
intellectual activity began at the imperial Court the results
of which no longer lagged behind those of Toledo.   When
Constantinople was conquered by the Crusaders in 1204, and
a Latin Empire established there, the interest of Byzantium
decreased considerably and Greek studies began to be ousted
by Arabic.   What the Emperor himself enjoyed at first hand
he now proceeded to interpret to the Western world through
his numerous scholars.
   It was probably when Frederick II visited Bologna on his
coronation journey that he first met the most celebrated of all
the scholars of his later court : Michael Scot.   Little is known
with certainty about the Scottish scholar's life.   He began his
career at Toledo, where he translated the *Spherics* of Alpetra-

gius in 1217. Three years later he appears in Bologna, then was for some time in correspondence with the papal Curia, which recommended him to the Archbishop of Canterbury, and he probably came to Frederick about 1227. He had probably made Frederick's acquaintance first at the same time that the Emperor had made friends with the mathematician, Leonardo of Pisa. Michael Scot, translator, astrologer, philosopher, mathematician and augur, was reckoned a wizard by his age, and Dante consigns to Hell this master of magic and necromancy " practised in every slight of magic wile," and introduces him as a false prophet of the future with his head turned backwards on his shoulders. Innumerable marvellous and uncanny stories were current about him and the Emperor, and can still be found in the novels and tales of the Romantics. The shuddering awe which Frederick II inspired was shared by his Court Astrologer, whom people called a "second Apollo." They related that, knowing beforehand the manner of his own death, he always wore an iron cap, and that in spite of it he was killed by a falling stone, exactly as he had foretold. His death probably occurred in 1235 as he was accompanying the Emperor to Germany.

Michael Scot is credited with a considerably larger number of writings than he actually produced. It is, however, certain that he translated Aristotle's *De Caelo* and *De Anima* with the commentaries of Averroes, and also the Aristotelian zoological writings which Avicenna had grouped under the title of *Liber animalium : Historiae animalium*, *De partibus animalium*, and other treatises—nineteen books in all. This work was dedicated, like most of his others, to the Emperor. It introduced the Aristotelian zoology for the first time to the West. Master Henry of Cologne made a transcript of the Emperor's copy in 1232, and this may well have been the copy used by Albertus Magnus. Translations of the *Physics* and *Metaphysics* were also ascribed, probably incorrectly, to Michael Scot. His authorship of some obscure philosophical treatises such as the *Quaestiones of Nicolas the Peripatetic* and a *Systematic Philosophy* is more probable.

Other Aristotelian writings were known at the Court : the *Nicomachaean Ethics*, *Rhetoric* and *Meteorology*, and, decades later, the *Politics* also. Pseudo-Aristotelian writings were on the other hand even more numerous. King Manfred later had the treatise *De Pomo* translated into Latin (Frederick had already had it translated into Hebrew) and presented the *Magna Moralia* to the University of Paris. Frederick himself quotes in his Falcon Book the pseudo-Aristotelian *Mechanics*. The so-called *Problemata*, which a scholar staying in Greece had translated from the Greek, were dedicated to the Emperor. The so-called *Theology* or περὶ βασιλείας of Aristotle was also presumably familiar.

Another scholar, Master Theodore, prepared for the Emperor extracts from the *Secretum Secretorum* which was also ascribed to Aristotle. Master Theodore, like Michael Scot, bore the title of Court Philosopher, and probably succeeded to the latter's post at Court. He was later even granted a fief. Michael Scot represented the spirit of Spain and Toledo, Theodore rather that of the Arab East. He probably came from Antioch, was said to have studied in Baghdad and Mosul, and had been sent to the Emperor in 1236 by the " Great Khalif," probably al Kamil of Egypt. He was not allowed to be idle : in the course of a few months he was employed as astrologer to cast the Emperor's horoscope ; as chancery clerk to conduct correspondence with Arab rulers ; he was sent to Tunis as ambassador ; as a scholar he was set to translate an Arabic treatise, and, lastly—a less intellectual but not less important employment—he had to prepare violet sweetmeats for the court, some of which the Emperor sent to Piero della Vigna who was sick.

Peter the Spaniard described himself in a medical treatise as a pupil of Master Theodore. Nothing further is known about him, nor about the two other men who are styled Court Philosophers : Master John of Palermo and Master Dominicus, probably a Spaniard. Almost all these court scholars maintained close relations with the circle of Leonardo of Pisa, who introduced the system of Arabic numerals to the West. We know that Frederick II met this greatest of all medieval mathematicians in Pisa and conversed with him at length.

Leonardo never actually entered the Emperor's service, but he sent a revised version of his most important work, the *Abacus*, to Michael Scot, referred to the "great philosopher" Master Theodore, and dedicated his *Liber Quadratorum* to the Emperor, who it seems had in earlier years completely mastered the great mathematician's other writings. The Sultan, al Kamil, had sent a mathematician and astronomer, the learned al Hanifi, to the Emperor, for mathematics were very highly valued by the Emperor personally. The court scholars all found mathematics absolutely indispensable for their astronomical and astrological calculations.

The immense importance of astrology for this century is rarely appreciated. A hard and fast conception of "Time" prevailed, and to astrology fell the task of determining the right moment, the feeling for which was imperfectly developed or had been undermined by a belief in Providence. Hers also was the task of proving directly from an eternal source, the metaphysical necessity of a given event's happening at a given moment. There was as yet no room for the conception that events themselves bring their own moment with them and that the event gives the moment its eternal significance. Even Dante assured himself of the position of the planets at the time of every important occurrence, thus linking time with eternity. In this his position was akin to Michael Scot's, who declared: "The heavenly bodies are not the cause of events, but the sign thereof, as the compasses in front of the tavern are the sign that wine is within."

Astronomy and astrology played an important part in court life. One of the sultans had sent Frederick that costly astrolabe which, with his son and heir Conrad, was the thing dearest to him on earth. The Egyptian Sultan sent as a gift an Arab work on astrology, the *Book of the Nine Judges*. His son Manfred later had the *Centiloquium of Hermes* translated, another astrological work; and, finally, Michael Scot in his *Liber Introductorius* and his *Liber Particularis* compiled a wonderful encyclopaedia of the collective astronomical and astrological knowledge of his time. Michael, not undeservedly, ranked as THE ASTROLOGER of the Middle Ages, and the Italian towns were swamped with spurious prophecies supposed to emanate from him.

Wherever the Emperor appeared he was accompanied by a

number of his astrologers, and there was nothing the Italian princes were so ready to learn from him as the use of the astrological art. How far Frederick really believed in his star-gazers remains a question. Though he frequently inquired what would be the propitious moment for a certain weighty enterprise, the founding of a city or the start of a campaign, he may very well have reflected, like the Renaissance princes, that if the stars cannot lie the astrologers can. He puts them again and again to the test. Michael Scot had recommended : " When you seek advice from a wise man, consult him by a waxing moon," and had also adjured him to be mindful of the ancient medical maxim to avoid blood-letting when the moon is in the sign of the Twins. The Emperor wanted to prove him a liar, and sent for the surgeon on a forbidden day. The blood-letting went off successfully, but when all was over the surgeon accidentally dropped his lancet and pierced the Emperor's foot. For several days the swelling caused him extreme pain. Another time Frederick asked his astrologer how far the sky was from the palace. Whatever this exactly meant, Michael Scot promptly calculated the distance. The Emperor sent him away and had the floor of the room or court-yard of his palace sunk a hand's breadth, and when Michael returned requested him to reckon out the distance once again. His calculation at once revealed that either the sky had moved a hand's breath further off or else the palace had sunk. These anecdotes are characteristic of Frederick, and manifest his scepticism not towards things but towards people. His astrologers, like his " harem," must often have simply formed part of his *mise en scène*. Mystery, like magnificence, was to contribute its quota to the impression he created.

The Hebrew scholars of Spain and of Provence with whom Frederick established relations, or whom he even brought to court, contributed rather to the astronomical and philosophical than to the astrological interests of the court. Through them he became acquainted with Jewish philosophy, which then had reached its zenith with Maimonides. Frederick was said to be able to express himself orally in nine languages and to write

seven ; it is quite probable that among them he knew Hebrew.
He certainly had numerous works translated into Hebrew.   At
the age of eighteen Juda ben.Salomon Cohen came to his court,
and there compiled an Encyclopaedia on the works of Aristotle, Euclid, Ptolemy and the Spaniard Alpetronius.   A Jew is
mentioned as secretary to Michael Scot ; it was the custom
in Spain for Jews to collaborate with Latinists in translations
from the Arabic.   Jacob ben Abbamari, who translated five
books of the Logic of Aristotle with the Isagoge of Porphyry
and the commentaries of Averroes, came from Provence.   He
prepared a Hebrew translation of Ptolemy in Naples, and translated al Fargani's *Elements of Astronomy* into Hebrew.   These
translations are dedicated to the Emperor, and express the
hope that under Frederick " this friend of wisdom who maintains me," the Messiah, may appear.   This wish was not mere
rhetoric, for the year 1240 was, according to Hebrew chronology
the year 5,000, and people were looking for the coming of the
Messiah.   Frederick II was held in such high repute by the
Jews that in a Hebrew *Mirror of Manners* anecdotes and sayings
of his are recorded as models, alongside those of Aristotle,
Alexander the Great, Porphyry and Theophrastus.

Frederick was introduced to the works of Maimonides, who
died in 1205, by another scholar, Moses ben Salomon from
Salerno, who had written a commentary on the *Guide of the
Perplexed*.   Other works of this great Aristotelian were known
to the Emperor, and some of his conversations prove that he
knew them intimately.   The talk turned on Maimonides one
day, and his chief work was stated to be his *Interpretation of
the Old Testament and of the Talmud*.   The Emperor remarked
that he missed in it any explanation of the origin of the curious
Jewish ritual according to which the ashes of a red cow were
potent for purification.   For his part he believed the rite had
its origin in India, where a red lion was burnt for a similar
purpose, as he had read in the *Book of Indian Sages*.   The
Lawgiver Moses, reflecting on the great danger involved in
catching a lion, had substituted a cow as a burnt-offering
for the Jews.   Possibly astrological considerations might have
had something to do with it, which would be akin to those of
Egyptian magicians and conjurers of spirits ! Another time

they were discussing why, according to Bible precept, only domestic animals, never wild animals, were offered as sacrifices, whereupon the Emperor gave as his explanation that sacrifices are, as it were, gifts to heaven, and a man can only give his own property, not the free beast of the field that belongs to none.

It is suggestive to note how, in this " republic of scholars," each knew the other and all mutually assisted each other in work. The Jew, Jacob ben Abbamari, was a friend of Michael Scot and often appealed to him. He had leagued himself with the Scot, he writes, and received many learned suggestions from him about various Bible passages, mainly connected with questions of natural science. Moses ben Salomon of Salerno again conducted learned conversations with Margrave Berthold of Hohenburg, who in 1240 was a page in the Emperor's service, and to whom, later, young Manfred was entrusted. So it is clear that the scientific curiosity of the court infected the young nobles also. Another courtier questioned the Jew, Jehuda ben Salomon, about the construction of five bodies from a given sphere and was directed to Euclid. The Hebrew scholar from Salerno disputed with Peter of Ireland, the famous teacher at the University of Naples, who afterwards held an extraordinarily learned conversation about most varied topics with Manfred and his friends.

This Renaissance-like " Academy," with its head the Emperor as *primus inter pares*, demonstrated how the free human mind, bridging all gulfs of race, religion and rank, acted as a levelling agency in the secular world just as—in a quite different direction—the faith of the Church acted in the spiritual world. In his Charter, drawn up on the foundation of the University of Naples, and modelled in many of its features on that of Bologna, the Emperor had pointed to the uniting action of the mind. The proffered gifts of learning bring nobility and possessions in their train which make the affections and graciousness of friendship flourish. To characterise the free human spirit as friendship-building struck a new and humanistic note, which indicated that the clerical spirit had already been conquered. A new power was dawning here, and the Emperor valued on that account scholars and learned men who, as a courtier writes, "inhabit the circle of the earth from sea to sea." When Frederick sent to the teachers and scholars of Bologna the manuscript of a treatise of Aristotle on logic and mathematics, which with other manuscripts filled the coffers of his treasuries and which he had found again in pursuing his linguistic and mathematical studies, he wrote in the covering letter: " The recipients should accept these writings gratefully as a gift of their friend the Emperor . . . *amici caesaris*." They would know how to use them and " to draw new water out of the ancient well."

This is the happiest interpretation of the learned activity of the dawning Renaissance at the Hohenstaufen court. With the high value attached to everything intellectual a new problem presented itself to the court circle, one which had occupied men's minds since the troubadour days began, and the stirrings of unfettered secular thought: what is the true nobility amongst men? Nobility of race or of the spirit? The question was debated with quite peculiar zest at the Emperor's court, where town-bred scholars and lawyers worked in common with knightly and aristocratic officials, and mixed with and argued with Christian, Jewish and Muslim philosophers. On one occasion the courtiers turned to Piero della Vigna and Thaddeus of Suessa, the two High Court Judges, and requested them to decide it. The reply may have been given in the Emperor's own quotation from Aristotle. Nobility consists in ancient possessions wedded with noble conduct. Frederick expressed himself on similar lines in his foundation charter of Naples. To him, himself the grandson of emperors and kings, nobility of mind apart from nobility of race was inconceivable, and Dante took the same position in his *De Monarchia*. In his *Convivio* it is true he had sought to demonstrate the emptiness of " ancient possessions," and in his great educational treatise and the canzones that accompany it he had taken Frederick II's maxim as a text only to refute it, although he styled the Emperor " a great logician and a great scholar." However much people might dispute over the definition, the fusion of an aristocracy of blood and an aristocracy of brain had already been realised at the imperial court.

A conversation of King Manfred and his friend with Peter of Ireland has just been mentioned. Though it took place ten years after Frederick's death this conversation vividly reveals the type of question which occupied the court. The problem is the significant one : of a " purpose in Nature." Are the limbs present because of the functions they perform, or are the functions the result of the limbs, or, more exactly— someone may have asked—are the claws of the vulture, the fangs of the wolf, the teeth of the lion, provided by nature to tear other animals to death ? A devilish question, full of pitfalls. For if it is answered in the affirmative, that implies that Nature recognises the principle of destruction—recognises evil—that this is the will of nature, the will of God. According to this theory Providence would not be aiming at the " Good " in the Christian sense, and that hoped-for dispensation where lion and lamb would play together in the fields of Paradise would no longer be the order of the world as willed by Nature and by God. That is conceivable enough . . . for every statesman would feel a sabbath fraternisation of all animals, and the equalisation of all created things a hideous disorder, not least Frederick II himself who always pictured Adam as the " King."

The Emperor held very strong views about the due observance of rank and precedence even in the animal world. An anecdote illustrates this : he loosed one day a favourite falcon, " whom he loved more than a city," on a crane. The falcon rose and was above the crane, when far below he spied an eaglet, stooped and slew it. When the Emperor saw this he wrathfully summoned a justiciar and had his favourite falcon beheaded *perk' avea morto lo suo signiore*, because he had killed an animal of higher rank than himself and his master, a young eagle, king of the birds ! This does not stultify Frederick's dream of bringing in the " golden age." He dreamt not of listless peace, idyllic absence of desire, but the tension of supreme control and discipline, under which the lion would if necessary abstain from devouring the adjacent rabbit. Such was the Emperor's vision of a Paradise in which he could then himself relax.

Peter of Ireland rejected the dangerous enquiry whether claws and fangs were created for the rending of other animals.

He added : " The secret potency of this question has led many
to recognise two principles in everything, the principle of evil
and the principle of good. This, however, is heresy and bad
taste to boot." He directs attention instead to the necessity
inherent in matter which provides for everything that is
necessary. The learned man may have had more particularly
in mind the spreading heresy of Neo-Manichaeism. Everywhere sects of devil worshippers were springing up, amongst
them the Luciferians, who were said to maintain that God
had unjustly condemned Satan to Hell—for Satan was the true
Creator of all things.

Another set of problems—indirectly suggested by Aristotle—
are touched on in a talk of the Emperor's about the interpretation of a passage in the Bible. They were discussing
why Maimonides had described earthly matter as snow. The
Emperor opined : because white takes every other colour
readily, as matter takes the form imposed on it. Snow is,
therefore, a symbol of the malleability of matter. The moulding
of matter was a subject frequently present to the Emperor's
mind. It is touched on in the preface to the Book of Laws,
where God is presented not as the Creator but as the Moulder
of pre-existent matter. This problem was interrelated with
another : Whether the World, as Aristotle taught, existed
" from eternity " or whether it had been created by God.
Frederick sought light on these and other metaphysical questions from the learned men of Islam—on certain discrepancies
between Aristotle and his commentator Alexander of Aphro-
disias (whom the Emperor therefore also knew). The Emperor
despatched his queries to Egypt, Syria, Iraq, Asia Minor,
Yemen. Ultimately, through the medium of the Sultan of the
Almohades, they reached Ibn Sabin, a Moroccan scholar in
Ceuta, who, as he himself writes, " smilingly undertook to
answer the Emperor." He refused to accept Frederick's
numerous gifts ; he intended thereby to bring home his in-
significance to the Christian Emperor, " to the triumph of
Islam." His answers themselves did so too. The Emperor
had asked, amongst other things, " What is the proof of the
immortality of the soul, and is her existence eternal ? " Whereupon Ibn Sabin, in most mysterious language, gave the Emperor

to understand that he did not even know how to formulate a question correctly. " O prince, thou who seekest truth," he wrote, " thou hast posed thy question about the nature of the soul without exactly indicating what type of soul is the object of thy questioning. Thou hast thus neglected the essential and hast regrettably confused many things which should have been treated separately. It is thine inexperience in treating of speculative matters and instituting enquiries in an independent branch of science which has led thee into such confusion. Hadst thou but known the number of separate types which are comprised under the one word ' soul'! Hadst thou but been acquainted with Dialectics and the manner of distinguishing the Finite from the Infinite, between the Particular and the General, between the conceptions of ambiguous homonyms and that which is consecrated by the terminology of speech !—thou wouldest never have so phrased thy question. For when thou askest : ' What is the proof for the immortality of the soul ? ' thy question may be understood to apply to the vegetable soul, the animal soul, the rational soul, the soul of wisdom, the soul of prophecy. To which of these souls does thy question apply ? "

Ibn Sabin continues in this strain, proud of his immense knowledge and powers of hair-splitting and incapable of giving a real answer. He writes a separate dissertation on each type of soul and explains his position with regard to Plato and Moses, Avicenna and the Brahmins; finally, in a feeble anti-climax maintaining that Islam is the only true religion. There was a certain value in all this harangue, the reference, for instance, to the teaching of the Brahmins. Much of Frederick's knowledge about India must have reached him in this sort of way.

It was not merely as an intellectual pastime that Frederick directed such questions to learned men. He was seeking proofs for the rightness of his own way of life, and he often established such proofs by violent and remarkable methods. To prove the mortality of the soul he had a man imprisoned in a perfectly tight-fitting wine vat and left to perish, to demonstrate that the soul which could not escape from the vat must have perished with the body : such at least is the tale. Maimonides to a certain extent encouraged this type of speculation in so far as he, like the Averroists, though on other grounds,

denied any general immortality, and only accorded immortality
to the truly wise. Frederick's correspondence with oriental
scholars was certainly not all so fruitless as that with Ibn
Sabin of Ceuta. We learn from the Arabs themselves that
Frederick sent astronomical and geometrical questions to
Mosul, one of which, for instance, was to construct a quadri-
lateral of the same superficial area as a segment of a given circle.
Books were even exchanged. The Emperor made a collection
of the prophecies of Merlin and had it translated into Arabic
for the Sultan of Egypt, and he himself received from Tunis
the novel *Sidrach* and the *Book of all Knowledge*. Envoys of
the Emperor, remarking the immense wisdom of the Ruler of
Tunis, and learning that he owed it to *Sidrach*, called Frederick's attention to this work. The Emperor at once begged
permission to have a copy made of this book, which in the form
of question and answer deals with every sphere of heaven and
of earth. Much of it must have stimulated the Emperor to
further questioning.

This impulse to inquire was Frederick's most dangerous
quality, for he had a gift of dissolving fast-frozen axioms by a
casual question. As he once sought to undermine the spiritual
basis of papal rule by the maliciously-innocent enquiry whether
Pope Gregory, like himself the Hohenstaufen, could trace his
claims back through his father and grandfather. He attacked
the very roots of medieval faith by a series of trustful, innocent-
sounding questions addressed on occasion to Michael Scot.
Michael Scot in his encyclopaedia relates as follows :
" Once, when Frederick, Emperor of Rome, the ever-
illustrious, had reflected long in accordance with the order
he had himself established on the differences of the whole
earth, what they are and how they appear on, over, in and under
the earth, he then sent secretly for me, Michael the Scot, the
most faithful of his astrologers, and laid a number of questions
before me, secretly, as it pleased him to do, about the foundations of earth and the marvels thereof, speaking as follows :
' My dearest Master, we have often and in divers ways heard
question and answer from one and another about the heavenly

bodies, about sun and moon and the fixed stars, about the
elements, the world soul, about heathen and Christian peoples
and other created things that exist on and in the earth, such as
plants and metals.   Yet we have heard naught of those secrets
which delight the mind that is wedded to wisdom : about Paradise, Purgatory, Hell, the foundations and the wonders of the
world.   Therefore we beg thee by thy love of wisdom and thy
loyalty to our throne to explain to us the structure of the earth.

How is the earth fastened above the abyss of space ?
And how is this abyss fastened beneath the earth ?
Is there aught else that bears the earth save air and water ?
Or does the earth stand fast of itself ?
Or does it rest on the heavens below it ?
And how many heavens are there ?
Who is their director ?
Who mainly inhabit the heavens ?
How far is one heaven distant from another by our measure ?
And if there be many heavens what is there out beyond the last ?
By how much is one heaven greater than another ?
In which heaven is God Substance, that is in his divine majesty,
     and in what wise doth he sit upon the throne of heaven ?
And in what wise is he accompanied by the angels and the saints ?
And what do the angels and the saints do uninterruptedly in the
     presence of God ?
Likewise tell us : How many Hells are there ?
Who are the spirits who dwell in them ?
And by what names are they called ?
Where is Hell, and Purgatory where ?
And where the Heavenly Paradise ?   Under the earth ?   Over the
     earth ?   In the earth ?
And what is the difference between the souls who go to Hell and
     the spirits which fell from Heaven ?   And how many torments
     are there in Hell ?
And does one soul know another in the next life ?   And can a
     soul return to this life to speak or to show itself to anyone ?
And what of this : that when the soul of a living man passes over
     into that other life, naught can give it power to return, neither
     first love nor even HATE as if naught had ever happened ?   Or
     does it seem that the soul careth naught for what is left behind,
     whether it be blessed or whether it be damned ? ' "

These questions at once recall the apparently similar questions of the Scholastics; but theirs are mostly pure mental

gymnastics of this type : how would mankind have spread over
the earth according to God's wish if there had been no Fall ?
or whether at the Resurrection the toothless will again grow
teeth and the bald grow hair ? Frederick II, however, asks
about the appearance of that other world. He directs the
same practical curiosity to the conditions of that other world
as dictated his questions to the messengers of Muslim princes
about the conditions of their various foreign countries. The
kingdom of God was for him just such another. The thought
of the future life, which disturbed Frederick's contemporaries
to the core and hunted terrified men to penances and flagel-
lations, was to Frederick in the most amazing way simply an
innocent object of knowledge and "a delight of the mind."
He inquires because the tectonics of the world-structure seems
to him immeasurably interesting ; he longs to know just how
God sits upon his throne, because he must sit in like fashion ;
it is unquestionably useful to him as a judge to know the punishments of Hell ; and the statesman in him enquires for practical
reasons about the precedence of saints, angels and spirits.

Mysticism is entirely foreign to this method of approach,
which seeks objective representation. There is not a trace
of any personal, emotional interest, nor in the imperial soul
the faintest shadow of anxiety. Eternal bliss, everlasting
contemplation of God offer no allurements : "What do the
angels do uninterruptedly in the presence of God ? " That
other question, whether a return to this life is not possible " not
even for hate," corresponds to the Emperor's saying on the
defection of a certain town : " If I had one foot in Paradise
I would withdraw it to take vengeance on Viterbo ! " Dante
answered all these questions soberly and practically too, but
interested in every fibre in that world which he never ceased
to picture tangibly and visibly to himself day and night. His
questions are often the same as Frederick's.

People tell of Frederick II, himself the master of so many
tongues, that he was anxious to discover by research what the
primeval human speech had been. He, therefore, had a number
of infants reared by nurses who were most strictly forbidden
to speak to them. " He wanted to discover whether the children could speak Hebrew, or Greek, or Latin, or Arabic as the

original of all languages, or whether they would speak the
speech of their parents who had borne them." The experiment
failed, for the children died. This problem also attracted
Dante, who deals with it in his treatise on popular speech.
Dante also, in another little essay, *de Aqua et terra*, discusses
just such hydrological phenomena as Frederick II had cross-
examined Michael Scot about. " How does it come," asked
the Emperor, " that sea-water is so salt, and that in many
places far from the sea salt water is found and in other places
sweet water, although they all derive from the living sea ?
And how comes it that sweet waters are often spewed out by
the earth and often drop from stones and trees, like grape vines
when they are cut in spring ? And how is it that many waters
are sweet and mild and sparkling clear, and many are wild and
others again viscous and thick ? We marvel much about all
these things although we know long since that all waters come
from the sea and that they flow through lands and caves of many
kinds, returning to the sea which is the bed and womb of all the
streaming waters." Dante and his age shared this conception
of the unity of all earthly waters.

This " much marvelling " of the Emperor's is the vital
point. Things which for centuries everybody had seen and
accepted as facts challenged him to curious enquiry. When
he was staying at a place like Pozzuoli or Montepulciano he
immediately wanted to know all about the remarkable springs.
" Where do the salt and bitter springs come from, which in
many places gush forth with violence, and the foul-smelling
waters which are found in many baths and pools. Do they
spring up themselves ? Do they come from elsewhere ? And
those waters which in some places are hot or at least very warm
and sometimes even boiling as if they had been in a vessel over a
fire ? Has the earth a hole in its centre, or is it a solid body
like a living stone ? " The world was, as it were, a new discovery
to him fraught with questions. He must have observed the
winds on his crusading voyage : " Whence comes the wind
which blows from different parts of the circle of the earth ? "
He probably means the regular wind-currents. Volcanoes are
another subject of inquiry : " Whence comes the fire which the
earth vomits forth both out of plains and mountain tops ?

Smoke too appears now there, now here.   Where is it generated
and what causes it to burst forth ?   We see it in many parts of
Sicily and near Messina, as in Etna, Vesuvius, the Lipari
islands and Stromboli."   He is probably thinking of sub-
marine volcanoes when he asks : " How does it come that
such flaming fire appears to issue not only from the earth but
in many parts of the Indian Sea ? "

Other things that occupied the Emperor's mind were the
secret forces inherent in matter, in things themselves, forces
which Frederick II was so skilful in liberating in his State.
He had a particular love for precious stones that was not
unconnected with their magic properties, and he would purchase them even when the treasury was exhausted.   Prester
John was said to have given him wonderful stones ; and he
was brought the legendary jewels from the crown of the
Babylonian dragon which a fisherman had found.   He was intimately acquainted with the magnetic needle and its mysterious
power, that wonderful instrument of which Brunetto Latini
wrote at the end of the century to Guido Cavalcanti : " The
seafarer can steer correctly thanks to this magnet, but for the
present he must use it secretly . . . for no shipmaster would dare
to employ him lest he be suspected of witchcraft.   Sailors
would refuse to serve on the ship if they knew that their captain
had in his possession such inventions of the devil."   Michael
Scot had minutely instructed the Emperor about the different
properties of minerals and metals, a lore which verged on
alchemy, an art by no means unknown at court.   He learned, for
instance, that quicksilver, the wonderful *argentum vivum*, makes
a man deaf if dropped into his ear.   He also got Michael
Scot to teach him the properties of herbs and drugs (the
Botany of Dioscorides was known in Sicily) and the wonderful
qualities of lakes and rivers, and he sent special messengers
to Norway to investigate the petrifying properties of a certain
spring.

Frederick's great resource in all his questionings was the
enormous work of Michael Scot, which was not only an
astronomical, astrological encyclopaedia, but a compendium of

all the secret sciences. It was based in many points on dangerous sources, a *Liber perditionis animae et corporis* for instance,
which contained the names, dwelling-places and powers of the
demons, and the *Liber auguriorum* of which Michael Scot
(otherwise a most obedient son of the Church) writes that
he has seen and owned the book although the Roman Church
had banned it. His work does not neglect the symbolism of
numbers and their mystic values : the number seven rules the
world, for seven is the number of the planets, metals, arts,
colours, tones and smells. Everywhere we detect him striving
to relate everything in the Cosmos according to law to everything else. Michael Scot treats of the music of the spheres and
expounds *en passant* the old musical doctrines of Boethius, and
the newer ones of Guido of Arezzo ; on another occasion he
explains the calendar. His immense astrological and astronomical knowledge he owes not only to the Almagest and to al
Fargani, but much also to the ancients, to the obscure Scholia
of Germanicus, for instance, in which again Nigidius and Ful-
gentius, Hyginus, Pliny, Martianus Capella and Aratus are
included. Michael Scot took over the star pictures of the
ancient Scholia, and these astrological figures of Mars and
Jupiter, the Archer and the Centaur, which followed the
ancient representations, exercised in their turn an influence on
Renaissance painting, as can be demonstrated from Giotto's
frescoes at Padua. For his astrology Michael Scot draws
largely on the Arabs, above all on Albumazar in whom more
ancient works were collected, Hermes, Dorotheus, the Babylonian Teucer and also Indians and Persians. In short, at the
imperial court all the superstitions of the late Roman empire, a
prey as it had been to the stream of oriental influences, came to
life again, just as Gnostic teaching reawakened amongst the
heretics of this same period.

Frederick knew all these things, or had learned in conversation all that was worth knowing about them. " O fortunate
Emperor ! "—wrote Michael Scot—" I verily believe if ever
a man in this world could escape death by his learning, thou
wouldest be the one. . . ." Frederick's knowledge must have
been stupendous. His mind enbraced every line of culture in
the contemporary world : Spanish, Provençal, French, Roman,

Italian, Arab, Greek and Jew. Add to this his knowledge
of tongues, of jurisprudence, of ancient literature, of Roman
educational literature and the literature of Scholasticism, whose
methods were entirely familiar to him as his Falcon Book
shows.   His contemporaries, amazed and fearful, called him
STUPOR MUNDI.

More admirable even than the fulness of his knowledge was
the fact that with it all the Emperor never for a moment lost
his clarity of vision.   Even in scientific matters he knew exactly
what things were of importance for research.   He was himself
at home in the mysterious twilight of the prophets and star-
gazers and could not value their sphere too highly as, in a certain sense, a training ground.   His own aims, however, were
far too simple and straightforward to be understood by any
of these over-learned folk.   He depended only on first hand
ocular observation.   " No certainty comes by hearsay " was
one of his maxims.   He acted up to it.   To let people know
the Emperor's methods he once sent mutilated and blinded
conspirators on a tour of all countries, for " the sight of the eyes
makes more impression on men than the hearing of the ear."
He by no means despised the mental training that served to
sharpen the sight.   An Arab scholar Shahabu 'd Din has
preserved in an essay on Optics : *Attentive Observation of
What the Eye Perceives,* some questions of the Emperor's.
He asked why Canopus looked larger at his rising than at his
zenith ;   why eyes afflicted with cataract could see black
streaks and spots ;   why a lance plunged in water should appear
broken.   Deceptions of the eye had a disturbing importance
for the man who relied preponderantly on visual observation.

The sense in which Frederick believed that knowledge was
dependent on seeing is clear from his laws about doctors.   The
Constitutions of Melfi lay down : " Since the science of medicine cannot be mastered without a preliminary knowledge of
logic, we command that none shall study medicine who has not
first studied logic for at least three years."   All medical students of Salerno were obliged to devote five years to reading
Hippocrates and Galen concurrently with their surgical and
anatomical studies, for the purposes of which corpses were on
occasion placed at their disposal.   After they had passed their

examination the Emperor did not grant them an appointment as doctor until " they had practised for a full year beside an experienced physician." After that they became state officials. The apothecaries were also state officials, and were obliged to study physics for one year. The Emperor himself had a very exact knowledge of anatomy, both animal and human, and of medicine. The Arabs had a great admiration for his medical knowledge, and he quotes Hippocrates in his Falcon Book. Michael Scot wrote a medical treatise, so also did Master Theodore, who, when he was instructed to work out a new scheme of dietetics, wrote to the Emperor : " Your Majesty has commanded me to prescribe certain rules for the preservation of your health . . . but you are long since in possession of that most ancient letter from the " Secrets " of Aristotle, which he sent to the Emperor Alexander when the latter asked to be instructed about the health of the body. All that your Majesty desires to know is completely contained in that letter." A certain Adam of Cremona also worked out medical instructions for the Emperor. And in Italy for many a day powders, prescriptions and healing lotions passed under Frederick's name. In addition to anatomy and medicine the Emperor sought to master the science of human physiognomy. At his request Michael Scot compiled from Arab-Hellenistic sources an essay on Physiognomics which forms the third part of his great Handbook. In the dedication he assures the Emperor that with this knowledge in mind a ruler may know the vices and virtues of his entourage as surely as if he were himself in their skins.

Slowly people were progressing from mental blinking to physical seeing. Seeing, observing, exploring and researching into Nature and her laws became a passion with Frederick II. The innumerable anecdotes, the countless questions all betray the same craving to explore the living newly-discovered world, all disclose the same passionate curiosity concerning the laws of cause and effect, the how and the why of every sort of life. He shares this passion for knowledge, this curiosity, with Leonardo da Vinci, to whom Nietzsche compares him : he at the beginning, Leonardo at the end of the same epoch. Where mere observation was insufficient Frederick II proceeded to scientific experiment, which, like every attempt at experiment,

seemed to the Middle Ages abhorrent or insane. They tell
that he was anxious to discover which of two men had better
digested his food, the one who had rested after his meal or the
other who had taken exercise : he cut them open to see. To
ascertain the length of a fish's life Frederick inserted a copper
ring in a carp's fin and set it free. The story of the " Diver "
is told about Frederick. He made the man dive into the Faro
to learn about sea animals and plants. He organised the most
original experiments on his Apulian estates, where he bred
horses and sought to improve the breed by importing Barbary
mares. In Malta he established a camel-breeding station, not
to mention his breeding of hounds, poultry and pigeons. To
study the chick's emergence from the egg, the embryo's
position in the egg, etc., he built artificial incubating ovens.
Having heard that ostrich eggs are hatched by the sun in hot
sand he procured ostrich eggs from al Kamil and experienced
people along with them, and tried to hatch them out in the
heat of the Apulian summer. Al Kamil also sent him Indian
cockatoos and pelicans, in return for which Frederick sent him
presents of white peacocks and a polar bear. He tried to
determine whether birds of prey detect their quarry by sight or
smell. " We have often experimented in various ways. For
when the falcons are completely blinded (by stitching the eye-
lids) they do not even detect the meat that is thrown to them,
though nothing impedes their power of smell." He was the
first to institute systematic cultivation of game ; he established
close seasons, based on an accurate observation of the times of
pairing and breeding, for which the animals of Apulia were
supposed to have written him a letter of thanks. He had
animal reservations in various parts of his kingdom, and the
larger part of his menagerie, when not in actual attendance on
him, was kept in Lucera. On occasion he would divide a
number of captured cranes among his various castles. His
large vivarium was symbolical. Close to Foggia he had a big
marsh laid out with ponds and walled water-conduits which
was alive with all descriptions of waterfowl. A fantastic
picture—the great palace with its columns of marble and
serpentine, with bronze and marble statues, the Emperor within
attended by Moorish slaves and noble pages, visiting his pools

to study pelicans, cranes, herons, wild geese and exotic marsh fowl !

All these instincts of his culminated in his passion for the chase which cost him the gravest defeat of his career—before the walls of Parma. For Frederick's ancestors the chase had been a peacetime substitute for war ; for Frederick it was more, it was an art " entirely born of love " (*totum procedit ex amore*), an intellectual exercise on a par with his natural science studies. Only hawking, of course. The charm lay in the mysterious power of the falconer over the freest, most elusive of all birds—the eagle, the buzzard, the falcon. When six, eight, or even ten falcons circled free in the air, almost out of sight and yet bound as it were by some invisible thread, compelled by some mysterious power that brought them with infallible certainty back to the falconer's wrist, scorning the proffered liberty, it was not only an exciting marvel, it was for Frederick the *ne plus ultra* of perfect discipline. The discipline Frederick would have liked to see equally developed in man.

He despised the hunter who hunted with snares or nets or quadrupeds. The noble sport was hawking, because it is an art that can only be learnt from a teacher. " Hence it comes that while many men of noble birth learn the art, the uneducated rarely do so. Hounds and hunting-leopards can be tamed by force, falcons can only be caught and trained by human skill. Hence a man learns more of the secrets of nature from hawking than from other kinds of hunting," thus Frederick writes in his Book of Falconry. This saying of his explains why, after the decay of hawking, intellectual monarchs like Frederick the Great or Napoleon had no love for the chase. It is also the revelation of what Frederick sought in the chase : the secret workings of nature.

Frederick's great work is the product of years of observation : *de Arte venandi cum avibus*. " Thanks to his amazingly penetrative glance, directed especially to the observation of nature, the Imperator himself wrote a book about the nature and care of birds, in which he showed how deeply imbued he was with a love of knowledge," wrote a chronicler. This comprehensive zoological treatise is anything but the superficial indulgence of a princely caprice. Down to the minutest detail it is based on his own observations or those which friends and experts had made at his instigation. For twenty or thirty years the Emperor had meditated the writing of this Ornithology—for it is no less—and all the time he had been amassing first-hand material till at last, urged by his son Manfred, he set about the actual task of writing the six books in this branch of Zoology. " He must be reckoned the greatest expert who ever lived," so judged Ranke. And the statement is not unjustified. In the most vital points the book has not even yet been superseded. The most astonishing thing about it is its absolute accuracy and matter-of-factness, which contains more knowledge of the mysteries of nature than do the cosmic astral encyclopaedias of the court philosophers at which the Emperor was wont to smile, even though on occasion he participated in the current superstitions. In that age of intellectual starvation, which speculated how many angels could dance on the point of a needle, Frederick summed up his programme in the introduction in the clear-cut phrase : " Our intention is to set forth the things which are, as they are (*manifestare ea quae sunt sicut sunt*)." This stern sobriety, that seeks nothing before things or behind things, but the things themselves, when exercised by a wise man, contains the vision of all visions. Everything is, first and foremost, itself. Neither the philosophers of the East nor the philosophers of the West had taught this to Frederick. We reflect that, a century ago, when the rest of Germany was celebrating orgies of emotion and philosophy, many a one quitted Weimar in disillusionment because there everyone was " busy counting the legs of cockchafers."

The Emperor's book *Concerning the Art of Hunting with Birds* contains far more than its title promises. The first part is a general survey of birds, a classification of species, their habits, their breeding, their feeding, their distribution, their methods of nesting. The migration of birds is described in detail, their skeletal structure, the organs and their functions ; every detail of the plumage, the number and position of the wing feathers, the flight itself ; in what relation the hardness of the wing feathers stands to the frequency of the wing beat. It is surprising to note that here Frederick seeks explanation in the various works known to him, and refers, for instance, to the pseudo-Aristotelian *Mechanics*. Each beat of the wing, we learn, moves through a segment of a circle, in which movement the outer feather describe the largest circle. According to the laws of the *Mechanics* the larger roller lifts the greater weight. Since the outer feathers have the greatest burden to support and the greatest circle to describe they are correspondingly stronger in build, and the hardness of the feathers decreases in given proportions.

In the second of the six books the Emperor talks of the different types of hunting falcons, their capture, their training, their temporary blinding, by sewing the lids, the way to carry them and the way to cast them. Frederick used to get falcons sent or fetched from all corners of the earth. He once took a condemned criminal and sent him down into an abyss to fetch the nest of a white falcon. When he speaks of the birds of prey which were sent to him from Spain and Bulgaria, the Near East and India, Britain and Iceland (which he locates between Norway and Greenland), his immense knowledge of plant and animal geography is displayed. He remarks that the birds of the Arctic regions who are nearer to the North Pole are stronger, braver, quicker and more beautiful than those of more southern lands. He explains precisely why this should be so, and recognises that two falcons generally considered to be of two different species are really identical, and their differences are due only to climatic variations.

He collected observations from all countries. He got experts sent to him from Arabia and other places and he used their information where they " knew better." He only claimed to set forth " what our own experience has taught, or the experience of others," and he held that " no certainty is attained by the ear." Whatever he knows only by hearsay he seeks to verify. He institutes enquiries, for instance, about the " barnacle-geese," which is said to hatch out of worms or shells or the rotting ships' wood in the northern regions. He specially sent envoys to the north to fetch such wood and demonstrated the baselessness of the tale. From this he concluded that this type of wild goose had her nest in remote regions which were

rarely visited by man.   Reports which he could not check he
quoted only with reservations ;   when he writes about the
Phoenix described by Pliny he adds : " We cannot, however,
believe this."

Frederick II rated Aristotle very high as a philosopher, but
considers him a scholar wholly dependent on book-learning,
and does not hesitate to dismiss his statement with a curt
" It is not so."   " We have followed Aristotle where necessary,
but we have learnt from experience that he appears frequently
to deviate from the truth, especially in writing of the nature of
certain birds.   We have therefore not followed this Prince of
Philosophers in everything . . . for Aristotle seldom or never
hunted with birds, while we have ever loved and practised
hawking."   The Emperor frequently corrects Aristotle : " But
we, who have had some practice in the chase, think otherwise."
After he has minutely described how the chain or triangle of
flying waterfowl change their leader he adds " It is therefore
improbable that the leader should remain unchanged as Aristotle maintains. . . ."

The Emperor's book contains thousands of separate observations which are marshalled formally, clearly, and logically,
passing always from the general to the particular as scholastic
method demanded.   The sentence construction is usually
lucid, the language—in contrast to the rhetorical manifestos of
his Chancery—is simple, straightforward, matter-of-fact, but
always stately, always couched in the *pluralis majestatis*, and
clothed with a certainty that defies refutation.   It was often
difficult—as the Emperor says—to find Latin synonyms for the
Arabic or Provençal technical terms.   The eye is appealed to
by many hundred drawings of birds which are unquestionably
from the Emperor's own hand.   It has been expressly recorded
that he knew how to draw.   One of the first two-volume
éditions de luxe of this book, which in 1248 at Parma fell into
the enemy's hands, and later came to the Anjous, contains
illuminations which are repeated in later copies.   The drawings
are true to life down to the tiniest details, and the style of picture, the birds in flight, in various phases of movement, point
unmistakably to the eager observer himself, though the magnificently coloured versions may have been prepared by some

court artist or other. It is possible that Persian or Saracen drawings influenced Frederick, perhaps ancient codices also. However this may be, experts pronounce the drawings of the Falcon Book to be as amazingly " before their time " as is Sicilian plastic art.

The Emperor's book soon appeared in several French versions, and ousted all similar works. Short *Instructions to Falconers* of Norman and other origin had preceded the imperial Falcon Book, but they had not the same thoroughness or zoological knowledge, and were not nearly so comprehensive. Frederick justifiably dismissed them as " inaccurate and inadequate." What he was aiming at was to lift hawking to the level of an exact science, which none of the existing books was competent to do. The Emperor was doubtless acquainted with oriental works. A Persian falcon book was translated at King Enzio's command, an Arabic book of healing for hunting-birds was certainly not unknown to Frederick. He can scarcely have utilised them, however, since his own book was based entirely on personal observation. Wherever opportunity offered the Emperor worked at the writing of his book " in spite of the unspeakable number of claims upon our time," as he writes, and we learn incidentally that during the siege of Faënza he corrected Master Theodore's translation of an Arabic essay on hunting, written by the imperial falconer Muamin. A Cremonese translated the same essay for King Enzio into French. The Emperor wrote the book only a few years before his death, and King Manfred out of his own knowledge and from loose sheets of the Emperor's, posthumously filled many lacunae.

The most important thing about the Falcon Book is not the fact that Albertus Magnus for instance used it, nor the fact that other hunting books sprang up, like one by a German knight who called as witnesses to his prowess in the chase " especially the huntsmen of the illustrious Lord Frederick, Emperor of the Romans." Vastly more important was it that the courtiers of the Emperor and his sons (who resembled their father) acquired an eye for Nature so that they learned the imperial art of seeing, whatever they might choose to apply it to. The new element in the Falcon Book is the idea of seeing and telling " the things that are, as they are," and that this should be done not by an unknown settler or scholar but by the Emperor of the Roman-Christian world : a remarkable parergon of a great statesman. The Emperor's immediate influence asserted itself further in another work which was widely circulated, translated into many languages, and which acted as a model for succeeding generations : the *Horse Healing* of a Calabrian nobleman and official, Jordanus Ruffus. This was the first book of veterinary lore that the West produced, and it was written at the suggestion of the Emperor. The author expressly declares that he received instruction to a very large extent in all the matters treated, from the Emperor who was himself an expert.

It is a significant fact that the great scholars of della Vigna's circle, those of the type of Michael Scot, all failed completely when it came to the use of the eye. The Emperor, King Manfred, Enzio, the noble official Jordanus Ruffus, the Arab falconer Muamin, are the men with seeing sight. We may say that seeing " begins " once more with them ; not that the gift had been entirely lost ; even in the Middle Ages the peasant and the huntsman had used their eyes as shrewdly as in other ages. But those who could put in words what they had seen, the intellectual, the learned of every kind, the " educated " had in those days no eyes for the material world. Frederick II, the predecessor of the great empiricists of the thirteenth century, of the Dominican Albertus Magnus and the Franciscan Roger Bacon, was the first man to make his appearance who was at once a master of all current learning, and as a hunter had from infancy the use of his eyes. It has often been asserted that the Falcon Book marks a turning point in Western thought, the beginning of experimental science in the West. And here we must recall the Emperor's opposite, Francis of Assisi, back to whom they trace the new feeling for Nature. It is true that the two approached Nature with different sense organs. If we reckon Frederick II the first open-eyed mind who traced the eternal unvarying Law of Nature and of life in type and species and gradation, we may with equal justice account Francis of

Assisi, the first open-eyed soul who spontaneously experienced Nature and Life as magic and emotion, and traced the same divine *pneuma* in all that lived. Dante was both in one.

TRANSFORMER OF THE WORLD ! This was what contemporaries named Frederick. Not least "transformer" of men. For this intellectual court of his reared a new human species in whom philosophy was no kingly caprice, but a begetter of life. The spiritual knight of the epoch of the Crusade was gradually superseded by the intellectual knight who was to prevail in the ensuing centuries. Naturally the Founder was himself the first of the new species who undertakes a type of battle for centuries forgotten, which from later ages earned for the Hohenstaufen Tyrant of Sicily the name of " Herakles Musagetes."

Frederick II was a warrior and a fighter rather than a knight, and we miss the glamour of joust and tournament which surrounded Barbarossa even in his old age ; the " game " for Frederick was not the shock of knightly weapons, but the clash of noble minds. When actual fighting was afoot, however, he shirked no danger. Seizing a shield he led the attack against a besieged town ; in open battle he charged the enemy at the head of his horsemen, especially when wrath and vengeance stirred his blood. From boyhood he had trained his body in the use of weapons ; no hardships were too great for him, and to the last he was equal to all the varied demands made on his physique by camping in hot weather or in cold. He never even betrayed signs of fatigue. His body, though but of medium height was kept in perfect condition, strong and muscular, not thin, inclining rather to stoutness, never flagging in alertness, achievement or endurance. Apart from an occasional indisposition and the one attack of plague he had no serious illness, and with all his love of other types of luxury he maintained a Spartan régime that allowed him only one meal a day. He had learnt from the Orient a refined cult of the body which to his contemporaries appeared simply satanic : a mendicant monk querulously reports that he did not forego his bath even on the days of Church festivals. This will have helped to preserve a

certain freshness, elasticity and youthfulness which characterised
him.   His mode of life also assisted : he spent not less than one-
third of his time in the saddle, and of that full half was given
to hunting.   To the very end he felt equal to any exertion.
Two years before his death he was on his horse for fully twenty-
four hours.   His black horse, " Dragon," carried him at dawn
to the chase, at midday into battle, and then all through the
night at top speed from Parma to Cremona.   He was so little
fatigued that immediately on arrival in the terrified town,
though it was still dark, he started assembling troops with which
he set out to battle two days later.   Similar exploits were frequent.   Just as the *Puer Apuliae* swam a river on a barebacked
horse, the Emperor at the opening of his Lombard campaign
accomplished a forced march of eighty-seven miles with his
heavy cavalry in two nights and a day, and at the end of his
ride surprised and took Vicenza : a feat to which his contemporaries paid a due tribute of admiration.

There was nothing soft about Frederick for all his intellect.
His limbs were as powerful as they were well built.   He tore
open the side of the rebel Saracen Amir with a blow of his
foot, and his beautiful and powerful hands will have been
equally terrible in their grip.   They were famed also for their
skill and neat fingeredness.   Shapely fingers may well have
been part of Frederick's Hohenstaufen inheritance.   Even
the twelfth century had noticed and admired Barbarossa's
unwontedly well-formed hands !

We have no evidence of the changes Frederick's appearance
underwent with the lapse of years, especially as the most
valuable witness, the great marble statue of the Emperor seated
on his throne that adorned the gate of the bridge at Capua has
come down to us only as a fragment.   Apart from scanty literary
allusions we have nothing to go on but the golden coins,
the Augustales, in particular the very perfect coins of the later
mintages.   Every reference we have confirms the fact that
the Emperor retained throughout the " cheerful brow and the
radiant cheerfulness of the eyes " which had characterised the
Puer Apuliae.   To the very last all the chroniclers boast of

the cheerfulness of his open gaze, and all western observers agree
that he was handsome, with a noble and distinguished countenance. They all seek to define the extraordinary fascination
which he exercised, and which perhaps was not unconnected
with his mixed blood ; a brown-tinted skin with rosy cheeks
and auburn-blonde hair, which grew thinner with the years.
An indefinable something clung to him, and, since he remained
always cleanshaven, a something unaging, of eternal youth.
The lack of beard or moustache let all his features be clearly
seen, the short powerful arrogant nose, the remarkably strong
chin, the mouth with its full lips tightly drawn in (so at least
the coins imply), and its frequently mocking impression. The
countenance of a Caesar worthy of the sculptor's chisel, of
which no details recall the accustomed God-the-Father type
of earlier German Emperors as Barbarossa embodied it, and as
the Renaissance Emperors revived it after Frederick II.

One of his enemies described him as sudden, sensual, subtle,
crafty and evil, but adds " if he wished to show favour he could
be friendly, cheerful and gracious." A feeling of insecurity
overtook everyone in his presence. Whether his countenance
was expressing the most charming and winning friendliness or
the most terrifying severity and sternest cruelty, the glance of
his eye never varied, or at most varied by an imperceptible
shade. Part of his magnetism must have lain in this disturbing
effect of his timeless, soulless gaze, which let no man guess his
true feelings ; it was not dissimulation ; it was something much
more deadly. One of his friends said he had the eyes of a
snake, thereby expressing this uncanny fascination. No flashing
penetrating eye, but probably that serene reposeful glance which
perceived unwaveringly, and—in most unchristian wise—was
not directed inward. This unwaveringness must have been
more cruel and alarming, and a thousand times more uncanny,
than a sparkling, lightning glance. It was probably the
amazing calm of two eyes set perfectly parallel, working perfectly in accord, which at times produces almost the same
effect as *mal occhio* ; it is interesting to note that one Oriental
described him as " squinting."

None can say how the daring dauntless spirit, which ranged
through all the distances of East and West, lay behind those

all-perceiving eerie eyes, nor how the mighty brain shaped the
head and cheerful brow.   The total impression, in spite of its
broad-necked power and steel-like strength, is one of something
lyrical and inspiring, which breathes even from the half-
Romanised Augustales—a German trait to which neither a
Caesar nor a Napoleon could lay claim.

VI. GERMAN EMPEROR

VI. GERMAN EMPEROR

FREDERICK II had spent more than a year in reorganising and consolidating the monarchy in Sicily. In August 1230 he had made peace with Pope Gregory, in August 1231 the collection of the Constitutions had been concluded, and a few months later the Emperor felt free to quit his hereditary kingdom and devote his attention to the affairs of the Empire. His rule in the south seemed secure and would not easily be shaken, and he could now consider the measures necessary to restore imperial power and prestige throughout the Empire, and could carry his forcefulness and fame north into Northern Italy and Germany.

The Lord of the Empire must perforce sail under very different colours from the Tyrant of Sicily. The favour or hostility of the Pope was a matter almost of indifference in the Sicilian state, which indeed throve best in open fight : the whole constitution of the Empire, on the other hand, was based on the harmony of the two powers, and the Empire at its best required a perfect balance of the two in good will and in peace. The Imperium, pillared on its secular and spiritual princes, was not incorporate in the monarch alone, as was the Sicilian state with its officials, but in the dual power of Pope and Emperor, who together constituted " a species of individual " : " two swords in one scabbard," two vicegerents of the true King.

The picture which Frederick II strove to present to the world during the next few years was that of a Christian Imperator cooperating with the Pope in outward friendship. Never again did he so closely resemble his imperial ancestors, never was he so truly the heir of Charlemagne, Otto and Barbarossa as in these years of peace. His power, not spending its strength in threats of war, was able to make itself felt far and wide through all the countries of the Roman Empire, " whose length was vast and whose breadth ended only at the ends of the earth." The days of the noble emperors were drawing to a glorious close ; with Frederick II came the sudden crash. Just once more before the end, the world was to see what the Middle Ages considered the " correct conditions " established ; once again Pope and Emperor in unison, once again the Emperor amid his princes as *primus inter pares*.   For one last time those ideals were realised in all their fullness and maturity and clothed in classic phrases which echo pitifully as empty catchwords in later days of petty Kaisers and tiara-crowned mid-Italian landlords.   For one brief moment Frederick II appeared radiant in the full majesty of the ancient Holy Roman Empire ; once more, in the Pala-tinates of the Neckar and the Rhine, the brilliance of imperial glory lit with southern light flared dazzlingly, then was for ever quenched.   Only : the Germans kept a yearning for it all.

From Foggia the Emperor moved northwards to Ravenna. He took a very modest Sicilian retinue.   Berard of Palermo and Count Thomas of Aquino were the only well-known nobles who accompanied him.   His immediate task was to put Lom-bard and German affairs in order, and the German princes had been long since invited to a Diet at Ravenna, to be held in November 1231.   Frederick's first intention had probably been to march into Northern Italy at the head of his armies ; but the Pope offered him guarantees for the Lombards' behaviour, and he abstained from any military steps, with the result that the Cremona fiasco of 1226, was, as nearly as possible, repeated. Although the Emperor announced himself as the Pope's ambassador on a mission to suppress heresy, and although Gregory really endeavoured to influence the Lombards, the towns made not the slightest move to send envoys to the Diet which was to serve " the honour of God, of the Church and of the Empire, and the prosperity of Lombardy."   Quite the reverse.   On the approach of the Emperor the League which had been gradually disintegrating immediately reconstituted itself, the mountain passes were again seized by the rebels, and passage denied to the German forces.

The Emperor was not, at the moment, in a position to inter-vene effectively.   The Diet was adjourned till Christmas, and the Emperor killed time in the ancient town of Gothic Kings and Byzantine Emperors.   He collected valuable building materials, ancient columns and statues, and despatched them to Sicily.   With remarkable antiquarian zeal he instituted the first systematic excavation. This revealed the mausoleum of Galla Placidia, and brought to light the beautiful mosaics of this building which had been completely submerged under boulders and rubble. Three alabaster sarcophagi were also unearthed, containing the remains of this Empress, of her consort Theodosius II and of St. Elisha. Antiquarian research had not, however, been the Emperor's purpose in Ravenna. Gradually German princes began to assemble in considerable numbers. Some had come by sea from Venice, some had evaded the Veronese and crossed the passes in disguise. The German Grand Master, Hermann of Salza arrived, and Gebhard of Arnstein, a Thuringian nobleman, an old acquaintance of Frederick's who had recently been appointed imperial legate in Tuscany, came from Central Italy. The person, however, for whom more especially the Diet had been summoned was still missing : the Emperor's son, King Henry.

For some time past misunderstandings had been talked of between Frederick II and the young German King, now some twenty years of age. Frederick had no serious crime with which to reproach his son, whom he had not seen for over ten years. But he had noticed a certain general indocility in the German King's attitude, both in personal matters towards his father and in political matters towards the Emperor. He had been under the tutelage, first of Archbishop Engelbert of Cologne, and, after the archbishop's assassination, under Duke Lewis of Bavaria ; but three years ago, at the age of eighteen, he had begun to reign independently. He took after his father perhaps, who at twelve considered it " disgraceful " to be still under guardianship, and who had the good fortune to be his own master at fourteen. King Henry's first ambition was to get quit of every sort of wardship, and to enlarge his own independence, not in the first place at the expense of the Emperor but rather at the expense of the princes who were thorns in the side of every German king. To this end he necessarily leagued himself with their opponents, with the townsfolk who were increasing in importance in Germany, as elsewhere (the days of the town leagues were not far off), with the *ministeriales*, the lower nobility who with knightly minstrels were always to be found in great numbers in his entourage. If King Henry had in this choice been prompted by political acumen, realising that Germany's strength and hope lay in the knights and in the towns, he would have been able to come to some agreement with his father, or at least profitably to consult with him. Any such flair for a political situation was, however, wholly foreign to his nature. He had all the amiability and charm of·the Hohenstaufens, but with it an inconsequence and aimlessness which people called " frivolity." If he favoured townsfolk and *ministeriales* he did so from no better reason than opposition and hostility to the princes who hemmed him in.

It was not long until this line of action on King Henry's part became embarrassing. When the princes were staying in Italy in 1230, arranging the Peace of Ceperano between Emperor and Pope, at a moment, therefore, when Frederick was more especially beholden to the German nobles, Henry made an unmistakably hostile move. The citizens of Liège were engaged in a quarrel with their bishop, and King Henry took the townsfolk under his protection. The occasion itself was unimportant, but there was a principle at stake, and in a moment the princes turned on him to a man. Immediately after their return from Italy, in January 1231, forgetting all their mutual quarrels, united in resistance, they compelled the King to hold the unfortunate Diet at Worms in May 1231, and, confident in the Emperor's support, forced him to surrender a great privilege. Except for a few honorary royal rights the " lords of the land " were to have well nigh unrestricted sovereignty in their own territories, especially over the towns. King Henry, who had been so eager to strengthen the Crown against the growing encroachments of the princes, had thus succeeded in weakening it beyond all precedent.

The Emperor's policy was diametrically opposed to his son's at every point. Frederick II could not approve Henry's general attitude of hostility to the princes, still less this particular manifestation of it, directed against the princes who were absent in Italy in the Emperor's service. Nothing could be less opportune for him than unrest beyond the Alps, and his son's behaviour was calculated to conjure up an anti-

Staufen alliance of the princes.   On the other hand, by allowing the Privilege of Worms to be wrung from him, King Henry
had wantonly flung away valuable prerogatives.   Frederick himself had frequently, and that without undue regret, surrendered
royal rights in favour of the princes, but never without an
adequate *quid pro quo*.   The King by his lack of address
had on this occasion secured nothing.   There were personal
matters in question also.   Henry wanted to divorce his queen,
Margaret of Austria, although he had issue by her, and marry
a youthful flame, Agnes of Bohemia.   This had been mooted
against the Emperor's will, for Frederick had had definite
political combinations in view when he negotiated the Austrian
alliance.   The question soon became otiose, for Agnes of
Bohemia, to escape further discussion, took the veil.   The
affair contributed, however, to the general unpleasantness.
On all these counts the Emperor considered a personal talk
with his son to be necessary, and had therefore invited him
to Ravenna.   Whether King Henry was right or wrong his
failure to accept the Emperor's invitation was unwise.   So far
he might simply have passed for a somewhat unskilful diploma-
tist ; his absence from Ravenna (though he later excused it on
the pretext of the closure of the passes) made him in his father's
eyes a disobedient son.   And disobedience, as he might have
been aware, was not the road to Frederick's heart.

In the meantime Frederick had been negotiating in Ravenna
with the German princes and numerous Italian bishops, and
finally had again banned the Lombard League when it continued
to bar the passage over the Alps.   The Emperor may not have
been altogether sorry to see the Pope embarrassed by the un-
justifiable recalcitrance of the confederate towns, for whose
good behaviour he had gone bail while secretly fomenting their
resistance.   The Lombard action had clearly demonstrated that
it was impossible here to assert the authority of the Empire
without resort to force.   The tangled skein of Northern Italy
was obviously not to be unravelled by peaceful measures, for
every edict of the Emperor's introduced fresh complications.
He had, for instance, given orders when outlawing the League,

that the loyal towns of Lombardy should not elect their annual *podesta* from any of the rebel towns. This immediately caused friction with Genoa, who had just done him exceptional honour by sending a magnificent embassy ; for the Genoese had appointed a *podesta* from Milan, and were now faced by the delicate choice of offending the League by rejecting the Milanese or offending the Emperor by retaining him. The Emperor could not permit an exception immediately after issuing his command. In spite of the strong imperial feeling in Genoa the Milanese was installed. Though he was reluctant to disturb his good relations with Genoa the Emperor at once retaliated by measures which injured the Genoese trade in Sicily. It was frankly impossible to conduct politics in Lombardy without an army.

Pope Gregory had again volunteered to mediate between Frederick and the League. The Emperor cannot have built much on his offer, for he had had some experience of papal mediation and arbitration. His misgivings were not unjustified. Though Gregory ostensibly supported the Emperor his choice of arbitrators and their line of action showed clearly in whose favour the so-called impartial verdict was to be given. The arbitrators were declared enemies of the Emperor, cardinals who were natives of the League towns. Instead of bearing to the rebels the terms proposed by the aggrieved Emperor they treated first with the confederate revolutionaries, and finally set out for Ravenna with the cut-and-dried proposals of the Leaguers. The Emperor did not wait to hear their award : he knew perfectly what to expect, but he was unwilling at the moment to fall out with the Pope. When the papal arbitrators arrived in Ravenna at the beginning of March they were surprised to find the Emperor gone. He rode out to the town one afternoon, as he was in the habit of doing. A fully-equipped galley was at anchor off the coast ready to sail ; he embarked with a few attendants and disappeared. He had made all preparations long before. Foreseeing a protracted absence he had sent Thomas of Aquino back to Sicily as Captain of the kingdom, had dismissed the other participants in the Ravenna diet, only retaining the German princes, and adjourned his Court till Easter in Aquileia. He did not invite his son's presence ; he commanded his attendance in Aquileia, and betook himself thither by sea.

The princes who had been left behind in Ravenna soon heard the unexpected news that the Emperor was on his way first to Venice. Most of them made haste to follow him by land. As Frederick's relations with Verona were for the moment unsatisfactory he now sought to secure Venice for his ally, and to take advantage for his own purposes of the rivalry between the two towns in the East. He had other weighty incentives. As the mountain passes were under a constant threat the road via Venice and Friuli was the only certain route to Germany, and a good understanding with the Venetians was therefore of the utmost importance. He sailed by Comacchio, Loreto and Chioggia. He halted for a short time in Loreto, and there received the envoys of the independent Republic (no appanage of the Empire) who hastened thither to greet him. To them he confided his desire to visit Venice to worship St. Mark, their patron saint. The Venetians immediately convened their Grand Council and decided to grant the Emperor's request. Frederick, therefore, continued his journey to Chioggia. When Frederick landed on the shores of St Mark and stood beside the Doge, Jacopo Tiepolo, he brought all his charm and amiability into play. The Venetians received him with pomp and ceremony ; he presented costly gifts of gold and precious stones to their saint, and received from their rich store of relics a splinter of the True Cross : he loaded them, almost against their will, with privileges and trade prerogatives for Sicily ; but nothing dispelled the distrust of these traders and seafarers, a distrust equalled only by their unlimited arrogance. Thanks to their immense possessions in the Levant, especially in the Latin Empire, the Venetians felt themselves almost the Emperor's equals. They did not intend to be under any obligation to the Hohenstaufen. A Venetian goldsmith was commissioned by Frederick to make him a crown ; the Grand Council granted permission, only on the condition that no harm should arise from it to the Republic. The Emperor's power alarmed Venice ; they wanted no dealings with him. On the first opportunity the Republic joined Frederick's Lombard enemies : on the other hand, Venice was the first town to conclude Peace with the Emperor, when a Genoese became Pope.

At Easter 1232 the German princes were assembled in unusual numbers round Frederick II in Aquileia. King Henry at first attempted to evade his father's command. Some of the princes, however, who were on their way back from Ravenna met the king in Augsburg, and told him of the Emperor's mood. Their urgent representations induced Henry to appear, however reluctantly, at the Diet summoned expressly for him. The Emperor appointed the adjacent Cividale for his residence with some attendants, but ordered Aquileia to be closed to him. In a business-like way, as if negotiating with a foreign prince, Frederick conducted from Aquileia the discussions with his son. After Henry had submitted to the imperial conditions, and not before, he was permitted to see his father face to face, for the first time in ten years. As father he reproved the son ; as Emperor he made heavy demands on the disobedient king. In Cividale, where the Court repaired after some weeks, King Henry was compelled solemnly to swear, in the presence of his princely opponents, to obey all commands of the Emperor in future, and to treat the German princes henceforward with due respect, as "lights and protectors of the Empire" and "apples of the Emperor's eye." The oath was further reinforced by a written document in which Henry himself released the princes from their oaths of fealty in case of fresh disobedience, and adjured them in that event to rise against him on the Emperor's behalf. The Emperor pressed his advantage further, and compelled King Henry to write also to the Holy Father and inform him what oath he had sworn to the "divine Augustus," and beg Pope Gregory to excommunicate without further notice the German King if he should break the promise made to his father. Frederick II had thus harnessed to his will the two forces which were wont to strive against the Roman Emperor—at the expense, it is true, of his recalcitrant son. For Henry the Lighthearted, under the supervision of Princes and Pope, was granted only a period of probation : an intolerable position, in comparison with which deposition would have been kinder and less severe. All royal freedom of action was denied him, who had sought to be independent and self-sufficing. The Emperor treated him as he was wont to treat a rebellious town : demanding unconditional surrender to his will, an oath of obedience, and submission to imperial supervisors. King Henry would have been no Hohenstaufen if this end of his dreams had not proved the beginning of his tragedy.

The Friuli Diet, which dragged on till the end of May (being transferred from Cividale to Udine, and then to Pordenone so that the whole burden might not fall on one town), was immensely important to the German constitution. It is a commonplace that the results of decisions there taken are still to be felt. Since King Henry had allowed the Privilege of Worms to be wrung from him, the Emperor had no option but to confirm this " Edict in favour of the Princes." It thus came about that Frederick II, the last of the German Emperors who had been elected as Duke of a race in the old sense, saw the end of the Germanic kingship based on race and armies. From the point of view of constitutional history Germany may henceforth be styled a Confederation of Princes or a Princely Oligarchy.

Every German statesman is faced by the same problem : to establish the ideal relation between the Empire and its members. Each preceding answer seems to have been suitable as a momentary, but questionable as a permanent solution : each has been big with fate. In Frederick's day the problem might have been stated somewhat as follows : everywhere each state was pressing on towards immediacy ; the absolutism of such a state as the Kingdom of Sicily, for instance, must in some way be reconciled with the existing kingship of the Germans based on race and feudal force. Contrary to what might have been expected Frederick II never even contemplated the attempt to transform the whole of Germany into a unified officialised Germany, comparable to the Sicilian monarchy. It is true that in later days Frederick from his Italian base pushed forward his Sicilian bureaucratic régime as far as Burgundy and the Tyrol, and even in a modified form as far as Austria, so that the thesis might be sustained that Frederick had simply been unable to complete the "Sicilianisation" of the Empire, which was creeping steadily from South to North, because he died prematurely before he was sufficiently master of Lombardy. There is no sign, however, that the Emperor was planning to push his Sicilian official system further northwards. All historical and spiritual forces in the country would at once have failed him, and one essential was lacking: the cultivated lay-man and the cultivated townsman who existed in Italy ; the whole great stratum of lay jurists which' replaced the feudal system as the basis of the Sicilian-Italian State. Frederick II never contemplated undermining the feudal forces of extensive and deeply subdivided Germany, and ruling through officials without the intervention of the princes. The German princes, moreover, were not Sicilian barons and duodecimo clerics, they were the Emperor's peers.

Since the Emperor renounced all intention of exercising in Germany his new methods of rule, the task of ruling must fall on the German princes who were in any case striving for greater independence, and whose rights were long since steadily increasing at the expense of the rights of the Crown. Frederick II allowed the princes to continue in this path, nay even supported them, because this exactly fitted his imperial policy which was narrowing down into a Lombard policy. More than any preceding Emperor, Frederick was first and fore-most the super-national Roman Imperator, whose great mid-European Imperium stretched from Syracuse to Friesland and the Baltic. To strengthen the Empire his first need was an utterly submissive Lombardy. Without this the Empire was rent in two. To reduce Lombardy, Frederick needed the forces of Germany, but needed even more—as security also against the Pope—an assurance of peace in the North and the protection of his rear by the trusty princes of Germany, both spiritual and temporal. By the sacrifice of his own revenues and prerogatives he could purchase all this from the powerful nobles who had clipped the wings of so many victorious Emperors before him. For the sake of the cause he did not hesitate to make the sacrifice, the less because his Sicilian wealth and resources were ample compensation. Sicilian gold was potent in money-lacking Germany, and Frederick's generosity won the attachment of the princes to his person, an attachment which withstood amazingly the protracted intrigues and machinations of the Church.

It cannot be doubted that practical considerations and the higher necessities of the Roman Empire prompted Frederick to these sacrifices in favour of the princes. What followed, whether with or against his will, was the almost sovereign independence of each individual prince in his own territory. The concessions which Frederick in his early days had made to the spiritual princes were extended by the new charters of Worms and Friuli to the temporal princes also, so that a certain uniformity prevailed throughout Germany. The princes, being thus all on more or less the same footing, began to feel themselves more of a corporate body than formerly, and became aware of a community of interest, advantageous or disadvantageous for the Emperor as the case might be. Renouncing most of the Crown rights in the princes' territories, Frederick, according to the new privileges, had agreed to abandon royal rights of coinage, the right of building imperial fortifications, the royal jurisdiction throughout all the lands of the princes, or, as they now came to be significantly called, the " Lords of the Land." The princes' authority *vis-à-vis* their subjects was enhanced, for the inferior courts of law were placed under the immediate jurisdiction of the princes, and jurisdiction other than theirs was abolished or greatly limited. Other clauses pointed in the same direction, so that the princes exercised almost autocratic power in their own domains, or were on the high road to acquiring it. An intensification of state organisation was thus set on foot in Germany as in Sicily, not emanating from and re-enforcing the central royal authority, but strengthening the separate parts, the princes. It was now possible for them to consolidate their states, and the constructive forces inherent in unity of race and country were immensely easier to release, develop, exploit under the direct thorough-going rule of a minor monarch than under mediate rule of an Emperor hampered by the princes, or of a prince hampered by the existence of intrusive royal rights. This clean sweep of all the powers that interfered between the lord of the land and his

territories made it possible for the individual states to begin
government in earnest.

From this point of view the Emperor's policy of strengthening the prince appears as a simplication of the whole German
state, and of untold importance for the consolidation of the
loosely-strung widely-spreading German lands, in which from
of old all strength and statesmanship had lain in the individual
clans and not in the congeries of German races.   It was, however, a policy fraught with immense danger.   The stronger the
constituent states grew the less hope there was of unifying them
into one German super-state, and Frederick's course of action
prolonged the subdivision of Germany.   He definitely hindered
the amalgamation of the German people into one " German
State."   The policy, moreover, reacted injuriously on the
Empire as a whole, for the princes, each immersed in the
development of his own domains, displayed little active interest
in the fate of the Empire.   The important gain for Frederick
was that the princes kept the peace and were ready at need to
stand behind him to a man ; a state of affairs that lasted
twenty years and more.   It is common knowledge how disastrous this increased independence proved.   With the decline of
the Roman Imperium the last unifying impulse was gone.   Each
lord of the land pursued the aims and interests of his own
territory, and developed a narrow provincial outlook which took
no heed of the world at large, of Germany, or Emperor, or
Empire.   Cleavages and clefts that the pressure of the Empire
had kept closed now yawned and widened.

However ready Frederick was to subordinate Germany's
advantage to the World Empire, it is scarcely conceivable that
a statesman of his calibre can have failed to visualise one united
northern kingdom, suited to the conditions of the expiring
Middle Ages.   He would gain nothing from a mere semblance
of power, and if this was to be avoided he must re-organise the
whole kingdom on a new basis, with due regard to the new
conditions.   A few individual measures destined to enhance
the central imperial power show that he had some definite
scheme in mind.   If the Lombard struggle had ended quickly

and happily we can imagine that the Emperor would have introduced some uniform method of administration for all territories. While preserving their sovereignty intact he might have metamorphosed the princes into viceroys, parallel to the later Vicars General of Italy, with their princely, even royal state. Frederick is credited with the intention of making a collection of imperial law and legal procedure. He must certainly have had such a work in mind which would have guided the princely governments into definite lines. It was not long after this time that Frederick appointed a Grand Justiciar for Germany, thereby implying that the Emperor's supreme jurisdiction should be asserted, while the normal administration of justice in each country should remain with the individual princes.

The essential thing, however, was that the Emperor should have some positive force at his disposal to guarantee the good faith of the princes and to compensate for the securities he had foregone. He required a sufficient force to compel obedience at need and enforce the unity of the Empire. It is of the utmost interest to note what deductions Frederick II drew from the reshuffling of the German powers. The Emperor had divested himself of so many prerogatives that he could no longer claim to be the foremost and the mightiest in virtue of his privileges ; he must prove himself so by actual strength. The personal private resources of the monarch had to fill the place of the impersonal imperial property and crown rights. This change is foreshadowed in the efforts of the Hohenstaufens to secure for themselves a firm working basis in the south. Now for the first time Sicily provided an Emperor with just such a personal possession. It lay wholly outside the range of the German princes, and, secure in his Sicilian resources, Frederick had been able to abandon his German prerogatives. In securing Sicily the Hohenstaufen Emperors had not had this policy in view. Sicily, like the other countries, was there to serve the Empire as a whole. Frederick II, standing on the borderline between the two epochs, was the first to feel the need of founding a personal power in the North within Germany itself : setting the precedent which the Hapsburg was so happily to follow—a remarkable coincidence. In 1236 the

Emperor crushed the rebellion of the last of the Babenbergs, Frederick the Fighter, of Austria and Styria. The Emperor confiscated his dukedoms and retained them under the immediate administration of the Empire, instead of granting them to some new fiefholder after a year and a day, as custom was. Thus in the south-eastern corner of the kingdom, where Bohemia, Hungary and the dukedom of Austria still offered large unbroken stretches of territory, the Hohenstaufen Frederick, whose Swabian patrimony, though scattered, was still of considerable extent, sought to build up a new power. The war against the Austrian Duke was only a minor action in larger campaigns, and the Duke ultimately succeeded in recovering the bulk of his lands. An agreement was reached later, and at one stage the Dukedom of Austria was to be elevated into a kingdom. This plan, however, fell through. Frederick the Fighter, last of the Babenbergs, ultimately died childless in 1246 and his vacant fief fell to the Empire. Frederick II forthwith revived his original scheme, retained the dukedom for himself, entrusted its administration to Sicilian Captains General, and bequeathed it as hereditary Hohenstaufen property to his grandson. The Emperor's fighting was, in future, mainly confined to Italy, and the importance of the Hohenstaufen personal Austrian domain was slight. The amazing thing is the astounding foresight of this world-statesman and his unerring intuition of what was to come.

The Emperor thus sought to forestall the dangers conjured up by his own surrender of innumerable safeguards and by his strengthening of the imperial princes. Frederick's greatest power lay, nevertheless, in his own personality. At the zenith of his glory Frederick II, most Roman of all German Emperors, possessed not only the armed force, but the personal magic, to sway the princes to his will and direct their gaze to the great problems of the Roman world. In these glorious years the strengthened princes and the double renown of the ancient kingdom-in-arms and the new Empire brought about that unique fulfilment which preluded the end : that full perfection of the German Empire, a mighty Emperor surrounded by his mighty princes. The dream of their return lulled anaemic generations for centuries to come. Germany as Imperium was at that moment the symbol and embodiment of the great conception of a Roman Empire embracing and unifying all peoples and races of the world, conterminous and identical with a great Christian Empire. This was possible because Germany preserved, for weal or woe, the multitude of races and princes which corresponded to that ideal and imaginary community of Europe's peoples and kings. In contrast to her shrewd, practical neighbours in the West, Germany remained always " the Empire."

The ideal World-Empire of the Middle Ages did not involve the subjection of all peoples under the dominion of one. It stood for the community of all kings and princes, of all the lands and peoples of Christendom, under one Roman Emperor, who should belong to no nation, and who, standing outside all nations, should rule all from his throne in the one Eternal City. Only thus could the perfect Germany arise, setting before princes and races the idea : the Imperium Romanum—and yet : nations.

The domination of one race over the other would, therefore, have been a betrayal in favour of one peculiar type—Saxon or Frank, Swabian or ultimately Prussian. For in the State dominated by one race (in spite of the attainment of a genuine non-national unity) the best powers of all the races could never flourish equally, to produce the one world-embracing German. Less fortunate, perhaps, than Ionians and Dorians, no single race, whether Saxon or Swabian or Frank, possessed a world-sense, though each alone was well-equipped with state-sense : the feeling for the universal—divorced alas from the feeling for the state—was incorporate only in the super-national German whole. Frederick never contemplated such a betrayal, never aimed at ruling Germany with Swabian knights and esquires. He was no Swabian Duke, no German King, he was solely Roman Caesar and Imperator, he was Divus Augustus—as none before him and none since. As Roman Caesar, centring in himself and in his own person the German whole, he became the symbol, foreign though it was, which supplied the one possible form of the self-fulfilment Germany was then seeking : self-fulfilment within the Roman Empire.

L.F.S.

The great Empire of this great Emperor was not a German National State on the model of Sicily, or of France under the Capets. The true statesman does not apply one hard and fast scheme to all countries. Yet in a higher sense Frederick II perfected and completed the unified German Empire. He did not here pose as the priest-like Emperor and imperial Mediator who figured in the Sicilian bureaucratic State, nor yet as the Demi-God sent from heaven, nor yet as the Son of God. The oriental love of hero-worship is radically foreign to the Germanic mind, especially while the hero is still in the flesh. Amongst the Germans he aimed rather at creating the impression of the King soaring to heaven, borne aloft on the shoulders of the princes. The release of the princes from feudal fetters and their unlimited powers (which now for the first time united them in the " voluntary unity " of the late Middle Ages) made the Hohenstaufen autocrat, in literal truth, amongst his autocrats, *primus inter pares*—the first amongst his peers. Further, since all royal authority and all royal rights had been withdrawn throughout the princes' territories, his imperial throne had no longer any basis upon earth. As the German princes themselves phrased it at the Friuli Diet: " The imperial throne, to which we are attached as the limbs are attached to the head, rests like the head upon our shoulders and is firmly upheld by our body, so that the Majesty of the Emperor shines forth in glory and our princely rank reflects the glory back again." This is the traditional conception of the Empire, which at last finds ultimate expression and literal realisation ; for a brief span, and almost against the ruler's desire. Unlike his predecessors Frederick never weakened or oppressed the princes to make his own greatness look the greater by contrast with their weakness. He strengthened the princes' power, even created a new dukedom, with more exalted statesmanship believing that the power and the glory and the brilliance of his own imperial sceptre would not pale in giving forth light, but would gain in radiance and would shine the brighter the more mighty and brilliant and majestic were the princes whom Caesar Imperator beheld " as equals round his judgment seat." The princes are no longer columns bearing as a burden the weight of the throne. Like the officials of the South, and yet

very differently, they become piers and pillars expressive of
upward-soaring strength, preparing the glorious elevation of
the " prince of princes and king of kings " who is borne aloft
on the shoulders of his peers, and who in turn exalts both kings
and princes.

Life was always unthinkable for Frederick without the sense
of tension ; here is an incomparably daring gamble, in which
the slightest reshuffling of the cards will mean ruin. Frederick
faced the situation unflinching, with wide-open eyes. He
wrote later : " Germania's princes on whom hangs our elevation—and our fall." The danger was proportional to the
elevation, no more. The Germans recognised Frederick II as
fate incarnate and as doom ; they yearned for him, they
shrank from him. With him the Empire fell ; but more
enduring than a century of safety were the few hours during
which a German Emperor was privileged to tread such dangerous heights. The increased power of the princes was a necessary
factor therein. If the correct balance was to be maintained
in Germany feeble limbs could not support an over-weighty
head : princes and Emperor together represented that super-
national German, symbolised the " illustrious body of the
Holy Empire," the corpus mysticum of the " German-as-a-
Whole," which Frederick II justifiably identified with his own
body. For this stranger, this Roman of Swabian race, embodied that European-German personage whom men had
dreamt of, who combined the triple culture of Europe : the
cultures of the Church, the East, the Ancients. The Church
was to Frederick II something complete and finished, which he
had in himself outgrown, which lay behind him. Nietzsche
called Frederick " to my mind the FIRST EUROPEAN," and wrote
of " that magic, intangible, unfathomable Riddle of a man
predestined to victory and betrayal." The type was one most
difficult for the Germans to assimilate by reason of just
that Roman chiselling, that secretiveness, that complete self-
sufficingness.

The solemn speech-making of Friuli was the prelude to
Frederick II's personal intervention in German affairs, and it

was German business which here chiefly engaged attention.
Counsel was taken, however, about other countries of the
Empire, and much important business transacted. A favourable
turn was given to the Lombard question by Frederick's success
in winning over the brothers Eccelino and Alberigo of Romano,
who were just then acquiring great importance in the March
of Treviso. By a skilfully-engineered rising they succeeded
in making Frederick master of Verona, so that the Alpine passes
were now open to the Germans. The kingdom of Burgundy
also, which was very loosely attached to the Empire, was drawn
into closer relationship, and before long Burgundian forces
were, for the first time, commandeered for imperial purposes.
Envoys of the French King, Louis IX, St. Louis, arrived to
conclude a pact of friendship. And here the ambassadors of
the " Old Man of the Mountain," the head of the Assassins,
came to find Frederick, and the ambassadors of the Sultan of
Damascus, who brought a planetarium made of gold and jewels
to the Maliku 'l Umarā, the King of the Amirs. The Feast of
the Hijra came round. In honour of the Muslim envoys the
Emperor celebrated the day of the Prophet's Flight by a brilliant
banquet, attended by German princes and bishops.

After an absence of many months from Germany the princes
were finally loaded with costly gifts and dismissed in the middle
of May, amongst them King Henry, on whose behaviour the
peace of the North now hung. Frederick himself, with his
oriental escort, took ship to Apulia. On his way he made a
successful attack on the Dalmatian pirates, took many prisoners
and flung them into chains. His next immediate affairs were
negotiations with the Pope.

The outward vision of concord did not alter the fact that the
peace between the Emperor and Pope was a secret battle, conducted with the weapons of an infinitely delicate diplomacy.
The tension between Frederick II and Gregory IX, just veiled
for the moment, had reached a height unprecedented in the
long warfare between Empire and Papacy. Henry VI and
Innocent III had not held the stage together ; equal powers
now existed simultaneously and stood face to face awaiting the

outburst of the final battle ; but both postponing it a while and both willing for expediency to exercise moderation and control. Deadly enemies, each as capable as the other of savage passion, but for the moment unable to dispense with each other, and each benefiting by the momentary truce. The Emperor benefited perhaps even more than the Pope, his wish for peace with Gregory was certainly more sincere, was even too sincere, though his hate for the old man in Rome was deep.

No sooner was peace concluded than an amazing diplomatic game began between Court and Curia, a game which was to last for some years yet, though with ever-growing embitterment. In the eyes of the world the two powers still figure as Father and Son, and while both weigh each several step with utmost caution, and each watches lynx-like to exploit any chance of weakness on the other's part, each is equally eager to seize opportunities of offering civility and assistance, so as to place the other under an obligation. Each side had difficulties and to spare. Pope Gregory was openly at war with the Romans. He had had to quit the town because the citizens had risen against their bishop, as had been occurring long since in the other communes of Italy. The thought of the ancient republican freedom of Rome was not without influence on men's minds, and they craved territorial expansion. The Romans always cast covetous glances on the Campagna and the Patrimonium. As enemies of their bishop they were the natural allies of the Emperor, yet Frederick, at the Pope's request, had sent a detachment of troops to Viterbo, which was usually the first point of their attack.

Frederick on his side was not without serious embarrassments. Apart from Lombard problems he had to assure himself of the Pope's concurrence in all questions relating to his son Henry, so as to be secure against surprise. The kingdom of Syria, too, provided endless difficulties. Not that the Saracens had broken the truce, but because the Christians raged against each other. The Syrian-Cypriot nobles, under the leadership of the sometime administrator of Cyprus, John of Ibelin, and supported by the Patriarch Gerold and the people, had inflicted a severe defeat on the imperial marshal, Richard Filangieri, who had enjoyed some initial successes. It ended within a year with

the loss of Cyprus. Pope Gregory had now at last granted
the Hohenstaufen Emperor the long-withheld title of King of
Jerusalem. It cost him nothing to take the Emperor's part on
the distant, now indifferent, oriental scene, and it laid on Frederick the obligation of some return service. So Pope Gregory
loudly denounced Patriarch Gerold, whom we know of old, and
abruptly recalled him ; the Curia having been suddenly as-
sailed with misgivings about his behaviour during the·Crusade.
" People whisper in secret and openly proclaim that the Syrian
kingdom of our well-beloved son in Christ, Frederick, the ever-
exalted Emperor of the Romans, King of Jerusalem and Sicily,
has been unsettled by thy means, for thy hand has lain behind
the hands of the disturbers of the peace." This was the new
note in the Pope's letters to Gerold, whom he replaced by the
Patriarch Albert of Antioch. The Pope was similarly ready to
go to any lengths against King Henry ; his reasons were transparent. The ruin of the German King, if skilfully exploited,
might mean the collapse of the whole Hohenstaufen rule north
of the Alps. On Frederick's side it was the usual game of
harnessing opposition forces, when he himself requested the
Pope, nay even—to enhance the effect—compelled King Henry
to request the Pope to excommunicate the son if he should
prove rebellious to the father. Emperor and Pope were here
able to indulge in the amusement of mutually obliging each
other—each secure in the faith that he would ultimately outwit
his foe—and of presenting to the world the edifying spectacle of
their affectionate harmony.

Frederick was perfectly aware that this untroubled amity
would not last a day longer than Gregory's Roman embarrassment, and he was therefore in no hurry effectively to end this,
hoping to derive some advantage for himself in his Lombard
affairs from the present favourable situation. The Romans
themselves increased the pressure on the Pope so greatly that
by the end of July 1232, shortly after Frederick's return from
Aquileia, Pope Gregory decided definitely to request the Emperor's help against the Romans, though knowing well that he
would have to requite his imperial ally by concessions in other
spheres. The Emperor received the papal letter exhorting him
" to dash to the ground the pride of these overweening Romans

with his triumphant and illustrious right hand, to scatter the demon hosts and break the horns of the ungodly." Frederick was obliged, most reluctantly he said, to refuse. He had, in fact, the luck to hear at the same moment of the rebellion in Messina, which imperatively recalled him to Sicily, and claimed all the fighting forces of his kingdom. So the most the Emperor could do was to place his good friends the Romans under the imperial ban. But he immediately summoned the Germans, the feudal knights of Provence, and of the whole kingdom of Burgundy, to come to the assistance of the harassed Pope. The imperial diplomat killed several birds with this one stone. It was the first time in history that the feudal army of Burgundy had been summoned for service in Italy, and Frederick created this weighty precedent not in his own but ostensibly in the Pope's sole interest. Further, this summons gave Frederick an opportunity of sending an imperial plenipotentiary to the Burgundian court, with the remark that it was a very long time since Burgundy had performed any service for the Empire ; not indeed that he wished to cast this fact in her teeth, since she had not been offered the opportunity. Thirdly, Frederick had great hopes that, though he personally had displayed the utmost promptitude, it would be a considerable time before help actually reached the Pope. Meantime, he had not antagonised the Romans whose friendship might at any moment be valuable, and amongst whom he had built up a strong aristocratic party. Finally, he could now devote himself in peace to restoring order in Messina and the other towns in the island of Sicily.

The Pope had hoped that Frederick, the King of Sicily, the feudal vassal of the Holy See, would appear in person before the walls of Rome ; he expressed himself, however, grateful for the assistance promised. A remarkable correspondence now set in between Pope and Emperor, taking its rise in the immediate circumstances, but laying down in the most perfect form the ideal relationship between Empire and Papacy and the principles of their mutual assistance. It was a remarkable feature of the time that in treating any question of the moment the eternal order of the universe was always included. Pope Gregory expressed his thanks that " the Emperor's spirit had been illuminated and rightly directed by a ray of divine radiance and the inspiration of God himself, who had united the son to his mother (the Church) and the mother to her son, to restore the rights of Church and Empire." The wily Gregory supplied precisely the phrases that Frederick had long and eagerly awaited; for in view of the triangular struggle of Emperor, Pope and Lombards, nothing was so dear to Frederick's heart as a *rapprochement* with Gregory that would loosen the Pope's disastrous attachment to the towns. Frederick hastened, therefore, to answer in similar style in a lengthy letter, which the writer, Piero della Vigna and the Grand Justiciar Henry of Morra, both of them negotiators in Lombard affairs, were entrusted to carry to the Pope. This masterly composition, enriched by all possible resources of style and playing on words, formulated a universal doctrine : God, the all-foreseeing physician, had in time diagnosed the double oppression of the Church by heretics and rebels, and to combat these two diseases had prepared not two separate medicines but a double treatment: " The ointment of the priestly office by which the inner infirmity of false servants is spiritually healed, and the might of the imperial sword which cleanses with its edge the suppurating wounds, and with its whetted blade of worldly Empire hews off from the conquered foe all that is infected and decayed." Again : " This, Most Holy Father, is in truth the one, yet dual, healing for our sickness. Although Holy Empire and Holy Priesthood from their names appear two separate entities yet they are in the effective sense one and the same, being of like origin, consecrated by the divine power. They are to be guarded by the same reverent homage and—I shudder to say it—annihilated by the same overthrow of their common faith."

It is worth noting that there, in writing to the Pope, as elsewhere in speaking to the princes, Frederick alludes to the downfall of the Empire. He was perfectly aware that his throne was a volcano. His statecraft in Sicily is based on a knowledge of the insecurity of existing institutions. The interdependence of Empire and Papacy has never been more clearly expressed than by Frederick II. It is Dante's vision of the two Suns of Rome, based on the immediate relation of the Emperor to God, which Frederick here emphasises, and which the Church never recognised. We shall see later that Frederick's picture of the ideal Pope anticipates Dante's most exactly. This doctrine, however, apart from its general, eternal, universal validity, had a very present practical application : " Therefore, Most Blessed Father, since we are one, and assuredly feel alike, let us take thought as one for the common service : let us restore the Church's impaired freedom, and while we renew the rights of Church and Empire let us sharpen the swords entrusted to us against the underminers of the faith and the rebels of the Empire. . . ." This return to present affairs meant, in fact, would the Pope be so good as to enforce obedience on the Lombard rebels with the same zeal as Frederick showed against heretics—" for time is pressing and quibbling out of place ! "

Frederick II had entrusted to the Pope the mediation in Lombardy. The Emperor's general position, after the Friuli Diet, and after the alliance with Eccelino and Verona, and after various imperial successes in Northern Italy, seemed so unusually favourable that the Lombards were prepared to make many concessions. Only on two points were the parties irreconcilable : the Emperor demanded satisfaction for the closure of the Verona passes, and refused to recognise the Lombard League as such. For the confederation was to him a rebel state within the State, which split the Empire in two and severed Sicily from Germany. This was why the Lombard question was the fountain head of all quarrels between Court and Curia : Frederick needed an unconditionally submissive Lombardy to round off his Empire ; while the Pope, to stave off this encircling power, was bound in defiance of right or custom to look with favour on such a buffer as the League provided. Since the Pope at the moment wanted Frederick's help he skilfully evaded contentious matters and put off the whole Lombard question. This expedient was probably not unwelcome to the Emperor, for it left all possibilities still open. They were thus partially at one on the subject of Lombards and rebels, and even of heretics, though they held different views on the methods of the Inquisition. After the Sicilian insurrection Frederick permitted his imperial officials and a few docile clerics to carry on an Inquisition of a markedly political type, but he excluded all papal assistants ; whereas in Lombardy the Inquisitors were all the Pope's creatures, Dominicans for the most part. The Pope was none too well pleased with the imperial methods of heretic-hunting, while Frederick strongly objected to the Lombard Inquisition's proceeding without the presence of imperial officials, for he had sound reason to fear disturbance of the loyal towns. For Emperor and Pope alike utilised the edicts against heretics as a welcome political weapon, and ere long the papal interdict lay heavy on Verona, with her new imperial leanings, and on her ruler, Eccelino. Anyone, in fact, who failed to accommodate himself to the papal or the imperial will was a heretic : for this was manifest rebellion against God.

While Pope and Emperor, each in his own way, persecuted the heretics, an event suddenly took place which can only be compared to some great natural cataclysm. The entire North of Italy succumbed simultaneously to the madness and confusion of the penance mania. This movement is probably not unconnected with the Dominican persecutions in the North. Dominicans were amongst the chief leaders of the penitents, and rivalry with the Franciscan Order may have been another factor. Francis of Assisi had long since been canonised, and in July 1232 another Franciscan, Anthony of Padua, had been beatified, whereas twelve years had elapsed since the death of Dominic, and no one had yet officially recognised his saintliness or honoured him by canonisation. A bishop who was in close touch with the preaching monks even challenged the brothers : " Now that ' Brothers Minor ' have a saint of their own, get yourselves one somehow, even if you have to throw him together out of wooden stakes." People took saints very seriously in Italy. The penance-movement was so successful that the other great Founder, Dominic, was presently canonised too (in 1234).

The most natural ambition of the Dominicans, to know that their Founder was a Saint, set no doubt a certain goal for some of the leaders. Other impulses, however, underlay the move-

ment as a whole.   For over thirty years prophetic sayings had
stirred and terrified Italy with words of dread, and the populace here more than in any other region was kept in a state
of continuous excitement in anticipation of the Last Trump.
Abbot Joachim of Flora had introduced the turn of the century
with terrifying visions of the Last Day, which profoundly
influenced the whole thirteenth century till Dante.   The
greatest effect was exercised by his remarkable doctrine of the
three ages : the first begins with the Creation of the World and
the creation of Adam ; the second with the birth of Christ ;
the third was just about to dawn.   Similar divisions of time
were not new.   Joachim, however, referred the three ages to
the Trinity and named the first the Age of the Father, the second
the Age of the Son on which should follow the third, the Age
of the Spirit.   As the three members of the Trinity are co-
equal it follows that the three ages must be essentially identical
and the courses of the three must correspond.   The world
situation at the opening of the third age must resemble that of
the dawn of the first and second, the ages of Creation and
Redemption.   This was the same conception as Frederick had
employed in order to place himself on a par with Adam and
with Christ as the bringer of the third and last age.

From this starting point people began to reinterpret the
Bible.   If the three ages were exactly to reproduce each other,
the prophets of the Old Covenant who associated all the
terrors of destruction with the coming of the Saviour, must
again be valid for the present age which was once more expecting the Messiah.   The sayings of Isaiah, Jeremiah and Daniel,
prophesying destruction and salvation, raged once again
through the towns of Italy ; the awe-inspiring visions of John's
Revelation and other apocryphal Apocalypses broke in upon
the terror-stricken world, which took all these sayings as applying to itself and to the immediate future.   Abbot Joachim, with
his interpretations of the Apocalypse and the Commentary on
Jeremiah which was ascribed to him, had set the ball rolling,
and in a short time he found innumerable imitators, especially
amongst the mendicant monks.   Matters reached such a pitch
that every occurrence on earth was interpreted as the " fulfilment " of a Bible dictum, and the chronicles of the mendicants

are full of such interpretations : this and that word of Scripture was accomplished in this and that event, the Law has been fulfilled. When Frederick II announced that he had come to fulfil the Law, and found the salvation of the world in the fulfilment of the Law, he was speaking to an age that was craving this fulfilment.

Where Abbot Joachim's sayings were insufficient other joachite promises and interpretations were speedily invented. Genuine and false sibylline verses, magic sayings of Merlin, prophecies of Michael Scot, oriental oracles, Spanish forebodings, all contributed to confuse and excite minds which were already living in terror of the imminent coming of Anti-Christ, the End of the World and the Day of Judgment, and were yet buoyed up by lingering hopes of the approach of the Messiah, the peace of the world and the golden age of Apollo. For though Anti-Christ would woefully assail the Church he would yet be overcome by the effective intervention of an Order, living a life of Apostolic simplicity. Such was the promise. And not long after Abbot Joachim Francis of Assisi made his appearance : the fulfilment of the prophecy. With similar weapons Dominic took up the war against heretics. In Padua Anthony was worshipped as a Saint. The Italian people were thirsting for peace and weary of neverending feuds. In this time of crisis and confusion, tortured with the throes of a new birth, all spiritual and other forces were tense and at fever heat, and men fell an eager prey to any miracle that promised easier and better things. In the midst of all this the preachers appeared everywhere simultaneously, calling to penance, and coupling their terrifying words with the message of peace they stung the people to raving and madness. The epidemic spread like wildfire. "All were drunk with heavenly love, for they had quaffed of the wine of the spirit of God after testing which all flesh begins to rave." The peace and penance mania of the year 1233 is known as the " Great Halleluja ! " because the penance-preachers overran the country with this cry in praise of the Three-in-One. Externally it was everywhere the same. In Parma a preacher appeared in fantastic garb who belonged to no Order : wearing a black beard and with a high Armenian cap on his head, shrouded in a

sacklike garment and bearing a gigantic red cross on breast
and back. The brother played on a little copper trumpet,
from which he drew now sweet now terrifying sounds. He
lured the people, especially children, after him like the Pied
Piper of Hamelin. They followed with boughs and burning
tapers through streets and market-places, joining loudly in the
brother's Halleluja. On his arrival all enmities were suddenly
forgotten, all battles abandoned: "A time of happiness and
joy began ; knights and people, burghers and peasants struck
up hymns and songs in praise of God ; people fell on each
other's necks, there was no wrath, no strife, no confusion : only
Love and Peace."

Almost the whole of Italy fell under the spell of the Halleluja. Sicily was an exception : one such penance-monger was
ejected across the border by imperial officials. Florence also
greeted these proceedings with witticism and merriment, and
met the miracle-working of the preachers with practical jokes.
In Milan the multitude was led by the Dominican Peter of
Verona, the same who was later murdered and honoured by the
title of "Martyr"; in Piacenza by Leo the Franciscan; the
Dominican, John of Vicenza, worked north from Bologna upwards, and in Parma Brother Gerard, a Minorite, took the
apostolic office, performing many miracles. Another Minorite
brother, Salimbene of Parma, relates vividly the manner of these
miracles. Every here and there all the great preachers must
have held conferences and agreed on the day, hour, place and
theme of their sermons, and then gone their several ways
and preached. "There stood Brother Gerard in the Piazza
of Parma on a wooden stair which he had had made for his
addresses as I saw with my very eyes, and while the people
hearkened he ceased and drew his hood over his head, as
if he sank himself in God. After a long time, to the admiration of the people, he removed the hood and continued his
speaking, as who should say ' I was in the spirit on the Lord's
day.' " And then he informed the amazed populace he had
been hearing Brother John in Bologna speaking on such and
such a text, and Brother Leo on such another. The people
of Parma assured themselves by messengers of the truth of his
visions and many entered the Order. What the preachers

achieved, by whatever means, was, in fact, a complete and sudden cessation of all hostilities.

In some towns matters went so far that mendicant monks snatched the reins of authority, like the Dominican Savonarola 250 years later, and ruled according to mendicant principles. The Minorite Brother Gerard, who was an admirer and supporter of Frederick II, did so in Parma, for instance, and Brother John of Vicenza, the Emperor's foe, who was worshipped as a saint in Bologna, cast the whole town under a spell, and thereupon continued his campaign of peace in the March of Treviso. Finally, at Verona he mounted the *carroccio* of the town and preached to the multitude who streamed in from Padua, Treviso, Ferrara and Mantua ; thousands were assembled, who acclaimed him Duke and Rector of Verona. None dared oppose the will of the excited populace and their leader. The authorities were impotent. In a moment the rule of Eccelino in Verona was at an end : he, " Satan in person," was compelled to swear obedience to the Brother, and did so with tears in his eyes—tears of emotion, opined the multitude.

The service of penance of 1233 was only a foretaste of the much wilder and more savage outburst of the Flagellants in 1260 after Frederick's death, fanatic figures who are not far removed from the cycle of legend that centres round Frederick. For the still living Emperor the Great Halleluja had the most inconvenient political consequences. The only person who profited was Pope Gregory. With the loss of Verona Frederick had again lost his mountain pass ; the Pope had seized this opportunity of making peace with the Romans. He was now triumphant in Rome without the Emperor's help, and had now not the smallest intention of meeting Frederick half-way in the Lombard question, just at the moment when it was peculiarly acute. The Lombards did not stand by their concessions, and though the Pope did not accede to their more outrageous demands he evolved an expedient. He revived in essentials the treaty, none too favourable to Frederick, that had been concluded by his predecessor Honorius III, and instead of achieving a settlement everything was, as before, in the melting-pot. This procedure of the Pope's stirred to bitterness and resentment not only Frederick but several of the Cardinals. The

Cardinals made no secret of their feelings ; they refused to
follow Gregory to Rome, but remained in Anagni, and when
the Pope returned to Anagni they immediately betook themselves to Rieti. To everyone's amazement the Emperor,
though not recognising the League, acquiesced in the Pope's
proposals, partly for expediency, partly because he had other
schemes brewing. He had not yet received satisfaction for the
interference with his Diet.

The Halleluja came to an abrupt conclusion. At the last
and greatest feast of peace in Paquera 400,000 North Italians,
it was computed, assembled round Brother John of Vicenza.
Solemnly a pact of eternal peace was sworn. Four days later
in Lombardy and the March of Treviso the war of the towns
broke out again. All flew at each other's throats, and Brother
John, " Duke " of Verona, sat in the dungeon of one of his
innumerable foes. The balance between Emperor and Pope
was gradually restored when the Romans had sobered again
after their orgy of peace. In 1234 Luca Savelli was elected
Senator of Rome. He declared papal Tuscany and the
Campagna to be the property of the Roman people, and he
demanded homage from the towns of these areas. The Pope
fled to Rieti, and excommunicated the Romans, who were
looting the Lateran and the cardinals' houses, and called the
whole Christian world to his relief.

Now was Frederick's opportunity. In the sight of the
whole world he could pose as *Advocatus* of Rome and Protector of the Pope. He could draw the temporal sword to
defend the Church, exactly as world-ideals demanded, exactly
as he had pictured in his recent letter to the Pope. He offered
active assistance to the Pope and joined him in Rieti, taking
his six-year-old son Conrad with him to hand over to the Pope
as a hostage for the purity of his motives. Then he entered
Viterbo with his troops to besiege the Roman fortress of
Rispampani from this base. The gesture was here the thing.
The Pope, of course, could not accept the hostage, and the Emperor, who had no desire for a fight with the Romans, preferred
to loose his falcons in the Campagna and hunt in papal purlieus.

As the siege grew protracted he returned to Sicily, while his troops, after a while, forced the Romans to make peace. The Emperor had accomplished all he wanted. It was no trifle. The latest news from Germany indicated that the moment had arrived to assign to the Pope his rôle in the coming events.

The Sicilian Book of Laws depicted the Emperor as Fate itself. The Emperor's own son was the first victim. Since the day when King Henry opposed his father's wishes by absenting himself on the first occasion from Ravenna his fate had been sealed; slowly, steadily, inevitably he moved towards his doom. When decision was forced on him at Cividale he had no choice but to bow unconditionally before his father's might, to swear obedience, and to treat the princes with respect. When once he had returned to Germany he felt the full pressure of the fetters he had donned. He sought, cautiously at first, to slip them from him. It was not long till circumstances compelled him to defy Princes, Pope and Emperor. There is no riddle here to read ! In forfeiting his father's confidence he had forfeited his own freedom of action. Spied upon by a host of hirelings, looked upon with suspicion and often thwarted by the Emperor, the very aimlessness of his movements often lent them a compromising air. Henry himself felt insecure, he gave orders, countermanded them ; whatever he did, right or wrong, turned at once to his own destruction.

It is unnecessary here to pursue in detail the successive phases of his fall. One episode will show the luckless star under which the young king sailed. Roughly about the time that the Hallelujas of the penance preachers were echoing through the towns of Northern Italy, the German Inquisitor, Conrad of Marburg, a narrow gloomy fanatic, distinguished himself in the papal service as a heretic-hunter. The chief German heretics appear to have been the various sects of Luciferians who magnified Satan as the Creator. The Emperor, in the edicts we already know, had commanded the eradication of heresy, and King Henry and the German princes were at first whole-heartedly on the side of the Inquisition. Before long, however, Conrad of Marburg began to behave like an irresponsible maniac ; he accepted every denunciation and accusation as a proof of guilt ; he declared burghers heretics and flung them to the flames till the Rhine towns gazed in paralysed horror at his rage, not knowing how to avert it. Finally, Conrad without rhyme or reason accused several of the German nobles of heresy : the Counts of Arnsberg and Solms, and, especially, Henry of Sayn, thus trespassing on the jurisdiction of the bishops. At this point King Henry, with the concurrence of the princes, called a halt to the increasingly savage behaviour of the Inquisitor and sent a protest to the Pope in Rome. This document unfortunately reached Pope Gregory at the same moment as the news that Conrad of Marburg had meantime been murdered by embittered enemies. The Pope, in a fury, tore up King Henry's letter. In the meantime Henry at a Diet in Frankfurt had declared himself opposed to all such courts as Conrad's, and had complained that the Bishop of Hildesheim was preaching a heretic-crusade.

In all this the King's procedure had been above reproach, but the fact that he should just at this moment draw down on himself the Pope's wrath was in the highest degree inopportune for the Emperor. Just at this moment the consequences of the penance epidemic had given the Pope an advantage over the Emperor, and he had been able to return to Rome, while Frederick saw his whole position in North Italy undermined by the activity of the preachers, and he was particularly anxious to be on good terms with Gregory. He, therefore, strongly disapproved of his son's course. At the same time King Henry had most unhappily mixed himself up in almost treasonable doings, had made friends with the Emperor's enemies, and had contrived, most unjustly, to injure his father's special friends, the brothers Godfrey and Conrad of Hohenlohe, and the Margrave of Baden. Finally, something very like anarchy was beginning to spread through Germany. The princes compelled Henry to proclaim a Public Peace : which altered nothing. Just as Frederick was taking the field against the Romans the son, after having been severely reproved by his father, raised the standard of insurrection. He was in Boppard with a handful of trusty friends, a heterogeneous group of all ranks, united only by the most various impulses of opposition. Some townsfolk and *ministeriales* and a few bishops, such as

Augsburg, Würzburg and Worms, the Abbot of Fulda, and a few secular lords, were on his side. It is hard to see what success King Henry can have hoped for. The Emperor had all the real power behind him, the Princes and the Pope. Frederick designated his son's behaviour as " boyish defiance," and his son as " a madman who imagined he could hold the northern throne in our despite." It was really an act of utter despair when Henry was tempted to a further and final folly. In the late autumn of 1234, in order to hinder or delay the Emperor's return to Germany, he allied himself with the deadly enemies of his father and his forefathers and of the whole house of Hohenstaufen : with Milan and the confederate Lombard towns. After this no accommodation was possible.

King Henry could no longer stem the tide of events. Frederick II wrote once : " The power of the Empire takes no account of individuals. . . ." Foreseeing the future he had long since prepared the net for his son, he now drew it slowly in, mesh by mesh, without speed or haste. King Henry's alliance with the Lombards was rendered valueless before it was concluded. When the first disturbing rumours from Germany reached Frederick, just as he was visiting the Pope in Rieti, and offering his youngest son as a hostage, he himself negotiated the excommunication of his eldest. Pope Gregory IX was pleased, only too eager, to accede to Frederick's wish, and issued the papal ban. With that move Gregory lost the game. He sat firm in the Emperor's snare just when he was preparing a trap for Frederick. For when the alliance of his Lombard friends, Milan and her train, with King Henry became known, the Pope was in an extremely delicate position. He could not join this Lombard-German conspiracy to overthrow the Emperor or gravely endanger him, for by his excommunication of King Henry he had declared himself his enemy. Far from being able to stand by the Lombards he ought by rights to have damned them also as the allies of the excommunicated king. He did not go quite so far as this ; nor did the Emperor press the point. Frederick, however, was not slow to take advantage of the Pope's embarrassment. It was impossible now for the Pope to uphold his Lombard friends, guilty of high treason. Frederick could find no delegate more apt to his purpose than the astonished Pope, so he entrusted to the faithful hands of the High Priest himself the task of exacting satisfaction and inflicting punishment for the new treachery of the League, which could not this time be explained away. The Pope was paying dearly for Frederick's help against the Romans. And Frederick could set out for Germany with an easy mind. He had already written to the German nobles " there is no doubt of our fortunate arrival."

The news of the Emperor's arrival in Ratisbon was enough. The quite considerable insurrection in Germany at once collapsed, and King Henry was quickly persuaded by Hermann of Salza to unconditional surrender. Fear of the Judge, though approaching alone from the south, exercised a paralysing effect. Without an army, without a train of Sicilian nobles (whom he dismissed at the frontier), Frederick had set out in the spring of 1235, using his galleys to convey him from Rimini to Aquileia, northwards through Friuli and Styria. He took the seven-year-old Conrad with him and his personal exchequer, whose coffers he had replenished by a new tax, well knowing what means would avail him best in Germany. Just as on that former occasion when the *Puer Apuliae* arrived almost alone in Constance to be soon surrounded by thousands, so now the Emperor's following grew from day to day, and the number of adherents who streamed to him. As often before, in Germany, in Syria, in Sicily, Frederick II trusted once again to his personal presence, the glory and the magic of his name. He was master of the various arts that cast men under a spell, and according to circumstances used now one method, now another. In Syria he had captivated the Orientals by learned talk about mathematics and astronomy ; in Sicily he conjured up the fear of the Divine Power, incarnate as Law upon the earth, charms which were too close and immediate to be potent in Germany, which unfailingly reacted to the magic of the far-away. The marvel of southern strangeness had helped the *Puer Apuliae* whom men called David to victory, and now the great Charlemagne of tale and story seemed bodily risen again, and came as one of the wise kings of the East, wealthy, magnificent, the

Emperor of the End, with his train of exotic animals—and conquered once again.

The German chroniclers tell of Frederick's magnificence with bated breath. " As befits the imperial majesty, he progressed with the utmost pomp, and many *quadrigae,* chariots, followed him laden with gold and with silver, with byssus and with purple, with gems and costly vessels. He had with him camels, mules, dromedaries, apes and leopards, with Saracens and dark-skinned Ethopians skilled in arts of many kinds, who served as guards for his money and his treasure." All the fairy-tale magnificence of the south, the exotic treasures and the marvels of his treasury, " of which the west has scanty store," the Emperor displayed in the towns of the Danube, the Neckar and the Rhine. And when by chance the uncanny monarch flung to his leopard-keeper a few commands in Arabic, the foreign words were not without effect on the people nor on his train of princes, knights and nobles. This picture of the Emperor stamped itself indelibly on the German mind : In the days of Rudolf of Hapsburg a "false Frederick " arose : he sought to prove his authenticity by possessing three Moorish attendants and some heavily-laden mules. And the pictures of the divine majesty in Berthold of Ratisbon's sermons are unquestionably coloured by memories of that triumphant imperial progress.

When Frederick with his magnificent escort rode from Wimpfen into the Swabian Palatinate on one of his noble Andalusian or Barbary steeds he found that King Henry had hastened thither before him, to cast himself at his father's feet. His life was forfeit for insurrection. The Emperor did not permit his son to enter his presence. Henry was first compelled to accompany as prisoner his father's triumphal progress down the Neckar valley to Worms. Frederick was solemnly welcomed by the people, and twelve bishops waited at the portals of the cathedral to greet him. The Emperor saw amongst them Landulf of Worms, one of the chief supporters of the rebellious king. He ordered him out of his presence and commanded them to strip his bishop's robes from him. King Henry was flung into prison, and the troubadours tell that in the morning when his armour was taken from him he was still singing; but when at evening they brought him food he wept.

Not till some days later did Frederick sit in judgment on his son. In the presence of many nobles, counts and princes, the Emperor sat enthroned in *sacra majestas*. King Henry entered the hall and flung himself at the feet of his judge, and as a traitor to his sovereign who sues for pardon bowed his forehead to the ground before the Emperor's unchanging glance. Amidst an oppressive silence he was obliged to retain this position for a long time, and no one bade him rise. At last, on the prayer of several of the princes, the Emperor allowed the command to be given that he should stand up. Shocked and bewildered he stood and commended himself to the Emperor's mercy, renouncing his kingly dignity and all that he possessed. His submission saved his life, but he had forfeited his freedom. He had made all hope of this impossible by at first refusing to surrender the castle of Trifels which his supporters were defending and in which the crown jewels were lodged; he had even attempted flight. He was first imprisoned in Heidelberg and then despatched to Apulia. Any rebels who had not yet surrendered were defeated. Frederick showed great leniency to all; he even took Bishop Landulf into favour again and released, after a short time, the Lombard envoys captured in Trifels. Only the son felt the full severity of father, emperor and judge. For weary years he remained a prisoner in Rocca San Felice near Melfi; then he was transferred to Nicastro. After a further six years of imprisonment he was to be again transferred. The story is that he was about to be released but had not yet been so informed. Weary of life and fearing yet severer treatment King Henry on the road from Nicastro to his new place of confinement rode his horse over a mountain precipice. He was thirty years of age. He was buried in the church of Cosenza in a marble sarcophagus, clad in a shroud of gold and silver tissue into which eagles' feathers were woven. A Minorite preached the funeral sermon, according to Apulian custom, and chose as his text: " And Abraham stretched forth his hand and took the knife to slay his son." The sermon concluded with a peroration in praise of *Justitia*, the God of the State, to whom Frederick had had to sacrifice his first-born. We must not forget how severely Frederick himself suffered. In the mourning letter he wrote when giving orders for the obsequies there echoes still the sorrow of that judgment day in Worms, when the father had to pass sentence on the son according to his own saying : human nature must of necessity bow to justice. "The pity of a tender father must yield to the judgment of the stern judge : we mourn the doom of our first-born. Nature bids flow the flood of tears, but they are checked by the pain of injury and the inflexibility of justice."

To describe the imperial stay in Germany is to describe a series of most brilliant festivities. For when the great attain the summit of their fame they love to hold stately review of all the forces and the spirits they command. The first celebrations honoured the occasion of the Emperor's re-marriage. Conrad, King of Jerusalem, was now the sole remaining legitimate heir to the throne, and Frederick determined to take him a third wife. Pope Gregory, like his predecessors, chose the bride. She was Isabella, sister of King Henry III of England. Soon after the Emperor's meeting with Pope Gregory in Rieti, Piero della Vigna had been despatched to London to negotiate the marriage treaty. It was a most important step in view of both home and foreign politics, for Frederick had hitherto on strictly German grounds always inclined to the side of France against England, lover of the Welfs. The marriage with the English Isabella was the first step in the solemn renunciation which was soon to follow, of the ancient Welf-Hohenstaufen feud.

While King Henry was still a prisoner in Worms awaiting his sentence people were already making preparations. It was the beginning of July, and Isabella had been in Cologne since May awaiting the Emperor's arrival in Germany. Matthew Paris, the English chronicler, with the Englishman's love for the "intimate" details about the great, cannot relate with sufficient minuteness the whole story of the wedding of the beautiful young Empress of scarcely twenty-one, scion of the ancient house of Plantagenet. He begins even before the engagement. After the English King had given his consent to his sister's wedding the imperial envoys had begged to be allowed to see the princess, and Isabella was escorted from her home in the Tower of London to the Palace of Westminster to show herself to them. They had gazed long upon her with delight, esteeming her in all ways worthy of the Emperor's bed, had placed the engagement ring on her finger in Frederick's name, and greeted her as Empress of the Roman Empire. All the details are now recorded of her jewellery and the individual items of her clothing and of her plenishing, down to the gay silken counterpanes and soft cushions of the bridal bed, and the cooking pots which were of unalloyed silver, " a thing that seemed to all superfluous." Then the Empress's journey and sea-voyage are described, and especially the festive and joyous reception which the people of Cologne prepared for her. Tens of thousands flocked out to welcome her with flowers and palm branches and music. Riders on Spanish horses had performed with their lances the nuptial breaking of staves, while in ships which appeared to sail upon dry land, but were drawn by horses concealed under silken coverings, the clerks of Cologne played new airs upon their instruments. The matrons seated on their balconies sang the praises of the Empress's beauty, when Isabella at their request laid aside hat and veil and showed her face. Six weeks later, on the fifteenth of July, with all conceivable pomp and ceremony, the wedding was celebrated in Worms.

People told each other with amazement that the Emperor did not consummate the marriage the first night, but waited till early the next morning till the hour which the astrologers had indicated as the most favourable for procreation. Then Frederick handed over his consort to the care of Saracen eunuchs (a state measure as important as, but no more significant than any other) telling her that she was pregnant of a son, a fact which he also set in writing in a letter to the English King. In contrast to his predecessors Frederick II looked on his consorts simply as mothers of his legitimate heirs and successors ; they had no importance as Empresses. His imperial forefathers, especially in making pious foundations, habitually drew up their charters in the name of the royal pair : Henry and Kunigunde for instance, Frederick I and Beatrice, even

Henry VI and Constance. With the sole exception of the few
documents relating to marriage settlements the records of
Frederick II, the last Emperor, contain no allusion to his
consorts. Frederick II stands alone, a fact that was not
without influence on his sons. Although he himself frequently
referred to his parents, and celebrated his Divine Mother in
phrases such as no German ruler had ever used before, his
sons called themselves only *Divi Augusti Imperatoris Filius*.
This cold-blooded attitude to his wives has often been made
responsible for Frederick's " lack of sentiment." Be that as it
may : any other relation was unthinkable. For Frederick was
in an unprecedented way on the pinnacle of the world, which
none could share with him. The picture of an imperial pair
was possible for a German Emperor, but inconceivable for a
Tyrant of Sicily or for a Roman Caesar. Even the appearance
of sentiment and domesticity was out of the question for Frederick, who could more readily be seen in company with a
Saracen beauty than with his royal consort. The English
King complained that after years of wedlock the Empress had
never worn the crown in public. Enemies accused the Emperor
of imprisoning his wives in the " labyrinth of his Gomorrah "
(that is in his harem, as contrasted with Sodom), rendering
them almost invisible and making them strangers to their
children. This was all true enough. There was no room round
Frederick in which a woman could strike root. All his wives
died after a few years of marriage, and, as far as we know, his
mistresses shared the same fate : none of them survived him.
In the rarefied atmosphere of these brilliant heights no human
being but himself could thrive : none even of his friends could
hold out for long ; no woman could have breathed there.
Hence, the English Isabella, surrounded by her imperial household and dignities, watched by eunuchs, disappeared forthwith
into the " harem."

The happy Hohenstaufen days saw an unprecedented outburst of artistic creativeness in Germany in which all races in
common found their own characteristic expression : human
forms were created in a perfection never since attained : it is

the only period in which German plastic art spontaneously and unconsciously approaches the antique. In August 1235, soon after the wedding festivities of Worms, Kaiser Frederick held a great Diet at Mainz. Never was the " better nature " of the Germans, the reconciliation of their great eternal contradictions, so strikingly realised as on this occasion. This great imperial celebration must have awakened many memories of that " incomparable festival " in which Barbarossa celebrated the sword-investiture of his sons with a noble and chivalrous ceremonial never before seen in Germany. Barbarossa, though well over sixty, had himself taken part in the tournament, and was hailed by the minstrels as a new Alexander, Caesar, King Arthur. The fresh glory of this beginning of courtly chivalry in Germany was happily symbolised by the exchange of greeting and handclasp between Henry of Veldeke, one of the earliest of German singers, and a French troubadour. The next fifty years, the period of Gottfried and Wolfram and Walther von der Vogelweide, brought blossoming and promise, and full in the midst of all this outburst of German genius the *Puer Apuliae* was wafted into Germany from the South, and was caught up and transfigured by its glory. Now Frederick II, himself in the forties, revisited Germany after twenty years and found the Springtime over and the moment ripe for him to garner the first fruits. Now seemed the time to give permanence to the beautiful Roman-German form that had been just evolved, to help it to a still finer perfection, to weld the whole into a conscious unity : princes and races into one people. To strengthen and harden into an enduring state, as sculptors then were fashioning enduring monuments of stone, this German growth that bore the impress of Rome, neither by cutting it adrift from Rome nor by abolishing the princely power, but by persistently inspiring princes and races with the thought and the spirit of state-building.

Frederick II's great *curia solemnis* of Mainz was the beginning : law, speech, blood and feudal faith (which here had more weight than in the south) were the links of the chain the Roman Caesar forged. He appeared in exotic magnificence before this dazzling assembly, at which almost without exception all the German princes were for once united, with all the solemn dignity pertaining to the God-appointed Provider, Protector, Preserver of peace and justice. He opened the Diet with a proclamation of Public Peace, from the opening words of which there echoes the pride of the Law-giver who for the first time erects Tables of the Law, "for men throughout all Germany in private quarrels and in legal suits at present live according to the age-old traditions and customs and according to unwritten Law." The Proclamation of the Landpeace of Mainz contained both old and new laws, and far excelled in importance all previous pronouncements of the sort. It was to form the basis of all future imperial legislation, a foundation which all later lawgivers must build upon, and to which they must ever and again recur. Town confederations and princes and kings like Rudolf of Hapsburg, Adolf of Nassau, Albert of Austria have frequently renewed the Landpeace of Mainz in its entirety. The nine-and-twenty sections dealt with the juris-diction of princes and bishops, rights of mintage and transport, the abolition of unjust dues, the prohibition of self-vindication, the limitation of ordeal by battle, and much else.

The Emperor, as himself the Law. Incarnate, always con-ceived his personal actions as constituting a precedent, he there-fore created an imperial law out of his own sentence of perpetual imprisonment against his son, and the Landpeace begins with the decree : "Whatever son shall drive his father out of his castles or other property, or shall burn it or shall plunder it, or shall conspire with his father's foes, or plot against his father's honour or seek his father's destruction . . . that son shall forfeit property and fief and personal possessions and all inheritance from father or mother, and neither judge nor father shall be able to reinstate him, for ever." And it con-tinues with a sinister note ringing through the Middle High German of the original words : whatsoever son lays hands upon his father's body or criminally attacks him " he shall be without honour and without right for ever, so that he may never again come into his own."

An important innovation, copied from Sicily, was the installation of an Imperial Grand Justiciar, who was daily without fee to preside over the High Court and represent the Emperor. He was to hold office for at least a year, and he was given the services of a special notary, who must be a layman, " so that he may pay the penalty " if he does wrong. We can detect here and there echoes of Sicilian laws, but nothing that does violence to natural German Law, rather another offshoot from the same root, clothing itself in forms that have proved useful elsewhere.

The Proclamation of Mainz was presumably only a preliminary regulation, as in Sicily the Capua Proclamation had been the forerunner of the great Constitutions of Melfi. Frederick may well have planned a similar work for Germany. We know that he had Sicilian High Court Judges in his train, and that the idea of a great imperial codification of law was in the air at the time. The English poet, Henry of Avranches, who was an ardent admirer of the Emperor, adjured him to win everlasting renown by publishing a Summa of the numerous scattered number of imperial laws which should be a companion to the Pope's Collection of Decretals which Gregory IX had published a year before.

It was a matter of the highest significance that this " Italian " Frederick published his proclamation in German, and recorded it in writing in German, and had it translated from the German into Latin. It was the first time that German had been utilised for a proclamation, and the importance of the fact that it was thus recognised as on an equality with Latin for an edict of the Roman Emperor needs no emphasis. It proves that this most Roman of Emperors was also the most German. It was the beginning of an individuality in the State as a whole (not only in the subsidiary states), the first record of German law in German, the first laying aside of the Latin scaffolding as no longer indispensable to speech.

It would be difficult to overrate this first tentative of Frederick's to raise with the co-operation of the princes a German state structure comparable to the contemporary German achievements in art and literature. This historic Diet was rich in memorable and symbolic events, but the pan-German legislation might easily rank as the most important of them all, were its pride of place not disputed by the termination of the age-old racial feud of Welf and Waibling. Otto of Lüneburg, the Welf nephew of Kaiser Otto, was present. Frederick announced : " At this solemn Diet of Mainz, with the princes ranged round our illustrious throne, Otto of Lüneburg hath done us homage, and unmindful of all hate and harassment that existed between our forefathers hath placed himself under our protection and at our service." Frederick confirmed Otto in all his Lüneburg possessions, which he first took over for the Emperor in order to grant them back as an imperial fief. Further, he augmented the Welf territory by the gift of Brunswick which he had acquired by purchase for himself, and created a new dukedom of Brunswick-Lüneburg. When Otto the Welf above the imperial crucifix placed his hands in Kaiser Frederick's and swore the oath of allegiance, voluntarily committing himself and his possessions to the good faith of the Waibling, to whom he showed respect in every manner possible, Frederick in return entrusted him with the newly-created dukedom as a hereditary imperial fief, and solemnly bestowed on the Welf the banner that custom demanded. The racial feud of earlier days had become an anachronism in a Germany flooded as far as the Baltic and the North Sea by the glory of Imperial Rome. There was no longer Welf nor Waibling in the North. The age-old prophecy had been literally fulfilled which laid down the correct constitution for Germany : the Welfs should ever provide mighty Dukes, but only Waiblings should be Emperors, Frederick II was well justified in giving command : " This day shall be recorded in all the annals of the Empire because it has added another duke to the Empire. . . ." This also gave him a reason for proceeding next day to the cathedral, crowned with the imperial diadem, and after high mass giving a royal feast to all the German princes and the 12,000 knights of their escorts. This was the last great imperial feast of the old aristocratic régime of the Holy Roman Empire, before the onset of a duller bourgeois world which Frederick was trying to hold at bay by strengthening the princely power ; a world which lacked the spaciousness of an Empire, but from its own narrow confines reached upwards, seeking to win the empire of the skies.

Frederick had come to Germany as the Judge, showing himself for the first time in this capacity to all Europe, and presently an opportunity offered to figure as the highest judge of all the Christian world in a case which aroused much interest and excitement and which he himself contrived to magnify into an affair of the whole Occident. It must have been shortly after the great day of Mainz that the case was brought before him while he was halting in Hagenau in the imperial Palatinate. The Jews of Fulda were accused of having committed a ritual murder on a Christian boy at their Easter festival. The first result of this was a massacre of Jews in Fulda and several other German towns. Then the people had waited till the Emperor's arrival to seek a decision in all the unrest, and both parties, Jews and Christians, now appealed to Frederick in Hagenau. As a witness against the Jews the Christians had kept the child's corpse and dragged it along to Hagenau. Frederick heard the case and passed a sentence worthy of Solomon. First he pointed to the body, and said drily to the Christians : " When they are dead, bury them. It's all they're fit for." He satisfied himself that the Jews were innocent, but imposed a large fine on them, because—innocent or guilty—that had been the cause of a disturbance. Thus peace was restored in Germany.

The case, however, did not end here. The Emperor vowed if ritual murders were possible he would slay every Jew in the Empire, and he instituted a full and complete enquiry to elucidate the truth. His first step was to apply to princes, nobles, great men, abbots, and various Church dignitaries in the Empire to ask their opinion. The complete contempt, however, which the autocrat and the scholar felt for the findings of such a body finds voice in his ultimate decision : " These men, being different all, expressed different opinions in the matter, but showed themselves incompetent to give an adequate judgment in the case. We, therefore, out of the secret depths of our own knowledge perceived that the simplest method of procedure against the Jews, who were alleged guilty of the aforementioned crime, would be through such men as had been Jews and had been converted to the Christian faith. They, being opponents, would not conceal what they might know against Jews or against the books of Moses or through the

Old Testament. Now, though we ourselves in our wisdom, acquired from many books which our Majesty has learned to know, intelligently consider that the innocence of these Jews has been proved, yet we are anxious both to satisfy the law and to appease the unlettered populace. Hence we have decided with wholesome foresight and in concurrence with the princes, nobles, great men, abbots and Church dignitaries, to despatch special messengers to all the kings of the Western lands, and request them to send us from out their realms the greatest possible number of newly-baptised who are learned in Jewish law."

This really took place. King Henry III wrote from Windsor that he had received the Emperor's messenger, an imperial marshall, joyfully and with honour as was seemly. His illustrious and imperial Majesty had earned the king's deepest thanks since His Majesty had been pleased to impart this hitherto unheard-of case which had recently occurred in his imperial territories. So far as in him lay the King of England would endeavour to meet the imperial desires, and he was therefore sending the two most eminent of the newly-baptised whom he had been able to find in England, who would be happy to obey all imperial commands. The other European monarchs must have replied in much the same strain. It was a case which concerned them all. This " royal commission," assuredly the first that any Emperor ever summoned, expended no little time in consultations, of whose tenor the Emperor kept himself exactly informed. Finally, they announced as their certain conclusion that, as the Emperor had supposed, the Hebrew scriptures contained no such suggestion, that they rather forbade all blood sacrifices, and that the Talmud and the Bereshith laid heavy penalties on bloody animal sacrifices. On the basis of this finding the Emperor granted the Jews a pronouncement which severely forbade any similar accusation in future throughout the entire Empire.

Frederick's main purpose in all this inquiry was to summon as Emperor a judicial court for the western world, and, secondly, to display before such a gathering his own immense learning, which he was never at pains to conceal, well knowing that the European kings would hear of it from their delegates. It made

no small impression in Germany, though in some quarters
they took it ill that the Emperor had given his decision against
the Christians. With what curiosity and amazement these
foreigners must have made the acquaintance of the Emperor
who showed himself not only surrounded by exotic brilliance
and luxury, but who held discussions about the Talmud, who
seemed more completely master of Arabic than of German, and
who gave visible proof of the truth of those reports that he made
use " of these Saracen augurs and soothsayers whom people
call mathematicians and astronomers." Philosopher in those
days meant much the same as wizard and magician, master of
all secret arts, and even a man like Albertus Magnus was reputed
to deal in magic. Later German legends relate that Kaiser
Frederick visited Albertus in his magic garden at Cologne, as
others tell that Averroes lived at his court. The Germans,
indeed, always felt the Emperor to be somewhat uncanny; but
their awe was blent on the whole with profound admiration
rather than repugnance, and with a secret yearning to love him.

Frederick II spent the winter in Hagenau, a place he preferred to all the others. He always designated Alsace, in climate
and in customs the most southern German province, as the
favourite of his German hereditary lands. He stayed here
for months with short interruptions, surrounded by numerous
princes, settling quarrels, making agreements, receiving ambassadors. Some came from Spain, bringing valuable horses,
and the Russian Duke (of Kiev ?) had sent messengers with
gifts. During this period in his own personal German
domains where he was " Lord of the Land " he seems to have
carried through some constitutional measures and at least
established a centralised customs department, probably not
very different from his Sicilian one. Otherwise he occupied
himself with increasing his private and imperial possessions.
With Sicilian money he redeemed certain claims on Swabia
exercised by the King of Bohemia, and he acquired imperial
rights in Uri which were so far important as they gave him the
land at this end of the newly-opened St. Gothard Pass and thus
secured him an alternative passage across the Alps. It was
scarcely possible yet to use the pass for troops to attack Milan
in the rear, for instance. Frederick will have had the ancient

route over the Septimer or Julier passes in mind when he conceived the plan, at the beginning of the Lombard campaign, of invading Lombardy with two armies at once.   The Rhenish and Low Country knights were to assemble in Basel, and those who were crossing by the Brenner Pass in Augsburg ; perhaps the first great strategic conception of the Middle Ages.

The Lombard War could no longer be averted.   At Mainz the German princes had unanimously voted for the campaign against the Lombards, whose alliance with King Henry was treachery to the Empire.   According to German custom they pledged themselves by shout and lifted hand, instead of oath, to be ready for war in the spring.   Frederick had not only right but might on his side.   Pope Gregory suddenly found himself completely deserted.   He had informed himself by a courier of German affairs.   His position was desperate.   An alliance with the Emperor against the Lombards meant the strangulation of the Papacy as a political power : the States of the Church would be wedged into an imperial Italy and would in all likelihood soon fall an easy prey to the Emperor.   Neither could Gregory declare openly for the Lombards.   They had undeniably offended in the highest degree against the majesty of the Empire, and when the Pope sought to treat with them the towns cared as little about his commands as about the Emperor's. Gregory himself now began to complain of their " insolence." To maintain neutrality was practically to declare for Frederick and to abandon the towns to the imperial vengeance.

Pope Gregory's first effort was, therefore, directed to trying to postpone for a little the punishment threatening his Lombard friends.   There was suddenly nothing so urgently vital for the Christian world as a new crusade and the regulation of affairs in general in the Holy Land, where the Christians, to the Emperor's detriment rather than to that of the Curia, were mutually fighting each other.   The Pope wrote to the princes still assembled in Mainz and begged them to abandon the Lombard War for the sake of the Holy Land.   He begged in vain.   Frederick would not, in any circumstances, have consented to breaking the ten years' truce with his friend al

Kamil, which was not to terminate till 1239. Nevertheless, he gave the Pope one more chance. If he, as arbitrator, could persuade the Lombards between the August and Christmas of 1235 to offer terms satisfying to the honour of Emperor and Empire no armed intervention need take place. Whereupon Pope Gregory made the utterly impossible demand that Frederick should pledge himself beforehand to accept unconditionally the Pope's award in the matter, whatever it might be. The Emperor, in view of his previous experience, returned an emphatic refusal, but sent the German Grand Master as negotiator to the Pope, to rejoin Piero della Vigna who had been for a long time in charge of the imperial cause in Rome.

Hermann of Salza now began his great rôle of go-between. He enjoyed a high reputation with Pope Gregory, who always recognised his honourable disinterestedness, and he was almost Frederick's friend. The Pope had untruthfully asserted the Lombards' unconditional readiness to abide by his arbitration, but week after week the Grand Master awaited their messengers in vain. At length he returned to his master—not wholly empty-handed. Pope Gregory had been endeavouring to wean Verona from her imperial allegiance by suddenly installing there, without the shadow of right, a papal *podesta*. Hermann of Salza, accompanied by the imperial legate, Gebhard of Arnstein, had arrived in the nick of time, and rescued the most important town for the Emperor, of which Gebhard now took control. No sooner had Hermann quitted Italy than the ambassadors of the Lombard League appeared before the Pope, in no wise minded to submit. Gregory despatched an express messenger to urge the Grand Master's return! Hermann of Salza's reply was that his master's orders were to proceed, and he went on his way to Germany. The period allotted by Frederick II had meantime run out, and all hope of peace was wrecked by the intransigeance of the Lombards, who were fully aware how dire was the Pope's need of them and took liberties with the Curia accordingly.

Pope Gregory now had recourse to another weapon which had served him at the time of Frederick's first excommunication. Then the real cause of friction, the delay of the Crusade, was pushed into the background and Sicilian politics were made the rock of offence. Similarly now the Pope dropped the Lombard question. He unexpectedly made complaints about the conduct of Sicilian officials, about Sicilian taxes on churches and clerics, about the Saracen colony of Lucera, and other kindred topics : he joined battle on another field. The complaints now raised bore no relation to the burning Lombard question and, right or wrong, had not arisen since Frederick had quitted Sicily in complete harmony with the Pope a few months ago. As if nothing had been on the tapis for a long time past but the state of affairs in Sicily, Pope Gregory closed his letter with the ominous words : " We can no longer lock such matters in our breast without injury to the majesty of God, without detriment to our reputation and our conscience."

Ere long a second letter followed. This time it was the Crusade which had to serve the Pope's turn. Pope Gregory suddenly found it absolutely essential and wrote in conclusion : " The Church cannot, with equanimity, be a witness of any oppressive measures towards the Lombards, who have trusted themselves to her protection, for in this way the Crusade is being delayed. . . . In a case where the glory of the Redeemer is at stake the Pope cannot be a respecter of persons.". . . This was the flimsiest of pretexts. When the Crusade later was in progress, and it seemed that the result might strengthen the Emperor, Pope Gregory was the first to prevent its setting forth.

The German princes were solid behind Frederick, and this time the Pope had tried their patience once too often. In a letter of unspeakable bitterness Frederick goes through the Sicilian complaints point by point and seeks to refute them. But even if, in his absence, irregularities had taken place, it was not possible for him from Germany to keep the eyes of a lynx on his Sicilian kingdom and make himself heard there in the thunder ! He would be coming soon enough to Italy, and would then be ready to discuss such matters. The imperial reply to the second letter stated briefly that foreign excursions were excluded until peace was restored within the Empire. This cast the die for an imperial campaign against the Lombards.

As Frederick's relations with the Roman Curia grew tenser and more doubtful he seemed to wish visibly to demonstrate once more the essential unity of Church and Empire, Emperor and Pope. At his coronation in Aix as a mere boy he had set the seal of sanctity on his German-Roman kingdom by unexpectedly taking the Cross and by the solemn re-interment of the sainted Charlemagne. Now that he was about to leave Germany he closed the circle with a kindred ceremony. He went to Marburg to exhume and re-inter the childlike St. Elizabeth, Landgravine of Thuringia.

St. Elizabeth, the chaste and beautiful princess of the Wartburg, is still remembered. The greatest miracle she wrought was to combine a tender love for husband and children with a life devoted to the poor and the sick ; to temper dignity and pride of race with gentleness and humility. The memory of the penitent of Marburg, clad in the robe of a Brother Minor, girt with a cord, flogging herself, is forgotten in the picture of the gracious lady. Elizabeth was a daughter of the King of Hungary, she had spent her childhood at the Thuringian court and was, at an early age, betrothed to the Landgrave Lewis. Later centuries related miracles of her childish days. The generous-hearted girl had filled a basket with food for the poor ; some one reproved her severely for her generosity, and lo ! beneath its covering cloth the basket was full of fragrant roses. When Elizabeth first met the disciples of Francis of Assisi in Eisenach she was fifteen years old. The teaching of the Tuscan-Umbrian saint fell on well-prepared soil. His demand for chastity and humility, and above all for poverty, pointed the path which the princess resolved to tread when presently she found herself a widow. Landgrave Lewis had always been benevolently tolerant to her enthusiasms, and when he fell a victim to the plague in Brindisi on his way to Frederick II's Crusade, Elizabeth ardently desired to exchange her life as a princess for that of a beggar woman. Her confessor was Conrad of Marburg, the same who, after her death, developed into the nightmare-haunted fanatic of the Inquisition. He persuaded her to avoid excess. She quitted the Wartburg, renounced her children, and built herself a hut of wood and mud, as St. Francis had commanded his followers to do ; but she retained her princely rank and used her widow's riches to help and to feed the poor and suffering. She housed diseased and leprous children, washed their wounds and cared for them, and even kissed them, overcoming her revulsion with a smile. One Good Friday in an ecstacy she was granted heavenly visions. She did not abandon herself to visions, however, still less gave them publicity and she claimed no miracles in her short life of twenty-four years. When she was about to die, and lay on her pallet in an intensity of joy, people said that the sweetest sounds of angelic music were heard from her throat though her lips were tightly closed. The very day after her burial the saint began to work miracles, and people came from far to secure scraps of her garment, of her hair and nails as relics. Not long afterwards the Pope canonised her at the request of Landgrave Conrad of Thuringia, who himself entered the Teutonic Order. Kaiser Frederick came to Marburg in May 1236 to give his sainted kinswoman royal burial.

An uncounted multitude—people spoke of twelve hundred thousand !—had streamed into Marburg when Frederick II, in the presence of many bishops and princes and especially knights of the Teutonic Order, lifted the first stone from the grave of the young saint. Forthwith from the sacred body oil began to flow, which the Teutonic knights collected and distributed to churches and monasteries. The corpse was then enclosed in an oaken casket overlaid with skilfully wrought gold, and richly adorned with silver figures and antique gems. Frederick presented the saint with the golden beaker from which he was wont to drink, and crowned the head of the Landgravine with a golden crown, thus doing homage to the saint and princess, his kinswoman. The foundation stone of the Church of St. Elizabeth in Marburg was laid at this time ; its stained-glass windows represent their patron saint as the daughter of the Queen of Heaven, receiving a crown from the Virgin Mother, while St. Francis at her side is being crowned by the Son of God himself. They give no picture of the barefoot servant of the poor, clad in white flowing garments, distributing alms.

Frederick's interest in the exhumation of any chance mendicant saint would have been scarcely seemly. People seem to

have hinted this, for Frederick defends himself against the
innuendo that his homage was paid less to the saint than to
the princely kinswoman. The two things—he wrote—are not
easy to dissociate : " For it fills us with joy to know that our
Saviour, Jesus of Nazareth, was a shoot of King David's royal
stem ; and the tables of the Old Testament bear witness that
the Ark of the Covenant might be touched only by the hand
of the nobly-born." Thus Frederick expressed himself in a
letter about the Marburg ceremonies to the Minister-General
of the Franciscan Order.

Marburg marked the close of this German period. They
were days of solemn festival, happy days of brilliance and of
peace, a peace which lay over the whole of Germany and over
almost all the lands of the Roman Empire. An atmosphere
of world peace prevailed ; the chroniclers report an overwhelming wine harvest and a mild warm winter ; all signs
which seemed to prove that the Prince of Peace, the Emperor
of *Justitia*, was reigning. It might well seem so, for Frederick
had always succeeded in conquering without weapons ; all the
great successes that had raised him to these heights had been
won by peaceful means, at most by a threatening gesture.
If the Lechfeld this summer was echoing to the clash of arms
as the warriors assembled round their Emperor this army was
to bring the world the gift of peace. The Emperor called the
coming campaign an " Execution of Justice," and he failed
to understand how Pope Gregory could damn with so ugly
a word as " war " the " peace-restoring intentions " of the
imperial Judge. The peace which God designed to fill the
world under the Emperor of Justice was nigh at hand, disturbance flickered here and there only in the Lombard corner.
It was now his duty to bring peace to this quarter also, this easily-
excited, bloodthirsty region which had brought on itself the
punishment of the Judge and the Avenger. He was bringing
peace with the sword—but only because the Lombards would
not have it otherwise.
All the Emperor's letters at this time are full of similar
statements : the ten or twelve towns of the Lombard League

are the disturbers of the peace, and the task has been assigned
to the Emperor by God to compel them to repose. " In the
eastern world the kingdom of Jerusalem, the inheritance on
his mother's side of Conrad, our most well-beloved son, is,
in obedience to the will of heaven, steadfast in its loyalty to
our name ; and the Kingdom of Sicily no less, the glorious
inheritance of our mother's race, and also the mighty overlordship of Germania. We therefore believe that the Providence
of the Redeemer has guided our steps so mightily and won-
drously to this one end alone, that we should bring back to its
allegiance towards our illustrious throne that centre of Italy
which is on all sides surrounded by our strength, and that we
should thus restore the Empire's unity." The conquest of
Lombardy, that centre of the Empire, has been set him as a
task by Providence, and God has directed his steps towards the
goal. " We believe therefore that we are rendering the most
welcome service to the living God when we think the more
joyfully on the peace of the whole Empire as we more clearly
read the portents which indicate the heavenly will."

It is rare to find Frederick thus expounding his political
actions. This one instance is all the more illuminating. The
punitive campaign against the Lombards is in the Judge's eyes
a service to God, and happily that which God has foreordained
corresponds remarkably with the passionate personal impulse
of the Emperor. He can fulfil the divine purpose and renew
the peace of the peoples, and gratify at one and the same time
his ancient, inborn hatred of Milan. He writes to the King of
France : " No sooner had we, in the years of our ripening
adolescence, in the glowing power of mind and body ascended
the highest peaks of the Roman Empire against all expectations
of men and by the aid of Divine Providence alone . . . than all
the acuteness of our mind was continually directed to one end
. . . to avenge the injury offered (by the Milanese) to our Father
and to our Grandfather, and to trample under foot the offshoots
of abhorred freedom, already carefully cultivated in other places
also." Such hate has in it something Providential, something
God-intended. Everything therefore points to one goal : Providence, the world's weal, and personal impulse : peace must be
imposed on the Lombards.

The Lombard war against heretics and rebels becomes no less a Holy War than a Crusade to the Holy Land, and it is again inconceivable to the Emperor why Pope Gregory should arrest the arm of imperial justice. The completion of his purpose is the first pre-requisite for fighting in Syria : " For on our side we have frankly no other aim behind our procedure than to take up the cause of the Crucified One. This, however, cannot occur until the peoples round are by the might of Justice reduced to peace." So he wrote to King Louis of France, and on other occasions he resolutely denied that he was waging war for his own advantage : " When once the discord in the bosom of this Italy is triumphantly brought to an end, to the glory of God and of the Empire, we hope to be able to lead forth a powerful army to the Holy Land." Had the Emperor here other things in mind ? Those prophecies perhaps which had often been interpreted as referring to him, the redeemer of the Holy Sepulchre ? That after the pacification of the West the Messiah-Emperor should return to the East, and there in the Holy of Holies lay aside the Crown of all the World, and hang up lance and shield on the dry tree as a token of the last Judgment ? Did Frederick hope literally to fulfil this prophecy also ?

Frederick took extremely good care not expressly to say this, nor to bind himself too exactly. The nearness of the Last Day, however, and the Empire of Peace are implicit in all he said. It was a question of peace . . . not only the peace of the actual Roman Empire but in this fulness of time the peace of the whole Christian world. The Lombard war, therefore, concerned the world. The Emperor invited the ambassadors of all the kings of Europe to a Lombard Diet in Piacenza in order, in common with them, to reduce the few remaining disturbers of the world's peace—behind whom, though not always openly, the Pope had taken his stand. Frederick had struck the right note. Europe's Christian kings now rallied to his side, though they did not send their armed assistance till his success in the war was assured. The King of England wrote : he would have preferred to gird on his sword and come himself. At the same time he spontaneously sent letters, in which he expressed himself very forcibly about the Lombards'

arrogance, to the Pope and some friends of his who were
Cardinals : they really ought to take up the Emperor's cause
against the confederate towns.   Even more emphatic was the
document which King Bela of Hungary directed to the Pope
in the June of this year 1236 : he had heard that the insolence
of the Lombards was seeking to induce the Pope on the pretext of necessary service for the cause of the Holy Land to
oppose the imperial measures for strengthening the Empire.
He would beg the Pope not to give ear to the Lombards.
Unquenchable dissension between Empire and Papacy would
be the consequence.   He added that such an encroachment by
the Pope on the secular rights of the princes would be a
warning to himself and to the other princes of Europe.

These manly words of the Hungarian King show how warmly
the other western monarchs felt the Emperor's cause to be
their own, and show also how high Frederick's reputation stood
amongst them ; he is felt to be by far the first amongst them,
not in virtue only of his imperial crown but in virtue of his
actual strength.   It now became the ultimate political goal of
the Empire to cement the unity of the Christian kings of the
west.   There was nothing insincere in his statement, just on
the eve of the greatest display of his power : " More than ever
the whole world lives by the breath of the Empire ; grows
feeble if the Empire is enfeebled, and rejoices when the
Empire thrives."   Again : " The Roman Empire must strive
the more earnestly for peace, must the more urgently devote
itself to establishing justice among the peoples, because it stands
before all the governments of the world, as before a mirror."

Now that his goal is an Empire of Peace, now that the *aurea
aetas* beckons, the Emperor feels himself more than ever as
Justice incarnate, and uses the phrase " our Justice " as synonymous with " our illustrious majesty."   He is about to arm
" his Justice," and the Lombards shall see his face which he
would fain have shown them in peace, and " they shall not be
able to look on it unmoved, from fear before *Justitia*."   Hitherto
Justitia has been the organising and regulating power leading
men in the path of reason, now for the first time it becomes
the punishing and avenging force that works for world peace
and perfect world order.   Another ten years will pass and

avenging Justice, filled with hate, shall rage solely for its own ends through the length of Italy.

Hopes of a world peace and the conception of a universal Roman Empire find expression at this time in yet other contexts. Frederick writes some remarkable letters to the populace of Rome. These are all full of the belief that the fulness of time is at hand and the world is about to be renewed. Renewal would mean reconstruction of the world in exactly the state in which it stood at the moment of the Redemption in the days of Augustus. The Messiah-Emperor who is expected and who shall set up an Empire of Justice must show himself the revivifier of the ancient Roman Empire, the re-incarnation of Augustus, Prince of Peace, restoring imperial Rome to her old position in the world.

As early as Barbarossa's day the Arch Poet, like his predecessors, had sung of this " Renovatio " expected from Roman Law and from his Emperor :

> Iterum describitur orbis ab Augusto,
> Redditur res publica statui vetusto,
> Pax terras ingreditur habitu venusto,
> Et iam non opprimitur iustus ab iniusto.

All the preconceptions which lent a tangible reality to the expected Messianic King : the tone and manner of the ancient Caesars and of the Augusti were adopted by Frederick when writing his magniloquent letters to the Romans to shake into wakefulness these people " all too content with the shadow of a great name," " to arouse this later posterity to scale once more the peaks of their ancient greatness." The Emperor's words fell resonantly on the Romans' ears : between domestic cares and enervating self-indulgence they have forgotten their mighty past, " Behold, the arrogance of Milan has set up a throne in Northern Italy, and not content to be Rome's equal, she has challenged the Roman Empire. Behold these folk who were bound of old to pay you tribute—so men say—fling insults at you in the tribute's stead. How sore unlike the deeds of your forefathers and the virtues of the ancients ! . . . that one town alone should dare to bid defiance to the Empire of Rome. In olden days the Romans were not content to subdue their neighbours only, they conquered all provinces, they possessed far

distant Spain, they laid fair Carthage in ruins ! " The contrast between the old Rome and the new, he continued, amazed
all who had heard the fame of Rome or had read the monuments of the past and looked now upon the present. And
thinking of the Roman communes the Emperor writes : " Ye
reply perhaps that Kings and Caesars accomplished these
great deeds. Behold, ye also have a King and Caesar who has
offered his person for the greater glory of the Roman Empire,
who has opened his treasuries and has not spared his travail !
Ye have a king who with his constant calling stirs you from
your slumbers. . . ."

In these ways the Emperor sought to arouse all the mental
powers of the time, that the world might see what was at stake
when he drew the sword against the Lombards. They were
opposing the clearly-manifested aims of God : a world peace
and an Empire of *Justitia*. Frederick was, therefore, justified
in proclaiming that the Lombard rebels were in revolt, not only
against him, the Emperor, but directly against God, against
the Catholic faith, against Nature. He himself spoke very
cautiously and only of his imperial peace mission, adding but
one phrase : " The glory of the Emperor's sceptre shines out
from Rome across the darkness *not in temporal affairs alone*."
His friends in Italy, however, lauded the coming " Deliverer."
Piero della Vigna addressed the people of Piacenza, announced
the Emperor's impending arrival and, not wholly by accident,
nor yet wholly by design, he took as his text the prophecy of
Isaiah which recurs in the Gospel for Christmas Day : " The
people that walked in darkness have seen a great light : they
that dwell in the land of the shadow of death, upon them hath
the light shined."

Such were the signs and tokens under which Frederick II
metamorphosed himself from Law Giver into Leader of
Armies and prepared men's minds for his appearance in the
new part, fulfilling the formula of the Caesars : *arma et leges*.
He had called the approaching campaign an " Execution of
Justice," and this conception made serious strategy impossible,
for the armies were only an instrument of the Judge to punish

law-breakers and rebels. Frederick had no large continuous stretch of territory to conquer. Like all medieval rulers he lacked space, and he lacked foes against whom to carry out campaigns in the style of Alexander, Hannibal or Julius Caesar. The Middle Ages saw on occasion kings and princes at the head of their armies, but—except perhaps in Byzantium—knew no generals, no strategists on a large scale. Any brave man could head an army, a cardinal or justiciar as well as a king, and none could be a good general or a bad general, because there was no art of war. An art of war began slowly to be evolved when the days of the condottieri came and the professional armies. The endless fighting of the preceding ten years had developed Frederick's army till it was showing indications of becoming a professional one : the troops serving as feudal levies became gradually subsidiary to the soldiers recruited and paid directly by the Emperor. Frederick showed the adaptability of all great men by developing into something of a condottiere himself. There was no opportunity, however, for great strategic combinations, whether on his side or his opponents'. In the Middle Ages every battle was a more or less accidental impromptu affair, needing an immediate decision. Frederick used to the full the advantages of speed, surprise, cunning and superior strength. He could, however, rarely induce the enemy to risk pitched battles in which they were always defeated. The siege technique of the day was so imperfect that when they ensconced themselves behind the stout walls of their fortresses they could only be starved out, or very occasionally the place could be carried by storm. These sieges dragged on for many months and were as far as possible avoided by Frederick, for the cost of maintaining the besieging forces was enormous. Compared with the vast conceptions of universal Empire and universal Papacy the armies of the time seem ludicrously small. It is the characteristic of the period descending from the universal and the spiritual to the material, that a very minute concrete object might be charged with a great idea, and a most trifling deed with overwhelming spiritual significance. It is probable that Frederick II never assembled more than twelve thousand, at the utmost fifteen thousand men, " under the victorious eagles of the Imperium Romanum." Even this

force will have consisted of a heterogeneous assembly of the
most disparate components : German, Italian, Sicilian feudal
knights fighting alongside Saracens, infantry levies from the
loyal towns beside mercenary knights, and archers of the most
miscellaneous origin.   The Emperor was probably superior to
the enemy in cavalry, but the confederate armies as a whole
were probably equal to his, and possibly even larger.   In open
battle the cavalry invariably won the day, but in siege operations
the heavily armoured knights were valueless.

The army which the Emperor took with him for the campaign
of many months in Lombardy was unwontedly small, even for
those times.   He had had to detach a strong German army
against the Duke of Austria.   The " Quarrelsome " Babenberg
had not put in an appearance at any of the appointed Diets ;
he had imprisoned imperial ambassadors ;   had indulged in
provocative acts against all his neighbour princes, and, finally,
had refused obedience to the Emperor.   He had now been
placed under the ban of the Empire, and the King of Bohemia
with the Duke of Bavaria were detailed to enforce the decree.
They were able to overcome him within a few months and drive
him back into his last fortresses.   The Emperor had told off
several of his German divisions for this subsidiary campaign so
that at least he need not weaken his Italian troops.

The whole campaign of 1236 which only lasted a few months
was, therefore, only a preliminary canter to clear the air in
Lombardy.   Frederick was anxious to have certainty about the
Pope's attitude.   He, therefore, begged that since the war was
against heretics, and since there was peace between Empire and
Papacy, the Pope should take a hand, by spiritual proceedings
against the rebels.   It was not too much to ask the Curia to
support this punitive campaign.   Gregory IX sent no reply.
Taxed with his silence he later wrote that he must have failed
to answer " out of a kind of dreamy forgetfulness, as it were."
Instead, he sent the Emperor a new list of complaints about
the Sicilian government and scarcely alluded to Lombardy.
Finally, when for a moment the Emperor's military progress
seemed to have come to a standstill, the Pope suddenly un-
masked, abruptly shattering the dream of unity :   " Thou
seest "—he wrote—" the necks of kings and princes bent under

the knee of the priest, and Christian Emperors must subject
their actions not to the Roman Pontiff alone ; they have not
even the right to rank him above another priest." This is the
famous, the notorious phrase of priestly omnipotence, which
Gregory was the first to formulate, and which he launched,
somewhat prematurely, against Frederick II. He far exceeded
the claims made by his predecessors, for he subordinated the
Emperor to every petty cleric, and in matters other than
spiritual. The verdict of the Apostolic See was supreme
throughout the world, declared Pope Gregory, which was the
equivalent of saying that Frederick must submit without protest to the Pope's decree in the Lombardy affair, although this
quarrel between the Emperor and the rebels had in the last
resort nothing whatever to do with the Pope. Pope Gregory
derived the right of the Papal See to decide all questions,
especially Italian questions, from that famous forgery, the so-
called " Donation of Constantine." He elaborated : " Constantine, Sole and Only Ruler over all regions of the World, in
agreement with the Senate and People of Rome, who possessed
authority not only over the city but over the whole Roman
Empire, had found it seemly that the Vicegerent of the Prince
of the Apostles who held sway over the priesthood and over the
souls of men, should also possess supreme power over the affairs
and persons of the entire world." And Constantine had believed that he, to whom the conduct of heavenly things had been
on earth entrusted by the Lord, must also lead all earthly
affairs on the bridle of justice. The symbols and the sceptre
of the Empire were, therefore, handed over by Constantine to
the Pope for all time ; the city of Rome with the entire duchy,
and also the Empire, for ever placed under his jurisdiction.
Constantine had placed Italy completely at the disposal of the
Apostolic Chair, and sought himself a new residence in Greece.
For it seemed to him unseemly to possess power as earthly
Emperor where the Head of the Christian faith sat on the
throne on which the heavenly Emperor had placed him. Without in the least impairing the quality of its judicial supremacy
the Apostolic See had transferred the Empire to the Germans,
to Charlemagne, and had granted him the power of the sword
by his coronation and anointing.

We need not here further pursue the papal doctrine. For the moment it served Pope Gregory to claim that his award in all Italian disputes was final and binding even against the Emperor. Frederick found it superfluous to answer this letter. If he had had any doubts before, he now knew where he was. What need of words ! No doctrine of the judicial supremacy of Pope or Emperor, no theories of papal overlordship in Italy or in the Empire could argue away the fact that the Lombards in conspiring with King Henry had been guilty of high treason. The negotiations which Hermann of Salza was conducting with the Pope might drag on to the accompaniment of military campaigns. In this affair only deeds could decide.

In August 1236 Frederick had reached the neighbourhood of Verona. Gebhard of Arnstein had been sent on in advance with five hundred mercenary knights and one hundred mercenary archers to invest the town, and Frederick himself brought a further thousand knights and some infantry. Considerable additional forces were to join him in Italy, in particular the levies from the loyal towns. The important thing was to enlarge in every direction the exit of the pass. Eccelino was to work eastwards towards the Treviso March : against Padua, Vicenza and Treviso, which were already being supported by Venice. The Emperor himself turned westward into Lombardy proper. Mantua had declared for the League, so communication with Cremona, Frederick's most valuable north Italian base, was cut. The town levies from Cremona, Parma, Reggio and Modena could not join Frederick because a hostile Confederate army was doing its utmost to prevent the junction of the two forces. By making a northern détour, and invading the hostile territory of Brescia, the troops from the imperial towns succeeded in effecting a junction with the Emperor, which was accounted a great success for his cause. The most important task was now to open the road from Verona to Cremona. The two minor fortresses of Mercaria and Mosio were held by Lombard garrisons. These were taken. An effort was then made to tempt the Mantuans into the open by a three-day siege, but when they refused to come out the march to Cremona was continued. One goal had now been reached, and the Verona base secured.

The Emperor spent nearly the whole of October in Cremona, waiting. Negotiations with Pope and Lombards were in progress, and the Diet was to be held in Cremona which had first been summoned for Piacenza. Piacenza was no longer eligible, for a papal " action of peace and mediation " had succeeded in detaching the town from Frederick and inducing it to join the League. The town was lost to the Empire for the next ten years. On the other hand, the town of Bergamo threw over the League and joined Frederick. Lombard politics were always kaleidoscopic.

The Diet was destined not to be held at all. At the end of October the Emperor suddenly quitted Cremona. Eccelino on the Adige in the Legnano region was holding a hostile army in check, composed of combined troops from Vicenza, Treviso, Padua and Mantua. He saw the Verona passes threatened again, and called Frederick to the eastern scene of war. The Emperor hastened to his assistance in a forced march that has become famous, probably intending to take the confederate troops in the rear by approaching from the north via San Bonifacio and Arcole. Accompanied only by his heavy cavalry Frederick quitted Cremona on the evening of the 30th October, and in a march of one day and two nights covered the whole distance from Cremona to San Bonifacio, east of Verona, close on seventy miles, at full speed," like a swallow cutting the air." On the morning of November 1st he reached San Bonifacio, halted " as long as it takes a man to eat a piece of bread in haste " and hastened on at once, not southwards to Eccelino but still east to attack Vicenza. The position had suddenly altered. When the confederate army heard of the Emperor's unexpected approach it dissolved at once, for the towns themselves seemed threatened. The Vicenzans led the van, abandoning tents and baggage in hasty flight for home, since Vicenza lay more exposed to attack than any of the other towns. They came too late. A few hours took Frederick the additional eighteen and a half miles to Vicenza. He arrived on the afternoon of that same first of November, stormed the town which had refused to surrender, and gave it over to plunder. Eccelino meantime came up, the town was handed over to his care and put in immediate charge of an imperial captain.

The story runs that Frederick II gave his friend Eccelino a brief demonstration of how he would like the government of the town to be conducted. The two were walking up and down in the bishop's garden in Vicenza when the Emperor drew his poniard and said : " I will show thee how thou mayest without fail maintain thy rule," and thereupon he beheaded with his dagger all the longer blades of grass. Eccelino understood. " I shall not fail to note the Emperor's instructions," was his reply. Before long he began by a reign of terror to build up Italy's first seigniory.

The immediate result of the taking of Vicenza was the surrender of Salinguerra, with his capital of Ferrara and the surrender of the district of Camino. The other towns of the East were so shaken that Eccelino and Gebhard of Arnstein were able, in the course of the winter, to capture Padua, after which Treviso under the Margrave of Este also surrendered. The whole of Northern Italy, east of a line running from Verona to Ferrara, had thus been won for the Emperor. Eccelino under the Emperor's protection now organised the whole territory into one kingdom or "Tyranny": which Venice felt to be a grave menace to her. The brief campaign of 1236 had not brought a final decision, but had at least achieved notable successes : above all the exit from the Alps and the approach to Cremona were secured.

We have already anticipated the chief events in Austria. The overthrow of the Babenberg had only been temporary, for Duke Frederick had been able to maintain himself at certain fortified places. Nevertheless, peace had been for the moment restored. The Emperor lingered for weeks in Vienna ; declared the Babenberg deposed, and laid the foundation of those private Hohenstaufen possessions already mentioned. He granted a great privilege to Vienna which was henceforth to be a direct appanage of the Empire. He held a Diet there at which once more a large number of German princes were assembled. Nothing bears more eloquent testimony to Frederick's increased prestige and power than the fact that without any special concessions the German princes at once consented to choose the nine-year old Conrad, King of Jerusalem, as Frederick's successor; and, more, as "King of the Romans and future Emperor," thus satisfying the ancient ambition of the House of Hohenstaufen. The electoral decision of the princes is couched in haughty language. They fell in with the Hohenstaufen tradition, and felt themselves in fact the successors and heirs of Roman Senators. "In the beginning of Rome's history, after the memorable defeat of the Trojans and the destruction of their noble city, the highest power and the electoral franchise for the Empire rested with the senators of the new race of the new town. Yet with the gradual ever-increasing growth of the Empire and its ever-growing strength, the height of such great fortune could not remain for ever with one single city—though she were the royallest among them all. After the Empire's power had pilgrimaged through the most distant regions in a certain circular wandering it came to rest at last for ever among Germania's princes—in a manner not less beneficial than inevitable—that from amongst them, who secure the safety and prosperity of the Empire, the ruler of the Empire should be chosen."

The royal succession was thus assured in Germany and in the Roman Empire. The Emperor, however, abstained from crowning King Conrad IV. His experience with King Henry, in whose stead Conrad was now chosen, "as David for Saul," had demonstrated that too great independence on the part of the German King was dangerous. King Conrad, or the Regents appointed for him, were, therefore, to rule simply as delegates of the Emperor. The first regent was Archbishop Sigfrid of Mainz, and, later, Henry Raspe of Thuringia. In spring Frederick moved from Vienna to Speyer to assemble other princes there for Whitsuntide and permit them to confirm the King's election. The Emperor's time was mainly occupied in extensive preparations for continuing the Lombard war, and in August he was again encamped on the Lechfeld with fresh troops. A brief letter informed the Romans of his proceedings. No matter which concerned the Romans should be concealed from them (he wrote), since every undertaking of the Emperor's was specially planned on their behalf. He was now striking his tents on the fields of Augsburg before again seeking Latium's

borders with the assembled fighting forces of Germany under
the fame-crowned banner of the imperial eagles.

When marching at the head of his armies Frederick felt himself more than ever one of the Caesars. He had opened the
Lombard campaign by seizing one of the Roman eagles in his
hand. This year, even more than last, he hoped the genius
of Rome would accompany him on his campaign.

At the request of the German Grand Master negotiations
with the Pope were again opened this year. Hermann of Salza
had a difficult task. At a big Chapter in Marburg, where over
a hundred of the Teutonic knights were assembled, the brothers
of the Order showed themselves quite as impatient as the
German princes at the thought that their Master was treating,
and for ever treating, instead of striking. The Emperor was
not optimistic about these fresh efforts, though, in fact, Hermann
of Salza accomplished on this occasion more than ever before.
Frederick's successes in the March of Treviso had intimidated
both Lombards and Pope. Gregory even withdrew from Lombardy his legate, Cardinal Jacob of Palestrina, whom the Emperor
cordially disliked, and replaced him by two more congenial
cardinals. The Lombards also were becoming more amenable,
and perhaps a treaty might have been arranged if the Venetians
had not torpedoed the peace negotiations. A Lombardy united
under the Emperor, an Eccelino at their back in the March of
Treviso : they must have felt that this would be a perpetual
menace. After Piacenza deserted the Emperor's cause a
Venetian had been put in as *podesta*. On instructions from
the Doge he made the Piacenzans swear that they would never
accept an imperial *podesta*. This was one of the Emperor's
most important conditions, and the negotiations fell through.

In the middle of September 1237 the Emperor arrived in
Verona with two thousand German knights. Gebhard of Arnstein joined him soon after. He had hastened on ahead and
called up the Tuscan levies in the greatest haste, and joined
forces with the Sicilian army consisting of seven thousand
Saracen archers and the Apulian knights. A few days later
the levies from the loyal towns came in, led by Cremona, and
the auxiliaries of Eccelino. The chivalry of individual towns
like Bergamo and Tortona mustered also, and other volunteers

poured in, so that the Emperor ultimately had at his disposal an army of some twelve to fifteen thousand men. Success speedily followed. The fortress of Redondesco, west of Mantua, was conquered in September, followed by two other castles in the Mantuan region, so that Mantua itself surrendered on the first of October. Preliminary negotiations with the *podesta*, Count Richard of San Bonifacio, had paved the way for the surrender of this important town.

The Emperor now turned north into Brescian territory. Montechiaro, strongly fortified and strongly garrisoned, was taken by stratagem after a siege of fourteen days. The fortifications were destroyed and the fifteen hundred foot-soldiers and twenty knights of the Lombard League captured here were taken to Cremona. The road to Brescia was now open. But a Lombard army about ten thousand strong lay close before the walls, and the problem was to attack the enemy forces as far as possible in the open. The Lombards skilfully evaded a battle, which was a simple matter as long as they could use Brescia as their base. The Emperor tried to lure them off. He marched through the Brescia territory southwards, laying waste, captured four castles and compelled the Lombards to follow, for they feared an attack on one of the other defenceless towns if they lost touch with the imperial army. The story of Vicenza might well have been repeated. By the middle of November the two armies finally lay face to face near Pontevico, separated by a marshy little river which there flows into the Oglio. Operations came to a standstill. The Emperor could not allow his heavy cavalry to attack across the marshy land, the Lombards accepted no challenge. November was almost over. Negotiations had been unsuccessful—in spite of considerable concessions by the towns. There seemed no hope of dealing a decisive blow at the Lombards before the year was out.

Then Frederick II had recourse to stratagem. The Oglio, a small river that traverses Lombardy from north to south and flows into the left bank of the Po, lay behind his position, which probably filled the angle made by the marshy little tributary

and the Oglio.　On the further side of the Oglio lay Cremona,
three or four hours' march away.　The Emperor made a feint
of setting off to take up his winter quarters in the town, a move
which the advanced season made entirely plausible.　While the
watching Lombards remained, covered by their marshes, the
Emperor crossed the Oglio by several bridges, broke these
behind him, as the enemy could observe, and sent in fact a

THE BATTLE OF CORTENUOVA

large part of his army, including the town infantries and the
baggage, southwards to Cremona,　He himself, however, now
separated from the Lombards by the Oglio, marched off northwards with his striking force : the entire cavalry and his light
Saracen archers.　He followed the Oglio upstream.　The
Lombards, certainly the Milanese, were bound to cross the
river somewhere, and the Emperor intended to intercept them.
For two days he lay in vain in ambush at Soncino ; at last news
came.　The Lombards, feeling perfectly secure, had moved off
further north, crossed the river and were encamped at Pon-
toglio.　Frederick immediately struck camp, left Soncino on
the morning of November 27th, and his vanguard of German
knights fell on the amazed Lombards that same afternoon.
The Lombards had only just time to rally round the *carroccio*,
the standard-bearing chariot of Milan, which had been set up
at Cortenuova.　Meanwhile Frederick's main force, marching
up in several columns, one of which the Emperor himself com-

manded, soon compelled a decision. Darkness set in early owing to the season, and there was not time to take Cortenuova by daylight. The Lombards abandoned the place in the night and fled, leaving the Milanese *carroccio* behind. The pursuit began at dawn ; the Lombards lost an immense number of prisoners : 3,000 foot soldiers and over 1,000 knights, amongst whom was the *podesta* of Milan, Pietro Tiepolo, son of the Doge of Venice. The standard itself, which the Milanese had sought to save, got lost in the flight and was found by the victors and made a great trophy in the conquered camp.

Cortenuova, one of the few great battles of the Middle Ages, was a complete victory for the imperial arms and a glorious climax to Frederick's empire in Germany. It belongs entirely to his German period. For the last time an Emperor's Italian campaign, voted and supported by the German princes took the form of an imperial war. Coming from the North, Frederick, like his forefathers, had once again crossed the Alps and conquered in the Lombard plain. The victory was won mainly by the German knights, but was immediately translated by Frederick into Roman phraseology to give the success its spiritual value : " Germanic victory " would have created a false impression, " German victory " would have as yet had no meaning. The victory was therefore turned to the glory of Roman arms, it was won in the name of imperial Rome and of her Caesars as Frederick truthfully wrote to the people of Rome. Even during the battle the *manes* of the Roman Imperators had accompanied the Hohenstaufen, yea, even victorious Roma herself, when he gave his warriors their new battle-cry, their new slogan of victory :

MILES ROMA !   MILES IMPERATOR !

And in order to lose nothing of the glamour and glory of ancient deeds of arms the Emperor followed up the victory, which he had won with the battle-cry of Rome, by a triumph which deliberately and intentionally revived prehistoric and forgotten ceremonies. People said that he was planning to elevate Cremona to the position of a second Rome. When Frederick a few days later entered Cremona with his immense booty, his numerous prisoners and his victorious army,

he did so after the fashion of the Roman Emperors celebrating their triumphs : the captured enemy commanders
followed in fetters ; Pietro Tiepolo, son of the Doge of Venice,
sometime *podesta* of Milan, was bound upon his back to
the lowered mast of the Milanese *carroccio*. This noblest of
trophies was drawn by an elephant through the streets of
Cremona to the joyous cheering of the people. The Emperor's
yellow banner with the Roman eagles floated aloft, while from
a wooden tower on the elephant's back trumpeters made
known the triumph of the new Divus Caesar Augustus. The
Emperor himself told the Romans that his triumph was a
reversion to the original Roman form.

The intoxication of this exotic, pagan-Roman, assuredly
most unchristian, celebration of victory, marked a turning
point in Frederick's life. All the magnificent Roman titles
which he, like his predecessors bore, were justified. The
empty formula, meaninglessly used, " Imperator Invictus,"
suddenly meant once more what it had meant of old. Without the need of transcendental interpretation he was now in
the naked literal sense :

FELIX VICTOR AC TRIUMPHATOR.

The shades of Rome, of the Romans and their Caesars, had
tasted blood : they began to stir again and to be visible in the
flesh once more ; a genuine breath of antiquity revivified by
life itself.

VII. CAESAR AND ROME

VII. CAESAR AND ROME

ROME, golden, eternal, mighty, glorious, world-conquering. . . .
Rome, the Mistress, the City of Cities, the fortunate, the royal,
the holy city. . . . THE CITY, seat of empire and of fame . . . !
No adjective was too august to be used in antiquity and in the
Middle Ages to do honour to the still-radiant glory of the one
capital of the world. Through the centuries the magic worked
on, at first the magic of glory, later the magic of glorious ruin.
The name of Rome and the possession of Rome, much striven
after, was one with the rule over the Roman world. If it was
desired to honour the mighty, Rome was shown offering them
homage on bended knee. Each of the Emperors in turn showed
honour to Rome by making a pilgrimage to the town in which
the crown of the world was given away.

Since the decline of Rome the wish to renew her ancient
glory had never died out. The Roman Empire of the Germans
was itself the idea of the *Renovatio*, and the inscription of
a Carolingian seal read : *Renovatio Imperii*.

The Emperors were the first and the most powerful of those
who sought to achieve the renewal of Rome, but two rivals soon
arose—first the Popes, then the Romans. The Caesar-Popes
of the Middle Ages felt themselves to be the successors of the
Roman Divi, just as much as did the Emperors, for the Donation of Constantine had entitled them to the imperial insignia :
pallium and purple, sceptre and standard and tiara ; had
endowed them further with the imperial palace of the Lateran,
and the rule over Rome, Italy, even the whole Empire. The
world-rule of the imperial Papacy was to renew Rome's ancient
greatness and power. It is a straight line from Gregory VII,
the founder of the imperial Papacy, through Innocent III, the
verus imperator and protector of the Byzantine-Latin Empire ;
through Boniface VIII, who called himself Caesar and Imperator, down to that Prince and General, the last of the
imperial Popes who chose Julius II as his name. The Romans

were slower to re-discover themselves, but a new era began even for them in the middle of the twelfth century. It was closely connected with the doctrines of Roman law and the Lombard conception of freedom. For a long time to come they dated their documents from the year 1144, in which the Senate and Equestrian Order were renewed and the Roman *respublica* ruled once again through a *sacer senatus* from the Capitol, reminding the first Hohenstaufen, Conrad III, that the Caesars of old ruled the world only in virtue of the Senate and Roman people. *Senatus Populusque Romanus* was now about to rule the world again.

In spite of these two rivals the dream of a Rome renewed remained alive in the German Empire until the fall of the Hohenstaufens, now weaker, now stronger, now ebbing, now surging up as in the days of the third Otto and of Barbarossa. The changefulness of the Roman idea is a testimony to its life : each of the Emperors who took it up gave it the impress of his time. Certain elements in it remained constant : from the very beginning this idea of rebirth involved rivalry with Byzantium, the capital of the Eastern Empire. Roman law had inculcated the subjection of all peoples under one Roman Caesar. Its resumption under Barbarossa set a goal for the Roman dream : to establish once again the Roman world of the days before Constantine in its whole undivided comprehensiveness. The Crusades enlarged the world indefinitely towards the East. Finally, Henry VI, as heir of Robert Guiscard, of whom they wrote " it might have been his to renew the ancient Empire of the Romans," had planned to give the *coup de grâce* to languishing Byzantium. The West-Roman German Emperor was to be sole monarch of the world. Such was his will. Such was granted, in fact, not to him but to his son.

No Angelus and no Comnenus challenged the rivalry of Frederick II. Before his rule began Byzantium had been conquered by the Crusaders. Titular Emperors, vassals of the Pope, reigned on a Latin Bosporus. What was left of the Empire of Nicaea was ruled by an impotent Basileus who had been given to wife a natural daughter of the Hohenstaufen

Emperor. Frederick II was unquestionably the last emperor of the ancient Roman Empire, the one and only head of the Christian world. If he took up the thought of a Renewal of Rome—and how could he fail to take it up !—he must give it a new meaning against internal rivals, for outer rivals there were none.

The triumph of Jerusalem had exalted the Hohenstaufen to be the Son of God : the bloodier victory of Cortenuova made him also a Son of Earth. The former was followed by the formation of the Sicilian monarchy : the celebration of the latter by Frederick's *Renovatio Imperii*. A secondary consequence was that Frederick II as *triumphator legibus et armis* stepped into the circle of the Caesars, attained the rank of a World Monarch though not that of a conqueror of distant worlds. In the signs manifested by Providence Frederick had read his task : " After the pacification of the surrounding peoples to bring the centre of Italy into the service of the Empire." This call to subdue " the province of provinces " accorded marvellously with the personal and private wish of the Emperor himself : " From the very beginning of our days, since the illustrious nature of the Caesars with happy violence overcame our royal disposition, ere yet a higher fortune had fallen to our lot, our heart has ever burned with the desire to reinstate in the position of their ancient dignity the Founder of the Roman Empire and the Foundress, Rome herself, . . . and this unquenched desire was fused with the dignity of Empire which ensued."

Retrospectively we see the boy and king, then the Emperor, enthroned in Palermo, in Aix, in Worms, in Mainz and in Jerusalem, straining from childhood towards the one great goal : by his own deeds to beget anew the ancient greatness of the Caesars and of Rome. Impelled by this passionate desire Frederick II journeyed through his realms with pride : " David in Syria ; Guiscard in Sicily ; Charles in Germany," as Henry of Avranches phrased it. From each of these countries the Hohenstaufen took something, but each of these rôles he exalted by the inspiration and impulse of a Caesar, and each he brought to ripeness and fulfilment. Others had prepared the ground, others had sown and watered ; the fulness of

time had come, and Frederick was chosen to reap the harvest
of centuries.   The form of one great Ruler was to be conjured
up anew less by magic than by force : the flattering poet had
sung " and Caesar art thou in Rome ! "   It seemed that the
victory of Cortenuova might perhaps make this promise
good : here was the key to Italy, the land of the Caesars, not
the provinces alone.   Sicilia—Germania—Syria—Frederick
wrote to the Romans that he hoped to see again the borders
of Latium and to be Caesar in the home of the Caesars : that
would be for himself and for the world the ultimate fulfilment.

ROMA CAPUT MUNDI !   This age-old phrase graced like a
challenge a seal of Frederick II's.   If this rune was as tangibly
and literally fulfilled as the ancient claim of the Emperors
to be the successors of David ; if Frederick II was Maximus
Imperator of Italy and with the Pontifex, a Caesar again in
Rome ; if Rome was, in no spiritual, transcendental sense, but
in sober actual fact, the capital of Italy and of the Roman
Empire, then the Empire of the Caesars, so oft invoked in
manifesto, had become tangible once more and the Empire had
been perfected as befitted the time.   It was the opinion of the
time that as a matter of course :

Roma caput mundi frenas regit orbis rotundi.

An Emperor celebrating a triumph in Rome itself would, in
some mystic way, become possessed of all the kingdoms of the
West.   Rome was the key to the ultimate Empire of Peace :
He who should renew the Augustan Age on earth must reign
in Rome and judge the peoples of the earth according to Roman
Law.   People expected the world's salvation to flow from
Roman Law, from one Justice in all countries : *legibus antiquis
totus reparabitur orbis*.   Such had long been the hope—the
Arch-Poet had sung the same for his master Barbarossa.   More
recently another poet had promised Kaiser Frederick that a
collection of imperial laws would make him *orbis terrarum
salutifer*.   The idea of renewal was doubtless at all times
quickened by such speculations about salvation ; but now they
are all finally engulfed in the belief in the imminence of the
Last Day, which so completely dominated the time.   Everything

was straining back to the same origins, the origins of Church and Empire: the expected Prince of Peace, the *Justitia-Imperator* and the Renewer of Caesar Augustus were ultimately, not radically different.

" His heart beat with no other purpose than to be Lord and Master of the Whole World . . .", Brunetto Latini declared later, and other contemporaries exchanged similar whispers. The world-dominion of which Frederick II dreamed, however, contained no threat to neighbouring rulers. " At the height of imperial fortune, content with our own lot, fulfilled with supreme happiness, we envy none. . . ." The Roman world-dominion of this Hohenstaufen was not to be won on the battlefields of Gaul or Spain, of Egypt or of Poland, but in Rome. Frederick II concentrated all his plans on Rome. The modern mind expects organic growth to proceed centrifugally, its ever-widening circles stretching further and further into actual space. In contrast this last Emperor in his ascent to the dominion of the world drew his centripetal circles ever narrower and closer. His task was to penetrate to the innermost recesses of the Empire, as his office entitled him to do, and condense all the widely-diffused spiritual influences of the Empire at its very heart. In proportion as his power increased he must, therefore, avoid the danger of dissipating his strength afar, and must concentrate it all at the central point. The ultimate result was an intolerable strain which, lacking an outward safety valve, grew in the centre more and more intense. Frederick II provides the only historical example of a World Ruler aiming not at expansion but at condensation.

The distant spaces of empire were closed to Frederick II by Cortenuova. Often as he sought to escape again from Italy he never left the peninsula. Italy consumed him. Cortenuova was also the beginning of his Caesarship, of his metamorphosis from the Law-Giver of great dominions into the Leader of tiny armies, a reflection of his personal pilgrimage from the spiritual spaces of a world-empire back to the core of Italy, " the province of provinces," the City of Cities. During the very battle itself and in the triumph after victory Frederick was mindful of the customs of ancient Rome and of the Caesars. His titles now ring truer, more sonorous : Victor, Felix, Triumphator.

They are no longer mere symbols of an idea ; they are the sober statement of its realisation. The imperial Chancery now multiplied the Caesarean titles. It was a venerable custom to speak of the Empire of the Caesars. Now unceasingly the swords of Caesar are victorious ; glorious and all-conquering are Caesar's standards, and the Roman Eagles, and Caesar's army. This flood of resonant adjectives exceeds all custom, as does also the " unquenchable will " by very deed to re-awaken to new life the Roman Caesars. It is idle to ask whether Cortenuova was a victory comparable to those of ancient days. People wanted to see Caesar. And the living history—deed and gesture and spectacle—was interpreted in the ancient Roman mood and brought more of the genuine Caesarean atmosphere into the time than scores of learned treatises could have done.

It was remarkable the connotations that " Caesar " brought : fame, glory, triumph, of course ; but also, rooted perhaps in Roman law : vengeance as function of the Caesars ; their hate, their savagery, their lion's wrath, their force and passion, their unbending will. Della Vigna in his victory manifesto proclaims that " streams of blood dyed the swords of Caesar," and tells how " Caesar charged boldly at the head of his armies.". . . Again, the Emperor will show the world " how Augustus proceeds against the foe and Caesar works his vengeance with the steel." "Augustus, the Avenger," a brilliant figure, wrathful, terror-inspiring, which Frederick showed the foe and which remained vivid and little-changed throughout the Renaissance.

Earlier Emperors had been freely enough compared to the Caesars, it is true. Frederick II, however, now began in quite a new strain to measure himself against their individual quali-, ties. " You may turn over and search through the history of the Caesars, starred with deeds of incomparable greatness, described in ancient chronicles and annals, you may scan the acts of individual Emperors, but the most diligent seeker will not find a gentle generosity comparable to ours wherewith God hath inspired us," thus Frederick wrote to all the world when he released a deeply-hated Cardinal from imperial im-

prisonment : convinced like many another despot of his
own overflowing benevolence. In the celebrated mourning
letter on the death of the discrowned King Henry, David and
Caesar, the Biblical and the Roman prototypes, must justify
the mourning father's tears : " Neither the first are we, nor
shall we be the last to suffer injury from sons who have done
ill, and none the less to weep upon their grave. David
mourned three days for Absalom, his first-born ; and that
illustrious Julius, the first Caesar, stinted neither duty nor
the tears of fatherly affection over the ashes of his son-in-law
Pompey, who had sought to compass the ruin and to take
the life of his wife's father." This is a new way to envisage
the past : the great figures live again when the man in action
is called up behind the high-resounding name.

The picture for which Frederick II posed and which the
imperial Chancery painted was quickly apprehended near
and far. The times were ripe, and ready to see the Emperor
under the symbols of the Roman Caesars, though, in fact, the
statuesque and empty Roman of their dreams was as far removed
from Frederick's living Caesar-incarnation as classicism from
Napoleon. But the shades had tasted blood again. The
Emperor took rank in the Caesars' heroic company. Poets,
chroniclers and writers began to compare Frederick with Caesar
and with Augustus and to seek resemblances in individual
episodes. A poet expressly recalls the victor in civil war, and
apostrophises Frederick thus : " Greater than Julius, thou,
when the rebellious people challenge thee to battle." They
quote Lucan to compare Frederick's treatment of his soldiers
with Caesar's. An historian in Florence not long after writes :
" From the first Imperator, Julius Caesar, called in the beginning Gaius Julius, to the mighty Lord, the all-wise Frederick
II, whom Merlin and the Sibyls had foretold. . . ." All the
adjectives and all the superlatives which all the carefully re-
capitulated ancient Emperors had borne were heaped upon
the Staufen.

The Emperor's relation to Piero della Vigna is compared
with that of Augustus to Vergil, of Theodoric to Cassiodorus,
and on a verse of Vergil is based the eulogy which runs :
" Jointly with Julius, Caesar guides the Empire." The poet,

Orfinus of Lodi, taking the name of Caesar for his title, rattles
out in threadbare phrase endless strophes of the type :

> Nullus in mundo Caesare grandior. . .
> Nullus sub sole Caesare fortior . . .

If it was possible for Frederick II to pose as Caesar amidst
the fragments of the ancient world and in the new intellectual
world that was awakening, it was much more possible in relation to Rome herself and to the Romans who, like the Emperor,
were jealous for the revival of their ancient greatness.
Frederick II wrote once that the Goddess Fortuna hailed
Caesar more joyously in the neighbourhood of Rome than in
any other place. The victory of the imperial, the Roman,
arms at Cortenuova brought Rome within nearer reach, and
Rome promised the Triumphator a triumph of a quality
Cremona could not give. Frederick II could strike a fuller
note in celebrating Caesarism to the Romans, the music of his
fame and theirs could ring more clear and true. The moment
had not yet quite come to bring Caesar back to Rome.
Frederick, however, could anticipate a little, could convey a
harbinger of future glory, could transfer some reflection of his
triumph to Rome, the home of imperial triumphs. To give
richness and reality to the gesture of his ancient Roman triumph
he sent, soon after the victory, to the Senate and People of
Rome, the Milanese *carroccio*, the standard-bearing chariot,
with banners, and standards and trumpets, as the *spolia opima*
which victorious Caesar, after the manner of the ancient
Emperors, laid at the feet of Rome. A solemn and magniloquent letter accompanied the trophies : " Nature and all-
powerful Reason whose commands kings must obey, make it
our duty in the days of our victory to exalt the fame of the
city which our forefathers enhanced by the glory of triumphs,
and humbly, in not unworthy phrase, we acknowledge our duty
in this matter. Look ye, if the triumph be traced back to the
inevitable nature of its origin, we could not exalt our imperial
glory without exalting first the honour of the city whom we of
old recognised as the fountain head of our power. Our wishes
would verily be far removed from Reason if we, illumined by
the radiance of the Caesars, were to tolerate the Romans' being

left without a share in the rejoicings over a Roman victory. . . .
If we were to rob you of the fruits of a venture which was
conducted in your name, when we conquered the rebels of the
Roman Empire to the battle-cry of the Roman name . . . if we
failed to bring home to the Royal City the fame and glory of
our exploits, that city which sent us forth to Germany to scale
the heights of Empire, as a mother sends her son.   We ascribe
to your renown whatever, under favourable auspices, we have
subsequently achieved, we turn again in the fame of our most
glorious success to the city which as a boy we quitted with the
anxiety born of an unknown future.

" Thus we recall the Caesars of old to whom the Senate
and people of Rome awarded triumph and laurel for deeds of
arms performed under victorious standards, preparing from
of old the paths according to your wishes by the present
illustrious example which we give : for we send herewith after
the victory over Milan, assuredly the Head of the Confederation
of Italy, we send to you the standard-bearing chariot of that
commune, as booty of the vanquished enemy and prize of
victory, and for you a pledge of our valorous deeds and of our
glory, in the intention of safely accomplishing all that remains,
when oncewe see peace restored in Italy, the seat of our Roman
Empire.

" Receive therefore with gratitude, O Quirites, the victory
of your Imperator !   The fairest hopes may smile on you, for
dearly as we love to follow the old ceremonies, yet more eagerly
do we aim at renewing the ancient nobility of the City. . . ."

Frederick II intended by triumphal ceremonies and by his
example to re-awaken in modern Rome the ancient Roman
spirit, as we also learn from the verses " of Caesar Augustus
the Just " which accompanied the triumphal gift :

" And mayest thou thus, O City, be mindful of earlier triumphs
    Destined aforetime for thee by the kings, the leaders in battle."

The City of Cities, battening still on its ancient renown, responded to the mood of the new Caesar.   The Romans led in
solemn procession the captured chariot, which to the shame of
Milan had been dragged for a spectacle through the awe-struck

towns of Italy, drawn by a team of mules instead of its own white oxen. According to the Senate's instructions the booty was escorted to the Capitol amidst the rejoicings of the people. There the chariot was mounted on five marble pillars. Then a relief was carved in white marble depicting this token of victory, with an inscription which sang in many distichs the fame of the Emperor and his love of Rome which had prompted him to send his trophies to the City.

This whole episode marks a new feature of the time, not only of Frederick himself : the ancient Roman triumph already heralds the Renaissance, and no less the lust for *trionfi*, for laurels, for personal fame, for the immortalising of the hero. Frederick II had already celebrated a triumph in Jerusalem, the fountain head of his Christian kingdom, but that Eastern triumph had been offered to God (not to the Church, who was angry). It had been a mystical *Gloria in Christo*, " accomplished more by miracle than valour." The new triumph of arms glorified only the Roman Imperator, Caesar, the man, as Victor.

In vain did Piero della Vigna, in the proclamation intended for the Pope and for the Christian monarchs, seek to lift the victory into the realm of the miraculous : the triumph on the Capitol—which Christians believed to be the seat of heathen demons—the celebration of the victory itself, which lacked all Christian consecration, subserved no longer the eternal glory of God but the everlasting fame of a mortal, who, it is true, bore himself almost as a demi-god. But the glory of man grows pale ; henceforth the thirst for fame grew stronger in Frederick and ever stronger. " That the might of Augustus may not lack occasion for fresh triumph ! " he writes once during these fighting years. For his subjects the fighting was to bring the end of their burdens, " for ourselves the highest victory . . ." ; for his subjects victory was to bring desired repose, " for ourselves the wreath of the battle." For the " fame and praise " of his name Frederick at this time contemplated restoring the tunnel of the Emperor Claudius by which he had drained the Fucine Lake. " For eternal and everlasting memory " he had a statue of himself carved in stone, a figure in the round standing free, to ornament the gate of the bridge at Capua ; reliefs all round celebrated the Emperor's victories and gave the whole the character of a Porta Triumphalis. To attach so much importance to the perishable body, so shamelessly to do it homage, was unheard of in the Middle Ages.

This Caesar-like gesture was no doubt the Emperor's personal caprice and carried its own meaning, but a statesman's most private act is not without its political purpose. Barbarossa, the first German Emperor after an interval of many years to intervene effectively in Italian affairs, found himself obliged sonorously to reassert his dignity as Caesar with the Roman law behind him, for the German feudal kingship with its armies which had sufficed the Ottos and the Salians no longer bore his weight in Italy. What had been true of Italy was truer still of Rome. A Cardinal writing in late Hohenstaufen times maintained that he who seeks to rule the Romans must show them : *et gestus magnificos et verba tonantia et facta terribilia.* The Romans had felt this craving for a century or more, since they re-awakened to self-consciousness : this lust for greathearted gestures and words of thunder and awe-inspiring deeds was heightened by Frederick. The Romans were for him the people of his imperial capital at whose feet he hoped to lay once more the empire of the world. Besides : he needed the Romans in his duel with the Pope.

The year 1236 brought the whole Italian-Roman question to a head. And in that year begins Frederick's wooing of the Romans with rhythmical high-sounding phrase. He had long since secured a strong party for himself in Rome, so that he was certain of finding some response. Probably during his first quarrel with the Pope about the Crusade, when Roffredo of Benevento had to read his explanatory manifesto from the Capitol, his first political alliances with the Romans had been established. Frederick had gathered about him the most powerful patrician families of Rome, headed by the Frangipani, and had made them his vassals by buying up their immovables in Roman territory and granting them back again as fiefs : landed estates, farms, vineyards, but, above all, towers and solid buildings in the town, most of which dated from old Roman times.   The Mausoleum of Augustus belonged to the Colonna, the Colosseum to the Frangipani ; the Arches of Titus and of Constantine, the Septizonium of Septimius Severus were all structures which had been fortified at an early date and served the town aristocracy as castles.   The Emperor had acquired possession of all this, and the Romans were well pleased with the transaction : they remained in enjoyment of their property and received no small sum in ready money, and their freehold became a fief.   For a long time to come Roman nobles were selling their possessions to the Emperor and becoming his vassals.

In addition to this Frederick had granted fiefs in his Sicilian kingdom to many of the Roman patricians, a Frangipane received one in the Principata, John of Polo was granted the County of Fondi, and later Alba.   It is probable that Frederick also took a wife for his son from the family of these adherents of his.   The consort of Frederick of Antioch was said to have belonged to the Polo family.   Yet other Romans drew regular annuities from the Emperor and enjoyed—rare privilege—untaxed commerce with Sicily.

The Emperor's party in the town of Rome, therefore, was by no means inconsiderable.   It had been disconcerting for him to have to take the field on the Pope's behalf against the Romans : a double game by which at the moment he purchased quiet in Germany.   The citizens' hate for their spiritual head, however, drove them back into Frederick's arms, and within a year of his campaign against the Romans the imperial party was uppermost in Rome once more.   Whether spontaneously in order to please Frederick, or whether at Frederick's direct instigation, the nobles now stirred up the populace against the Pope just at the moment when the Lombard question was acute between them.   In 1236 it again happened that a pro-Kaiser senator was elected, and Frederick now addressed his letters to this imperially-minded Rome.   Pope Gregory's complaints, therefore, that the Emperor was recklessly expending money in order to foment strife were not without

plausibility. Frederick's reply was that, on the contrary, peace
had reigned in Rome since, and not before, the appointment
of an imperial senator.

It is a striking fact that Frederick II supported and turned
to his own advantage in Rome the very same revolutionary
anti-government impulses which in Lombardy he fought with
fire and sword. But in Rome the movement was hostile to
the Pope. The Lombards' ambitions, moreover, were wholly
individual and selfish, whereas the Romans were aspiring to
their ancient and traditional world-dominion. Earlier Emperors had resented the suggestion that they exercised imperial
rights in virtue of the Senatus Populusque Romanus, and had
felt an enmity towards the Roman people. Conrad III had
simply left unanswered the Romans' invitation to make Rome,
the *caput mundi*, his capital, and to restore the Roman Empire
to the position it had held in the days of Constantine and
Justinian, who had ruled the world from Rome. When Barbarossa was coming for his coronation the Romans made him
a similar proposal and asked for certain assurances. With the
magnificent arrogance of a Caesar, not lacking a touch of naïveté,
Barbarossa thundered at the ambassadors of Rome : the
Senate and the Ordo Equester were naught to him : " Do you
crave to see the glory of your Rome ? the dignity of your
Senators ? the valour and discipline of your Knights ?   Behold
our empire ! We have your Consuls, we have your Senate, we
have your armies. I am the legitimate successor ! Let who
will snatch the key from the hand of Hercules ! The prince
issues orders to the people, not the people to the prince ! "

Nothing could more clearly illustrate the resemblance and
the difference between Frederick and his grandfather. They
had in common boundless pride and arrogance, but their attitude to Rome was radically different : one was the imperial
warrior-knight, the other the imperial statesman-diplomat.
Frederick II did not for a moment question that the imperial
dignity was divinely his, having been bestowed on him by the
Senate and Roman people. He loved, on the contrary, to
recall that it was the Romans themselves who had chosen him,
who had collauded the boy of seventeen, who " in all the
anxieties of ambiguous fate was setting out to Germany to scale

the heights of imperial fame." He did not weary of repeating
that the Romans of their own motion had entrusted to him all
the offices and dignities of the Princeps according to the *lex
regia*. The deduction which he drew was that the Romans
who had spontaneously invested him with the imperial dignity
were henceforth in duty bound adequately to support their
King and Caesar, their Knight and Imperator, the *pater imperii*,
the Princeps whom they themselves had chosen. He by
no means deduced a right of the Romans to act against him.
The reward that he held out to them was a share in their
Emperor's fame and triumph, a sample of which they had
received in the spoils of victory sent by their Triumphator.
" The same *Felix Roma* who had bestowed all office and owner-
ship on the Roman Princeps must stand by him, sharing
burdens and toil, nor fail to share the honours she herself had
helped to heap on him."

Frederick II thus made the Romans sharers in his responsibility for the greatness and permanence of his Empire, and
he had yet another thought in mind. He promised fulfilment
of their ancient dreams : their wishes for the revival of the
ancient Roman power. His Caesar titles meant a great deal
to him, so did the revival of ancient forms and ceremonies, yet
" gladly though we follow the rites of old we seek yet more
eagerly to revive the ancient nobility of the City." These
words cannot be interpreted too literally or too exactly.

The old idea of *Renovatio* connoted for Frederick less the
revival of titles and ceremonies than the regeneration of the
Romans themselves, the Roman citizen and the Roman
patrician who should again be worthy to rule an Empire.
Romans had to be made anew. Frederick II could not, single-
handed, effect a re-birth of Rome and of the Empire ; could
not alone call to life a Roman State in the ancient sense. He
required the co-operation of a Roman aristocracy who had at
least as great an affinity with the Fabii, Cornelii and the Tullii
as he himself with Augustus and with Caesar. In this also he
gave the Romans a lead : " We recall the ancient Caesars to
men's minds by the ensample of our own Person ! " This was

but the first preliminary of what he sought: "That in our auspicious days the honour of the blood of Romulus may revive, the imperial Roman speech be again heard in its glory, the ancient Roman dignity renewed and an inseparable bond by our grace be tied between the Roman Empire and the Roman people themselves." To quicken the old instincts of rule and statesmanship by a share in the responsibility for the fate of the Empire, the Emperor now gave orders that Roman nobles and distinguished Roman citizens should be sent to him in order that offices of various kinds might be allotted to them. Some were to receive state offices at Court in his own immediate entourage. He would make others responsible for the conduct and administration of districts, and provinces, yet others would find a place in varied offices suited to the rank and qualifications of the individual. He summons to his service by name Proconsuls from the aristocratic families that were loyal to him, the Orsini, the Poli, the Frangipani and the Malabranca.

It was now clear what Frederick had had in mind when he invaded Lombardy. The new pan-Italian State which he was planning was going to be ruled by Romans of the blood of Romulus, the Provinces were to be governed by Roman proconsuls, as of yore the mighty Imperium Romanum had been held in leash by a small number of Roman officials. "We shall no longer delay the execution of the plan we have evolved : that to the honour and glory of Rome distinguished Romans shall preside over the business of the State and shall be resplendent in dignity." The Roman Empire, Italy, " the seat of Empire," should be for the Romans, for the blood of Romulus ! That was Frederick's idea of *Renovatio*. Once Milan had been eliminated, " the head of all dissensions in Italy," the central point and the fountain of strength in the Italian Roman state should be Rome herself. The contemporary Dominican, Bartholomew, interprets Frederick's intentions thus : Frederick wished quietly to leave in Rome the symbols of his mercy and his might, that the strength, the " virtue " might flow from the head of the world into the limbs. This implied a complete displacement of the centre of gravity of the Empire which under the olden German-Roman Emperors had been in Germany. It was more vital for Frederick to call the ancient Roman Caesar-Empire to new life from its very origins. True Roman blood should course again through the veins of the Roman Empire.

Frederick had chosen the Romans for great tasks : but they must not slumber lest they miss the flow of the tide : " Awake ! awake ! Sleep not ! " was the burden of those exhortations full of zeal and power, the aim of all this recalling of the famous deeds of ancient days. Fame, hard to earn, easy to keep, was almost lost to these Romans, so far estranged from their noble origin. The Emperor approaches them with a human touch otherwise reserved for his Apulians : now he calls them Fellow-Romans, *Conromani*, and recalls their origin from the ashes and ruins of Troy, now he harks back to the great names of old time and calls up the hosts of the *Quirites*, the tribes of Romulus, the *Patres Conscripti*, and the tens of thousands of the *Populus Romanus* : now he exhorts them to have in remembrance the triumph and the glory of their ancestors, the laurels of the conquerors, the ancient *fasti* of the Empire, the rods of the lictors.

Rome is more to him than the origin of his imperial title ; the Rome of the Caesars, like the Church herself, is his spiritual mother ; he himself the son of Rome. A son was born to Frederick in these weeks following the victory of Cortenuova. All the world was informed of this auspicious event ; the young king was celebrated " already conceived under a lucky star, whose birth has been heralded by such triumphs, which are pledges of the strength of the longed-for peace and justice that shall prevail in the Empire renewed under the ancient fasces, symbols of law and order."

The age-old revival dream of the German Emperors thus flamed up once more in Frederick, and as he sought to re-quicken not merely Roman forms (like his predecessors) but Roman life, the ancient state-life of the Romans, his *renovatio* ended by heralding the Renaissance. From the revival of the ancient State, Italy was led to the re-birth of the ancient man. Rome was to be the capital of a united Italy, and Italy herself the centre of the Roman Empire. Frederick, it is true, realised his dream only in part, but the vision never faded—Dante took it up and gave it a soul.

The poet also conceived Italia Una as the centre of the Roman Empire, as the province of provinces, not only as the realm of the Caesars but as a national Italy. Frederick had sought to re-awaken the dead Roman, but Dante to call into life the Italian people, whom Frederick for a decade had been forcibly welding into one in his imperial State. This was the cause of Frederick's great breach with the Curia, who also desired the rule over a united Italy and continued on into the period of the Borgia and Medici Popes to cherish the dream.

Frederick II was not content with securing for himself the Rome of the Caesars : he sought to win also papal Rome, and he thus kept Pope Gregory in perpetual unrest. Since the victory of Cortenuova the Pope's position seemed in any case well-nigh hopeless. He had but recently returned to Rome, and Frederick's undisguised intention of capturing Rome, his episcopal seat, followed by the intrigues amongst the Roman nobility, had hit him hard. Moreover, the concluding words of the triumphal proclamation which Frederick had addressed to the Romans contained a threat to the Curia that could not be misunderstood. The Romans should beware, he wrote, of those who saw with envy the imperial victory and pondered the destruction of the spoils ; they should carefully guard the Emperor's gift, and if necessary put their *lex plebiscita* in force which prescribed in such cases the penalty of death ! Finally, in an emotional manifesto—a copy of which was sent to the Pope—Frederick interpreted his victory over Gregory's pro-tégés the Lombards as a triumph of the Lord over Satan ! Nor was this all. Frederick II was a dangerous enemy, skilful to seek out the weak points in the armour of his foe. He formed a rallying-point for all enemies of the Papacy, and was able to find support amongst those most closely associated with Gregory : in the very college of Roman cardinals.

The relation existing between the cardinals and the Pope has very justly been compared to that borne by the German princes to the Emperor : as the Emperor was elected by the princes so the Pope was elected by the cardinals, and the Bishop of Rome was, in certain matters, as much tied by the *consilium* and *consensus* of the cardinals as the Emperor in certain circumstances by the advice and concurrence of the princes. Similarly, in the Roman Curia it depended wholly on the personality of the Pope for the time being, whether he would rule more autocratically or more constitutionally, and the cardinals opposed excessive claims of the Caesar-Popes as strenuously as the princes those of the Emperor.

Pope Gregory IX, kinsman and disciple of the great Innocent, was an autocrat in every fibre. To assure himself of a complaisant College of Cardinals he had nominated six new cardinals immediately after his elevation, men whom he knew to be wholly devoted to himself and prepared to support his policy as a whole. Individual cardinals, however, concerned for the welfare of the world and recognising a peaceful co-operation of the two powers as necessary, early began to deprecate Gregory's excessive hostility to Frederick. The Emperor was always kept well-informed about the course of affairs at the papal court. A favourite device of the Pope's was to encourage the German princes against the Emperor ; imitating this, Frederick skilfully drove a wedge into the almost invisible rift. He expressed on occasion a doubt whether the Pope had acted with the concurrence of the cardinals, and sought to play them off against their master with gradually-increasing success. As his relations with Pope Gregory grew worse over the Lombard war Frederick began more and more to make use of the cardinals, even to negotiate with them directly, over the Pope's head. In a quarrel about the allegiance of a certain Italian town he accused the Pope of having refused to restore this place to the Empire, against the advice of almost all the cardinals. He complained direct to the cardinals against the activity of the papal legate in Lombardy, and the King of England wrote to individual cardinals urging the imperial claims. The Emperor's success in arms was the ultimate cause of the final breach. Circumstances gave the verdict too plainly against Pope Gregory, and the majority of the cardinals saw with anxiety and concern the danger into which their master's intransigeance threatened to plunge the Church. The peace party, who sought an accommodation with Frederick if at all possible, gained in numbers quite apart from Frederick's wooing. John Colonna, for instance, complained to a cardinal who was residing in England that the Church had committed herself " all too violently, all too unreflectingly," to the waves . . . that no heed was paid to the dissatisfaction of the cardinals and others . . . that the advocates of peace were rebuffed, the College of Cardinals divided, and that he, the writer, had been shamelessly betrayed and left unsupported whenever he had tried to restore order. . . .

The mood prevailing in the Roman Curia was dangerous for the Pope. The condemnation of his policy by the " pillars of the Church " soon received a public confirmation which could not easily have been more annihilating. When Frederick II sent to the Roman people the Milan *carroccio*, the spoil of a victory which spelt the Pope's defeat, many cardinals of the Roman Church joined the Senate and people of Rome in escorting the standard-bearing chariot in festive procession to the Capitol, Gregory having strained every nerve to prevent its entry. They attended the solemn installation of the imperial trophy, and thus gave in some measure the Church's benediction to the ancient Roman celebration of victory. The Pope, deserted by the discontented cardinals and by the Romans, who were intoxicated by the gift from their Triumphator, was suddenly alone in Rome, " grieved unto death." This Rome the Emperor was about to make the capital of the Empire and of Italy, " as soon as we have first reduced to peace the seat of our Empire, Italy." This reduction of Italy to peace—or to subjection—could not, after the Emperor's recent successes, be far off ; to hinder it, the beginning and the end of papal policy, was scarce now possible. Yet the old man, reaching in these last years an almost eerie grandeur, indomitably daring, fate-defying, did not despair. Opportunity might come : the Emperor might trip. He waited, ready for a counter-thrust with sword and ban, to break though the fatal encirclement.

The Emperor's victory over the Lombard armies had, in fact, dissolved the League. Ten days after his triumph in Cremona Frederick was able to enter Lodi ; a little later, in January

1238, he received the submission of Vigevano at a Diet in Pavia ; soon after that the submission also of Novara and Vercelli. In February he entered Piedmont. In Turin he held a second Diet at which the nobles of these regions did him homage, Savoy, Montferrat and others. Hereupon Savona, Albenga and other towns of the Riviera were occupied, so that western Lombardy, the upper reaches of the Po, were obedient to the Emperor. The influence of the victory immediately spread southwards. The legate Gebhard effected an agreement with Florence : the Florentines dismissed their Milanese *podesta* and took instead a Roman, Angelo Malabranca, one of those proconsuls whom Frederick had designated for imperial office. Imperial Tuscany was now in Frederick's hand. " As when new waters stream into a dried-up river-bed and all the fish begin to live again, the Emperor's supporters sprang everywhere to life . . ." so spoke a chronicler on a similar occasion. The success of Frederick's arms had been potent throughout Italy for intimidation or good cheer.

The war was not yet over. No peace had yet been made with Milan. The Emperor's behaviour since the victory had stiffened instead of breaking the resisting power of this commune. Frederick imagined that a Triumphator should not stoop to treat with rebels : they must offer unconditional submission. To preserve this attitude, which was bound up with his abysmal hate of Milan he flung to the winds all political expediency. The Emperor had indeed defeated the Milanese army, and there had been severe disturbances in the city itself after the battle : the heretic rabble had stormed the churches, defiled the altars, hung the crucifixes upside down . . . but the kernel of Milan's strength, her impregnable city, was unimpaired. For the sake of peace at last Milan would have offered conditional surrender : Lodi had submitted on demand to accepting an imperial captain, to delivering hostages, and had been prepared to undertake yet other obligations. Frederick, however, appears to have rejected all suggestions from Milan, and obstinately demanded complete and unconditional surrender. The conquered must put themselves and their town unquestionably at his mercy. He sent the Milanese the equivocal oracle : he would do only what he must.

What punishment the imperial judge destined for Milan was not to be guessed at. Other towns that had surrendered at discretion Frederick had spared, displaying his imperial indulgence, but it was at least questionable whether the specially-hated Milan could count on clemency. The Milanese would not take the risk. Mindful how Barbarossa had destroyed their town, and reflecting accurately that an unconditional peace could be concluded any day, Milan rejected the Emperor's demand. They instructed their messengers to say that " their wits sharpened by experience, they feared the Emperor's savagery." Faith in their own strength and in their trusty walls enabled this single town successfully to bid defiance to the victorious Emperor. Five other towns, scattered fragments of the Lombard Confederation, followed the heroic example of Milan : Alessandria, Brescia, Piacenza in Lombardy, and Bologna and Faënza in the Romagna.

The war went on, and the Emperor was now faced with the necessity of overcoming these six towns or taking them by storm, a difficult feat, though not impossible, if Frederick had only had to do with the townsfolk. No sane political reason explains what urged the Emperor to such severity towards Milan that he would not content himself with a humiliation of the town, especially as he knew that by far his most dangerous enemy was in Rome. If Milan was his, on any terms whatsoever, the whole of Italy was his, and the Pope remained in very deed merely Bishop of Rome. But hate for rebels in general and for Milan in particular animated him, and the inexorable sternness of a judge who had come to exercise justice, and the arrogance of a victor in the first flush of triumph who saw himself a tool in the hands of Providence. These things may all have contributed to the Emperor's attitude. He had, moreover, good reason to hope that another successful campaign would break the resistance of the six remaining cities. If the imperial arms were again victorious the Pope need no longer be feared, he was dangerous only in conjunction with the Lombards.

Frederick at once set about unprecedented preparations for the new campaign. The whole world was laid under contribution to chastise the few rebellious towns. Frederick II even

begged friendly foreign monarchs for assistance, on the remarkable plea that the Lombards were attacking and endanger-
ing not so much Frederick himself as the whole principle of
monarchy.   It was usual enough for an intractable noble to
revolt against his overlord, but the Emperor was right in
detecting a far graver menace in a rebellion of his subjects the
town-dwellers, seeking independence.   " This matter touches
you and all the kings of earth," he wrote to the King of France.
" Keep open, therefore, your sharp eyes and ears and studiously take heed what encouragement to revolt would be given
to all them that would fain throw off the yoke of authority, if
the Roman Empire were to suffer loss through this kind of
insurgence."   The Lombards were for Frederick no commonplace insurgents.   He scented in their recalcitrance a principle
hostile to monarchy and majesty, pregnant with heresy which
it should be " the desire and the honour of all rulers in common
to combat and to extirpate."   Woe worth the day when such
aspiration, such craving for " abhorred freedom," confined as
yet to Italy, should flood the world !

All monarchs must stand shoulder to shoulder with reciprocal obligation to help each other against such overthrows of
the State, and, therefore, was the Emperor asking support from
the kings, not because he was himself too weak, but in order
that " sheer terror may pursue rebellious subjects far and wide
when they see that royal armies re-enforce imperial troops and
feel that in similar case imperial help will be due unto the
kings."   " Therefore, if the imperial arm," runs the message
to King Bela of Hungary, " is supported by the power of the
kings, if various allied princes are voluntarily bound together
for mutual help : then every impulse to revolt and conspiracy
will cease among the subjects.   So seriously had this increased
in the provinces of Italy that though they failed to tear up our
sovereignty by the roots, the rebels carried their vicious example
into the most remote and distant regions, more especially
amongst our neighbours ! "

It is idle to contend that Frederick missed the deeper
meaning of the Lombard insurrection.   It was precisely because he fully plumbed the danger that he at all times sought
by the natural alliance of nobility and clergy to rear a bulwark

against the emergence of the *tiers état*. Hence the emphasis he laid on his community of interest with the monarchical, aristocratic Church. He did not succeed in realising the unity of Empire and Papacy. It lived on in letters and in formulas only. To meet the menace that threatened the principle of monarchy, Frederick was, therefore, now obliged to turn to the secular rulers of Europe in default of the Church. He now sought to unite all the monarchs of the world in an alliance under the primacy of the Empire, and win them for a crusade against the unbelievers and infidels of the State and of *Justitia*. The enterprise did not lack a religious element, for the rebels were setting themselves against the reign of peace which God had willed : were, therefore, in a sense heretics. Frederick, logically, re-issued his edicts against heretics. The alliance of monarchs to combat the principle of freedom from authority which had come to birth earlier amongst the enlightened Lombards—the Alemanni at the southern base of the Alps —constituted the first SECULAR OECUMENICAL ACTION FOR POLITICAL ENDS in history : a forerunner of the coalitions of hereditary monarchs against the Jacobins.

Frederick's warning and Frederick's demand met with response. Extraordinary auxiliaries would be forthwith at his disposal, first and foremost the forces of the Empire itself which he had called up at the beginning of the year. Sicily and Germany were arming, and Diets in Turin, Cremona and Verona had set everything in motion from Burgundy to the March of Treviso. King Conrad with his German contingent reached Verona from the North in the Spring of 1238, and by the summer an enormous mass of troops had assembled, the largest and the most heterogeneous army that Frederick ever commanded. There were the mercenaries, the feudal knights and the Saracens from Sicily, King Conrad's German Knights, the forces of Florence and Tuscany, the knights of Northern Italy, warriors from imperial Lombardy, from Rome, the Marches, the Romagna, besides foot-soldiers from the imperial towns, and an army of Burgundian knights who, under the Count of Provence, were to fight for the first time in the service of the Empire. In addition to these almost all the monarchs of the world had sent auxiliaries : troops from the kings of England and of France, from King Bela of Hungary, and from the King of Castile. The eastern monarchs were not to be outdone, John Vatatzes, Emperor of Nicaea, had sent his Greeks, and the Sultan his Arabs to fight in the Emperor's armies.

This mass of troops was followed by the entire, exotic train of the imperial court, with its menagerie of strange beasts. People said that since the old days of the circus the like had not been seen in Italy, and they recalled the war-elephants of Alexander and Antiochus which they had read of. This was not the army of a Roman general in whose wake followed the thunderous tramp of well-drilled legions, but the levy of a Cosmocrator who commanded men and animals from every corner of the earth, comparable perhaps to the hordes which the mighty Persian led of old against the towns of Greece. Frederick II first led his hosts against the small, high-lying town of Brescia. A siege was contemplated, and the Emperor boasted his great stores of siege implements. He had, moreover, commandeered the services of a Spanish engineer, Calamandrinus, who was pre-eminently inventive in the construction of battering-rams and the like. Eccelino had despatched him to the Emperor : in fetters, so that he might not escape. Fate willed, however, that the captive should fall into the hands of the Brescians. They made him welcome with gifts of hearth and home and a Brescian bride, and he was forthwith employed in exercising his skill in the service of the beleaguered town against the Emperor.

The campaign had begun with this stroke of ill-luck and the Emperor sought in vain to bring about a change of fortune. In spite of successful skirmishes near Brescia, in spite of great gallantry amongst individual contingents—the English particularly distinguished themselves—the siege made no progress. Numerous assaults were made, none were successful. The missiles of Calamandrinus, which found their mark with great accuracy, destroyed the Emperor's siege equipment. In order to protect his instruments of war Frederick tied captured Brescians to his attacking towers. The townsmen showed no weak consideration for their fellow-citizens, but retaliated in similar wise on their imperial prisoners. The fighting continued savagely for weeks. After a fortnight of it, the Emperor, who had counted on the rapid victory of his immense army, opened negotiations, but the townsfolk refused to treat. A plague broke out amongst the cattle in the imperial camp, bad weather and deluges of rain made the enterprise more difficult. Frederick's peace-envoy, Bernardo Orlando di Rossi of Parma, appears to have betrayed his master : instead of persuading the Brescians to surrender he encouraged them to hold out. After two months of useless sacrifice, and a final unsuccessful attack, the Emperor finally broke off the siege in October.

The failure of this elaborate undertaking was almost equivalent to a defeat. A crisis was imminent. Frederick dismissed all his foreign auxiliaries and retained only the German knights. Success had recently emboldened the Emperor's friends, failure now offered encouragement to his foes. The Lombards perceived how strong their towns were to resist such forces, and trusted more than ever in their strength. All Italy had breathlessly awaited the outcome of the struggle, none with greater attention than Pope Gregory IX. As long as the siege of Brescia was in progress he prudently refrained from siding openly with the Lombards. He had even seemed to lean towards a reconciliation with Frederick, had sent the Minister-General of the Franciscan Order, Brother Elias of Cortona, a friend of Frederick's, to the Emperor's court with assurances that the Pope was anxious to be *unus et idem* with Frederick. Scarcely, however, was the end of the siege known than the Pope threw off his preceding restraint. Frederick II had skilfully been stirring up all anti-papal forces and gathering them round him. Pope Gregory was now able to repay him handsomely in kind.

The imperial fiasco released the Pope from an extremely unpleasant position, and in spite of his great age he developed an amazing activity. He must provide what Frederick's foes had hitherto lacked : a rallying-point and a great common idea. With fiery zeal Pope Gregory set about retrieving the delay.

The fuse had long since been surreptitiously laid.   The intimate sympathy of the Pope with the Lombard heretics, rebels
and enemies of the Emperor, was an open secret.   He now
appointed Frederick's bitterest enemy, Gregory of Montelongo, as Legate of Lombardy.   This prelate had begun his
career as a notary of the Roman Curia, and was to end it as
Patriarch of Aquileia.   He was cunning and resourceful, well-
versed in every type of political intrigue and subterfuge, and
possessed a knowledge of war unsurpassed in his day.   His
skilful manipulations succeeded in uniting all the anti-Kaiser
elements in Lombardy and reconciling the most varied interests.

His great achievement was the creation of a consolidated
opposition to the unified imperial power in Italy.   All aspira-
tions of the towns and the town parties, by whatever name they
might be called, which were hostile to the Emperor, could be
sure of his assistance, and their short-sighted and hitherto self-
centred squabblings of every kind suddenly gained dignity and
import by being associated on equal terms with a great world
idea, the Papacy.   The miscellaneous imperial enemies of
all camps and ranks and strata were no longer rebels and
revolutionaries, but champions and defenders of the oppressed
Church.   The name of " Guelf " became a general term for
all enemies of the empire under the leadership of the Church :
patrician and plebeian, heretic and orthodox, layman and priest
rallied together, so that the party division of Ghibelline and
Guelf by no means tallied with the natural, social, religious, or
national cleavages.   Very much the reverse : as people rightly
felt, the whole world was involved : no order, no town, no
rank, no family, no individual even, but was rent asunder by
the warring principles of Empire versus Papacy, as the one or
the other in turn prevailed.

The anti-imperial coalition under the Church's leadership
was not merely defensive.   Frederick II was, of course, the
challenger, because his very existence was war and battle,
though he sought peace ; but the aggressor who repudiated
every compromise, who aimed at war to the knife was, as has
been generally recognised, the hasty, hot-headed Pope Gregory.
Before he declared himself as an open enemy he had effected
in the Lateran an offensive alliance between Venice and Genoa

against the Emperor. The two maritime towns who had so
often been at war undertook to render reciprocal assistance, and
swore to make no peace with the Emperor without the Pope's
consent. The papal party, under their Milanese *podesta*, had
the upper hand in Genoa at the time, and, apart from the threat
to the Trevisan March, the Venetians were feeling peculiarly
embittered by Frederick II's treatment of their Doge's son,
who had been captured at Cortenuova, dragged in Frederick's
triumph, and was still, to the disgrace of Venice, prisoner in
an Apulian dungeon.

Pope Gregory exploited the resentment against the Emperor
to the full. When he had left the capital in July 1238 to go
to Anagni, at the very moment that the Emperor's powerful
army was marching on Brescia, Rome was almost wholly pro-
Emperor. On his return in October the papal party was
dominant once more. Pope Gregory hastily made up his mind
to breathe more securely by destroying a number of castles
belonging to the Emperor's adherents, palaces dating from
ancient Roman days that were now flying the colours of Antichrist. Their marbles and mosaics were destroyed. Later,
Frederick II commanded a Sicilian official to restore as far as
possible the ruined buildings at his expense.

Although the Pope was undisguisedly bent on war and working up for a breach he nevertheless resumed negotiations with
the Emperor, not with any intention of an agreement but to gain
time. After the Brescia failure nothing could be less opportune for Frederick than a resumption of open hostilities with
the Curia. He did all that in him lay to avoid a fresh rupture
until a new victory should have altered the situation to his
advantage. He, therefore, displayed the greatest self-restraint.
He called a halt to the organisation of the Italian State already
begun in Western Lombardy, and submitted to an enquiry
before a number of prelates. The Pope lodged a complaint
against the Emperor under fourteen heads. Though the sus-
pension of hostilities was to depend on their being disposed of
not one of them dealt with the questions at issue. From the
beginning of his arbitration Pope Gregory had deliberately
forgotten that the Lombards' support of King Henry had been
the *fons et origo* of the new strife between Court and Curia.

He had preferred to ignore the Emperor's justifiable complaints, and pick holes in the administration of Sicily. The issue was at first perfectly clear, but Pope Gregory had contrived, as of yore in the Crusade question, to conceal and distort it, and had even been able to lend a religious colour to the purely political question : who should be master in Italy.

There is little need to labour the question of the essential inevitability of the struggle. The personal courage of Pope Gregory, which led him, in spite of his age, to force his foe to battle by every means in his power, compels admiration. These means aimed at so distorting facts that the Emperor might appear to have injured the Lombards. Ultimately these methods did more harm to the Pope than to the Emperor. The fourteen points, whose enunciation was intended to mask the designs of the Curia, were completely unimportant. They dealt with the alleged oppression of churches, monasteries and clergy in Sicily, with the treatment of the Templars and Knights of St. John, with a Muslim prince whose conversion to Christianity Frederick was supposed to have hindered, and similar petty accusations which the Emperor was in many cases able to disprove. It was certainly true that his friends had stirred up disaffection in Rome against the Pope, though the Emperor skilfully excused himself : the Pope also had underlings in Rome who served his ends. Gregory only touched on the Lombard question, the core of the whole situation, casually and as a side-issue : he reproached the Emperor with allowing the cause of the Holy Land to suffer by his Lombard war— the same old complaint which two years before had stirred the German princes to indignation.

An understanding might have still been possible on all these points, especially as the Emperor promised speedy correction for Sicilian irregularities, but Gregory's whole attitude made it obvious that he did not want an understanding. Discussions grew more and more acrimonious. On the Emperor's side Hermann of Salza, the trusty peacemaker of years, began to fail. The German Grand Master had come with King Conrad's troops to Italy, already seriously ill, he was now trying to recruit his strength in enforced inactivity in Salerno. He could no longer be counted on. Meantime the air in Italy grew thunderous. Frederick's own behaviour did little to relieve the prevailing tension : as the signs of coming conflict grew plainer he gave fresh cause of offence. That October saw in Cremona the festivities that accompanied the knighting of his beloved son Enzio.

Of all the sons Enzio must have been the most like his father. Frederick himself called him " in face and figure our very image." Enzio was the son of a German lady of noble rank whom Frederick had loved in his early days as German king, and the proud, handsome boy, with his lithe body, his medium height, his long golden curls falling to his shoulders, may have well recalled the picture of the *Puer Apuliae* men might otherwise have forgotten. Well built, alert and light of foot (people even called him *falconello*), incomparably daring and fearless, the first in every fight, a hero rejoicing in danger and bearing many a wound—such is the picture that contemporaries paint.

The easy freedom and elasticity of his mind matched his agile body, and the courtly training of the day had given it full development. He was far from being so learned as his father, but he was thoroughly cultured, intellectually most receptive, and a poet to boot. Joy in life and joy in living ring from his lyrics even when the singer was in prison mourning his fate. If the father appeared as a Caesar reincarnate, something of Achilles was reborn in Enzio. A simple straightforward soldier, singer and king, the mind conjures him up seated outside the royal tent during a pause in the battle playing the harp amongst his lighthearted companions.

Enzio's unique charm, which has so often been recorded, probably lay in this natural grace and simple heartiness : his enemies even fell victims to it, and it is rare that spite or malice even graze this handsome lad, though no slander is hateful enough for the opponents to heap on the rest of the Hohenstaufens. Legends and tales were woven round this imperial son, even in his lifetime. They have an epic simplicity, happy, simple, less " profound " than the anecdotes, always a shade

uncanny and sinister, that gather round the father.   A German
dream was Enzio—such as life too rarely yields.

Hard upon Enzio's knighthood at about twenty followed his
marriage with Adelasia, the heiress of two Sardinian provinces,
by right of which he was entitled " King of Torre and Gallura,"
or King of Sardinia.   This marriage had been arranged at
Frederick's wish, but was destined to accentuate the quarrel
with the Roman Curia.   For Sardinia was reckoned a fief of
the Church which long ago Pisa and Genoa, with papal encouragement, had plucked from the hands of the Saracen.
Barbarossa, on the other hand, during his struggle with the
Papacy, had granted Sardinia in fee to the sea towns, so that
the Empire now laid claim to the island, and it became like the
Matildine inheritance, a perpetual bone of contention between
popes and emperors.   By marrying Enzio to the heiress of the
greater part of the island Frederick expected to acquire new
rights, and he was not to be turned aside by Pope Gregory's
express veto.   He had vowed, he said, to win back for the
Empire all the possessions it had lost, and the main factor in
the Pope's wrath at Enzio's marriage was, he hinted, the fact
that Pope Gregory had coveted the handsome boy for one of
his nieces.

Whatever the rights and wrongs of the case the Emperor's
procedure embittered the Pope afresh, and peace was not
easily maintained.   Frederick II repeatedly sought to re-establish good relations with the Pope.   Gregory, however, only
dallied with the Emperor's envoys, most distinguished men
like Archbishop Berard of Palermo, Count Thomas of Aquino,
Thaddeus of Suessa.   He had been long since planning a
breach.   The embassy was fruitless.   Frederick saw clearly
what was coming.   He had taken up his winter quarters in
Padua, intending a lengthy stay, and there the beginning of
1239 found him.   He was living with his court in the monastery
of Santa Justina.   It was a great honour for the monks, of
course, but no small burden, for they were expected (as were
later the monks of San Zeno in Verona) to entertain an elephant,
five leopards and twenty-four camels, as well as an emperor.

The Emperor had summoned Eccelino to Padua. His government of the Trevisan March had been threatened by the intrigues of his brother Alberigo of Romano, Azzo of Este and other nobles, who were jealous of Eccelino's growing power. The situation must have been eased a little by Frederick's arrival in person, and by his giving his daughter Selvaggia in marriage to Eccelino. Similar unrest in Parma had shortly before been quelled and peace quickly restored by Frederick's appearance on the spot, the strengthening of the imperial palace, and Frederick's taking over the office of *podesta* himself.

Frederick tried to improve matters with the Pope by reissuing his edicts against heretics, but he must have known the case was hopeless. A couple of weeks later he tried a new expedient to avert the threatening ban. He addressed himself no longer to the Pope but to the cardinals, availing himself of their divided counsels. In order to subordinate the Pope's position to the College of Cardinals Frederick evolved a remarkable new theory, in reality an old well-nigh forgotten theory revived : an expedient which later generations took up again. The Emperor recalled that the cardinals, the lights and true representatives of the Church, were also successors of the apostles. Peter had been only spokesman and executant among the apostles, not their despotic master, and similarly the Pope, as successor of Peter, was in all questions of Church policy and jurisdiction only the president and executive officer of the cardinals, his equals. Frederick thus sought to appeal to an oligarchy of the cardinals, amongst whom he had many friends, instead of to the rigid papal autocracy. It was, he wrote, the cardinals' business to avert the imminent offence. The ultimate responsibility was theirs if the Pope, whom they had elected to proclaim the gospel, chose to wield the spiritual sword in the interests of Lombard rebels and heretics against the Advocate of Rome. For their own prestige, which the Emperor highly valued, he must beg the college to dissuade the Pope from his rash enterprise ; the whole world possessed irrefutable proof that it was based on injustice and domineering caprice. The cardinals who shared responsibility for whatever occurred would feel his imperial vengeance : he would have to take steps against them, for neither this Pope himself nor his kin were worthy that the illustrious Empire should waste attention on him or them. Frederick II was already dubbing the Pope " unworthy." He himself, he added menacingly, was willing to bear injustice from the Holy Father, but actual violence he would requite with the measures " which Caesars are wont to use."

This ambitious document was the Emperor's last attempt to preserve peace by threat. He knew exactly what was now at stake. Deposition and excommunication awaited him as soon as the breach with Pope Gregory should come. He had no further power to influence the Pope's decisions. Things must take their course. He could do nothing but outwardly preserve an unruffled calm. No one could have divined from his manner of life the weight of the burden that lay on the whole court. Those were many care-free days—to all appearance—which he spent in Padua. Banquets and hunting parties succeeded each other, and when on Palm Sunday the Paduans, in accordance with ancient custom, were making merry on the town common with every sort of sport the Emperor appeared among them. From his raised seat as from a throne he watched the proceedings with cheerful good-fellowship, while Piero della Vigna made one of his magnificent speeches, in which he dwelt specially on the Emperor's affection and goodwill towards the people of Padua. None could have guessed that at that very moment the Pope's ban had fallen. Frederick's letter to the cardinals, from which he had expected great things, arrived too late. It is quite possible that the Pope had got wind of it, and fearful perhaps of the cardinals' intervention, had anticipated Maundy Thursday, which was the usual opportunity for proclaiming excommunications. Determined to postpone the fight no longer he acted swiftly, perhaps over-hastily.

On that same Sunday, while Frederick in Padua was watching the amusements of the people, Gregory IX excommunicated the Emperor for the second time. From henceforth at every High Mass, in every church throughout the world, every priest, to the accompaniment of bell and of burning tapers, should proclaim Frederick's extrusion from the community of the faithful. Simultaneously all subjects of Frederick were released from their oaths of fealty. Not one syllable of Gregory's pronouncement hinted that the Lombards had been the cause of strife : the whole cause of the ban was sought in the Sicilian differences.

The die was cast. By a fateful coincidence the great German Grand Master, Hermann of Salza, died on that Palm Sunday in Salerno. His life had been devoted to preserving the unity of Empire and Papacy. It had lost all meaning. The ideal picture of a Pope and Emperor perfectly balanced and perfectly united in a perfectly-organised world, that had floated before the mind of Europe for centuries, was shattered for ever. The ruthless, savage combat *à outrance* between the two powers began, though the monstrous strife that overstrained the strength of both antagonists, and in a few years devoured the hoarded wealth of centuries, was destined to remain indecisive. The Interregnum and Avignon are the graves of the Middle Ages and of Christian world dominance.

When the news of the excommunication reached the Emperor in Padua a week later there was a moment of consternation. Frederick summoned the Paduans to the town-hall. Piero della Vigna had to address them a second time in the name of the Emperor, and scarcely had he ceased speaking than, to the amazement of the people, the monarch himself lifted up his voice from his elevated seat to defend himself against the precipitate action of the Pope. The tension was relieved. The Emperor quitted Padua. The paralysing uncertainty that had condemned him to inactivity during the leaden-footed months of suspense was ended, and was replaced in the twinkling of an eye by an almost feverish activity. He could now develop without let or hindrance. In those last months of oppressive strain, when everything had to be done with the utmost silence and caution, Piero della Vigna had warned the Grand Justiciar of Sicily to beware of irritating the sensitiveness of the Roman Curia by any measure not expressly sanctioned by the Emperor, lest he should thereby pour oil on the fire and set the whole of Italy ablaze. No such consideration now prevailed. The long-dammed wrath burst forth. The Emperor addressed the world in thunderous manifestos and pamphlets full of passion, provoking thereby from the Curia reproaches and retorts not less vehement. These were the flourishes of the trumpets before the battle. Actions soon succeeded each other headlong. Frederick at last was free to develop all his rich resources in their full magnificence.

To turn to the fighting.... The campaign against the Lombard rebels had become a side issue. In spite of it an unprecedented work of reorganisation was accomplished within a few months. Hither and thither, to and fro, in every direction Frederick crossed and re-crossed Northern Italy. The announcement of the ban had cheered the rebels, the Curia intrigued through its legates everywhere, and conflagrations were breaking out in various places. Frederick hastened from Padua to Treviso, then back to Padua, and off again to Vicenza to make sure of the nobles of the Trevisan March who, under Margrave Azzo of Este, Eccelino's enemy, were inclined to quit the Emperor's cause. The Emperor could do little to prevent it. The Margrave, who had recently sworn good faith, betrayed him. In the middle of May Treviso was surprised, and the imperial *podesta*, Jacob of Morra, driven out. In the middle of June Azzo of Este went over to the enemy, and other nobles with him. A solemn session was held in Verona, and Piero della Vigna, seated on horseback, was commanded to proclaim the imperial ban against them.

At the end of June the hitherto completely loyal town of Ravenna suddenly seceded. The Emperor himself hastened to Cremona, where Cardinal Sinibald Fiesco, later Pope Innocent IV, had stirred up the people, and Paulus Traversarius, *podesta* of Ravenna, had driven out the Emperor's adherents, though his only daughter was said to be a hostage in the Emperor's hands. The protection of Ravenna had been entrusted to Bologna and to Venice. Frederick rapidly marched out from Cremona into the Romagna for a campaign against the Bolognese. The territories without the town were laid waste, and two fortresses, Piumazzo and Crevalcore, were conquered within a fortnight. By the end of August the Emperor was again in Parma, where signs of unrest had shown themselves the year before, and, finally, from mid-September till the beginning of November, he was prosecuting the war under circumstances of the gravest difficulty against Milan and against Piacenza, the Curia's latest ally. Frederick had no intention of trying actually to take these towns any more than Bologna. He had no time for long-drawn sieges. He had weightier tasks in hand.

He did his best to compel the town troops to accept battle in the open. If they evaded it he wasted their town lands, which caused them sensible loss. He did not succeed, however, as with his considerable superiority in force he had doubtless hoped, in repeating Cortenuova. Each time he advanced against Milan, after conquering and burning down several fortresses on various sides, the Milanese simply gave way or retreated to their town under cover of trenches and hastily drained water-courses. Frederick was in this way successful in inducing Como and some neighbouring towns to forsake the Milanese and come over to his side. This was an important gain, for Como was " the key to the passage from Germany to Italy," as the Emperor wrote to King Conrad. The Julier and Septimer Passes, and possibly the St. Gothard also, were now open to him as well as the Brenner. Just before the onset of winter, Frederick had hastily undertaken a new venture, the capture of a new bridge-head which Piacenza had recently built on the Po. Continuous rain fell for days, the Po flooded its banks, the bridge-head was inaccessible, and the effort had to be abandoned.

The fighting had only just begun, the Emperor was still in the Bologna terrain, when the Curia compelled him to turn his thoughts to other things. The alliance which Pope Gregory had engineered between Venice and Genoa was widened by the inclusion of Piacenza and Milan, and, finally, of the Roman Curia itself. The agreement was that none of the contracting parties, not even the Pope, should make peace with the Emperor without the concurrence of the others, and, further, that Venice and Genoa should land troops—their own and the Pope's—in Sicily. A great attack on Sicily, the basis of the imperial power, was planned. They reckoned that six months would suffice for the campaign, and the distribution of the spoils had been agreed upon.   The Pope would keep the whole kingdom *quod est beati Petri patrimonium*.   Venice would be rewarded by the harbours of Barletta and Salpi, and Genoa by the restoration of her bitterly-mourned Syracuse, and both should receive compensation in other ways also for their expenses.   This was the programme of the group of compact allies whom Frederick had now to face.

The Emperor saw his Sicilian kingdom gravely imperilled. Even if he was at first unacquainted with these secret arrangements, which is most unlikely, he must from his previous experience have been fully prepared for the invasion of Sicily by a papal army as soon as one had been mustered.   He could not break off the war in Northern Italy, but he must seek at the same time so to secure his territories on every side that they would be strong enough not only to ward off attack but to pursue the even tenor of their way.   Sicily must surpass her previous achievements in raising money and war-material. Complete reorganisation was necessary to put the kingdom on a war footing, for the country was at the moment being governed by a Council of the Household Officers (consisting of the Grand Justiciar Henry of Morra, Count Thomas of Aquino, the Archbishop Berard of Palermo and two other prelates) to whom Frederick had entrusted the regency during his absence.   This independent council would no longer be serviceable.   The outbreak of war with the Church involved Sicily's meeting the ever-varying demands of the Emperor fighting in the North, in addition to her own normal requirements.   The Council could not divine what Frederick's needs might be.   The Emperor must, therefore, resume the direct government of Sicily himself.

One difficulty of his doing so was that since he had left his hereditary dominions for Germany nearly five years before he had not set foot in them again ; another, that he could not for the present dream of returning ; and, finally, that the communications with Sicily by land were still severed by the Papal State.   The reorganisation and mobilisation of Sicily had, therefore, to be conducted under circumstances of the utmost difficulty in accordance with instructions sent by the Emperor from North Italy.   Nothing but the well-planned, well-oiled machinery of the Sicilian State made this possible.

It was soon manifest what the will of one individual could accomplish in a minimum of time when backed by a brilliantly drilled, unspoiled bureaucracy, working at high presssure. The Household Officers were superseded, the central authorities of Sicily : Administration, Justice, Chancery, were linked up directly with the Court, as it hastened to and fro in North Italy from one battle to another.   Earlier pledges to the Curia to keep the administration of Sicily separate from that of the Empire were no longer binding.   There was now one uniform imperial administration, one Supreme Court, one common imperial Chancery, one imperial Treasury ; no longer a Sicilian, but an Imperial Fleet, under an Imperial Admiral.   The highest official of Sicily, the Grand Justiciar, Henry of Morra, could no longer represent the Emperor in Sicily, because his permanent presence with the Court was necessary.   In order that the justiciars might not, meanwhile, lack supervision, the Sicilian justiciarates were divided into two groups, each of which was under a Captain or Grand Justiciar : peninsular Sicily, under the tried and trusty Andrew of Cicala, who frequently submitted independent suggestions to the Emperor ; island Sicily, under Roger de Amicis, already well known as one of the poets.   To avoid " confusion of numbers " and " permanence of appointments " the number and the tenure of the officials was normalised for each province on the simplest possible basis : one Justiciar, one High Treasurer ; with each Justiciar, one Judge and one Notary ; all with tenure for one year only.   The kingdom had, therefore, a tighter grip than ever on its officials ; the constitutional structure was more symmetrical, more rigid, more transparent than ever.   It is to this period that Frederick's phrase belongs : " Sicily shall be the envy of princes, the pattern of monarchies "—*invidia principum et norma regnorum.*

The entire Sicilian administration was now centred in the Emperor's court in Northern Italy.   The burden was lifted from Frederick's shoulders by the Chancery, which was admirably organised under its two heads : Piero della Vigna and Thaddeus of Suessa.   The mass of work to be dealt with was stupendous. All orders had necessarily to be in writing. All imperial instructions had to be issued through the Chancery, which, therefore, had to follow the Emperor hither and thither in all his campaigning, whether his headquarters were in town or camp. Not for a day was the flow of orders interrupted. The name and date on the documents show that on marching days the Chancery worked all morning till the moment of starting, and resumed work immediately on arrival. The notaries had countless other business to attend to, since the Sicilian and Imperial Chanceries were not amalgamated. When we reflect that dozens of written orders of every description were issued daily (some days up to thirty or forty or even more) all drafted in careful style, all in two or three copies ; that there were in addition constant circulars to the Justiciars, we get some idea of the labour which fell on the six or eight writers and six or eight transmitters. In these days of crisis all work must have been done at the highest possible pressure and at a speed that contrasts with the leisureliness of earlier Chanceries.

The Emperor showed not the smallest compunction about overworking his secretaries : at least one-third of the orders issued were concerned solely with his personal hobbies : horses, hounds, falcons, and the chase. Frederick, however, truly said that he worked night and day, and that " his majesty, ever ware and waking, slumbered not neither slept." The characteristic of the new life was speed : its watchword : *non sit quiescendum*, *continue sit agendum*, and the whirring pace of the court corresponded. The courtiers streamed in and out unceasingly, mostly Sicilian messengers. The land route through the papal patrimonium was for the most part unsafe—the greatest caution was enjoined on all who used it—and a sort of express service was arranged by sea from Pisa to Naples. Pisan galleys, imperial galleys, and swift sailing yachts were utilised. Troops, corn, cash, and courtiers with important despatches were sent to and fro by sea, and depots established at Naples and Pisa. The swift conveyance of despatches was highly prized, and officials reaped rich rewards for speed. To deal the more rapidly with the whole, the subordinate personnel and the writing staff were increased.

The prime necessity was to secure Sicily against attack. All the important fortresses, which in peace time were garrisoned by one chatelain and a few men, were well manned, partly by mercenaries, partly by fiefholders. Monte Cassino, for instance, near the papal frontier, was allotted one hundred men, other castles were speedily equipped with cross-bowmen and missile-throwing engines. Every means was taken to get possession of important fortresses. Prudence must be exercised and scandal avoided, but Castle Cerro must here be taken over, and there certain border strongholds in the Abruzzi which belonged to a Sicilian knight or abbot. The participation of Genoa and Venice in the war gave increased importance to coast defence. The watching towers, which were always manned against pirates during the shipping season, were more strongly garrisoned, and the construction of coast castles at Bari, Trani, and Otranto was expedited.

As a preliminary to all other measures the entire kingdom must be bolted and barred and transformed into a single mighty fortress. The frontiers throughout Sicily were rigidly closed. Every communication with the enemy was dangerous and must be prevented. People wishing to enter the kingdom needed a passport. The Emperor would permit no stranger to travel, buy or sell in his territories unless he bore on his right hand the mark and the number of his name, till enemies made merry about the passport regulations. Ships might only enter certain specified harbours ; even to enable merchants more conveniently to load or unload, no exception was permitted. The ships arriving in harbour were strictly searched by imperial officials, the crew and passengers minutely cross-examined— the birthplace of each, whence he came, whither he was going and why. None might leave the ship before the examination, none might leave the kingdom without the Emperor's permission. Above all, papers and letters were forbidden. To bring a letter into Sicily required the imperial permission in each separate case. If such permission had not been obtained the bearer was hanged.

All communication with Rome was strictly forbidden. A man from Caserta was carrying a perfectly harmless letter from the Pope about a benefice for his son. He was imprisoned and his property confiscated " on account of his audacity." A non-Sicilian bishop who had some important documents to hand over was instructed to deliver them to the Justiciar at the frontier, but not to set foot in the kingdom. The Emperor sought above all to prevent the intellectual poisoning of his hereditary domains. Hence, students from the rebel towns were forbidden to study in Naples.

Concurrently with the sealing up of Sicily against the outer world the country itself had to be cleansed of suspicious elements. Within a few weeeks of the Emperor's excommunication the necessary orders were issued relative to suspect Sicilian clergy. The mendicant friars, the Pope's favourite spies and agents for stirring up insurrection, were expelled. At first only those who were natives of the rebellious towns were banished, later all without discrimination. The lands of the non-Sicilian clerics were confiscated. No priest might go to Rome without the Emperor's orders. The loyal Sicilian clerics who happened to be in Rome on any business must return to Sicily without a moment's delay, on pain of losing their possessions and forfeiting the right of subsequent return.

In addition to all this the justiciars were instructed to assemble all the bishops and clerics of their province and to tell them in the name of the Emperor : the Emperor wished the services of the Church to be continued, in spite of the papal ban ; no priest would be compelled to celebrate High Mass, but if any pretermitted the services the worldly possessions of his Church would be forfeit. Further, the omission to conduct service was considered suspicious, a sign that the priest was more ready to obey Pope than Emperor, and this often sufficed to lead to banishment or the gallows. There was a humble cleric who had begged the Emperor to grant a rescript making his bastard sons legitimate. When the document came he whimpered that now perhaps the Emperor's excommunication would invalidate it. Frederick banished him " for his shameless impudence " and confiscated his property.

Pope Gregory had complained about the oppression of the Sicilian clergy, and professed to have excommunicated the Emperor on this account. Frederick now gave him some oppression to complain about. Since he had had his first quarrel with the

great Innocent as a boy of fourteen, the Emperor's desire had
been to build up in Sicily an episcopate independent of Rome.
He could now proceed to do so without remorse. Amongst
some one hundred and forty-five sees in the Sicilian kingdom
there were at the moment thirty-five vacancies. These were
either left vacant or filled by trusty supporters of Frederick,
here a notary, there a nephew of the chamberlain Richard, in
another see another loyalist. Archbishop Berard of Palermo,
who as the most faithful adherent of Frederick, had also been
excommunicated, became the head of the Sicilian Church.
Rome had here lost all weight, and the longer the ban lasted
the more unimportant she became. A priest who applied for
a bishopric without the Emperor's leave was called on to answer
for it to the Court. The sternest watch was kept to see that
all imperial orders were carried out.

By such measures the Sicilian Church was rapidly purged.
All who remained were loyal to the Emperor, and the future
proved them completely trustworthy. A large number of
bishops had first to be got rid of on the most various grounds :
unquestionably all who had sided with the Pope in Frederick's
first breach over the Crusade. In this matter the Emperor
dealt out banishment and confiscation of property to clergy and
laity alike. The justiciars were ceaselessly commissioned to
investigate all cases against suspects of this sort, and the little
notebook which all suspects were obliged to carry about with
them must have considerably lightened the task of the officials.
The feudal nobility who had participated in the rebellion of
1229 were mercilessly banished with their families. As
Frederick punished all relatives of heretics to the second
generation " that they might know God to be a jealous God,
visiting the sins of the fathers upon the children," so he turned
out the relatives of the rebels whether clerics or laymen. The
measures adopted towards the feudal nobility were, however,
varied. Some of them were despatched to join the imperial
armies in Lombardy and some shipped off to the army
in Palestine. Pope Gregory had already complained that
Frederick was misusing his sacred kingdom of Jerusalem as a
penal settlement for political criminals and suspects, and the
process naturally did not now cease. A knight who had quitted

the Syrian army without permission was imprisoned. Another who had left the Court without leave shared his fate, while a third for similar reasons was sent in chains to Malta. In such cases the Emperor also banished the families of the exiles, while, on the other hand, he held the families of his own supporters as hostages for their good faith. The instructions to send fighting men or subordinate officials to Italy " who are of loyal stock and who have brothers and sons in Sicily " becomes a recurrent formula. These were then his hostages on whom he could if necessary wreak vengeance. He had a sufficient number of hostages from every town, and it is to be understood that he never hesitated a moment to avenge himself on them. When the Venetians gave him trouble he immediately hanged the Doge's son, Pietro Tiepolo. He is said to have burnt the daughter of Paulus Traversarius, the renegade *podesta* of Ravenna. When an opportunity offered to take Pope Gregory's brother prisoner Frederick immediately responded and wrote that the proposal pleased him and would please him still better if successfully carried out : the official in question could not render him a more welcome service. He is alleged—but the accusation is probably unfounded—to have hanged all Pope Gregory's blood relations. He admitted himself that he hated the whole " breed."

This system undoubtedly breathed immense suspicion and mistrust. But Frederick II would have been lost without these qualities, which he shares with every great man whose position has been equally precarious. It was the Tyranny in action, but it is impossible to conceive Sicily or Italy without tyrants. Under this system denunciation flourished more and more luxuriantly, which had both drawbacks and advantages. The accusers were frequently prompted by purely personal spite (a blood feud, for instance, once entered into the matter), but each case had to be exactly investigated. In this process all sorts of facts came to light, even corruption and deceit on the part of the officials who, especially in the later phases, frequently allowed themselves to be bought off by the accused. These denunciations were part and parcel of the secret service which the Emperor urgently required. " I have messengers and envoys everywhere, and hear all that is going on," Frederick once stated to the General of the Dominicans.   It was perfectly true that he enjoyed that omniscience which goes with greatness.   From his camp before the walls of Milan he was able to inform the justiciar of the Abruzzi that a number of people quoted by name had secretly exchanged gifts with the rebels. Would the official kindly look into the matter and hang the guilty " as a punishment for themselves and as a terror to others."   At about the same time he pointed out to the justiciar of the Terra Laboris that a Capuan from his province was resident in Rome : his property should be sequestrated.   He learnt that certain Templars in disguise were bringing moneys to assist the rebels : he begged the Grand Master of the Order to put a stop to this.

His purification of the kingdom would have been incomplete if he had not eliminated the papal enclave at Benevento.   As the focus of the Curia's hostile propaganda, whence resistance to the Emperor was organised, Benevento must have been in very deed " a stone of stumbling and a rock of offence." Numerous Sicilians who were adherents of the Pope had taken refuge there till Frederick finally commanded that no one should be allowed to return from Benevento into Sicily, the town should be besieged, all exit prevented, and all supplies cut off.   " May she perish of hunger and rot in the pestilent freedom she herself has chosen. . . ."   In 1241 Benevento was completely destroyed.

By such measures the security of Sicily, internal and external, was assured in the shortest possible time.   The kingdom was not only to enjoy peace but to employ its peace to find money and war-material for the Emperor.   Again and again he wrote that his coffers were empty and he needed money.   He had already raised loans in every direction at incredible rates of interest : in Siena, in Parma, from a certain Henry Baum, merchant of Vienna, and especially from the Romans.   He may have had a political motive in applying to them.   It was useful to make the widest circles possible interested in the success of the imperial arms.   If the Emperor failed, the Roman creditors would stand a good chance of losing their money.   The merchants thus harnessed to the Emperor's fortunes could help in many ways to forward his Roman plans. There were many small groups of three or four merchants who combined to advance a couple of hundred ounces, an ounce of gold being approximately two and a half guineas. The total number of ounces borrowed from Rome ran into tens of thousands, so that a proportionate number of merchants were involved : from one statement of accounts alone we learn close on eighty names of creditors.

The Emperor's need of money, if only to pay his mercenaries, had grown immense. This is where Sicily had to help. First a new tax was instituted from which neither clergy nor officials were, as heretofore, exempt. New coins were struck, which did not, however, necessarily imply any debasement of the currency. The old coins had to be exchanged for new, and the commission charged for the exchange brought in appreciable sums, since money-changing was a state monopoly. The Emperor gave orders that the precise proportion of alloy in the new coins was to be kept secret so that foreign merchants might not assess them solely on their intrinsic metal value.

The Emperor further called in without exception all arrears of taxes due. According to old law the incomes of all vacant bishops' sees flowed direct into the coffers of the State except so far as they were expended on the upkeep of the churches. On financial grounds the Emperor was not unduly keen on new appointments, though political considerations sometimes outweighed economic ones. The whole financial administration was now more strictly organised. A Court of Exchequer was set up in Melfi, and all officials had to submit their accounts back to the year 1220. The entire official expenditure of the past twenty years was carefully re-examined, and the officials were personally liable to make good any deficit out of their private means. All balances in hand were simultaneously checked. In addition, the Emperor commissioned an expert to seek for buried treasure.

The Emperor's trade in corn was a further source of revenue. His transactions were extensive. That shipment to Tunis which brought in almost £75,000 had been arranged from Lodi. The Emperor raised large sums in Vienna in exchange for mere orders on Sicilian corn. The galleys which conveyed Lombard prisoners from Pisa to Apulia were instructed to use their empty space to bring back corn on their return. Part of this supplied the army's needs and part was sold to the Pisans, though the Emperor did not want to profiteer at the expense of that loyal town. He had no scruple on the other hand about making money out of the Venetians. For, although he was at war with them, the Emperor did not want to lose a paying customer, and he permitted the export of provisions to Venice, "but prudently, so that it may not appear a general permission." The Venetians had equally little scruple in buying from "the enemy." The Genoese were at first also allowed to use Sicilian harbours. Under strict supervision this involved little danger to the Emperor, but later all trade with both towns was forbidden. The State also made money out of pilgrims : one-third of the fare to Syria had to be paid into the Treasury. All sale of horses out of the country was strictly forbidden. Mention has already been made of the great workshops which manufactured armour and equipment ; they were kept working at full pressure.

All the resources of Sicily were now strained to supply the Emperor with what he needed for the Italian war. Thanks to the efficient and well-disciplined officials the entire reorganisation of the kingdom was possible, without any serious hitch, in spite of the absence of the ruler. But the Emperor could not leave the pick of his younger officials in Sicily : he wanted large numbers for Italy. Sicily began to suffer the fate that always overtakes the homeland of a conqueror : she was unduly drained of strength which served the monarch's world dominion but not the State herself. Frederick II had had, as a young Emperor, to reconquer his ruined kingdom ; during his lawgiving period he had shown himself in wonderful harmony with his new-created State ; now, as Caesar, he had far outgrown the State in which he had his roots, and he now drew means and might from her to overcome and harmonise the larger world without. With other rulers of the same calibre that would have meant at his age an overflowing into distant regions : Frederick II's case was different. His world-empire was Italy, and he poured means and men not into distant lands but into the core of the ancient *imperium* which more and more sucked the life-blood of the universe.

At the same uncanny speed and in the same masterful fashion the Grand Seignory of Italy was now established whose capital was to be Rome. Soon after his excommunication Frederick announced " our heart yearns to see Italy re-established under the imperial banner." No further consideration need be extended to the Pope. As priest Gregory had excommunicated the Emperor ; as Italian prince and Ruler of the States of the Church he had declared war by allying himself with Venice, Genoa and the rest ; Frederick could, without scruple, extend the boundaries of his Italian domain even further than he had originally intended. There was no need for tenderness towards the States of the Church, least of all the two imperial provinces, the March of Ancona and Spoleto which Frederick had been compelled as a boy to renounce, and which most inconveniently barred his passage from Italy to Sicily. Frederick declared these two " natural provinces of the Empire " confiscate, and in accordance with Roman law justified this resumption of the two districts of which a gift had been made to the Pope, by the simple phrase " ingratitude of the recipient." By the time that Frederick made this announcement the organisation of the new realm was already well under way.

The creative construction was speedy, thorough and drastic ; within a few months, lo ! the State stood there complete. It usually required decades if not centuries during the Middle Ages for much slighter reconstructions gradually to work themselves out. Frederick II suddenly evolved a new, rational constitution for Italy and carried it through at one swoop. It is true that certain preliminaries had been disposed of some years before. At the Diet of Turin, immediately after the victory of Cortenuova which opened Italy to him, Frederick had instituted the first Vicariate General or Captaincy General (the new provinces were called by either name and their governors were either Vicars General or Captains General). This was the province known as " Upper Pavia," which embraced West Lombardy and Piedmont. The main work was done now, however, as a counter measure to the Pope's attack.

The excommunication silenced the last of Frederick's scruples, and he immediately completed, with the utmost speed, what he had already begun. His hasty journeys to and fro through Italy were not only campaigns against the rebels : wherever he appeared a new province sprang, fully organised, to life. The news of the excommunication reached him in Padua at the beginning of April 1239. On May 1st he inaugurated the Vicariate General of the Trevisan March, in June, probably during his stay in Cremona, that of " Lower Pavia " with Cremona roughly as its centre. The kingdom of Burgundy was at the same time constituted a Vicariate General and incorporated into the Italian system, though less strictly dragooned than the other provinces. Still in that same June, at the time of the Bologna campaign, Frederick added the Romagna to the others, first as an immediate Vicariate and later as a Vicariate General. The campaign against Piacenza and Milan caused a short interruption till a successful winter campaign opened central Italy. Under circumstances similar to the Romagna's Frederick in December 1239 incorporated the Ligurian coast province under the name of the " Lunigiana " ; this was later enlarged by the addition of the Versiglia and Garfagnana, and raised to the rank of a Vicariate General. In January 1240 the Vicariate General of Tuscany followed, and in the same month two further creations, that of the Ancona March and of the Duchy of Spoleto. In February the conquered portions of the States of the Church, papal Tuscany, in particular, with Viterbo as its centre, were formed into a Vicariate General, " from Amelia through the Maritima to Corneto." A year later Frederick created the province of Narni also from Church territory. If we add to these the two new provinces of Sicily which adjoined on the South we find the whole of Italy, with the exception of a few remaining fragments of the Patrimonium and the few rebel towns, clearly and consistently organised in one solid block, and working under one unified imperial administration ruled by the iron will of the Italian Super-Tyrant.

The whole organism of this State, which the excommunicate

Emperor had fashioned under war conditions, was fluid and elastic for all its massiveness and solidity, and according to the fortunes of war or other needs could be regrouped as necessary. The large Captaincies General like Tuscany, Upper Pavia and others were subdivided as required into Captaincies, somewhat as the justiciars' provinces were. The new State was fashioned with some exactness on the Sicilian model, only the new creation was incomparably more powerful. Beside the mighty machinery of this imperial State Sicily appeared like some finely chiselled toy. A few indications will reveal the character of the world-monarchy that was enshrined in Italy.

Every great man meets sooner or later with world opposition, a united resistance from the peoples who feel themselves threatened. Frederick II met this coalition of hostile powers not on the periphery of his domains, on the unthreatened frontiers of the Roman Empire, but in its innermost recesses in the Caesar-Papacy and the Lombard towns. He had to operate with all the human and material resources of his outlying lands and peoples, even seeking support from foreign kings in East and West, in order to consolidate the universal state in the very centre of his Empire. The narrow compass of Italy saw the concentration and accumulation of these forces. This is the beginning of that concentration of a maximum of might in a minimum of space which characterises the Renaissance. In the centre of it all towered Rome, the capital of the world, the goal desired. Centering on Rome there arises that unique Super-seignory of Italy which shows in incredible concentration all the characteristics of a world-empire like Napoleon's. Dignity and importance were lent to this creation of a State by the passion and intensity with which the hostile powers organised their opposition, in whose despite Frederick II succeeded in establishing his despotism in its naked simplicity and grandeur.

The spirit of the new State was akin to that of the Sicilian Tyranny ; the commissions of the officials expressed the same state philosophy and doctrines of salvation ; but apart from such byelaws as the organisation of the bureaucracy rendered necessary there was no need for fresh legislation. Frederick II's Grand Seignory revived the Imperium Romanum, Italy was to live again under the standards of the Caesars ; it was axiomatic that Roman law should rule in the new Roman provinces.

The Italian towns had long ago adopted and administered Roman law. The new event was that a great State, fulfilled with the spirit of the Roman law, had come again to birth in the very heart of the Empire ; that the provinces of Italy were again parts of a monumental whole which a new Caesar, with his officials, held firmly in his grip ; that a new Augustus again administered justice according to ancient formulas, from whose rule the salvation of the world should spring. The *Renovatio Imperii Romanorum* had been accomplished on Italian soil. Frederick II had quietly abandoned his first intention of filling all the provincial governorships with Romans " of the blood of Romulus." Handicapped by the papal ban he needed the most trustworthy agents he could command, and only Sicily supplied them.

The new government had been speedily and drastically introduced, its strict and exact operation was no less drastic. There was no existing constitution to which it could be linked, as there had been in Sicily, so existing institutions had for the most part simply to be swept away. Imperial authority in Italy had hitherto been exercised solely through the imperial legates, invariably German bishops and German nobles. There had originally been one single legate only for the whole of Italy, but as early as 1222 Frederick II had divided this unmanageably large district into two legations, one for Northern and one for Central Italy. These German imperial legates with wide powers and long terms of office enjoyed considerable independence, but their influence was nevertheless limited by having no substructure of subordinate officials. They floated vaguely as it were in space. There was no place for them in the new efficient intensive administration of the Emperor, and they were abolished. Their wide districts were broken up into the various Vicariates General, which permitted firm and immediate action. Instead of the independent legate, representative of the Emperor, dependent officials were installed to be the Emperor's executive officers, probably enjoying the civil and military powers of a justiciar. Finally, instead of the lengthy tenure of office which had been the prerogative of the legation, the short term usual in Sicily was introduced even for Vicars General, and exchange of officers was frequent, if not invariable, to avoid any fraternisation with the ruled. When these imperial officials were posted as *podestas* in an important town the town was most strictly forbidden to elect a successor at the expiry of their year of office, as had been the Italian custom.

The old title of Legate was preserved in one case only : King Enzio was styled Legate General for the whole of Italy. He was tied to no province, but free to act where circumstances made action desirable. He was the Emperor's viceroy. Frederick was thus able simply to double throughout Italy the influence of his presence and personality by his son, his " living image." Enzio was placed over the Vicars General, who had to accept his orders as his father's, though they derived their authority like Enzio himself direct from the Emperor and not through the Legate General.

With few exceptions the appointment of officials even of the lowest grades was reserved for the Emperor alone. This was in Italy as in Sicily the basis of Frederick's absolute monarchy. Through the length and breadth of Italy the will of the Emperor must be supreme down to the lowest strata in the State. There was no room in the imperial State for independently elected authorities, whether feudal or municipal. Henceforward, with due allowance for varying local conditions, one uniform imperial administration was to prevail. Marches and Palatinates were as far as possible incorporated in the Empire, especially if their holders were disaffected. Many of the great nobles, especially in the North, were given office in the service of the State. The rights of feudal lords and the rights of towns, however, were recognised only with reservations, and only in so far as they did not run counter to the general organisation of the State. The custom which the Communes had had of choosing from a friendly town an independent *podesta* for themselves had now to be given up. The annual governor of the more important towns was now appointed by the Emperor from amongst the Vicars General, or else the Emperor took the post in his own name and appointed a representative. Here and there the right of electing a *podesta* was conceded, but hedged by such restrictions that in fact the actual choice was the Emperor's. No loophole was left by which a *podesta* could be elected who was not *persona grata* to the Emperor.

Frederick II had thus in a short time extended his imperial bureaucracy over the whole of Italy. In addition to the Vicars General and imperial *podestas* an army of sub-vicars, fortress-captains, finance officials, judicial and chancery officers, and various subordinates held the country in subjection. The official discipline was as usual extremely severe. To facilitate supervision the Vicars General were obliged to submit lists of all posts vacant in their provinces, and also salary-lists. For the officials were paid direct from Frederick's treasury or else from the revenues of the towns entrusted to them, but subject to fixed standards. Officials were instructed to be satisfied with their salary, to keep their hands clean and to avoid simony, which was sternly penalised. An official hierarchy was established throughout Italy in opposition to, or more accurately in supersession of, the clerical hierarchy. The position of Church and episcopate was unambiguous : the Caesar accursed of the Church had created the State, and no writ but his could run therein.

The most radical change was in the personnel itself of the new government. Hitherto the imperial services in Italy had employed one or two German legates, and the government of the towns had been directed by *podestas* from the aristocracy of Northern Italy. Suddenly a horde of Apulians flooded the country. Every stratum of the service was mainly, if not wholly, staffed by Apulians experienced in the work, whose loyalty was guaranteed by the property and families they had left behind in Sicily. The students of Bologna taunted the cities whose internal dissensions had brought them to such a pass that " they must render tribute to Caesar and weep under the Apulian yoke." It was a foreign rule—but the rule of South Italians, not of Germans—which spread through the land. With the exception of the two quondam pages, the Hohenburg brothers, who were appointed to governorships, no

German had any share in the administration. The two Hohenburgs, like the Apulian nobles, had been schooled in the Emperor's immediate entourage, and Frederick now made the general pronouncement that he was entrusting these important offices for choice to those who had grown up at his own Court " because they are moved to accept the provinces entrusted to them by their zeal for our imperial honour." Everything now hung on the utter trustworthiness, the personal loyalty and the blind obedience of the officials, since the Church by releasing all subjects from their allegiance to the Emperor invited them to disloyalty, and, indeed, rewarded it by benefits in this world and the next.

Thus all the familiar names suddenly reappear in the Italian administration, the young Sicilians, for the most part highly-gifted : the Filangieri and Eboli, Acquaviva and Aquino, Morra and Caraccioli. Besides these the Emperor's sons ; Enzio and Frederick of Antioch, the little known Richard of Theate and later King Henry, son of Isabella of England ; further, his sons-in-law, the husbands of his natural daughters : Eccelino of Romano, Lord of the March of Treviso, and Jacob of Caretto, Margrave of Savona, Richard Caserta, and Thomas of Aquino the Younger. Finally, Manfred's relations by marriage, the Margrave Galvano and Manfred Lancia and Count Thomas of Savoy. Italians of loyal families or from loyal towns were also sometimes employed, chiefly as *podestas* but sometimes in other offices ; very rarely as Vicars General. Apart from Italian relatives of the Emperor the only ones so honoured were Percival Doria, already mentioned amongst the poets, and the wild Margrave Hubert Pallavicini who, with Eccelino, later became the first of the great Italian Signors in the Renaissance sense.

A contemporary styled the imperial Vicars General " princes," *principes*, and this described the demeanour of these petty despots who called themselves " By the Grace of God and of the Emperor, Vicar General of Upper Pavia," or merely " By the Grace of God Vicar General of Tuscany." Their dependence on the Emperor was absolute, but in every other way their position was one of unlimited princely power, especially in the later days when the Vicars General were almost

exclusively imperial Princes, sons-in-law and near relatives of
Frederick II. These became, especially Eccelino and Pallavicini, who grew daily more and more independent, the very
" mirror " of their imperial master down to the minutest
external traits. They aped his love of luxury, of astrologers
and menageries and Saracen satellites, even his intellectual
activities and his flippant jests about Church dogma. The
podestas of the great towns such as Florence, Pisa, Verona and
Cremona, trod closely on their heels. In other circumstances
these imperial representatives would probably have ruled as
kings over vassal monarchies like the Napoleon relatives. It
was characteristic of this intensive rather than extensive state
that wide kingdoms were compressed into small vicariates, or,
rather, that these minute vicariates ruled by the sons of an
Emperor should swell to the importance of duchies and of
kingdoms. In this connection a remarkable scheme of the
Emperor's must be treated of later.

Meanwhile the historical importance of this last and greatest
Germanic state foundation is to a certain extent already manifest, a state founded on Italian soil, founded, moreover, by the
last Emperor of the Romans, with whom the old Imperium
ceased to be. For these imperial Vicars General and these
imperial *podestas*, these representatives and vicegerents are the
direct ancestors of the Signors and Tyrants of the Renaissance.
The office of *podesta* with its unlimited despotic power,
especially when it became a life appointment, gradually came
to equal the position of a prince. The great Signors of Italy,
imitating the early Vicars General Eccelino and Hubert
Pallavicini, for centuries styled themselves " Vicars " of the
Emperor, until, about 1400, the German Emperors created
Dukedoms of the Vicariates of the Visconti, the Este, the
Gonzaga, etc. Let us grasp the full significance of Frederick's
Italian-Roman State : a mighty pan-Italian Seignory, which
for a short time united in one State Germanic, Roman and
Oriental elements. Frederick himself, Emperor of the World,
being the Grand Signor, or Grand Tyrant thereof, the first and
last of these princes to wear the diadem of Rome, whose Caesar-
hood was not only allied with German kingship like Barbarossa's but with Oriental-Sicilian despotism.

Having grasped this we perceive that all the tyrants of the Renaissance, the Scala and Montefeltre, the Visconti, Borgia and Medici are down to the tiniest features the sons and successors of Frederick II, the *diadochi* of this " Second Alexander." A mendicant monk tells of a wonderful nut-tree which sprang from the altar of a ruined church in Apulia, and which, when they felled it, showed the countenance of the Saviour in the cross section, which recurred in every section of every branch even when the tree was hewn into a thousand fragments. When the imperial autocrat was dead, and the Grand Seignory of Italy was shivered to fragments, a similar phenomenon occurred. Each of the princely courts bore the image of Frederick's court ; and all the princely sons which " Ausonia's sacred soil " bore in succeeding centuries, reflected, as noble or ignoble bastards, the countenance of their great unknown ancestor : Frederick II, this German Emperor by whom the " Maid Italia, Lady of Brothels " (Dante), had once been seized and overborne and got with child.

The despotism which Frederick II and his officials exercised in Italy, though often arbitrary in its severity, was by no means in principle exotic in Italy. The constitution of the towns had clearly shown a leaning towards dictatorship. Up till the turn of the twelfth and thirteenth centuries the towns had been ruled by two consuls. These were either subordinated to, or super-seded by, a radically foreign importation, the *podesta*, whose functions resembled more and more those of a dictator. The Lombards' conception of " freedom " will have been an indi-vidualistic striving for independence which tilted against any authority imposed from outside, but did not resent the stern-ness of its own chosen authorities. Hence it came that the individualism was able to mate so kindly with despotism. Frederick fought against the separatist impulse : he and his officials pointed the path to despotism. In many respects the Emperor brought the towns exactly what they themselves wanted, and the individualist spirit was thus for a while over-come. The towns who supported Milan were drawn together by the bond that united them against their great foe ; the others were unified by the Imperium and the hope of the general peace which might be expected from the Emperor's powerful rule.

Frederick II hit the nail on the head when he wrote at this time : " The Italian towns would be unmindful of their own advantage if they preferred the luxury of an uncertain freedom to the repose of *Pax et Justitia*." For many men were heartily sick of this " uncertain freedom " which continually involved them in internal and external wars, and they longed for such order as the Emperor promised. The speculative and mystical hopes of the time, the faith in the saving mission of the Imperium Romanum and of its Emperor went out to Frederick from another side. He had exploited this faith years before. When he was embarking on the " Execution of Justice " in Lombardy, Piero della Vigna heralded his coming with the Scripture words : " The people that walked in darkness have seen a great light. . . ." This was, however, only the prelude. When the Pope, with his excommunication and his encyclicals, threatened to shake men's belief in the Emperor's mission Frederick began seriously to work up these little-used forces and was able with their help partially to paralyse the full potency of the ban. He succeeded in fanning to a blaze the enthusiasm for the long-promised Messiah-Emperor, but only because the highest spiritual authority, Pope Gregory IX himself, had been at pains to surround the Emperor with the atmosphere of the Apocalypse.

If the time had not already been steeped in the belief that the Day of Judgment was at hand this last frenzied battle between the two leaders of the Christian world, fought out at first in pamphlets and manifestos of unprecedented savagery, might well have begotten the idea that an era was expiring in delirium. For ten years the Christian peoples were bewildered by the thunder-laden accusations launched by both parties, each proclaiming to the listening monarchs and their peoples that he was the highest authority alike in secular and spiritual spheres : that the Destroyer himself was seated on—as the case might be—the papal or the imperial throne.

Not many days after Pope Gregory IX had with his excommunication " committed the Emperor's body to Satan, that his
soul might at the Last Day be saved alive," Frederick II opened
the spiritual battle by a great manifesto to all the kings and
princes of the earth : " Lift up your eyes, prick up your ears,
O ye children of men !   Mourn for the woe of the world, the
discord of peoples, the exile of justice, since the abomination
of Babylon goeth forth from the elders of the people who had
the appearance of guiding them, but into wormwood they
turned the fruits of justice, and righteousness into gall.   Take
your seats, O ye princes, and hearken unto our cause, O ye
peoples !"   Thus Frederick's document began, in which he
expounded in detail his conduct towards the Pope during the
whole course of his reign.   At the same time he exposed Pope
Gregory's behaviour to detailed criticism.   Since the day when
he mounted the chair of St. Peter this Pope had, from unknown
motives, relentlessly persecuted the Emperor and shown himself an implacable foe.   Frederick here laid the foundation of
all his attacks on Gregory IX.   He was challenging neither
Papacy nor Church, but denouncing solely the present Pope,
whom he could not acknowledge as his judge, since Gregory,
by leaguing himself with the Empire's enemies, had become a
deadly foe.   Finally, Frederick proclaimed to the world certain
details of Gregory's procedure as Pope and revealed certain
abuses of the Curia.

In so doing Frederick catered for a prevailing mood.   The
materialism of the spiritual power had long been abhorrent to
the best minds, and to ordinary men the Curia's insatiable
thirst for money was burdensome.   Public opinion was ready
enough to find in the Emperor's words confirmation of all that
songs and satires, parodies and pamphlets had long since openly
betrayed.   This vigorous century had seen a multitude of
squibs and skits on Pope, Cardinals and Curia, parodying
hymns and litanies and masses, and pillorying above all the
greed of the Church and of her head.   Witty bogus gospels
were broadcast in which the rôle of St. Mark is taken by the
silver mark, in others the cardinal becomes the *carpinal* (the
" snatcher "), and money reigns as king of kings.   The secret
of the papal entente with usurers who were counted heretics

was common knowledge. Speaking at the Council of Lyons
Frederick's ambassador warded off an attack on his master as
a heretic by retorting that it was not the Emperor who tolerated
usurers in his dominions. The western powers were deeply
embittered by the papal demands for money. England, in
particular, resented the payment of tribute, and ceaselessly
protested against the plague of papal money-hunters.

This critical attitude towards the Roman Church and its
abuses had first found voice in the threatening words of Abbot
Joachim at the beginning of the century, and criticism had
been quickened by contrast with the frugal life of St. Francis.
Frederick II now seized on it and exploited it, not in an attack
against Church or Curia or Papacy, but solely against the
person of Pope Gregory IX, from whom he strove to detach
cardinals and Curia. He accused Gregory of issuing dispen-
sations without the concurrence of the cardinals but in exchange
for money. Like a huckster who acts as his own clerk and sets
his own seal, and mayhap is also his own paymaster, Gregory
sits in his closet, binding and loosing. Frederick added some
specific examples of the unworthiness of the present Bishop of
Rome. The same line was taken by a pamphlet that emanated
from Frederick's circle which attacked Pope Gregory sharply
and with effect. " Thou who as Shepherd of the Sheep
preachest poverty according to the commands of Christ,
why dost thou so diligently flee the poverty that thou com-
mendest . . . ? " Frederick II's most serious accusation
against Pope Gregory was his alliance with the Lombard
heretics, more especially the Milanese. The Pope himself had
accused them of heresy, and responsible spiritual authorities
had judged that the town was mainly inhabited by heretics.
By making common cause with Milan Pope Gregory had
forfeited all claim to be worthy of the priesthood.

The Emperor felt moved by anxiety lest " the flocks of the
Lord by such a shepherd be led astray." He, therefore, urges
the cardinals to summon a General Council composed of the
clergy of the whole Christian world, not excepting the secular
princes. Let this Synod then judge both Pope and Emperor.
This proposal seemed monstrous, for since the days of Gregory
VII the Church Councils had ceased to be above the Pope and

had become his instruments. Frederick II reiterates that he is fighting only against the person of this Gregory. " The Church in general and the Christian people must not marvel that we fear not the verdict of such a judge : not that we lack reverence for the papal office nor for the apostolic dignity, to which all orthodox believers do homage and we in particular above them all, . . . but we accuse the degeneracy of this one person who hath manifested himself to be unworthy of a throne so illustrious." Frederick II thus scrupulously distinguished between the papal office and its present incumbent : a refinement which his contemporaries noted and felt to be extremely skilful. For the Emperor thus avoided a quarrel with the Church and her institutions and prosecuted his campaign solely against a personal enemy. And Gregory had displayed enmity enough by the alliance with Venice, Genoa and Milan. On the other hand, this discrimination of office and incumbent brought Frederick into conflict with the dogmas of the Church, which taught that the sacramental virtue was independent of the personal worthiness or unworthiness of the priest. This gave Pope Gregory his opportunity.

The imperial manifesto had been forceful. In comparison, however, with Pope Gregory's answer the Emperor's most savage outbursts appeared tame. Gregory piled up all the most terror-fraught images of the Apocalypse against " this scorpion spewing passion from the sting of his tail," against this dragon, this hammer of the world. The opening words of his frenzied encyclical were calculated to awaken horror at this apocalyptic monster, already Satan's prey : " Out of the sea rises up the Beast, full of the names of blasphemy who, raging with the claws of the bear and the mouth of the lion and the limbs and likeness of the leopard, opens its mouth to blaspheme the Holy Name and ceases not to hurl its spears against the tabernacle of God and against the saints who dwell in heaven. With fangs and claws of iron it seeks to destroy everything and to trample the world to fragments beneath its feet. It has already prepared its rams to batter down the walls of the catholic faith. . . . Cease ye therefore to marvel that it aims at us the darts of calumny, since the Lord himself it doth not spare. Cease ye to marvel that it draws the dagger of

contumely against us, since it lifts itself to wipe from the earth
the name of the Lord.   Rather, that ye may with open truth
withstand his lying and may refute his deceits with the proofs
of purity : behold the head and tail and body of the Beast, of
this Frederick, this so-called Emperor. . . ."

The Pope called uncanny forces to his aid in this warfare
against the Emperor.   Distorting every fact with magnificent
effrontery he accused him of crime after crime, careless of
everything save the effect he hoped to produce on the minds
of Christian people.   Frederick had intentionally doomed to
death the crusaders in the pilgrim camp of Brindisi, had
poisoned the Margrave of Thuringia, had made peace with the
Sultan in the Holy Land to the detriment of the Christians,
had in his own absence directed the war against the peace-
loving Pope, while for greed he allowed his own kingdom to be
wasted by fire and sword.   Pope Gregory met with humility
the reproaches directed against his person and his conduct:
" Freely we confess our lack of merit and that we are all unworthy to be the Vicar of Christ.   We acknowledge our impotence in face of such a burden which the nature of man, save
with divine assistance, is unable to sustain."   Nevertheless, so
far as human fragility permits, he has conducted his office in
singleness of heart and according to the command of God.

Far otherwise Frederick II, continues Pope Gregory, doomed
to perdition he, with his craftiness and wiles, who has sought
to add the functions of the priest to those of the prince, who
rejoices to be called the Forerunner of Antichrist and blas-
phemously denies the Church's power to bind and to loose.
Frederick in his own writings had brought the darkness into
light, and with his own hand has torn the veil from his own
hideousness.   " For while he obstinately declares that he cannot be bound by the fetters of our ban who are the vicegerent
of Christ, therewith he declares that the Church does not
possess the power transmitted by the Holy Peter and his followers to bind and to loose . . . thus he sets the seal on his own
heresy and thereby shows how evilly he thinks of the other
clauses of the true faith. . . ."   Having thus, out of his own
mouth, convicted the Emperor of heresy, Pope Gregory hurls
against him the most terrible of all accusations : " This King

of the Pestilence has proclaimed that—to use his own words—
all the world has been deceived by three deceivers, Jesus Christ,
Moses and Muhammad, of whom two died in honour, but
Christ upon the Cross. And further, he has proclaimed aloud
(or rather he has lyingly declared) that all be fools who believe
that God could be born of a Virgin, God who is the creator of
Nature and of all beside. This heresy Frederick has aggravated by the mad assertion that no one can be born save where
the intercourse of man and wife have preceded the conception,
and Frederick maintains that no man should believe aught but
what may be proved by the power and reason of nature."

Pope Gregory had saved up his deadliest weapon for the last,
for behind this monstrous blasphemy could be discerned, however distorted and disguised, the radiant features of the man
who sought to see in Nature " the things that are, as they are."
On this point there was no doubt. There is no hope of proving
whether or no Frederick had made the infamous statement
about the three deceivers. He was certainly capable of saying
that—and worse. . . . The phrase would not, in any case, be
his own invention. A generation earlier a Paris doctor of
theology, Simon of Tournai, had propounded the thesis in
order to prove his dialectic skill in its disproof. The Popes
never again laid this blasphemy to Frederick's charge, and even
Pope Gregory never renewed the charge when once the poison
had done its work and the accusation had been taken up by all
the world. Little did Gregory reck whether it was false or
true. The assumption that Frederick's friendship with the
Muslims would have restrained him from any blasphemy
against Muhammad will not hold water, though his contemporaries distrusted the papal statements on this ground. How
could Frederick, they asked, have named Muhammad as a
deceiver along with Moses and with Christ when the same Pope
Gregory had based his first excommunication of the same
Emperor on the accusation that he was a servant of Muhammad,
and addicted to Saracen, no longer to Christian, customs?
Pope Gregory could not, of course, prove his statement. But
Frederick was equally unable to refute it, and he must, therefore,
seek by some other means to neutralise the effect of the papal
document that painted him as Satan and as Antichrist. He

repudiated the speech about the three deceivers.   Such a phrase
had never crossed his lips.   A mere denial, however, proved
nothing, and even a solemn profession of the true faith carried
little weight.   The most effective course was to cast doubt on
the Pope's veracity and to turn against him the most deadly
accusation of all : that of heresy.

The Emperor had little difficulty in presenting Pope Gregory
as the real heretic and the friend of heretics.   The Pope's
alliance with the Lombards was known to all the world
and lent weight to the charge.   The spiritual princes of
Germany, who still to a man stood firm behind the Emperor,
wrote soon after this to Pope Gregory.   They had examined
all the reasons for the excommunication, and with all respect
they begged to counsel the Pope not further to embitter so true
a son of the Church as this Emperor.   For such vexation would
add new dangers to those already seriously threatening the
catholic faith.   Moreover, the Pope's attitude lent colour to
the general belief that the Pope's severity towards the Emperor
was prompted by a desire to protect the Milanese, these enemies
of the Empire, and their following.   Little as they themselves
could credit that the " Vicar of the Truth " could be abetting the
manifest baseness of recalcitrant rebels, yet appearances were
against him, for the papal legate in Lombardy was doing his
utmost to entice the towns from the allegiance they owed the
Emperor.   They openly stated, therefore, that they, who as
limbs of the Empire must not fail her, would be reluctantly
compelled to mourn for the Church.   For the Emperor truthfully contended that he had offered himself and all he possessed
to the Church, and they, therefore, begged the Pope to make
peace without delay.   They were ready themselves to act as
intermediaries.

Frederick II was still, in the eyes of all the world, primarily
the liberator of the Holy Sepulchre, who had, in fact, sacrificed
himself and his wealth for the good of the Church.   As a
persecutor of heretics, too, he had shown himself an orthodox
prince.   It was, therefore, not easy to shake his position or men's
faith in him.   " We know "—they wrote in England—" that

he faithfully set out to war for our Lord Jesus Christ, and exposed himself to the perils of the sea and of the fight. We have not up to now observed an equal piety in the Pope." Frederick II must still be accounted innocent and unconvicted in England. Moreover, they said, an enemy's word is in no wise to be trusted, and all know that Pope Gregory is the deadly enemy of the Emperor. That the Pope dared to protect imperial rebels and heretics from the punishment justly due, and even excommunicated the victorious and fortunate' Emperor solely for their sakes, is sufficiently remarkable.

Frederick II expressly returned to this point, that he himself had only been the fortunate instrument of the divine will : "In truth, however, the Emperor's good fortune has always awakened the hostile envy of the Pope. When Simonides was asked how it was that none were jealous of him he answered, ' because I have never successfully accomplished anything.' But because by God's grace all has prospered with us and we are pursuing the Lombards our rebels to the death, this apostolic Priest who wishes them to live, heaves a sigh and seeks himself to obstruct our good fortune." By thus representing the Pope as envious of others' good fortune and a disturber of the world's peace Frederick appeared as the champion of the oppressed Church.

To illustrate the confusion which the Pope was causing Frederick had recourse to the doctrine of the two luminaries, the familiar parable of the Sun and the Moon, which were typified on earth by Papacy and Empire. Both were directly appointed by God so that man who is always drawn hither and thither might be bridled by a double rein—both, however, were independently created so that neither should disturb the other in his orbit. As the Sun and Moon exist in heaven side by side, so on earth the Papacy and the Empire. Frederick made no attempt to assert imperial superiority over the priest ; he contentedly equates the Empire to the Moon :

" But, O marvel of unheard-of arrogance ! The Sun would fain steal from the Moon her colour and rob her of her light ! The priest would bait Augustus, and with his apostolic greatness would obscure the radiance of our majesty whom God has set upon the pinnacles of Empire ! " Thus the Pope has brought confusion into the world : instead of loving the peace which the Emperor seeks, Peter becomes a rock of offence and Paul turns again into Saul and corrupts the world. " And there he sits in the seat of the Pharisees and of false doctrines, anointed by his comrades with the oil of evil unrighteousness, the Roman priest of our day. Insolently he tries to stultify the order of things decreed by heaven, and perchance believes that the laws of nature will be governed by his heated will. He seeks to darken the radiance of our majesty by perverting truth to lies. . . . He, who is the Pope in name alone, has said that we are the Beast who rises from the sea full of the names of blasphemy and spotted like the pard. And we maintain that he is the monster whereof it is written : another horse rose from the sea, a red horse, and he who sat thereon stole peace from the earth, so that the living slaughtered one another." The Pope himself was the great dragon. The Pope himself was Antichrist, whose forerunner he had called the Emperor, a prince among the princes of darkness, who abused the gifts of the prophets, a false vicegerent of Christ who transformed his priesthood into a beasthood.

Thus Frederick stamped the Pope as a heretic. A heretical Pope was a much more revolutionary thought than a heretical Emperor. This new insight suddenly metamorphoses all the relationships in the world. For without more ado the " true believer " is the friend of the Emperor, and the " infidel " is like the Lombard heretics, a follower and comrade of the Pope. The Pope can no longer protect the Church. It is the Emperor who upholds his credit as her God-appointed protector, since the High Priest " acts against the faith, the false vicar of him who though he was cursed yet answered not again." It is the Pope who brings discord into the world and snatches peace away which it was the Empire's mission of salvation to bring. The cardinals as Roman Senators will no longer find it their duty to help the Pope but will be helpers of the protecting, rescuing Emperor. They will even have to act as opposing forces " as the planets circle in opposite directions to temper the speed of the firmament." The Emperor writes to the cardinals, " Call ye back our roaring lion from his purpose, the beginning of which was abhorred." In similar strain to the

kings of Europe : they also as defenders of the true faith should
rise as one man for the sake of the world's peace against this
Pope and stand shoulder to shoulder with the Emperor. " Ye
princes, ye beloved princes, reproach not us alone, reproach
also the Church which is the community of the faithful : for
her head is weak, the leader in her midst is as a roaring lion,
her prophet is a madman, her bridegroom an infidel, her priest
a defiler of the Most High, who acts unrighteously and con-
temns the law. In the sight of the other princes of the world
we must mourn as is due the failure of such an High Priest,
we who enjoy honour and bear burdens and who in space are
as it were nearer to him and in office more akin." The fact
that Pope Gregory had protected the Empire's rebels should
also be a warning to them : " Urgently and without ceasing,
we exhort you, Beloved, to see in this outrage to us an injustice
likewise to yourselves. Haste ye to your houses with water
when the fire flames in the house of your neighbour ! " There
was no ordinance of the Church, no word of Scripture, no
legend from which Frederick failed to draw new strength, seeing
everything from new standpoints, till, finally, the Donation
of Constantine itself was turned to account for the Empire's
behoof. This dangerous document was a monument of the
gratitude which was owed to the Empire by the Papacy.

It has often been remarked that in this duel of the Chanceries
the genuinely productive side was the Emperor's. The Curia
exhausted itself in biblical turns of thought and speech that
had been worn threadbare for centuries, while the manifestos
of the Emperor sparkled with new ideas, some of which ripened
after centuries. One reason was, that whereas Pope Gregory
was solely negative and destructive, aiming at the annihilation
of his foe, Frederick had a constructive aim. Without so
expressing it, Frederick countered each negation of the Pope's
by pointing to himself, the Emperor of *Justitia*, the Rescuer,
the Bringer of Salvation in a day of chaos. Frederick II, whose
very name spelt a gospel of peace,[1] might well seem by his deeds
as by his power the long-awaited Prince of Peace : he who had
worn the royal crown of David in Jerusalem, he to whom men
had long applied promise and prophecy—as they had not to

[1] The Germanic root *fride =*peace* and *rīk =*rule*.—*Tr*.

Pope Gregory. Men looked for a messianic Pope as they looked for a messianic Emperor, but he would come in the guise of Peter the Fisherman, or the simple beggar Francis, the Bridegroom of Poverty, not as an Emperor-Priest like Gregory or Innocent.

What Frederick had only indicated was explicitly claimed by a pamphlet which represented the Emperor as the Saviour. " The High Priests and Pharisees assembled a Council and came together against the prince and Imperator of the Romans, ' What shall we do,' said they, ' since this man thus triumphs over his enemies ? If we do not prevent him he will overthrow the whole fame of Lombardy, and coming like a Caesar he will not stay till he have driven us from out our land and have exterminated our people. . . .' " Thus the pamphlet opened, verbally recalling the words of scripture where the High Priests and Pharisees decide on the Saviour's condemnation. The parallel is pushed far : the Pope is compared to Pilate because what he has written he has written, and is reproached with his breach of the peace since he " as a friend of discord . . . against the honour and the right of the Roman prince protects heretics who are the enemies of God and of all believing Christians." As for the Pope's pious pretext : his protection of the Lombards is to serve the cause of the Holy Land. This is scornfully turned against Gregory himself. His ban has so sorely damaged the cause of the Holy Land that Jerusalem might well fall again a prey to the infidel : "And thou, the vicegerent of Christ sleepest the while and carest naught that our inheritance has passed to others ! For the city which once was full of people and beautiful among cities lieth waste . . . she who was wont to flow with milk and honey floweth now with the waters of bitterness." The guilt lies with the Pope. Jerusalem, the city of Christ, uncomforted by the Pope, is awaiting another Lord, " Without ceasing she waits for him, the Roman prince, the comforter of her captivity, the redeemer of her destruction. But thou on the other hand, thou foe, thou Godless Herod, thou fearest to go thither . . . thou stone of stumbling, thou rock of offence, thou hast thrown into confusion the ways by sea and land that this Caesar, this wondrous light of the World, this mirror without flaw, might be

unable to hasten after the manner of the Caesars to the help
of the land of God." Let the Pope, concludes the pamphlet,
receive the Emperor again, the " true born son," once more
into the bosom of the Church, " for otherwise our great-hearted
lion which now feigneth sleep, will with his dread roaring draw
unto himself the fatted kine from all the furthest corners of the
earth, tearing out and breaking asunder the horns of the proud.
He shall establish justice and bring the Church into the right
way."

Visions of the Last Day are thus associated with Frederick.
His figure was destined to live on in myth through the centuries
as this pamphlet pictures him, in the saga of the messianic
Emperor, in his mountain fastness, who will one day return,
establish the reign of Justice, castigate the Church and lead the
people of Christ into Jerusalem. Herein lay something positive,
above and beyond accusations against the Pope. While the
Emperor's partisans saw in Gregory the High Priest and the
Pharisee, the Pilate who condemned the Christ, the Emperor
stood before them as the true Redeemer, promised by the Sibyls,
praise-deserving, " the wondrous light of the world, the mirror
without flaw," the Saviour chosen by God to renew the peace
and order of the world. The more he felt compelled to deny
the worth of this individual Pope the more insistently the
Emperor pointed to the sacred and exalted mission of his own
Empire and the sanctity of his own Caesar-majesty.

Frederick found the rôle easy to sustain. Not only his friends
and adherents but many of the orthodox recognised in him the
long-awaited messenger of God who had come to chastise a
corrupt priesthood. They trembled before the face of this
" Hammer of the World," but well they knew from the sayings
of the prophets that a MAN was needed who should smite with
iron fist both papacy and priesthood, to lead the world again
into the state of peace and of salvation which had blessed mankind in the reign of Augustus when Christ himself had walked
the earth. In the mystic circles of the Franciscans, amongst
whom Abbot Joachim's teachings were still alive, these fears
and hopes were centred more and more in the person of the

Hohenstaufen Emperor who as the Pope's bitter foe threatened to fulfil the prophecies. In these Franciscan convents, which in apostolic purity were awaiting the reform of the Church, the belief soon found credence (in spite of their hostility to the Emperor) that Frederick II was in very deed the herald of the End, and that no man, but only God himself, could remove or slay God's messenger.... In Frederick's circle the legend later grew that God's own hand had shaped him.

The most various dreamings were here blended : the Church visions which dreamed of a Scourge of the peoples which should restore the primitive Church of apostolic times ; the imperial visions which dreamed of the revival of the Augustan Empire under a new Caesar Augustus ; and, lastly, the more human cravings which dreamed of a return to the primitive innocence of man before the Fall under the rule of a *Justitia* Emperor. These mystic dreams flourished in more and more riotous luxuriance, and year by year Frederick II became more and more the centre of the hopes of every camp. Judge of the World, *Justitia* Emperor, Redeemer of the Holy Sepulchre and Messianic Prince of Peace, all blent into the figure of Caesar Augustus who himself expressed the ideal of a *rex justus*.

By the minting of his Augustales Frederick II had already shown that his Caesar gestures had a deeper significance than the merely personal or political. The more he resembled the Roman Caesars and Augusti in triumph and word and deed the greater grew his similitude to the Saviour Vergil had foretold, with whom Roman Empire and Christian epoch were to begin : and end. Seeds of the Renaissance lurk in this eschatological faith : the Rebirth of the World both by the cosmic rebirth of the natural man and by the return to the origins of Church and Empire. Even for Dante these, however, lay in Roman antiquity in the time of the apostles and the golden age of Rome.

From all the inextricable confusion of vague, mysterious, terrifying or idyllic visions of the time Frederick II had hitherto seized only on those features which could be baldly and clearly represented in the State : first, the establishment of his imperial world-redeeming *Justitia* in all his domains, even in Italy, and then the demeanour of a Roman Caesar Augustus, both of which things were without ulterior motive, instinctive in his blood, inherent in his office. The interpretation was left mainly to others. Now all was changed. The Pope made inevitable that religious speculations should play a part in his life. If Frederick was to take the field against the Pope as the Saviour of the Church, it was not enough to oppose the Reason of the State to the Faith of the Church. Frederick II must win for himself the transfiguring halo of God's messenger which must surround the head of a Ruler of the Faithful. Unexplored mysteries lay to the hand both of Empire and Papacy. Caesar could look for his divine nimbus to the great peace movement of these days of crisis with their expectation of a Messiah-Emperor, days filled with peace-services, hallelujahs and flagellation. . . . The great movement bore Frederick on its crest. He made himself its hero and became its God. So it was said that the French took the Revolution for their religion, and for their God, Napoleon.

When Frederick left Lombardy at the beginning of 1239 he had months of intensive activity behind him. The more manifold the tasks, the more comprehensive the demands, the swifter the progress of events, the better it suited the Emperor's mood and the more certain was his success. Frederick had fought the rebels in the Romagna and in Lombardy ; from his camp before Piacenza and Milan had issued the orders that transformed Sicily into a fortress ; from Lodi had radically recast the Sicilian constitution and set in motion the most elaborate shipping transactions ; had sent orders to outlaw these, hang those, exile others, and deprive yet others of their goods. With it all he had kept leisure enough to make daily minute enquiry about the game, the baiting of cranes, the breeding of horses, the destruction of vermin, to occupy himself with horses, hawks and hounds, to draft and superintend drawings for one of the most beautiful and luxurious castles of the Middle Ages, for the first Renaissance gateway, for a triumphal arch whose detached figures mark the beginnings of secular plastic art. He has not lost the taste for costly purchases: a dish of onyx, curios, precious stones. He sends antique statues home to his Sicilian castles by porter: he issues instructions for the University of Naples. Within a few months his Italian Seignory stands as a monument of creative genius and of organising skill, and he is able to write to a friendly prince that he is rejoicing in the best of health, everything is succeeding just as he wishes and he is now planning something new. This new project was the resolve, after the many challenging pamphlets, to assume the offensive against the Pope and to invade the States of the Church.

Coming from Lombardy the Emperor marched by way of Parma and crossed the Tuscan Alps by the La Cisa Pass. Here he was joined, it is said, by the Minister General of the Franciscan order, Brother Elias of Cortona, to the further confusion of parties. This was a clear proof of the change in relationships that had taken place, and the first indication of that secret sympathy which united the Franciscans and the Ghibellines, and which is so strongly characteristic of Dante and the first century of the Renaissance. Brother Elias had been one of the earliest and most intimate disciples of St. Francis, who had named him as his successor. His stern piety was entirely free from weakness or sentimentality. He was not strictly a mendicant friar in the original meaning of the term, rather : a statesman, prince and scholar, with a touch of genius leavening his haughtiness and love of pomp. The general held somewhat aloof from the brethren and rarely ate with them. He took his meals in his private room, and that not only because he relished better fare than the brothers were accustomed to. He lived either in his handsome house in Cortona or in the papal palace at Assisi, for he was an intimate friend of Gregory IX. He was never seen save on horseback, even though he had only a few steps to go, and then escorted by a handsomely-dressed page. Like a true autocrat he repudiated the suggestion that such magnificence was contrary to the Rule of the Order : the Minister General was above the Rule. As befitted a spiritual noble, Brother Elias was a great builder, and the magnificent Lower Church in Assisi which he erected to his Master was his work. He was said to have got the money for this through his knowledge of alchemy, about which he had written a treatise. If this had been the case it might have silenced the religious murmurings of many of the brothers, although the horror of money was still vivid amongst them. But since, in fact, he raised the money by provincial taxes on the Order itself they began to grow restive under him. He was hated as a despot and a tyrant : the brothers partly yearned for the simple freedom of the early years, partly feared his harshness, for to their great indignation Elias had appointed stern " visitors " to stiffen the discipline of the order.

At this point they rebelled. The inclination of the Minister General to consider only the worldly aims of the Order as a State—a point of view akin to Gregory's—finally brought about his fall. Delegates were sent from all the provinces to Pope Gregory to compel Brother Elias's removal from office. The messenger from the Order's province of Saxony particularly distinguished himself by excess of zeal. Brother Jordan, on his arrival in Rome in a state of high excitement, contrived by some means or other to force his way into the Pope's bedroom ; he paid no heed to the command to leave the room, but joyfully hastened to the bed and fetched out from under the bedclothes the aged Gregory's naked foot to apply the necessary kiss, remarking to his companion, " We have no sacred relics like this in Saxony ! " Brother Jordan himself tells the tale. This same brother must have taken part in the great assembly held in the Spring of 1239 which removed Brother Elias from the post of Minister General of the Brothers Minor, though Pope Gregory strove to retain him.

The fall of the well-known Minister General of the Minorites naturally caused a stir throughout the world. What amazement when Brother Elias, who after his deposition at first remained in Assisi doing penance, suddenly appeared in the train of the excommunicate Emperor ! The inevitable result was to draw on him the papal ban. The Franciscan was for Frederick a most welcome recruit. The Brother's intimate knowledge of Gregory IX was invaluable, and his presence amongst Frederick's followers demonstrated to all that the closest disciples of St. Francis were turning from the heretic Pope. As a chronicler said : Frederick loosed those whom the

Pope had bound, and sons of the Church became through the papal behaviour the Church's step-children.

Under such auspices Frederick embarked on his new, perhaps fantastic adventure.   It began with a short stay in Pisa.   Here Frederick proclaimed himself the Peacemaker his name implied, and succeeded in effecting a reconciliation between the wildly warring Pisan parties of the Gherardeschi and the Visconti. A remarkable scene followed.   Christmas was at hand, and his own birthday followed hard on that of the Saviour.   To celebrate the season, he, the excommunicate, whose mere presence brought an interdict upon the town, not only caused a service to be held and the mysteries of the mass consummated, but himself mounted the cathedral pulpit on Christmas Day and preached to the assembled people.   He promised peace and the reign of peace to the astonished worshippers.   This sermon brought down on him the papalists' accusations of blackest blasphemy.   A few days later he invaded the Pope's dominion as the Prince of Peace.

King Enzio with some force had been sent on a few days earlier into the papal provinces that had of old belonged to the Empire : the March of Ancona and Spoleto.   Frederick following him will not have met with much resistance.   Cardinal John Colonna, whom the Pope had placed in charge of the defence of these regions, was one of Frederick's most ardent supporters, which increased the confusion.   The Emperor thus won once again one of his bloodless victories : his last.   He had contrived, as in the dramatic actions of his earlier years, to make a masterly entry, so that the gates of towns and fortresses sprang open as if by magic at his approach.   He trod the soil of the papal states as the Liberator, nay, the Saviour, whom his own were awaiting in Jerusalem.   Summonses addressed under the sign of the Cross to the various communities preceded the invading Caesar with his Saracen escort.   These appeals were designed to give the right tone to his arrival. Never before had Frederick II so undisguisedly proclaimed himself in the very words of the scripture as the Promised One :

" Since the great and acceptable day is come which ye can make yet more acceptable to us and to the Empire we beg of you : Arise ! direct your eyes to see the wisdom and the might of the Empire ! And know ye us, your prince and gracious possessor ! Prepare ye the way of the Lord, make his paths straight ! Take the bars from off your doors that your Caesar may come, gracious unto you and unto rebels terrible, at whose coming the evil spirits shall be silent which have so long oppressed you." Similar were the words with which the Baptist announced the coming of the Lord and promised that the kingdom of heaven was at hand. It can only be the messenger of God who silences the evil spirits : him especially " whom men call the Pope." To another town he calls : " The moment of your redemption for which we and you have yearned is nigh ! " And the town's joining him he styles its " conversion."

Frederick's identification of himself with him whom the kings of the east came to seek in Bethlehem appears more unmistakably than elsewhere in the famous letter to his own birthplace, Jesi : " The instincts of nature compel us to turn to thee, O Jesi, and embrace thee with heartfelt affection, noble town of the March, the place of our illustrious birth, where our Divine Mother brought us into the world, where our radiant cradle stood : that thy habitations may not fade from our memory, that thou, our Bethlehem, birthplace of the Caesar, may remain deep-rooted in our heart. Thou, O Bethlehem, city of the March, art not the least among the cities of our race : for out of thee the Leader is come, the prince of the Roman Empire, that he might rule thy people and protect thee and not suffer that thou be in future subject to a foreign hand. Arise then, O our first mother, shake thee free from the foreign yoke. For we take pity on thy oppression and on the oppression of the Faithful. . . ." A more solemn cult of the birthplace could hardly be conceived than this, couched in the words of Holy Writ. The like had not been heard since Justinian had raised his birthplace to be a bishop's see, second only to Rome alone. Foligno is also honoured, " In whose radiance our childhood began and which we revere as the home which nourished us." The worship of his Bethlehem and the phrase " Divine Mother," taken in conjunction with the legend that the nun his mother had miraculously borne him, had a quite peculiar significance.

On the Emperor's arrival in these regions the papal authority instantly crumbled both in Spoleto and in the March of Ancona. The towns, with few exceptions, opened their gates most gladly to this Caesar who came " accompanied by Salvation." And wherever the Liberator entered he was received with rejoicing, for " one and all were right glad to find themselves under the protection of a master's hand." Deep emotion and astonishment must have gripped the people of the Papal States at the sight of the Emperor, especially those who were papalists at heart. One of these reported this blasphemous march of the Messiah : " He has the Cross borne before him, himself the enemy of the Cross, while he paces through the land of the accursed. In Foligno and in Gubbio he shamelessly presumes to bless those whom the Church has cast forth, consecrating them, so eyewitnesses assure me, with his godless right hand. And in these and other regions in spite of the ban he has caused masses to be said and has celebrated the other holy offices . . . he, the forerunner of Antichrist."

Frederick II appears, in fact, to have halted in Foligno in considerable state. The ambassadors of many towns and many of his own nobles, amongst them King Enzio, were assembled round him while he made a speech, and in accordance with his office restored peace between Gubbio and another community. It is probably true enough about his blessing the people. For a court was held in Foligno with all the elaborate ceremonial which had been customary of late since Cortenuova, and a firm and lasting peace proclaimed throughout the Empire. The Emperor was enthroned in serene detachment above the multitude, while like an officiating priest Piero della Vigna stood by his side and communicated to the audience the oracle of the imperial Godhead while the people bowed the knee before his majesty. This type of ceremony was exotic in the west and aroused redoubled stir and amazement in the Papal States, especially since the Emperor's retinue included Mussulmans.

The re-occupation of the imperial provinces was one uninterrupted triumphal march. His success exceeded expectation, and decided Frederick to push on into the Patrimonium proper, papal Tuscany, " where on all sides the peoples' prayers call for our presence and arrival." The same scenes are repeated. The people of Tivoli, Orta, Sutri, the fortified Montefiascone, and many other towns went over with banners flying to the Emperor, at their head the most important of all : Viterbo. By the middle of February the Emperor was installed in Viterbo with his whole court and had been greeted with rejoicing. The imperial plenipotentiaries whose duty it is to receive oaths of allegiance can scarcely keep pace with their task, writes the Emperor at this time.

More and more narrowly, more and more closely, Frederick drew his circles round the centre of the Empire : suddenly he stands before Rome. The road from Viterbo lies open before him. Shall he now end his fantastic tour of victory with the sack of Rome, take the Pope prisoner like any ordinary enemy general—and make the Church the gift of another martyr ? To Frederick this road was barred. Only as the Caesar Augustus of prophecy, only without a blow as Prince of Peace, could he enter the city of cities. This he planned to do. " One deed is left to do : if the whole Roman people is in our favour and greets our coming with rejoicing as it has begun to do, then we should prepare joyfully to enter the city and revive the ancient festivals and the triumphal laurels, to show the victorious eagles honour due. . . . Then shall our contemners feel belated shame, when they see us face to face, then they shall fear him whom their loose lips roused to wrath."

The Roman populace was, in fact, well disposed. Roman nobles had again got into touch with Frederick, who had himself addressed new letters to the Romans full of reproaches. Sunk in ignoble lethargy not one of the tribe of Romulus, not one of the Quirites, not one of the many nobles, not one of the ten thousands of the Roman people had dared to hinder the Pope when this Roman priest in Rome itself pronounced the ban against the Roman Emperor. That Emperor who derived his name from their city had come once more to make the name of Rome glorious again and famous as in the days of old. Frederick called himself the benefactor and father of the

Romans, and immediately responded to the request of Senate and People to spare the conquered town of Sutri. His influence in Rome was increasing and grew with his success.

The Emperor's partisans in Rome intrigued all the more ardently against the Pope, whose position became from day to day more untenable. All portents were against him. Far from attacking Frederick in Sicily or repressing him in Lombardy Pope Gregory was losing province after province of the States of the Church left to him by his predecessors, and while he warned his towns against the machinations of Antichrist he saw town after town opening its gates to the Saviour. The revolution which he himself had conjured up was not to be stayed and was victorious all along the line. Not only the Roman people turned their backs on the aged fanatic. His cardinals were no longer to be trusted. The majority were hostile. Some had already left him. By his passionate obstinacy the old man had brought himself and the Church to the verge of destruction. He stood alone. His cause seemed lost.

Meanwhile the excitement in Rome was at its height. The Emperor had left Viterbo and started on the march to Rome by way of Sutri. Only one or two days' march separated him from the city. The papalists spread the wildest rumours. What did that avail ! The Antichrist, the Monster had sworn, they cried, to turn St. Peter's into a stable and to make the altar of the apostles a manger for his steeds, to cast the body of his Lord to the dogs . . . he was approaching with his wild Saracens to overthrow the chair of St. Peter. With his new rites he would outvie the " three impostors," revive the practices of heathen times, would have himself installed as Pope or even God in the holiest of holies ! None of these terrifying suggestions carried weight. The Romans intoxicated themselves with the " resounding words, the mighty gestures, the awe-inspiring deeds " of their Caesar and Imperator, and shouted for joy at the approach of the laurel-crowned Deliverer :

ECCE SALVATOR ! ECCE IMPERATOR !

VENIAT VENIAT IMPERATOR !

The fate of the world was balanced on a knife's edge.

But Rome, " the harlot who offers herself for sale to any man who draws near," as a contemporary chronicler phrases it, had not been vainly depicted on the seals as a woman with a palm branch in one hand and in the other a globe, reposing on a lion, symbol of world rule which Pope or Emperor could exercise only in her name. He was the victor who first won her favour. Pope Gregory IX had waited long. Now in the hour of utmost need he turned for help to the saints of Rome, the two apostles. It was the festival of Peter's Chair. In spite of riot and unrest the Pope ordered the usual ceremonies to be carried out : the heads of the Princes of the Apostles, Paul and Peter, splinters of the True Cross, and other relics of Christian Rome were borne in solemn procession to St. Peter's. He himself, the aged man—reputed to be a hundred—paced along shrouded in incense amidst his prelates and the faithful cardinals. The crowd greeted him with boisterous mockery. Pope Gregory, however, at other times so hot-headed, preserved a royal calm. He pointed to the heads of the apostles : " These are the antiquities of Rome, for whose sake your city is venerated ! This is the Church, these are the relics, which it is your duty, Romans, to protect ! I can do no more than one man may ; but I do not flee, lo, here I await the mercy of the Lord ! " And taking the tiara from his head he placed it protectively over the relics of the saints. " Ye Holy Ones ! Protect ye Rome when the Romans care for her no more ! " Whereupon the mocking multitude broke into sobs, snatched from their garments the imperial eagles, tokens of Antichrist, and replaced them by the sign of the Cross, prepared to fight for their threatened Church. Caesar in the purple of the Triumphator was forgotten. Frederick II passed by the capital of the world, and proceeded to his kingdom of Apulia.

VIII. DOMINUS MUNDI

Cult of the Emperor——The *sacratissimum ministerium*——
Outburst of Sicilian art——Capuan Gate——Nicholas of
Pisa——St. Francis and " Gothic " painting——Diet in
Foggia, 1240——Inefficacy of papal ban——Princes' effort
to mediate——Surrender of Ravenna——Resistance of
Faënza——Cost of prolonged operations——Issue of
leather coins——Hostilities against Venice——Gregory's
General Council——Frederick's counter-measures——
Gregory's pact with Genoa——Fall of Faënza, April 14,
1241——Destruction of Benevento——Victory at sea, 1241;
capture of 100 prelates——Mongol threat——Battle of
Liegnitz, 1241——Pope hinders Crusade——Muslims re-
take Jerusalem, Nov. 1240——Frederick negotiates reco-
very of Jerusalem——Advance on Rome ; death of Pope
Gregory——Status of Empire in Europe——Relations
between Frederick and brother kings——Saint Louis——
Stirps caesarea——Deification of the Hohenstaufens
——Conclave of Terror, 1241——Innocent IV elected
Pope——Defection of Viterbo——Treachery of Cardinal
Rainer——Provisional peace, 1244; breaks down——
Flight of Innocent IV——Lyons——Diet of Verona
——Rainer's hostile propaganda——Council of Lyons——
Thaddeus of Suessa——Deposition of Frederick II

VIII. DOMINUS MUNDI

" Tho' we cannot everywhere be present in the flesh, yet our restraining hand is felt even to the remotest frontiers of the earth." This phrase of Frederick II's is characteristic, for himself and for his *sacrum imperium*. All the while that he was concentrating his Empire at the core in Italy, the land of its origin, his invisible influences were potent in the world at large and with mysterious power sucked the whole globe into the vortex of his strife with Rome. His dash for the City of Cities, whose possession would magically have assured his world dominion, had unfortunately failed. What the upshot would have been if he had succeeded none could guess. The mere attempt had filled the world with sudden unrest : the Emperor before the walls of Rome ; the Pope in direst need. A sudden misgiving was felt : what unthinkable development might be expected from this excommunicate Emperor whom the Church cursed as Antichrist, but whose followers acclaimed him as the Saviour and Messiah while they prepared his paths before him ?

For the moment Pope Gregory had averted Fate, but the whole of Christendom lived in continuous anxiety of what this Emperor and the morrow might bring forth. The deafest began to hear, the blindest to see and to perceive something fateful in Frederick's mission. Prophetic verses quivering with apocalyptic horror filled Europe with a shudder of uncertainty. They reached Pope Gregory. Men said that Frederick was the author. The world held its breath to catch the wing-beat of those birds of fate which in the starry heavens should hover round the Prince of the Last Days :

Fate is still as the night. There are portents and wars
In the course of the stars, and the birds in their flight.
I am Frederick, the Hammer, the Doom of the World.
Rome, tottering long since, to confusion is hurled,
Shall shiver to atoms and never again be Lord of the World.

With what designs was Frederick credited who had uttered dark threats against the Romans, " drunk with draughts from the cup of Babylon ! " " Your Babel shall be dissolved, Damascus shall fall, the bellows shall be consumed with fire, the throne erected towards midnight shall crash and the apron hung about your loins shall rot in the zeal of our exalted glory which the eye of God ceaseth not to illumine, which causeth the ulcers of darkness to perish, and to which well-nigh the whole universe doeth homage."

Neither camp had failed to realise the epoch-making nature of Frederick's mission : whether with rejoicing or with paralysing fear people saw the power of the Divus Augustus ever growing, saw the dizzy heights which he was scaling and the abysses which were yawning at the Pope's feet. Friend and foe alike believed that the wearer of the imperial diadem was sent by God himself and was striding through the world for a blessing or a curse to Christendom. None was insensitive to the extraordinary something. For decades the world had been busy seeking to interpret the imperial manifestation : was Frederick, fulfilling the time as Tyrant and King to the confusion of the peoples, Antichrist himself ?—or was he the Prince of Peace, the Saviour bringing in the reign of Justice ? The world recognised only these two mythical possibilities for a ruler of this stature. Every act and phrase of Frederick was forced into one or other of these ready-made moulds. Every event was interpreted as the fulfilment of a biblical or sibylline prophecy pointing either to Christ or Antichrist. Even the complimentary form of address which now became frequent, DOMINUS MUNDI, was full of ambiguity, for Satan also was " Lord of the World." According to taste, therefore, Frederick II was the Bringer of Absolute Good or of Absolute Evil. In either case he was the " Expected One," and this he remained for centuries in the faith of the peoples.

Since none even of his foes failed to appreciate the exceptional character of Frederick's mission it is easy to understand the veneration he evoked amongst the " Faithful." The phrase of his own that concluded the threats against Rome : " The earth obeyeth us and the sea doeth homage and all that we desire cometh forthwith to pass " indicated the type of tribute which was seemly. The resistance of Rome seemed incomprehensible to Frederick's adherents. A long Greek poem against the Romans written by the Chartophylax Georgios of Gallipoli, runs : " Rome who of old had her Caesars and her kings and her satraps and rendered glory for glory. . . . Alas ! we must mourn that she has driven forth her Caesars, the trebly-blessed . . . since Fate has plunged the best and the mightiest Rule of One into an evil Rule of None . . . but He the mighty trebly-fortunate Frederick, the Radiant, the Wonder of the World, τὸ θαῦμα τῆς οἰκουμένης, whose bow is of brass, whose lightnings blind the foe ; earth is his servant and the sea and the vault of heaven, the Just in fame, the Exalted . . . his voice thunders and the noise of his chariots . . . his lightnings flame from on high annihilating the enemy's arrogance. What trembling at such a campaign ! . . . Murmur, therefore, O Rome, wholesome words of divinely-inspired determination . . . exalt him above every cedar . . . and expel for his sake the whole race of corruption." The Calabrian official utilising the resounding metaphors of the Byzantine court diction here represents the Emperor as Jupiter, the angry Thunder-God ; not seriously different from the phrases which the Imperial Chancery was wont to lavish on the Ruler : " Of a truth earth and sea revere him and the winds of heaven praise him whom the Deity has granted to be the true Emperor of the World, the Friend of Peace, the Protector of Love, the Founder of Law, the Preserver of Justice, the Son of Power who ruleth the World."

In his great Crusade manifesto from Jerusalem Frederick had praised God, " who commanded the winds and the waves and they obey him." Now the same phrase is used of him as if he were himself the incarnate God : " Who bindeth the corners of the earth and ruleth the elements." Even the foe recognised his supernatural quality—for evil. His adherents worshipped him as a God : " Thy power, O Caesar, hath no bounds ; it excelleth the power of man, like unto a God," writes one of his courtiers. A second says : " Wear the crown that beseems thy supernatural position." A third praises him as the *co-operator Dei*, the coadjutor of God. Such phrases were, of course, the current coin of this Hohenstaufen court,

but they characterise the monarch.   Behind the adulations of
the courtiers, often grossly overdone, we can see the truth : the
impression the Emperor wished to make, especially on his own
followers.   The language of a court coterie is always two-edged,
by turns veiling and revealing.   If the phrase of the worshipper
is taken too seriously it immediately becomes a jest, but if it is
treated merely as a courtly game it suddenly is fully and literally
intended.

This homage shows at least that Frederick enjoyed a degree
of supernatural reverence that was unique.   Nothing proves
this more clearly than the deep anxiety which the Emperor-cult
evoked on the papal side.   They reproached him with allowing
himself to be worshipped like a God, with letting men call
him holy and kiss his feet, with aiming at founding a priestly
Empire.   None of these accusations is strictly true, but none
is entirely false.

Earlier Emperors had been praised as *deus de prole deorum*,
vicar of God, second David, holy, divine, the anointed of the
Lord, *Christus Domini*, *Salvator Mundi*.   There was nothing
far-fetched in this because the Christian Middle Ages—unlike
pagan antiquity—had only one type of God in human form :
the Saviour.   What seemed to the Church so satanic, so
acutely dangerous, was that in addition to the stereotyped and
relatively harmless formulas previously in use men spoke of
Frederick as " versed in the divine plans," " ceaselessly illuminated by the eye of God," as a real, active, divine force.
Apparent humility took a step back and conceived him as an
emanation of the true God, a son of God, and continually
placed him on the same plane as the Redeemer Christ himself.
Perpetual reiteration gave these claims a peculiar ring, and their
effect was enhanced by the fact that the world was at the
moment wrought up to an hourly, vivid expectation of an
imperial Messiah.   Frederick II was the only Emperor of whom
posterity cherished the dream that he would return as Saviour
at the End of the World.

The Emperor himself, and Piero della Vigna earlier, had
given the courtiers the note : the letter to Jesi, the Emperor's
Bethlehem, is the best example of the style.   An echo was only
to be expected.   A few years later an imperial governor with

his troops was surrounded, and in need he wrote: "Our fore-fathers looked no more eagerly for the coming of Christ than we do for thine. . . . Come to free and to rejoice us. . . . Show thy countenance and we shall find salvation ! . . . This it is for which we groan, this for which we sigh : to rest under the shadow of thy wings." An imperial notary goes even further in numerous appeals from prison to the Emperor : "O harbour of salvation to them that believe . . . lead the children of Israel out of Egypt . . . we endure torment for thee such as the martyrs endured for Christ. . . ." One of the faithful Sicilian bishops, when summoned to court, writes : "Walking on the waters I shall come to my Lord."

After the second excommunication it became the fashion for the courtiers to keep up this "style" even in conversation amongst themselves. It is noteworthy, indicating the plane on which the Emperor moved, that all their allusions are either to Caesar or to Christ, never to Charlemagne or any of the great medieval Emperors. Piero della Vigna had had the largest share in creating this figure of his master. The vital thing was that Frederick II found spirits to praise him and recognise him : that he not only felt himself to be the emissary of God but was believed to be so by his followers.

It is Piero della Vigna and his circle of jurists, stylists and literati who supply the enduring expression of this conception. The time believed that the first and second ages of Adam and of Christ were overpast and that the third was drawing on. Piero della Vigna boldly pointed to his imperial master as the hero of the third and coming age, the ruler "whom the Great Artificer's hand created man," "into whose breast all virtues are poured, on whom the clouds rain justice and the heavens send their dew." And della Vigna praises in this last Emperor of the ancient Empire the "ideal of good," "who is free from crooked sight, who bindeth the corners of the earth and ruleth the elements, that frost is mated with fire, and wet with dry, and rough with smooth, and the pathless is wedded to him whose ways are straight."

The marriage of opposites had been from of old the token of an *aurea aetas*, a Golden Age in which strife and war shall cease : an age of peace which the Saviour-Emperor shall bring.

The Logothetes, therefore, praises his master: " In his day
shall the bonds of evil be loosened and with might shall security
be sown : men shall beat their swords to ploughshares for the
bond of peace causeth all fear to cease." Piero della Vigna was
not alone in his belief that the reign of peace had come again
under Frederick II. A North Italian sings : "*cuius ad imperium redit aetas aurea mundo*." Another Italian poet in his
enthusiasm over Frederick's great victory at sea hopes that this
severe defeat will teach the Pope the kind of peace which awaits
him at the end of the strife :

> Et Puer Apuliae terras in pace habebit.

The youthful name of Frederick II is revived again to link the
Vergilian prophecies of the divine peace-bringing boy with the
Messiah whom men now were seeking or had found in Caesar
Augustus. Thus myth and poem and prophecy were inter-
woven in the life of that Emperor who had redeemed the Holy
Sepulchre and was now waging war on a corrupted clergy.

The fusion of the Messiah-Emperor and the Sicilian God of
Justice in the person of Frederick II gave a peculiarly practical
and human character to the new Emperor-cult. In turning
over the letters that passed to and fro between the courtiers
we find such unanimity of tone and phrase as almost amounts
to a " secret dogma," which grows more concentrated and
forceful in proportion as the Pope is seen as the false and
Frederick as the true Vicar of Christ. It was natural to turn
to Piero della Vigna as the Peter and Prince of the Apostles of
this new imperial Saviour. Della Vigna became " like unto
the new Law-bearer, Moses, descending from Sinai, bringing
the tables of the law from Heaven to men," or, again, " a second
Joseph to whom as a true interpreter the mighty Caesar whose
power the Sun and Moon admire has handed over the direction
of the kingdoms of the earth. He was the Peter who bears the
keys of Empire and locks what no man may open, and opens
what no man again may lock." " Peter, the humble fisher, the
Prince of the Apostles, who left his nets and followed God . . .
but this law-bearing Peter quits not his Master's side. The
Galilean thrice denied his Lord . . . far be it from the Capuan
to deny his Master once." The trend of courtly thought is

even more clearly revealed in the half serious letter which was written to Piero della Vigna. " And the Lord said : ' Peter, lovest thou me ? Feed my sheep,' and thus the Lord who loveth Justice wished to build justice on this rock and give the reins of law into the hands of Peter, making you the custodian of justice. To show this the more clearly the Lord hath placed you over against the face of him who is the President but also the Perverter of the Church, that the true vicegerent Peter may rule through Justice while the false Vicar of Christ perverts his vicegerency to the injury of many in body, goods and name. . . . If such a charge oppresses you, since you are unaccustomed to it and never sought it . . . you can only answer ' Lord thou knowest that I love thee. If I can serve thy people I refuse not the service : Thy will be done.' "

This was not, as has sometimes been assumed, a serious suggestion that Piero della Vigna should be, in fact, elevated as a real Anti-Pope, but it contained the idea that the Head of the " imperial Church," the jurist hierarchy, should be in a special sense an " Anti-Pope." Below the half-serious, half-jesting flattery with which the courtier recalls the master to his lofty duties, urging : " the Pope is useless, do thou, as the true Peter, discharge his duties," we detect the lofty sense of dignity and responsibility which inspired the Court, and the clear consciousness that the imperial hierarchy of jurist and official formed an independent spiritual order like the Pope's Church, and quite as good. Napoleon's thought: " Gown against gown, esprit de corps against esprit de corps, judge against priest," was anticipated, in other words, at Frederick's court. To express ideas such as these was in those days only possible by using the symbols of the only spiritual kingdom then known : the Church with Christ her King.

To establish the worship of a spiritual ruler without the Church men were fain to employ the Church's methods : while to celebrate the warlike triumphs of the Emperor their thoughts leaped forthwith to the pagan Caesars. Thus it is that the State is called the *imperialis ecclesia*, the provinces are conceived as bishops' dioceses and the purchase of office as simony. At moments men went further and stated that the Emperor's Church, founded on Peter, was manifest whenever

" the spirit of the Illustrious Emperor draws strength from a supper with his disciples." We recall in this connection the High Mass of *Justitia*, the mystery and the *sacratissimum ministerium*, the solemn exotic ritual of the High Court when the Law Incarnate was revealed in the Emperor's person, when the Emperor whispered his sentence to his Logothetes, who announced it to the kneeling multitude, while the tinkling of the bell betokened the mystic communion that was consummated. The essential result of the identification of Frederick with the Son of God is the reintroduction of the human element. The State was cemented by the direct belief of his disciples in a living man and his divine mission. Such a faith as saints evoke by miracles, but never an Emperor inspired save Frederick only. He wrought no miracles, but he was called " Transformer," " Wonder of the World." He was inevitably glorified into a saint, and men gave him the title of the Byzantine Emperor : " Long live the name of St. Frederick amongst the people ! "

There would be no need to pay so much attention to the inflated homage of the courtiers' writings if this worship of Frederick had been confined to the rhetoric of the Vigna circle. This, however, was by no means the case. This extra-ecclesiastical " sacred cult " of a living man had other and very different consequences : it led to the representation and immortalisation of this divine person in art. The remarkable outburst of south Italian plastic art, an early breath as it were of the Renaissance, that suddenly blossomed as if by magic in the carefully-tended Paradise that was Frederick's Sicilian kingdom, gave more open and more unmistakable expression to the feelings which the elaborate metaphors of the courtiers' letters half obscured.

This new art formed no exception to the law that representational art is dependent on a living worship—certainly in primitive times. The great works of Hohenstaufen sculpture in Sicily date almost without exception from the last ten years of Frederick's life, from the period after Cortenuova when the Emperor-worship began to take more definite shape and play a more ceremonial rôle. Amongst court circles it began to strike a more human and personal note and gradually to develop into a Frederick-worship. The sculpture was inspired by the worship of the Hohenstaufen God : at no moment was this " ruler, wrought and made man by the Great Artificer's hand " more vividly present to men's minds than in that solemn ceremony in which he, clothed in the awe of his divine majesty as highest judge and lawgiver, consummated in the eyes of all his communion with God when God, incarnate as Law, became man in the stainless Son ! "

The literary records tell of that High Mass of the Emperor's, the " supper with the disciples," the founding of the *imperialis ecclesia* on Peter, his nearest intimate, and the works of art themselves, representing man in his " ideal," *i.e.* his divine moment, can mean no less. In those days when the solemn ritual was evolved and della Vigna, under the exotic title of Logothetes, officiated, as intermediary and speaker for the Emperor, there was created in Naples a representation, probably a relief, picturing the scene. It has not been preserved, but has been described with considerable exactness : In the background the Emperor was seen high and lifted up, seated on his throne, beside him at a more modest elevation Piero della Vigna, and in the foreground, at the Emperor's feet, the kneeling people. The multitude was demanding Justice from the Emperor, the chronicler declares, and the inscription tells the same tale :

CAESAR—AMOR LEGUM.   FREDERICE PIISSIME REGUM
CAUSARUM TELAS   NOSTRARUM SOLVE QUERELAS.

The person so addressed who is to loose the web of strife, and who in his Book of Laws describes himself as weaving the woof of Justice, points to Piero della Vigna, the transmitter of the divine commands, as who should say : " Turn to this man in your strife. He will give judgment or beg me to do so. Vigna is his surname . . . he is called Peter, the Judge."

Even without the explanatory verses of the inscription the arrangement of the scene would have indicated what was here represented : this was the Emperor " *in cultu Justitiae.*" Justice, poured forth in due gradation. As Justice reigns as mediatrix between God and the Emperor, so *Petrus Judex* is represented as mediator between the Emperor of Justice and the people. Men were accustomed thus to see their ruler holding his High Court. The vitally important point is that we have here a representation of no abstract thought, but of real, actual life as it was known and seen. We have no knowledge how far this relief in the palace of Naples approached the antique, but under Frederick II all plastic art turned towards antiquity, driven by an inner necessity, quite independent of the Emperor's personal predilections. For the sculpture that came to birth in Sicily was a " profane " art. Here, in the Pope's fief, in scorn of the Church, came to birth the first great non-religious art of the West such as served to celebrate the State and the State Gods in the days of the old Roman Divi, if by " profane " we understand a contrast to ecclesiastical and religious representation. The secular art of the Hohenstaufen State was in its own way no less " sacred."

In the Middle Ages all creative art had been exclusively ecclesiastical ; the outburst of new creativeness, and the new style associated with the secular state, inevitably meant reversion to the antique, and the dependence was surprisingly intimate. For a whole millennium all pictorial representation had served the glorification of the Saviour or his followers, the Saints. Pictures of rulers formed no exception : they were confined to chapels and cathedrals and were designed to magnify the Redeemer. Now for the first time plastic art was given a meaning, a life, a consecration, a *raison d'être* by the secular State. Only the worship of the Emperor Frederick makes this possible. Here, in the secular world, outside the Church, another son of God was glorified.

From another point of view this ultimate dependence on antiquity and its method of seeing and portraying was entirely logical. The hieratical-ecclesiastical art had devoted its first attention to the relation which the presentation bore to the God of the other world, and its second thought only to the object represented. Here a bodily presentation of the World Ruler himself was possible : a portrait of the man who was, as he was. Truth and reality in art, which a heavenly subject rendered superfluous and which could be replaced by signs and symbols and frozen symmetries, now became the important aim. The beautiful golden coins indicate that even a " likeness " was by no means to be despised: " In order that the form of the money may bring our name to your memory and our illustrious image to your eyes . . . that the frequent sight thereof may strengthen you in your loyalty and fire your devotion." Above the image on the seal is written : " The human impulse to fulfil commands received, faith in the message sent, these things are only justified by the image stamped in wax or metal of him who issues the commands." On the seals the image is still mainly a mere " sign," but this image speaks like a command, and the more it resembles the commanding person the greater will be the force it carries. This was the point to which the Emperor attached importance : the imperial image would be potent by recalling the PERSON, and power would radiate from it as grace from a sacred picture through religious faith.

Emancipated from the rigidity and symbolism of religious convention and once more in touch with life, everything in Hohenstaufen plastic art turned towards antiquity, whose achievements in a " profane " self-sufficing State had no need of Christian or mystic interpretation to be sacred. The recognition that every thing existed in its own right, was in itself divine and god-devised, was reinforced by the new conception of art for which Frederick stood. He had an eye for the bodies of man and beast such as no man before him had possessed, and his strong feeling of affinity with the Caesars had given him a keen appreciation of the art of their times. He filled his Apulian castles with ancient sculptures. From Grottaferrata, near Rome, he had a bronze cow and a bronze male statue transported to Apulia. From Naples slaves had had to carry on their shoulders ancient works of art to adorn the castle of Lucera. Almost all his castles boasted similar treasures. High on a wall of the inner court of Castel del Monte a relief may even now be seen, on which horses and riders can still be distinguished. Perhaps it was a Meleager hunting-scene such as was a favourite subject for sarcophagi . . . such as adorns the tomb in which Frederick buried the remains of his first consort, Constance of Aragon, in the cathedral of Palermo.

The Emperor by no means contented himself with such works of art as were already to hand. His sculptors were commissioned to make more. Many heads and fragments of sculpture in Castel del Monte are probably copies of antique originals. Imitation, however, was not good enough. The Apulian stone masons received remarkable commissions and were set to work from real life, though in antique style. At times one might imagine that these were genuine relics of Roman days did not some detail betray the thirteenth century. The Emperor's " unquenched desire " to renew the greatness of the Caesars, to take his stand beside the Augusti and measure himself against them, called forth these wonderful creations : figures in the round more like the antique than any preceding medieval work. Since the days of the Roman Emperors no state divinities had called for representation. What Christian ruler would have thought it necessary to build a great triumphal arch to glorify himself and his State, and decorate it with the figures of his trusty followers. Who would have dared to crave it ! Who would have dared to execute it !

We need not here further emphasise the boldness of an earthly warrior's celebrating his own triumph in a day when men recognised only One as victor. A strongly fortified bridge-head had been in course of construction since 1234 in front of the town of Capua, to guard the Via Appia where it crossed the Volturno. The fortification itself, the plan of which the Emperor had sketched with his own hands, seems to have been roughly finished by 1239. It was probably about this time, when Frederick was returning as Triumphator to his own kingdom, that he decided to adorn the gate of the bridge with sculptures and develop it into an ornamental arch. " The magnificent marble portal " which has been so much praised was not completed till 1247. This work of art, begotten of the Hohenstaufen rule in Sicily, was much admired throughout Renaissance times.

It must not be compared with the Arch of Trajan in the adjacent Benevento. The combination of fortification and triumphal arch recalls rather the gate of the Castel Nuovo in Naples which was erected two centuries later by Alfonso I of Aragon, a ruler who in many points is a true heir of Frederick II.

We are told that " two towers of astounding size, beauty and strength " flanked the entrance to the Capuan Gate. Everything was faced with marble or a stone resembling marble ; the hewn stones, as in all Frederick's buildings, were so skilfully fitted that the joints secured by molten lead were practically invisible. The victories and triumphs of Frederick were portrayed in relief. The side that faced the town was adorned with figures of Mercury, and the keystone was a laurel-crowned head of Jupiter (possibly plundered from the neighbouring amphitheatre of Capua). The outer side that faced the traveller who was approaching Capua along the Via Appia was more ornate. Gigantic statues, all carved by Frederick's own sculptors, filled the niches. We are not absolutely certain of the arrangement of the figures, but everything indicates that in the highest place of all there stood a female form, double or even treble life-size, whose powerful and beautiful head is still extant. The features recall the majesty, the reflective power, the serenity of a Farnese Juno. In spite of the general antique effect of this colossal figure the details are not indebted to antique models. The hand of this goddess is pointing to her breast, where instead of a heart the imperial eagle stretches his wings and claws—perhaps the scarcely-tamed eagle of the coins.

This figure probably stood alone, crowning the summit of the structure. The eagle is not the only indication that this figure stands in intimate relation to that of Frederick himself in the niche immediately below. The armies of the French Revolution shattered the head of this figure and have left only the trunk, but much can be deduced from even the fragments of this life-size statue. Frederick was represented, as on the Augustales, wearing the mantle of the Roman Imperator, but otherwise the usual dress of his day ; his beardless, still-youthful face (deduced from a gem) looking straight before him, scanning the new arrival with his calm unruffled gaze. His forearm is stretched out in an attitude half of menace, half of benediction, familiar in certain pictures of Christ. Two fingers of one hand were raised " as if," says the chronicler, " his mouth were about to give voice to the resonant threatening of the verses " which are engraved in a semicircle above his head. They form a distich : the hexameter is apparently spoken by the Goddess above :

> At the bidding of Caesar I stand, guarantor for the peace of the kingdom.

The pentameter is assigned to Frederick himself :

> In wrath I shall ruin the man whom I know to be faithless.

This couplet forms a second link between Frederick and the Goddess.

Two other figures give the clue to the identity of the exalted figure who is represented as larger than the Emperor, and stands above him and yet with him forms a unity. Right and left of the Emperor and probably slightly lower, very possibly one on each of the towers, are two busts which are usually interpreted with extreme probability as two High Court Judges : the one Piero della Vigna, the other Thaddeus of Suessa. Each of their niches bears a hexameter. The one offers the invitation :

> Enter with confidence all who purpose to live without trepass ;

while the second threatens :

> He who is faithless may fear to end as an exile in fetters.

This more than human female form, which later patriotism interpreted as a representation of the town of Capua, can have been no other genius than the "Justitia Augusti," one with Caesar and yet greater than man, and exalted even above the Emperor : Justice communicating her commands through the Emperor to the Judges. Frederick II in life : "Father and Son of Justitia."

The composition of the three-storied Capuan Gate tells the same tale as the relief in the palace at Naples, where the multitude, awed by the fear of the Lord, kneel before incarnate Justice. There was no need to portray the multitude on the triumphal arch ; they were represented by the living passers-by, who if they did not pause to kneel would yet shudder before the threatening Judgment Day. It was certainly Frederick's intention here to inspire the people with fear of the divine imperial power by this image of himself, by the impression on the eye—"whose sight is more potent than aught that the ear perceives." The chronicler confirms this hypothesis, for he himself felt the effect the Emperor intended : " The threatening verses were inscribed to inspire fear in those who passed through the gate and fear in those to whom the figures themselves spake."

We recall the Sicilian representatives of the " Pantocrator " or " Immanuel," " famous in his majesty, terrible in his glory," figures of Christ still Byzantine in style, with unmoved gaze, slightly oblique, almost cruel, compelling perhaps a shuddering love through the fear of sword and lawbook which the threatening-blessing figure holds in its hands.

Such fear Frederick II definitely sought to evoke. The Sicilian Kingdom of Peace and of Justice whose threshold was marked by this Gate of Judgment could only be maintained, to quote Piero della Vigna, " by the fear which the Emperor inspired who was skilled both to correct and to chastise by the rod of his victory ". . . a spirit close akin to Dante's, who inscribed the verse : " All hope abandon ye who enter here," over the gate that led into the realm of God's Justice.

People of those days were ready to give an ecclesiastical-allegorical turn to the interpretation of the gate of Capua. The *Gesta Romanorum* first describe the portal with accuracy, and then provide a strange interpretation : the Emperor's figure becomes that of our Lord Jesus Christ. The marble gate represents Holy Church through which men enter into the Kingdom of Heaven. The female figure of Justice becomes the Saviour's Virgin Mother and the Vigna bust John the Evangelist. Even the courtiers could scarcely have given an interpretation more flattering to their imperial master. The pious writer, however, had another end in view. This building and these figures which display no solitary Christian symbol— the Emperor has not even a cross upon his crown but is wearing the simple Roman pointed diadem—must be robbed of their dangerous pagan suggestion and ecclesiasticised. As a cardinal wrote about Frederick, however, in another context, " The stones hurled against him by the Pope turn to straw, like filth he scatters the gold of the papal anathema, he lets the rays of the sun fall upon him, and he fears the God of the Lightning as little as an archer with his bow."

The Church looked askance at this new art, and amongst the papalists it became an obsession to accuse the Ghibellines of idol- and image-worship. Even Dante did not escape : he was said to have placed wax figures in smoke. It must have seemed an unspeakable *hubris* that the same Emperor who denied the general immortality of the soul should cause the perishable body to be carved in stone " for eternal and undying memory." " Frederick dares to alter laws and epochs " was the papal verdict on the " Transformer of the World."

Sicilian plastic art would have been unthinkable without the glorification of the World Ruler and the World Judge, and was indeed so entirely grounded thereon that, apart from a few late echoes, monumental art in the antique style died with the death of Frederick II. A Gothic reaction set in everywhere, superseding the antique which had been reawakened by the State for the glory of the State.

For many decades to come there was no call for the representation of godlike man ; only one Emperor had been able to inspire and to compel this homage. After him no one individual was sufficiently pre-eminent ; without the Emperor, the unique ruler who is " the one thing that exists in its own integrity and forms no part of another," the life-giving breath was lacking. Thus it fell out that the magic glory of the Caesars that had suddenly blazed up in the south with Frederick perished with him and died away like a terrifying but seductive emanation of Lucifer.

Not the least part of the miracle lay in Frederick's finding the artists who could carry out such unwonted tasks in a form so perfect. For the products of these imperial sculptors reached a level which Italian art did not soon regain. The amazing thing was that Frederick drew these artists from his own Sicilian kingdom, and begot as it were his own sculptors, as he had earlier begotten his own poets. How he conjured this ability from his simple Apulian stone-masons is a mystery. He required it for the glorification of his State and his State Gods, and what he required he was wont to get.

The names of some of these masters are known. They were for the most part natives of Apulia and the Capitanata. Their names throw no light on the mystery. The creative force was not theirs. These masons were instructed to follow closely the antique models ; the first school of art that worked systematically from the antique, directed by one master mind, was the imperial School of Sculpture in Apulia. Without the compulsion which the Emperor exercised the work of the Sicilian sculptors ceased, though a son of the imperial master-craftsman, Bartholomew of Foggia, was still able to carry out a noble work, the bust of Sigilgaita at Ravello. Only one exception might perhaps be made in favour of Nicholas of Pisa.

It seems no longer in doubt that this artist, though later settled in Pisa, was a native of Apulia. Vasari, who counts him as the earliest master of plastic art in the Italian Renaissance, relates him vaguely to the Sicilian school and to the master of the Capuan Gate. It is by no means impossible that Nicholas had learned and worked anonymously amongst the imperial sculptors of his native country before, in 1260, he created his first masterpiece, the pulpit in the Baptistery at Pisa. Whether Nicholas of Pisa was directly or indirectly the bringer of new vision to Italy, there is no doubt that sculpture after the antique spread, as vernacular poetry had spread, from south to north, from Sicily to Upper Italy. It was noticed from the beginning that poetry and the new plastic art alike struck their first roots in the imperial towns of Italy. Nicholas's first works were created in Pisa, Siena, Pistoia, at a time when these towns lay under papal interdict.

Vasari records that Nicholas of Pisa learnt his craftsmanship by copying ancient vases and sarcophagi. Where was this done elsewhere in Italy, and where, with such method as in the imperial School in Apulia, in which this exercise was imposed by Frederick as a duty ? Who opened the eyes of the Apulian, and indirectly, therefore, of the Italian masters, to see and appreciate the works of the ancients, if not the man who in other spheres taught men " to draw new water from old wells " ? Frederick did not himself wield hammer and chisel, yet the sculptors are his creatures and his pupils. A recent French art-critic exclaims : C'est l'empereur qui a été le vrai sculpteur !

There is no reason to doubt that the true statesman can evoke a new art of poetry, of architecture and of sculpture, the more that the magic of the chisel thrives best in the ordered atmosphere of a living state, in which the voice of the community begins to make itself heard.   Thus this Hohenstaufen Emperor, whom men hailed as the image of God, who was the first human incarnation of Universal Law, became by the glorification of his state and of his person the founder of a new plastic art, consciously drawing its inspiration from the pagan.   Almost contemporaneously a new school of painting was born within the Church, which based itself immediately on the reanimated myth of early Christian worship.   The recent theory is that the glorification of St. Francis fired the new " Gothic " painting.

In March 1240 Frederick II returned to his Sicilian kingdom, but all his thoughts and plans were now directed to the development of the Italian monarchy.   In spite of having been absent for five years, in spite of having spent four in almost continuous campaigning in Upper and Central Italy, he allowed himself only a few weeks of rest in his beloved Sicily.   " Such yearning and care for the pacification of Italy impels us . . . that neither the need of rest nor recreation, nor yet the delights of our kingdom can hold us back.   When with diligence and perseverance we had accomplished the great tasks which were inherent in our greatest task of all, we speedily quitted Sicily without rest, which would have been fatal to our activity, and fared forth in the heat of summer and the dust of the camp, eschewing dangers neither to our faithful followers nor to ourselves."

After a Diet in Foggia, the complete restaffing of all Sicilian offices, and the promulgation of a number of new laws, Frederick was in May 1240 actually again encamped near Capua with the newly-levied army.   In June he advanced against the frontier of the Papal States.   His intention was to compel the Romans to open their gates and the Pope to make peace if possible, by a campaign of devastation in the Roman Campagna.   At the last moment the Emperor had to change his plans.   The new Grand Master of the Teutonic Order, Conrad of Thuringia, arrived as envoy from the secular and spiritual princes of Germany who hoped as intermediaries to negotiate a peace between Emperor and Pope, as they had been successful in doing after the Crusade.

The Pope's proceedings against Frederick had completely failed in their effect. From over-frequent use the ban had lost its edge, and was no longer the formidable weapon it had been of yore ; the release of subjects from their allegiance had likewise worn thin. The sentence of excommunication was, it is true, to be pronounced anew every Sunday from every pulpit in the world with burning of candles and tinkling of bells. This, no doubt, took place in foreign countries, though often under protest. In those very countries, however, where the reading of the papal bull was most vital to Pope Gregory, within the Empire itself, there was no lack of resistance and obstruction. Innumerable communities in Italy were themselves under the ban for the most various reasons, and no Church service was being held in them in any case. Every town which Frederick visited fell automatically under an interdict, and we may fairly doubt whether in any case any bishop throughout Imperial Italy would have dared to read the ban : and in Sicily it is improbable that any single priest was found to incur the risk to life and property. Moreover, all adherents of the Emperor's, like the Archbishop of Palermo, were also excommunicate, and any Sicilian bishop who was not an adherent was speedily banished.

In Germany also numerous spiritual princes refused to proclaim the excommunication from the pulpit. The bishops of Germany were as reluctant as the secular princes to imperil their rights as lords of the land by taking sides against the Emperor to whom they owed so great an extension of these rights. They rarely went so far as to make any move against the Pope, and certainly not against the Emperor : for the most part they calmly looked on.

Pope Gregory may well have hoped to win over the princes, usually so ready to revolt against the Emperor, and to turn them against this Hohenstaufen, as Innocent III had so successfully done against the Welf Otto. But Gregory's expectations were disappointed, as at the time of the Crusade. His attempt to set up a rival king failed utterly ; the envenomed letters in which he posed as the protector of princely privilege which Frederick was seeking to undermine fell on deaf ears, as did his insinuations that Frederick was seeking to destroy all Christian princes and magnates by the hands of his assassins in order to rule alone. Frederick II had succeeded beyond belief in attaching the princes to himself, and they viewed the situation clearly. First the spiritual and then the secular princes wrote unanimously to the Pope, and stated in the clearest and most unequivocal language that the sole cause of the ban was the Pope's having espoused the cause of those arch-traitors, the Lombards. The princes recalled that their position was a dual one : on the one hand as prelates they were sons of the Church, on the other hand as princes of the Empire they were vassals of the Emperor, and that they must not fail in their duty as members of the Empire ; they would greatly grieve if they were driven to mourn for the Church. At the same time they offered the Pope their assistance in re-establishing between him and the Emperor the peace they most earnestly desired to see. All the princes joined in one great common declaration, and, further, each wrote separately, describing the confusion into which the world had been plunged by this new quarrel, and imploring the Pope to release the Emperor from the ban.

The German Grand Master had just at this moment reached the Pope bearing the princes' proposals, and Frederick did not care to jeopardise the arbitration by a new invasion of the Patrimonium. The Emperor had, it is true, no hope that the stiff-necked Pope would accept any peace that was not wrung from him, and the negotiations in fact proved fruitless.

With unblushing effrontery the Pope suddenly announced that he could release the Emperor from the excommunication incurred by his heresy, godlessness and persecution of the Church, only if the enemies of the Emperor, the Lombards, were included in the peace. Though Pope Gregory had always firmly denied that the Lombard question was in any way connected with the excommunication, and had made the most far-fetched allegations in his bulls and manifestos (though it was known in the market-place that he had banned the Emperor to save the Lombards from his vengeance), yet now Frederick's release was to be effected, not by penance for acknowledged

sin, but by political concessions to the Lombards. We can
hardly wonder that the negotiations broke down; not even
an armistice was achieved. All subsequent peace overtures
foundered on the same reef ; the Curia clung to the Lombard
clause, and Frederick with perfect justice refused to buy his
absolution at the price. The German Grand Master died a
few weeks after his arrival in Rome, and Frederick meantime
had resumed the fighting in the Romagna, though not in the
Patrimonium.

The Emperor's position had grown less favourable since the
defection of Ravenna in the preceding year. The imperial
cause was gravely endangered in the Romagna. The papal
legate, Gregory of Montelongo, had rallied Venetians, Bolognese and others and conquered Ferrara, while Bologna and
Faënza had throughout belonged to the League. The Emperor now marched north along the Adriatic through the March
of Ancona. It was summer and he was attacked by a slight
fever in the swampy country which, however, "we so overcame by the might of the spirit that it did not presume to stay
our victorious progress after the end of the critical day." By
the middle of August he lay with a modest force of Germans,
Tuscans and Apulians before Ravenna. He had originally
intended to march on Bologna, but hearing that Paulus Traversarius was dead, who had been the leader of the anti-imperial
party in Ravenna, and that feeling in the town was veering
round, he changed his plan and appeared before Ravenna.
The water supply was cut off, and the town after a six-day
siege surrendered and gave hostages. It was then received
into favour.

Frederick was now free to turn to Bologna. If he had
invested Bologna, however, Faënza lying further to the south
would have threatened his rear. It, therefore, seemed prudent
first to take Faënza. Frederick counted no doubt on succeeding as quickly here as at Ravenna. But a mere siege effected
nothing. The town offered an unexpectedly strong resistance,
the garrison having been heavily reinforced by Venetians and
Bolognese, and the defence was conducted by a young

Florentine of twenty-three, Count Guido Guerra. The Counts
Palatine of the Guidi family were usually staunch imperialists,
but this one grandson of " the chaste Guldrada " (whom Dante
praises as a fine soldier though a sodomite) had broken with
the tradition of his house.   He plays an important part in the
anti-Hohenstaufen campaigns as one of the bravest Florentine
leaders on the Guelf side.

The Emperor soon got into difficulties at Faënza. September had slipped by without a decision. October came
and still the end was not in sight.   Frederick now decided to
blockade Faënza completely and spend the winter before the
town.   He struck his tents and to everyone's amazement built
strong wooden huts.   Before long a complete wooden town,
protected by trenches, stretched in a wide circle round the
beleaguered fortress.   Winter undertakings of this sort were
unprecedented.   It had not hitherto been Frederick's way to
show this bulldog tenacity.   He had usually achieved success
at the first onslaught with comparatively little trouble, and if
that did not succeed he preferred to withdraw as he had done
from Brescia.   At this juncture a spectacular failure would have
been fateful, and in spite of innumerable obstacles he must
carry the siege through to the end.

The Emperor's aversion from long-drawn military enterprises which involved large numbers of troops had a very
practical basis : the cost was enormous.   The imperial army
was largely a mercenary one.   The only unpaid troops were
the Saracens, who were probably indemnified by grants of land.
All the other Sicilian troops were paid either from the very
first, or after a certain number of days.   The feudal system had
been almost wholly superseded in Sicily.   At best the vassals
served within the kingdom for a short time at their own expense.   If this period was exceeded, or if they were employed
outside Sicily, they received pay, and that at a very high rate.
The difference between vassals drawing pay and ordinary
mercenaries was slight.   The Italian towns gave the Emperor
troops on somewhat more favourable terms.   The infantry
militia and the knights received pay from their commune for
the first four or six weeks.   If this was exceeded, which it
almost always was, then the payment fell on the imperial

Treasury, and this question naturally was of prime importance in waging war. The storming of a town was often fixed for a certain day, say November 10th, not with reference to the military situation but because November 12th was the day on which several thousand men ended their term of service, and a prolongation of the siege would mean expense. Considerations of this sort probably accounted for the speedy abandonment of the siege of Brescia by the immense army.

Want began to be felt outside Faënza. In order to make the blockade complete it was necessary to call up large forces, especially infantry, which the Italian State had to find. The surrounding towns, Imola, Forli, Forlimpopolo, Ravenna, Rimini, were first drawn upon, then Florence and Tuscany in general, where King Enzio was in charge of recruitment; finally, troops were even brought from Western Lombardy, from Lodi, Vercelli, and Novara. As the blockade grew more and more protracted money grew scarcer than it had ever been. At the beginning of the campaign the Emperor had had recourse to the expedient of collecting the taxes from the Italian towns in advance for the coming year, remitting one-fifth as interest. He next helped himself to the treasuries of the Church in Sicily, as the leaders of the papal troops had done on a previous occasion. Gold, silver, precious stones, costly brocades, silken garments, were taken over against a receipt and stored in the imperial Treasury. Then the ingenious Emperor—perhaps on the credit of this large treasure—hit on the expedient of issuing leather money showing the head and the eagle of the golden Augustales. This leather money was everywhere accepted without protest, and was later redeemed by the imperial Treasury.

On the other hand there was no shortage of provisions, for the routes to Sicily were open to the Emperor. The favourite sea-route from the Apulian harbours to Ravenna was not wholly safe. The Emperor's siege of Faënza involved Bologna and Venice also, and the Venetians had succeeded in plundering and burning to the ground the two Apulian coast towns of Termola and Vasto and in capturing an imperial galley near Brindisi which was returning from Jerusalem. Frederick at once instituted reprisals; he requested the Emperor John

Vatatzes of Nicaea to raid any Venetian possessions within his
reach and the Sultan of Tunis to break off all commerce with
Venice for the moment. He also subsidised the Dalmatian
pirates of Zara and despatched ships from Ancona against the
Venetians. His Apulian fortresses and dungeons were, moreover, full of hostages from almost all Italian towns, on whom
he could wreak his vengeance. It was at this period that
Pietro Tiepolo was hanged, the son of the Doge of Venice, who
had been taken prisoner at Cortenuova. These measures put
a stop to the attacks of Venice.

The Emperor lay for eight months before Faënza in enforced
idleness while his troops constructed underground tunnels to
the beleaguered town, and the provisions of the besieged began
gradually to be exhausted. He occupied himself by reading
and correcting the translation of an Arabic treatise on hawking
which Master Theodore had made. Weightier matters than
his falcons, however, claimed his attention in this winter camp.
Pope Gregory had schemes afoot that Frederick could not
ignore.

Immediately after his excommunication Frederick had
written to the cardinals and conjured them, " the coadjutors of
Peter, the Senators of the City, the hinges of the World," to
invite the whole Christian world, kings and princes, bishops
and church dignitaries alike, to send their delegates to a General
Council. He himself would be prepared to submit his case to
this council, even to appear before it in person to prove his
complaints against Pope Gregory, who had in the most serious
manner infringed imperial law in Italy. He might himself
have had recourse to the age-old imperial right to summon
such a council. To preserve the impartiality of this tribunal,
however, which was to judge between him and the Pope, it
seemed to him right that neither he nor Pope Gregory should
approach the world in his own cause ; the College of Roman
Cardinals should issue the invitations.

This eagerly-desired Council never met. Pope Gregory had
sound reasons for preventing it : no Council should sit in
judgment on the Vicar of Christ. He notified instead a Church

Council to be held a year later. His letters of invitation sug-
gest a commonplace agenda : certain affairs of Church and
State are to be discussed : as if one of the usual, not-infrequent
synods was in question. The Pope's real intentions, however,
were not to be misunderstood. The Council was to be summoned by the Pope and to be his instrument, and its first duty
would be the deposition of the Emperor. Pope Gregory had
already been canvassing for a successor to the Hohenstaufen :
without success. He first sounded a Danish prince ; when this
candidate refused the Pope tried to win France over by playing
on her historic yearning to fill the imperial throne : a dream
that had not slept since the days of Charlemagne, which lived
in Louis XIV and was realised by Napoleon. Pope Gregory
suggested Count Robert of Artois, brother of Louis IX of
France, as Frederick II's successor. France declined with the
proud remark that a man in whose veins ran the royal blood of
France was greater than any Emperor whose throne depended
on election. Further, that the Count of Artois had informed
his friend the Hohenstaufen Emperor, a man whom France
beyond measure respected, of the Pope's proposal, and that the
Emperor Frederick had called on the God of Vengeance to
requite His Holiness.

No one could for a moment mistake the intention of this
Council, summoned by Frederick's personal enemy, the Pope,
to which Milan and the other rebel towns were invited to pass
sentence on the Emperor. This Council, usurping the place
of the Council which Frederick desired, must not take place.
Immediately on learning of the Pope's design Frederick started
his counter-measures. He addressed innumerable letters to
bishops, princes and kings, declaring that this Council summoned by his personal enemy had only one aim : to decide the
Lombard question. He would, however, never concede the
principle that a spiritual power should adjudicate in state
affairs. He had no quarrel with the Most Holy Church of
Rome, but a grave one with the existing Pope, and as long as
Gregory IX acted as a foe of the Empire he, Frederick, as
Emperor, would take steps to prevent any Council of the High
Priest. He would refuse safe conduct to all delegates attending
the Council, and he warned the whole world against sending

representatives thereto.   He had secured all routes by sea and
land and no one would reach Rome against his wishes.   Simultaneously with these warnings he issued stringent orders to his
supporters in all countries of the Empire to refuse passage to
any seeking to attend the Council, and offered rewards for each
delegate captured.   No one could question the possibility of
this blockade, for it was well known that remittances of money
to the Pope merely swelled the imperial coffers.

Frederick II cannot be accused of having made a secret of
his intentions.   He always made a practice of making his plans
known beforehand down to the minutest details.   He was not
believed ;   no one credited him with the serious intention of
carrying his threats into execution, and the world was immensely surprised when he did so.   The Emperor's strict
command deterred the prelates of Germany, Italy and Sicily
from attending.   The western powers, however : England,
France and Spain could scarcely turn a deaf ear to the papal
summons, and proposed to send the heads of their churches to
Rome.   Since the Emperor at Faënza could block most of the
land routes Pope Gregory recommended the sea routes to these
western travellers.   He put himself in touch with Genoa.   A
fleet composed of cargo-boats and war-galleys was to await the
prelates in Nice and Genoa and conduct them to the Tiber
mouth.   Corresponding recommendations were made to the
prelates :   they would find sea-travel the safer, and might confidently trust themselves to the Genoese, with whom the Pope
had made all arrangements and had concluded the necessary
agreements.   The sea-republic was to profit by three thousand
five hundred pounds, of which one thousand was to be paid at
once.   The papal legate to whom the negotiations had been
confided had to raise the money from Genoese merchants who
demanded two hundred pounds as interest.   The balance was
to fall due for payment a month before the departure of the
fleet, and if Pope Gregory broke the contract he was to pay
five hundred pounds as penalty.   The property of the Roman
Church was pledged as security.   Genoa was not giving her
assistance for love.   Gregory IX accepted all the terms proposed, but begged that the preparations might be secret, so that
no hint of them might reach the Emperor.

Frederick II, however, had, as it happened, more adherents in Genoa than in any other enemy town. The upper nobility like the Spinola, Doria, Grilli and de Mari were almost exclusively Ghibelline (the Margrave Caretto was later to be the Emperor's son-in-law), so that Frederick was in constant communication with the town. One letter of the Emperor's which had been hidden in an imitation loaf made of wax was intercepted by the enemy, and created great excitement in the town, but other despatches safely reached their destination. However it was achieved, the Emperor in his winter quarters before Faënza learned exactly what the Pope had planned.

Quietly he made his counter-preparations. First Sicily was instructed to mobilise and man the fleet. The Emperor was now to reap the benefit of the sea-power he had so steadily built up. For years past ship after ship had left the royal wharves, and Frederick was now in a position to command at need a fleet of sixty-five galleys. For comparison's sake it should be mentioned that Genoa could, with difficulty, man a contingent of fifty boats of war. The Sicilian crews were brought up to strength by levies on the maritime peoples who were compelled to serve as sailors, but in return were relieved from other obligations. The ships' captains were sea-counts, feudal vassals. Frederick II's whole organisation of the fleet was so admirable that the Aragonese in Sicily later exactly repeated his decrees and re-issued his instructions about the duties of the Admiral, which included regulations for every branch of the service. The previous Admiral, Nicolas Spinola, a Genoese, had recently died. From Faënza Frederick II appointed in March 1241 another Genoese, Ansaldus de Mari, first as Admiral of the Kingdom of Sicily. Shortly after, the Emperor sent him an imperial banner and his warrant as Admiral of the Roman Empire, an office which Frederick created. The strength and equipment of the squadron which was destined for the transport of the prelates was known in its minutest details to the new Commander of the Fleet, who, being an imperialist, had thought it discreet to escape secretly from Genoa in February 1241. His powers as Admiral left him completely free to take what measures he deemed best. He immediately assumed command of the Sicilian fleet, which was in readiness to put to sea, and sailed that same March with twenty-seven galleys to Pisa to join forces with an equal number of Pisan ships.

Frederick II had been instant in warning the invited guests to refrain from attending the Council. The Pisans even sought to dissuade their rivals, the Genoese, from the undertaking, and other voices also made themselves heard, pointing out the grave danger of visiting Rome against the Emperor's wishes. One pamphlet—a product perhaps of the imperial Chancery—purporting to be addressed by a well-meaning cleric to his friends the prelates was particularly urgent. The author dwelt at length, with evident glee, on the general miseries of a sea-voyage, describing sea-sickness in its minutest consequences with the satanic pleasure of a non-sufferer, and, finally, demonstrating that Frederick II, " a second Nero, a second Herod," was " miserly in mercy, prodigal in punishment, full moreover of wrath, and entirely lacking in piety." He was in command of all harbours from sea to sea with the sole exception of Genoa ; from Pisa, Corneto, Naples or Gaëta, he could lie in wait for all vessels sailing the Ligurian Sea, and who could tell but that this man of pre-eminent acuteness and cunning might have bought over the sailors of Genoa ! " Ye are no gods or saints," cried the author, " to have power over his powers." The Pope, moreover, had embarked on this quarrel without the prelates, let him conclude it also without them. " But since the Pope sees that his undertaking against this mightiest of Tyrants has been unsuccessful he is now anxious further to sharpen the sentence pronounced against him, or to threaten him with deposition and to instal another Emperor in his room, and ye forsooth are to give your advice and concurrence whether it seemeth to you good or ill, ye are to be the organ pipes which echo to the touch and at the good pleasure of the organist."

The town chronicler of Genoa opens his entries for 1241 with the remark " In this year it pleased the Lord that great misfortunes should overtake the town." The Sicilian fleet set out for Pisa at the end of March, and the prelates were to sail from Genoa at the end of April. The intervening weeks saw the fall of Faënza. Several times during the winter Frederick had foretold the certainty of its capitulation in the spring. The heroic town had defended itself with the courage of despair, and its resistance was strengthened rather than weakened by fear of the Emperor's wrath and the Emperor's vengeance. In the extremity of famine the Faëntines tried to send away the women and girls. Frederick ordered them to return at once and to remind the besieged of the unforgotten insult that Faënza had done him of old: half a century before they had mortally offended the Empress Constance, his imperial mother, and fifteen years before they had sought to assassinate him as he entered Lombardy on his way to the Diet, though they had in fact mistakenly slain a knight in his stead who had been wearing the imperial clothes.

This was the voice of the World Judge who, if he is to be just in the day of judgment cannot and must not forget, and for whom Time is naught in face of his own Eternity. Since Faënza hoped for no mercy it had resisted to the utmost. The siege had lasted eight months, food was completely exhausted, the walls were destroyed, and the imperial forces had entered the city by underground tunnels, then—and not till then—the valiant town surrendered without awaiting the Emperor's *coup de grâce*. Their lives had been promised to the *podesta* and the foreigners in the town, but not to the citizens themselves, who now awaited their fate with natural anxiety. Frederick, smiling, showed his magnanimity: "Thus we enter the town in our overflowing gentleness and with the outstretched arms of inexhaustible clemency we greet the conversion of the believers . . . that they may know that nothing is juster and lighter and easier to take on them than the yoke of the Empire."

Faënza fell on April 14th. Frederick remained for a few weeks in the devastated town and arranged for the construction of a fortress and a palace. While he was still there several items of good news arrived. At about the same moment the papal enclave of Benevento in the kingdom of Sicily had been conquered, destroyed and obliterated. In the west of Northern Italy the Emperor's generals were harassing the outlying lands of Genoa to disorganise the preparations for the Council. The Apulian Marinus of Eboli, Vicar General of " Upper Pavia,"

had invaded Genoese territory from the North and the Margrave Uberto Pallavicini attacked from the East. He had had
several successes and had conquered two fortresses, and the
Emperor, whose arms were now everywhere victorious, wrote
these handsome words to him : " Continue therefore in the
same path and thou wilt assuredly bring to a successful issue
those royal services of ours which thou didst with honourable
intention undertake. Success and Fortune will wait upon thy
deeds, since thou art fighting with the guidance of wisdom in
a fortunate cause, and under a prince whose star is fortunate...."

The culminating success was still lacking. Shortly before
the surrender of Faënza Frederick II had sent his son, King
Enzio, on a special mission to Tuscany, " representing the
person and the likeness of his father." In Florence King
Enzio received the news of the Emperor's victory. The
Florentine infantry and cavalry had so long served in the
Emperor's armies that the town shared in the glory of his
victory, and the son must have received in his father's place
their testimonies of exultant homage. Enzio hurried on after
a few days. He travelled by way of Prato, giving instructions
for the enlargement of the imperial castle (whose beautiful
entrance gate recalls that of Castel del Monte and anticipates
the Renaissance), and thence to Pisa. He must have reached
Pisa just before the departure of the united Sicilian-Pisan fleet.
He will have brought just the final orders for the Admiral.
He did not himself take part in the naval action, but in Pisa
awaited the outcome.

The prelates had embarked at Genoa on the 28th of April.
Only a few of the spiritual princes, amongst them the English
with their knowledge of the sea, had decided to be warned in
time after seeing the overcrowded vessels and the imperfect
equipment of some of them. These either remained behind
altogether or, at best, sent on their procurators. All the rest,
however : French, Spaniard and Italians from the League
towns had sailed from Genoa amid the blaring of trumpets and
the cheers of the people. They passed Pisa in safety and the
narrow strait between Piombino and Elba. They were approaching their goal, the Roman harbour of Civitavecchia.
After eight days at sea, on the 3rd of May, the festival of the

Elevation of the Cross, they were attacked by the Emperor's fleet, which had been lying in ambush between the islands of Monte Christo and Giglio. A short and bloody battle decided the victory : three enemy ships were sunk and the passengers drowned, amongst them the Archbishop of Besançon. Twenty-two ships were captured, and only three sailing ships with Spanish passengers succeeded in escaping to Genoa. It was a complete victory for the Imperialists, who took over four thousand ordinary prisoners and over one hundred Church dignitaries of high rank : three papal legates, including the Emperor's *bête noire*, Cardinal Jacob of Palestrina ; the abbots of the celebrated monasteries of Cluny, Citeaux, Clairvaux and Prémontré, and a host of archbishops and bishops were in Frederick's hands.

King Enzio welcomed the victors and their captives in Pisa. He ordered a mild detention for the highest prelates till an order from the Emperor arrived commanding him to proceed with the utmost severity : the prelates had not asked his mercy ; they had defied his warning. The inferior clergy remained in the prisons of Pisa, the more important were first sent to the imperial castle of San Miniato and afterwards for the most part despatched to Apulia, where they were kept in strict confinement. Frederick II now held pledges of the utmost value and utilised them with skill. After a short detention he released the French, though he had in the first instance met King Louis' haughty demand for the release of his prelates with a courteous but decided refusal : " Where persecutors of the Empire exist, the Empire's defenders must not be lacking. The Empire is greater than individuals, and the single animals tremble at the sight of the lion's spoor. Your exalted majesty will therefore not marvel that Augustus keeps the prelates of France in fear, since they sought to compass the Emperor's downfall."

Frederick interpreted the victory as the judgment of God " who looketh down from Heaven and fighteth and judgeth righteously." A judgment against the Empire's deadly foe, against Pope Gregory whom God himself had smitten. The faithful followed the Emperor. The will of God had been revealed to the World : the Emperor Frederick's office was to castigate clergy and church, and to renew Justice on the Earth and Peace. Songs were composed in praise of the Child of Apulia, victorious, world-conquering. A Dominican announced that in this sea victory " the God of the Earth and of the Sea had testified that He Himself was the ally of the victorious Caesar . . .", and people recalled a prophetic saying, or perhaps invented it for the occasion : " The sea will be incarnadined with the blood of the saints." This event made an enormous impression on the world. Nothing that any previous emperor had ever dared or done was comparable to this capture of cardinals and a hundred priests. Frederick's power seemed boundless, but a certain horror was blended with the admiration. Enemies recognised therein the ruthlessness of Satan. Nothing had so strongly ministered to the conviction that Frederick was the herald of Antichrist as the capture and continued captivity of the princes of the Church in the prisons of the Emperor. Many of them died in his dungeons, and their blood cried out against this enemy of the faith.

Possibly Frederick hoped to be able to bend the Pope by this deed of violence and to move him to peace. He presumably hoped to barter the release of the prelates against his release from the papal ban. The prisoners themselves implored the Pope to make peace at last, and the general opinion in Italy was that this blow would compel Pope Gregory to do so. Gregory was at the point of death and suffered indescribably from this rain of heavy blows, and felt himself, moreover, personally responsible before God for the death and imprisonment of so many priests, but he was less ready to make peace than ever before. More than ever must the fight be fought and the dragon laid low ! He besought the captives for the sake of God and of the Church to bear their sufferings with patience and to endure to the end. Even when a new visitation came that shook the whole Christian world to its foundations, and imperatively demanded the peace and co-operation of all the western powers—even then the aged man clung to his hate, unbending and unbent. Nothing could shake him in his faith that he was called by God to fight against Frederick II, though victory after victory waited on the eagles of Rome, which the Emperor was bearing against the City.

Whilst Frederick was still encamped before Faënza, and the fleet still lay at anchor in the harbour of Pisa, Europe had, as by a miracle, escaped the direst fate. The strangest rumours were current, fed by the Crusaders who brought back tales they had heard : far in the East there was a mighty king who ruled over an enormous Empire and was moving towards the west and conquering one by one the princes of the Mussulmans. The Christians thought to see in him again the legendary Prester John, a king after the order of Melchizedek, who had so vividly appealed to the imagination not only of the people but of Innocent the Great himself. He was coming to obliterate the teachings of Muhammad, to unite in Jerusalem with the King of the West, and to fulfil the time. The Jews, on the other hand, believed that this King of the East was King David, who was returning as the Messiah to redeem them. Their faith was strengthened by the fact that the year 1240 was, according to their calendar, the year 5,000. The Messiah was to appear in the first year of the sixth millennium. Christian sources tell the same tale, and the identification, in his most victorious year, of Frederick with the Messiah, was not unaffected by this belief. The Jews gave free rein to their joy at King David's approach and even dreamt of going forth to meet him with sword and shield and spear. In many places they were bitterly persecuted and massacred for their obstinacy in clinging to this belief.

Suddenly the West recognised its error and armed itself in terror-stricken fear against the tumultuous hordes of Chingiz Khan. We now know that it was not Chingiz Khan himself who was leading his hosts against Europe. This Earth-Shaker of Asia, for sheer power the most appalling phenomenon of historic time, the man who conquered and organised the most extensive empire the world has ever seen, who amalgamated peoples, gave them religion and laws, and let loose the greatest human hurricane that the force of one man has ever conjured up, Chingiz Khan, had already closed his unique career of conquest. But his will lived on. That will which had issued orders to his son who sought to check the hordes who were plundering Herat : " I forbid thee ever, save at my direct command, to treat the inhabitants of any land with leniency. Pity belongs to weaklings, only severity keeps men in servitude.

An enemy merely conquered is not tamed, and only hates his
new master."

In the year 1227, when Frederick II was setting out on his
crusade, the Great Khan was buried in the Karakoram. He
had divided up his Empire in his lifetime between his four sons.
The West fell to the lot of Batu, who had his capital at Sarai

THE MONGOL PERIL

on the Volga and was himself the founder of the " Golden
Horde." The momentum generated by Chingiz Khan continued uninterrupted in this son. The Russian principalities
had succumbed to him by 1240, and by the beginning of 1241
he was approaching Hungary. Another section of Batu's army
had conquered Poland and was proceeding against Silesia.
The danger seemed overwhelming. The whole of Asia was for
once united ; Europe, on the other hand, divided, disintegrated, rent by a thousand mutually-hostile forces. The West
at last began to mobilise, Germany in breathless haste, for the

Mongols were swarming over Hungary. An army which the King of Bohemia recruited came too late : on the 10th of April he made a stand at Liegnitz, but on the 9th, 30,000 men (it is computed) under Duke Henry of Liegnitz had been cut down by the Mongols on the battlefield. The Duke, a son of St. Hedwig, with Slav, Polish and German nobles, had flung themselves against the Tartars. His army was defeated and he himself was slain : Germany lay exposed to the onrush of the foe, but the sacrifice had not been made in vain. In spite of their victory the Mongols were shaken, and could not face another encounter with the forces of the King of Bohemia. They turned sharply south, devastating the greater part of Moravia, and thrust forward as far as Vienna, but then withdrew to Hungary. The conquering invaders had only for a short time pushed beyond the territories whose natural conditions and features resembled those of their homeland. The death of Ogotai, the Great Khan, far away in Eastern Asia, ended the danger.

The news of these events spread like wildfire throughout Europe, which conceived a new attack imminent. Minor quarrels were forgotten in face of the graver danger and the whole of Germany united—the last time for centuries. King Conrad held a Diet at Esslingen in May 1241 and proclaimed a Landpeace, preached a Crusade against the Tartars and took the Cross himself, stipulating only that this involved him in no obligations towards the Pope but only in a campaign against the foe. Otherwise the papalists would have led the Crusaders, as was now their habit, against the Emperor.

The news of Liegnitz must have reached Frederick in May, just as he was advancing on Rome from Faënza. King Bela of Hungary in his need offered Emperor Frederick suzerainty over all his lands if he would free them from the Mongol threat. This alluring offer was not needed to summon Frederick to the North East battlefields. He might have become in very deed the saviour of Europe in this year of grace 1241—King of the West he had himself united. His manifestos, masterpieces of the imperial Chancery, were despatched to all the Kings and great ones of the earth. The Christ-like Imperator, throned above the clouds, sounded the blasts of his trumpet to rally

" powerful imperial Europe " against the foe before whose
victorious eagles the pride of the Dragon should be laid low
and the Tartar hurled to Tartarus. Each and every nation
should despatch with speed her chivalry to fight under the two
standards of Europe, the imperial eagles and the banner of the
Cross : Germany fiery and furious in arms, France the mother
and nurse of chivalry, Spain valiant and warlike, England fertile
in men and ships, Allemania full of daring warriors, Dacia
strong on the sea, untamed Italy and Burgundy unacquainted
with peace, restless Apulia with her Adriatic and Tyrrhenian
and Greek islands of unconquered sailor-folk, Crete, Cyprus,
Sicily, bloodstained Hibernia with lands and islands ocean-
bound, quick Wales and marshy Scotland, icy Norway, and
every noble and renowned land under the Western sky.

Had Frederick hastened north he would have stilled the
voices which were murmuring everywhere, that he himself had
called the Dragon forth, lusting by the aid of Tartarean allies
to make himself *Dominus Mundi*, and to destroy like Lucifer
the Christian faith. These rumbling murmurs were doubtless
strengthened by the intimate knowledge of Mongolian habits
and customs displayed in the manifestos. Frederick II had
probably made it his business, with eager curiosity, to acquire
all the information he could about these unknown Mongols, a
people " whose origin and first home we do not know," who
were fabled to have lived hidden beyond the seven climates under
burning sun. They are described with ethnographic exactness,
not without an implicit side-glance at the Emperor himself,
"A wild people are they and lawless and without ruth, but
they have a lord whom they follow and whom they obey, and
whom they honour and whom they call Lord of the Earth.
The bodily frame of this man is small and undersized, but
powerful, broadshouldered, hardy and enduring. Stout of
heart and courageous they plunge into any danger at a sign
from their leader. Their face is broad, their gaze is sinister,
they utter a terrifying cry that is like their heart. They wear
untanned hides of oxen, horses and asses. Into these they
stitch sheets of iron and use them as armour, or have heretofore
done so. Alas, they now bear handsomer and better weapons
from the spoils of conquered Christians. These Tartars are

incomparable archers, and have ingeniously inflated skins in which they swim across lakes and flooded rivers. The horses they have brought with them are said to be content with roots and leaves and bark when other fodder fails, and yet they are swift and, at need, long-enduring." Thus writes the Emperor of their customs, and he counsels his correspondents to avoid open battle, to provision their fortresses and to arm their people. But he did not himself set out against the Mongols.

The unity which Frederick so strongly recommended to the peoples of Europe he was unable to attain in his own Empire. Even the Mongol peril brought no peace with the Church ; and as long as the war with Pope Gregory lasted he dared not quit Italy, especially as on all sides he was now victorious. His previous experience had been too bitter. " The painful memory of ancient days recurs : once of old we sailed to the rescue of the Holy Land and the destruction of the Saracens, who were no less persecutors of our religion than the Tartars of to-day, and while we were thus active beyond the sea our beloved Father, having raised troops amongst the Milanese and their allies, subjects all of our Empire, broke forcibly into our kingdom of Sicily and by the mouth of his legates forbade all followers of Christ to help us in the cause of the Crucified." The Emperor was within sight of final success, he dared not imperil the harvest of years unless Pope Gregory, whether voluntarily, or under compulsion, would consent to peace. The Pope was unmoved by the crisis ; since the capture of the prelates he was less than ever inclined to make peace. The imperial despatches kept the world informed that only the Pope's lust for strife prevented Frederick from taking an active part in the campaign against the Mongols.

The Pope's behaviour in other affairs was no less ambiguous. Frederick II designated his supporters as " faithful Christians " and the papalists as heretics whose " heresiarch " was Gregory IX. Other events justified his terminology : the state of affairs in the Holy Land.

Frederick had previously declared that there could be no thought of a new crusade till the expiration of the ten-year

truce : that is not before 1239. In March 1239 he was excommunicated by Pope Gregory amongst other reasons because
his Lombard war was making a crusade to the glory of the
Redeemer impossible. The Crusaders were summoned to
meet at Lyons in this same March, and numbers duly assembled
there under the leadership of the King of Navarre. Suddenly
a papal messenger arrived, forbade the Crusade for this year,
ordered the pilgrims to return home, and fixed the start for
March 1240. The journey was to be made not to Jerusalem
but to Constantinople to bolster up the Latin Empire, a papal
creation, of which Baldwin II of Flanders was now Emperor.
The disobedient were threatened with spiritual penalties. The
luckless Crusaders who had equipped themselves by the sale or
mortgage of their possessions felt themselves befooled, and were
so enraged that they nearly attacked the messenger. They did
not know where to turn. The Emperor came to their relief.

It seemed that the Curia was determined on principle to
permit no crusade to Syria, and did not abandon this attitude
as long as Frederick lived. A little later the papal legates in
Germany went so far as to excommunicate all who entertained
even the idea of crusading against the Saracens or the heathen
of Prussia. In England, likewise, the Curia sought to prevent
a crusade to Palestine. It was perfectly obvious that the Pope
was bent on wrecking the crusade he had begun by proclaiming. His motives were clear. In the previous year he had
concluded an offensive alliance with Venice and Genoa against
the Emperor. Both these maritime towns had interests in the
Holy Land and both were at war with the Emperor. A crusade
against Syria would have strengthened Frederick's position in
Jerusalem, which was none too secure, just at a moment when
Venice and Genoa were hoping to drive him out of all his
territories, including Sicily. It would, therefore, have stultified
Pope Gregory's whole policy : hence the crusade must be
abandoned, even though the Holy Land should thus be lost not
only to Frederick but to Christendom. The same indulgences
could lure the crusaders to war with Frederick in Italy. It is
said that when Frederick captured rebels fighting against him
and wearing the sign of the Cross that he forthwith crucified
them so that they might realise the meaning of the symbol.

This may be untrue, but Frederick would have been quite capable of it and would have held that the responsibility fell on the Pope, who was misusing Crusaders for his own ends.

Frederick had again and again deprecated a campaign against Syria till he should be free to lead the crusade, from which only the quarrel with Pope Gregory was detaining him. And the crusaders well knew that without the Emperor they would be " as sand without lime or a wall without mortar." Nevertheless he put no obstacles in their way and helped them where he could. He urged them to travel by way of Sicily, where they would find shipping facilities, and he gave immediate instructions to his Sicilian officials to look after the pilgrims, many of whom had to winter in Sicily waiting for the new date proposed. The imperial marshal in Syria, Richard Filangieri, received the necessary instructions. In the spring of 1240 the pilgrims set forth for Syria, where, as was to be expected, they increased the existing confusion. The lack of a common leader, the proverbial disunion of Christians in the Holy Land, the untrustworthiness of the Knights of St. John and of the Temple, contributed to a severe defeat in November 1240, which was immediately followed by the conquest of Jerusalem by the Muslim prince of Kerak.

Frederick II was encamped before Faënza. He bestirred himself to salvage what he could. He hastened to get into touch with the Sultans of Damascus and Egypt and to negotiate at least the release of the prisoners. He despatched his Sicilian captain Roger de Amicis to Egypt to conclude a treaty with the Sultan Malik Salih, the son of al Kamil. For al Kamil had died in 1238, deeply mourned by Frederick, who wrote to the English king: " Many things would have been very different in the Holy Land if only my friend al Kamil had been still alive." England was to espouse his cause in the East. Despite the Pope the Emperor's brother-in-law, Richard Earl of Cornwall, sailed to Palestine with the English pilgrims. Frederick provided him with plenary powers and instructions, and he succeeded, thanks to dissensions no less acute in the Saracen ranks, in renewing the truce and in recovering Jerusalem for the Emperor and for Christendom. In the eyes of the world Frederick was once more the protector of the Holy Land and

Pope Gregory its destroyer, and the pamphlets of the time openly express this view.

Meantime, in the face of the Mongol peril, Frederick had been striving to reach an understanding with the Pope. When this failed he invaded the Papal States to compel the Pope by force to make peace. When the Earl of Cornwall returned from the Holy Land negotiations seemed possible once more. He landed in Trani in July 1241, met the Emperor and betook himself to Rome with full credentials to act as mediator. Frederick had no hope of success, but the Englishman would not be dissuaded. After a short time he returned empty-handed, and much annoyed by the stiff-necked obstinacy of the Bishop of Rome. Richard of Cornwall, not improbably, met Count Rudolf of Hapsburg at the Emperor's court on this occasion. If so it was a remarkable rencontre: for these two noblemen were later the two chosen successors of Frederick II in the tarnished splendour of the Roman throne.

Frederick now gathered all his strength for a final thrust against Rome. His prospects were on the whole better than last year; the Pope's position was hopeless. To add to his misfortunes, one of his cardinals, John of Colonna, had openly deserted to the Emperor and was prepared now to take arms against the Pope, of whose policy he had long disapproved. While Colonna's adherents in Rome fortified themselves in their towers and palaces, the Baths of Constantine and the Mausoleum of Augustus, against the papalists, who at the moment had the upper hand in the city, the cardinal betook himself to Palestine, and besieged several positions in the Emperor's name. Frederick hastened to comply with his call to join him. The Emperor wrote to the cardinal that he had at first been surprised to find in him an upholder of plans for renewing the Imperium. No cardinal and no priest had previously given such encouragement to the Eques and Imperator of the Romans, and he attributed this " to the noble anxiety of a noble race and the fire of noble blood." It proved to be the fact that in many particulars the Colonna were the inheritors of Frederick II's plans for the rebirth of Rome.

Nothing now lay between the Emperor and his longed-for Roman triumph. He had now determined, whatever might be the outcome, to use open force against the Pope, and he had no lack of fighting strength. In June he had captured Terni and then lay before Rieti, and was now advancing nearer to Rome itself. In August Tivoli opened its gates to him, and his troops were laying waste the country up to the walls of Rome. Frederick was already comparing himself to the "Libyan Hannibal" before the gates of Rome. By the middle of August his headquarters were in Grottaferrata, nine miles south of Rome. Piero della Vigna wrote "the path of peace which base obstinacy has hitherto kept closed will now be opened by the pressure of the Pope's advancing enemies." At this moment, when Frederick was about to strike the final blow, news came from Rome that Pope Gregory IX was dead. The Pope had for the second time snatched the certain conquest of Rome from the hand of his hated foe : Frederick's sword a second time smote empty air. Pope Gregory had played his last card. No enemy was left, for the Emperor was fighting neither Church, nor Pope, nor Rome, but only Gregory : and Gregory was dead.

The Pope's advanced age had long since made his death a contingency to be reckoned with. The fever-laden air and the burning heat of a Roman August, and the impossibility of seeking healing in the baths of Viterbo or elsewhere, may have hastened the end. There were some who did not hesitate to dub Frederick the murderer of Gregory, and others who said the Pope had died "unable to bear the sorrow he had brought upon himself." Just as the Pope refused till the last moment to grant peace to the foe, so Frederick's hate against this "disturber of the world's peace" lasted beyond the grave. "And so he who refused to make peace or to treat of peace, who took upon himself to challenge Augustus, was fated to fall a prey to the avenger August. And now is dead indeed ! Through him the earth lacked peace, the strife was great and how many perished !"

Such was Frederick's epitaph on his dead foe. He had little cause to feel magnanimous towards Gregory IX, who had persecuted him till his last breath as the "Beast of the

Apocalypse." One of the Pope's last letters had been directed to the prelates imprisoned through his fault, bidding them take courage though they languished in the hands of Pharaoh, of the snare-devising Satan. His very last conjured the Genoese " to arise with the might of their galleys, and avenge the new injustice which the Church was suffering." Hate was Gregory's greatness and he hated to the end, though it seemed as if his hate might wreck the Church. Frederick returned his hate. During the fourteen-year war in which the two monarchs strove each with every nerve to wrest the world-crown from the other they had both grown in stature. These deadly enemies were the incarnation of two hostile worlds who in each encounter outvied and re-outvied each other. Gregory IX was never so great as in his last years, and Frederick II would never have attained the heights he did without his abysmal hatred of the Pope. Nothing less than Gregory's double power, as Caesar-Pope and disciple of St. Francis, would have compelled Frederick to put forth his utmost effort. Even in his age we can only picture Gregory with eyes flashing in the passion of unbridled wrath, and yet this savage obstinate old man was attuned to the sublime ecstasy and mystic rapture of St. Francis. As an aged man he wrote beautiful hymns in praise of his friend, in one of which he celebrates Francis as the Archangel Michael who slays the mighty dragon. Both as St. Francis' friend and as the papal politician of the decretals, Gregory was bound to consider Frederick II as the dragon whom the Devil had sent to the confusion of the Christian world. The weapons Gregory used had little resemblance to those of St. Francis, nor was he destined to become the *papa angelicus* for whom the world was waiting. The fact that Gregory wielded the " dragon weapon " transformed Frederick in the eyes of the world into a " saint," and Frederick, stung by the power of such a hate, had Gregory to thank for his elevation.

The death of Gregory brought relief from intense strain. Frederick II abandoned his attack on Rome and marched into Sicily, which he scarcely quitted again for the next two years. He had no remaining enemy, but neither was there any Pope to release him from the ban. For two and twenty months the orphaned chair of St. Peter remained empty and no absolution was possible. No warlike events demanded Frederick's presence in Italy. People always feel respect for well-proved force, and the capture of Faënza, the victory at sea, the conquest of a further part of the Patrimonium had all had an intimidating effect. Finally, Gregory's death had produced calm. King Enzio was able to hold the Lombards in check, and the imperial fleet inflicted injury on Genoa's trade. A strange repose brooded over Italy. From his Apulian castles Frederick watched events. Without the Pope the Emperor was sole Lord of the West, in very fact the Dominus Mundi.

As such he needed to find a responsive world. The imperial mantle with its heavy folds, embroidered with the symbols of the Macrocosm, was no mere ornamental robe, accidental perhaps, or even burdensome. Being what he was and honoured as he was, he might have been lord of a few hundred acres and yet he would have dominated the world. Everything, from the conception of a re-birth of Rome down to Sicilian sculpture, was interwoven with the Empire and the Emperor : " Our influence is felt to the remotest corners of the earth. . . ." The suzerainty of the Macrocosm is in its nature spiritual. Frederick's task was now to translate into reality this spiritual overlordship.

The conception of a spiritual overlordship is a commonplace in the ages of the Church, though it may seem strange in relation to an Emperor. Frederick II had been the ward and pupil of the great Innocent, founder of the Church as a State. He was an intellectual man, and we need not wonder to find in his conception of Empire a reflection of the Church. The whole Italian-Sicilian State which the Popes coveted as their Patrimony of Peter became as it were the Patrimony of Augustus for this gifted monarch, who sought to release the secular and intellectual powers that were fused into the spiritual unity of the Church and to build a new empire based on these. The Popes with their encyclicals summoned the whole of Christendom to arms, and now Frederick II with his circulars stirred the whole Roman world to battle with the Pope. The priesthood had laid claim to men or money from the kings, but

Frederick begged rather the moral backing of the European rulers against the clergy. Each of the opposing powers, Empire and Papacy, sought what it needed to complete itself, no longer representing moon and sun, but the " two suns " that Dante styled them. The empire of the sword, however, was uplifted by becoming an intellectual State, while the Church degraded herself by " secularisation." The Hohenstaufen sought to rouse and rally round him all the statesmanlike instincts of his fellow-kings against the ever-spreading organisation of a world-church, to lead the Empire to battle as a spiritual, not as a political unity. Such was the sum of all Frederick's communications to the Christian kings of Europe.

Up till about 1236 Frederick's relations with the Christian rulers of the West had been confined to casual interchanges. The first excommunication and the Crusade, events which touched the whole of Christendom, made the Christian kings appear to form a sort of forum. When Frederick took rank as a world ruler by entering on the Lombard war his relation to the kings of Europe assumed another colour. Active diplomatic exchanges took place between the imperial and the various royal courts, a regular interchange of news concerning the most diverse affairs became established, imperial envoys often remained a considerable time at foreign courts, and Frederick could count on the sympathy of the kings in his actions and in his plans ; for what concerned the Emperor of the West now concerned also the western kings. The theatre was enlarged and all the world was touched by whatever happened in the imperial sphere.

Frederick did not cultivate " foreign politics." He would not have recognised their existence. For him there was one " Europa imperialis," one *res publica universae christianitatis*, one Imperium Romanum embracing the whole of Christendom. He held himself aloof from all quarrels of the kings amongst themselves. England distrusted him when with the help of France he won the Empire at the battle of Bouvines. France distrusted him when he married the Englishwoman. They were both unjust. Not that he observed " neutrality " ; this idea also was foreign to him. As Roman Emperor he had a super-national character which he prudently would not forego.

England offered him an alliance which he steadfastly refused. It would have been treachery to the still-valid conception of a universal empire to form an alliance with one of the European kings. It would also have been unwise, for a counter-alliance would inevitably have followed, and the world which should be one would have split in twain. An alliance would have been to fling away the Empire and descend to the level of a territorial king of Germany, Italy and Sicily, as inevitably happened with the later Emperors, even Charles V. Frederick II's task was rather that of Dante's Emperor : to command sufficiently superior force to preserve peace and with it the unity of Europe. Such ideas were powerful in an age in which the idea carried as much weight as the fact, or more. The feeling never arose that there was a discrepancy between the Empire as a divine world-embracing institution and the actual imperial territory of political realities.

For Frederick and for the world at large the hegemony of the Roman Emperor was a matter of course : suzerainty and leadership, but not by any means the exercise of ruling power. All his contemporaries, kings included, acknowledged the imperial superiority, but they would all have instantly and vigorously repulsed any attempt by him to interfere in the life of their states. The Emperor could issue no orders to the kings of Europe, in which his position was inferior to the Pope's, as a chronicler has shrewdly remarked who puts these words into the Emperor's mouth apropos of the Council : " The Pope is my inveterate foe and open enemy, and he moreover has the power to deprive any man of his dignity who opposes him, and even to fetter the deposed person with the bonds of his curse, and to hurl him into the abyss of yet more terrible punishment. Our position is endangered, the position of the Emperor is that of all the princes, and I alone stand as the champion of all. The kings of the earth and the princes whose cause I defend, who have made me their counsellor and representative, would not answer my summons nor obey my command. They are not my subjects that I could compel them or could punish the disobedient."

The earlier Hohenstaufens had, indeed, attempted to compel the kings to obedience. Barbarossa called his fellow-monarchs

" heads of provinces," Henry VI considered them his vassals, and both sought to trample on the petty kings to augment thereby their own greatness. Things had changed by Frederick's time : the " nations " had come to birth, and the stronger national feeling grew in the western dominions, the more difficult it became to maintain at all a universal empire : even in the abstract. If Frederick II had shown hostility to the national impulses and sought to limit the independence of the kings, he would infallibly have come to grief and had the royal pack at his heels as well as the Pope. He had to take another line if he was to bridge the gulf implied in the challenge : a Roman Empire and yet nations.

Frederick's policy towards the kings was not unlike that which he pursued towards the German princes or the Roman citizens : instead of swimming against a powerful living current he sought to turn it to account, to let it sweep him on to greater greatness. Far from suggesting, as his forefathers had done, that the western kings should sacrifice their national independence on the altar of a universal empire, Frederick used his most eloquent manifestos to adjure them jealously to guard their independence, their nations and their separate states, not against the Emperor, who " filled with highest happiness and content with his own lot, envies the life of none," but in co-operation with the Emperor to defend them against the two enemies of all kings and of all states : the rebel and the priest.

A common cause against the attacks made by rebels and by clerics on the majesty of the State is the beginning and the end of all the political relations of Frederick with the kings of Europe. Instead of trampling on the kings Frederick sought to enhance their self-consciousness. He considered them as, like himself, immediate under God. He sought to enlist them in the same cause and be himself merely their leader, their counsellor, their champion. This solved the question of peace amongst the kings themselves. By compelling them continually to keep their minds on world-questions which equally affected all, he left them no opportunity for strife, so that apart from a peripheral quarrel, even the eternal war between England and France was laid for a time to rest. " By God, most well-beloved brother," he wrote to the King of

England, who was despatching money to the Curia, " let not
such procedure take place, least of all against us, that monarchs
should voluntarily fight against monarchs. Let not the yoke
of papal authority press so heavily on the neck of kings ! "

Frederick rallied the kings against the common foe : first
against the rebels who threatened monarchy itself ; next
against the Pope, who was in league with the rebels and undermined the independence of the secular power, even challenging secular by spiritual jurisdiction. There was no western
ruler who was not entangled in similar conflict with his church
and with the Roman Curia, none who had not to protect
himself against similar encroachments on his royal power.
The question of lordship in Italy merely provoked the quarrel
earlier and more fiercely between Frederick II and the Pope.
" All of us kings and princes, especially those of us who are
jealous for the true religion and the true faith, suffer from the
open and secret hate of our peoples, and the special but secret
strife with the princes of our Church. For our peoples hunger
to abuse this pestilential freedom, but the priests misuse our
benevolence to injure us in our possessions and in our privileges." Hence Emperor and king had the same interests to
defend, and all the monarchs should form a " sodality " under
imperial leadership. If Frederick had insisted on claiming
imperial power and titles he would have accomplished nothing,
and assuredly have awakened resistance. On the path he chose
he achieved much. He had flung a new idea to the dynasts :
the corporate unity of kings. The echo of the ancient Roman
Imperium was still clearly to be heard and lent breadth and
meaning and cohesion to the idea. This community of kings
was something new, non-hieratic, non-feudal, independent of
force, firmly based on the common secular interests of the
State and on the ever-growing national power and consciousness. This separate power of the several nations might prove
the ideal cement for a super-national Empire—or its solvent.
Universal monarchy was almost on its deathbed, but Frederick
II at the beginning of the thirteenth century was able to give
it again, for the last time, a short new lease of life, a complete,
practical and genuine *raison d'être*, by converting it into a voluntary co-operation. He could only succeed by emphasising the

contrast between Church and State and rallying all secular forces to his banner.

Frederick took his stand on this commonwealth of western kings, and strove to bind them together into a royal corporation. An insult to the Emperor was an insult to his fellow-monarchs. "Hasten with water to your homes when fire flames in your neighbour's house . . . fear the same danger in your own affairs. The humiliation of other kings and princes will be a little thing, if the power of the Roman Caesar whose shield bears the brunt of the first onslaught should crumble under perpetual attack. . . . We conjure you, nobles and princes of the earth, and cry you the alarm, not because our own weapons are unavailing to ward off such shame, but that the whole world may know that the honour of all is touched when insult is offered to any one of the guild of secular princes."

As Germany had her " Illustrious Body of the Holy Empire " Frederick saw the ideal Imperium as a *corpus saecularium principum* under the leadership of the Emperor—a Corpus which he was the first to call to life. He thus set himself to awaken the non-ecclesiastical but spiritual instincts of the west and (as he had done on a smaller scale in Sicily) to marshal them as one universal whole against the Church. Again and again he utters his warning cry, " the affairs of the secular power should not be subordinated to the Church," and explains that that is why he prevents the papal Council which was intended to decide the Lombard question. His theory that with the fall of the Emperor, the head of all, the whole world would fall, was quite in tune with the mental atmosphere of the time. " They begin with us, but be assured of this they will end with the other princes and kings whose might they will no longer fear when once we are overcome. Defend therefore your own rights in defending ours." He summons the kings to vigorous resistance, for the Pope is bent on subduing to himself all the dominions of the faithful.

Such exhortation was by no means unjustified. Pope Gregory's successor, Innocent IV, met with some resistance in France, Aragon and England, and is said, " with rollings of the eyes and curlings of the nostril," to have thus addressed the messengers of England. " It is better for us to make a treaty with your prince to crush these recalcitrant kinglets. When once we have quelled or destroyed the great Dragon the petty snakes will easily be trodden under foot."

The world feared some such treatment by the Pope if the mighty Emperor Frederick were once laid low. The Curia would boast : ·" We have trampled on the great Frederick, and who then art thou that thou dare hope to resist us ? " If the Pope acted thus the fault lay with the kings themselves and with them alone. The Emperor's words are menacing : "Neither the first are we, nor yet the last, whom priestly power opposes and seeks to hurl from the seats of the mighty. And the fault is yours who give ear to these hypocrites of holiness whose arrogance would fain believe that into their gullet all the Jordan floweth."

What the Emperor perceived as the gravest danger, threatened not indeed by the Church but by the new hierarchy, was the sacrifice of original loyalties made by the Roman priest. He writes in wrath to one of the kings : " These who call themselves priests now turn oppressors, grown fat upon the alms of the fathers and of the sons. Although they be themselves the sons of our loyal subjects, yet do they render no reverence to Emperor nor king when once they are ordained as apostolic fathers." Napoleon felt the same bitterness.

Frederick II was the first to feel the fact acutely and express it freely. With diabolic ingenuity he turned the tables and challenged the whole conception of spiritual authority. He wrote to the Christian kings that he considered it base of the Pope to hinder him, the Emperor, from marching into Lombardy, the historic inheritance of the house of Hohenstaufen. Especially base since the Pope had claimed his imperial help against the Romans, who owed no allegiance to Gregory's father, nor to his grandfather, nor to his kin. One argument of Frederick's in particular carried great weight with the national nobility of England and of France. A movement of the French barons against the clergy adopted bodily the Emperor's ideas, and rebelled particularly against the fact that priests " aforetime the sons of slaves presume according to canonical precept to judge free men and the sons of free men." They demanded that all jurisdiction should be withdrawn from the priests in favour of the king.

Although Frederick II never ceased to emphasise the community of Emperor and kings, he did not fail in his letters duly to stress the unique and eminent position of the Roman monarch and the comprehensiveness of the Empire. What was an individual king beside an Emperor ! A pitiful figure, standing alone, surrounded by danger on all sides. " Ye single kings of single countries what have ye not to fear from such a High Priest who dares to depose us . . . , us, whom God hath singled out by the imperial diadem, us who mightily hold sway over illustrious dominions." The exalted character of the Imperium is again expressed not less haughtily and clearly. An English or French bishop who crowns and anoints his king has thereby acquired no right to depose his king. No greater right has the Pope to dethrone the Roman Caesar whom he has anointed and crowned. This sentence sets clearly forth the difference in status between king and Emperor. Frederick was fond of describing himself as " geographically nearer in space and in office more akin " to the Pope than to his fellow-monarchs.

What was the reaction of the western kings to these theories of the Emperor ? Though Frederick reiterated his absence of envy towards the kings they did not wholly trust him. In England it was considered not impossible that Frederick might cross the narrow Channel to avenge himself if England resisted his request and continued her payments to the papal overlord. In spite of assurances of friendship the King of France was prepared at any moment to leap to arms to defend his frontiers. Not till the very last did they consider themselves wholly safe from possible conquest. Nevertheless, a feeling of fellowship with the Emperor was strong, as was shown at the outset of the Lombard War when the kings intervened with the Pope on the Emperor's behalf, and two years later actually sent auxiliaries for the campaign against Brescia. On the other hand the idea of a league of secular monarchs against the Church awakened little direct response. No active common resistance to the Pope was organised, though in all countries the aristocracy sympathised with the Emperor. None of the kings was anxious

wantonly to attack the Church, though each was engaged with
her in open or in secret strife. It was, however, an extraordinary triumph of imperial policy that none of the kings
allowed himself to be seduced into alliance with the Pope, none
of them stabbed the Emperor in the back, and none recognised
his excommunication or deposition. Passively the solidarity
of the kings was perfect.

Any sign of partisanship for one side or the other was made
impossible in France by the strict, unerring uprightness of
King Louis IX, known as St. Louis. He was by far the
most important royal contemporary of Frederick II, and one of
the noblest figures in the roll of the kings of France. His
reverence and simple humility made him a saint, but with these
he combined all the knightly pride of a Western Frank, and that
genuine royalty of kingship which left its impress so deeply on
the land of France, down to the days of le Roi Soleil. Germany
was the land of Emperors, and France was the cradle of kings.
The Valois and the Bourbons may well have outshone St. Louis
in royal pomp ; as little more than a boy he had forsaken all
outward show. He was second to none, however, in royal
pride ; and in royal sincerity he outshines most of his successors. As founder of the Law-State of France he seems to
have learnt more from Frederick II than is generally recognised,
and he had the clear eye of a great man for the problems of
Christendom whose confusions frequently distressed him. As
he lay at nights on his plank bed pondering eternity he never
lost sight of the universal meaning of the western powers, he
was never seduced by expediencies, he never forgot what the
honour of his country demanded.

The importance of St. Louis lies in this : that at a time when
Christian chivalry was beginning to crumble and peter out in
the petty and the commonplace, this Frankish king set her to
new and universal tasks, inflamed the torpid for the last great
Crusade with the same fire and enthusiasm as he brought to
conquer his own bodily weakness, which was never allowed to
deter him from midnight prayers or matins. The world saw
in him something of the spirit of the early Templars : a combination of pride, humility and joy in work, transfigured by the
same faith. A generation later this Order was abolished ; its

degeneration had caused him bitter sorrow. The last symbol
of its greatness perished with St. Louis off the Tunisian coast.

On a royal plane St. Louis had the same significance for
Frederick that the German Grand Master, Hermann of Salza,
had had on the more modest stage of earlier days. As all-
Christian King, Louis IX was the God-given peacemaker
between two warring powers, Empire and Papacy; for a
decade he strove indefatigably to fulfil his task. His failure
brought him grief, for his dream of freeing again the Holy Land
was shipwrecked on the arrogant obstinacy of the Curia. Yet
with strict impartiality he rendered unto the Pope the things
that were the Pope's and unto Caesar the things that were
Caesar's. He permitted the proclamation in France of Frederick's excommunication, but forbade all armed assistance for
the Pope, and he threatened to confiscate the goods of the
Church when he found his clergy raising money in France for
the war against Frederick. The French prelates who were
setting out to attend the Pope's Council seem to have been forbidden to undertake anything against Frederick II, even if
Gregory should demand it. On the other hand he wrathfully
resented the Emperor's retention of French clerics in his
prisons. " The kingdom of the Franks is not so weak that it
is wise to goad it with the spur," thus he writes to Frederick.
As confidant of both parties he was ready to fly to arms against
either, if either sought to lure him from his neutrality. He
succeeded in preventing a decisive predominance of either Pope
or Emperor.

Beside King Louis the other kings make a poor showing.
King Henry III of England is, in comparison, characterless and
poor-spirited. He was a puppet, unable to hold his own with
Emperor, Pope or peers. Beyond other kings he had ties to
each of these powers : the Emperor was his brother-in-law,
the Pope his feudal overlord, and the peers took their stand on
Magna Charta. Cowardly and undecided, Henry agreed with
whoever at the moment happened to be his interlocutor. His
phrase " I do not wish to contradict the Pope in anything : I dare
not," might *mutatis mutandis* equally apply to Emperor or barons.
On occasion he gave in to the Emperor when Frederick, supported by the peers and their spokesman Richard of Cornwall,

demanded that he should refuse the papal tribute. For Henry
III, to the indignation of many of his subjects, had permitted
the Pope to raise money levies, and had allowed the country
to be mercilessly exploited, besides thus supplying the Pope
with money for his war and indirectly injuring the Emperor.
Under pressure from Frederick and the barons he defied the
Curia for a little while. Henry of England and Sancho II of
Portugal, whom the Pope had deposed, supplied the Emperor
with two classic instances of the way in which Roman priests
sought to suppress the secular royal power. He constantly
pointed out to the other kings how dearly England paid for her
subjection to the priest.

The *corpus saecularium principum* under the Emperor's
leadership was entirely a creation of Frederick II's, and a completely new way of conceiving the world as a sort of corporate
State. The conditions precedent for this were a very considerable independence of the individual kings on the one hand,
and on the other the emancipation of the secular state from the
Church, an emancipation which had everywhere begun to set
in. By striving to kindle this corporate spirit in the kings,
which was everywhere in evidence in Europe, Frederick was
taking the only line by which the maintenance of a world
monarchy was possible. When we dream to-day that we have
approached nearer to a community of equal nations, such as
Frederick II and Dante had in mind, let us not forget that the
bond that then united them was the dignity and nobility and
supremacy of the worthiest among them.

Amongst the elements which the western monarchs had in
common, their royalty, their intellect, their secularity, Frederick
laid stress on another common tie, valid until very recent times :
their common blood. This was another bond which Frederick
valued highly, the more because it lay outside the Church.
Frederick liked to boast that he was connected by descent or
by marriage with almost all the royal houses of Europe.
Hohenstaufen blood was almost synonymous with imperial
blood. People had ceased to look for the scion of another
house fitted to wear the imperial diadem. For Frederick was,

in fact, the fifth of his family to reign as Emperor in this elective kingdom, and the succession of Conrad, his son, the sixth, was well assured.

Frederick, therefore, treated the royal houses of Europe as one great princely family, within whose circle, however, the Hohenstaufen was the imperial branch, the " Empire breed " as Manfred called it. A special virtue resided in the race, and to their offspring it was given " to know the mysteries of the kingdom of God . . . but to the others only in parables." " What German, what Spaniard, what Englishman, what Frenchman, what Provençal, what man of whatever nation or tongue, could, without our will rule over thee, O Rome, or to thy glory exercise the imperial office ? The inexorable necessity of the Universe replies : None, save the son of the greatest Caesar whose gifts, inborn in his imperial blood, ensure him force and fortune."

These words of Manfred's clearly indicate the new line of thought that Frederick had initiated. The Hohenstaufens rule the world not as the old Germanic, Frankish, royal stock—what weight could that carry in England or France, in Spain or Hungary ? In the person of Frederick II the *regia stirps* of the Waiblings had become the *stirps caesarea*, the imperial race of Rome ! The divine stock of the Roman Caesars appears once more in the Hohenstaufen, " the heaven-born race of the God Augustus, whose star is unquenched for ever," a race which springs from Aeneas, the father of the Roman people, and descends through Caesar to Frederick and his offspring in direct descent. All members of this imperial race are called divine. The predecessors on the imperial throne are *divi* and the living no less, finally all members of the Hohenstaufen family. By a coincidence King Conrad from the very day of Cortenuova drew up his documents as " Conrad, son of the divine Frederick, the exalted Emperor, chosen by God's Grace King of the Romans," whereas before he had styled himself simply, " Conrad, son of the glorious and exalted Frederick." Frederick's own letter to Jesi, his reference to the divine imperial mother in Bethlehem of the March had an almost embarrassingly definite ring about it, and he addressed his son Conrad as a " divine scion of the imperial blood." Decades after Frederick's death the Margrave of Meissen, who had married the Hohenstaufen princess, Margaret, Frederick's daughter, was flattered as the " father of divine children." Even at the end of the century a daughter of Ottocar II of Bohemia was celebrated as " an offshoot of the divine blood " whom fortunate Bohemia had begotten, because Ottocar's mother had been a daughter of Philip of Swabia, and another great grandmother had been " of the race of the Roman Gods." So deeply rooted was this deification of the Hohenstaufens in Italy that Boccaccio, arch-Guelf that he was, lodged a protest against the prevailing assumption that the imperial Hohenstaufen race was the noblest that ever breathed. The " blood of Barbarians," he contended, could never exceed in worth the matter which Nature had used to shape the Italian !

The imperial office had been held divine by Barbarossa ; now gradually not only Frederick's person but the Hohenstaufen race and the Hohenstaufen blood was Caesarean and divine. Yet one half-century of Staufen rule, the longed-for THIRD FREDERICK whom the Sibyls had foretold, and the West would have seen the God Augustus marching in the flesh through the gates of Rome, would have burnt incense on his altars and offered sacrifice. In the Hohenstaufens the son of God had appeared for the last time on earth.

The Roman Curia was right that she dare neither slumber nor sleep till this accursed race had been exterminated down to the last bastard of the second and third generation. For the Church recognised the Staufen as a race apart in whom a mysterious intangible power resided, a race of priest-haters and priest-persecutors, a house on whom the Church's ban rested for all time. Each separate member was equally accursed, not for his personal guilt but for the crime of belonging to the "tribe of the ungodly"! "Destroy ye name and fame, body and soul, seed and sapling of the Babylonian !" was for decades the battlecry of the vengeful, hate-haunted priesthood of the Church of Christ. For the first time since ancient days a curse was to overshadow a whole house, cruel, unrelenting, terrible, executed by the priests of a wronged and jealous God. The priests had no alternative. They were faced by the *hubris* of a race, growing from generation to generation more youthful

and more beautiful, approaching near and nearer to God and
to the Gods.

A Cardinals' conclave frequently takes time. An earnest,
solemn assembly of reverend men, meeting in the seclusion of
a luxurious room in some papal palace, to treat in peace concerning the person of a new Pope : such is it normally—but
not always. The history of the Roman Church records many
a meeting long-drawn-out and many marked by wild excitement,
but scarce another to compare in savagery with that first real
" Conclave " which took place in 1241.

Rome and the Church were in acute danger at the moment
of Gregory's death. Emperor Frederick was at the gate
" with an army like the Libyan Hannibal " ; the Church lacked
leaders ; two cardinals were in prison since the fight at sea,
Cardinal John Colonna was a deserter in the imperial camp,
the remaining cardinals in Rome were split into two factions :
the stronger peace-party inclining to the Emperor, the weaker
war-party bent on continuing the fight. It was clear that a
unanimous vote was hardly to be hoped for and that the election
business would be protracted. This was little to the liking
of the Senator of Rome. For the safety of Rome and of the
Church he wanted a new Pope chosen with the minimum
delay. The sole Senator of the day was Matthew Orsini, a
papalist whom Gregory IX had helped to power, and who now
ruled Rome like a Dictator. He reflected that uncomfortable
quarters would promote speed, and laid his plans accordingly.

Immediately after the Pope's death Orsini had the cardinals
seized by his myrmidons and dragged to the election like pick-
pockets to gaol. Their treatment was harsh enough, the cardinals were driven along with kicks and blows, one feeble man
was thrown down and dragged by his long white hair over the
sharp stones of the street, so that he arrived all battered and
torn in the council chamber whose doors were closed on him

for many weeks. The election room as on previous similar occasions was in the so-called Septizonium of Septimius Severus on the Palatine. This had been in its day a fine building with fountains and waterworks and nymphs, but it was now a ruined sort of tower which had suffered considerably in recent earthquakes.

Only one single apartment with a kind of alcove was placed at the disposal of the ten cardinals, and the soldiers of the Senator kept the prelates so strictly in confinement that the place resembled a prison. The guards accepted large bribes, but no amount of bribery permitted the entrance of servants or of doctors, and doctors were sorely needed before long. The whole building was faulty and the rain dropped through the fissures in the roof, and not only rain but revolting filth, for the guards who were quartered at night above the conclave chamber facetiously used the faulty floor as a latrine. The cardinals contrived by improvised tents to keep their actual sleeping quarters reasonably clean and dry, but it is unnecessary to labour the insanitary conditions and the resultant stench. Add to this the fever and heat of a Roman August, inadequate food, lack of medical attendance, and an overbearing soldiery ; it was not long till almost all ten cardinals fell seriously ill, and three actually died in consequence of hardship.

The Senator's calculations were so far correct : the cardinals were anxious to agree as soon as possible on a new Pope and quit this hell. The difficulties, however, were unusually great. The peace-party was numerically stronger, but not one of the other side would allow himself to be converted, and the necessary two-thirds majority could not be attained. The result was a dual-election : five of the peace-cardinals chose a sixth, one of their own number, the Milanese Godfrey of Sabina ; three of the war-cardinals chose a fourth of their party, Romanus of Porto, a man peculiarly hateful to Frederick.

At this point Frederick intervened. Reviving an ancient imperial right in cases of indecisive election he rejected Romanus of Porto and confirmed the election of Godfrey. The peace party might perhaps have succeeded in winning the one vote they lacked, but unfortunately one of their number, the English Robert of Somercote, died in the conclave. The conditions attending his death were disgusting, as can well be imagined. While he was still alive the soldiers flung him into a corner to die, sang mocking songs at him and spat on him and left him without medical attention or the rites of the Church. When the purgatives which he had taken began to act they dragged him on to the roof, and there in public, in full view of the Eternal City, the poor man relieved the last necessities of nature.

The Englishman's death removed the last hope of a two-thirds majority, and finally all agreed to choose an outsider. But the Senator Orsini would have none of him. He wanted to parade the new Pope at once before the Roman people. He began to storm and rage, and threatened if the choice did not fall on one of those present he would dig up Pope Gregory's corpse and put it in the council chamber to complete the misery of the half-dead cardinals. Further, he would carry the Cross through the city and massacre every adherent of the imperial party. The cardinals after what they had already gone through had no reason to doubt that he was prepared to put these threats into execution, so at last after two months' deliberation they decided in favour of the Milanese Godfrey, whom the Emperor also had supported. He ascended the papal throne as Celestin IV.

Whatever hopes centred in the name of Celestin, " whom God himself had sent down from his table in Heaven," as Frederick later phrased it, the Pope himself died on the seventeenth day of his pontificate, before he had even been consecrated. He had fallen ill at the conclave, and his only act as Pope was an unsuccessful effort to excommunicate Matthew Orsini.

A new conclave was necessary. The cardinals did not wait. Terror seized them at the thought of a repetition of what they had suffered and still were suffering from. Some of them fled the town and took refuge in Anagni. The three anti-Kaiser cardinals remained, as well as Cardinal John Colonna whom the Senator had captured and imprisoned after the close of the conclave. The feud between Orsini and Colonna continued thereafter for generations.

The College of Cardinals was thus dispersed. Four were in Rome, four in Anagni, two still in the Emperor's hands. How could a new Conclave be held ? It was not possible to agree even on a meeting place. Negotiations on this point dragged on for months between the Anagni and the Roman group. Those in Anagni refused emphatically to return to Rome and those in Rome would not, or could not, on any terms leave the city. No progress was made, and the fault lay chiefly at the door of Senator Orsini. The world did not grasp the reason for the long delay, but noted only the fact that the cardinals were not choosing a Pope. Abuse began to be heard on all sides, contemptuous rhymes suggested that the fathers should toss for the tiara. Another suggested Frederick II as Pope. Frederick was reproaching the cardinals for not concluding the election. In the summer of 1242 the Emperor even advanced on Rome ostensibly " to free his friends the cardinals," for since two of the pro-Kaiser cardinals had died it was important to Frederick at least to set John Colonna at liberty again. This demonstration against Rome was without result, however, and a year later the position was still unchanged.

In these circumstances the Emperor's two prisoner-cardinals assumed great importance. The College of Cardinals was not only scattered but sorely depleted, especially as yet another cardinal, one of the war party, Romanus of Porto, died of the consequences of the Conclave of Terror. The two groups of cardinals in Rome and Anagni joined the prisoners in demanding their release so that the election might proceed. The moment had come for Frederick to turn his valuable hostages to the best account, with practical wisdom and slow deliberation. One of the captive cardinals, Jacob of Palestrina, was a bitter enemy. The other, Otto of St. Nicholas, had begun by being hostile, but Frederick had been so successful in casting his spell upon him that Otto became, like Cardinal Colonna, an intimate friend of the Emperor. Negotiations for the release of the cardinals appear to have begun at the time of the first conclave, and Frederick was probably willing enough to release Otto of St. Nicholas on the condition, it is true, that Otto would return if not himself appointed Pope. These negotiations were now re-opened, with the result that Frederick brought himself to

set Cardinal Otto free, the more readily that Colonna's imprisonment had left the pro-Kaiser party without a leader.
Otto was now to go and use in the Emperor's favour his influence on the College of Cardinals ; he quitted his prison
richly laden with gifts.

No conclave followed. All through the winter of 1242-3 the
negotiations dragged on. In the spring the Emperor again
undertook a campaign against Rome to waken up the cardinals
there, but abandoned it with speed when they complained that
the imperial troops were blocking the roads and preventing
their joining their colleagues in Anagni. This complaint was
wholly baseless, but Frederick withdrew at once to avoid even
the appearance of interfering with the papal election. From
the same motive he ultimately released Palestrina on receiving
certain assurances from the College.

Matters seemed now beyond measure favourable for the
Emperor. In return for the release of the cardinals—" and
that without ransom " as a chronicler admiringly records—
Frederick was promised the immediate withdrawal of the
Lombard legate Gregory of Montelongo whom he hated.
They had probably also agreed on their choice of a Pope, while
Frederick on his part had promised to restore the Patrimonium
and release the remaining prisoners if a *persona grata* were
elected. Frederick could anticipate the result of the election
with equanimity. He had, it seemed, played his cards to the
very best advantage. He was, therefore, not at all surprised
to learn that at a brief Conclave at Anagni on June 25th, 1243,
the Genoese Sinibaldo Fiesco, Count of Lavagna, had been
unanimously elected.

Joyfully the Emperor announced a few days later that now
the general peace of the Christian world was assured, the welfare
of the Empire and the friendship between father and son were
guaranteed, since the chosen Pope was one " of the noble sons
of the Empire, and has ever been well-disposed towards us
in word and deed." Frederick ordered thanksgiving services
throughout his Sicilian kingdom and wrote in the same vein
his congratulations to the new Pope, who assumed the name of
Innocent IV : he was a noble scion of the Empire and was now
chosen as a new father to his old friend, and his god-inspired

name of Innocent was a pledge of the protection he would accord
to innocence. The noblest representatives of Frederick's
Court, the new German Grand Master, Gerard of Malperg, the
imperial Admiral Ansaldus de Mari, Thaddeus of Suessa, and
Piero della Vigna were despatched as imperial ambassadors to
convey Frederick's congratulations in person to the new Pope.

One of the nobler sons of the Empire ! That the new Pope
was, though the Fieschi could hardly be reckoned among the
pro-imperialist families of Genoa. But Sinibaldo Fiesco who
long ago, after studying and teaching in Bologna, had spent his
early prebendary years in Parma, was intimately related to the
best known partisans of Frederick II. Parma itself was always
an imperialist town of which the Emperor himself was *podesta*.
Bernard Orlando di Rossi of Parma, a brother-in-law of Pope
Innocent IV, was even a godfather of Frederick's, and might
be accounted a leader of the Ghibelline party. And Sinibaldo
Fiesco's favourite nephew, Hugo Boterius, the son of a sister
who was married in Parma, was devoted to the Emperor in
genuine affection and admiration, till his death and after.
Frederick attached at all times great importance to blood-
related hostages, so that the new Pope's Ghibelline relations
carried great weight with him.

At last Frederick saw a Pope with Ghibelline propensities in
Peter's Chair, and might with some justice consider this man,
whom he himself had chosen, as a personal friend or at least no
enemy. Though not like the Roman Colonna a passionate
partisan of Frederick's, this polished Genoese with his urbane
manners and non-committal courtesy might certainly be
reckoned as one of the friendly cardinals. Warm partisanship
would have been out of character in this citizen of a seaboard
trading town, who weighed in the balance the things of this
world, shrewdly, with heart of ice. In addition, he was one
of the most brilliant jurists of the day, extremely cultured and
the author of a famous commentary on the decretals. In
Frederick's eyes all this was in his favour. The Emperor saw
with relief at last a completely unbigoted priest, a man who saw
things naked, as they are, without mysticism or exaggeration,
a man entirely free from passion, ecstasy or fanaticism, a man
the absolute antithesis of Gregory IX, who was fire and passion

personified. True, Fiesco lacked also the regal bearing and
gesture, the commanding majesty of Gregory ; he lacked the
dauntless personal courage of that indomitable greybeard. He
was in his own way daring and unscrupulous enough, as a
physical coward often is when he knows his own skin is safe.
The motto of the wily Genoese was eminently expressive :
sedens ago.

It is easy to understand that after a struggle of fourteen
years with Gregory IX, Frederick II should have sought
at all costs to avoid the election of another wild fanatic.
The courteous Cardinal Fiesco, politician rather than priest,
with his worldly interests and free-thinking mind seemed by
contrast a friend. In all this Frederick was right. His terrible
mistake lay in thinking that a sober, intellectual Ghibelline was
less dangerous on the papal throne than a fanatic, that a half-
friend was preferable to a whole-enemy. When he recognised
this, too late, he exclaimed " No Pope *can* be a Ghibelline ! "
" Woe when the Pope is a Ghibelline ! " would have been
better, for the Pope now wielded the same weapons as Frederick
himself. The Emperor might often have cried, as Napoleon
did of Blücher " He has learnt ! " It might in a sense be true
to say that Innocent IV was Frederick's most remarkable pupil.
From the immensely many-sided achievement of Frederick, the
Pope had broken off merely a single splinter, had copied one
only of the methods of his master's genius, but this with clear
intent he practised and perfected and turned deliberately
against the Hohenstaufen : the concentration of all forces to
one end, unhampered by pity or piety or scruple. Whereas the
Emperor's lack of scruple was wedded to the passion of a creator
building a new world, Innocent IV's was a practical " method,"
coolly devoted to the annihilation of one man, whose existence
threatened to shatter the foundations of an age-old institution.
The one-sided efficiency of the Genoese speedily brought a
kind of anti-climax to the mighty struggle which had raged
between Frederick and Gregory. The fight against the politician Innocent was of a wholly different quality from that
against the priest, and lacked all fruitful mutually-stimulating

elements. The struggle was now wholly a mundane one. All spiritual tension between Emperor and Pope gradually died out : though some survived between the Emperor and his adherents. A consequence was that the previous methods of attack failed Frederick. Other symptoms also indicated that the quarrel had entered its last phase : Frederick was suddenly driven into the defensive. His passages of arms with Pope Gregory had often enough been forced on him, but they always were fights in a cause where he was willing to fight. His finest achievements were the product of this duel which brought his gifts to their full fruition. Now, however, the Emperor found himself continually in check to his opponent, and driven to fight a battle which he had not foreseen and did not want. He lost enthusiasm and the fighting lost its meaning. He was no longer the champion of a given world-order willed by God, but was spending his strength merely in self-defence. The one thing he craved was peace ; and peace was the one thing denied.

Frederick's delicate web of diplomacy had accomplished the forbidden thing and influenced the papal election. He now saw on the papal throne the cardinal he wanted, whose Ghibelline relations stood in some measure surety for him. It does not appear to have struck him just at first that if the Pope were able to effect a change of atmosphere in Parma these hostages might prove a Nemesis. Frederick had blunted his favourite weapons, the intellectual. For the resources of an individual are more quickly exhausted than those of a system such as the Papacy. His fantastic faith in himself as Caesar, in his unchangeably victorious star, in his divine mission, is now fraught with doom. His faith does not lose its strength, even though the mission is fulfilled, even though—to quote Goethe—" Every remarkable man has a certain mission to fulfil. When it is accomplished he has outlived his usefulness on earth . . . and the Fates lay for him snare after snare. So with Napoleon and with many another."

The name chosen by the new Pope might have given Frederick more than a hint of the line that Innocent IV was likely to pursue, but it was long before he allowed himself to be convinced that Innocent was not the whole-hearted friend whom he had hoped at all costs to find. Frederick's chief weapon had broken in his hands : he had not been fighting against Church or Papacy but against " the unworthiness of the present Bishop of Rome." He had perhaps succeeded during his duel with Gregory IX in convincing the world that this was so ; he could not hope a second time to distinguish the office from the office-bearer. If the Pope was not to be the personal enemy then he must be the personal friend of the Emperor. Frederick II flung himself into an imaginary friendship of long-standing with Sinibaldo Fiesco and enthusiastically proclaimed it to all the world, hoping thus to call a friendship into being. He wanted to be friends with the new Pope and by sheer force of will to compel him to goodwill, and doggedly he clung to the belief that this Genoese would free him from the ban and give him peace. Even when appearances looked black against Fiesco the Emperor held to his optimism, and sought the cause of unsuccessful negotiations everywhere else rather than in lack of goodwill on the part of this Pope whose election he had secured. Later, when he realised the full irony of the situation, he turned against himself the bitter wit that he loved, and penetratingly remarked that in the Cardinal he had lost a friend but thereby gained an enemy in the Pope. Without an enemy a man like Frederick II would have ceased to be.

It seems probable that Pope Innocent at first genuinely wanted peace. For, as recent events had testified, the war which had so heavily taxed the Emperor's resources had pressed even more severely on the Church. A certain amount of pre-liminary negotiation with the cardinals had preceded the papal election, and discussion was resumed immediately after the Pope's enthronement. We need only pick out the essential facts from these wearisome and complicated negotiations.

The first thing to note is the conciliatory spirit of the Em-peror. He made one concession after another to shake off at last the burden of the ban. It was soon manifest that an amicable solution would not be easy to find, and the Pope embarked on a double game. He did not abandon the serious negotiations, he fought every point with Frederick's envoys, but at the same time he endeavoured to evade the peace question altogether. Frederick had sent to the Pope as his representatives Piero della Vigna and Thaddeus of Suessa, by far the most experienced diplomats of his court and skilled in every variety of subterfuge. With them was associated the indefatigable and ever-faithful Archbishop Berard of Palermo to hold a watching brief for the ecclesiastical issues. These three imperial envoys were released from the ban in order that they might treat with the Pope. Innocent had rejected Frederick's proposal that the negotiations should be conducted at the imperial court ; he knew too well, and feared, the Emperor's eloquence and his power over men.

A great deal of the business was quickly and easily disposed of. The Emperor had always recognised the papal authority in spiritual affairs and acquiesced unconditionally therein. He declared himself prepared to render any satisfaction to any degree that the Church might demand : alms, pious foundations, even the penance of fasting. When he had received absolution he was prepared to restore the Church's Patrimony on condition of himself being the Advocate, in exchange for which privilege he was ready either to pay interest far exceeding the actual revenue or to undertake the re-conquest of the Holy Land at his own expense. This would, however, have been a new victory for Frederick, and Innocent refused to entertain the suggestion. In this, as in every agreement between Emperor and Pope, the most difficult question of all was that of Lombardy. Frederick took his stand on the indisputable fact that his excommunication by Gregory IX had nothing to do with the Lombard question and that his absolution should not depend on it. Innocent was perfectly aware that the Emperor's legal position was unassailable and that in any legal discusssion the Papacy would be the loser. On the other hand neither he nor any other Pope could afford to sacrifice the Lombard alliance. Moreover, the Milanese were nervous about a hasty peace, which was sure to be unfavourable to them, and Innocent had reassured them by a promise not to negotiate without them.

Innocent's hands were, in fact, tied by Gregory's agreement with Venice, Genoa, Piacenza and Milan, that none of the contracting parties should conclude a separate peace. The Pope, therefore, demanded that the Emperor should accord peace to the whole Christian world, not only to a part. The Emperor was prepared for this, and after some hesitation announced that he was anxious not to let all the negotiations be shipwrecked on this one reef, and that as regarded the Lombards he would be willing to revert to the situation as it had been at the moment of his excommunication in 1239. Just as this concession seemed about to secure an agreement an event occurred which, for the moment, interrupted all discussions. The loyal town of Viterbo suddenly yielded to papal machinations and deserted the Emperor.

It is quite possible that the defection of Viterbo at this particular moment was not wholly welcome to the Pope. He had not himself directly brought it about, though he knew what was going on. The anti-Kaiser cardinals had good reason to distrust a peace. Their leader was the fanatic Rainer of Viterbo, a man of the school of Innocent III and Gregory IX, who hated Frederick with all the fire and passion of the dead Pope. He was a soldier by instinct and one of the first cardinals of Rome to win glory and honour in the field as warrior and general. The one thing he dreaded was peace. He, therefore, made it his business so to widen the breach that in future any compromise with this hated Emperor (whom at one time he had revered and even loved) should be impossible. He devoted himself to this task with singleness of heart. Cardinal Rainer of Viterbo was the cause of all the most grievous breaches of faith of which the Church was guilty, the author of the most venomous and malicious pamphlets to which this quarrel gave birth. He had his way.

With the assistance of some friends he had long intended to organise a rising of his native town of Viterbo against the Emperor, though he was by no means unpopular there. Pope Innocent was not in favour of this scheme, but gave the cardinal ambiguous powers to work in the Tuscan Patrimonium for the advantage of the Church. The Pope was thus covered and yet had avoided a breach with the cardinals, who had grown somewhat too independent during the papal vacancy. If the enterprise were successful it might always be turned to advantage. The revolt was successful. The imperial garrison had, perhaps too precipitately, retreated into the citadel of Viterbo, where they could hold out for several weeks. The populace in general looked on indifferently. Those citizens who were imperial partisans were overcome after heavy fighting.

Frederick was in Melfi when he got the news of the loss of Viterbo. " He leapt like a lioness robbed of her young or a she-bear bereft of her cubs. Clothed in the fire of his wrath he rushed like a midnight tornado to punish the town ; like a courier for speed he rode, and with no royal pomp. Mounted on a red horse he came to snatch peace from the earth." Thus Rainer describes the Emperor's coming. He hastily gathered an army of Apulians and of his ever-ready Saracens and dashed to Viterbo. At the same time he sent the alarm to the Vicars General of the surrounding provinces to bring their town infantry to his help without delay. He thus got together a fair army in a short time, but the interval was sufficient to give the people of Viterbo, egged on by Rainer, opportunity to throw up strong entrenchments. On a certain Sunday the imperial forces mustered for the attack. The ever-resourceful Piero della Vigna helped to organise the troops. The Emperor in person led one wing against the entrenchments, the second was commanded by the young Count of Caserta. In spite of spirited attacks however—the Emperor leaped from his horse and seizing a square shield wrathfully led the charge—the strong town was not to be taken by storm. Siege machinery had to be fetched. Some weeks later the attack was renewed at dawn. In an attempt to employ Greek fire against the fortifications one of the attacking towers caught fire. The wind, which at first had been blowing the flames against the town, suddenly veered, so that the other attacking towers caught fire and were finally burnt to ashes. This second attempt was, therefore, unsuccessful.

The Pope chose this moment to resume the negotiations. He was impelled to this because friends of the Emperor's, the Count of Toulouse and the Emperor Baldwin of Constantinople, were working at the papal court for peace, and the Viterbo question was causing Innocent uneasiness, for it wore an air of illegality. He, therefore, despatched Cardinal Otto of St. Nicholas, the Emperor's new and trusty adherent, to Frederick to come to terms about Viterbo. He was possibly empowered to offer the Emperor absolution on more favourable terms if he would abandon his attacks on the town. Frederick had no wish to embark on a second prolonged siege like Faënza. Moreover, since Viterbo was situated in papal territory, he would have to give it up again as soon as he was released from the ban, and peace now seemed at hand. He quickly came to terms with his friend Cardinal Otto and agreed to withdraw into Apulia, stipulating that the half-starved imperial garrison should be allowed to go free. This agreement was ratified also by the people of Viterbo on oath. Then the unforgivable occurred. Cardinal Rainer, haunted by visions of the hated peace, hounded the citizens of Viterbo against the exhausted garrison, and as the imperialists sought to leave the city they were cut down almost to a man, though Cardinal Otto sought to control the mob and with his own body strove to stay the slaughter.

Frederick II knew perfectly that Rainer of Viterbo was the sole culprit. This flagrant breach of the cardinal's oath shocked him profoundly : it undermined his faith in all human statutes. It was not, he wrote to Otto, the massacre of his people nor the injury to himself that so deeply moved him ; he must beg to know " What expectations can we have of success if human good faith is so despised, if all shame is cast aside, if conscience is powerless, if no respect is paid to the honour of spiritual fathers ! What bond will hold amongst men ? To whom can we look for reconciliation in so serious a quarrel, in which almost the whole world is involved, if the promise of a holy legate, nay, of a cardinal—a name which should be venerable amongst the peoples—is suddenly violated ? " The catastrophe was monstrous. Frederick at first could scarcely realise it. It was a foretaste of what was yet to come. His wrath against Rainer and the people of Viterbo was unbounded. Ten years before he had enquired of Michael Scot whether hate would not suffice to give the soul power to return after death. He is said now to have prayed that his bones might arise from the dead to destroy Viterbo ; he could not slake his thirst for blood unless he might fire the town with his own hand, and though he had one foot in Paradise he would withdraw it to take vengeance on Viterbo. Only for the sake of the world-peace which was now at stake he would turn the key on righteous wrath and lock his just grievances in his heart. Thus he wrote to Cardinal Otto, freely exonerating both him and the Pope.

The events in Viterbo appeared to cause the Pope great pain. He exacted a fine from the town, and to ensure its collection he entrusted the execution of the sentence to : Cardinal Rainer. He also commanded the release of the surviving ill-treated imperialists. With the Cardinal's connivance the order was disobeyed, and Innocent blandly apologised : he would have been glad to put the matter right, but he did not want to risk the loss of the town that had so recently been (so treacherously) recovered. In face of such effrontery did Frederick still fancy Innocent his friend ? Apparently he did. He still relied on the Pope's fair dealing and wrote that he hoped through him to arrive at peace and compass his own release from the ban.

King Louis of France was now directly interesting himself in the peace negotiations, which set them moving again. On both sides an effort was made to settle knotty points in order that when Maundy Thursday came again the Emperor's name might no longer appear on the Pope's list as an outcast son of the Church. An elaborate formula with detailed clauses of reservation had been evolved to meet the Lombard difficulties : the Pope was to appoint the satisfactions to be rendered, but without prejudice to the imperial rights in Lombardy. On Maundy Thursday 1244 a provisional peace was sworn, the final form of which was still held over. The ceremony was public and was performed by the Count of Toulouse, Piero della Vigna and Thaddeus of Suessa in presence of the Cardinals, the Emperor of Constantinople, the Senator and the people of Rome. The Pope on his part named the Emperor in a public sermon as " a devoted son of the Church and a believing Prince." Both sides were thus committed, and Frederick II joyfully acclaimed the event in addressing his son Conrad. He also informed the German princes and invited them to a Diet at Verona for a date to be determined later.

Everything now seemed in equilibrium, but Pope Innocent had still the task of expounding the arrangement to the Lombards. Their envoys arrived in Rome, saw the draft treaty and rejected it. They demanded that the Pope and the Pope alone, should have unconditional and unlimited power to settle their differences with the Emperor. Frederick II refused to go back on the conditions already sworn. Innocent thereupon made arbitrary alterations in the fair copy of the treaty intended for ratification ; Frederick refused to accept them. Hesitations on the Pope's part followed. Suddenly the wind veered. It was no longer a question of the Lombards. The Emperor was to restore the territories of the Church before his absolution. With all his complaisance the Emperor could not concede this point. Who would be his surety that he would be absolved ? The Pope had no need of sureties, for he could again excommunicate the Emperor if he failed to restore the Patrimonium according to treaty, and the *status quo ante* would be restored. It would have been madness for the Emperor to throw away his weightiest security—especially after the Viterbo experience. This phase of the negotiations is important, for the Pope now accused Frederick of perjury for refusing to evacuate the papal territories before receiving absolution. No time had been specified for the evacuation, simply because it was self-evident that it was to follow the Emperor's release from the ban.

Frederick II now requested a personal interview with the Pope and suggested their meeting in the Campagna. He would forthwith surrender this section of the Patrimonium. Innocent suspected treachery. He feared that the Emperor intended to get possession of his person. He first refused, then suddenly accepted, but preferred to meet at Narni rather than in the Campagna. The Emperor, therefore, moved to Terni, while Innocent with his court quitted Rome and halted first in Civita Castellana, sending Cardinal Otto to the Emperor. The subsequent negotiations were a pure mockery on the Pope's part. He agreed to Frederick's wish that he should repair to the Campagna. Frederick II had probably received some disquieting information and wanted to have the Pope near at hand.

He was building everything on a personal interview. Before
this took place the difficulties solved themselves in another way.

Since Innocent had recognised that no negotiations could
end in a manner wholly satisfactory to the Curia he had planned
his flight. He did not love the clash of weapons. Suppose
that the negotiations finally broke down, suppose that war
broke out again, suppose that he were still in Rome. . . . The
events of Gregory's day might repeat themselves ; the capital
might be besieged. The Genoese was taking no risks. Though
he was Pope he had hidden in one of the back rooms of the
Lateran for days and not ventured to appear at meals, because
he feared the faithful in some matter of £3000. How would
he have borne himself at the approach of armed men !
Throughout the negotiations with the Emperor, Innocent had
been only playing for time to complete his preparations. As
soon as he was apprised that all was in order he fled from Civita
Castellana to Sutri ; thence by night, in disguise, accompanied
only by a few followers, to Civita Vecchia, where a number of
Genoese galleys lay at anchor ready to sail as arranged by him
weeks before. While the Emperor awaited his arrival in Narni
he put out to sea in the dawn of a certain morning. The story
ran that imperial horsemen were hunting for the Pope. On
the 7th of July, 1244, Innocent landed in his native town of
Genoa, where he was enthusiastically welcomed. He was
seriously ill from excitement and anxiety. He remained some
months in Genoa to recuperate, but he did not there feel himself safe enough. In the late autumn he left the town, and after
a severe winter journey arrived in Lyons in the beginning of
December. This town nominally belonged to the Empire but
was really independent. Here Innocent IV remained until his
opponent was dead. It was the *lever de rideau* for Avignon.
" I was playing chess with the Pope and was about to mate
him or at least to take a castle when the Genoese burst in,
swept their hand across the board and wrecked the game."
In these words Frederick II announced to the Pisans a few
weeks later what had occurred. He was deeply moved by his
opponent's flight. He was normally mistrustful enough ; this

time he had trusted too long, and for the first time had been deceived and beaten on his own field of diplomacy. He knew only too well that it was no victory for him to have driven the Pope to quit Rome and Italy. With one manœuvre Innocent had captured a whole series of important positions, and the consequences of this flight—his only personal exploit—would forthwith be felt in many directions. The Pope had only been able to escape the persecutions of a savage tyrant by speedy secret flight: such was the interpretation put on the matter by many. Innocent did his best to confirm this view by posing as a luckless fugitive, a hapless exile whose life was endangered by a crazy Emperor. He was surrounded by guards to protect him against imaginary assassins. In contrast to the Pope's later procedure Frederick never intended to employ poison or dagger. The Church was not dependent as was the Empire on the life of one. A new Pope would have replaced the murdered one and the Church would have gained a martyr. " Who in his senses would imagine that we would seek the death of one whose death would bring undying strife on us and our successors ! " Even yet the Emperor did all in his power to end the quarrel, but it was far more difficult to exert pressure on the Curia when the Curia was not in Rome.

The flight to Lyons had not only rescued the Pope from the fruitless fluctuations of the negotiations but had given him personal liberty. He was practically beyond the Emperor's reach. Lyons, instead of Rome, became the focus of the Roman Church, and without let or hindrance the Pope could get into immediate touch with all the world. The Emperor could no longer cut his communications. He was able from Lyons to summon the Council which Frederick had prevented four years ago. Within a few weeks of his arrival the Pope invited the princes of the Church and the ambassadors of the kings for the Feast of St. John 1245 to a Synod to arrange for the deposition of Kaiser Frederick.

A possibility of peace again presented itself. Through the folly of the Christian knights in the Holy Land Jerusalem had been conquered in August 1244 by a Turkish tribe, the Khwārizmi, and for ever lost to Christendom. This misfortune demanded co-operation between the two powers, Empire

and Papacy, and the Patriarch Albert of Antioch, supported on
all sides, undertook the difficult task of bringing about a reconciliation. Above all Frederick wanted peace. The terms he
now offered were equivalent to a complete surrender : the Pope
should arbitrate unconditionally on the Lombard question,
Frederick would evacuate the Patrimonium; he would depart
for three years to the Holy Land to reconquer it ; he would not
return earlier without the Pope's express permission ; he would
forfeit all his territories if he broke his vow ; he would appoint
kings and princes as his sureties. King Louis of France, who
had also taken the Cross, supported Frederick by refusing
permission to the Pope to reside in France. Innocent could
hardly hold out longer without himself appearing as the disturber of the peace. On the 6th of May, 1245, he commissioned the Patriarch of Antioch, who was with the Emperor,
to release him from the ban if the conditions were fulfilled.

It is not completely clear why Frederick II was suddenly
prepared for such a capitulation ; at one point he even contemplated abdicating in King Conrad's favour and going to the
East for good. His position was certainly growing more and
more difficult ; he was now fifty years of age and the craving for
peace must have become overmastering. The phase of life is
clearly visible in his constant toying with the thought of going
to the East for a long period : or for ever. Besides, for his
heirs' sake he wanted peace lest the quarrel should become
immortal for his successors. He himself could defy the world ;
he could hardly ask his successors to do the same. The fall of
the Empire seemed to lie ahead unless an end could be put, at
whatever sacrifice, to this quarrel.

Frederick was spared this humiliation. Once again the warlike *manes* of Gregory IX awoke. Cardinal Rainer of Viterbo,
on whom had fallen the mantle of Gregory's hate, succeeded
in dashing to the ground the last possibility of peace. Pope
Innocent intended to hold his Council in Lyons in June. It
happened that Frederick had invited the German princes for
the same date to a diet in Verona. In April 1245, while the
Patriarch of Antioch was still wrestling for peace, the Emperor

set out from Apulia with his whole court and a large army and marched north. His route lay through the Papal State, close by Viterbo. He could not refrain from laying waste at least the country round Viterbo and even indulging in a short siege. On the representations of the Patriarch that hostilities would imperil the negotiations that were in train he at last consented to move on. He did so on that very 6th of May which Innocent had appointed for his absolution.

Now Cardinal Rainer had been left behind as the Pope's vicegerent in Italy. He had followed with deep vexation the course of the Patriarch's overtures, which appeared likely to bear fruit. As Frederick II devastated the Viterbo domains it happened that the imperial troops here and there crossed into papal territory. This gave Rainer of Viterbo a pretext for again wrecking the threatening peace ; he made a report to the Pope, and under his pen these trifling trespasses became a serious breach of the treaty. At the same time he despatched numerous pamphlets to the prelates assembling in Lyons, all of which bore the hall-mark of the school of Gregory IX.

These pamphlets of Rainer of Viterbo were destined to fix for all time the hostile portrait of Frederick II as the della Vigna letters fix the contrasting portrait for his friends. In his decree of deposition Pope Innocent only reproduces in moderated terms and with more coherence the contents of Cardinal Rainer's unbridled and hate-ridden pamphlets. Pope Gregory's awe-inspiring manifesto of excommunication was, in comparison, a mild and harmless document. The Pope had been the first to treat Frederick II as an apocalyptic figure. Rainer utilised all the terrifying imagery of the Revelation and the Prophets to prove that Frederick was, in fact, the forerunner of Antichrist. All previous accusations are raised to a monstrous and inhuman power, each one is corroborated by the phrases of the prophets employed with savage fury. No single feature of Antichrist must be missing ; all must be found in Frederick's life. Rainer rehearses all Frederick's activities, and finds in all symbols of the Antichrist : his friendship with the Muhammadan princes, from whom he accepts gifts in spite of their slaughter of the Christians ; the heretical sayings of his courtiers, repeated as his own ; the existence of the Saracen colony ; the outrages committed by these warriors, who are alleged to violate Christian women and girls before the altar of their God ; the murder of Pope Gregory and of his own imprisoned son, all these crimes are laid at Frederick's door. Further, it is recounted how he had kept his three consorts (the third of whom had recently died) imprisoned in " the labyrinth of his Gomorrah," and, finally, had poisoned them ; how he and his warriors spread death and destruction throughout the world, how he savagely pursued even the prelates with his ships. " But because his accursed raging and his fearsome stiff-necked wrath are like unto the foaming sea that cannot rest but stirs up with its waves the mud and slime in the eyes of all that see, he charged against the Lord with the uplifted neck of his pride and with the broad shoulders of his riches and his power he destroyed the cities, ravaged the habitations and recked so little of men that he slew them like lambs. But the foe and the pursuer set his hand to yet worse evil. He carried the war further against the saints and constrained them. Lifting himself up against Heaven he flung down from the firmament and from the stars the holy ones of the Most High and tore them in pieces. He hath three rows of teeth in his jaws, for the monks and the clerks and the innocent laity, and mighty claws of iron hath he, and some he hath devoured, consigning them to death, and others he hath slain with other torments, and the remnant he hath trampled in his dungeons under foot. Hell-hound shall he be called like Herod, yet Herod thought only to slay the Christ, while this man blasphemes the body of the Lord and strives to overturn the law of God and hath slaughtered exalted members of the clergy. Crueller than Nero shall he be known, for Nero slew the Christians because they sought to abolish the worship of his idols, but this man is crueller and baser than Julian the Apostate who seeketh to destroy the faith he doth himself profess."

Every deed that Frederick had wrought marks him as Antichrist : the closure of Sicily and the passport regulations are tokens of Satan, and now this glorification of his own person. " And thus this new Nimrod, a raging hunter before the Lord, steeped in vice, who loveth the lying word, hath as his servants abandoned men who delight the king with their wickedness, and with lies rejoice their prince. . . . He despises the ban and gulps down his punishments like water from a brimming goblet and misprises the power of the Keys, this Prince of Tyranny, this overthrower of the Church's faith and worship, this destroyer of precept, this master of cruelty, the transformer of the times, this confounder of the earth, this scourge of the universe. He is like unto the fallen angels who would fain be the equals of God and seat themselves on the mountains of the Most High. Like Lucifer he essayed to scale the heavens to establish his throne above the stars and the candlesticks of the Bride, and his seat over against midnight, that he may be equal to, yea higher than, the vicegerent of the Most High. And while he sits like Very God in the temple of the Lord he alloweth priests and bishops to kiss his very feet, and while he commandeth that they shall call him holy, he hath all them beheaded as enemies of the State and as blasphemers who dare to utter truth about his manifest untruths. When the apostolic chair long time stood empty, the heart of this evil prince became uplifted to the destruction of the Church, and like the Prince of Tyre he would fain have sat upon the seat of God as if he were God indeed, and he sought himself to choose the High Priest and to fasten his yoke upon the apostolic chair, and had in mind to break the right divine and to alter the eternal precept of the Gospel. Since he hath in his forehead the horn of power and a mouth that bringeth forth monstrous things, he thinketh himself enabled to transform the times and the laws and to lay truth in the dust, and hence he blasphemed against the Highest and uttered contumelies against Moses and against God."

The aim of these half-insane, abusive trumpetings was to cause the priests assembled in Lyons to forget the very possibility of peace and induce them to agree to Frederick's deposition. " Sacred vessels and holy places dedicated to God hath he put to shameful uses, as of old Belshazzar the Babylonian defiled the vessels of the temple of Jehovah what time the prophetic finger wrote on the wall *mene tekel upharsin*, who in that same night lost his Empire and his life. This criminal deserves no less to lose his kingdom of the Church." Cardinal Rainer quotes dozens of biblical parallels, " The men of Bethshemesh were destroyed because they looked upon the ark of the covenant ; Uzzah was slain because with unclean hand he sought to support the ark of the Lord ; Uzziah the king, who sought symbolically to burn incense on the altar of incense, was marked with leprosy on his forehead, and the word of the priest drave him from his throne ; Korah, the shameless, with his kindred was devoured by fire because he sought to snatch the privilege of the priesthood. Of a truth whoever could be proven to have transgressed the law of Moses was without mercy condemned to death." How much more does Frederick deserve such a fate : " Have therefore no pity for the ruthless one ! Cast him to the ground before the face of the kings that they may see and fear to follow in his footsteps ! Cast him forth out of the holy place of God that he may rule no longer over Christian people ! Destroy the name and fame, the seed and sapling of this Babylonian ! Let mercy forget him ! "

Cardinal Rainer knew how to get his effects. The pamphlets contain nothing doctrinal, nothing about the supremacy of the Pope over the Emperor, no learned hair-splittings. In the main their contents consisted in rehearsing the Emperor's well-known behaviour with interpretations which turned everything Caesarean into anti-Christian. How ripe the moment was for such bogeys needs no elaboration. The appearance of Antichrist had been independently and confidently predicted for the year 1260, and we recall how the dawn of this year of terror brought the outbreak of the Flagellants throughout Europe. Rainer of Viterbo played for his own ends on the unreasoning terror which this event inspired. The Emperor's downfall was the goal of his existence. When the Council met in Lyons at the end of June men lent a willing ear to these extravagant outbursts.

Frederick II was also summoned to appear in Lyons, though it is true that the Pope had only indirectly invited him in the course of a sermon. The position was an impossible one : the Roman Emperor could not appear as the accused before a council consisting almost wholly of hostile bishops. If he had appeared escorted by an army the situation would have become even more acute. Frederick, moreover, knew nothing of the altered atmosphere produced by Rainer's reports and writings, and still imagined that his position was favourable. At the end of May 1245 he reached Parma on his march to Verona, and from thence he despatched his representative and advocate to Lyons, the tried and trusty Thaddeus of Suessa. We know frankly nothing about this renowned jurist and orator. He may have been a replica on a smaller scale of Piero della Vigna ; his name indicates that he was a native of the Campagna. He was always one of Frederick's most faithful adherents and was killed fighting his battles. This man was now entrusted with the most responsible and difficult task that can be conceived—the hopeless defence of his master before a court of hostile priests.

While Thaddeus journeyed to Lyons Frederick proceeded to Verona. Here, after many years, he again met Eccelino, and here King Conrad with the nobles of Germany awaited his father. The most important business before the Verona Diet was the Austrian situation. Frederick was contemplating a marriage with the heiress of the last of the Babenbergs and was prepared to create Austria a kingdom in return for his bride. The papal Curia had other plans for the Duke's daughter, and apparently succeeded in terrifying Gertrude of Austria at the thought of marrying the excommunicated Antichrist. One of Rainer's pamphlets represented Frederick as a Bluebeard who had already murdered three wives, and some legate would appear to have put this in her hands. However this may be, the seventeen-year old girl refused at the last moment to follow her father to Verona. So this Austrian scheme fell through. When the Duke died in the next year 1246 Austria was annexed as a vacant imperial fief and administered by a Vicar General.

This was the last Diet of Frederick's at which the German princes put in an appearance, and there were already serious gaps in the ranks. King Conrad, Frederick's son and heir, remained some weeks with the Emperor ; it was the last time his father saw him. The boy was only seventeen, but he had matured early according to the Hohenstaufen habit ; joyless years of inglorious fighting lay before him in which in spite of his ability he could only hold his own. All that was brilliant in Frederick seems to have been handed on to his bastard sons, and beside Enzio, Manfred, Frederick of Antioch, the fate of the legitimate heirs seems drab indeed. Burdens too heavy to be borne had been laid on their young shoulders.

From Verona the Emperor sent an embassy to Lyons to bring the new peace proposals. An arrangement had been made with Thaddeus of Suessa that the Emperor would halt in Turin in July so as to be the nearer to Lyons in case of a reconciliation with the Pope for which he still hoped. When he left Verona in haste on the 8th of July, later than had been agreed upon, the first two meetings of the Council were over.

The Council was not well attended. Innocent III's Lateran Council had rallied 405 ; scarcely 150 prelates attended at Lyons. The German and Hungarian bishops were absent almost to a man, so were the Sicilians, for Berard of Palermo attended only in his capacity of Emperor's representative ; very few Italians appeared. There remained only the clergy of England and of France to be the Emperor's judges, and the bishops of Spain, who since the sea-encounter of 1241 nourished an indescribable fury against Frederick, though they were the only victims who escaped. After their arrival in Genoa the Spaniards had at once written to the Pope, Gregory IX, to take every possible step against Frederick II, for he is setting a bad example to other kings. Nevertheless, the Council styled itself a " General Council," though Frederick sturdily disputed its claim to the title. According to the testimony of friend and foe, Thaddeus of Suessa's defence of his master during the sittings of the first two days was brilliant. Cardinal Rainer had summarised the various accusations under the incongruous title of " lese majesty." His reasoning appears to have been somewhat on these lines : the clergy are members of the Church, hence members of the Body of Christ ; the majesty of Christ is above the majesty of man ; whoever, therefore, injures a priest is guilty of lese majesty. We need not pursue in detail the defence of the High Court Judge. By the end of the second day the most important thing that he had accomplished was the adjournment for twelve days of the final session. He was awaiting plenary powers, or even the Emperor's personal attendance, for Frederick had already reached Turin. Not to appear intransigeant Pope Innocent agreed to the delay. He did not, however, wait for the arrival of the envoys. All that was necessary had been arranged in secret session with the prelates, and the blow was timed to fall on the 17th of July.

The concluding session of the Council was introduced like the earlier ones by a solemn ceremonial. The Pope sat on a raised throne in the choir of the Cathedral church of Lyons, the nave of which was filled with archbishops and abbots. A few serious complaints of the English prelates against the money-hunters of the Curia, a topic unwelcome to the Pope, were speedily disposed of. The refusal of Thaddeus of Suessa to recognise the assembly as a General Council was " humbly and benevolently " waved aside by the Pope. Protests on Frederick's behalf by envoys of the French and English kings received no hearing, and the Patriarch of Aquileia, venturing to take up the Emperor's defence, was threatened with the loss of his ring if he broke silence.

Thereupon the Pope read the decree of deposition. Frederick had been proved guilty of perjury, breach of the peace, sacrilege and heresy. He was perjured because he had not fulfilled the treaty sworn in Rome ; he had repeatedly broken the peace with the Church ; he had committed sacrilege in taking prisoner the prelates ; and, finally, he was a heretic who was even yet bound in the bonds of friendship to the Saracen kings ; he had put his consorts in the charge of eunuchs ; he had permitted Muhammad to be proclaimed in the Temple of the Lord at Jerusalem ; he had utilised Saracens as warriors against Christians ; he had entered into marriage relations with the schismatic Emperor, John Vatatzes ; he had cleared princes from his path by assassins ; he had caused the sacred mysteries to be celebrated in his presence when he was excommunicate. Apart from the irregularities of his harem he despised the morals and manners of a Catholic prince, and took no pains to secure his good repute or the salvation of his soul by pious deeds ; he gave no alms ; he was ready enough to destroy churches and oppress the clergy, but he had built neither church nor cloister, neither hospital nor any other pious building. In virtue, therefore, of his papal power to bind and to loose, the Pope declared this Emperor, so sunk in sin, deposed—and his territories released from their allegiance. A new Emperor must be chosen. Whereupon Pope and Prelates extinguished the torches which they bore, and while Thaddeus of Suessa, weeping and beating his breast, left the cathedral with the other supporters of the Emperor, Pope and Prelates intoned the Te Deum.

With pain and wrath and scorn Frederick received the news. How could the Roman Emperor, the Lord of all majesty, be accused of lese-majesty and deposed ! Sternly he bade them bring his royal treasure. Choosing amongst his many crowns he selected one and himself placed it on his head and grimly remarked : he had not yet lost his crowns and would not let papal baseness nor council's decree rob him of them without most bloody battle. His position now, he said, was better than before. Previously he had to obey the Pope, now he was free ; without obligations.

Pope Innocent himself had saved Frederick from a second Canossa, from a humiliating peace and a decline from the heights of Empire. The pamphlets had unwittingly pointed the way which the last Emperor of the Roman Empire no longer hesitated to tread. In Lyons they had called him " Proteus," who was not to be caught because he constantly changed his form. He was now ready for the final metamorphosis thrust on him. Something of that northern defiance and northern horror which formed part of his make-up now found vent, when Frederick II, whom men had called Antichrist and Scourge of the World, turned to his followers with a new saying : " I have been anvil long enough . . . now I shall play the hammer ! "

IX. ANTICHRIST

Dual interpretation of Frederick's life——Frederick's posterity——Satellite giants: Eccelino, Guido of Sessa, Hubert Pallavicini——" Labour of Love " : to purge the Church——Reform manifestos——Pope's counter-activities——Increasing savagery of Frederick——Lure of the East——Conspiracy of intimates, 1246——Distrust of subordinates——Punishment of conspirators——Complicity of Pope——Henry Raspe——Italy partitioned amongst the Hohenstaufen——March on Germany; threat to Lyons——Defection of Parma——" The Cardinal "——Siege of Parma——Saracens as executioners——Victoria——Defeat before Parma——Money shortage——German knights in Italy——German influence on Renaissance art——Renewed threat to Lyons ——Fall of Piero della Vigna——Attempt to poison Frederick——Piero della Vigna's suicide——Enzio taken prisoner——Manfred's rise and fall——Death of Enzio ——Conradin's coronation——Tagliacozzo ; Conradin's execution——Curse on the Hohenstaufen——Parma avenged——Death of Frederick, December 13, 1250—— Burial at Palermo——The Frederick myth

IX. ANTICHRIST

" Nemo contra Deum nisi Deus ipse."

" Now I shall be hammer ! " This was the characteristic cry which led Nietzsche to hail Frederick of Hohenstaufen as " one of my nearest kin." Nietzsche, the first German to breathe the same air as Frederick, took up the cry and echoed it. Frederick had struck a new note, and passed into a supernatural world in which no law was valid save his own need. He had long realised that he would be compelled to loose terrible and savage forces ; he shrank from it and had sought to avert it by the humblest offers of peace, even by complete submission to the Pope; nay, by actual abdication. He did not seek the rôle of the Scourge of God, compelled to lay the recalcitrant " between hammer and anvil and to smite their obstinacy with blows so thick that they shall bow their necks to the yoke of commandment, and whatever their thoughts may be, shall recognise their true master."

Innocent IV had not recognised that a man like Frederick II could be bound only by fetters of his own forging and would take on him the yoke only of his own choosing. Innocent trusted to his papal power of binding and loosing, to excommunication and deposition, and had thus released from bondage the Antichrist, whom the Lord himself had held in fetters for a thousand years. The chains had worn thin ; they had grown rusty ; the Pope had subjected them to a strain too great. The " Lord of the World " might polish them till they shone like gold, and voluntarily adorn himself therewith, but they could not bind him against his will. He laughed them to scorn.

Since Antichrist it had to be, Frederick accepted his fate. All that had gone before now wore an air of preparation and seemed to indicate a readiness to welcome the inevitable with open eye. Though he had been (Frederick wrote) unalterably convinced that this Pope, like all others, would be opposed to him, yet he had worked to compass the elevation of Innocent.

Why ?   " Solely in order that our hand might hold him whom
we should overcome or—if the fates had been kinder—him
whom we should love ? "

That is to say with open eyes to co-operate with mysterious
fate, to create his own foe since fate so willed.   This is the
clearsighted fatalism of the man of action : a survival of the
heroic age.   A thousand years of Christianity lend it a Christian
colouring : almost to the point of self-immolation Frederick
had hoped that he might love his enemy.   But the Norns which
ruled the career of this Hohenstaufen recognised no such
solution.   Love was barred ; he must fulfil himself through
hate.   If he might not as a Saviour-Emperor join hands with
an Angel-Pope to draw the peoples under the gentle yoke of an
Emperor of the End, he was ready with scourge and sword,
with axe and halter, to compel the recreants to bow under the
yoke.   " Because they above all others have cut us to the HEART,
therefore shall we pursue after them with greater zeal and fury,
we shall the more mightily deploy our powers to compass their
destruction, we shall wield the sword of vengeance the more
cruelly against them . . . and the HATE that consumes us will
be slaked only by their utter annihilation."

At every stage of his career it was clear that Frederick was
full of primeval hate for any disturber of his sacred order.
Hatred and revenge—virtues both in Frederick's eyes—are
characteristics of the priest, who asks quite other reparation
from the desecrator of his Holy of Holies than that which the
warrior exacts from his enemy.   Hatred and revenge are qualities of the *Justitia* and of the judge of whom it is said " the
righteous is as a glowing coal."   Frederick II was the sacred
judge in a degree undreamt of by Emperors before or after him,
hence gratitude, tolerance, kindness, magnanimity, had no
more right than their opposites to a place amongst his qualities.
Gentleness and mercy he recognised as forces at the disposal
of *Justitia*, in the same way as revenge and hate, but henceforward he displays almost exclusively the avenging power of
the state-founding *Justitia*.   Hatred becomes to him the breath
of life.   In proportion as the foe no longer seeks to overthrow
the Emperor's order, but aims solely at his person, this hate
becomes a personal imperative.   As the Scourge of God he

recognises no law, divine or human, save his own advantage and his own caprice. None knew, none guessed what he was fighting for, what he still hoped to gain—perhaps he knew himself—except the assertion of his own personality. He became the battle-cry of the West ; bloodier and more savage than before the strife raged through the Christian world round his person alone. Never before in Christian times had one single individual achieved such personal importance—Frederick the man, not Frederick the Emperor. Times had changed. Those lofty ideals for which Frederick had fought of old : the rebirth of the Roman Empire, the reign of *Justitia*, the mission of World Peace—at most their distant echoes faintly sounded, as " revolution " and " enlightenment " echoed faintly round Napoleon in his last years. They no longer supplied the driving force. The person of the Emperor was now the World-Idea. If Frederick had been unable thus to exalt himself the Curia would still have given the struggle its œcumenical importance. With magnificent single-minded concentration the Church laid aside all other tasks and devoted her entire world-organisation to the destruction of one man. The Church magnified the Hohenstaufen into a giant. The Papacy, with all the forces of all the countries of Europe, was now fighting not the Emperor nor the Empire, but one demon in whom all the evil of the world was incarnate, one Hohenstaufen, by name Frederick. Only once again has the world seen such a fight against a single man in which, perhaps, greater numbers were involved, but scarcely greater forces, the final death-grapple with Napoleon. This was the atmosphere in which Frederick let his new note be heard. The air of Attila was round him which he alone could breathe. Attila's mission was his, which none but he could comprehend. Instinctively his contemporaries bestowed on him the cognomens that Attila had borne, " Scourge of the Peoples," " Hammer of the World." With hushed voices his own followers styled him no longer merely " him who ruleth over earth and sea " or " him who maketh the winds of heaven to rejoice," but " him whose might tramples the mountains and bends them." All Europe suffered terribly under him, friend and foe alike, Italy and Germany more particularly. Except for those who worshipped and followed him, Frederick now became in very deed the incarnation of evil.   He possessed, indeed, a capacity for evil rare in a ruler of his greatness.   Nor has any man ever felt a greater joy in ill-doing than Frederick in the rôle the hostile Church had thrust upon him.   Where the State was at stake Frederick had always been capable of every meanness and cunning, of every violence and severity, of every deceit and ruse, of every malice and of every scorn.   " I never reared a pig but I was prepared to eat his bacon " is one of his sayings.   Hitherto whatever evil he had done had been done for the sake of the State.   The world was now at war over the body of the Hohenstaufen.   State necessity had of old constituted right : now his personal exigencies.   Law was bent to his will not to serve the state or the world at large but at the apparent bidding of imperial caprice.   Theoretically he had often proclaimed that the welfare of the Empire, of the other peoples, of the kings, of those who believed, hung upon his private weal or woe.   Every act of his now appeared more tyrannical, more monstrous, and was, in fact, more ruthless since it seemed to serve the preservation of one single individual. Just because Frederick II had so nearly been the Saviour (and indeed in the eyes of the faithful still was) he had the opportunity to be the very Antichrist.   Since as a priest he knew all mysteries no mystery was safe from his fearless mocking attack. No spirit among all the thousand demons of the world was a stranger to his cosmopolitan mind.   All the supernatural magic of the East was at his command and the elusive *jinns*, and all the satanic poisons of Italy and the immeasurable daring of the German Mephistopheles, who crosses the Alps " and believes that all is his."   The great saying of Luther might well have been applied to him :   " An Italianised German is the devil incarnate ! "

It is hardly necessary to mention that ecclesiastical principles, excommunication and dethronement decreed by a Council, broke powerlessly against this genius and ruler of the Opposition-world : " The stones hurled by the papal catapults were changed to straw."   The blasphemies with which he was credited are without number ; whether authentic or not, they

were believed. The Church in her own defence circulated the
wildest exaggerations and the most fatuous lies, and spread them
more widely than Frederick in speech with his friends could
possibly have done. Not only the speech about the three
deceivers, but mockeries about the sacraments were ascribed
to Frederick as to every heretic. At the sight of a cornfield he
is said to have remarked with jesting reference to the Eucharist :
" What a lot of gods are ripening here ! " And another time,
" even if God had been bigger than the biggest mountain the
priests would surely have devoured him before now." And
when he saw a priest bearing in haste the viaticum to a dying
man : " how long will this humbug continue ? " It is known
that he made merry over the virgin birth as contrary to nature,
and that he denied the immortality of the soul. Cardinal
Rainer was, therefore, not without some justification when in
his pamphlets he asked : What was to restrain the Emperor from
the most devilish infamy since he had no craving for eternal
bliss, which he was prepared to sacrifice to slake his thirst for
vengeance in the blood of the people of Viterbo, and since he
had no fear of hell. For he had taught his courtiers to believe
that " the soul passes away like a breath and is consumed like
an apple plucked from off the tree, man and apple composed
alike of the four juices."

What recked he of the Church's means of grace—confession,
penance, absolution—since he and his astrologers believed in
fate determined by the stars, and such a belief in fate precluded
remorse ! How was a man to be bridled who counted human
blood as naught, who could, with impunity, hang or behead,
drown or imprison bishop, monk or priest, whom men reproached for pulling down churches to build privies in their
place and using the stones for fortresses for his beloved
Saracens !

Councils and popes could certainly now erect no barriers
that Frederick would have hesitated to break down. The only
limits he could recognise were those he set himself. He had
taken on himself a new mission, the office of Hammer of the
World and Scourge of God : not without the demonic joy of
creative genius in being free to destroy : not without the pain
and sorrow of preserving genius in being forced to destroy.

Pope Gregory had once said that Frederick loved to hear himself called Antichrist ; but Frederick had endured to the last limit of endurance before becoming Antichrist indeed. He was capable of any sacrilege, of any blasphemy, of any depravity, but whatever rage or revenge he might indulge was never wanton, it was always necessary for his self-preservation, and with it all he preserved always unimpaired the proud gesture of a Caesar, the noble bearing, the exalted dignity which stooped to nothing mean, the self-control, the poise that became a Christian Caesar. Woe to the heretic who dared to draw near him as a " fellow heretic ! " He remained to the last the Christian Emperor in style and bearing, without prejudice to his personal system of dogma. " Even dogmatic orthodoxy is false if the correct bearing is lacking," he once wrote. The phenomenon was remarkable : however violently his terrible and primitive force broke forth it was always controlled by the restraint of a Roman Augustus, who might tolerate vice but not indiscipline. He once described his own ambition : " to repress even the most righteous impulses of the spirit, and in virtuous self-discipline to preserve a Caesar's calm." Thus we too must picture him. A Scourge of God not in the aberrations of Ivan the Terrible, not sunk in sinister and brooding gloom, but in a more eerie windless calm, the detached aloofness of a timeless God. Thus under the figure of Caesar Augustus, Kaiser Frederick is reflected two-fold in a double mirror as Antichrist and as the Messianic Judge.

Caesar, Messiah, Antichrist : these are the three fundamentally identical manifestations of Frederick II since Cortenuova, since the beginning of his World Rule. He remained unchanged ; only the fluctuations of circumstance show us his form lit with a different glow. The more he genuinely approximated to a Roman Augustus from whom salvation was to come the more he resembled the very antithesis. A genuine Roman Emperor reincarnate who erected statues to himself, inevitably appeared as Nero or as Antichrist beside the Galilean.

The whole life of Frederick II could be interpreted either in the Messianic or the Anti-Christian spirit. The Antichrist begotten in sin shall be surrounded by astrologers and augurs, wizards and magicians, shall re-introduce demon worship, shall seek personal fame and call himself God Almighty. He shall come to Jerusalem and set up his throne in the Temple. He shall restore the temple of Solomon, and shall lie, and call himself the son of the Almighty. He shall convert the kings and princes and through them the peoples. He shall send his messengers and preachers over the whole earth, and his message shall reach from sea to sea, from East to West and from South to North. With him the Empire of Rome shall end. He shall accomplish signs and wonders and unheard-of deeds, but confusion shall reign upon earth the like of which was not before. When men shall see his deeds then even the perfect and the chosen of God shall be in doubt, whether he be Christ who shall come again at the End of the World according to the scriptures or whether he be Antichrist. For both must be like and equal.

Frederick's manners and methods were always open to two interpretations. His menagerie and exotic pomp made some to think of a world-king who ruled over all beasts and kindreds and tongues, of the Messiah under whose sceptre all the animals of earth should lie together in peace ; while some saw in this train of owls and pards and dark-skinned corybantes, sweeping through the towns of Italy, the hosts of the Apocalypse. Frederick could not mount a horse but some symbolic meaning was forthwith attached thereto : if he rode a white horse he was aping the Saviour and was accused of blasphemy ; if a chestnut, he became " the rider on a red horse " who bringeth strife ; if he chose a dun, he was death : and if he was mounted on a black horse men trembled before the judge with his balance. Frederick probably aggravated things himself by calling his favourite horse " Dragon." When Cardinal Rainer spoke of the " horn of power in his forehead," and when the Cistercians, after his deposition, dated their writings according to the years of the reign of " Fridericus Cornutus," the horn is thought of as the sign of Satan. But two horns are the token of the Messiah, symbols not of evil but of power as Moses shows and Alexander. Frederick was reputed invulnerable ; in later days this was accepted as conclusive proof of a pact with the Devil ; but others believed that only God could summon back his own. Some called Frederick the fallen angel whose countenance had once been likest God's ; others thought of the God-likeness of the Messiah, and Piero della Vigna celebrates his master as " like unto God." Riches marked the Antichrist, but again Christ was lord over all the treasures of the earth. Frederick's knowledge of tongues, so that " he was wont to speak in many languages of many kinds," was also satanic : or divine. Points in which Frederick quite unquestionably appeared as the Christian ruler caused most discussion of all : for deceit and disguise were the chief characteristics of Antichrist. Frederick was then more dangerous than ever. There is irony in the fact that this temperate man, who preserved his health by a régime of one meal a day (so that he was even accused of stultifying the penance of fasting), should have volunteered to win absolution by fasting.

Frederick's life was a consistent unity, though capable of a dual interpretation ; yet some have sought to find a " conflict " in it and to trace this throughout his life : the freethinker persecutes heretics ; the friend of Saracens goes a-crusading ; the man whose very atmosphere generated freedom must nip freedom in the bud as he fights the freedom-loving towns ; the man born to rule the world must confine himself to Italy ; the man who poured scorn on the priesthood must call himself a priest; the Christian Emperor must needs by penetrating query undermine the Christian faith ; and, finally, he who would fain be like the Messiah was yet prepared to play the Scourge of God and Hammer of the World. It is depreciating genius to expect it to be transparently simple to construe.

The conception of a Roman-Christian Caesar implied the fusion of two worlds ; the tension of two extreme forces. Each perpetually denied the other, each owed the other the fullness of its vitality. A smaller man than Frederick II would have succumbed under the strain, but at such altitudes the same miracle is ever renewed and ever challenges man's admiration : " the glaciers shone on by the fiercest sun become not warm, neither do they melt, the sunlight lends them brilliance only." Frederick summed up the situation in his fundamental dogma of the secular State : true freedom exists only under the yoke of the Imperium.

For once these antitheses could co-exist in one form and shape without thus losing firmness of texture or of outline : Emperor and Galilean ; Pagan and Christian ; Saviour and Antichrist. For the Christ whom Frederick the Hohenstaufen represented, who was for the last time incarnate in this German Emperor, was the almost pagan Christ of the Old Saxon Heliand, the Iesus Rex of the royal house of David, who wore the diadem of the Roman Emperors and ruled the Germanic year with fame and glory ; who founded the new Christian Imperium which ended with him. This Saviour, blent of Germanic, Greek, and Christian elements, wearing a crown of light, holding in his hand the orb, the lance, the book, enthroned in the aloofness of the *mandorla* that knows not time nor space : this was the Saviour whom Frederick in actual fact released, fulfilled and lived, lending him bodily existence in his own flesh. Christ once more had become man : God was again to die. St. Francis had vouchsafed a new glimpse of the same God : a picture of a gentle not a jealous God, a sufferer with wounds and crown of thorns, beside whom the stern judge and un-approachable, the fame-crowned king, inevitably appeared as Antichrist. For yesterday's God is ever the Satan of to-day.

For nearly three hundred years—the era of the Renaissance —the strife of the one yet dual God was the spur of mankind. Dante was the first to fight it to the end and overcome. Dante who reconciled the Eagles and the Cross, the kingdoms of this world and the next, ended the opposition which had begun with Vergil, and growing ever stronger had lasted for a thousand years. The tension between the Empire of Caesar and the Empire of Christ was symbolised in the two contemporaries, Francis and Frederick, preceding the great singer with whom the Empire closed. Another great singer Vergil, whom Dante claimed as master, had heralded the era of tension and cleavage, the age of the dual Saviour, Christus-Augustus.

Frederick's influence partook of this dual character. His legacy was most potent in Italy, and the reverberations of his career were felt there for three hundred years. New giants grew up around him. Through his son-in-law Eccelino of Romano, the Devil of Treviso, he became the ancestor of Sigismondo Malatesta and of Cesare Borgia. Eccelino, the admirer and the creature of the Hohenstaufen, was one of the many who seized on one trait only of the Emperor's many-sided character and exaggerated it into a colossal caricature. The ruthless assertion of personality, the unbridled lust for power, became with Eccelino an end in themselves and therefore evil. After the death of the Emperor had removed all restraint, this tyrant developed his vices to their uttermost. The two men were of the same age, but Eccelino survived Frederick for nine years. Long before the end Romano was the most feared and most hated man in the East of Northern Italy, which, in the Emperor's name, he had subjected to his power. Eccelino had ripened in the party quarrellings of the towns, had at an opportune moment rallied to the Hohenstaufen banner, and been given a free hand in those regions without any definite imperial office. Basing his operations on Padua, Verona and Vicenza, Eccelino had built up a self-contained despotism. He added town after town to his possessions, raised taxes on his own authority, promulgated new laws, appointed his own relations to office, at times against the Emperor's wishes, and even enlarged his territories at the Emperor's expense. His power was based wholly on terror. From pure self-seeking he remained faithful to Frederick, and, as he was a trustworthy guardian of the Brenner, Frederick left him unmolested. Eccelino, in spite of the Emperor's backing, was the first of a new type of ruler, a type which Manfred later dignified by referring to the precedent of Caesar : the illegitimate prince who founds his throne on power and cunning, and maintains it with severity, cruelty and fear, relying on his personality alone.

Dante represents the tyrant Eccelino expiating his sins in a stream of boiling blood : " that brow whereon the hair so jetty clustering hangs." He is said to have been covered all over with black hair like an animal's coat. His outward appearance was sinister, his bearing assured. He was only of middle height, but the sight of him inspired terror. He always appeared to be trembling with wrath and arrogance. Though for political reasons he had frequently been married, he held aloof from women. He despised them and rarely approached one. Yet he poniarded on the instant a German soldier whom he caught raping a woman at the storming of Vicenza. He liked to call himself a " scourge sent for the punishment of sinners," seeking the sinners rather among the aristocracy than amongst the common people, whom he kept sternly under his heel. Eccelino believed that his fate was linked with the stars and relied on the learned Guido Bonatti and the long-bearded Saracen, Paul of Baghdad, to read his fortunes in the sky. He loved magnificence, but his Padua court displayed only the oppressive pomp of the tyrant, and his Saracen bodyguards served more for awe than for grandeur. " This state must be kept pure " was the motto of the despot, who grew more and more stony as the years went on. The faintest breath of suspicion spelt rack or stake, castration or the dungeon. He is said to have sacrificed 50,000 men by murder, torture or execution to maintain his power. He acted, no doubt, on the principle of his brother-in-law, Salinguerra : " The whole heavens are the Lord's . . . but the earth hath he given to the children of men." He died faithful to his principles. He was sixty-five when uncounted enemies suddenly surrounded him, and brave though he was and tried in battle, he was stunned by the blow of a club and taken prisoner. He refused food and doctors and died within a few days. He repudiated confession and the last sacrament, jesting that he had but one crime of which he repented, having let himself be overpowered and being unable to take vengeance. Whereupon he dismissed the priest. His voluntary death may well have saved him from an end as gruesome as his brother's. Alberigo of Romano had at first been hostile to Eccelino, but later became his ally. He was quite as cruel, and lustful to boot. They made him creep on all fours to the place of execution with a bit in his mouth, serving as a mount for the mob. He was made to witness the tortures of his family, then the flesh was torn from his body with pincers, and while still living he was tied to a horse and dragged to death.

Eccelino was by no means the only giant in Frederick's circle. Another was Guido of Sessa, who cynically refused the last rites to some condemned papalists, assuring them that as friends of the Pope they were sure of immediate access to Paradise. Taking flight, one night, he and his horse plunged into the lepers' *cloaca* and perished in the filth. Yet another was the one-eyed Margrave Hubert Pallavicini, who began as Eccelino's friend but betrayed his rival and took him prisoner. He rivalled Eccelino in vice and practised the same unscrupulous violence to maintain his rule. He had less demonic fanaticism and remained always a sly calculator without a conscience. His whole appearance was uncanny. While he was still in the cradle a cock had picked out one eye, but the remaining one glittered " like a black coal " from a face framed with blackest hair and beard. He also was of middle height, but immensely powerful and tough. Like all the Emperor's intimates he made merry over the Church and her dogmas. He looked on the Roman Church purely as a political power and the Pope as a ridiculously petty Italian landowner, scarcely on a par with a Pallavicini. This materialist point of view was usual amongst men of his type in Renaissance times. The Emperor had entrusted him with the Vicariate-General of Cremona and had made him a gift of numerous places in these, his native territories. After Frederick's death the Margrave continued the war against the Papacy and the Guelf. Like Eccelino he fought nominally for the Empire, but with the parts of Lombardy which he conquered he swelled his growing Seignory and styled himself " Vicar General in Lombardy and permanent lord of Cremona, Pavia, Piacenza and Vercelli." Crema and Milan, Alessandria, Tortona and Parma also obeyed the despot, whose immense domain ultimately fell to pieces as rapidly as it had been thrown together. When he died at seventy (also, so the legend runs, refusing the ministrations of the Church) the Margrave Hubert Pallavicini possessed nothing but the single castle Busseto near Parma from which he had been wont to sway the destinies of Lombardy.

These comrades of Frederick II were large-scale criminals, men who made mock alike of the bliss of heaven and the pains of hell. And each of them showed features of the Hohen-

staufen Emperor distorted into caricature. Frederick was the
only one of them who bore God in his breast as well as
the Devil. His immense potentialities are seen in the way
in which he developed as Hammer of the World and Scourge
of the Peoples, and yet might worthily have stood beside
Francis of Assisi and with him fought the common foe, the
degenerate Church. Frederick took care at first not to attack
the Church ; he sought to confine his quarrels to the individual
Pope. When this became impossible he changed weapons
with lightning adaptability and began to emulate the wrath of
Elijah, who "jealous for the Law slew the greedy priests of
Baal in the storm of the spirit " and embarked on a campaign
against the worldliness of the clergy. His great Reform Manifesto followed hard on the Council of Lyons : " It was ever
our intention and our will to induce the priesthood of every
rank, not least the highest, to endure ' to the end ' as they were
of old in the early church : leading an apostolic life and
emulating their Master's humility. For such are the men who
see visions and work miracles, who heal the sick and wake the
dead, who not by force of arms but by their holiness make
kings and princes to serve them. Our priests on the other
hand are slaves to the world, drunken with self-indulgence, who
put God in the second place : the increasing stream of their
wealth has stifled their piety. To take from them these
treacherous treasures which are their burden and their curse :
THIS IS A LABOUR OF LOVE." Thus Frederick wrote to the
kings of Europe and exhorted them to relieve the servants of
God of all superfluity. In this Frederick was in accord with
the mood of his time. This was the doctrine which well-nigh
caused Francis of Assisi to be condemned as a heretic : the
doctrine of return to the simplicity of apostolic times, the
Church's re-marriage to her long-forgotten spouse, poverty.
The moment seemed opportune, for the end should be like the
beginning, as Frederick expressly emphasised.

The Emperor pressed his demand further : " Whence have
our priests learned to bear arms against the Christians ? To
don their coats of mail instead of sacred garments, instead of a
shepherd's crook to wield a lance, to carry the bow and arrows
of bitterness instead of their writing reed, to think lightly of

the weapons of salvation ?   What assembly of God-fearing men
has commanded this and sealed it with its seal ?   If anyone
doubts us let him behold the holy cardinals and archpriests who
brandish warlike weapons in the land where we bear sway !
The one styles himself a duke, a margrave another, yet a third
a count, according to the province where he rules.   Did the
first disciples of Christ so arrange it ?   O foolish multitude !
Ye attribute holiness unto them, ye create saints unto yourselves as imaginary as the giants of myth ! "

Frederick in this document demanded nothing less than the
abandonment by the Roman Church of all her worldly property and of all her worldly dignities : duchies, margravates
and counties.   The French Revolution first brought these
demands to general fruition, though in Sicily Frederick had
succeeded in establishing the desired state of affairs.   For in
his own kingdom most of the Church treasures had been confiscated and Frederick had long since ceased to bestow official
rank on his Sicilian clergy.   It is obvious that Frederick was
not preaching the poverty of the Church from the motives of
urgent faith and piety that inspired St. Francis.   It has been
the fashion to make it a reproach that Frederick wanted the
Church to be poor, not because of his zeal for God but because
he was a bad Catholic.   The Emperor certainly did not espouse
the cause of Church reform for its own sake, yet reform was
part of his office, and in pursuing it Frederick was boldly ahead
of his time.   St. Francis and the reforming Emperor are suddenly near akin.   Whoever sought to bring again the Augustan
age had need of a church as it had been in the days of the early
Empire.   The Saint demanded the return of the primitive
Church, and his Order yet more imperatively demanded it
(for that they hoped " as a new breed of men " to oust from
office the degenerate clergy), and in so doing they unwittingly
conjured up the Augustan as well as the Apostolic age.   St.
Francis, intent only on the Church's weal, had no thought for
such logic.   Frederick II, however, with wider vision, saw that
his empire could absorb the greatest movement of the time,
saw indeed that the Empire of Rome could co-exist only with
a Franciscan type of pope.   Frederick here anticipated the
vision of Dante : a penniless Peter as pope, side by side with

him, an emperor of boundless possessions, both immediately appointed of God. To such a pope, who by his holiness made kings and princes to serve him, Frederick was prepared to render—as Dante demanded—" that reverence which a first-born son must show his father, that in the light of his father's grace he may be more powerfully resplendent throughout the world. . . ."

We must draw attention to a remarkable turn of phrase in one of the reform manifestos. " Our conscience is pure and therefore God is with us," Frederick announced to the European kings. This is a kind of spiritual communion with God different from that of St. Francis. A communion in virtue of conscience, which is based on the imperial doctrine that the Emperor is responsible for his action to God alone. This is the layman's claim to immediacy of intercourse with God, which not without good reason was first formulated by the last Emperor of the Middle Ages. This doctrine preludes the later notes of the Reformation. Yet there could hardly be a greater contrast than lies between the two points of view. The appeal to purity of conscience which, when taken up by the many, served to obliterate all ranks and grades, was here a privilege of the all-responsible Emperor who claimed it for himself in full consciousness of his own uniqueness and accorded it otherwise to none. In judging others Frederick held their actions only of account. But the imperial attitude was challenging; how challenging we see from the gloss on this passage by an astonished monk: " Believe in deeds ! "

Frederick had described his campaign against the Church as a " labour of love," and we need feel no surprise that the mendicant orders hailed his tribunal as just, and hoped that the final era of peace and repose was now about to dawn. The growing hostility between the regular clergy and the orders became Frederick's ally, and many, both Franciscans and Dominicans, supported him against the clergy. In opposition to the prevailing belief that Antichrist would come from without to attack the Church, many saw the destroyer within the bosom of the Church herself.

One of the mendicants, Brother Arnold, demonstrated in a document bearing the title " Innocent IV, Antichrist," that the words "Innocentius Papa" yielded the number 666, and that, therefore, the Pope was Antichrist. In another highly emotional pamphlet the same writer espoused the Emperor's cause. He asserted that God had revealed to him in a vision that it was the divine intention to renew Holy Church and to lead her back to her original purity. Thus instructed, Brother Arnold had, he reported, betaken himself to Kaiser Frederick, who had investigated the vision with the advice of wise and learned men, and being himself a Catholic free from all unfaith, the Emperor had approved the reformation of the Church as a most pious work. After forty days of mystic rapture Christ himself vouchsafed a vision to the monk, and revealed to him that the Pope and the papalists were the real enemies of God and the destroyers of the Gospel, and that the Lord had expelled them from the community of the faithful.

Many shared Brother Arnold's belief, and the cry " Heretic Pope " was heard unceasingly till the Reformation. It was particularly loud in Germany. In Hall in Swabia and in other places wandering preachers announced to thronging listeners : " the Pope is a heretic ; the prelates are simonists ; the priests are unworthy to bind or to loose ; papal indulgences are value-less and the Pope leads a perverted life and sets an example of evil." " Pray therefore," the preachers concluded, " for the Lord, Kaiser Frederick and for Conrad his son, for they are perfect and they are just."

The Emperor's reform manifestos were particularly popular in Germany. Wild abusive pamphlets attacked the clergy, "spouses of luxury who shirk marriage " ; one in its wrath struck the very note of imperial utterances : " O the blind unenlightened simplicity of you Christian people! Why be ye deceived by such trickery ! Arise, arise, ye monarchs of the earth. Arise, ye princes ! Arise, ye peoples, open your eyes and see ! Endure no longer the disgrace of such enmity. Root out this diseased multitude from the earth who bring confusion and contamination ! Reform Holy Church disfigured by such crimes ! And when the evil leaven of crime and wickedness is swept away may a new yeast begin to work in purity and truth and faith ! "

Such voices could not alter the outcome of the strife and no rising of the masses was at that period to be hoped for. But it is idle to pretend, as some have done, that Frederick was " misunderstood " by his contemporaries. Frederick must have been perfectly aware that his reforming manifestos could not shatter the Papacy ; he probably did not even wish that they should, for without a World Church the World Empire would cease. But he pushed the campaign to the uttermost, and the seed he sowed took root even in his own day. With his instinct for a living force Frederick seized on these ideas and flung them into the conflict between mind and might, to germinate for centuries. The hopes of earnest men in Germany who sought reform were for all time linked with the name of Frederick II Hohenstaufen. Men dreamt that he would some day return, in all his glory, to reform the corruption of the Church, and would pursue the Roman hierarchy so savagely that they would hide their tonsures with cow dung if they could find no other covering.

Perhaps it was especially to make impression on the Germans that Frederick let loose the terrors of the Angel of Death and of Antichrist. Germany is quicker to recognise the good than the beautiful ; perhaps it would not otherwise have recognised the Emperor as Saviour. The Pope's procedure gave new food for such reflections. Germany was drawn into the strife to a greater degree than before and suffered bitterly under the Curia's persecutions.

Up till the Council of Lyons Germany had felt relatively little of the great strife between Papacy and Empire. The church agitation had exercised little influence, although in 1239, just before the Emperor's excommunication, the papal legate, Albert of Bohemia, had succeeded in organising an opposition amongst the princes : Bohemia, Bavaria and Austria had formed the Confederation of Passau against Frederick. But it broke up within a few months. Bohemia and Austria came to terms with the Emperor, and the Duke of Bavaria was left alone. Not even the Bavarian clergy had gone over to the Pope, doubtless because the bishops were hostile to the Duke and therefore remained imperialist. The bishop of Ratisbon openly defied the Pope's legate ; the bishop of Brixen barricaded the street against the papal messenger ; the bishop of Freising denied the Pope any jurisdiction whatever in Germany, and the archbishop of Salzburg trampled a papal letter under foot. Princes and towns sent auxiliaries and money to the Emperor in Italy. Finally, even the Duke of Bavaria abandoned his hostility, for the Mongol peril which threatened his neighbours Bohemia, Hungary and Austria, diverted his attention. The propaganda of the Curia seemed to have been in vain.

A slight weakening might, however, have been observed in quite another quarter : on the Rhine. The great archbishop of Cologne, Conrad of Hochstaden, is famous as the founder and builder of the great cathedral, whose foundation-stone he laid in 1248. In those days he was no less famous as a warrior, a wild quarrelsome fellow who, like all the German princes, bent his whole mind to his territorial policy and lived in perpetual conflict with his neighbours on the lower Rhine. Through these quarrels he presently fell foul of the imperial government, which lent an ear to the complaints of the princes, and the Archbishop of Cologne was declared an enemy of the Empire. Finding himself single-handed Conrad of Hochstaden ultimately found an ally in the scarcely less powerful Sigfrid, archbishop of Mainz, whom Frederick had appointed Regent in Germany. The archbishop of Mainz had long been at odds with the Duke of Bavaria about the Abbey of Lorsch, which Mainz had hopes of retaining as long as Bavaria was hostile to the Emperor. When, however, the Duke of Bavaria began veering towards friendship with the Emperor the archbishop of Mainz saw his Abbey of Lorsch imperilled. Weighed against this he recked little of the regency. He and Cologne could both be certain of papal support if they deserted the Emperor, and so the two formed an alliance. Henceforth they both proclaimed the ban against Frederick and invaded the Hohenstaufen territory of Wetterau with fire and sword. Thus Innocent IV found a German group hostile to Frederick among

the Rhine archbishops and their suffragans.   It was now one
of the chief aims of papal politics to increase their adherents.
Innocent systematically began trying to seduce the German
Church in every rank from its loyalty to the Hohenstaufen.
The papal methods were forceful.   The imperialist bishops
were deposed where possible, and in the cathedrals the
imperialist canons degraded.   After the Council of Lyons the
following dignitaries were involved in deposition proceedings :
the archbishops of Salzburg and Bremen ; the bishops of
Passau, Freising, Brixen, Utrecht, Prague, Worms, Constance,
Augsburg, Paderborn and Hildesheim ; the abbots of St. Gall,
Ellwangen, Reichenau, Kempten and Weissenburg.   Further
proceedings were pending against the bishops of Magdeburg,
Chur and Trent, and against innumerable priests.   Many, like
the bishops of Olmütz and Passau, were deposed, and many
voluntarily resigned so as not to turn traitor.   Their places
were filled by creatures of the Pope.   Others went over to
Innocent and were duly rewarded.   The German clergy speedily
became wholly dependent on the Curia, as the great Innocent
had once intended.   Any free election by convent or chapter
was expressly forbidden, and the bishops were nominated by
the Pope just as were Vicars General and *podestas* by Frederick.
The Emperor exercised his right of appointment down to the
lowest ranks, and now Innocent also supervised the appointment of the meanest clergy.   Even before a benefice was vacant
its next incumbent was frequently designated.

These reversions to posts in the Church were often granted
in exchange for payment of a tax, a procedure not far removed
from simony.   Other measures again led to the infamous traffic
in indulgences.   Masses of mendicant monks were carefully
instructed and despatched to spread the news of the excommunication and deposition far and wide, for which purpose they
were to make use of every convenient opportunity : processions,
fairs, markets and the like.   They were to follow each sermon
by a summons to all to take the cross against Frederick.   In
order not to stultify the crusade against Frederick and his sons
Pope Innocent most strictly but secretly enjoined on them not

by any chance to preach a crusade to the Holy Land : and this at the very juncture when Louis of France was preparing to set out on the sixth Crusade. An indulgence of forty to fifty days was earned by merely listening to a crusading sermon against Frederick, and those who took the cross received the same indulgences as those who fought the Saracens. If they later chose to redeem their vow by a money payment the indulgence for sin still held good, and many took the cross solely with the intention of acquiring the indulgence and then repurchasing their freedom. This procedure was not an entirely novel device. It had long been possible to purchase absolution from a crusading vow. Hitherto, however, the moneys thus amassed had been devoted to the prosecution of the crusade, whereas now they simply spelt a new source of revenue for the Church and a new weapon against the Emperor. The moment the fiction of a crusade was at an end, and indulgences were simply bartered for money, that traffic was in full swing which ultimately gave the impetus to the great schism of the sixteenth century, the Reformation.

The Pope's activities extended far beyond Germany. He had at his command the highly-ramified organisation of the Roman Church extending through the whole Christian world, and, between promises for this world and threatenings for the next, all kinds of hitherto unexploited sources of supply could be tapped and new partisans be won. There was no command in the Canon from which Innocent would not grant dispensation, no Church law which could not be circumvented, no ecclesiastical crime which could not be condoned if it seemed profitable for the campaign against the Hohenstaufen brood. To procure adherents the Pope began to distribute the property of the church as a feudal prince his fiefs : whoever performed a service for him received a " promissory note " so to speak on the next vacant benefice or see wherever situate. Spaniards might thus acquire a church in England or Germany, or the revenues thereof. Needless to say most of these foreign benefices fell to Italians whom the Pope himself required for the immediate war against the Emperor. These Italians frequently never even saw their cures, they were concerned only to collect the revenues, and the multiplication of benefices, which was an ancient abuse sternly condemned by canon law, became a favourite device of the Pope's to attract new or to fortify old loyalties. The fifths, tenths and twentieths which the Pope issued were endless. These creatures of the Pope were strangers and entirely indifferent to the fate of the flocks allotted to them ; they found no fault with the principle. They acquiesced readily enough in the demands made on them for money, for by such levies they could reap advantage for themselves.

These interferences of the Pope aroused acute bitterness in England and in France. Innocent, however, had not so free a hand in those countries as in Germany, where the spiritual princes were " pillars of the State " to a degree unknown elsewhere in Christendom, and where, therefore, systematic resistance was scarcely conceivable. In Germany, therefore, the papal rod was severely felt. In dioceses whose incumbent was not a papalist, all divine service ceased for years together, and no baptism, no marriage, no confirmation and no burial service could take place. No member of an imperialist family could take holy orders, and all supporters of the Hohenstaufen were cut off from Church fiefs and leases. In such circumstances everything fell far more seriously into decay in Germany than in Italy, where interdicts were frequently in force for years, but where people took a more commonsense view of religious matters. Similar conditions produced, therefore, very different consequences north and south of the Alps.

All these arrangements were made on a uniform system by the Curia from the base of Lyons, which was now the centre of the ecclesiastical web, whose threads Pope Innocent manipulated with consummate mastery. The Pope, indeed, showed himself an expert ; he also was a transformer of energies, skilled in utilising intangible forces, in translating spiritual into temporal advantage : into political, military and financial power. One thing was needful : an unscrupulous readiness to turn every available force to account. If we conceive the Church as a purely political power which was face to face with unprecedented political and military tasks, we must reckon the

Genoese as one of the most brilliant politicians who ever occupied the papal throne. Without a shadow of misgiving he put out his spiritual talent to usury and opened for the moment innumerable and unexhausted sources of revenue. There is something truly great in the way Pope Innocent silenced every scruple, stifled every sentimental qualm in pursuit of his one goal : the annihilation of the Hohenstaufen. He was no hypocrite ; he did not even seek to keep up appearances ; he did not even trouble to mask his features, which expressed frank scorn for every rule of canon law. He broke or evaded or altered every canon at will, introducing into the Papacy a " macchiavellian " trait which placed immediate expediency before all law, human or divine. This was a new type of pope, who had little in common with his warlike Caesar predecessors. The various reactions of the world at large to this new tendency are characteristic. In Germany this betrayal of ideals awakened bitterness, sorrow, detestation. The materialisation of the Church provoked by contrast the more intensive spiritualisation of religion and led ultimately to the Reformation and the renewal of Christendom. Whereas in Italy this conduct of the Popes gave birth to an unfathomable cynicism which brought with it the rebirth of paganism : the Renaissance.

Meanwhile the main theatre of war was Italy, where after the Pope's flight the mighty figure of the Emperor Frederick held the field and fought the fight for life and empire. North of the Alps Pope Innocent's efforts aimed at undermining the Emperor's sovereignty, south of the Alps his covert attacks were directed against the Emperor's person. In Italy the papal machinations were secret and difficult to counter, and the personal danger necessitated the most terrible severity. It was hard enough at any time to impose internal order on Italian party strife, and the Pope's myrmidons had no difficult task to stir up opposition. All the forces of disorder which had at such cost been calmed and quelled were released again by the papal agitators. Every political, social, religious, economic discontent was fostered and exploited by the Church, which distributed gold and promises without stint. In these circumstances the Emperor could keep up any semblance of control in the State only by extreme harshness and even cruelty. Discipline became more and more difficult to maintain ; treachery and defection were rife, and murder instigated by the Pope threatened the Emperor's life.

All the communes with few exceptions were untrustworthy. Even in the Ghibelline towns the opposition party was strong, and if the Guelfs gained the upper hand in one town a whole series of friendly and related towns forthwith fell away also. Conversely, of course, the accession of an important town to the Emperor's cause exercised widespread influence. Yet when one town was with difficulty reduced to allegiance, rebellion fanned by the Pope flamed up in three others, and no sooner had the Emperor gathered a stronger force than usual for some big undertaking than an unforeseen revolt broke out in another quarter, and his efforts were frittered in fruitless fighting. He made oath " never shall we sheathe the sword we have un-scabbarded till the hydra of rebellion whose reborn heads are charged with overflowing ruin, challenging the very existence of the Imperium, shall have been visited with mighty punish-ment . . .", but nevertheless he could not alter the fact that for long periods whole provinces like the Romagna or the Marches were lost to him. At moments during the last five years the general situation in Italy seemed more favourable to the Emperor than ever before. But such conjunctions of the stars were dearly bought !

The repressive measures of the Emperor grew severer year by year. The mistrust of a naturally mistrustful monarch was nourished by one ugly occurrence after another. Any town that he entered had immediately to give hostages, and these were carried off to Apulian prisons to be slaughtered at the first symptom of revolt. Anyone who showed letters from the Pope lost hands and feet. The Emperor recognised rebels only, not enemies ; hence every non-imperialist found armed was hanged. Places that were suspect might expect any fate. Occasional miscarriage of justice was not unknown : a pair of knights from the March were caught and hanged—they had been on their way to join the Emperor's army. It is said that a tiny mark was sometimes put on a suspect's back without his knowledge so that the imperial spies might keep their eye on him. One nobleman fell under suspicion because when his native town went over to the enemy his tower was left standing. Frederick sardonically opined that both he and the tower-owner must be much beloved since the imperial palace was also spared. The noble smiled a forced smile but disregarded his friends' warnings, and on the next breath of suspicion found himself at the bottom of the sea with a millstone round his neck. Even the good faith of loyal towns like Pisa and Lucca had to be purchased. The Emperor handed over to them the territories of the Lunigiana and Garfagnana which King Enzio had promised them. He even promised the Cremonese to make their town the capital of Italy in place of Rome. His treatment of prisoners was ruthless. In his manifestos he boasted, for instance, that he had had three hundred Mantuans hanged along the banks of the Po, or again that he had prevented the defection of Reggio by publicly beheading a hundred revolutionaries. Before the end the word " mercy " had been deleted from his vocabulary. Some noble Florentine Guelfs defended themselves in the Tuscan fortress of Capraio and surrendered after a short siege. Some were hanged on the spot ; some were taken in chains to Naples, blinded, mutilated and flung into the sea. Only one of the most distinguished was blinded and released and sent to the barren island of Monte Christo to end his days as a monk.

Frederick thus sought to defend himself by terror against the host of minor foes. Since the Pope's flight he had no " big enemy " in Italy and the struggle had changed its character. He was no longer fighting as in the days of Gregory IX as Emperor against the Pope in person. Frederick II and the House of Hohenstaufen were now fighting with tangible weapons against intangible opponents : Papacy and Church. Formerly the Italian continent had been too narrow for the two world powers, now Frederick II filled the space alone, while Innocent had vacated the scene of battle and from Lyons was driving his subterranean tunnels, mining the very ground beneath the Emperor's feet, instead of meeting him in the open field. Frederick lacked a visible enemy and a definite point of attack. He could no longer cross swords with the Pope ;

the fight now raged to and fro between the Emperor and his own subjects whom the Pope seduced. Whenever Frederick attempted a march towards Lyons or into Germany, so as to be again face to face with the foe and to escape the almost intolerable tension—" would that our hand had someone to conquer! "—some insurrection or another drew him back into the vortex of Italian strife. He remained for ever chained to the Apennines. Never again was he able to try his strength in the more distant spaces of the Empire. Whether or not he groaned " O felix Asia! " the worm gnawed remorselessly at his vitals.

Under this strain, in the hampering conditions of this ignoble struggle against the plots and intrigues of rebels and priests, a craving suddenly flashed out to bid the west good-bye and to seek again the alluring spaces of the east. The later Napoleon felt it too : " I should have been wiser to have stayed in Egypt. By now I should have been Emperor of the whole East," he exclaimed at the sight of St. Helena. In a letter to the Nicaean Emperor Vatatzes, after various complaints against revolutionaries and deceitful priests who dared to depose a king, Frederick wrote : " But such things happen more easily in our western lands! O happy Asia! O happy rulers of the Orient! who fear neither the dagger of the rebel nor the superstitions invented by the priest! " Such an outburst of personal feeling was rare in Frederick's state correspondence. It tallies with the legend that he had contemplated abdication and dreamt of betaking himself for ever to the east, promising to conquer the whole of Syria. A new Empire in the Orient, now that he had exhausted what the narrow west could offer ; intercourse with Muslim friends ; subjects whose only thought was blind obedience even unto death—these were the Emperor's castles in the air. Such a journey to the east as he desired was not to be. In another fashion, more bitter than the resignation of a throne, than a gradual retreat towards the east, he was to be gradually weaned from the men and things and states of this world.

Within a few weeks of the Council of Lyons Frederick saw

in what quarter the danger-clouds were gathering. Treacherous documents, including plans for the assassination of the Emperor and of King Enzio, were discovered in the monastery of Fonte-vivo near Parma. Parma was implicated, and when Frederick hastily repaired thither to prevent the defection of this important town he made the further discovery that Bernardo Orlando di Rossi, the Pope's brother-in-law, with a number of Guelf knights had fled from Parma in the direction of Piacenza and Milan.

Orlando di Rossi had been hitherto one of the professed supporters of Frederick II. He was an important personality, well known throughout upper Italy, for he had frequently held the office of *podesta* in imperial towns. His countryman, Fra Salimbene, the mendicant of Parma, describes him thus : " I never saw a man who looked so perfectly the part of an illustrious prince." Orlando had a most impressive exterior which his courage did not belie. When he appeared, armed, in the battle, and laid about him right and left, felling the foe with a heavy iron club, men fled as from the devil incarnate, and Fra Salimbene was fain to recall the exploits of Charles the Great : " according to what is recorded of Charlemagne and what I with mine own eyes saw of Orlando." Orlando di Rossi belonged to the cultured men of his time. As *podesta* of Siena he instituted a sort of town history in which he proposed to record : " the victories and triumphs for undying memory," as the Scipios had painted the deeds of their forefathers upon their doorposts to be inspired thereby to the conquest of the earth. Orlando has taken this anecdote with misunderstandings from Sallust. With such style and bearing and mentality it was natural that Orlando should be one of Frederick's more intimate circle—they were, moreover, related—and it was one of the contributory considerations influencing the choice of Sinibaldo Fiesco as Pope that Orlando di Rossi was his brother-in-law. Soon after the papal flight a breath of distrust towards the Pope's friends in Parma must have crept over Frederick. He certainly despatched Piero della Vigna to Parma at the time to ensure the town's allegiance. But in spite of misgivings Frederick acquiesced in the choice of Orlando di Rossi as *podesta* of Florence for 1244. It could only produce a reassuring impression during the progress of the peace negotiations if the Pope's brother-in-law was holding office in one of the most important of the imperial towns. But this time the game went wrong. Instead of Orlando's winning the Pope over to the Emperor's side the Pope converted his brother-in-law to the Guelfs. Orlando di Rossi openly betrayed the Emperor. Frederick felt the blow severely, but this was only the prelude to the great conspiracy amongst his intimates which followed a few months later.

There is no doubt that service under a ruler like Frederick II was anything but a sinecure. All private life came to a standstill for the imperial vicars as it did for the marshals of Napoleon. Their life was consecrated wholly to the service of the State and of the Emperor, and that service was wearing, difficult and dangerous. The relationship of vicar to Emperor was one of extreme delicacy. On the one hand the vicar had the fullest responsibility and almost unlimited powers, on the other Frederick never abandoned towards any man a certain suspicion, all officials were watched, and the Emperor would intervene at any moment in the administration. Considering the great independence of the officials and the precariousness of Frederick's exalted position this was most natural, but friction was inevitable. Sometimes the Emperor was over vigorous ; sometimes the official was unduly sensitive. Most of the vicars had known their master from their youth up ; they knew his distrust, they knew his watchfulness, and on their side they brought suspicion to bear, often most unfairly, on every utterance of the Emperor's. The nagging and the eternal discontent of the Napoleonic marshals offer a parallel. The sensitiveness and querulousness of his trusty intimates indulged even at critical moments aroused at times Frederick's impatient wrath. In a letter referring to some question of accounts the Emperor wrote to Piero della Vigna the innocent words " be diligent and attentive in the matter as is thy wont." Della Vigna was deeply hurt by the phrase and wrote back that all the praise contained in the imperial letter amounted to the exact opposite. Frederick would seem to consider him lazy and careless, which must be based on slander. . . . Whereupon Frederick only threatened his friend with his serious anger for daring to bring such ridiculous accusations against his Emperor.

It is quite possible, however, that the Emperor was at times really unjust to one or another, especially in those years of strain and stress. This was only to be expected, but there often reigned at Court a dangerous atmosphere, and visitors used with foresight to inform themselves about the current temperature. Frederick was neither obstinate nor petty. He never clung to a mistake, and there is something deeply moving in the words he writes at a time of terrible anxiety to a well-beloved Captain of Sicily, Andrew Cicala, soothing and encouraging him, acknowledging a blunder and apologising for it unreservedly and with gracious dignity : " The unfortunate words which caused you pain and so suddenly upset the calm of your firm mind, sprang from a mood of wrath and irritation. We are all the more rejoiced that thy well-tried uprightness and good-faith remained unshaken by such idle words. The more strongly thou feelest such unjust phrases the more steadfast and sure is thy constancy, one of the bastions of thy incorruptible loyalty, the proof whereof lies with thine own memorable deeds and with our pure and constant trust— more solemn testimony than any outside witness ! Need we say more . . . canst thou still find room to doubt . . . apart from the subtle signs of affection which the eyes cannot see, thou must be conscious of our trust since we leave our cares in thy hands and rely on thee as on a second self. If aught of thy vexation still remain banish the last remnants thereof, and when the rust of doubt has been polished away, believe in the constancy of our unaltered regard. As we on our side trust that thy good faith to us is immutable, thou for thy part must not doubt that our favour and our grace are thine unchangeably."

The distrust of his officials ! The fact that distrust was possible ! In this Frederick saw the greatest menace of all. Nothing is recorded of the Emperor's grief at the petty irritability of his friends, the deeper underlying causes of which he did not fail to fathom ; we are not told how often he comforted them by a letter like the foregoing, or oftener yet by a talk, many a time by a mere glance, and once again renewed the

spell that bound them to him, the charm by which he first had
won them. It is one of the fateful penalties of greatness that
the magic of a personality by becoming a daily commonplace
loses its power most readily over the nearest intimates. The
spell that still can bind the stranger plays false at home. No
great monarch but has been the victim of a friend's treachery.
Such treachery springs not from hostility and hate but from
weakness and cowardice. The traitor too incompetent to
sustain for long the demands of office ; too weak to bear the
continuous presence of the great man ; too cowardly to avow
weakness and incompetence ; and, again, too vain and self-
seeking to resign the service, not lacking withal in genuine love,
admiration, reverence for the Master—the intolerable burden
of such a conflict drives sometimes the nearest to deceit and
treachery. One renegade who at a critical moment thus
throws scruple to the winds easily becomes the seducer of the
wavering. Such was Orlando di Rossi's rôle.

From Parma Frederick II had taken steps to avert the
threatening defection of Reggio. He had then embarked on a
campaign of devastation against Milan, but he did not succeed
in coming to grips with the Milanese army, and during the
winter of 1245-46 he made Grosseto on the coast of Tuscany
his headquarters for several months. The district of the
Maremma promised good hawking, and at the same time the
Emperor could supervise Tuscany more closely. Various
irregularities had appeared in the administration, and the
venality of several authorities had come to light. Frederick
was obliged first to recall the Apulian Pandulf of Fasanella, who
for many years had been Vicar General of the difficult province
of Tuscany, and to replace him by the imperial bastard Frederick of Antioch, whom people soon styled King of Tuscany.
Frederick of Antioch must have then been a youth of about
twenty : competent, energetic, cautious, equal to the delicate
conditions in Tuscany, a courageous warrior, a poet who could
write tender canzones, a man of such gracious and charming
personality that people forgot that he was lame. Men liked to
believe that his mother had been the sister of al Kamil, a lady

whom the Emperor had met on his first Crusade, but who had refused his advances until Frederick arranged for a black-sailed ship to sail into the Syrian harbour bearing news of the Empress's death. . . . This was pure fiction. Nothing was known of Frederick of Antioch's mother.

The following events stand in intimate relation to the removal of Pandulf. The preceding year he and Orlando di Rossi, who was then *podesta* of Florence, had worked together in Tuscany. It was the custom that the higher officials when temporarily unemployed should take up their quarters at Frederick's court and place themselves at the Emperor's disposal. Pandulf, therefore, betook himself to court after his recall. Some weeks passed. In March 1246 a boat arrived in Grosseto, sent in haste by Count Richard of Caserta, the Emperor's son-in-law. It brought word of a widespread conspiracy against the life of Frederick and King Enzio. It arrived at the eleventh hour. The crime was scheduled for the morrow. Natural phenomena were already foretelling some monstrous catastrophe, which the astrologer Guido Bonatti claimed also to have foreseen. Sun and moon disappeared, the stars turned pale, the heavens rained blood, the earth was enveloped in thick darkness amidst lightning and thunder, the sea ran mountains high. Terror seized those of the conspirators who were at court. Before the Emperor could institute investigations they fled to Rome, having been warned in time. Amongst them were two of the most distinguished leaders, Pandulf of Fasanella and Jacob of Morra. The latter was one of Frederick's most trusted intimates, Vicar General of the March, a son of the recently deceased Chief Justice, Henry of Morra.

The flight of the two conspirators confirmed Count Caserta's warning. The Emperor learnt at the same time that the conspiracy had spread through much wider circles. The prime mover in the plot was Orlando di Rossi. He had not only enlisted Pandulf of Fasanella beforehand in Florence, but had induced the imperial *podesta* of Parma, Tebaldo Francisco, to join them. Francisco, who had been for years Vicar General of the March of Treviso, one of the most eminent of Frederick's officials and one of his most intimate friends, was generally

considered to be the head of the conspirators. When Tebaldo
got news that the Grosseto scheme had failed he fled to Sicily,
being in secret correspondence with Andrew of Cicala, Captain
of Sicily. Apparently Roger de Amicis, Captain of the Island,
was also in league with the conspirators. Like Jacob of Morra
he was famous as one of the first poets in the Sicilian vernacular.
The conspirators were thus one and all men who had for years
discharged the highest offices in the State, and ruled the most
important provinces, men who on the human side stood nearest
to the Emperor and enjoyed his fullest confidence. A few were
subordinate officials, relations for the most part of the bigger
men : Richard and Robert of Fasanella, William Franciscus,
Godfrey of Morra. In Sicily itself some non-officials had
joined the plot from personal motives : the Counts of San
Severino ; they had unquestionably always been badly treated
by the Emperor.

The discovery that his nearest friends had been seeking his
life had, naturally, a profound effect on Frederick. It made
him shudder, he wrote, to think that these men were actually
plotting the deed of shame at the very moment that they were
dining at the same table with him and conversing amiably with
him in his rooms at court. With a father's pride he had watched
them grow up, he had exalted them from the lowliest stations
to the highest posts of honour at Caesar's court, he had treated
them with so much affection that he kept no secrets from them,
he trusted them as fully as he trusted the sons of his body, he
had even chosen them to be his bodyguard, and many a time
had laid his head in their lap. " Parricides " he called the
recreants, stepsons, not sons. . . . They were men recognising
no human tie, miscreants who criminally plotted the death of
their benefactor. With them a new human type had come to
birth : a human form with animal instincts only.

Faced with danger the Emperor showed himself possessed
of all his old vigour and power : as he had need to be. The
plan had wide ramifications. Frederick and Enzio and Eccelino were to have been murdered at a banquet ; Parma was to
have gone over to the enemy. Already the Emperor's old foe,

Rainer of Viterbo, called in by one of the traitors, had invaded
the imperial territories at the head of a papal army. He was
completely defeated with heavy losses at Spello by Marinus of
Eboli, Vicar General of Spoleto, who had remained faithful.
The worst was, however, that the traitors had stirred up an
insurrection and produced general confusion throughout Sicily
by the news which they spread broadcast that the Emperor
was dead. They had got possession of the fortresses of Sala
and Capaccio and the town of Altavilla. Thus the centre of
the revolt was in the heart of Frederick's hereditary kingdom
in southern Campania between Paestum and Salerno.

Frederick immediately hastened southward from Tuscany :
" the apple of his eye must not suffer harm ! " The loyal
Sicilians, even before their master's arrival, had independently
cut off the two fortresses, so that Sala surrendered to the
Emperor after a few days. Altavilla was taken by storm and
razed to the ground, and anyone related even remotely to the
conspirators was blinded and burnt alive. The Emperor's
arrival in person immediately quelled what remained of the
revolt. Only the citadel of Capaccio, which the ringleaders
were defending, still held out, although the town was in the
Emperor's hands. The heat of July was extreme, water supplies gave out, and the besiegers' catapults began to do greater
and greater execution. The citadel could not be saved ; the
garrison surrendered. To his amazement Frederick found
amongst the hundred and fifty prisoners the leaders of the conspiracy themselves, especially Tebaldo Francisco. Frederick
seems to have expected that they would have fallen on their
own swords or leapt from the crags, preferring self-chosen
death to the vengeance of their outraged master. Since they
did not, he felt them at his mercy.

Their punishment fitted their crime. They were blinded
with red-hot irons that they might not see their lord, and
mutilated in noses, hands and legs, and thus the sometime
friends were brought before their ruthless judge. According
to the Lex Pompeia Frederick had them condemned for murder
and treated them as parricides. They had committed a crime
" against nature " and therefore were put to death by all four
elements. Some were dragged to death by horses over stony

ground, others burnt alive, others were hanged, the rest sewn up in leather sacks and thrown out into the sea, following the Roman treatment of parracides. Frederick added a symbolical refinement by having poisonous snakes sewn up in the sacks with them.

Frederick made an exception of Tebaldo Francisco, the arch-villain of the piece. He and five others were to be blinded and mutilated and dragged through all the countries of the earth from town to town to all kings and princes so that the earth might see the monster. " Let the punishment of this accursed criminal instruct your minds and spirits by the sight of the eye which makes more impression than what is heard by the ear. Let no forgetfulness obliterate what ye have seen, let the memory of a just judgment be remembered." A papal bull was tied to the traitor's forehead so that all the world might know the instigator of the murderous plot : Innocent IV.

Frederick had long had no doubts left in his mind that the High Priest was the ultimate assassin. The threads of the conspiracy were spun in Lyons. " We would fain," he wrote, " have kept silence about the name and title of our foe, but transparent facts make the accusation, and public opinion lays it bare and declares the name our silence is shielding, and the cloak of our words excusing." The Emperor was able to announce that the first prisoners, not under torture but volun-tarily in making their last confession, had admitted that they had taken the cross against Frederick from the hands of men-dicant monks, and that they had been authorised to act as they did by letters from the Pope.

The Emperor further made known that his enemy the Bishop of Bamberg, coming from the Pope at Lyons, had openly declared in Germany that Frederick II was about to die a shameful death at the hands of his friends and intimates. Other indications : Orlando di Rossi's leading part ; the par-ticipation of the *podesta* of Parma, the instantaneous invasion of Cardinal Rainer, and many another thing pointed clearly to the papal Curia's being implicated. The extant documents of the cardinals leave no doubt alive to-day that Innocent IV, who had been inviting everyone " to wash his hands in the blood of this sinner," had at the very least minute knowledge of the plan. No one else could so promptly profit by the Emperor's death.

It is unprecedented in medieval history that a pope should actually set out to have an Emperor murdered. Within the framework of Innocent's total policy this attempt on Frederick's life is only one ingredient in a great scheme. The spring of 1246 was to mark the opening of a general papal offensive destined to smash the Hohenstaufen influence simultaneously in every country of the Empire: in Sicily, in Germany, in Italy. With the battle-cry "to free the oppressed" papal legates with troops furnished by the citizens of Rome were to invade the kingdom of Sicily immediately on Frederick's death —an easy matter since the Vicars General and the highest officials were among the conspirators. Parma was the centre for Italy, where Tebaldo Francisco was the faithless imperial *podesta*. He had been promised the rule of Sicily, ostensibly in the Pope's name. The inclusion of Enzio and Eccelino in the plan shows that the fall of the Hohenstaufen rule was the real goal. The murder of the Emperor himself was the task allotted to the nobles remaining at court. In Germany the establishment of a rival king was expected to produce the fall of Conrad. No one seems to have reckoned with a possible miscarriage of the plot.

The Pope's whole elaborate plan was wrecked by the timely discovery of the conspiracy, at least as far as Sicily and Italy was concerned. In Germany the Pope had a momentary success. Gregory IX's efforts to set up a rival king had all fallen to the ground. Innocent IV had now set the election to work. He had closed the decree of deposition with the request that the electors should forthwith proceed to choose another prince to fill the place of the deposed Emperor. Pope Innocent even found an aspirant: the Thuringian Landgrave Henry Raspe, whom the Emperor had appointed a few years before to succeed the Archbishop Sigfrid of Mainz as Regent of the Empire. Raspe at first protested, but Innocent appears to have overcome his reluctance by the news of the impending murder of Frederick. The Landgrave ultimately consented to his elevation, and in May 1246, while the Emperor was still fighting in Campania against the conspirators, Henry Raspe was elected in Veitschöchheim, near Würzburg, King of the Romans, or Rex Clericorum as the people mockingly said, for no single secular elector was present, and only a small number of spiritual princes.

The Landgrave was never either anointed or crowned. For his acceptance of the crown the rival king had received from the Pope the not inconsiderable sum of 25,000 silver marks. The number of his supporters was negligible, but with further subsidies from the Curia he contrived to achieve a surprising though short-lived success. A few months after his elevation the " Battle of the Kings " took place near Frankfurt. The Thuringian king, Henry Raspe, and the Hohenstaufen king, Conrad IV, strove for victory. King Conrad's army was superior in numbers. But immediately before the onslaught two-thirds of the Hohenstaufen forces, led by a Swabian noble, went over to the enemy. The Pope had bought them for 6000 marks and promised them the Dukedom of Swabia, as he also promised Sicily to the unhappy Tebaldo Francisco. The Landgrave won the battle of Frankfurt, and forthwith a victory proclamation on the imperial model went forth to " our faithful Milan," prophesying a speedy victory over King Conrad's father. It concluded with a familiar turn of phrase " we shall triumph as the Emperors of Rome are wont to do." Even the puppet king had " learnt."

The victory decided nothing. The Landgrave's recognition was strictly limited, and a few months later, in February 1247, Henry Raspe died, to the great inconvenience of the Church. It is unlikely that he would have accomplished anything of real value. King Conrad at this point married Elizabeth of Bavaria, to put an end once and for all to the Bavarian-Hohenstaufen friction, and in this same year the Duke of Austria died and the Emperor resumed his territories. The route to Italy was thus barred by an unbroken Hohenstaufen barrier from Alsace to Austria. Yet there was no peace for King Conrad. The German situation grew yearly more difficult, and in the endless fighting almost the only allies on whom the young king could count were the towns who were the natural enemies of secular

and spiritual nobles.   That internal battle which the Italian
communes had already fought out still lay before the towns of
Germany which were still seeking support from the Empire,
were even eager to become "imperial towns" and hoped by
this means to achieve their independence.   King Conrad sorely
needed help.   In October 1247 a new rival king had been set
up, again a protégé of the great archbishop Sigfrid of Mainz.
Sigfrid's mighty tombstone represents two miserable little
dwarfs of kings, one on each side, while in the centre the
haughty prince of the Church almost unheedingly places with
his finger tips a tiny crownlet on the head of each.   This
corresponds exactly to reality.   The new King of the Romans
was Count William of Holland—the first mere count, who was
not even one of the princes of the Empire, to bear rule in
Germany.   William lacked neither courage nor chivalrous
qualities, but his power never extended beyond the Rhine
country, the sphere of the great archbishops.   Still, he contrived from there to keep King Conrad amply occupied.   The
world in general, however, had no use for a nineteen-year-old
Count William of Holland as substitute for the mighty figure
of Frederick II !

   The danger of the conspiracy being overcome, Frederick's
position south of the Alps was almost stronger than before,
and his reputation of invulnerability against human assassins
was finally established.   The confusion of a few weeks died
down in Sicily, and the skill with which Frederick had countered
the papal machinations had not failed to impress Italy, where
the episode was considered a triumph for the Emperor.   Even the
Musulmans showed the warmest interest in the latest events
in Tuscany and Campania.   In Northern Italy the Emperor's
power was growing.   The Venetians had long since begun to
lean towards him.   They had little to hope from a Genoese
pope.   Several important nobles in Western Lombardy and in
Piedmont allied themselves to Frederick, and he now controlled
a large unbroken block of territory stretching almost as far as
Lyons.   The importance of these regions to Frederick was very
great, and so he hastened to attach the nobles more firmly to

his person and his cause by establishing family relations with them. He married one of his natural daughters to the Genoese Margrave of Caretto, and Manfred, the son of his well-beloved Bianca Lancia, he married to the daughter of Count Amadeus of Savoy, thus establishing relationship with Thomas of Savoy, to whom he afterwards entrusted a Vicariate General.

Circumstances were also favourable in central Italy. Tuscany was firmly held, and Frederick of Antioch ruled like a Signore in Florence after displacing the captains of the popular party. Finally, Viterbo voluntarily submitted. The people of Viterbo had always liked Frederick's rule ; they now timidly sought Frederick of Antioch's mediation. In response to his son's request the Emperor again accorded his favour to this once-hated town, opining that its treachery had been the work of Cardinal Rainer. To forestall any recurrence of earlier events he sent his nine-year-old son, whom Isabella of England had borne him, to reside in Viterbo, as " King " they said.

This precaution is noteworthy because it formed part of a general reorganisation of the whole Italian administration, which was the immediate consequence of the great conspiracy to which it finally put an end. The principle became established that the Vicars General should be, as far as possible, relations of the Emperor. The constitution henceforth depended on primary personal relationships, and it was abnormal for any post of eminence to be held by anyone outside the imperial house. Hubert Pallavicini was one of the rare exceptions. During the years following, Italy became simply a family possession of the Hohenstaufens. Imperial Italy was thereafter partitioned more or less as follows : the north-east is held by Eccelino, central Lombardy by King Enzio, followed later by Pallavicini, who at first administered the coastal province of Liguria ; west Lombardy by Thomas of Savoy, whose unmanageably large domain was later divided between the Margraves Lancia and Caretto ; Tuscany by Frederick of Antioch ; Spoleto, the Romagna and the March (a region which later shrank considerably in size) by Richard of Theate, a natural son of the Emperor, and Viterbo by the nine-year-old Henry.

A thoroughly experienced administrator was essential for

Sicily, and Walter of Manupello was appointed. No official was now so tried that Frederick would trust him with complete independence, so the new Vicar was given as " Counsellors " the two juvenile sons-in-law, Thomas of Aquino, the younger, and Count Richard of Caserta, to whom Frederick wrote on one occasion that " as a blood relation of the Emperor you must be wholly faithful." Thomas of Aquino was later employed as Vicar of the Romagna and Spoleto. Now that the Vicars General were for the most part members of the imperial house their independence was robbed of its danger. This system held good till the Emperor's death.

Other alterations were effected at the same time : Richard of Montenero was appointed Lord Chief Justice and Piero della Vigna Logothetes of the Kingdom of Sicily. The Emperor seems to have been working out another unified scheme ; to equip each of his sons with his own court and ceremonial, assign to each an endowment and to make each a real " King " over a certain Vicariate General. A fragment is extant of the Emperor's will dating from 1247, drawn up apparently under the impression of the conspiracy or in anticipation of a campaign towards the north. Its contents are confirmed by certain entries of the chroniclers in the same year : Frederick of Antioch with the County of Alba was to be King of Tuscany ; King Enzio of Lunigiana ; King Henry of Sicily and the Province of Viterbo ; the Emperor's grandson Frederick, son of the unfortunate German King, Henry VII, was to be king of Austria and Syria. Finally, in the same year, Manfred was to be invested with the Vicariate General of Burgundy and West Lombardy. This scheme was never actually put into execution, but it shows how Frederick was endeavouring to strengthen his Italian Empire which he felt rocking under his feet. It also shows how by this distribution of his inheritance he was gradually loosening himself from earthly ties which were exercising less and less force on the Antichrist and Scourge of God. He announced at this period to his friends that he had handed over the fatigues of Italy to his sons. He was, however, planning another stroke.

In the spring of 1247, after a stay of several months in Sicily, the position south of the Alps seemed so favourable that Frederick felt he might safely leave Italy and march to Germany once more, where the pretender Henry Raspe was creating unrest. He had long since promised King Conrad, who was a lad of only twenty and who had been carrying on the fight on hopeless outpost duty, remote from his father and his brothers, that he would ere long be with him, and the preparations for his German campaign occupied the winter of 1246-7. This time he did not intend to rely solely on exotic pomp and imperial riches which had been so effective when he crossed the Alps alone with the boy Conrad twelve years before. A great army was to accompany him as well as his Court, and it was remarked that the Emperor summoned the knights of the Italian towns to join the campaign. The suggestion was supposed to be Piero della Vigna's. This was an unheard of thing! Many a time had the Emperors led German warriors to Italy, but since the days of the Caesars no Italians had been enlisted for trans-Alpine service in Germany. It appears that the Italian knights acquiesced without a murmur.

In March 1247 the Emperor quitted his hereditary kingdom. He travelled by the usual route northwards through Tuscany, met Frederick of Antioch in Siena, marched by way of San Miniato to Pisa, without approaching Florence. Frederick always avoided this town, they say, because the astrologers had foretold that he was destined to die " sub flore," and the oracle had been interpreted as relating to Florence. From Tuscany he continued his march to Lombardy. Only one of the Apennine passes was open to him : the Cisa Pass, which was covered in the south by Pontremoli and in the north by Parma. The other route, down the Reno valley by way of Pistoia, was commanded by the hostile town of Bologna. Frederick reached Parma in April, intending to push straight on to Cremona. His original plan was to hold a one-day Diet in Cremona and to proceed straight by Verona and the Brenner into Germany. Before quitting Tuscany, however, the Emperor had heard of the death of Henry Raspe, and this news, which the court received with rejoicing, probably modified his plans. He now decided to march through the Arelate instead of by the Brenner

and from Burgundy to make his appearance on the Upper
Rhine, taking this opportunity not only of visiting his kingdom
of Burgundy but also of paying a call on Pope Innocent IV in
Lyons.   Counting on the mediation of King Louis of France
he hoped either to induce the Pope to conclude a friendly peace
or by a siege to wring peace from him, as he had once tried to
wring it from Gregory in Rome.

It was a daring undertaking which held great prospect of
success.   The plan of appearing on the Upper Rhine shows
foresight.   He could count on many supporters there and
could immediately march on to the lower Rhine which was
the focus of the German revolt.   His personal appearance in
Burgundy would have greatly strengthened its attachment to
his service ;   he had already made more impression on this
western frontier kingdom than any preceding German Emperor
had done, and he was now apparently intending to establish
Manfred there as a Burgundian king.   The undertaking against
Lyons was not less promising.   The recent alliances with the
Count of Savoy and his neighbouring magnates had extended
his power up to the very gates of Lyons, so that Innocent IV
would indeed be in serious straits if Frederick II really appeared
in Burgundy.   The King of France and his brothers would,
of course, have shielded him from actual armed attack, but
Lyons belonged not to France but to the Empire, and King
Louis had not given permission for the Pope to cross into
French territory.

In this spring of 1247 Pope Innocent IV was in considerable
distress.   He was a partial prisoner.   The fate of his pre-
decessor besieged in Rome, the very fate he had sought to flee
from, seemed about to overtake him.   Preparations for the
Emperor's reception were proceeding apace.   The Count of
Savoy and the Dauphin had already prepared the pass south of
the Mont Cenis ;   the Gallic nobles were invited to a Diet in
Chambery for the second week after Whitsun, and the trans-
Alpine populace was eagerly awaiting the arrival of the
" Caesarea Fortuna."   After a brief meeting with Eccelino in
Cremona, Frederick had turned his face westwards in the
middle of May, had marched through Pavia with great pomp
and reached Turin in early June.   While the imperial house-

hold and the whole attendant train marched on into the mountains Frederick remained behind for a few days in Turin at
the foot of the Alps to meet the Count of Savoy. Just as he
was about to set out to overtake his vanguard a cry for help
reached him from Enzio. Parma had been surprised and taken
by the Guelfs.

Orlando di Rossi had again taken a hand in the game. Some
seventy Guelf knights of Parma, who had fled to Piacenza with
Orlando two years before, had seized their opportunity to
appear suddenly one Sunday before the gates of their native
town. They knew the Emperor was in Turin ; Enzio was
besieging a fortress in the Brescia region ; the Ghibelline
knights of Parma has just assembled for a big wedding and were
" full of wine and of good cheer." Nevertheless they leapt to
horse on hearing of the Guelfs' approach. Led by the imperial
podesta, Arrigo Testa of Arezzo, the knightly poet and the
Emperor's friend, they flung themselves on the foe before he
reached the town. The imperialists were worsted in the first
bloody encounter. Arrigo Testa fell " fighting like a king,"
and with him many another, so that the Guelfs unhindered
entered the open city. Frederick had always feared the internal treachery of Parma, and with a refinement of shrewdness
he had had the fortifications destroyed. The German garrison,
though fairly strong, was therefore unable to make a stand, and
the victors met with no other resistance, for the townsfolk
remained indifferent. No sooner had the surprise been successful than Parma by arrangement received help from all sides.
The other Guelf towns sent help ; the Guelf partisans who had
been banished from the imperial towns hastened to Parma ;
Milan sent a strong body of auxiliaries under the leadership of
the papal legate Gregory of Montelongo. With them came
Orlando di Rossi. All the Emperor's enemies who had long
been chafing in inactivity had now one rallying point ; in the
shortest possible space of time the struggle for Parma had
become the affair of all the Guelfdom of Italy.

Frederick recognised the danger involved. The journey to
Lyons and the German campaign were abandoned and the

return march hastily begun. The Emperor's prestige demanded the most severe punishment of the treacherous town, which was of the highest strategic importance because it commanded the only route of communication with the south. The command of Italy outweighed every other consideration. "Only one anxiety occupies our mind: to restore Italy's severely-shattered government." Within two weeks of the catastrophe the Emperor reached Cremona, where he was met by Eccelino with six hundred knights. Two days later he camped before Parma, where King Enzio was awaiting him. He had abandoned his luckless expedition against Brescia, hastened to Cremona, and marched on Parma with all men capable of bearing arms. Enzio had not ventured to attack with such meagre forces, though according to the chroniclers' account the town might even then have been re-won for the Emperor. He had fortified his camp in front of Parma and was awaiting his father's arrival. It is not now possible to divine why Frederick did not immediately storm the town, which had scarcely had time to throw up serious defences. He seems to have overestimated the strength of his opponents, and waited to bring up reinforcements from every side. Hugo Boterius of Parma was one of the first to arrive ; he brought the levies of Pavia. He was a nephew of the Pope and of Orlando di Rossi, but in spite of his two uncles he remained faithful to the Emperor to the last. Frederick of Antioch was soon on the spot with the troops of Tuscany. The Emperor had himself had a large army going to Turin, mainly composed of Sicilians, Saracens, Italian and German mercenary knights. Eccelino had brought Burgundian knights. Altogether Frederick must now have had a very considerable force at his disposal. Having missed the initial opportunity of storming the town without waiting to besiege it he could not keep this large army together before Parma.

The defection of Parma was the signal for an almost universal revolt of the Guelfs of Italy. In every province the Emperor's authority was suddenly endangered. There was not a single Vicariate General where the Guelfs did not rise against the

Emperor, usually supported by papal troops, and even Sicily seemed threatened by the Genoese. Within a few weeks the whole of Italy was ablaze, and innumerable minor theatres of war sapped the strength of the main army. Every great power in its death-throes is exposed to the same danger. Never before had Frederick's case been so desperate. It was no small achievement that he did succeed in repressing the insurrection in spite of the infinite dispersion of his forces.

A hard and fast siege of Parma was from the first impossible. The Emperor must be in a position to release troops as required for minor campaigns. He, therefore, set about cutting off all lines of communication with the town in a wide arc, while his strong cavalry detachments swept the country round Parma. The Emperor himself closed the road to the Guelf town of Piacenza by camping west of Parma on the Taro. The imperial towns of Reggio and Modena blocked the eastern road to Bologna. The road to the north, and with it the communication with the Po, had to remain open for the moment, for nothing competed in importance with the southern route over the Cisa Pass. This pass over the Apennines was as good as lost. The northern exit had been at once secured by Margrave Lancia, but confusion reigned on the further side. Garfagnana and Lunigiana had fallen at the same time as Parma, the Imperial Vicar had been taken prisoner and the Malaspina Margraves had revolted, hoping thus to recover their territories which the Emperor had confiscated. Communication with Tuscany was, therefore, actually cut. King Enzio had just returned with Eccelino and Hubert Pallavicini from a raid—he had been sent to strengthen Modena and Reggio against Bologna. He was now entrusted with the task of opening up the Cisa Pass. With the assistance of Pallavicini, and supported by the loyal Pontremoli, he succeeded in taking the fortress of Berceto and pushing on far beyond Pontremoli. One of the Malaspina Margraves submitted. This most important route was thus at the Emperor's disposal once more.

Frederick was now free to complete the encirclement of Parma on the north. As long as the besieged town had free access to the Po the garrison was able to secure provisions sent from Mantua and Ferrara by boat. Enzio and Eccelino, who now usually worked in concert, were ordered to make a bridge-head on the Po west of Guastalla, both to put an end to river traffic and to close the roads leading from the river to Parma. They took Brescello, a fort upstream from Guastalla, and threw a bridge across the river which they strongly fortified. This drew the Mantuans and Ferrarese into the quarrel. They tried to relieve Parma, and Enzio and Eccelino had to keep this new enemy at bay. This they did without difficulty, but presently a strong army from every possible Guelf town, accompanied by a great fleet, was known to be approaching. Eccelino's brother, Alberigo of Romano, was in the Guelf camp. But they did not venture to attack the imperial forces, and for two months the hostile army lay at Guastalla. Enzio and Eccelino felt no need to attack. They were holding a whole army in check and ful-filling their task of closing Parma's last line of communication.

We have no clue to the inactivity of the papal-Guelf army. The rumour inevitably spread through the besieged town that the papal general, young and charming Cardinal Ottaviano degli Ubaldini, was secretly in league with the Emperor. This was certainly untrue, for this particular scion of the powerful Tuscan family which played so important a rôle in Florentine history, never was in league with anyone. He made this a matter of principle. This highly-gifted, "most unpriestly priest," had been made acting-bishop of Bologna at twenty-six, was fully consecrated when he reached the prescribed age of thirty, and at once created a Cardinal Deacon by Pope Innocent. He was neither Guelf nor Ghibelline but just him-self: THE CARDINAL! Every child in Tuscany knew him under this title, and Dante introduces him into the Divine Comedy under this name. The poet saw him side by side with Frede-rick II in the fiery tombs of the Epicureans "who with the body make the spirit die." Dante made them neighbours no doubt also because the Cardinal, like Eccelino and many another, was under the intellectual spell of the great Hohenstaufen whom he took as his model in many ways.

Once when he lost a sum of money through the Ghibellines the blasphemous Ottaviano remarked with a sigh, "If there happens to be a soul I have lost mine to the Ghibellines." Ubaldini did not make ruthless power an end in itself—he was a complete failure as a general—but he pushed to its ultimate limit another method of the Emperor's : the game of political diplomacy. He did not pursue imperial politics, nor church politics, nor Ubaldini family politics, nor cardinals' politics, but just "politics"; sometimes pro- and sometimes anti-Guelf; sometimes with, sometimes against, Florence; there was no Ghibelline party, no political group with which he did not maintain continuous relations, no intrigue in which his ringed hand did not play its part always holding the last card in reserve. Far above Empire or Papacy he rated his own attractive, capricious personality which everyone in Italy cordially distrusted. This lighthearted artist, epicure and prince of the Church sought every stimulus that the times offered. He was one of the first Tuscan vernacular poets, closely related to Hohenstaufen circles, not only in matters of belief. When the handsome Cardinal Ottaviano apostrophised " my master, Cupid," in a very perfect sonnet he sang of what he knew. His mistresses and his posterity were well known. The luxury indulged in by the amorous poet, who was also an enthusiastic huntsman, in his magnificent country seat in the Mugello, rivalled the Emperor's. He had had his silver table-service wrought in Paris ; he sent for ornaments and costly stuffs from Spain and Tripoli and Greece ; his buckles and brooches were set with cameos and pearls and precious stones ; his apartments were lighted by candles in candelabra of mountain crystal ; as well as the rarest and most select works of art, such as the first goblet worked in *niello*, his treasure included a magnificent crown set with sapphires, rubies and carbuncles. The pomp of Ubaldini exercised nearly as great a fascination over the young aristocrats as the Emperor's court had been wont to do, and the Cardinal was well skilled in finding high positions for his young chaplains. These protégés of his were infected as a matter of course with his amazing religious indifference, still remarkable amongst the spiritual princes of the day, and with the Epicurean doctrines of Averroes which Ottaviano expiated in his tomb of flame. He raised his chamberlain, Otto Visconti, to the see of St. Ambrose, making him archbishop of Milan when this town turned Ghibelline. Otto Visconti, to whom the Galeazzo and Bernabo owed their power, was such a perfect heretic that his chiselled tomb of red marble turned black of itself, and when his nephew Matthew Visconti had it painted red again turned black once more, so the story ran. Cardinal Ottaviano was, in short, the first of a type of cardinal which perished with Ippolito Medici.

While the Cardinal remained quietly in his camp at Guastalla his reluctance to attack produced ere long unpleasant consequences in Parma. The blockade which Enzio and Eccelino had succeeded in establishing began to make itself gradually felt. Parma was cut off from all external assistance, and nothing was to be got from the immediate neighbourhood, for cavalry and raiding parties of the Emperor's scoured the country without ceasing, and devastated and laid waste everything which they did not themselves require. Famine became so acute that they were baking bread of linseed, and were suffering severely from lack of salt. The townsfolk began to lose heart when the Cardinal's promised reliefs on which they had been counting were still delayed. The courageous and resourceful defender of Parma, the papal legate Gregory of Montelongo, who knew the Lombards better than most men, was driven to every conceivable stratagem to persuade the inhabitants to hold out. The most distinguished knights of Parma were assembled when a mendicant monk suddenly appeared in their midst, travel-stained and in the last stages of exhaustion, and took from his knapsack a letter with the joyful news that help was at hand. The letter had been written overnight by Montelongo. In spite of all promises the general opinion was that Cardinal Ottaviano was betraying the papal cause, and Fra Salimbene, who at this point escaped from Parma, even carried the rumour to Lyons, where the upshot of the siege was awaited with intense anxiety: "for as in a duel the whole fate of Rome and of the clergy hung thereon." The story ran that the red-legged cardinals who swarmed in Lyons had pressed round Fra Salimbene in such numbers that one climbed the shoulders of another in their eagerness to hear the latest news of Parma.

In spite of the greatest exertions on both sides a speedy decision was not forthcoming. During the winter of 1247-48

the Emperor was fighting everywhere in Italy. December
brought especially heavy battles in the provinces. Margrave
Boniface of Montferrat, who had recently submitted to the
Emperor, had turned his coat once more, and with the support
of Vercelli and Milan had seized Turin, where only the garrison
of the Emperor's palace still held out. The Emperor despatched thither his grandson Frederick, a youth of twenty or
so, who succeeded in driving the Margrave out and rescuing
Turin for the Emperor. At about the same time Count
Richard of Theate defeated a papal army under Hugo Novellus
at Interamna, and Robert of Castiglione, imperial Vicar of the
March, inflicted an overwhelming defeat on the papal legate,
bishop Marcellina at Osimo, south of Ancona, chiefly by the
assistance of German mercenary knights. The bishop was
taken prisoner, four thousand papalists were reported slain,
numerous standards and banners were captured, amongst them
one which Manuel Comnenus had presented to the people of
Ancona when they betrayed Barbarossa. Hubert Pallavicini
with Jacob of Caretto, the Emperor's son-in-law, was preparing
an attack on Genoa in which the fleet took part.

Conditions in Florence, and indeed in Tuscany in general,
were nevertheless very critical for the Emperor. Even without
going himself to Florence Cardinal Ottaviano had an easy task
to urge the Guelfs, especially the nobility, into open rebellion.
They had been everywhere excluded from office and jealously
watched. The common people, artisans and merchants, were
by no means exclusively anti-Kaiser. Thanks to skilful Ghibelline policy the famous imperialist party, well known as the
primo popolo, had been formed, which included both the pro-
Kaiser nobility and the people's party. Their case was not
unique. The popular movement in Siena had years before
been given an imperialist bias and a Ghibelline had put himself
at the head of the people. In Florence both parties now proceeded to woo the crowd, and although Orlando di Rossi may
have worked against the Emperor while still keeping the mask
of loyalty during his term of office as *podesta*, there were probably not many of the popular party on the occasion of this rising
fighting under the lily-banner of the Guelfs against the Hohenstaufen eagles.

Frederick of Antioch had hitherto treated the Florentine Guelfs with tolerance and had permitted their remaining in the town. This lightened their task of capturing the reins of government in the town with the help of the Bolognese and causing Florence to desert the Emperor. The most terrible street fighting took place, in which the rage of the Guelfs was chiefly directed against the imperialist family of the Uberti. They, however, were able in their powerful towers to defy all attack and even to take the offensive. The head of the Uberti was the great leader Farinata, who, in Dante's hell, is a neighbour of Frederick II and of the Cardinal. After the victory of Montaperti his Ghibelline friends wanted to wipe Florence off the face of the earth, but Farinata intervened and won thereby the eternal fame of having saved Florence. His gigantic shade recognising a fellow Florentine in Dante's speech revealed the future to the poet:

> His breast and forehead there
> Erecting, seemed as in high scorn he held
> E'en Hell.

Farinata had been preparing the ground for an attack on the Guelfs when Frederick of Antioch, having assembled his forces in Prato, arrived and penetrated into Florence. He soon had the town in his power, and while the Guelfs fled to various minor rallying points in Tuscany the crash might be heard of the Guelf towers which Frederick of Antioch was pulling down. The lofty tower of the Adimari, some 230 feet high, crashed down on the Piazza, missing the Baptistery by the thickness of a hair.

The tale of Florence was repeated everywhere, and even when the imperial officials contrived to drive the rebels from the towns, the " fugitives," as they were called now, formed a definite class in the population (one to which Dante was later to belong) which was nearly as dangerous without the walls as within. For they leagued themselves with the fugitives from other towns and constituted a standing menace to every imperialist city, as, conversely, fugitive Ghibellines from the Guelf towns fought in the Emperor's army and threatened their native places. The defection of Parma was the signal in Italy for a

fight of all against all, which was to rage for decades with un-
diminished fury. The chronicler complains that none could
plough nor sow nor reap nor gather in the vintage, nor live in
the country villas, for all was too unsafe. Only quite close to
a town under the protection of armed men a little agriculture
could be carried on. On the high road one traveller shrank
from another as from the devil incarnate, for each suspected
the other of wanting to hold him to ransom. Merchants could
only move about in large caravans, and even then the Florentines who were reckoned to be imperialists were by no means
safe from, for instance, the papalist folk of Piacenza, who on
occasion looted an entire Tuscan caravan. The Middle Ages
looked on this general unrest only as a sign that the reign of
Antichrist, of the *rex tyrannus*, had come, and that, as the
chronicler adds, " all hath fulfilled itself in its time from the
moment that Parma fell away from the side of the Emperor to
the side of the Church."

Day by day Frederick was indeed growing more and more of
a *rex tyrannus*. While he was encamped before Parma he saw
his whole Italian state aflame in raging revolt and the Church
lashing men on to treachery. How could he master these
intangible spirits ! Thanks to the valour of his sons and his
vicars he was at first victorious in the provinces, but it
became more and more difficult to get to grips with the foe.
Men of Florence, Parma, Ferrara, Mantua, and other places
were fighting : some in the imperial army and some for the
Guelfs ; and Frederick was now pitted not against the hostile
feeling of whole communes, but against individual and isolated
persons, whose adherence to this party or that was dictated by
the petty accidents and advantages of the moment. The impulses that actuated them were confused, incalculable, making
a mockery of any comprehensive policy. Thousands of single
foes and single traitors constituted no commensurable enemy
for an Emperor. All the while, as the great conspiracy had
proved, Frederick's life was not safe. Surrounded by his bodyguard of Saracens he came more and more, though against his
will, to resemble the " Tyrant " who, with treachery spreading

round him like a plague, the defection of yesterday's friends
for ever imminent, grew hourly more suspicious, more severe,
even malicious, in his punishments, and often by fear terrified
men into disloyalty and rebellion.

Frederick now began to have recourse to all the cruel re-
finements of oppression which are forced on a government
threatened by betrayal. The principle of taking hostages had
long been in force, but the system was now carefully extended.
It was not possible to transport all hostages at once to Apulia, so
those of one town were handed over for safe custody to another.

The hostages of Como, for instance, were lodged with Siena,
those of Spoleto with Poggibonsi and San Gimignano, so that
each town went bail for the other and the towns were linked
together by a network of hostages. Further, so far as Guelfs
did not of their own accord fly from the Ghibelline towns,
suspects were banished in masses and every imperialist town
was forbidden to accord them refuge. The evils of denunciation followed, for anyone could thus get rid of a rival or
opponent. The imperial officials, breathing the air of treachery,
dare not neglect any accusation. They had to take up any suspicious case brought to their notice, and in order, if necessary,
to extort confession, torture came into play. The Sicilian
Book of Laws forbade the use of torture save in a few
restricted cases, but all safeguards were now thrown to the
winds in Italy, and nothing short of a miracle (the repeated
breaking of a rope for instance) could set a victim again at
liberty. The application of torture had a further consequence.
It was natural to employ " the cyclops of Avernus, the slaves
of Vulcan," that is to say, the Emperor's Saracens, as executioners, and the vicar's courts were usually provided with a
Saracen hangman, whom saint or priest could not intimidate.

The case of bishop Marcellina of Arezzo, who was taken
prisoner in the battle of Osimo, will show how these " myrmidons of Satan " discharged their office. The Emperor had
issued general orders that no more prisoners should be spared
and held to ransom, they should be without exception hanged.
The fact that Marcellina of Arezzo was a priest and a legate

of the Pope's was certainly not an extenuating circumstance in the Emperor's eyes. On the contrary, he had often inveighed against weapon-bearing priests, and Marcellina was, moreover, a vassal who had broken his oath of fealty. Yet his case was looked into and he was imprisoned for several months before being handed over to the hangman. His execution aroused great indignation. Cardinal Rainer of Viterbo gave vent to his hate shortly before his own death in a horror-inspiring pamphlet recording in letters of fire the martyrdom of Marcellina and the abominations of Frederick II. The Saracen devils had first bound the saint's hands and feet and tied the bishop to a horse's tail to drag him through the mire to the place of execution. But the bishop sang the Te Deum and the pious horse stood still, and even blows would not induce him to move till the Saracens had silenced further singing. After various torments the bishop was hanged. Three days later some mendicant monks buried him. The Saracens exhumed the corpse, defiled it, and hung it on the gallows again. This continued till the Emperor put an end to it.

The episode gave a handle to hostile agitation. In Würzburg a crusading sermon against Frederick was preached. In England the opinion was that this deed of shame would have been more scandalous if the papalists had not sullied their cause with deeds more heinous. The Emperor will not have been greatly stirred by the news that Marcellina's bones performed miracles. Saints who were still alive were always, with good reason, highly suspect : Peter " the Martyr," who later became the patron saint of the Spanish Inquisition, stirred up a revolt in Florence, and St. Rosa carried on her activities in Viterbo till the Emperor banished her and her following. Frederick now issued instructions against the monks and priests of Italy similar to those he had formerly levelled at the clergy of Sicily. No cleric was to presume to change his dwelling without the written permission of the *podesta*. Every bishop who obeyed the Pope's command and ceased to hold divine service and administer the sacraments was banished and his goods confiscated. A ten-days' respite was granted them in which to resume the services. This put the priests into an awkward position. The Pope's advice : patiently to endure martyrdom was probably not always taken. The mendicant monks, whom Innocent sternly segregated from all other orders, developed a Jesuitical theory that it was lawful for them to hold services and avail themselves of imperial passports in order to get about their business. Frederick, therefore, tightened up the regulations against the mendicant orders : any receiver or conveyer of a papal letter, anyone even knowing of such a letter, was forthwith condemned to a fiery death. One suspect procurator of the Sicilian Minorites was arrested, and eighteen separate tortures were appointed for him. The chroniclers were never tired of recording the cruelties and outrages committed by this " Pharaoh drunk with the blood of the saints " who had persecuted the clergy above all others.   Frederick showed in reality little of a bloodthirsty tyrant, though he would execute a number of Parma prisoners every morning in front of the city to intimidate the besieged.   His reign of terror was inspired not by madness but by direst need.

Meanwhile matters were progressing favourably round Parma. As winter drew on, Frederick II repeated his Faënza procedure on a much larger scale and built a fortified camp-town, bringing wood and tiles from all the neighbourhood round. The Emperor was determined that when Parma fell it should be wiped out and in its stead this new town should remain. He laid it out according to a well-thought-out plan, and in anticipation called it "Victoria," a name not unworthy to rank with his other foundations : Caesarea, Augusta, Aquila. He copied the methods of classical town-planners : the new town was to arise under the sign of Mars : astrologers and augurs had to calculate an auspicious moment while the site of the new town was marked out with the plough. It was to have eight gates, with walls, moats and drawbridges ; nothing was lacking : a canal brought water to it, and mills were built on the new river. And in Victoria one of the very few places of worship was erected of which Frederick was the founder. This temple was dedicated to St. Victor. The coins of the new town bore on the one side the Emperor's head, and on the other the town with the legend "Victoria"; they were known as

Victorines. This new foundation was to resemble a town of long standing, with streets and houses, market-place and palace, shops, and everything which a town could require, while outside it the Emperor laid out villas with gardens and vineyards and orchards for his Saracen maidens and their host of eunuchs. Frederick had installed himself with his entire court, his chancery and treasury, his courts of law and household, his menagerie and his huntsmen, so as to await in peace and comfort the starvation of Parma. The world looked on in amazement. Not a chronicler but records at least the building of Victoria. One who was learned in astrological lore remarks that the Emperor had failed to note in founding his town that Cancer was very close to Mars ; the town was doomed.

Here in Victoria the Emperor felt himself safe for the winter. He had, as usual, at the beginning of the cold weather, dismissed a part of the town levies or sent them off to other theatres of war where the fighting this December was very brisk. In the Spring the town ought to be nearly starved out and could be stormed. The privation in Parma was increasing. Just once the Mantuans and Ferrarese had succeeded in getting a supply of corn into the famine-stricken town. During a short absence of Enzio and Eccelino these allies of Parma had destroyed the fortified bridge at Brescello, and when Enzio in revenge besieged Colorno, which lay on Parma's own little river, they opened the sluices and flooded the country so that Enzio had to withdraw. The king of Sardinia soon equalised the account. He threw a new bridge over the Po at Bugno between Colorno and Brescello, and from this position he was able to repel all attacks. Parma was thus once more completely shut in and its surrender imminent. Frederick could feel his success assured, and when messengers came out to him to beg his mercy in case Parma should surrender, he sent them back, so the story runs, " with the acid advice ironically imparted in confidence that they had better be economical with their corn, because as long as he lived Parma should get nothing more to eat."

But, as a chronicler puts it, " confidence is the mother of misfortune," and the imperial camp let itself be lulled into culpable carelessness. The Emperor was normally distrustful

enough ; for once he was too trustful.   Certainly Parma had
spies in his army and were exactly informed of his movements.
Thus they knew that on the eighteenth of February, 1248,
Victoria's garrison was weakened by many small diversions ;
that Enzio was away ; that the Emperor according to custom
had ridden forth at dawn with his falcons and his hawks and
his buzzards, accompanied by his sixteen-year-old son Manfred
and some fifty knights : the marshes round Parma lent themselves to the chase of waterfowl.   Only Margrave Lancia was
left behind in command.   The Parma garrison made a sortie
as they often did, this time towards the south in the direction
of the Apennines.   The Margrave with a portion of his army
set off in pursuit.   The sortie had only been a ruse.   No
sooner was Lancia gone than the population of Parma, followed
by their wives and children, flung themselves suddenly on the
almost unguarded camp, rushed over the drawbridges into
Victoria, set the town on fire and mowed down the unprepared
troops in masses.   The Emperor, listening to his falcons' silver
bells, heard suddenly the great alarm bell of Victoria.   He
galloped back at full speed with his following and found the
Margrave heavily engaged.   The Emperor came to his assistance, forced his way into Victoria and tried to save what still
remained.   But he was soon in difficulties himself with his few
huntsmen : he could only just cut his way out, and when he
saw that all was lost he escaped with barely fourteen horsemen
to Borgo San Donnino.

It was the severest defeat of his life.   Fifteen hundred of his
men were slain, and twice that number taken prisoners—
Thaddeus of Suessa, his friend and Lord Chief Justice, was
dead, and with him others of the very best : one Aquino and
one Hohenburg among them, it would seem.   The whole
treasury was gone: gold, silver, pearls, gems, solitaires, purple
cloths, ceremonial robes ; gone was the sceptre, the Royal Seal
of Sicily, the heavy giant crown with its many figures like a
piece of masonry, which was intended on solemn occasions to
be suspended over the head of the world-ruler.   A little man
from Parma, who was nicknamed " Corto passo " from his
tripping gait, had secured this as his booty and brought it in
triumph back to Parma.   Much other booty from the light-

hearted camp-town : the menagerie, the eunuchs, the harem, must have excited interest ; other things awakened horror and curiosity : there was, for instance, a statue supposed to be made of Church treasures melted down, which the Emperor was said to have adored. They found experimentally that this idol healed neither the maimed nor the blind ; at most it contemned the scriptures. There were magic drawings, charts of the heavens and animal circles which " Beelzebub and Ashtaroth, the Consuls of Darkness," the astrologers and magicians, made use of. The most important trophy was the *carroccio* of Cremona, which to Cremona's shame was drawn by a team of donkeys in triumph into Parma—following the example the Emperor had set.

The impression which this defeat made on the world at large was annihilating. This was the end of the Emperor's power people said, and numerous songs of clergy, townsfolk and wandering minstrels sang the brilliant victory of Parma. It was Frederick's first serious defeat. Things had gone against him on previous occasions, but he had never before been conquered by the towns, and now his most priceless asset was at stake : the tradition of his invincibility. Frederick diagnosed the situation exactly. Instead of being crushed under the blow he drew new strength from defeat through his fanatic belief in his star, in the Fortuna Augusti. Even defeat must turn to advantage since Fortune dwelt with him, and this defeat spurred him to maximum effort, as at other times victory was wont to do. Under this blow the fifty-year-old warrior showed the tense vigour of his prime. With the scanty following that had followed him to Borgo San Donnino he galloped to Cremona and arrived late that night, having been in the saddle since dawn, " in no wise out of heart." The terrified populace, men, women and children, poured into the streets and crowded round the Emperor, thanking God with tears that he at least was safe. Frederick spoke to them words of good cheer. Within three days he had assembled a new army, mainly composed of men of Pavia and Cremona, and on the fourth he resumed the offensive. Victoria had fallen on the 18th of

February ; on the 22nd the Emperor led his forces across to the Po to attack Parma. The mere sound of his name had still such potency that the victors who had intended, under Montelongo, to invest the bridge at Bugno which Enzio was still holding, took to their heels in terror at his approach. King Enzio was consequently able to loot a fleet of some hundred ships which was bringing provisions from Mantua and Ferrara to the half-starved town, and to take three hundred prisoners whom he promptly hanged on either bank.

Frederick could now have restored the previous state of siege, and this was undoubtedly his first intention, for he wrote that he was now laying waste the country round Parma with fire and sword and inspiring courage in his troops by his own presence, and the town should not evade her fate. A council of war was held in the ruins of Victoria, but the vote was against a resumption of the siege. Frederick still camped near in order to secure the road to Pontremoli and the pass which was again threatened. Incidentally he was able to take a preliminary revenge. The Parma forces were pressing on after the Emperor when they were attacked by Lancia with the loyal knights of Parma, sixty Guelf knights were captured and over a hundred slain, amongst them Bernardo Orlando di Rossi, who was hewn in pieces, " our infamous traitor of long standing, the head and tail of the entire opposition." The most dangerous result of the defeat of Victoria was its effect on opinion at a distance. Parma's defection had breathed hope into the Guelfs, how much more Parma's victory ! Almost the whole of the Romagna was lost ; Ravenna surrendered to Ottaviano, and her secession brought in its train the loss of a number of other towns in the neighbourhood who were her dependents. It is believed that an imperial vicar had here been in league with Pandulf of Fasanella and Jacob of Morra, the two fugitive conspirators who were now fighting in the papalist ranks.

Nevertheless, the Emperor succeeded in restoring the equilibrium of the tottering state. Richard of Theate seems to have won another victory over the papalist general, Hugo Novellus, at Cittanuova in the Ancona March. Novellus was slain and with him Matthew Fasanella, the traitor's brother. A conspiracy was detected in Reggio and nipped in the bud by

Enzio, who had a hundred conspirators publicly beheaded. A
Milanese army going to Parma's assistance hastily turned back
when the Emperor moved against Milan. At the same time
Feltre and Belluno in the north-east submitted to Eccelino,
and a revulsion in Frederick's favour began to be felt in
Vercelli. Frederick was to appear during the summer in Piedmont and take possession of Vercelli. He wrote to his loyal
Sicilians that " Fortuna who is ours and who is wont to smile
more graciously when we challenge her favours has turned
once more on us a smiling face, though lately she had seemed
to cold-shoulder us a little." He told his friends in confidence
that he had "thrice thrown a six" at dice, and Fortuna was
promising not only invincibility but certain victory.

The Emperor's confidence was never shaken, though
numerous minor annoyances occurred at this juncture. It was
peculiarly irritating that the entire imperial treasury had been
lost at Parma. He was in such straits for money that he maintained that he and his court lacked for the moment the barest
necessities, he had scarcely enough to eat, let alone the means
for winning victories. New taxes must be raised. The taxes
now imposed were double or more than double the average :
60,000 ounces had been levied in Sicily in 1242, 130,000 were
raised now. Frederick further commanded all his Italian
vicars to impose a tax extraordinary on all monasteries and
churches. The Emperor was not wont to consider the tax-
payer overmuch ; yet when one Sicilian town offered to make
a proportional freewill contribution towards replacing the
state treasury he declined to accept it. He thanked the citizens
warmly for their good will, but in view of existing hardships,
and of the intolerable burden which the town was already
bearing, he would take the will for the deed. On the other hand
he again mortgaged, as he had done once before, the Montieri
silver mines at Volterra. Either he or Frederick of Antioch
borrowed 12,000 Pisan silver pounds (roughly £6000) from
Siena at 80 per cent. interest. The Emperor absolutely had to
have cash, and had to resort to extreme measures. New coins
were struck in Sicily which, with exchange fees, etc., brought

in some 8000 gold ounces (say £21,000). These expedients must have mitigated the money shortage, and we learn that considerable consignments of money reached Frederick with other assistance from the Greek Emperor, John Vatatzes. It must have been about this period that a certain amount of grumbling was heard among the mercenary knights who were drawn from every corner of the Empire, but more especially from Italy and Germany.

The German knights, who came in ever-increasing numbers to serve in Italy, were in these last years almost Frederick's only link with the North. Since the diet of Verona, which Frederick had held at the time of the Council of Lyons, the German nobles had ceased to attend Frederick's camp and court ; and the feudal knights whom they should have supplied were also missing. "We do not wish to overtax our princes either in personal service or material contribution for the conquest of Italy, though some, thirsty for the glory of the Empire and greedy of our presence, have voluntarily shared our labours and been with us all the time . . .", wrote the Emperor once. Except the brothers Hohenburg no German princes had sought to share the Emperor's labours ; and conditions in Germany : the papal oppression which lay heavy on the spiritual princes ; the rival kings who divided the secular loyalties ; the civil wars in Germany and the general misery, made absence from Germany well-nigh impossible even if they had wished to go to Italy. Frederick could dispense easily enough with the German princes ; but he would sorely have missed his German knights. Although the town infantries were taking an increasing share in the fighting, the heavily-armoured knight still formed the flower of every army. The brilliance and the power of the higher command depended on the number of the knights, declared the Emperor, and he naturally valued the German knights above them all. " We want to have Germans as knights, for we rely on their war experience. They must receive their pay and whatever they require without hitch." Early Hohenstaufens had used mercenary knights as well as feudal cavalry for their short journeys to Rome and campaigns in Italy, but Frederick was permanently in Italy. He was the first, therefore, to establish a permanent corps of German knights as a regular institution. His principle was that Sicily must provide the money and Germany the men. Frederick's need met a complementary need in Germany. Love of adventure and many another motive drove the German knights into Frederick's arms. In large and ever-increasing numbers the lower nobility crossed the Alps and joined the imperial armies ; counts and gentlemen, *ministeriales*, made the pilgrimage and hired themselves out, at first to the Emperor only, later to other Ghibelline leaders, and, when the Empire had fallen, to the Guelfs also. Presently counts and dukes also, whose gifts found no scope in Germany, followed the lead and became commandants of large mercenary bands. These independent " Marshals " foreshadow the later type of great mercenary leaders, John Hawkwood for example, or Duke Werner Urslingen (Guarneri) with his " Great Company " of three thousand German lances, who bore on their silver breastplate the motto " Enemy of Pity, of Mercy, and of God." Under Frederick II one such German force, said to have amounted to eighteen hundred lances, was serving under Count Jordan as Marshal, Frederick having no doubt appointed Jordan to the command.

It is possible either to regret that so much German strength flowed into Italy, or to rejoice that at least some ten thousand German knights escaped the cheerless constriction of Germany after the fall of the Empire. Whichever line we take, Frederick II and the Hohenstaufens must answer for it. Through her mercenary knights Germany played no negligible part in the Italian Renaissance, for the appearance of these northern warriors made a great impression in Italy. The Italians of the late thirteenth century, and still more of later days, would have had no conception of a knight if it had not been for the French and the thousands of young German nobles whom first the Hohenstaufens attracted to Italy. What an impression King Manfred's victorious Germans of Montaperti left behind them ! " Powerful figures, expert in the use of weapons, expert on horseback, they charge like lions let loose, and their war horses are like moving mountains in the flash of the weapons." They went into battle on the Arbia singing, with the name of God and St. George, their patron saint, on their lips. We learn in

great detail how these Germans under the black and silver
banner of King Manfred charged against the red lily of Florence :
" Never did Hector perform such slaughter among the Greek
host as Marshal Jordan this day amongst the Florentines."
After the victory the eight hundred German knights, with
wreaths of olive on their helmets, rode behind the trumpets and
the royal banner in triumph into Siena and dismounted before
the cathedral to thank the Virgin for their victory. In later
days the impression made by the Germans was even stronger.
Somewhere about the beginning of the Trecento a body of
fifteen hundred knights rode into Lombardy, "excellently
armed and cast as it were in one piece with their chargers," and
the Italians said " these are the most handsome men that
Lombardy has ever seen and all down to the very last of them
. . . fearless knights of lofty stature, still in the flower of their
youth, but practised in arms and dauntless in courage."

A Roman cardinal of those days still called the Germans
"the handsomest warriors in the world." In all the larger
towns they erected to their " San Giorgio " altars, chapels and
churches. We need not, therefore, be surprised that Donatello
in the opening of the fifteenth century, in creating his St.
George, unwittingly quickened from the marble a noble German
boy. In these forms we still catch the echoes of Germany's
heroic age, the Hohenstaufen age that gave birth to the regal
horsemen of Bamberg and Magdeburg, now echoing to its
close in Italy. The tortured, distorted, thought-tormented
Germany of later Gothic had no eye for the noble pride and
aristocratic freedom of such forms. It almost seems as if these
young warriors were driven south so that their beauty might
not perish fruitlessly, unhonoured and unsung. These home-
less heroes were doomed to perish whichever way they turned :
" if they mixed too long with the Italians they became inocu-
lated with their vices . . . but from their homes they come
simple and loyal and true hearted." Their simplicity struck
the over-refined, indescribably corrupt Italy of the Renaissance
much as of old that of the Germanic tribes had affected the
Rome of the Caesars. The Germanic heroic age closed, therefore, as it had begun : singly at first, then in groups, then in
ever-growing numbers their warriors had gone to Rome to

serve the divine Emperors; they then had conquered Rome, and then—beginning with Dietrich of Bern and ending with Frederick II—they had founded their own States, and then fought on as mercenaries till towards the close of the Renaissance the stream dried up : to Italy's loss.

Within four months of the defeat of Victoria, Frederick II to some extent quieted Italy. Indeed, he felt the situation so secure that he began to toy again with the plan of the preceding year : to march on Lyons. New possibilities of peace seemed open. King Louis of France was just about to start on his Crusade, and that strife at home might not imperil his great undertaking he wanted to see the Empire and the Papacy at peace. Saint Louis had never recognised the Emperor's deposition, and for all his piety had throughout maintained a correspondence with Frederick, although the Pope assured him that Frederick sought to abolish all worship of God so that he himself might be worshipped alone throughout the universe : an idol of the most revolting depravity. Moreover, Louis wanted the Emperor's co-operation, for Sicily was always the base for any overseas expeditions. Other important people also interested themselves in securing peace, but all attempts failed. The Pope refused to contemplate any peace which left the Hohenstaufen Empire standing. Disappointed by his failure the French King set sail from Aiguesmortes on his fatal Crusade. These negotiations and the plan of a possible move to Lyons had led the Emperor to enter Piedmont in July 1248, where the accession of Vercelli gave affairs a favourable turn. Pope Innocent IV saw the Emperor again drawing near the Alps and had himself well guarded in Lyons. A papal attempt to divert some Crusaders for an attack on Sicily instead of on the Holy Land fell through. Frederick held a diet in Vercelli and remained many months in Western Lombardy. Towards the end of 1248 he returned to Cremona by way of Pavia. Here he was to meet the bitterest disillusionment of his life.

Frederick had allowed his followers to worship him as the Son of God ; his loyal adherents captured in Parma implored him to set them free with " his sacred hands," for they were

suffering for him " as the martyrs for Christ's sake." He had
shared the honour and the glory of the Son of God. There was
a pitiless logic in the fact that at the end of his life he had to
a certain degree to share Christ's fate. It was probably from
Cremona that he wrote to the King of France that he felt it
particularly embittering that the Pope should send Crusaders
against Sicily," as if the mystery of the life-giving cross had
been wafted from the Holy Land to Sicily, as if Christ were
crucified again in Apulia." This mournful comparison is
uncannily close to facts : Judas Iscariot's rôle had just been
played by his most trusted friend, Piero della Vigna.

The details of the occurrences at Cremona are obscure. The
Emperor drew a veil over them and gossip distorted them.
Contemporaries heard little more than the fact of della Vigna's
sudden fall and his arrest. The obvious guess was that the
Protonotary and Logothetes of Sicily had been bought by the
Pope, like so many others. So much, however, seems certain
that della Vigna was not conspiring with the Pope. No change
of thought prompted his treachery, no suddenly awakened
papalist spirit, no fanatical love of freedom stirred him against
the Tyrant whom yet he reverenced and loved : della Vigna was
no Brutus. Neither was he guiltless. It was not only envy,
" that harlot of courts," that brought the Capuan to his fall.
He sinned not as the defender of a lofty idea but as one who
sold his master for thirty pieces of silver.

As far as the evidence goes, it seems that the inconceivable
repeated itself : della Vigna betrayed his Lord for a handful of
silver by selling justice for money. Only once did the Emperor
quite briefly, in a confidential letter to Count Richard of
Caserta, betray his feeling about della Vigna's guilt, calling
him a " second Simon," who " that he might fill his purse or
keep it full, turned the rod of justice into a serpent." Della
Vigna had always been exposed to terrific temptation. All
letters and petitions went through his hands, he decided what
must be referred and what might be independently disposed
of. Princes and kings, prelates and popes who had business
to transact with Frederick approached him through della
Vigna. Abusing his absolute discretion Piero della Vigna may
have taken money to let things pass which at this highly critical

moment involved danger to the Emperor. Or, perhaps, as
overseer of the entire accounts of the Sicilian kingdom he may
have connived at embezzlements by his subordinates, or himself
committed them. He left an immense fortune, and how far it
was honourably acquired the Emperor must have known pretty
exactly. Embezzlement at such a time of money-famine would
not be far short of treason. Apart from the major defalcation,
della Vigna may well, as Frederick further wrote to Caserta,
" by systematic swindling have driven the Imperium into such
danger that Empire and Emperor like the Egyptian chariots and
the hosts of Pharaoh might have been drowned in the depths
of the sea."

Bribery and embezzlement must have been indulged in by
the majority of the officials, but this does not lighten della
Vigna's guilt ; it aggravates it rather. The other officials were
merely disobeying the laws. Della Vigna had himself in the
Emperor's name promulgated those laws. He had formulated
and defined them ; with his own words as the mouthpiece of
the Emperor he had condemned the bartering of Justice and
stigmatised it as " simony." He had for money betrayed the
whole worship of the *imperialis ecclesia* which was based on
" the lawbringer Moses " and the " Vicar Petrus " which he,
like a very apostle had evolved and represented. If Piero della
Vigna himself could not preserve clean hands, could not himself live the laws that he proclaimed, it was calculated to shake
the world's faith in the Emperor, as the shortcoming of a
justiciar or a vicar could not do. A crime that an ordinary
official might unobtrusively expiate by loss of office became in
della Vigna's case a fall that shook the world.

There is no doubt that Frederick would have overlooked
many little irregularities as long as it was possible to do so in
order to retain his nearest counsellor, his ablest intimate.
Arrest will not have occurred until Piero della Vigna's behaviour
had become a danger to the State, and the jealousy of the other
courtiers may well have precipitated the climax. What amazes
the observer is the disproportion between the advantage gained
and the advantages lost by this treachery. On the one hand
the master, honoured as the Saviour, perhaps at last believed
and proclaimed a Saviour by della Vigna alone . . . on the other

the silver. . . . There is something grotesque in this incom-
mensurability : there is something sinister. The power and
magic of great men are shattered not by the world's great
resistances, on these they thrive, but by the pettiness of human
frailty.

The discovery of Piero della Vigna's breach of faith and the
arrest were terrible for Frederick, the more because at this same
moment he escaped poison by a hair's breadth, poison proffered
by one of his entourage. His physician, whom he completely
trusted, and whom he had ransomed from Parma because he
could not do without him, prepared a poisoned bath and a
poisoned draught to meet some trifling indisposition. At the
last moment the Emperor was warned. When the doctor
handed him the goblet Frederick said—so the story goes—that
they must be careful not to give him poison instead of medicine.
The doctor sought to reassure him. Frederick looked at him :
" Drink to my health and share the draught with me." The
doctor feigned to stumble, and, falling, contrived to spill most
of the contents of the goblet. The Emperor's guards seized
him. What was left was given to a condemned criminal to
drink. He died on the instant. The Emperor is said then,
reflecting on what had passed, to have wrung his hands and
groaned aloud : " alas for me, my very bowels fight against me !
Whom can I trust ! Where can I again be happy and secure ! "
And his friends sat round and sighed with him and wept.
After this the words of Job were often in the Emperor's mouth :
" All my inward friends abhorred me, and they whom I loved
are turned against me."

Contemporaries associated the doctor's attempt with Piero
della Vigna's sudden fall. They were two quite independent
episodes which happened to occur at the same time. The
doctor had been captured at Parma and had been won over by
the Pope's legate ; " the Pope's reputation was blackened not
a little," a chronicler writes. Frederick informed the kings
and people of the world of this new effort of the Pope's. " This
priest, this shepherd, this peace-loving director of our faith is
not content with the innumerable intrigues and shameful

machinations with which he has disgraced the rule of his order
to do us injury but—O shame !—he has just attempted to
murder us by secret means ! " After the events of the last few
days the Emperor can no longer doubt that the end of the times
is near. The doctor's fate matched his crime. Blinded and
mutilated, with continuous torture, so that no rest was given
him even on Sundays or on holy days, he was taken to Sicily
for execution.

A similar fate hung over Piero della Vigna. When the
Cremonese heard of his treachery they nearly tore and hacked
in pieces the man so lately feared. But Frederick prevented
mob justice and had the prisoner taken by night to the neighbouring Borgo San Donnino. In March when the Emperor
started for Tuscany he took Piero della Vigna with him mounted
on a donkey, amongst the baggage train. They took him to
San Miniato. They say that Frederick made use of his former
friend for a stratagem. The Guelfs in San Miniato would not
permit the entrance of armed men. They were assured that
only the prisoners and the imperial exchequer were being
brought to the fortress. The baggage animals were, however,
loaded with weapons instead of treasure, and the ostensible
prisoners were imperial men-at-arms whose fetters could easily
be struck off. To disarm the Guelfs' suspicion, however, Piero
della Vigna had to lead the procession of prisoners. If the tale
is true, it was Frederick's last vengeance on his friend. Piero
della Vigna knew his master well enough to know that some
terrible death awaited him. He put himself beyond the fear
of torture : he, also, "went and hanged himself." The story
is that when the blinded prisoner was being led into the dungeon
of San Miniato he asked the guards whether anything lay
between him and the wall. They said not. The blind man
forthwith flung himself with such violence against the prison
wall that he split his skull. After these days of horror Frederick
proceeded to Pisa. On the Arno he embarked on his Sicilian
galleys to return to his mother country : for ever. He never
saw Italy again.

For more than a decade Frederick II had reigned and ruled

and raged in Italy as the Judge, the Caesar, the Antichrist, and he had left his mark indelibly on the land. He had left a legacy of " the majestic and the terrible." Italy had altered more in those ten years than sometimes in a century. The times had gone mad with the intensity of life, with the enormous expenditure of power, and Italy stood under the shadow of Dante in the sign of the rising Renaissance. The Hohenstaufen had not only a share in the change : he had been himself the *immutator mirabilis* who dared to alter laws and times, a fact which the Church cast in his teeth. It was high time that he should now pass on. His mission was fulfilled. The sap was in circulation. Condottieri, signori, tyrants, as well as the wise, learned and magnificent dukes of Florence, Urbino and Ferrara, finally the towns and the city-states also, were all the heirs and inheritors of Frederick II.

The image of Frederick as ruler and the image of Frederick's state survived actually only in miniature. Spiritually they received immense extension through Dante : in the *de Monarchia* as well as in the state structure and cosmogony of the *Divine Comedy*. It has often enough been demonstrated that Dante only proclaims what Frederick II had lived. Since the heretic Frederick II, his life, his acts, his thought, all determined Dante's picture of a State, it was inevitable that the poet should also be reckoned as a heretic. The implications of his poem were not wholly understood, but the *de Monarchia* was clear to all, especially as this dangerous Ghibelline document seemed about to be fulfilled by Louis the Bavarian seven years after the poet's death. The papal legate thereupon condemned the treatise as heretical and burnt it publicly, and they even wanted to take the poet's remains out of their Franciscan vault at Ravenna and burn them to "the eternal disgrace and the ruin of his memory." The *de Monarchia* was put on the Index of Forbidden Books and was not removed therefrom till the days of Leo XIII in 1897.

Frederick II had created in Sicily the " mirror of likeness for those who admire it," a visible mirror of princes for the days to come. It was the structure of the State that was the vital thing. The kingdom of Sicily itself lost all importance for the world at large. This last Emperor was not destined, like

Caesar or like Charlemagne, to be the *heros eponymos* of a new epoch, which bore his stamp on its secular statecraft and was irradiated by his indwelling spirit. Frederick II dominated the Renaissance anonymously and illegitimately. The establishment of the Norman despotism itself had been illegitimate, and so, therefore, were the small Italian town-states which were offshoots of the Sicilian parent state. The tyrants, too, were illegitimate : the bodily or spiritual bastards, sons or grandsons, of the Hohenstaufen, had each to win anew *sua virtute* the Emperor's immediacy, since Frederick had only usurped it by right of genius through an illegitimate priestship.

The Emperor's rule in Italy might easily have become legitimate if the Lombards had been complaisant. It rested, however, in fact, not on the privileges or rights of the excommunicate monarch but on his genius : what Machiavelli called *virtu*, this combination of strength and talent, not incompatible with evil. After this each of the Renaissance tyrants had to show *virtu* or genius if he was to maintain his illegitimate rule over his tiny State. Frederick II, statesman and philosopher, politician and soldier, general and jurist, poet and diplomat, architect, zoologist, mathematician, the master of six or it might be nine languages, who collected ancient works of art, directed a school of sculpture, made independent researches in natural science, and organised states, this supremely versatile man was the Genius of the Renaissance on the throne of the Emperors, was the Emperor of Genius. It is not without deeper significance that this first genius of the Renaissance wore the actual diadem of a world ruler, which in a sense still crowned the later geniuses but no longer kept them within the Empire.

So Frederick left Italy. The year of horror did not end with his friends' death. He had lost within one year his two best statesmen and most trusty comrades, in whose company he had had his image carved over the triumphal gate of Capua, Thaddeus of Suessa and Piero della Vigna. Now he lost two sons. Soon after the Emperor's arrival in Naples, Count Richard of Theate seems to have died. He had been Vicar

General of the Romagna and of Spoleto, and had just recently distinguished himself by his victories over Hugo Novellus. We do not know how much attached the Emperor was to him. The news about King Enzio which shortly followed certainly touched Frederick more.

Enzio had remained behind, as usual, to represent his father in Lombardy. His marriage with the Sardinian heiress Adelasia had been declared void, and Frederick had been present at his marriage to a niece of Eccelino's at Cremona. This relationship set the seal on the comradeship in arms of two gallant men. The ceremony had taken place just about the time of Piero della Vigna's arrest. The active young king had no idea in life except fighting; for ten years he had been continuously crossing swords with the Lombards, and soon after his wedding, in January 1249, he marched against the Guelfs of Reggio to undertake a campaign in the neighbourhood of Parma. He had returned to his headquarters at Cremona when he got an appeal from Modena for help against the Bolognese. Off he hastened with his bodyguard, his " cohort " and the knights of Cremona across the Po by his own bridge at Bugno in the direction of Modena. At Fossalta in the frontier of the Modena territory he got entangled in a small skirmish ; suddenly the main forces of Bologna arrived and took a hand. In the *mêlée* Enzio's horse was killed under him, his troops began to waver, and he was taken prisoner with four hundred knights and twelve hundred foot-soldiers. Marinus of Eboli, well-known as *podesta* and vicar, shared his fate.

The skirmish had in itself no serious importance, but the loss of Enzio was for Frederick more severe than the loss of an army or a province. The later battles of the Hohenstaufen heirs might have worn a different complexion if King Enzio had been there to keep the Ghibelline flag flying in Lombardy. The Emperor at once set about procuring his son's release. He first wrote a beautiful letter to the people of Bologna about the Goddess Fortuna. " We read in the most various writings that Fortuna knows many final acts. The evil fortune that now weighs a man to earth may presently lift him to the heights. And fortune often smiles on those she raises and yet casts them down at last and scourges them and pierces them with wounds incurable. If ye, therefore, on this day, see fortune smiling on you with unclouded brow ye would yet be wise to refrain from being puffed up, for he who rises to the greater heights is the worse broken by the fall. Fortuna often promises success at first . . . but overfills the middle and concludes the end with manifold misfortune." There breathes here a spirit of foreboding. There is no longer any word of the Fortuna Augusti, the Goddess who obeys the Caesar. The Emperor, however, is not bankrupt of proud words as he demands Enzio's liberty. " Ask ye of your fathers and they will tell how our grandfather of most happy and glorious memory, the all-conquering Frederick, drove out that generation of Milan from their *lares* and divided up their town into three parcels. If ye surrender Enzio our beloved son, King of Sardinia and Gallura, from his prison, we shall exalt your town above every town in Lombardy. But if ye hearken not to the voice of our commandment then expect our triumphant and unnumbered army. The traitors of Liguria shall not avail to deliver you out of our hands, but ye shall become a fable and a disgrace to the nations and this shall be held as a reproach against you for ever."

The Emperor's letter bore no fruit. Bologna's answer was that *a cane non magno saepe tenetur aper*, and Frederick must know that they had held, and did hold, and would continue to hold, King Enzio. The suggestion of exchanging Enzio for the son of the Count of Montferrat whom Frederick had captured was not acceptable, neither was the offer to buy his freedom by laying a ring of silver round the town for ransom. King Enzio was fated to live and die a prisoner. The early fame of the young warrior formed henceforth a halo round the royal captive. The people of Bologna had chained the imperial king with golden fetters when they led him in triumph through their town, following the fashion set by the Emperor. Legend tells us that the young king in his royal dress, with his long golden hair under the flashing helmet-crown, set the hearts of the populace afire, not only of the beautiful womenfolk. The men of Bologna no less met with admiration and respect the young hero who bore with justice a lion in his shield. His confinement was strict but never degrading. A large hall in the *podesta's* palace was assigned to him, in which he and his

well-born fellow-prisoners could spend the day. Only at night
he was shut into a small chamber of wood and iron that had
been erected in the middle of the apartment. This is the
origin of the legend that he was kept in an iron cage. He was
allowed to correspond freely with the outside world and to
receive as many visitors as he would. In later times he lived
at the expense of the commune, for he was so extravagant that
in spite of his large means he was presently reduced to poverty.
His fellow-prisoners soon left, and only one German count,
Conrad of Solimburg, shared his captivity. The Bolognese
themselves counted Conrad an intolerably effeminate little
creature. The king found him at last so wearisome that he
begged his captors to spare him this companionship.

Except for his own servants Enzio's only friends were the
Ghibellines of Bologna, the Lambertacci, who frequently
visited him and with one of whom, Pietro Asinelli, he formed
an intimate friendship. Visitors of the other sex were not
lacking. People tell how the beautiful Lucia Viadagola took
pity on him, and his two natural daughters probably belong to
the twenty-three years of his captivity.

In the early days his imprisonment was quite endurable.
He bore it with unclouded serenity and was often able to cheer
his guards or visitors by singing his songs to them. He
guarded the volume of his poems as a treasure and mentioned
it in his will. His songs were pretty if not profound, such
as befitted this gifted but simple warrior, singer and king.
Gradually, as all hope of freedom died away, they lost their
lightheartedness. There is a sad sonnet about the ever-
changing demands of changing time . . . there is a still sadder
canzone which Enzio sent to Tuscany, the land of noble living,
where he had worked in the most brilliant days of his father's
reign, in the days when Faënza fell and the prelates were caught
at sea.

> Va, canzonetta mia . . .
> Salutami Toscana
> Quella che de sovrana
> In cui regna tutta cortesia,
> E vanne in Puglia piana
> La magna Capitana
> La dov' è lo mio core nott' e dia.

Enzio was probably familiar with Apulia and the Capitanata from childhood, for these were his father's favourite provinces. Here the captive king's brothers and nephews were presently to fight a losing fight against Frenchmen and priests, and were to succumb one after another while still scarcely out of boyhood.

Enzio had to witness, from his prison, the whole tragic disappearance of the imperial House of Hohenstaufen, ever hoping for freedom, ever doubly disappointed and deceived. A year after the Emperor's death the news reached him that his half-brother, King Conrad, the heir of the Empire, was coming to Italy. Conrad had been spending Christmas night in the monastery of St. Emmeram in Ratisbon, and had only by a miracle escaped a treacherous attempt on his life by the abbot, his host. He had abandoned the lonely, hopeless fight in the north, had precipitately mortgaged, sold, or given away all his German possessions and come south. He hoped to make Sicily a base, as his father had done, for war against the Church on behalf of the Empire. From the first the cause was lost. The burden of intolerable responsibility on his young shoulders had made the boy prematurely bitter and gloomy. He knew very little about Sicilian conditions. Though he was the son of the Syrian Isabella and had been born in Apulia he was unaccustomed to the climate. After more than two years of joyless undistinguished activity he died of fever at scarcely twenty-six. The corpse was taken to Messina and before the consecration was consumed in a great conflagration. Other people said that Manfred was jealous and had poisoned his brother, and that enemies had thrown the body into the sea. In those first years, when the Emperor was no longer there to bear the brunt of fate, other Hohenstaufen sons fell victims to the doom of their house. King Henry, the son of the English Isabella, had died at the age of fifteen, and here the rumour ran that King Conrad had had his brother assassinated by the black Grand Chamberlain, Johannes Maurus. Two years after Conrad's death Frederick of Antioch, who had had to give up the attempt to maintain himself in Tuscany, was killed in battle against Foggia (1256), which Cardinal Ottaviano degli Ubaldini had garrisoned.

Just at this time Manfred's star began to mount. He was prince of Taranto. With the help of relatives and friends he won by force or cunning or genius, with or without right, the crown of Sicily. With snow-white skin and pink cheeks and eyes like stars (Dante calls him " comely and fair and gentle of aspect," and praises him as the pattern of an Italian prince) he restored something of the old brilliance to his father's court. Hohenstaufen wit sparkled once more ; Hohenstaufen hospitality and *joie de vivre* blossomed again in the southern kingdom ; again the royal falcons rose and stooped ; the king conversed again with oriental and western philosophers. Almost more numerous than the warriors were the minstrels and fiddlers who hummed around the irresponsible young prodigal, who with his friend Manfred Maletta himself composed airs and canzones, crowding the fulness of a lifetime into the space of a few years. Manfred seemed to be reviving the Italico-Sicilian rule of the Hohenstaufens as well as the brilliance of the court. The victory at Montaperti on the Arbia was full of promise and made Manfred dream even of the imperial crown. He did not know, however, how to follow up the victory, and before long he was busy defending his kingdom against Anjou, whom the Church had called in.

The young king was said to possess a magic ring with which he could conjure demons (Pope Boniface used later to wear it) ; but this did not avail. If the Hohenstaufens loved life they also knew how to die. The battle of Benevento was as good as lost when Manfred, armed by a tearful aged servant of the Emperor's, plunged into the fray in which he perished. Not for some days was his body found under the pile of corpses. They knew it by its beauty. His friends, captives now themselves, drew it forth with trembling hands and covered their dead king's feet and hands with kisses. Victorious Anjou gave King Manfred a grave beside the bridge over the Liris at Benevento. But the revengeful Pope, so runs the tale, would not permit the body to rest there. The archbishop of Cosenza dug up the royal corpse and gave it shallow

burial in the sand close by the river, so that the remains were
washed away :

> . . . but the rain now drenches them
> And the wind drives, out of the kingdom's bounds,
> Far as the stream of Verde, where, with lights
> Extinguished, he removed them from their bed.

Thus Manfred in Purgatory tells the poet.

Manfred's consort, Helena, was some twenty-four years of
age. With three sons and her one daughter she fell into the
hands of Anjou and died after five years' imprisonment. The
daughter, Beatrice, after eighteen years of confinement in the
Castel dell' Ovo at Naples was set free by the Sicilian Vespers.
The sons grew up literally in chains. They were unfettered
after thirty years but still kept prisoner. Half-starved, reduced
to beggary, driven to madness one after another, the two heirs
of Manfred died in prison : " the brood of poison-swollen
adders."

Before leaving his wife Elizabeth behind in Bavaria King
Conrad begot a son called Conradin. This nephew of Enzio's
now came to Italy. Once more the Ghibellines took heart.
The tall slight boy was hailed as " the most handsome child a
man could find." He was received with enthusiasm in the
quondam imperialist towns of northern Italy, Verona and Pavia,
Pisa and Siena. He was fifteen when he left his Swabian home
with his friend Francis of Baden, who was three years older.
" In order that the glorious race to which we belong may not
degenerate in our person," the proud boy said as he journeyed
south. It seemed as if the ancient Hohenstaufen dreams were
to be at last fulfilled. What had lured on the *Puer Apuliae*
from afar, but what the giant Emperor and Caesar Frederick II
had never achieved, was granted to young Conradin. He rode
beside his friend into Ghibelline Rome as Felix Victor ac
Triumphator. His cousin, Henry of Castile, Senator of
the Eternal City, handed over the town to him. Triumphal
arches stretched across his path all the way from the Bridge of
S. Angelo to the Capitol, ropes were slung across the streets
from house to house, on which carpets, silks and purples were

hung. Choirs of Roman women sang songs of welcome to the last Hohenstaufen king, while the men already acclaimed him Emperor as they led him to the Capitol. It was Ghibelline Rome welcoming the Hohenstaufen, and the Romans whom the thunder-voice of Frederick had so often roused from their lazy slumber remembered now that they were of the blood of Romulus, remembered the triumphs and the laurels Frederick won for them of old, and did homage to his grandson. In Sicily the Saracens of Lucera revolted against the hated Angevin as soon as they heard that a Hohenstaufen was coming again to his hereditary kingdom.

Less than four weeks later catastrophe followed triumph. Conradin had scarcely entered Sicily when he was defeated by cunning at Tagliacozzo and betrayed as he fled. He fell a captive into the hands of Anjou, and with him the rest of his family, Conradin of Caserta, Thomas Aquino, Henry of Castile, whose brother Frederick had educated at his court, and several Lancias. Only Conrad of Antioch escaped and carried on a relentless guerilla war against the French. All the others were victims of a cruel fate. Aquino was condemned to death. Conradin of Caserta spent thirty-two years in prison at Castel del Monte, Henry of Castile was captive for twenty years, the Lancias, Galvano and Frederick, were executed, the father after his son ; a half-brother of Conradin's, yet another Conradin, was hanged in Lucera. Conradin, sitting playing chess with his friend Frederick of Baden, learned the fate reserved for them both. An unheard-of decision of Anjou's—to send to the scaffold a king taken in battle. The majority of the judges refused to concur in the sentence. The execution took place in the Frenchman's presence in the market square of Naples, witnessed by a thronging crowd, curious to see a king's decapitation. As the head fell to the ground an eagle swooped to earth, trailed his right wing in the blood of the last of the Hohenstaufen kings, and thus stained soared again to heaven —so men said.

" How can the Germans bear to live "—queries a Venetian troubadour—" when they think upon this end ! They have lost their bravest and their best and have reaped disgrace ! Unless they avenge themselves they are dishonoured ! " The night after the death of Conradin the earth trembled; but the Germans felt no earthquake. They thought not of revenge. Nay, Rudolf of Hapsburg, to gratify the Pope, solemnly renounced the right of vengeance on Anjou. Never has the blood-stained eagle yet been purged; never have German vespers followed the Sicilian. " The southern peoples seemed more moved and grieved than the Germans," the German chronicler confesses with surprise, when the royal corpses were shovelled into the shallow sand " as if the sea had spewed them forth." The German princes shuddered, and Conradin was mourned in Worms and Strasburg on the Upper Rhine, but all the great body of Germany lay dull and stupid and unmoved. Better this, perhaps, than imitating the Meissner poet, who patted as it were the fallen king patronisingly on the shoulder with a " pride goeth before a fall " and a " why fly so far afield," or the schoolmaster who wrote a comic poem on Conradin who had been playing the children's game of " peep " and " heads off " with Anjou and had lost it. This characteristically German obtuseness in face of greatness, fate, and human dignity, makes the miracle the more astounding that such heroes could have sprung from such a people.

The hapless Enzio, forgotten in his Bologna prison, lived to hear the tale of Conradin. He was now himself the last of all that brilliant race. He must take up the thread again and spin it on, avenge the blood of the slain, sacrifice himself and die like them. He had been twenty years a captive, he was over fifty, but he must escape since there was no Staufen left alive but he. He negotiated with friends and bribed a gigantic cellarer named Filippo to carry him forth one evening in an empty cask. Pietro Asinelli was to be in waiting with horses for the king. Everything worked according to plan. Filippo had reached the street with his burden when a woman spied a long lock of golden hair flowing from the bung. In all Bologna was no such hair but Enzio's! She shrieked; all was discovered; the cellarer was beheaded and King Enzio more strictly watched. Not for long. He died within two years, in 1272.

The Bolognese accorded him a royal funeral. In scarlet robes, with sceptre, sword and diadem, he was buried in San

Domenico according to his own request. The curse on the Staufen house did not perish with him. His children were swept into the tragedy of another race. His only legitimate daughter was married to Guelfo da Donoratico della Gherardesca of Pisa. An old nobleman, a relation of Guelfo's, had already shared Conradin's fate. A grandson of Enzio's shared the fate of his father's father and perished with Count Ugolino in the dreaded hunger-tower of Pisa.

The unforgiveable sin was Staufen blood. Never in historic times had a jealous God demanded through his priesthood such expiation : " Root out the name and fame, the seed and sapling of this Babylonian ! " Frederick had no presentiment of what Fate had in store for his sons. If he had he could scarcely have challenged Nemesis by writing to cheer his family after the battle of Fossalta and the capture of Enzio : " Though this misfortune—since we must call it so—seems as in fairytale or nightmare terribly severe, yet is our cause not lost. We accept this reverse as slight or even negligible, nor is our proud head bowed. The accidents of war are manifold but OUR ILLUSTRIOUS QUIVER IS FILLED WITH MANY SONS. We learn such news therefore with calm ; and our powerful right arm is thereby strengthened the more vigorously to pursue the destruction of our rebels."

The doom of the house of Hohenstaufen is comparable to the fate of the children of Niobe. Frederick was spared the sight of his sons' long martyrdom. One of the uncanny " Antichristian " things about him is that in spite of the heavy blows fate dealt him in the later years the arch-offender himself escaped anything like adequate expiation of his guilt. His life and strife to the last hour did not lack glory.

" Nor is our proud head bowed," Frederick had written. It is a fact that his last year showed neither weariness nor dejection, nor any relaxation of his tense activity. An actual rejuvenation seems rather to have renewed his powers. He wrote in friendly wise to his contemporary Eccelino how fully he realised that Eccelino's loyalty grew warmer with the years " as a renewal of mental vigour accompanies the ageing of the body." In reply to Eccelino's kind enquiries he could assure his friend that while thoughts of the Empire and the rebels were ever with him, he was happy, and his physique which had been somewhat severely taxed by the Italian campaigns was now responding to the comfort and treatment of home.

Frederick was even contemplating a new marriage with the daughter of Duke Albert of Saxony. His return to Sicily had had a double purpose, first to restore order in the administration and finance which under Piero della Vigna had of late fallen into confusion, and, secondly, to make the necessary preparations for the following year " to turn his steps joyfully to Germany " as he expressed it. He had long been promising King Conrad a visit.

The political situation seemed every month to favour such plans more. A few ugly items of news had followed King Enzio's capture : the defection of Como, the capitulation of Modena, which the Bolognese took after a siege, the renewed loss of the Cisa Pass. The beginning of 1250, however, saw the fortune of war set again in the Emperor's favour   It began in the Romagna. Ravenna, which had twice proved false, had once more been won for the Emperor by the loyal Counts of Bagnacavallo and the March of Ancona was following suit. The papal legate of the March, Peter Capoccio, had been instructed to invade Sicily, but before the banner of the Keys could cross the Sicilian frontier he was utterly defeated with a loss of two thousand dead. Two of his nephews were taken prisoner. A few months later the imperial troops took Cingoli in the March and the Cardinal escaped capture by the skin of his teeth. A whole series of towns returned to their allegiance, so that Frederick was able to announce to his Byzantine son-in-law that Spoleto, the Romagna, and the March were his once more.

Frederick of Antioch's position in Florence was not so happy. The imperial government of Tuscany could only be maintained by perpetual petty fighting. Some Florentine troops in Frederick's service were surprised by the Guelfs on a campaign in the Arezzo neighbourhood, and in the autumn of 1250 a distinct change of atmosphere was noticeable in Florence. Not that the Florentines went over to the Pope or rebelled against the Emperor, but they were the first commune to form a non-party *popolo* regardless of Ghibelline or Guelf.   Henceforth all the forces which Frederick had hitherto sacrificed on the altar of the Empire should be diverted to the service of the town itself.   The imperial *podesta*, however, remained for the duration of Frederick's life.   The very night following the Emperor's death the house fell in and the imperial official was buried in the ruins.

Central Lombardy was the scene of really big successes. The one-eyed Margrave, Hubert Pallavicini, was proving a most distinguished successor to King Enzio.   Possibly Hubert's despotic savagery was more effective than Enzio's chivalrous battle-loving bonhomie.   Hubert was famous as the inventor of new tortures : he would hang a victim up naked by his feet and break his teeth one by one.

Frederick knew just how to handle this most ambitious man. Eccelino enjoyed practical independence and guaranteed the Brenner ; similarly, the Count of Savoy was guardian of the passes into Burgundy ; Hubert Pallavicini was in like manner to cover the Cisa Pass.   Frederick, therefore, made over to him some fifty small villages and hamlets in the neighbourhood, so that the Emperor's cause was his own.   A number of these estates lay in the Parma domain, and the Margrave took the field with his Cremonese against this hated town.   On the very spot where the Emperor's care-free town of Victoria had stood a battle was fought in which Parma lost three thousand dead and captured and lost also their standard-bearing chariot, Cremona was avenged for the *carroccio* she had lost at Victoria. Parma long remembered this " Black Thursday."   Dante once, in a letter to Florence, exhorting his townsmen not to oppose the advancing Henry of Luxemburg, recalls the episode : " Let not yourselves be lured to foolhardiness by the incredible good fortune of the people of Parma who in ill-advised passionate greed . . . burst into Caesar's camp in Caesar's absence. They brought home victory from Victoria but they also drew down on themselves sorrow from sorrow."   The effects of this victory of Pallavicini were felt also in the Bologna direction.

The men of that city sent messengers to Frederick to treat of peace. But Frederick refused to negotiate about anything save Enzio's release.

Hubert Pallavicini was successful in other matters. He reduced the political confusion of Cremona by a firm re-organisation of the imperial partisans who called themselves "the Beardless" *Barbarasi*. He soon got into touch with Piacenza also, a town traditionally anti-Kaiser. Ere long it renounced its old alliance with Milan and elected to be ruled by Pallavicini, whose strength men feared and trusted.

The fleet now came once more to the fore again. Peter of Gaëta, the new Sicilian admiral, succeeded in conquering seventeen Genoese ships with their crews, by an attack in the neighbourhood of Savona.

The Pope's prospects began to look bleak in Italy. Nor were things brighter for him in Germany, for in the summer of 1250 King Conrad had undertaken a great Rhenish campaign against William of Holland, which had happily led to a truce with the archbishops on the Rhine. In Avignon and Arles the inhabi-tants had renewed their oaths of fealty to the imperial envoys in spite of the Pope's utmost efforts to alienate them from the Hohenstaufen cause. Pope Innocent IV had little stomach left for further fighting. His money and his troops were almost exhausted ; less than ever could he count on the French king even for the most trivial service. King Louis had had some initial successes in his Egyptian Crusade, but had been taken prisoner at Mansurah with almost his entire army. In com-mon with countless others he laid the blame for this disaster at the Pope's door. For in spite of Louis' instant entreaties the Pope had refused peace with the Emperor, and hence prevented Frederick from lending " an assistance more potent than letters " in these overseas adventures. The Pope, moreover, still diverted, as far as he was able, those who had taken the cross to war against Frederick and thus robbed the Crusade of full support.

Frederick skilfully exploited the spreading discontent. From the beginning he had furthered Saint Louis' undertaking to the utmost of his power, and when the news of the French King's capture reached him in Apulia he wrote immediately to the Egyptian Sultan, the son of al Kamil, and begged the king's release. The commander-in-chief of the Saracen army was Frederick's old friend Fakhru'd Din, and the French were not a little surprised to see the Roman eagle flashing in the shield of the infidel, an early gift of Frederick to his friend.

A change of dynasty in Egypt, however, had enabled Louis to purchase his freedom for a large ransom without awaiting Frederick's intervention. He then proceeded to Acre. The hopes of the French king and of the Crusaders were centred in help from Frederick, the chosen Leader of Crusades. Even one of the Templars (whose order Frederick had bitterly persecuted for years) wrote from the Holy Land that Christian and Saracen alike believed that the Emperor could have averted the fiasco of this Crusade if the Pope's conceit had not prevented his participation. "Truly all our hope lies in Frederick's bosom," wrote the Templar. The whole world agreed. King Louis charged his brothers, whom he sent back from Acre, most insistently to demand that the Pope make peace with the Emperor, otherwise the French would drive him out of Lyons. Innocent, in perturbation, addressed himself thereupon to the English king, begging him to offer the Curia asylum in Bordeaux. The English king hesitated to permit this change of domicile, for Innocent IV had filled England with unfathomable hate.

Frederick II seemed near the goal of his desire, an alliance of all the secular princes against the Pope. At the beginning of 1250 the Greek Emperor Vatatzes had sent considerable auxiliaries, and only the stirring events in Egypt, so Frederick wrote to the Castilian king, had detained Frederick so long in Apulia, that he might be near at hand. The journey to Germany and a call at Lyons were plans ever present to Frederick's mind. His power had not for many years been so assured as now. Victory waited on his banners everywhere, and he was able to send one jubilant message after another to Vatatzes, "To let one letter follow on another, bringing good news of victories, rejoices not only those who are related by ties of blood and of unfeigned affection but rejoices every friend," he

wrote, concluding with full assurances of success : " and thus
our divine glory re-inforced by the providence of heaven, leads
and directs the Empire in order and in peace."

In this moment of brilliant, almost unhoped-for, fulfilment,
when the power of the Empire seemed unimpaired and the
Imperator himself rejoicing in action and ready for the fray ;
when east and west alike were turning their gaze with eager
expectation on the monarch of the world, at this moment of
suddenly intensified glory the Emperor was reft from the arena.
Frederick II died on the 13th of December, 1250, the feast of
St. Lucy, shortly before the completion of his fifty-sixth year,
an age that seems to belong to a certain group of heroes and
rulers.

In the early days of December he had been staying at Foggia.
He seemed perfectly fit in spite of several slight indispositions
during the year. Then he had left the palace, presumably on
a hunting expedition, and later legends tell that while hunting
he had turned on his finger the magic ring of Prester John and
suddenly disappeared from sight. The fact was, however, that
a severe attack of fever drove him to take refuge in Castel
Fiorentino which he had never visited before. The dysentery
which he had foolishly been neglecting turned to gastric in-
flammation, and he seems to have realised from the first that
this illness was to be his last. He must himself have summoned
at once his chief state officials, for within a day or two he had
with him Archbishop Berard of Palermo, Lord Chief Justice
Richard of Montenero, several High Court Judges, notaries,
etc. The other faithful adherents who were with him in these
last days were probably part of his permanent household.
They included the eighteen-year-old Manfred, who was then
the nearest and dearest of all his sons ; Count Berthold of
Hohenburg, to whose friendship the Emperor commended the
boy ; Pietro Ruffo, Master of the Royal Stables, with his nephew
Folco Ruffo, one of the young poets of the Sicilian school to
whom Frederick had recently been showing marks of great
favour ; his son-in-law Count Richard of Caserta ; and, lastly,

the physician John of Procida whose name is linked with the Sicilian Vespers that spelt the fate of the Anjous.

Frederick II never left Castel Fiorentino, and the oracle that had foretold that he was destined to die *sub flore* was here fulfilled. The man who had, they said, hoped " to defy Nature " and live for ever, had in vain avoided Florence all his life. The illness lasted a few days only. Shortly before his death Frederick II, in the presence of his faithful friends, drew up his last testament: Conrad was to be heir of the Empire as a whole; Manfred, Prince of Taranto and Vicar of the Italian-Sicilian state. Arrangements for legacies, pious foundations and the like were made. All prisoners were to be released, except traitors. The Church was to recover her possessions on condition of rendering to Caesar the things that were Caesar's. Frederick anticipated that his sons would carry on the fight. The witnesses signed the will : first among them the octogenarian Archbishop Berard of Palermo, who had accompanied the *Puer Apuliae* on his first dash to Germany, and was now about to render him the last rites. Then Frederick, showing himself therein a greater man than the giants Eccelino and Pallavicini, asked for absolution, donned the grey habit of a Cistercian and received the last sacrament from the hand of Archbishop Berard, in death as in life preserving the restraint and dignity that beseem a Christian-Roman Emperor.

Frederick had given instructions that his obsequies should be carried out without ostentation. He probably also gave orders that the news of his death should be kept from the public as long as possible to avoid premature disturbance throughout the Empire. Manfred, however, did not allow the ceremonies to lack pomp or reverence as the body was conveyed first to Messina and then to Palermo. In the cathedral of Palermo, beside the tombs of King Roger II and the imperial parents Henry VI and his great consort Constance, Frederick was laid to rest in the majestic sarcophagus of dark-red porphyry which more than twenty years ago he had himself transferred from Cefalu to Palermo to await his mortal remains. The sarcophagus is borne on four porphyry lions carved with mysterious south-Italian pagan symbols dating from prehistoric times ; one of them with his claws is guarding a Hercules. The lid is

ornamented with the symbols of the four evangelists and the
figure of the Emperor himself. The ruler was no longer
shrouded in the Cistercian habit, but wrapped in a garment of
Arabian silk into which were woven the symbols of world
lordship and writings in exotic script.

Frederick had passed away in the full glory of imperial power.
The faithful hailed him as the *vas electum Dei* . . . " overcome
by the might of God alone whom the might of the children of
men had not availed to overcome " . . . " the unconquered "
. . . " the mightiest of heroes " . . . " the greatest of the princes
of the earth, the admiration of the world and her most marvellous transformer." Frederick suffered no martyrdom, nor
bore the wounds St. Francis bore. The last Emperor of the
Romans disappeared from amidst his followers in the radiant
glory of the Imperator Invictus, and was spared the knowledge
of the tragic fate that overhung his house. His life closed with
the " transfiguration " into the Emperor of the End. His imperial career had described no curve, had known neither climax
nor decline. From birth his line of life ran arrow-straight to
its zenith, then quitted earth and vanished like a comet in the
ether : perchance to reappear once more in fiery brilliance at
the end of time. Ere long the sibyls spake : HE LIVES AND HE
LIVES NOT.

Frederick was the last emperor to be deified or to find a place
among the stars of heaven. In life they had hailed him as a
" Sun King." A notary and master of Frederick of Antioch
writes " a new Sun is born : peace and fame, and haven and
way." At the time of the great conspiracy another had written,
" they sought to rob the world of her Sun," and again " Satan
would fain have erected his rival throne beside the Sun God
(*deitas solis*)." These are not the traditional commonplace
metaphors applied to any powerful Emperor, they are comparisons belonging to a certain cycle of thought. The poet has
in mind the great Vergilian prophecy of a Saviour and when
he celebrates the Emperor's " sacred posterity," " like a radiant
sun begotten by the sun," or praises Conrad the imperial heir

as the "unifying king at whose feet lieth the universe and to whom God smileth"; these and countless other turns of phrase belong to the messianic idea.

Manfred writes to King Conrad of their father's death : " the sun of the world has set, the sun which lightened the peoples ; the sun of Justice has set, the treasure of Peace." Within a month the Emperor's followers are writing in the style of the Tiburtine Sibyl, " like the sun when he sinks from the heaven into the Western Sea, Frederick has left a son-sun in the west and already the crimson of the dawn begins to glow." Here is the age-old cult of Sol Invictus, revivified by prophecy, which a thousand years before had fused with the cult of a Saviour and had now lent itself to an Emperor, Frederick II, who himself was born within a day of the birth of Christ and of the Sun, who had died in December and would return in his own time at the end of time to establish the kingdom of heaven.

Prophecies and sibylline sayings multiplied themselves without end. Men knew that the Roman Empire closed with Frederick ; it was said and said again. The people did not believe that Frederick was dead. The Pope had too often announced the Emperor's death and the fall of the Empire. After great promises people were still awaiting greater deeds ; they were readier to believe in a ruse of the resourceful Emperor than in his death. Many years after his death wagers were still laid in Florence as to whether Frederick was alive or not, since the prophets had promised him a life of two hundred and sixty-seven years. For decades to come impostors gave themselves out for the returning Emperor, who was believed to be in concealment in Etna or where not. Mons Gebellus was clearly the appropriate dwelling-place of the Ghibelline Emperor and philosopher whom men feared like Satan. One of these sham Fredericks established himself there and was styled Emperor, and was honoured and worshipped as the Lord. A Sicilian Franciscan told how he had been sunk in prayer beside the sea and had suddenly seen a mighty train of five thousand armed horsemen riding towards the shore and plunging into the sea. Then the sea hissed as if all the riders had been armed in glowing metal, and one of the horsemen said to the astonished monk " that was Kaiser Frederick, riding into Etna with his men." This vision, which recalls the death of the great King of the Goths Dietrich of Bern, was said to have visited the brother at the very moment that Frederick died.

The rumour of a mysterious disappearance of Frederick was not slow in reaching Germany. The Sibyl had foretold : " The Empire shall end with him ; his successors, if any he shall have, shall be bereft of the Roman throne and the imperial name." The chaos of the Interregnum saw the literal fulfilment of the prophecy. Germany had kings enough and to spare : William of Holland, Alfonso of Castile, Richard of Cornwall ; but no ruler. The world had never seen before on such a scale the spectacle that followed the death of the Emperor : the complete disintegration in a night of the proud structure of government, the incoherence of all German happenings. The dismay which gripped the Germans is even more evident in art than in history : the glorious pride and freedom of Hohenstaufen days lay in the dust.

South of the Alps Frederick's legacy was the image of the " terrible " blent with the " majestic " which stemmed the inflowing tide of the God of Souls. Nothing of this touched the Germans in the North. Goethe's saying already held of them : " they are more apt to perceive the Good than the Beautiful." To them Frederick was no Apollo, no Sol Invictus, neither the God of the Sibyls nor the Bringer of the kingdom of the Sun God. The terrifying vision of Antichrist sweeping in storm above the clouds carried more conviction, for here only the degenerate Church stood at the judgment bar. Germany also refused to believe in the death of this great Emperor, and decades later impostors would still appear as the risen Kaiser. The pre-Christian God with whom men here identified Frederick was not Apollo but Woden. He appeared as " The Wanderer " to the peasants to announce :

> Once again shall he come home
> The mighty emperor of Rome.

The reformation of the Church appeared the most important mission of the " Awaited One," to flog and scourge the priests till they should hide their tonsures with cow-dung. So persistent was the conception of the redeeming saviour as a figure of awe and horror that after the Great Plague people hailed the dread leader of the Flagellants as Kaiser Frederick.

Even in Germany other attributes, however, clung round Frederick's name, wisdom and majesty and glory, though the beauty and the radiance had not impressed themselves on the northern people as on the Italians. Frederick would come again, though he had been cut into pieces or burnt to ashes, he would come to raise the Empire of the Germans to glory and to brilliance. He would bring justice and peace, he would hang the shield on the dry tree and lay down the sceptre of the world. Until the hour should strike when he would sit in judgment on a corrupt Church and gloriously renew the Empire's might the northern peoples dreamt of him as withdrawn into some fastness of the mountains. The sagas pitched on Kyffhäuser in Thuringia as his hiding-place ; perhaps because a grandson of Frederick II's, Frederick the Peaceful, lived on till the opening of the fourteenth century, the son of the illustrious Henry of Meissen, and people longed to find in him the wished for Frederick III. Whatever associations of glory and brilliance the " Emperor " retained in the people's dreams even into the later barren years, were derived from the deposed and ex-communicated prince, the enemy of the Church, the Antichrist, the fallen angel.

Old prophecies had given Frederick 267 years to live, and 267 years after his death the Reformation dawned in Germany. Two years later, in the chapbook of 1519, Frederick II was for the first time confused with his grandfather Barbarossa. It gradually became superfluous to picture the long-hoped for Saviour-Emperor as persecutor of the Church. And almost no one in Germany had had an Italian eye for Frederick II Antichrist as Herakles Musagetes. Frederick II is gradually metamorphosed into the bearded Barbarossa, the immortal boy into the aged man. Germany's dream was changed, and change of myth reflects the changing life and longings of a people. The snow-white sleeper whose beard has grown through the table on which his elbow rests has no message for the German of to-day : he has had his fulfilment, in the greatest vassal of the Empire, the aged Bismarck. The weary Lord of the Last Day has naught to say to the fiery Lord of the Beginning, the seducer, the deceiver, the radiant, the merry, the ever-young, the stern and mighty judge, the scholar, the sage who leads his armed warriors to the Muses' dance and song, he who slumbers not nor sleeps but ponders how he can renew the "Empire." The mountain would to-day stand empty were it not for the son of Barbarossa's son. The greatest Frederick is not yet redeemed, him his people knew not and sufficed not. "Lives and lives not," the Sibyl's word is not for the Emperor, but for the German People.

FINIS

INDEX

[*v.* also Table of Contents]

691